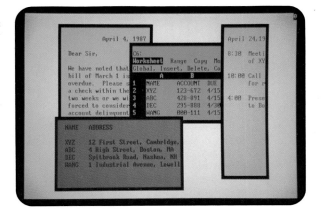

Figure 14–20 Use of color to communicate organization.

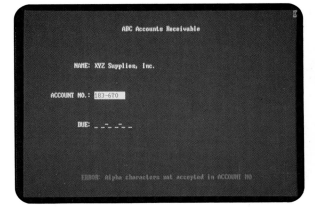

Figure 14–21 Use of color to indicate status.

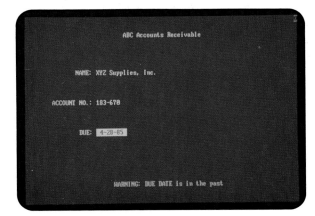

Figure 14–22 Use of color to indicate status.

PRINCIPLES AND GUIDELINES
IN SOFTWARE
USER INTERFACE DESIGN

PRINCIPLES AND GUIDELINES IN SOFTWARE USER INTERFACE DESIGN

Deborah J. Mayhew

P T R Prentice Hall
Englewood Cliffs, New Jersey 07632

Library of Congress Cataloging-in-Publication Data

Mayhew, Deborah J.
  Principles and guidelines in software user interface design /
Deborah J. Mayhew.
    p. cm.
  Includes bibliographical references and index.
  ISBN 0-13-721929-6
  1. User interfaces (Computer systems) 2. Systems design.
I. Title.
  QA76.9.U83M39 1992
  004.6′16—dc20   90-28454
                   CIP

Editorial/production and interior design: *Harriet Tellem*
Cover design: *Bruce Kenselaar*
Prepress buyers: *Mary Elizabeth McCartney/Kelly Behr*
Manufacturing buyer: *Susan Brunke*
Acquisitions editor: *Paul W. Becker*
Editorial assistant: *Noreen Regina*

Published by P T R Prentice-Hall, Inc.
A Simon & Schuster Company
Englewood Cliffs, New Jersey 07632

The publisher offers discounts on this book when ordered
in bulk quantities. For more information, write:
  Special Sales/Professional Marketing
  Prentice-Hall, Inc.
  Professional & Technical Reference Division
  Englewood Cliffs, New Jersey 07632

Printed in the United States of America
10 9 8 7 6 5 4 3

ISBN 0-13-721929-6

Prentice-Hall International (UK) Limited, *London*
Prentice-Hall of Australia Pty. Limited, *Sydney*
Prentice-Hall Canada Inc., *Toronto*
Prentice-Hall Hispanoamericana, S.A., *Mexico*
Prentice-Hall of India Private Limited, *New Delhi*
Prentice-Hall of Japan, Inc., *Tokyo*
Simon & Schuster Asia Pte. Ltd., *Singapore*
Editora Prentice-Hall do Brasil, Ltda., *Rio de Janeiro*

Dedicated to

My Family

Mom, Dad,
Jack, Sarah,
Betsey, Caroline, and Lucy

and

My Home Town

The Town of West Tisbury
on Martha's Vineyard

Contents

Contents

Preface

This book is about the software user interface to computer systems. It offers design principles and guidelines for all aspects of user interface design, including the high-level conceptual model, dialog styles, organization of functionality to support user tasks, and effective error handling. It provides both guidance for the design of traditional interfaces, such as menus and fill-in forms implemented on character-based screens, and for the design of state-of-the-art user interfaces, such as direct manipulation interfaces including graphics, color, windows, and pointing devices. The book is based on an extensive review of research and practice in human–computer interaction in the last ten years, as well as on the author's ten years of experience in this field. It is a synthesis of the current body of knowledge in this relatively young discipline, organized and presented in a manner digestible by the practicing nonspecialist.

This book is intended primarily for an audience of computer science professionals and students. This audience needs *concrete, practical assistance in making user interface design decisions*. The goal of the book is to provide these professionals with a fundamental and *immediately applicable* understanding of this aspect of computer system design.

Many software development organizations now employ "human factors" or user interface specialists, who participate directly in the design of software products. It is unlikely, however, that any development organization will ever have enough of these specialists to be involved in every product under development. It makes sense, therefore, for all software professionals involved in software user interface design and development to be at least fundamentally literate in this aspect of computer science. The purpose of this book is to provide a basis for this fundamental literacy and to provide a reference book that can be *used as a tool during design*. Such basic literacy should result in the development of higher-quality software products and in better communication between computer scientists and human factors experts.

The book has been carefully organized to meet the needs of the intended audience. Chapter 1 provides an introduction to and definition of the topic. Then Chapter 2 provides a primer on theories from cognitive psychology. These chapters provide a broad framework upon which the principles and guidelines offered in later chapters rest.

Chapters 3 through 17, each of which addresses a specific aspect of user interface design, are divided into two major sections. The first defines the topic and reviews and discusses the available research data and current theoretical models related to the topic. The second *synthesizes the available data and theory into a set of concrete design principles,* which are presented with examples and illustrations.

This book differs from others on this topic in that it includes not only principles and guidelines for design but also the research data and theory that they are drawn from. This is very important. Books providing only discussions of data and theory require the reader to synthesize complex technical information from outside their own field in order to make basic design decisions. This may be an appropriate treatment of the topic for human factors professionals, but it is not useful to computer scientists and designers. On the other hand, books offering only principles and guidelines for design provide little or no insight into their rationale, so the interested computer scientist and designer cannot begin to learn how to intelligently generalize and apply the principles and guidelines in novel contexts. This book offers *both* theoretical foundations *and* guidelines in a single source, thus providing immediate assistance in making design decisions on the job and the beginnings of a deeper understanding of the topic. Therefore, the motivated reader can become a more critical and intelligent user of the principles and guidelines.

While both theoretical foundations and immediately applicable principles and guidelines are included, these two components are *cleanly separated into different sections* within each chapter. This organization accomplishes an important purpose. By separating theory and guidelines, we permit the designer to use the book as both an educational resource and a reference tool on the job. The theoretical sections can be read initially as an educational exercise and to provide context. The principles and guidelines sections can then be referred to as needed during design projects as a kind of checklist. Ample cross references between the two sections in each chapter allow the reader to easily link the principles and guidelines back to the data and theoretical discussion that motivated them. Generous illustrations and examples for all principles and guidelines provide a more efficient and accurate understanding of their meaning and implications.

Finally, Chapter 18 provides an outline of a general methodology for designing the user interface during a software development project. Much more than principles and guidelines are required to produce consistently high quality user interfaces within a software development organization. Techniques for managing this aspect of software design and development are laid out and briefly described in this chapter. A full description of this methodology may be the subject of a future book by the author.

The words of some professionals in the field of computer–human interaction will help to summarize the main goals of this book. In the words of one:

> Although psychologists have brought to development efforts a dedicated professional interest in user problems, and have successfully acted as intelligent advocates of the interest of users, they have *not brought an impressive tool kit of design methods or principles,* nor have they effectively brought to bear a relevant body of scientific knowledge or theory. . . . Physics and chemistry have had engineering, physiology and biology have had medicine . . . . But cognitive psychology has had only limited associations with artifact invention . . . . We now have the opportunity, but we have not done much with it yet. (Thomas K. Landauer, in John M. Carroll, ed., *Interfacing Thought: Cognitive Aspects of Human–Computer Interaction,* The MIT Press, Cambridge, Mass., 1987, pp. 1–25; italics mine)

My hope is that this book will be one contribution to the "tool kit of design methods or principles" needed by software development professionals. As put by another pair of authors:

> What exactly is cognitive science asking developers to do? What would be required for a developer to apply the knowledge gained from cognitive science? Are they required to be familiar with the academic work in this area and to determine for themselves how to apply it? Experience suggests that such application is not straightforward or simple. Generalizing from an experiment or from a model is not an easy undertaking. *Guidelines are at least one attempt to concretize the results of experiments and models (and common sense) into easily followed recommendations.* Yet designers and developers find guidelines hard to use and complain that they are too general or too specific, and do not apply to the particular system being developed. (John Whiteside and Dennis Wixon in John M. Carroll, ed., *Interfacing Thought: Cognitive Aspects of Human–Computer Interaction,* The MIT Press, Cambridge, Mass., 1987, pp. 353–65; italics mine)

I felt that my intended audience needed a book *full of practical, usable, immediately applicable advice, organized in a way that would make accessing that advice easy.* Thus I have organized the book around guidelines, and I have striven to make these guidelines easy to find, easy to understand, easy to evaluate against current design goals, and neither too general nor too specific.

When using the guidelines offered in this book to help them make specific design decisions during a development effort, I hope that designers will also devote attention to the theoretical underpinnings that are offered in the initial sections of each chapter. After gaining a foundation of design skills through this book and from their practical experience, the more advanced and interested students and professionals can then move on to the many important and useful books on fundamental theories of human–computer interaction now available.

ACKNOWLEDGMENTS

I would like to thank the people who reviewed various chapters and sections of this book. Invaluable suggestions were offered by Phil Barnard, Raoul Smith, Jo Tombaugh, John Van Praag, Susan F. Ehrlich, Wanda Smith, and Steve Boyle. Thanks also to the reviewers and editors supplied by Prentice Hall for their expert advice.

FURTHER INFORMATION

The Author can be contacted at the following address concerning topics covered in this book.

> Dr. Deborah J. Mayhew
> Deborah J. Mayhew & Associates
> Box 248
> Panhandle Road
> West Tisbury, MA 02575
> (508) 693-7149

CHAPTER 1

Introduction

The three Doonesbury comic strips on the next page illustrate the historical problem of computer–human interfaces. The first strip caricatures the communication gap that has long existed between professional software engineers and the nontechnical users of software systems. Software professionals and, for example, business professionals simply do not speak the same language. Each lives in a different world, has a different vocabulary of specialized jargon, is challenged and stimulated by very different kinds of intellectual problems, and probably even has different cognitive styles or strategies for problem solving.

Software engineers have been extensively trained in ways of thinking that are very different from that of the average office worker or business professional (see Grudin, 1989). The software engineer tends to judge his or her own work by criteria that may have little to do with the needs and constraints of the end user. For example, efficiency of code and flexibility of architecture may be admirable engineering goals, but may have little or nothing to do with the success of a computer system in being accessible to and supportive of a particular type of user. The first comic strip nicely illustrates the difficulty that two specialists have in communicating: the potential user has trouble communicating his needs to the software professional, and the software professional cannot phrase what he or she has to offer in terms that the user can understand.

This communication gap is carried over to the computer–human interface, as illustrated in the second comic strip. A software engineer who does not understand

DOONESBURY   **by Garry Trudeau**

DOONESBURY   **by Garry Trudeau**

DOONESBURY   **by Garry Trudeau**

and cannot communicate well with his or her customer designs an interface through which the user will communicate with the system. Thus the communication problems that exist between people are designed into the communication between user and system.

One major stumbling block to improving communications between software professionals and users, and thus indirectly between users and systems, is attitude. This is caricatured in the third comic strip. It is difficult for any expert to put himself or herself in the shoes of someone totally uneducated in his or her own field. Software experts find it hard to imagine that their logical structures and jargon are obscure and alien to nonprofessionals. "Idiot proof" and "Dumb users" are terms one often hears, and the attitude implicit in such terms is that anyone who cannot make sense out of and learn to use a computer system is simply stupid and cannot be helped.

THREE STEPS TO IMPROVING INTERFACES

The first step toward improving computer-human interfaces involves *changing the attitude of the software professional*. Software professionals need to be convinced that a high-quality user interface is in fact important. A great deal is known about how to design better user interfaces. What has been missing is motivation. Designers need to think of designing a good human interface as just as challenging and stimulating a problem as designing elegant algorithms or well-structured and easily modifiable code.

The second step to good interface design is to *draw upon the fast accumulating body of knowledge regarding computer–human interface design,* to avoid "reinventing the wheel" or, worse yet, repeating bad designs. Often old interface techniques are carried over to new products simply because "that is how we've always done it" or to mimic competitive products. A growing body of research is available to software developers to guide them in their design decisions.

The third step to successful computer–human interface design is to *integrate user interface design methods and techniques into the standard software development methodologies currently in place.* In particular, it is critical to adopt testing and quality control procedures to evaluate interface designs, analogous to those procedures already accepted for testing other aspects of computer design, such as performance. Applying available design guidelines is a good start, but the bottom line is testing. Although we know a lot about user interface design, we do not know enough at this point to provide a "cookbook" approach to design, and what knowledge we do have tends to be somewhat technology specific. Thus, there simply is no substitute for testing a specific design against a specific set of intended users.

No software developer, no matter how expert, expects to design code correctly on paper. One always has to debug code. The same is true of user interface design. Applying known principles and guidelines makes for a significantly better first pass, but does not eliminate the need for testing. All user interface designs need to be debugged.

This book explicitly addresses the first two steps. Chapters 3 through 17 summarize for the software professional the state of the art in principles and guidelines for computer–human interface design. By applying these principles and guidelines, an initial design can be a good start toward a perfected design. It is hoped that, in the course of reading the whole book, the designer will come to appreciate the complexity and importance of the problem of good interface design. And perhaps this appreciation will provide the reader with the motivation and stimulation, the first ingredients to successful interface design, to take upon himself or herself the responsibility for this very important aspect of computer system design.

Finally, Chapter 18 provides a high-level overview of the third ingredient for good user interface design, integrating user interface design methods and techniques into the standard software development methodologies currently in place. Although not the primary focus of this book, these methods and techniques are absolutely key to good user interface design.

WHY THE QUALITY OF THE USER INTERFACE IS IMPORTANT

A 1984 marketing brochure put out by Apple Computer, Inc., for its new product, the Macintosh, heralded a new attitude toward the importance of the computer–human interface as an aspect of competitive edge in commercial products. In the past, such marketing brochures typically focused on technical specifications, functionality, and maintenance support. The Macintosh brochure, by contrast, focused decidedly on the human interface. A few quotes give the flavor of this then novel marketing approach:

> Of the 235 million people in America, only a fraction can use a computer. . . . Introducing Macintosh for the rest of us.
>
> Wouldn't it make more sense to teach computers about people, instead of teaching people about computers?
>
> Macintosh. Designed on the principle that a computer is a lot more useful if its easy to use.
>
> Macintosh is much more natural, intuitive, and in line with how people think and work. . . .
>
> The real genius is that you don't have to be a genius to use a Macintosh.

In 1984, the Macintosh interface was the latest generation in a line of interfaces that originated with the Xerox Alto, an internal research project, and the Xerox Star, a commercial product that was not very successful in terms of numbers of systems sold. Today there are many look-alike products that mimic the general interface style of these products. Whether or not the general interface style of all these products is as effective as is claimed remains to be seen. In fact, later research (Whiteside, Jones, Levy, and Wixon, 1985) cast some doubt on the kinds of claims made in marketing brochures for such products. The real importance of the Macintosh, however, lies in the attention and publicity it brought to the computer–human interface as a selling point. It signaled a new attitude on the part of the computer industry toward this aspect of software products. The motivation for this change in attitude, and the then new and still fast growing interest in computer–human interaction, came from a number of trends in the computer industry.

First, the costs of technology began decreasing while the power of technology was increasing. In the 1960s and 1970s, all the computer power available at an affordable price had to be dedicated to providing functionality and performance. Today, hardware is much cheaper and software more efficient and powerful, and more computer resources can be dedicated to the computer–human interface without sacrificing functionality, performance, or cost effectiveness.

Second, the technology emerged out of the data processing center and into the office, the professional's desktop, the home, and the classroom. The user of computer technology is now often a person who is technologically uneducated, unsophisticated, and unmotivated, rather than a professional technologist. Different kinds of interfaces to computing power are required for this new type of user. To penetrate these new markets, computer companies recognize that acceptable and appealing interfaces, as well as desirable functionality, must be offered. Certain kinds of users simply will not buy systems that require too much of an investment in learning. To sell to this kind of user, products must be very easy to learn.

Third, there is a never ending desire for increased productivity among computer users and their organizations. Even high-frequency, ''power'' users continue to seek interfaces that will allow them to do more, better and faster. Small improvements in productivity on a screen or task basis can add up to significant organizational benefits when the number of users and the volume of transactions are high. Consider the following.

Suppose that the expected number of users for a system being developed is 250 and that their salary is comparable to an hourly rate of $15. Suppose further that two or three major fill-in form screens in this system (each containing many fill-in fields) are expected to be used 60 times a day, 230 days a year by each user. Now make the assumption that these screens can be improved by decreasing throughput time by 3 seconds per screen as a result of applying human factors principles and guidelines, and techniques such as prototype testing. These facts and assumptions result in the following estimated benefit:

    250 users
   × 60 screens per day
   × 230 days per year

$\times$ processing time reduced by 3 seconds per screen $\div$ 3600
$\times$ hourly rate of \$15
= \$43,125 savings *per year*

This is a significant benefit and would justify the investment of significant resources to obtain. In general, it is usually easy to cost justify a significant investment of money and resources in better user interface design because of the very real benefits in increased productivity, decreased training time, decreased user errors, decreased development time, decreased customer support costs and increased sales that better user interfaces can produce. The reader is referred to several articles on cost justifying human factors activities for more detailed information on this topic (Mantei and Teorey, 1988; Mayhew 1990; Karat, 1990).

COMPUTER–HUMAN INTERACTION: A DEFINITION

Many software system designers fail to realize that the system they are designing is really more than the software alone, and the scope and purpose of the system is wider than the functionality provided by the software. In fact, the software is only one component in a larger system and provides only a subset of the functionality that is desired. This larger system includes at least one human user and may, in fact, include other users and other software systems.

Any subsystem that is designed and implemented in isolation from the larger system to which it belongs is likely to produce problems. Any system programmer understands the need to plan ahead so that system components will successfully communicate with one another. It is just as necessary to ensure that the user and the software, both components of a larger system with its own purpose and goals, will successfully communicate with one another. The importance of the interaction is less clear in this case, because users are so flexible, intelligent, and adaptive that they can often compensate fairly well for failures on the part of the software to optimally communicate with them. However, the overall effectiveness and efficiency of the whole system will not be optimized unless the relative strengths and weaknesses of each subsystem are taken into account.

Any plan for a new software system should begin with a definition of the whole interactive system that it is a part of. Decisions regarding functionality should be based on a clear and complete idea of the goals of the user's organization, and the job and tasks of the user. Similarly, any decisions regarding the design of the user interface to specific functionality should be based on a sound and thorough knowledge of the user. This includes an understanding of the general strengths and weaknesses of the human information processing system, as well as a general profile of the average level of ability and the specific knowledge and educational level of the intended user group.

Consider the Venn diagram in Figure 1-1, representing an interactive computer-based system. The rectangular border represents the boundaries of the whole system. The main system components include the human and the computer, each represented by a circle. The intersection of the two circles represents the **computer–human interface:** the means through which these two subsystems communicate with one another. (There are other subsystems as well, such as the physical environment, the organizational environment, and the social environment, but these topics are outside the scope of our text and are not discussed here.)

Considering the two main subsystems, the computer and the human, a few initial observations can be made. The human is flexible and adaptable. Most importantly, the human can learn how to operate in new environments. By contrast, the computer system is not flexible or adaptable; at least most commercial systems currently are not. Inputs must be made in a particular format. Outputs are predefined. Thus, for a given computer system the human can learn and adapt, while the computer cannot. This puts the burden of successful interaction totally on the user.

On the other hand, people build computers, and computers can be redesigned. Because we build them, we know (we in the collective sense) how they work, we understand how they operate, what they can and cannot do, and how they do it. By contrast, we cannot change the design of the human. We know relatively little about how the human information processing system works, indeed far less than our understanding of the computerized information processing system. And, although the human subsystem is intelligent and adaptive, we cannot change the basic properties that define its strengths and weaknesses.

In the past, the design of the computer–human interface was heavily biased to accommodate the weaknesses of the computer system. For instance, the computer could only recognize exact input, such as correctly spelled words and properly formatted numbers. Thus, the burden was on the user to provide correct

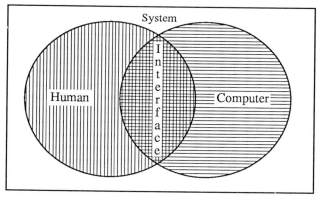

Figure 1–1 Computer–human interaction: a definition.

inputs. But humans are error prone and do not always have perfect knowledge of acceptable inputs.

Similarly, computers could not resolve ambiguity. They required precision. Thus, to communicate with computers, users had to learn precise, notational languages. The ambiguity and richness of human natural language could not be parsed by a computer. A considerable investment in learning was usually required on the part of the user before the two subsystems could communicate.

More recently, due to advances in technology, this bias toward accommodating the deficiencies of computers in the computer–human interface is slowly shifting. Initially, the idea has been to shift the responsibility for the success of the computer–human interaction to the computer designer, or the computer–human interface specialist. That is, without actually making computers more adaptable or more flexible, it is nevertheless possible to make them more compatible with the way people naturally work and communicate. The idea is that computers can be designed to support the weaknesses of the human.

The future in computer–human interaction technology will take things a bit further. Through the application of artificial intelligence technology, we may be able to design computer systems that literally do adapt to their users. Natural language interfaces are a step in this direction. So are other "intelligent" interfaces, which track the performance of individual users and present different interfaces to them depending on their level of expertise.

In the meantime, however, a lot can be gained simply by applying what we know about people in general, and potential users in particular, to the design of particular computer systems.

GENERAL PRINCIPLES OF USER INTERFACE DESIGN

The remaining chapters in this book are devoted to the definition and discussion of *detailed* design principles. But, first, it will be useful to provide some more *general* design goals, and this is done next. These goals are general characteristics that any interface should have, and they apply to all aspects of the interface. Chapters 3 through 17 provide specific ideas on how to implement these principles in different aspects of the interface. Figures 1-2 through 1-18 illustrate these principles.

User compatibility.   Perhaps the fundamental principle, from which all others derive, is to *know the user*. The most common error among software developers is to make two assumptions, illustrated at the left of Figure 1-2: that all users are alike, and that all users are like the developer. These erroneous assumptions lead to the conclusions that, if the interface is easy to learn and use for the developer, it will be so for the ultimate user, and that if an interface is acceptable to one or two users, it will be acceptable to all. Nothing could be further from the truth.

Designing something is very different from learning how to use it for the first time. The deeper that software designers get into an evolving design, the less they

User Compatibility

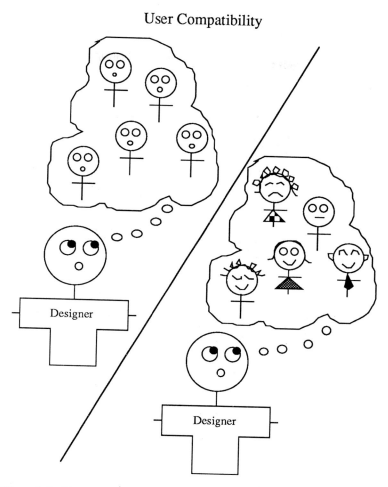

Figure 1–2   User compatibility: different interfaces for different types of users.

are able to imagine themselves in the shoes of a first-time user. Thus, even as designers strive to develop an easy to learn interface, they become, by definition, less and less able to assess the ease of learning of their own design.

Many users today differ significantly from designers in technical sophistication, education, and motivation. Designers should be familiar with basic **cognitive psychology,** or an understanding of the general strengths and weaknesses of the human mind. They should also know and understand the particular individuals in the user population of relevance and the details of their jobs. People are different more than they are the same. Perhaps the safest attitude for a designer is to assume that users are different both from the designer and from one another, as illustrated on the right of Figure 1-2, and to set out to understand them and define the variations among them. This approach will prevent the designer from making assumptions about the user that are probably not true and that may lead to inappropriate design decisions.

Product compatibility. Often the intended user of a new system is already a user of other systems, perhaps even of earlier releases of the new system under development. Thus the user has already invested a great deal in learning the previous systems and has habits and expectations that will be brought to bear when learning the new system. If these expectations are not met, users must start all over again learning the new system (see Figure 1-3).

Although across-product compatibility must always be carefully traded off against providing improved user interfaces, whenever possible, making new systems compatible, that is, similar to old systems in their user interface will exploit what the user already knows and minimize the necessity for new learning. It can be particularly confusing for a user of many different systems to remember how to perform simple operations common across all systems when each system has some arbitrarily different syntax or mode for performing those operations. Compatibility across systems can reduce both learning time and errors. Imagine if every time you bought a different kind of car you had to learn how to use very different kinds of controls and to read very different kinds of representations of information on the dashboard! In most consumer products, such as cars, telephones, lawn mowers, and kitchen appliances, we expect compatibility in interfaces across products. In the computer industry, surprisingly little attempt has been made to standardize interfaces even across products from a particular company. This places an enormous burden on the user. Compatibility should not be emphasized to the exclusion of improvement over suboptimal technologies, but it should be one of the many goals that a designer considers in making design decisions.

Task compatibility. The structure and flow of a system should match and support the task that is being carried out. For instance, on the left of Figure 1-4, a system has been organized according to the different data types that might be employed. However, most tasks the user will perform with the system involve all data types. Data types are not a meaningful organizational principle to the user. This system will force the user to navigate back and forth between applications in order to complete a task.

On the other hand, the right side of Figure 1-4 illustrates a system that is organized by task type. All data types would be accessible through each task type in this fully integrated system. This system will support the tasks of the user much more effectively.

Work flow compatibility. Systems should also be organized to facilitate transitions between tasks. Figure 1-5 illustrates the fragmented nature of the work of a typical manager. Managers often spend no more than 5 to 10 minutes on any

Product Compatibility

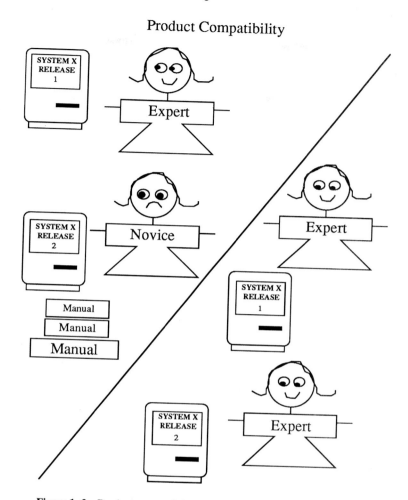

Figure 1–3 Product compatibility: similar interfaces across products.

given task before moving on to another. They are "interrupt driven," so to speak. A computer system that allows only single-task support and makes it slow and tedious to transition between tasks will not effectively support this kind of professional. On the other hand, a windowed, multitasking system, such as that illustrated on the right of Figure 1-5, will support the nature of this type of user's work much more effectively.

Consistency. Consistency is related to compatibility, but it refers to similarities *within a product,* rather than *across products.* Often there are similar operations in different parts of an application or in different applications of a system.

Task Compatibility

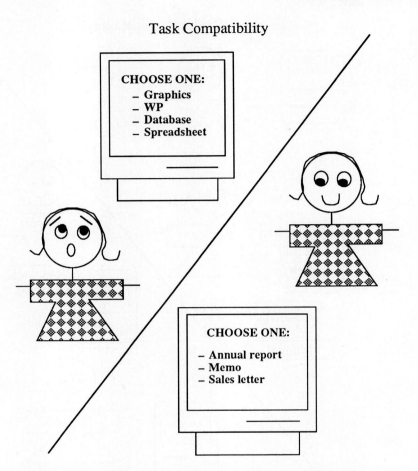

Figure 1–4   Task compatibility: an interface that supports users' tasks.

These operations should have interfaces that are similar, or even the same if possible. For instance, as illustrated in Figure 1-6, if there is a "move" command in the word processing application and in the graphics application of an office automation package, the same command and syntax should apply in both cases. Thus, once users have learned one application, they already know something about how to use other applications in the system.

People naturally assume consistency, and they reason by analogy. Exploiting people's natural reasoning processes and expectations will result in less of a learning effort for them. Consistency allows people to reason by analogy and predict how to do things they have never done before, thus minimizing the need to consult a manual. It improves both performance and user satisfaction, as it imparts a sense of mastery to the user.

Work Flow Compatibility

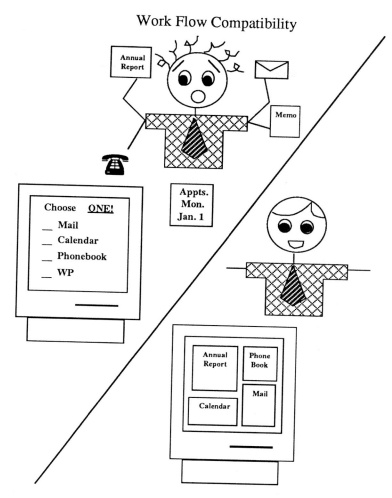

Figure 1–5 Work flow compatibility: easy switching between tasks.

On the other hand, the principle of consistency must be carefully applied. Grudin (1989) provides many examples where designing consistency into an interface actually made a system less usable. For instance, the letter keys on early computer keyboards were laid out in alphabetic order on the assumption that this familiar layout (consistent with past experience with the alphabet) would make a keyboard easy to use. More modern keyboards (for example, the QWERTY and Dvorak keyboards) are laid out in a fashion that is inconsistent with any past experience of a novice typist, but that better supports the task of typing letters in the orders in which they commonly appear in the English language.

Consistency

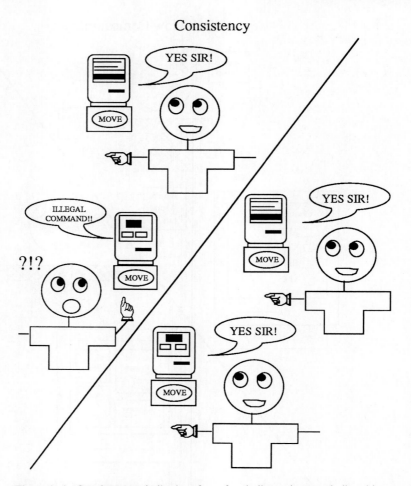

Figure 1–6   Consistency: similar interfaces for similar actions or similar objects.

In another example, Grudin points out that a system with default menu selections might in most cases base the default on which selection the user is most likely to select next. In the case where the most likely choice is also a potentially destructive and irreversible action, however, it might make more sense to violate the principle of consistency and have some other, less destructive or more easily reversible selection be the default. The point is that design decisions should be based on a clear understanding of users' tasks and work flow, not just on a blind application of the principle of consistency.

Familiarity.   Another characteristic that can greatly facilitate the learning of a new interface is familiarity. Concepts, terminology, and spatial arrangements that the user is already familiar with can be incorporated into the interface. One example of the exploitation of familiar concepts is the use of objects and terms from manual filing systems in the interface to automated filing systems. A system that presents the user with file cabinets, folders, and documents is more familiar than one that presents volumes, libraries, workspaces, indexes, workpads, and files (Figure 1-7). The latter are computer jargon and refer to technical concepts. The former can be used to present the same objects and functions in a form that is already familiar to the user and thus requires little or no learning of new ideas and terms. Again, exploiting the natural tendency to learn and reason by analogy is the human characteristic behind this principle.

Simplicity. One common mistake in interface design is to try to provide all the functionality, all the "bells and whistles," that any user could possibly ever

Figure 1–7 Familiarity: exploit already familiar concepts in the interface.

want or need. This is an admirable goal in and of itself, but often the result is a complex interface that is overwhelming and confusing to the new user and tedious to navigate for the expert. It is possible to provide very rich and complex functionality through a simple interface, although it is often quite difficult and challenging to do so. The main idea is to *layer* the interface so that novices need not be aware of the full complexity of the system on a first encounter, but can learn the fundamentals and then gradually add the more advanced and sophisticated functions to their repertoire at their leisure. One way to do this is to use **defaults,** as illustrated in Figure 1-8. For instance, when a novice is learning to use a word processor, invisible defaults for all the formatting options could be provided. This way the novice would not have to learn about footers and headers, justification,

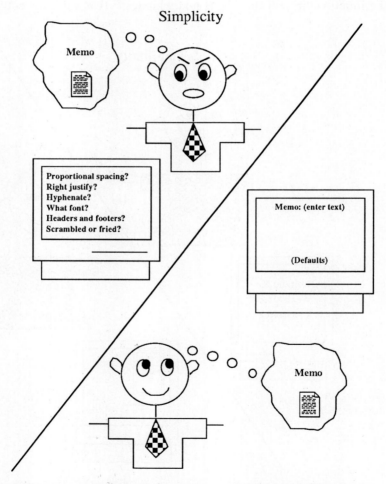

Figure 1–8   Simplicity: make simple things simple, complex things possible.

font choices and the like, while first learning to create and edit a one-page memo. Similarly, the expert would not have to make all these choices for every document, but could set defaults once.

Many systems provide functionality that is rarely or never used. This may be because the functionality itself is not very useful. More often it is because users never discover or remember how to use much of the functionality. Complexity in the interface is often to blame. It is better to provide less functionality that will get used than so much functionality that the interface is hopelessly complex and inhibits use of system. It is also true that systems with simpler functionality tend to be less ''buggy'' and easier to maintain. Although a simple interface to a rich and complex system is always the designer's ultimate goal, the former often should take precedence over the latter, since an overly complex interface will inhibit use of the additional complexity anyway.

Direct manipulation.   A direct manipulation interface is one in which users directly perform actions on visible objects. This is in contrast to interfaces in which users specify actions, parameters, and objects indirectly through language (for example, command language or menu interfaces).

For example, contrast old-fashioned text editors with modern word processors (see Figure 1-9). In a text editor, text is edited in a very indirect way through a command language. The user enters a command string invoking the ''change'' command and specifying the text to be changed by a line number and a character string. Then the user asks for verification by requesting a listing of the lines that have been changed. Both action and verification are indirect, accomplished through a command language.

By contrast, many modern word processors allow the user to ''point'' (using the traditional cursor keys) to the text to be changed and to simply type over it to change it. The user watches as the text from which the selected string was removed ''closes'' up and is reformatted and as the new text is inserted in its place, reformatting as necessary. Verification is automatic and occurs during the operation. This is a much more direct, easy to learn and use interface.

Control.   Users prefer to feel a sense of mastery and control over any tool at their disposal, and the computer is no exception. It is frustrating and demoralizing to feel that you are being controlled and directed by a machine. The interface designer should be sensitive to this and present a toollike interface. Users will soon gain a sense of mastery if the interface is simple, predictable, and consistent. They will feel more in control if the interface is flexible and passive. For instance, messages such as ''Enter command'' and ''Illegal command'' (see Figure 1-10) sound like commands and reprimands from the computer. Messages such as ''Ready for command'' and ''Can't recognize input'' impart more of a sense that the computer is a willing slave with limited abilities. This, of course, is actually the case. Thus these messages also impart a more accurate picture of the capabilities and limitations of the system.

Direct Manipulation

Figure 1–9   Direct manipulation: allow users to manipulate objects directly.

WYSIWYG.   WYSIWYG is an acronym for ''what you see is what you get.'' It generally refers to the degree of one-to-one correspondence between information displayed on the screen and information displayed on printed output or stored in files. For instance, older character-based terminals were incapable of displaying certain text attributes such as boldface and italics, while printers could print these attributes. Thus, special codes were inserted in the text on the screen to designate that these attributes should be applied at print time. The codes were displayed on the screen so that they could be edited, but not on the printed output, which instead displayed the attribute. The problem with this approach was that the codes themselves took up character positions on the screen that were not occupied

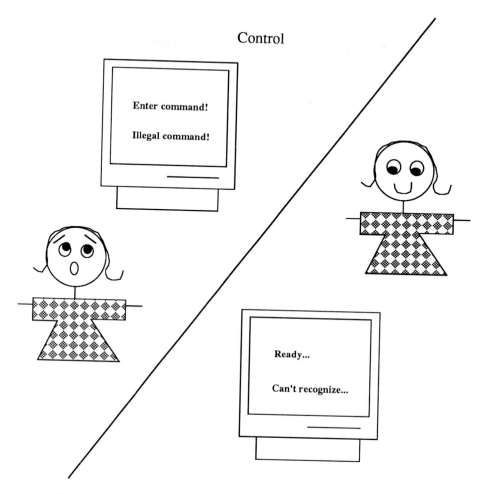

Figure 1–10   Control: users should feel they (not the system) are in control.

on the printed page. Word wrapping, tabs, and paging on the printed output might thus be different than they appeared on the screen, since a different number of characters were printed than were displayed. As illustrated on the left of Figure 1-11, what you saw (on the screen) is not what you got (on the printout). Bit-mapped screens whose display capabilities match more closely the capabilities of printers result in a much closer correspondence between screen displays and printed output, as illustrated on the right of Figure 1-11.

Flexibility.   Flexibility in a system allows more user control and accommo-dates variations in user skill and preferences. Flexibility is manifested in many

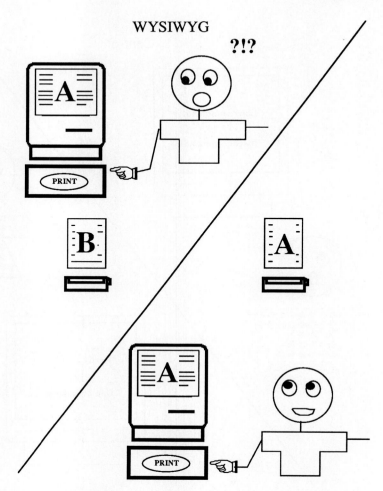

Figure 1–11   WYSIWYG: what you see is what you get.

different ways. Some dialog styles, such as command languages, are inherently more flexible than others, such as menus, because they allow more variations in user action at any point in time. Tasks that are inherently unstructured demand flexible user interfaces. Interfaces that allow user tailoring and user choices (see Figure 1-12) also offer an important kind of flexibility.

Responsiveness.   The computer should always respond immediately to a user's input. What the computer is doing internally is invisible to the user, and many users have no way of knowing how long the system will take to accomplish a task. Users will conclude that the system has crashed and start hitting keys on the

Flexibility

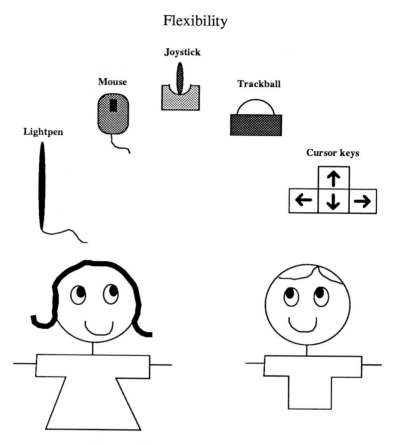

Figure 1-12 Flexibility: give users choices.

keyboard after very short delays with no feedback. Response time should be as short as possible, but even when long delays are unavoidable, it is usually possible to inform the user of the current status of the task in progress. At the very least, a simple message such as "Working . . ." or "Please wait . . . ," which repeats periodically, should be provided for any task that will take longer than a few seconds. It is even more desirable, especially for longer tasks, to give information regarding the exact status of the task. For instance, displays that count down on some meaningful unit (for example, number of pages processed or number of files loaded) give the user an idea of how much longer the task will take (see Figure 1-13). With this information, the user can turn his or her attention to other things temporarily, rather than sit idly by, eyes glued to a blank screen, waiting for something to happen.

Responsiveness

Figure 1-13 Responsiveness: give users feedback.

Invisible technology.   Generally, the user should need to know as little as possible about the technical details of how the system is implemented and operates in order to use it constructively. Anybody can drive a car without knowing anything at all about what goes on under the hood. The same should be true of a computer system. Technical jargon, obscure error messages, and unfamiliar concepts and representations all require users to have some technical background, and this is usually unnecessary (see Figure 1-14). What is actually going on inside the computer should be invisible to the user, or at least presented in simple and familiar ways so that the user is not confronted with unfamiliar symptoms of processes he or she does not understand.

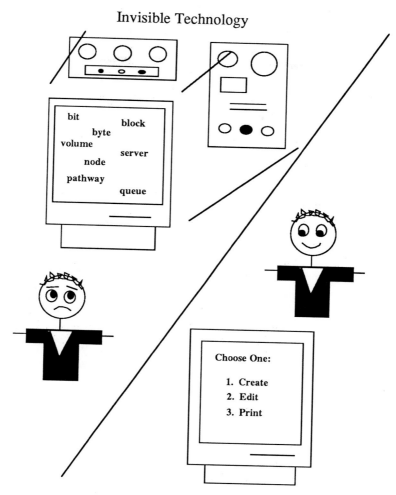

Figure 1–14 Invisible technology: hide the technology, present the functionality.

Robustness. A system should tolerate common and unavoidable human error. System crashes should be minimized, and simple to understand and execute recovery measures should be presented (see Figure 1-15). A system that is over-sensitive to erroneous input will quickly discourage a user from exploring and trying new things. Learning will be inhibited, and productivity will suffer because users will work carefully and slowly to avoid the kinds of common errors that cause crashes. The user should feel confident that the system is robust enough to handle any kind of input, including errors.

Robustness

Figure 1–15   Robustness: the system should never "crash."

Protection.   The user should also be protected against the catastrophic results of common human error. It should always be difficult and cumbersome to take actions that have radical results. For instance, it should take several keystrokes to delete all files. It should not be possible to inadvertently erase an entire session of editing. Recovery procedures should be simple and easy to execute when these things do occur by mistake (see Figure 1-16). People make errors, especially when they are working quickly or under pressure. This should be recognized and protected against.

Protection

Figure 1–16   Protection: protect the user from drastic results of common errors.

Ease of learning and ease of use.   Finally, systems should be both easy to learn for the novice (see Figure 1-17) and efficient and easy to use for the expert (see Figure 1-18). Many of the previous principles contribute to these two basic goals.

Ease of use and ease of learning are terms that are overused and casually claimed. Nevertheless, they sum up what we are trying to attain in any interface. These characteristics are extremely difficult to attain on systems rich in functionality, especially simultaneously. Often, designs that attain one violate the other. This is not necessary, however. One of the most challenging tasks for the interface designer is to provide both.

Ease of Learning

Figure 1–17   Ease of learning.

Trade-offs

There are two problems with our list of design goals. First, they are often in direct conflict with one another, as just mentioned and as illustrated in Figure 1-19. For example, increased ease of use might require sacrificing product compatibility across releases. Offering maximum user control may require sacrificing ease of learning. Simplicity may require decreasing power and ease of use. Making these trade-offs intelligently requires a thorough understanding of the intended user population. This is addressed in Chapter 2.

Ease of Use

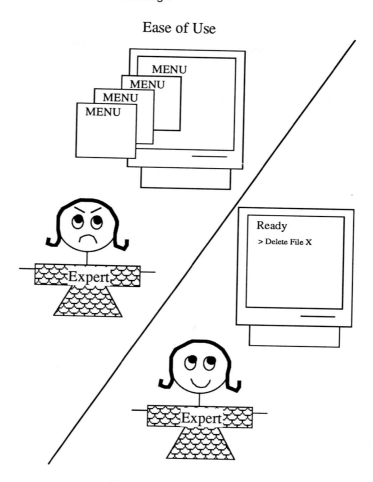

Figure 1–18 Ease of use.

Second, these goals are very general and, thus, not directly applicable by designers. How does one achieve ease of learning? How can a system be designed to be most flexible? How can a designer know if a design is consistent with the users' expectations? Chapters 3 through 17 provide the designer with many specific design ideas to achieve the general design goals described in this chapter.

Design Trade-offs

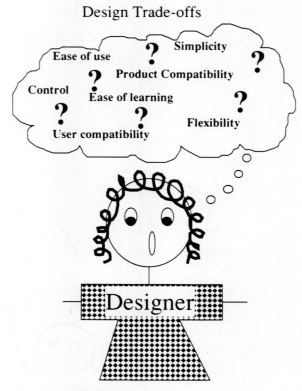

Figure 1–19   Design tradeoffs.

REFERENCES

GRUDIN, JONATHAN, "The Case against User Interface Consistency," *Communications of the ACM,* 32, no. 10 (October 1989), pp. 1164–73.

KARAT, CLARE-MARIE, "Cost-Benefit Analysis of Usability Engineering Techniques," *Proceedings of the Human Factors Society 34th Annual Meeting,* 1990, pp. 839–43.

MANTEI, MARILYN, and TOBY J. TEOREY, "Cost/Benefit for Incorporating Human Factors in the Software Lifecycle," *Communications of the ACM,* 31, no. 4, (April 1988), pp. 428–39.

MAYHEW, DEBORAH J., "Cost-Justifying Human Factors Support—A Framework," *Proceedings of the Human Factors Society 34th Annual Meeting,* 1990, pp. 834–38.

WHITESIDE, JOHN, SANDRA JONES, PAULA S. LEVY, and DENNIS WIXON, "User Performance with Command, Menu, and Iconic Interfaces," *CHI'85 Proceedings,* 1985, pp. 185–91.

CHAPTER 2

The User Profile

The ultimate purpose of an interactive system is to improve the efficiency and effectiveness of a **user's performance** in his or her job, where performance is defined as the *time and effort expended to complete tasks*. To improve performance, we must first know both how to measure it and what factors affect or determine it. With this knowledge, we can measure current performance, manipulate the identified determinants, and then measure the change in performance to confirm that improvement has occurred. This section describes some basic determinants of user behavior that are relevant to interactive system designers.

User performance may be described in terms of a number of general determinants, including

the human information processing system,
the user's psychological characteristics,
the user's knowledge and experience,
the user's job and tasks,
the user's physical characteristics,
the user's physical environment, and
the user's tools.

The first determinant tends to be relatively *constant* across individuals, while the last six may *vary* significantly across user groups or individuals. The first five are *internal* to the user (that is, characteristics of the user), while the last two are *external* to the user (characteristics of the environment). From the software designer's point of view, the first six are predetermined, while the last is under the designer's control. In the balance of this chapter, each behavioral determinant is discussed in turn.

THE HUMAN INFORMATION PROCESSING SYSTEM

Introduction

The most basic determinant of user performance is the information processing capabilities of the human mind. Understanding how people think, reason, learn, and communicate is critical to designing interactive systems to facilitate the **cognitive** (that is, the human information processing) tasks that involve these processes.

A simple and useful overview of the human information processing system can be gained by constructing a model based on an analogy between it and an already familiar information processing system: the computer. Figure 2-1 summarizes some of the similarities between models of the two systems.

Each system can be conceived of in terms of memory structures (storage), input and output devices, and basic processes. Computers have several types of **memory** structures. The primary memory component is known as **main memory.** This is where programs in execution and the intermediate results of operations are stored. Smaller memory buffers called **registers** actually carry out operations and store immediate results. **Hard disks** represent permanent internal memory buffers in a computer system.

The human mind is believed to have a similar set of memory components. In our model, the counterpart of registers is called **short-term memory,** or working memory. This is where conscious thought occurs. Here we perform calculations, interpret incoming data, and juggle information as we solve problems.

Permanent memory is called **long-term memory.** Here we remember everything that ever happened to us and all the information and skills we have learned over a lifetime.

Intermediate-term memory is the human counterpart to main memory. As in a computer, some part of our memory system keeps track of the problem-solving process we are currently executing by storing intermediate results of operations and remembering and modifying future plans.

Consider a person playing chess. In *long-term memory* are stored all the rules of chess and many experiences from past chess games. *Intermediate-term memory* keeps track of where one is in the current game, what future moves are planned, and what one has learned about one's opponent's likely behavior in this game. In

Basic Information
Processing Components

	COMPUTER	HUMAN
MEMORIES:	**Registers**	**Short-term memory**
	Main memory	**Intermediate-memory**
	Disks	**Long-term Memory**
	Tape, cards, optical disks	**Books, pictures**
INPUT DEVICES:	**Keyboard**	**Eyes**
	Touch screen	**Ears**
	Voice recognizer	**Touch**
	Mouse	
OUTPUT DEVICES:	**Screen**	**Hands**
	Voice synthesizer	**Voice**
	Printer	**Eyes**
PROCESSES:	**Operating system**	**Executive control unit**
	Compiler	**Pattern recognition**
	Applications	**Knowledge and skills**

Figure 2–1   The computer and human information processing systems.

short-term memory, calculations are performed to formulate the best move at the present time.

In fact, research has not been able to locate distinct, physical locations in the brain corresponding to these three types of memory buffers. They really are probably not distinct buffers at all, but rather represent the characteristics of one unified memory process that emerge under different learning conditions. Different theories of human memory have been put forth and are currently under debate (see Hitch, 1987, and Gardiner, 1987, for good reviews of memory research). However, there is ample experimental data establishing the constraints and capabilities of human memory, and the model of three different memory buffers is a simple and convenient one for our purposes.

Finally, people use external memory aids, such as books and pictures, analogous to tapes, diskettes, and cards on a computer system.

The **input and output devices** of the typical computer system include keyboards and other input devices such as a mouse or touch screen, a screen, and a printer. People also have input and output devices. We take in information from the world around us through the sensory organs of sight, hearing, touch, taste, and smell. We communicate with and manipulate the outside world with our hands, voice, and eyes. In one emerging technology, the user's eyes serve as an output device. Screen elements actually detect and respond to the position of the user's gaze.

Finally, each system has basic **information processes.** A computer has an **operating system** that controls all other processes. Similarly, the human mind must have a basic controlling process, which we might call the **executive control unit.** In a computer, a **compiler** translates information received through the input devices into an interpretable form. Similarly, we have a **pattern recognition system,** which serves the same purpose. Finally, whereas a computer system is provided with specific **applications software,** people acquire specific **knowledge and skills** that can be applied to new problems and modified in response to new learning experiences.

Although this is a greatly simplified model of human information processing, and perhaps even a bit misleading in that there are many important differences between computers and people, it is a reasonable way to introduce a computer scientist to human cognition and provides a useful model of the user for the software designer to keep in mind.

Like a computer information processing system, limited resources are available in the human information processing system, and processing is impeded when demands on these resources exceed supply. Baecker and Buxton (1987) provide a useful overview of the behavior of the human information processing system under conditions when task demands require more resources than are available. This overview is summarized and paraphrased here.

Cognitive resources include *working memory capacity* and various information processes (for example *attention* and *memory retrieval*). A given task is said to be **resource limited** if applying additional cognitive resources would improve task performance. For instance, a task that required concentrated attention or overextended working memory capacity would be said to be *resource limited*.

A task is said to be **data limited** if performance cannot be improved by providing additional resources, but only by improving the quality or quantity of available data. For example, a problem-solving or decision-making task might simply not be doable without additional or better information. Data might be missing or of poor quality in *long-term memory,* in which case we refer to **memory data limits** (for example, a lack of key information). Or, data might be in a low-quality form (or just plain missing) from the available *outside resources,* in which case we refer to **signal data limits** (for example, static on the phone line).

Resource and data limitations in the performance of a task interact in that, up to a certain point, task performance is improved by dedicating more cognitive resources to it, but after the supply of resources has been exhausted, only relief from data limitations will continue to produce improvements in performance. The implications of this for software user interface designers is as follows:

> In virtually all cases a primary design objective should be to *minimize resource consumption by improving the quality of the data.* Improved display quality and graphic design are techniques for pushing back signal data limits. Training and the use of appropriate mental models are means to push back memory data limits (Baecker and Buxton, 1987).

Cognitive resources are limited, and often when more than one task is presented simultaneously, degradation in the performance of one or more tasks occurs due to the competition for critical resources. This is known as **interference.** Sometimes all tasks suffer equally, but more often tasks with higher priority continue at the expense of the others.

People using computers are always performing at least two types of tasks: **functional** tasks, which have to do with the *content* of the problem at hand, and **operational** tasks, which have to do with the *means* of solving the problem, in this case, interacting with the user interface to the system. These two tasks will compete for cognitive resources and, if both are too demanding, will interfere with one another, thus degrading the performance of one or both and of the interaction overall.

Designers can optimize user performance by *designing interfaces that will demand minimal cognitive resources to perform operational tasks* (for example, by designing in consistency, standardizing interfaces across systems, and exploiting metaphors), and they can also *minimize the cognitive resources and maximize the quality of the available data required to perform the functional tasks* (for example, by applying principles of screen design or organizing functionality well).

Designers can also seek to minimize interference between tasks by *drawing upon different sensory modalities that utilize different processes.* For example, the use of voice or other sounds to draw attention in an otherwise visual and text-based interface will be more effective, because processing pictures, text, and sound do not draw upon the same processes and resources.

Finally, **skilled task performance** is overlearned, automatic behavior that differs from **problem-solving performance** in that it consumes negligible cognitive resources (for example, attention or conscious thought). Skilled performance is thus much less susceptible to interference than is problem solving. Consistent user interfaces improve performance by *allowing for faster development of skilled performance and by keeping the number of required skills to a minimum.* Interface designers can also exploit existing skills (for example, typing on the use of similar systems) in designing a new interface. These design techniques will improve overall performance on a system.

Designers should keep in mind this overview of the behavior of the human information processing system under different task demands when designing user interfaces.

The analogy between the computer and human information processing systems can be considered in still another way. Consider Figure 2-2, which represents the interaction between a computer and a human user. Each is an information processing system, represented by a circle. The interface between them is represented by the intersection of the two circles. As the two systems carry on a dialog, control is passed back and forth between them. On each side, the interaction can be conceived of in terms of three separate phases of information processing: read–scan, think, and respond.

First consider the computer, probably the more familiar information processing system to most readers of this book. When the user makes a response, such as a key press or mouse click, the system must first *recognize and interpret* the input. Usually, software modules called device handlers perform this function. This we will call the **read–scan phase.**

Then the input is *processed* according to the main algorithms of the application program. Files may be created or modified, calculations performed, or new data generated. This we will call the **think phase.**

Finally, *output is sent back* to the user in the **respond phase.** Displays may be presented, files sent to a printer, or sound output emitted. Usually, separate, specialized software modules handle formatting output to the screen or printer.

Now that the system has produced some output, control is passed back to the user. And the user's interaction with this output can be described in the same three phases. First, the user must *recognize and interpret* what has been displayed. This usually means reading text on the screen, but may also mean interpreting graphic displays or voice output. This is the **read–scan phase** of the human response. Then

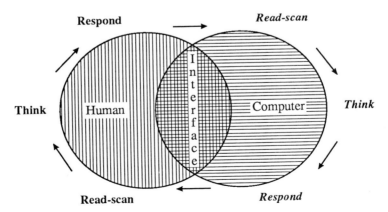

Figure 2–2   A three-phased model of computer–human interaction.

the user must *decide what to do* with the recognized output. Decisions are made, intentions formed, and actions planned. This is the **think phase.** Finally, the user must *respond* with some action to provide the system with new input to act upon. Keys are pressed, pointers moved, and commands issued. This is the **respond phase.**

What is important about this three-phase model of human–computer interaction is that, although all three phases contribute to the overall time it takes for the user to respond to computer output during a task, as designers we often *focus on one and fail to consider the impact of our design on the other two.*

For instance, designers of command languages tend to focus on minimizing keystrokes. Thus, command abbreviations are designed to require only one or two keystrokes so that time will not be wasted entering lengthy commands and making and recovering from typos. While it is true that shorter command names optimize the *respond phase* by minimizing keystrokes, they may also have an impact on the other two phases of human processing. Short command names are usually less **mnemonic,** that is, less easy to learn, remember and recognize, than longer ones. Thus, although the *respond phase* is optimized, the *think phase* and the *read–scan phase* may suffer. Users may take more time to remember commands or may even need to look them up in a manual because they cannot remember them. This might be true both during entering and in reading or reviewing past command entries. For some types of users (for example, low-frequency users), the added time recalling and recognizing commands may in fact be greater than the time saved in keystrokes. Thus, the *overall* time to enter or read a command may be increased, rather than decreased, by shorter command names. The designer has focused on optimizing a single phase of human response, whereas *the relevant measure is the total response time in all three phases.*

As another example, consider the trade-off between a menu hierarchy that has many choices on each screen, but only a few levels in the hierarchy, and a hierarchy that has many fewer choices on each screen, but more levels in the hierarchy. In the former case, the *read–scan phase* may be increased as users try to search through very busy screens for the desired choice, although the *respond phase* may be decreased because users need to respond to less screens. In the latter case, the opposite is true. The *read–scan phase* is facilitated by simpler screens with less choices to scan, while the *respond phase* is increased because there are more screens to respond to. Again, the different design options have different effects on the different phases of processing, and this must be taken into account when choosing an optimal design. The designer must keep in mind the *total task time,* rather than the efficiency of *simple, isolated operations,* when making design decisions. Keeping this simple three-phase model of the human response in mind will help the designer to remember this.

The three phases of processing presented in Figure 2-2 and just discussed in fact correspond to three major subsystems of the human information processing system: the **perceptual system** (read–scan), the **cognitive system** (think), and the **motor system** (respond). These are illustrated in Figure 2-3 and described next,

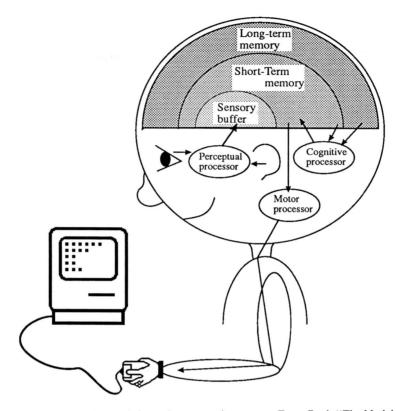

Figure 2–3 The human information processing system. From Card, "The Model Human Processor: A Model for Making Engineering Calculations of Human Performance," *Proceedings of the Human Factors Society 25th Annual Meeting,* 1981, 301–5. © 1981, by the Human Factors Society Inc. Reprinted with permission. All rights reserved.

with particular emphasis on the implications of the properties of each subsystem for user interface design.

The Perceptual System

The perceptual system may be discussed in terms of *memory structures* and *information processes*.

Memory Structures

Information first enters the human system through the sensory organs. One type of memory buffer is the **sensory buffer.** Its purpose is to hold a fixed image of the outside world within the system long enough for some analysis to be performed on it. This is especially important with auditory signals (sounds, such as speech) because they are frequently very short in duration. It is often important for visual signals as well because they do not always remain conveniently in our line of vision for study.

The sensory buffers hold a virtual, uninterpreted image of the external signal. That is, coding in the sensory buffers is *hard-wired,* or fixed. These buffers can hold a high level of detail, but the memory trace has a very short life: it decays very quickly (on the order of tenths of a second).

Processes

Information from the sensory buffers travels to the brain (at a rate of about 4.3 million bits per second), where successive levels of processing occur. At higher levels of processing, the image from the sensory buffers is recoded in a learned, rather than fixed, way by drawing upon the information stored in long-term memory. For instance, as you read your brain successively analyzes a signal of lines and angles as letters, words, phrases, sentences, and meaning. Once it is learned, this processing is automatic and primarily unconscious. Again, the memory buffers at this stage of processing hold a high level of detail but decay very quickly.

By the time familiar or recognizable information reaches our consciousness (short-term or working memory), it has thus undergone a very complicated process of analysis that we call *pattern recognition.* Human pattern recognition is an extremely complex and powerful process, which artificial intelligence experts have only barely begun to be able to simulate with computers. Consider the fact that you are able to recognize speech in your native language across enormous variations in tone, speed, accent and grammatical deviations, even when there is significant noise (for example, static on the radio) in the signal. Human pattern recognition is not a simple matter of matching a pattern in the signal to a template in memory; *it makes heavy use of context and knowledge.* It is a highly active type of processing, rather than passive or receptive, and is able to tolerate both ambiguity and incompleteness in incoming information. In the words of Baecker and Buxton (1987), ''The perceptual mechanism is not a sponge that simply soaks up stimuli. It is an active process that involves cognition. . . . We can't hear without listening, and we can't see without looking.''

To get a feel for the power of your pattern recognition capabilities, consider Figure 2-4. In the upper-left configuration, if you read across the row, you will have no trouble recognizing the number 13 in the middle. If you read down the column, you will recognize the middle letter as a B. In spite of the fact that the middle symbol is the same in both cases, the surrounding context helps you interpret the symbol in two very different ways. This you do unconsciously, without necessarily even noticing the ambiguity. In the second example in Figure 2-4, a single symbol is read as an H or an A, again depending on the surrounding context.

Now read the sentences in the upper half of Figure 2-5. Each pair of sentences is preceded by a sentence (in bold) that is ambiguous in meaning. Note that you

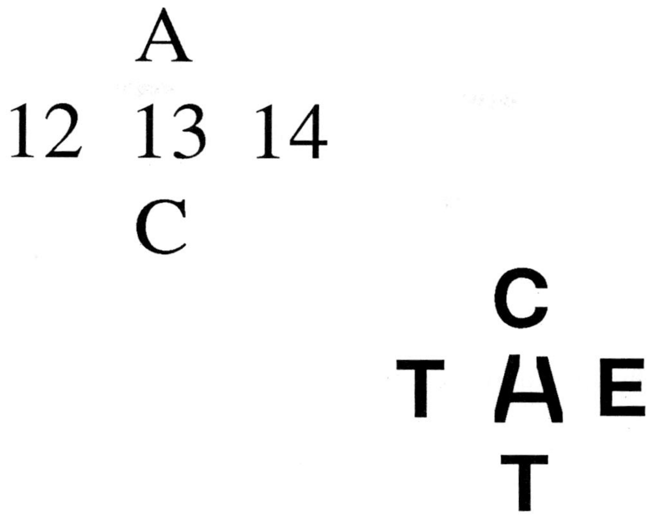

A

12 13 14

C

C
T A E
T

Figure 2–4   Pattern recognition.

We found a bat lying by a tree.

1.   We were playing baseball yesterday.

2.   We were studying rodents in science class and went on a field trip.

Fighting tigers can be dangerous.

1.   Have you ever fought with a tiger?

2.   Have you ever seen two tigers fighting?

"How is bread made?"
"I know that!" Alice cried eagerly. "You take some flour -"
"Where do you pick the flower?" the white queen asked.
"In a garden, or in the hedges?"
"Well, it isn't picked at all," Alice explained: "its ground -"
"How many acres of ground?" said the white queen.

Lewis Carroll, *Through the Looking Glass*

Figure 2–5   Pattern recognition.

interpret the ambiguous sentence differently depending upon which sentence in the pair follows. These examples illustrate that the context that allows us to resolve ambiguities in language is often received *after* the ambiguous information. Our system operates in such a way that the interpretation of incoming information can be partially suspended until additional information is received. Yet we are often not consciously aware of this fact. This points to the importance of the memory buffers involved, as well as to the sophistication of the pattern recognition process.

The quote from Lewis Carroll in Figure 2-5 plays upon the fact that human language is extremely ambiguous and that our interpretation of it depends highly on context. Our ability to use context to resolve ambiguities in turn depends on a very powerful and flexible pattern recognition system.

The Perceptual System: Implications for User Interface Design

Communicating with a commercial software system can be very frustrating for a user because the system's pattern recognition abilities are so much more primitive than the user's. The average system treats trivial typos, which a human probably would not even have been conscious of, as major semantic deviations from recognizable patterns. It is relatively unable to tolerate errors, ambiguity, incompleteness, and noise. If the user types in "Delate file," the system will respond "Unrecognized command."

A command language could use context to interpret simple typos. If the user typed "Delate file" by mistake, instead of giving an error message the system might respond with "DELATE: Did you mean DELETE? Y or N." With enough memory and a little bit of "intelligence," a computer might be able to respond to what a user *means,* as opposed to what a user *says.* This will make the interaction feel more natural to users.

An even more intelligent user interface would make more use of context in interpreting input, the way humans do. For instance, a command language could make use of defaults established by previous interactions. If the user had specified a file or object in a previous command, and then issued a command that required a file or object as a parameter but did not supply one, the system could assume the user meant the file or object last referred to. This is what a human would do in conversation with another human.

The Cognitive System

Like the perceptual system, the cognitive system can also be described in terms of *memory structures* and information *processes.*

Memory Structures

By the time information in the system reaches working or *short-term memory* (STM), it has been recognized (assuming that it is nonnovel, recognizable information). STM is a memory buffer with an extremely low capacity (7 ± 2 units) and only moderate trace duration (a matter of seconds). Consider how hard it is to remember an unfamiliar telephone number long enough to dial it. It is only seven to ten digits, yet the only way we can remember it is to rehearse it over and over again in our mind. Often we still cannot remember it long enough and must refer back to the phone book while we dial.

STM is not only a storage buffer, but also a processor; it is where we perform conscious mental operations, that is, where we think. It is a very slow processor, relative to the rate at which information is arriving from the sensory buffers: it receives information about 100,000 times faster than it can process it. Consider how long it might take you to add two 3-digit numbers in your head, compared to a calculator or computer. Not only does it take time, but you will likely make errors because you are also taxing STM capacity. You must keep in mind not only the six digits, but also parts of the solution and numbers you carry as you add.

The limited capacity and duration of STM is the major bottleneck in the human information processing system. We cope with this serious constraint by *organizing information into meaningful patterns*. Groups of associated information are treated as single units in STM, so we can hold more information here if it is meaningful and organized.

Consider the relative ease of remembering the following two phone numbers: 683-4952 versus 111-2222. The second is easier to remember, because instead of being seven unassociated units of information, it is really only three units: two numbers and a rule for generating the sequence. Or consider how much easier it is to add 100 plus 100 in your head than 429 plus 697. The nature of a *unit* of information is thus dynamic; that is, many units become a single unit if they can be associated in some meaningful way.

These characteristics of STM have major ramifications for the way we perform almost all higher-level mental processes. Since the primary channel for information to enter long-term memory is through STM, significant limits are imposed on the rate at which we learn and the way we solve problems. Because of the limited capacity of STM and the increased capacity if information is meaningful and well organized, the human mind has a natural tendency to seek meaning and patterns in the outside world. Stereotypes, superstitions, and other simplistic theories about causality in the natural world are all ways the human mind copes with a world whose complexity taxes its basic information processing capabilities.

Other known characteristics of human short-term memory are reviewed and summarized in Hitch (1987) and Gardiner (1987). Some of these may be paraphrased as follows:

1. Letters or words that rhyme are particularly difficult to differentiate in STM.
2. Even small, manageable amounts of information will be lost from STM in a matter of seconds if that interval is filled with distracting information or activity.
3. The rate of forgetting from STM increases with the complexity of the distracting task or activity.

4. The rate of forgetting from STM increases as the amount of information to be remembered increases.

5. The rate of forgetting from STM increases when similar material has recently been stored.

6. Recall from STM of names of items is usually better when they are presented as pictures, rather than words.

7. The probability of recall from STM increases as a function of the depth and elaborateness of processing at the time of encoding.

8. The older the user (especially after around 55), the less information can be held in STM.

Past the bottleneck in the system of STM lies an extremely powerful storage buffer and processor: our *long-term memory* (LTM). In contrast to other memory buffers in the system, LTM is both essentially *unlimited in capacity* and *permanent in duration*. We never in our lifetime become unable to store something new in LTM, and all evidence suggests that memory traces in this buffer do not decay.

In addition, information is stored in a *very rich, complex, and dynamic structure,* allowing constant reorganization to accommodate new information and learning and providing access to information through many different pathways or "keys." For instance, a given concept such as "game" may be retrieved based on an example (for example, tennis), a definition, a rhyming word (for example, "tame"), or associated objects (for example, a tennis racket). These cues or keys may be presented visually, auditorially, or verbally (for example, watching people play a game, hearing the sounds of a game, or reading the words game or tame).

On the other hand, both storage and retrieval processes are *slow, unreliable, and difficult.* Often we simply cannot remember (retrieve) something we know is there (such as someone's name or a movie title), and it generally requires effort and concentration to get things into LTM in the first place (to learn new information). It does appear that, in general, *information more frequently accessed is easier and faster to retrieve than information that is accessed only occasionally or has not been accessed in a long time.* In spite of its shortcomings, the structure and processes of LTM represent one of the most powerful resources of the human information processing system.

Other known characteristics of human long-term memory are reviewed and summarized in Gardiner (1987). Some of these can be paraphrased as follows:

1. The probability of retrieval of information from LTM increases as a function of the match between the cues and context present at the time of storage and the cues and context available at the time of recall.

2. The greater the compatibility between the operations carried out to store information and the operations carried out to retrieve it, the greater is the probability of successful recall.

3. If information stored in LTM was generated in response to some cue or rule,

as opposed to simply being read or seen, it is more likely to be successfully recalled.

4. Recall from LTM for dynamically interacting information is better than for independent, isolated information.

5. The more distinct and unique the information stored in LTM is, the greater the probability that it will be successfully recalled.

6. Recall from LTM is better for pictures than for words and is better for visualizable words than for nonvisualizable words.

Memory Structures: Implications for User Interface Design

Several implications for software user interface design result from the known properties of short- and long-term memory. Consider the low capacity and fast decay of short-term memory. This suggests that one should avoid requiring users to remember transient information as they move from screen to screen and avoid requiring complex translations and mental operations. The use of defaults, point-and-select mechanisms, and a WYSIWYG ("what you see is what you get") interface will help minimize the burdens on short-term memory. For instance, if a system allows users to point to and select file names on a directory screen and then enters them as defaults in fill-in fields on other screens, the user will not have to remember a file name while navigating from the directory screen to the fill-in screen. A system that displays different fonts and actual page breaks on the screen, rather than cryptic codes that users must translate to calculate spacing and paging on printouts, will not tax the low capacity and duration of short-term memory.

Also consider the phenomenon of "**chunking**," the fact that associations, meaning, patterns, and order in information facilitate learning and memory. This suggests that patterns and organization in screen design will facilitate recognition and comprehension and that consistency and analogy across an interface will facilitate learning.

Examples of the implications of other characteristics of human short-term memory are given next:

> *Characteristic:* Letters or words that rhyme are particularly difficult to differentiate in STM.
>
> *Implications:* Design labels (menu choice labels, captions, and the like) and names (icon names, command names, parameter names, and others) to be phonemically distinct, that is, distinctive in sound. For instance "Delete" and "Repeat" sound very similar, and may be confusable in short-term memory. "Get" and "Set" would be another example. "Erase" and "Repeat" and "Find" and "Set" might be better choices for tasks in which users must hold the name in memory while they navigate from one screen to another.
>
> *Characteristic:* Even small, manageable amounts of information will be lost

from STM in a matter of seconds if that interval is filled with distracting information or activity.

Implications: Minimize STM requirements when interactions must occur while information is being held in STM.

Characteristic: The rate of forgetting from STM increases with the complexity of the distracting task or activity.

Implications: Eliminate STM requirements when users must perform complex, nonroutine interactions with the system. Simplify interactions so that when users must hold information in STM, other requirements taxing STM are minimized.

Characteristic: The rate of forgetting from STM increases as the amount of information to be remembered increases.

Implications: Keep STM storage requirements at any given time to a minimum.

Characteristic: The rate of forgetting from STM increases when similar material has recently been stored.

Implications: Avoid taxing STM when highly repetitive tasks are being performed.

Characteristic: Recall from STM of names of items is usually better when they are presented as pictures, rather than words.

Implications: Add visual cues (for example, color) and icons to information that must be temporarily held in STM during interactions.

Characteristic: The probability of recall from STM increases as a function of the depth and elaborateness of processing at the time of encoding.

Implications: Avoid overtaxing short-term memory in simple transcription tasks (for example, data entry). The more important the meaning and details of information are in the task, the more users will be able to handle STM requirements.

Characteristic: The older the user (especially after around 55), the less information can be held in STM.

Implications: Be particularly sensitive to STM requirements in interfaces where a significant part of the user population is expected to be older.

Remembering that retrieval from long-term memory is slow and unreliable but facilitated by frequency of access, the designer will want to consider frequency of use in design decisions. If users are expected to be casual, low-frequency users, then memory aids such as prompting, on-screen instructions, on-line help, and menus should be designed into the interface. Given the rich, redundant, multi-keyed nature of long-term memory, the designer might use redundant cues for coding information on the screen, such as names, shapes, and colors. Icons with names provide richer information than icons or names alone. Adding color can facilitate recognition even more.

Examples of the implications of other characteristics of human long-term memory are as follows:

Characteristic: The probability of retrieval of information from LTM increases as a function of the match between the cues and context present at the time of storage and the cues and context available at the time of recall.

Implications: Structure training and learning experiences (for example, in manuals and on-line tutorials) to closely match real tasks. For instance, teach through example tasks, and teach users about operations in the order in which they are likely to be used.

Characteristic: The greater the compatibility between the operations carried out to store information and the operations carried out to retrieve it, the greater is the probability of successful recall.

Implications: Structure training and learning experiences so that users learn by doing, rather than just by reading about, operations.

Characteristic: If information stored in LTM was generated in response to some cue or rule, as opposed to simply being read or seen, it is more likely to be successfully recalled.

Implications: In training manuals, explicitly point out to users the rules of consistency behind the design of the interface. For instance, if all command name abbreviations are formed by simple truncation and editable fields always appear in bold, specifically point these rules out to users in the manual or training program.

Characteristic: Recall from LTM for dynamically interacting information is better than for independent, isolated information.

Implications: Teach users about operations in the context of some total, meaningful task in which all the operations interact to accomplish some goal. Do not simply teach users about operations in some random order so that the relationships between them are not obvious.

Characteristic: The more distinct and unique the information stored in LTM is, the greater the probability that it will be successfully recalled.

Implications: Design distinctiveness into the interface. Use colors maximally distant on the color spectrum, design names and labels to be distinctive in both sound and in keystroke sequence, make screens with different functions look visually distinct, and so on. This does *not* mean to avoid consistency. It means that when there *are* important differences these should be made distinct and easy to discriminate between.

Characteristic: Recall from LTM is better for pictures than for words and is better for visualizable words than for nonvisualizable words.

Implications: Use icons and visual cues when possible. Use concrete rather than abstract words.

Processes

Four primary processes of the cognitive system are of interest to the interactive systems designer. We have discussed how the human *perceptual* system recognizes familiar information (*pattern recognition*). The *cognitive* system includes processes that allow us to **attend selectively** to incoming information, **learn** new information, **solve problems,** and communicate with others through human **language.** The way these higher functions are carried out is determined and constrained by the basic characteristics of the system as described previously. Here we will briefly summarize a few details on each of these processes that are relevant when designing interactive systems.

Selective attention.   Because short-term memory is so limited in capacity and processing speed relative to the rate and detail of incoming information, the system has to have a way of selecting what to store and process or it would quickly be overwhelmed and incapacitated. Thus we have a process called **selective attention,** which acts as a sort of switch on incoming channels. It is not, however, a low-level switch that simply blocks information channels at the sensory level. Rather, it seems to be located very high up in the processing system, somewhere near the level of consciousness or STM.

We are able, for instance, to have a conversation in the middle of a very noisy cocktail party and be relatively unconscious of all the other conversations going on around us. That is, we can *voluntarily* focus our attention on signals of interest to us by tuning out irrelevant signals in the environment. However, if someone across the room speaks our name in a normal tone of voice, we usually hear it; it grabs our attention *involuntarily*. For this to have happened, we must have *unconsciously* been processing *all* the other conversations in the room at a **semantic** level (the level of meaning). This is a very powerful and adaptive mechanism, which allows us to concentrate our limited cognitive resources on a single important channel while monitoring most of our immediate surroundings for other high-priority (salient or novel) signals.

Selective attention: Implications for user interface design.   Given the *voluntary* nature of selective attention, we can design screens so as to facilitate this process. By using different visual attributes such as boldface, reverse video, color, case, and font, we can help users focus on types of information according to their attributes. For instance, if captions are always in bold and fields always in plain text, users will be more easily able to scan through captions while ignoring fields or scan through fields while ignoring captions. *Salient visual cues facilitate the selective attention mechanism.*

Considering the *involuntary* nature of attention, we can employ particularly salient visual and aural attributes to draw attention when this is important. For instance, blinking and beeping are particularly powerful attention-getting mechanisms. They can be used to *involuntarily* draw a user's attention to important messages on the screen, regardless of his or her current *voluntary* focus of attention.

Recent work in modeling attentional processes during computer-human interaction (Zachary, 1989) is being applied to the design of interfaces that anticipate and support the user's changing focus of attention during problem solving (Zubritzky, Zachary, and Ryder, 1989).

Learning.   The term **learning** encompasses a wide variety of phenomena from rote memorization to complex rule learning to the acquisition of complex mental or motor skills. Learning how to use an interactive system includes many of these phenomena. A user must *memorize* the vocabulary of the command language, *learn the concepts and rules* that relate the command language to the various functions of his or her task, and *acquire the motor skills* for efficiently operating the terminal.

Learning is facilitated by analogy. That is, if users can see some relationship between new information and information they are already familiar with, this will make it easier to learn and remember the new information. For instance, it is easier to learn a new programming language if you are already familiar with another programming language. On the other hand, the tendency to seek analogies is so strong that sometimes users will apply prior knowledge to situations where it is not really relevant (Carroll and Rosson, 1987).

Learning is also facilitated by structure and organization. This is due to the property of short-term memory discussed previously. When information can be viewed as a few associated pieces of information, rather than many unassociated pieces of information, it is easier to store that information in short-term memory. To get into long-term memory, information usually must pass through short-term memory (the exception is known as *incidental learning*). Thus, anything that facilitates short-term memory also facilitates learning.

Finally, *learning is facilitated if new information is presented in incremental, independent units,* that is, if information can be learned a little bit at a time at the learner's own pace.

Learning: Implications for user interface design.   Remembering that learning is facilitated by analogy, structure, and organization, we will want to design an interface that draws upon the user's current knowledge and skills as much as possible and presents information in a simple, well-organized way. We will want to avoid arbitrary or jargonlike function names and unnecessary new concepts, and we must not require that the user remember too much from one step in the system to the next. For example, the desktop metaphor for a filing and retrieval system draws upon the familiar analogy of office filing systems and the familiar operations of opening files and moving objects from file to file. The user does not need to learn new jargon or new concepts for computer filing mechanisms.

On the other hand, if making a software interface perfectly true to a metaphor from the manual world means failing to exploit the potential power of the computer, then this is probably not an appropriate goal. The design technique of metaphor must be applied intelligently (see Carroll and Rosson, 1987, and also Chapter 3 of this text).

Because information usually must be processed in STM to be effectively stored in LTM (learned) and because of the limited capacity of STM, information to be learned is best broken down into small, coherent units. This implies that system functions should be relatively independent (for example, the user should be able to learn and use the "Move" function without having to know about or understand the concept of "Supermove"), so that users never have to learn more than they immediately need to know. Learning is greatly facilitated if the user can learn small pieces of information and then continuously build upon and add to that core knowledge (Hampton, 1987). Consistency in the user interface and the use of mnemonic aids will also facilitate learning.

On the other hand, keep in mind that, although STM places constraints on the user's ability to quickly learn a set of complex, detailed information, other aspects of the human information processing system, such as the powerful pattern recognition system and the structure and capacity of LTM, mean that the human mind is capable of learning large amounts of very complex information. The key is presenting information in a manner that does not overtax memory and processing capabilities. If the information is presented in an organized and coherent manner, the mind expends less effort in organizing the information to facilitate memory and can thus expend more effort in simply comprehending and storing the information.

Work is currently being conducted to investigate how people learn to use computer systems in particular. Carroll and Rosson (1987) make two observations about users learning computer systems:

1. Users focus on getting a job done rather than on learning to effectively and efficiently use a system per se.
2. Users apply prior knowledge from what they see as analogous problems, even when it does not apply.

They suggest three strategies for accommodating these tendencies. To deal with job focus, they suggest (1) finding ways to make learning intrinsically rewarding, (2) making the system easy to learn, and (3) using user's goals to structure and drive the learning process. To deal with the tendency to use analogy, they suggest (1) explicitly discouraging the perception of inappropriate analogies in the interface, (2) building a complete and true metaphor into the interface, and (3) using a metaphor but departing from it when this can be accommodated easily by users. Carroll and Rosson point out shortcomings and disadvantages to each of these approaches, but their work represents progress toward a better understanding of the strategies users apply when learning about new systems and applying this understanding to the design of better learning environments.

Problem solving.   Problem solving is related to learning; however, it implies not only the storage of new information in LTM, but also the application of general knowledge stored in LTM to particular tasks or problems. Playing chess, solving algebraic equations, making marketing decisions, and creating documents on a word processing system are all examples of problem solving. They involve the application of known, general rules to a particular instance of a class of related problems.

The first time we encounter a problem from a new and unfamiliar class of problems (for example, our first encounter with a word processing system), we naturally draw upon our experiences with analogous situations (for example, typing). The strategies we use thus tend to be a function of the experiences we have had, and since we all have very different experiences, there are usually as many ways to solve a problem as there are people trying to solve it. In fact, there is very little that we can say about human problem-solving behavior that is general across people.

However, three general and related statements that are of relevance to interactive system designers can be made about human problem-solving behavior. First, *people are more often* **heuristic** *than* **algorithmic** *in their problem-solving strategies,* particularly in more complex problems. This is because, although *algorithms* guarantee solutions while *heuristics* do not, algorithms usually are very time consuming and often require more memory capacity and other cognitive resources than are available (resource limited tasks). Since the human mind is short on working memory capacity and speed, we often gamble that a heuristic will pay off, because it is potentially less expensive (in terms of cognitive resources) to execute.

For instance, when people play chess, they do not generate in their minds elaborate trees of possible moves and countermoves (an *algorithmic* strategy), computing the probable success of each, as computer programs do. Even if the player were allowed pencil and paper (to circumvent the limited capacity of STM), the time required to perform these calculations would probably exceed acceptable game behavior. So, instead, people use a variety of *heuristic* strategies, from remembering successful moves in similar situations, to guessing about what their opponent is likely to be aware of, and thinking through a few, hopefully representative, possible scenarios.

Second, humans do not always choose optimal problem-solving strategies, even when these strategies are available to them. People make decisions regarding the relative importance of a problem and the relative expense of different strategies and *often choose suboptimal strategies for lower-priority problems,* simply because the time and resources required to execute superior strategies are not available (resource limited tasks). For instance, a person may *estimate* their current tax status in order to make investment decisions, because *calculating* their tax status to the penny is not important enough for making a good investment decision to merit the extra effort required.

On the other hand, the third general point about human problem solving is that there is a *natural ability and tendency to learn better strategies with practice*. This applies to motor and perceptual processes as well as to mental or cognitive processes. People become better chess players the more games they play. They become better piano players the more often they practice. And they get better at recognizing symbols and other visual cues (as in an air-traffic control system) the more often they use them.

Problem solving: Implications for user interface design.   Because of the tendency of humans to be *heuristic* rather than *algorithmic* problem solvers, an interactive system that blindly forces a user to execute algorithmic procedures over and over again will quickly cause boredom and frustration. Systems should be flexible and allow shortcuts for experienced users. A robust system with good "help" capabilities will encourage users to experiment.

Because users will often adopt the first way they discover to do something, the system should make efficient strategies as visible as possible. An *active* help or **suggestions system,** as opposed to a *passive* help system may be useful. A suggestions system would note when users are consistently using inefficient strategies and suggest more efficient ones. For instance, such a system might note when users are consistently using the "Delete" and "Insert" commands in sequence and would suggest the "Replace" command. Or it might note that the user is doing a lot of smooth scrolling and suggest the "Search" command. This will allow users to become more efficient without requiring them to take the initiative, which they simply might not be motivated enough to do.

A suggestions system is a tricky thing to implement well, because not every user will appreciate interruptions that might seem judgmental and may in fact at times be inappropriate. A suggestions system is a good idea only if it is under user control and can be turned off and on as the individual user desires.

A good interactive system should not require more effort to learn than is merited by the problem to be solved. If it does, no matter how powerful a tool it is, it will be underutilized or not used at all. To avoid this, designers should have a good understanding of the user's job and how the task that the system is intended to facilitate fits into that job. For instance, executives might be willing to invest a considerable amount of time in learning a support system for making better high-level marketing decisions, but not in learning an electronic calendar. Designers must consider the level of task importance when designing interfaces to such systems.

Finally, given that users inevitably improve with practice, interfaces must be flexible enough to accommodate both novices and experts and to allow the transition from the former to the latter as smoothly as possible. Alternative interfaces, bypasses, and shortcuts provide this kind of flexibility.

Language.   What is known both about the structure of natural language and the ways in which we use it to communicate can be effectively applied to designing successful communications between people and information systems. Human language has particular structural properties that are related to the basic characteristics of the human information processing system. First, it is *rule based*. This is adaptive to the STM constraints of the system. For instance, instead of remembering entirely different words to express tense or plurality, we need only remember (in most cases) the base word and the rule for generating tenses or plurals. Learning language, which involves STM, is thus greatly facilitated.

Related to this property, human language is **productive.** That is, an infinite number of grammatically correct and meaningful utterances are possible, given a finite sets of vocabulary words and grammatical rules. We can generate grammatically correct sentences that we have never heard or spoken because of the consistent underlying structure of the language.

Third, syntax and semantics are related in a **keyword** as well as in a **positional** grammar. That is, we analyze the grammatical structure of sentences as much by recognizing the grammatical category of words as by the position of words in the sentence. For instance, we can understand the two sentences "Tom hit the ball" and "The ball was hit by Tom" to mean essentially the same thing in spite of the different position of subject and object in the two sentences, because we recognize "hit" and "was hit by" as grammatically different entities. Of course, there are some important positional rules or at least tendencies in human languages. But a keywordlike structure is an important aspect of natural grammars.

Besides what is known about the structure of natural languages, much is also known about the ways in which people use language to communicate. This is summarized in Hampton (1987) and paraphrased in part as follows:

1. It is natural for people to use a *variety of ways to say the same thing*.
2. Intention is most clearly communicated by following the basic conventions of *relevance, truthfulness, informativeness,* and *clarity*. Clarity is aided by:
   a. Taking into account the knowledge and understanding of the listener,
   b. Using vocabulary that will be familiar to the listener,
   c. Using an order of statements or arguments consistent with the intended effect, and
   d. Avoiding redundancy and repetition.
3. Successful communication is *cooperative*. This includes:
   a. The listener supplies potentially relevant terms or information when the speaker is having trouble doing so.
   b. The listener provides immediate but unobtrusive feedback to keep the speaker on track.
   c. The speaker matches speech to feedback received from the listener.
4. Successful communication depends on both sides of the dialog maintaining *common ground* and contributing new information.
5. Successful communication requires that both parties in the dialog maintain an accurate representation of the state of knowledge and *understanding of the other*.

6. Keeping track of information in a conversation is facilitated if both parties *use standard conventions* for marking changes in topic, temporary diversions to sub- or supertopics, and switches between foreground and background information.

7. Motivation to continue a dialog is maintained when *cooperation* (as in all the preceding points) in the dialog is perceived. Uncooperative dialog discourages conversation.

Language: Implications for user interface design.   There is controversy among interactive systems designers concerning whether or not command and query languages should attempt to mimic natural language (see Chapter 10). There are reasonable arguments on either side, and it appears that the type of user and type of task determine the advantages or disadvantages of natural language systems. However, it seems clear that, even when more concise, artificial command languages are in order, these languages can be improved on by designing in certain structural characteristics of natural languages such as those just discussed.

At the very least, a command language should have a **syntax** that is logically related to its *semantics*. This applies whether the command language is primarily through function keys or typed-in commands. For instance, the command for "super copy" (copy *across* documents) should be syntactically related to the command for "copy" (copy *within* a document), and the relationship between "move" and "super move" should be similar to that between "copy" and "super copy" because the semantic relationships are similar. If the command language has a consistent structure, it will be easier to remember, and the user will be able to predict how to perform new functions without consulting the manual.

There is some evidence that users make less errors using commands with a *keyword* grammar than with a *positional* grammar, probably because it is a more natural kind of grammar (see Chapter 7).

We can also design dialogs that will seem more natural and friendly to users by applying what we know about how people use natural language to communicate. Some examples are:

Characteristic: It is natural for people to use a variety of ways to say the same thing.

Implication: Allow synonyms in a command language, such as "Delete" or "Erase" or "Rubout" to execute a delete.

Characteristic: Intention is most clearly communicated by following the basic conventions of *relevance, truthfulness, informativeness,* and *clarity.* Clarity is aided by:

a. Taking into account the knowledge and understanding of the listener,
b. Using vocabulary that will be familiar to the listener,
c. Using an order of statements or arguments consistent with the intended effect, and
d. Avoiding redundancy and repetition.

*Implication:*Include only information relevant to users and tasks and avoid cluttering screens with redundant information; but always present all the necessary information, given the likely state of user knowledge and understanding and the task at hand. Do not mislead. Do not use unfamiliar jargon or terminology. State instructions in their order of execution, and present information in orders that are meaningful to users.

Characteristic: Successful communication is *cooperative.* This includes:

a. The listener supplies potentially relevant terms or information when the speaker is having trouble doing so.

b. The listener provides immediate but unobtrusive feedback to keep the speaker on track.

c. The speaker matches speech to feedback received from the listener.

Implication: In a command language, provide prompts rather than error messages in response to missing parameters or typos. Provide plenty of immediate feedback to users, such as instantaneous screen echo in response to keystrokes and highlighting of selected items. In a help system, offer suggestions to users in response to frequent errors or persistent inefficient use of commands.

Characteristic: Successful communication depends on both sides of the dialog maintaining *common ground* and contributing new information.

Implication: Make use of context-based defaults, such as assuming parameters in a previous command as defaults in a current command.

Characteristic: Successful communication requires that both parties in the dialog maintain an accurate representation of the state of knowledge and *understanding of the other.*

Implication: Display key context information to users at all times. Provide tailored interfaces to users based on past interactions with them. Protect novices from complexity and make simple things simple for them. Make complex things possible for experts.

Characteristic: Keeping track of information in a conversation is facilitated if both parties *use standard conventions* for marking changes in topic ("that reminds me," "by the way"), temporary diversions to sub- or supertopics ("anyway," "so"), and switches between foreground and background information ("you have to understand that").

Implication: Provide plenty of context information on screens (such as previous menu picks) to help users keep track of where they are in a dialog, how they got there, and how to get elsewhere. Design dialog flows to support the natural structure of user tasks.

Characteristic: Motivation to continue a dialog is maintained when *cooperation* (as in all the preceding points) in the dialog is perceived. Uncooperative dialog discourages conversation.

Implication: Cooperativeness, naturalness, and friendliness in computer–human dialog, as described in the preceding examples, are especially important for discretionary users who are low in computer experience and have low motivation and negative attitudes toward technology.

The Cognitive System: Summary

In summary, the human mind has certain characteristics that affect the way we process information. If we are to provide the mind with an effective and efficient tool, we must understand the constraints it operates under so that we can support its weaknesses and exploit its strengths. The major strengths and weaknesses of the human information processing system can be summarized as follows:

Strengths	Weaknesses
Infinite-capacity LTM	Limited-capacity STM
Duration and complexity of LTM	Limited-duration STM
High capacity for learning	Error-prone processing
Powerful attentional mechanism	Unreliable access to LTM
Powerful pattern recognition	Very slow processing

We can also compare the relative strengths and weaknesses of the human information processing system to those of the computer information processing system. When we do (see Figure 2-6), we note an interesting fact. *The strengths of the human* (capacity to learn, long-term memory capacity, powerful pattern recognition) *tend to be the weaknesses of the computer,* and the *weaknesses of the human* (low-capacity short-term memory, slow and error-prone processing) *tend to be the strengths of the computer.*

These facts are important to keep in mind when designing a user interface. The designer should allocate tasks to the user and computer depending on which does them best. For instance, the computer should retain data from screen to screen, while the user should make complex decisions based on heuristic analyses of data. Users should not be required to perform complex mental calculations and translations, and computers should not be expected to perform intuitive analyses.

Olson (1987) offers a framework for categorizing and allocating information processing activities to computers and users based on their relative strengths and weaknesses. First, different types of tasks are categorized, and then allocation is discussed:

Communicate: Transport Information
   The movement of information from one physical location to the next.

Transform Information
   Change information storage medium.

Process: Algorithmic Decision Making
   Sort information according to prespecified, stable rules.

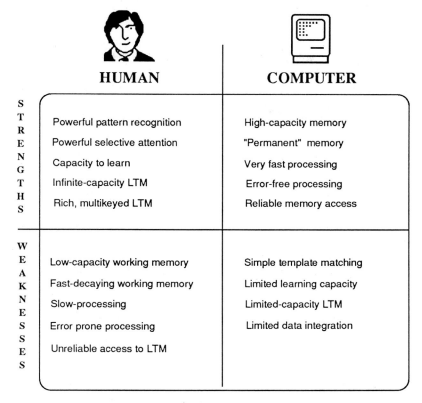

Figure 2–6   Strengths and weaknesses of the human and computer information processing systems.

Process: Judgment-based Decision Making
   Sort information according to multiple, complexly related dimensions.

Correlate Information
   Retrieve information from several sources and merge aspects of each into a new record.

Analyze Information
   Look for patterns in retrieved information.

Communicate: Negotiate
   Persuade, decide, teach, learn.

Create Information
   Organize, synthesize, add new information.

Those steps that require transportation, transformation, simple but accurate retrieval, algorithmic decision making, or merging are allocated to computer support or automation because they require actions that are difficult, inaccurate, or tedious for the human. Those that require recognition of patterns, appropriate multiattribute retrieval, judgmental decision making, learning, or creation of information are to be allocated to human processing because they capitalize on human strengths.

User interface designers would do well to keep these simple guidelines in mind. For a more detailed discussion of human information processing strengths and weaknesses the reader is referred to Card, Moran, and Newell, (1983, Chapter 2) and Bailey (1982).

The Motor System

It is believed that thought is translated into action through a series of discrete micromovements. Rapid behavioral acts such as typing and speaking are executed in bursts of "preprogrammed" motor instructions. Visual and tactile feedback during motor acts allows modifications of these instructions and facilitates accuracy (Card, 1981). Different sets of muscles are involved in gross motor movements (for example, moving the hand from the keyboard to the mouse) versus fine motor movements (for example, positioning the mouse on a target or typing).

The Motor System: Implications for User Interface Design

Motor movements relevant to user interface design include head, eye, arm, hand and finger movements. The designer should try to minimize gross motor movements, such as movement back and forth between the keyboard and mouse or movement from the keyboard to a touch screen. Frequent gross motor movements slow the user down and can be fatiguing, and transitioning from gross to fine motor movements requires concentration.

Adequate perceptual feedback should be provided to guide motor movements. For instance, an instant keyboard echo on the screen facilitates typing accuracy, as does the aural and tactile feedback from keyboard keys. Highlighting icons or other targets when a pointer is positioned on them is also important feedback for gaining accuracy with a pointing device.

Eye movements should be minimized to increase performance and minimize fatigue. For instance, screens can be laid out to minimize scanning and searching, and keyboard–screen eye movements can be minimized by the optimal placement of frequently used keys near the alpha "home row." An organized layout of keys will minimize scanning and searching for keys on the keyboard.

Easily discriminable motor sequences should be designed for different operations. For example, on the Apple Macintosh, the user clicks a mouse button once to select an object, but twice in rapid succession to "open" it. Users who frequently use the double click to open find that they often double click by mistake when they only wish to select an object.

Similarly, in a command language, users who frequently use the command "Sea" or "Search" may type it by mistake for the less frequently used "Sen" or

"Send" command. This error would be much less likely if the "Search" command were renamed "Fnd" for find. The similarity of the motor sequences for typing "Sea" and "Sen" induces the error. The preprogrammed nature of well-learned motor responses causes this kind of error, and such errors can be minimized by designing nonsimilar motor sequences for different operations.

The Human Information Processing System: Predictive Models

As pointed out many times in the forgoing discussions, knowledge of human information processing strengths and weaknesses leads us to a number of design goals for interactive systems. It is also true that knowledge of the characteristics of human information processing allows us to make *predictions* regarding human performance on interactive systems (Card, 1981, Card, Moran, and Newell, 1983).

One example of making such predictions is reported by Landaur (1987). Two well-established laws developed from research on cognitive psychology were applied to predict selection times on menus varying in the number of choices per screen and the number of levels in the menu hierarchy. One law (Hick's law) states that simple decision times are a linear function of transmitted information, and the other (Fitts' law) states that movement time to a target item is a function of both the distance and size of the target item.

Since menu selection is more or less a simple matter of making a choice from a set of options (decision time) and then making some motor response to actually select the choice (movement time), average performance times for navigating through menus with different numbers of choices per level and different numbers of levels can be computed. This was done, and the predicted performance times were then compared to several sets of empirical data that actually measured the performance times of real users performing the selection task.

In general, the predictive model was found to correlate well with the empirical data. The model predicted and the empirical data generally confirmed that menus with few choices per level and many levels took longer to navigate than menus with many choices per level and fewer levels.

However, it was also observed that the accuracy of the predicted performance times was influenced by various factors such as the "naturalness" of the categories in the menu hierarchy and the likelihood of different kinds of errors. This suggests that the model is too simple to be applied broadly without confirming predictions through empirical testing.

A more broadly applicable predictive model is offered by Card, Moran, and Newell (1981). The basics of this model, the Model Human Processor, were first published by Card (1981). The model includes, among others, three parameters representing basic units of processing time for each of the three basic information processing subsystems: the Perceptual Processor (t_P), the Cognitive Processor (t_C), and the Motor Processor (t_M). These parameters are estimated (with an average value and a range) as follows:

$$t_P = 100 \text{ (50 to 200) milliseconds (ms)}$$

$$t_C = 100 \text{ (25 to 170) ms}$$

$$t_M = 100 \text{ (70 to 360) ms}$$

Any simple user task can be broken down into components that can be associated with one of the three processors, and then calculations of the predicted task time can be made based on the parameters of the model. For example:

Example 5:   Simple Decision Times

The user is presented with two symbols, one at a time. If the second symbol is identical to the first, he is to push the key labeled Yes, otherwise he is to push No. What is the time between signal and response for the Yes case?

Solution.   The first symbol is presented on the screen where it is observed by the user and processed by his Perceptual Processor giving rise to associated representations in the user's Visual Image Store {sensory buffer} and Working Memory {short-term memory}. The second symbol is now flashed on the screen and is similarly processed. . . . Since we are interested in how long it takes to respond to the second symbol, we now start the clock at 0. The Perceptual Processor processes the second symbol to get an iconic representation in Visual Image Store {sensory buffer} and then a visual representation in Working Memory {short-term memory}, requiring one cycle, t_P. . . . If not too much time has passed since the first symbol was presented, its visual code is still in Working Memory {short-term memory} and the Cognitive Processor can match the visual codes of the first and second symbols against each other to see if they are the same. This match requires one Cognitive Processor cycle, t_C. . . . If they match, the Cognitive Processor decides to push the Yes button, requiring another cycle t_C for the decision. . . . Finally, the Motor Processor processes the request to push the Yes button, requiring one Motor Processor cycle t_M. . . . The total elapsed reaction time, according to the Model Human Processor, is

$$\text{Reaction time} = t_P + 2t_C + t_M$$

$$= 100 \text{ [50 to 200]} + 2 \times (100 \text{ [25 to 170]}) + 100 \text{ [70 to 360] ms}$$

$$= 400 \text{ [170 to 900] ms}$$

This analysis could be repeated for the case ("name match") where the user is to press Yes if the symbols were both the same letter, although one might be in uppercase, the other in lowercase. Here, an extra Cognitive Processor cycle is required to get the abstract code for the symbol (Computed reaction time = 500 [195 to 1070] ms). Likewise, if the user were to press Yes when the symbols were only of the same class ("class match"), say both letters, yet another Cognitive Processor cycle would be required (Computed reaction time = 600 [220 to 1240] ms). Experiments have been performed to collect empirical data on the questions presented in these examples. The finding is that name matches are about 70 ms slower than physical matches and that class matches are about 70 ms slower yet, a number in line with our 100 [25 to 170] ms value for t_C. (Card, 1981) (Braces, { }, are mine)

The idea behind a model such as the Model Human Processor is that a good, validated model or theory allows us to make predictions about behavior without actually having to collect empirical data. In this case, the model could be applied to a typical task, given one or more alternative designs, and it would allow us to predict the usability of a design or determine which of a set of alternative designs would result in the best performance, without having to actually implement and test the design alternatives.

However, identifying and responding to a letter on the screen is a rather trivial task compared to the interactions that user interface designers must design. The model has been used to predict performance in more relevant tasks, such as text editing and graphics editing (Card, Moran, and Newell, 1987a). But, it is important to note that the Model Human Processor provides predictions only for the *time* it will take *expert* users to perform *simple, routine tasks*. Obviously, much of interface design is directed at *nonexpert* users performing *complex, problem-solving* (nonroutine) *types of tasks*. And other measures of performance besides time, such as *errors, learning time,* and *recall* with low frequency of use, may be of equal or even higher importance (Card, Moran, and Newell, 1987a). On the other hand, more recent research has attempted to begin to apply this basic model to a range of broader but still basic activities common to all computer–human interaction, such as reading, visual searching, planning, problem solving, pointing, transcription typing, and command entry (John and Newell, 1989).

Another problem with the Model Human Processor approach to predicting human performance is that it assumes that users will always identify and choose the optimal interaction for accomplishing any particular goal. However, people tend to be *heuristic*, rather than *algorithmic*, problem solvers, and heuristics do not always yield optimal solutions.

Young and MacLean (1988) demonstrated this aspect of human performance. Users were given a choice between a mouse method and a keyboard and menu method for entering data into a spreadsheet. In some tasks, the mouse method was the optimal choice, while in others the keyboard and menu method afforded optimal performance. Users did not always choose the optimal method, probably due to a simple heuristic method of assessment that did not always yield the best selection. The authors offer a model to account for how users made such choices and suggest that "By using this approach, we could expect to be able to superimpose the notion of compensation schema onto such models [for example, Model Human Processor] in order to predict human behavior more precisely" (brackets are mine).

In fact, Card, Moran, and Newell (1987b) also propose a type of model, broader in scope than the Model Human Processor, called a GOMS model (which stands for *goals, operators, methods,* and *selection rules*), that addresses the fact that, when choosing between available methods to accomplish goals, users do not always choose optimal methods. In the GOMS model, users are said to apply specific *selection rules* for choosing between available *methods* in the pursuit of specific *goals*. Methods consist of *operators*, which in one form of a GOMS model, correspond more or less to the parameters in the Model Human Processor. Card, Moran, and Newell (1987b) found that with a small number of selection rules they could describe the choices between methods that users made and, for a given user, account for a large part of the performance data. The GOMS model, however, is primarily *descriptive* of *individual* behavior, rather than *predictive* of *average* user behavior; as such, is not particularly helpful to the designer trying to design an optimal interface for a population of diverse users.

The state of the science of computer-human interaction is not such that we can yet apply models such as the Model Human Processor or GOMS with complete confidence, eliminating all need for testing. Many different models are available, and each tends to focus on different mental processes (for example, memory, perception, motor behavior), thus highlighting the variety of potential problems and providing widely different metrics of usability (Olson, 1987). However, such models can be useful tools if applied intelligently and validated in specific circumstances, and they certainly represent an important step toward an applied science of human cognitive behavior in engineering environments.

On the other hand, it is important to point out that regardless of the accuracy and power of such models, they are by nature *descriptive,* rather than *prescriptive*. That is, they may allow a designer to *evaluate* a proposed design by predicting its usability, but they do not provide any framework to *guide* or *drive* design ideas in the first place. There will always be a need for *design tools* as well as *evaluation tools*. This book focuses on *design guidelines* rather than on models and other *evaluation methods* because its purpose is to provide a *design tool,* rather than an *evaluation tool.* Testing and evaluation are critical tools for the interface designer, but they are not the subject of this book.

The preceding discussion of the human information processing system and its implications for user interface design is meant only as an introduction to this topic. For a good basic text on human information processing, the reader should see Lindsay and Norman (1977). For good discussions of the implications of human information processing for interactive system design, the reader is referred to Card, Moran and Newell (1983), Gardiner and Christie (1987), and Carroll (1987).

THE USER'S PSYCHOLOGICAL CHARACTERISTICS

The human information processing system is a *general* determinant of human performance. But a number of additional determinants *vary* across individuals, and it is important that the designer of an interactive system know how the intended user population is influenced by these determinants. Some of these determinants are summarized in Figures 2-7 and 2-8, and these and others are discussed in this section and the sections that follow.

Certain *psychological characteristics* contribute to performance. It is a well-known fact that both **motivation** and **attitude** play a significant role in the performance of tasks requiring motor, cognitive, or perceptual skills. The designer of an interactive system cannot control the attitudes (positive, neutral, negative) or the level of motivation (for example, high due to fear, high due to interest, moderate, low) that users bring to an interactive system. However, interactive systems can be designed to *minimize the negative emotions* of fear, anxiety, threat, boredom, apathy, and the like, and *to maximize* job satisfaction, and thus *motivation and attitude* (for example, by empowering, challenging, or fascinating).

It has been found that emotional arousal affects performance in a U-shaped function, as illustrated in Figure 2-9. That is, too little arousal impedes performance (perhaps due to a lack of attention), a moderate degree of arousal improves performance (probably by increasing alertness), and a high level of arousal again impedes performance (perhaps due to an inability to concentrate). Users who feel anxious about their ability to understand computers and fear that computers are

User Profile Checklist

Psychological Characteristics

Cognitive style:
__ Verbal/analytic
__ Spatial/intuitive

Attitude:
__ Positive
__ Neutral
__ Negative

Motivation:
__ High
__ Moderate
__ Low

Knowledge and Experience

Reading level:
__ Less than fifth grade
__ Fifth to twelfth grade
__ Above twelfth grade

Typing skill:
__ Low
__ Medium
__ High

Education:
__ High school degree
__ College degree
__ Advanced degree

System experience:
__ Expert
__ Moderate
__ Novice

Task experience:
__ Novice in field
__ Moderate
__ Expert in field

Application experience:
__ No similar systems
__ One similar system
__ Some similar systems

Native language:
__ English
__ Other

Use of other systems:
__ Little or none
__ Frequent

Computer literacy:
__ High
__ Moderate
__ Low

Figure 2–7 The user profile.

User Profile Checklist

Job and Task Characteristics

Frequency of use:
__ Low
__ Medium
__ High

Primary training:
__ None
__ Manual only
__ Elective formal
__ Mandatory formal

System use:
__ Mandatory
__ Discretionary

Job categories:
__ Executive
__ Manager
__ Engineer
__ Secretary
__ Clerk

Turnover rate:
__ High
__ Moderate
__ Low

Other tools:
__ Telephone
__ Calculator
__ Adding machine
__ Other

Task importance:
__ High
__ Low

Task structure:
__ High
__ Moderate
__ Low

Physical Characteristics

Color-blind:
__ Yes
__ No

Handedness:
__ Right
__ Left
__ Ambidextrous

Gender:
__ Female
__ Male

Figure 2–8 The user profile.

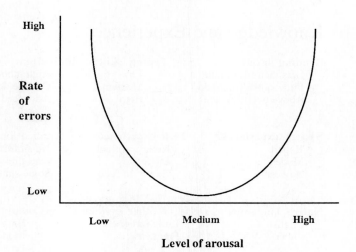

Figure 2–9 Arousal-performance relationship.

going to change or eliminate their jobs or to whom the computer appears to be dominating and inconsistent will learn less quickly and perform with more errors. People do not perform well in stressful, frustrating situations.

A third psychological characteristic of users is **cognitive style.** There is evidence that people vary in their approach to and ability in problem solving. Some people excel at **verbal** thinking, while others are better at **spatial** reasoning. That is, some work better with words and equations, while others are better at manipulating pictures, images, and symbols. Some are **analytic** thinkers, approaching problems systematically, while others are more **intuitive** thinkers, more comfortable with rules of thumb, hunches, and educated guesses than with equations and algorithms. Other dimensions of cognitive style include **abstract** versus **concrete** and **field dependent** versus **field independent.** People also vary in their visual memory skills and information processing rate (Vicente, Hayes, and Williges, 1987).

The User's Psychological Characteristics: Implications for User Interface Design

Only if designers are aware of the cognitive styles, attitudes, and motivational levels of users can they design interfaces to address differing cognitive styles, negative attitudes, and low motivation, or to exploit and maintain positive attitudes and high motivation. For instance, consider the following goals:

User characteristic	Design goal
Low motivation, discretionary use	Ease of learning
Low motivation, mandatory use	Control, power
High motivation, due to fear	Ease of learning, robustness, control, power
High motivation, due to interest	Power, ease of use

If users lack motivation (either in their jobs in general or to use computers in particular), then it is important to provide some incentives immediately. **Discretionary** users (who choose whether or not to use a computer) need to feel immediately that a system will not take too long to learn. **Mandatory** users (who must use a computer as part of their job) need to immediately experience some benefit from using the computer. Users who are highly motivated out of *fear* (for example, of losing their job or of appearing incompetent) need the reassurance that the system is not overly complex and will not be difficult to learn. Users highly motivated out of *interest* need to have this interest maintained by an immediate sense that the system will empower them and provide speed and efficiency. Any system should strive to achieve all the design goals given previously, but usually this is difficult to achieve. The user's psychological characteristics must be considered in the design trade-offs that designers must inevitably make.

Interactive computer systems, especially for naive users, should be consistent, predictable, simple to understand and operate, and toollike, rather than humanlike, in order to give the user an immediate sense of control, mastery, and achievement. This will reduce frustration, fear, and stress and increase motivation, thus allowing for better performance.

Interactive systems should also contribute to, rather than detract from, job satisfaction by providing a tool that facilitates and widens the scope of a user's job. Systems that detract from job satisfaction by narrowing the scope of a job (for example, by changing a job from customer service to data entry) will both decrease motivation and induce stress, frustration, and anxiety, all of which decrease performance. Systems designers do not always have control over the way their systems will be implemented (for example, a word processor as a tool for the traditional secretarial role versus for use by centralized word processing operators), but a good system design takes into account the job of the user as much as possible and attempts to increase, rather than decrease, job incentive and motivation.

Some studies suggest how cognitive style might be considered in design. Vicente, Hayes, and Williges (1987) found a significant relationship between spatial ability and performance on a given user interface and hypothesized that a different user interface could improve performance among users low in spatial ability.

Another study (Ambardar, 1984) investigated the cognitive style dimension of **field dependence** versus **field independence,** defined as ''the general processing strategy used to separate information from the context in which it occurs.'' This study found that field-dependent and field-independent users chose different strategies for interacting with a software system and showed significant performance differences when they used a preferred versus a nonpreferred strategy. Both these studies suggest that a flexible user interface that offers more than one way to do things will provide for better performance across all users.

Systems such as the Apple Macintosh that allow users the choice of representing objects as icons in a two-dimensional space or as words in a list would be an example of an interface that accommodates varying cognitive styles. A direct manipulation system with a command language alternative would similarly address the range of cognitive styles in a diverse population of users.

THE USER'S KNOWLEDGE AND EXPERIENCE

Designers tend to consider *user experience* as a simple binary dimension: novice and expert. In fact, the dimension of knowledge and experience is a *continuum*; and, there are a number of *types* of knowledge and experience that are relatively independent of one another and must all be considered in interface design. These are listed in Figure 2-7.

First, there is the general **educational level** of users. Have they completed high school? Do they have a college degree? Do they have advanced degrees in specialized areas related to system use?

Educational level is generally correlated with **reading level.** If much of an interface is verbal, then it is important that the vocabulary and grammatical structure be at a level that can be easily understood by users. Users' reading levels can be objectively measured, but if this is not possible, reading level can be inferred from educational level.

Typing skill is an important user characteristic to consider. Are users expert touch typists (135 words per minute), skilled touch typists (90 wpm), good touch typists (55 wpm), average touch typists (40 wpm), or "hunt and peck" typists (10 wpm) (Card, Moran, and Newell, 1987b)? Will they be familiar with the standard typewriter layout?

Designers should consider the users' general level of **computer literacy.** Are users highly technical and computer literate, such as programmers or highly experienced on-line data entry clerks? Or do they have no prior experience with computers at all? Will they be familiar with the use of such keys as the tab, enter, and backspace keys or not? Will they be familiar with computer jargon and concepts such as memory, saving, and queuing?

Task experience refers to knowledge of the task domain, that is, of the functions that the system is designed to help the user perform. For instance, to make use of an airline reservation system, a user has to know something about which cities have airports, the different rate structures for fares, the different airlines and their pricing policies, the common connecting cities between departure and destination points, and the like. To make use of a database of information on insurance policies, a user needs to know quite a bit about how the insurance industry works. Task experience is also called *semantic knowledge* (Shneiderman, 1980).

System experience, by contrast, refers to knowledge of the particular language or mode of interaction of a given system. Users may have been performing their job for years effectively by hand, but will be unable to perform the job when it is automated until they have learned the idiosyncratic language of the new system. In the example of the airline reservation system, system experience pertains to knowledge of special function keys on the keyboard, codes for airlines and airports, the syntax for entering a reservation, the commands for searching for flights with desired characteristics, etc. System experience is also called *syntactic knowledge* (Shneiderman, 1980).

Users may also have some level of **application experience**. That is, they may have used other similar systems before. Is this the user's first word processing system or have they used others? Is this the first airline reservation system new clerks have used or have they used others? Note that application experience is different from general computer literacy and other types of knowledge and experience. If a user has used a variety of word processors before, but this is their first time using a spreadsheet program, they have some level of *computer literacy*, but no *application experience*. If they are using the spreadsheet for an accounting application, they may or may not have *task experience*. And if they have never used this particular spreadsheet before, they do not have any *system experience*.

In many applications, designers have to consider the **native language** of the intended users. Obviously, if the native language of users is not English, then the system should not be in English. If a system must be translated into several languages, then this must be considered up front, as it will affect screen layout and design. And if most but not all users will be English speakers, then some provision for those who do not speak English or do not speak it well must be made.

The **use of other systems** is also an important aspect of users' knowledge and experience. If users will use other computer systems on a daily basis besides the one being designed, they will bring certain motor habits and certain interpretations of vocabulary and visual cues with them each time they go from one system to another. The more compatibility in the user interfaces across systems, the less learning burden there will be for the new system and the fewer the errors that will be made as users go back and forth between systems.

The Users' Knowledge and Experience: Implications for User Interface Design

Most of the various kinds of user knowledge and experience are relatively independent of one another. A given user may have high typing skill, high task experience, and low reading level or may have low typing skill, high task experience, and high reading skill. Almost any combination of different levels of different kinds of knowledge and experience is possible.

Users with varying degrees of the different kinds of knowledge and experience have different needs that must be accommodated by the system. For instance, consider just the two determinants of *task experience* and *system experience*.

1. Users with *little task or system experience* will need a system with *many prompts of both a semantic and syntactic nature* [for example, "Pitch (1) (1=Pica,2=Elite)"] and effective error recovery procedures.
2. Users with a high degree of *both task and system experience* may need *efficient commands and concise syntactic error messages, but not verbose prompting of a semantic or syntactic nature.*
3. Users with a *lot of system but little task experience* (for example, data entry operators) need *semantic help facilities and messages* (for example, "Press LIST for a list of department numbers") and an *efficient command syntax.*
4. Users with a *lot of task but little system experience* (for example, an experienced professional on a new system) will need *minimal semantic prompting but a lot of syntactic prompting and instructions* (for example, "Press TAB to move from field to field, Press ENTER to accept form").

Knowledge, more than any other performance determinant, is dynamic and changes within users across time. The novice may quickly become an expert, especially if the job requires using the system frequently and continuously. Unless a system is designed for a user whose frequency of use will always be low (for example, managers or the general public) and/or who does not have a lot of time to spend in learning (for example, jobs that tend to be transient, such as bank tellers), systems should be designed to accommodate the expert user, as well as the novice. Such a system might give the user a choice of levels of help and prompting and accept a variety of input modes from multiple-choice menus to a concise parametric command language. Again, the nature of the user's job and the frequency and importance of the task will ultimately affect their level of knowledge and experience over time. These factors, in turn, should determine the relative emphasis to be put on ease of learning and memorability versus ease of use, and thus the amount of syntactic and semantic assistance provided in the interface.

Other dimensions of expertise besides task and system experience feed into interface design as well. For instance, the complexity and abstractness of the interface should be compatible with the users' educational level, level of computer literacy, and reading level. The general interaction technique (for example, type in versus point and select) should take into account the expected typing skill. Icons, universal symbols, and/or a language option should be considered when members of the user population do not all have the same native language. And, if users frequently use other systems, some compatibility of the user interface across systems is important.

THE USER'S JOB AND TASKS

A number of the dimensions of the user's job in general and tasks in particular, have implications for interactive systems design. These are listed in Figure 2-8 and discussed next.

One of the most important determinants of user performance with an interactive system is **frequency of use.** Users might use a system 8 hours a day, 5 days a week (for example, a data entry system or word processor). Or they might use a system once in a lifetime (for example, an amusement park information system). These represent the extremes on the continuum of frequency of use. Use may fall anywhere between the extremes, with some interesting variations, such as everyday, but only 5 minutes per day.

Frequency of use has profound implications for interface design because it affects learning and memory. Frequency of use affects systems design in two ways. First, users who spend a lot of time on the system are usually willing to invest more time in learning, and therefore efficiency of operation often takes precedence over ease of learning. Second, frequent users have less difficulty remembering system commands between uses and, again, efficiency of operation takes precedence over memorability. Conversely, low-frequency users will be less able to remember interactive techniques between uses.

Another important consideration is **primary training.** Will users get a mandatory, extensive training program? Will they be expected to teach themselves from manuals? Or must we assume no training and no manuals will be possible or practical, such as with the amusement park information system? The amount of available training determines in part how easy to learn the interface must be.

Another determinant that guides us in the ease-of-use/ease-of-learning trade-off is **system use.** Is system use **mandatory,** that is, required, such as is the case in many job environments? Or is it **discretionary,** that is, at the choice of the user, as is the case for many systems for managers and executives or personal computers used at home? The type of use may be related to the level and type of motivation, which in turn lead us to different design goals.

Turnover rate is an important job factor. A system that requires a great deal of training and is difficult to learn would not be appropriate for a job with a high turnover rate. The expense of training time may outweigh the advantages of the automated system. When turnover is low, a greater learning burden can be justified and will be perceived as a reasonable investment.

Other tools used by the intended users of a new system might also figure into user interface design. For instance, whether or not users are familiar with adding machines and calculators might determine whether an adding machine layout (7-8-9 on the top row) or telephone layout (1-2-3 on the top row) for a numeric keyboard would be more appropriate. A system meant to automate and replace an existing tool, such as an appointment book or rolodex, might take such a tool as a metaphor in its user interface to exploit the familiar experience and reduce the learning curve (see Chapter 3).

Task importance will in part determine the level of motivation. The importance of the task automated by a new system will influence how much of an investment in learning users (especially discretionary users) are willing to make. For instance, an electronic calendar might be perceived as very important to a secretary, a decision support system might be very important to an executive, and electronic mail might be very important to a manager. These systems support key tasks in their jobs. On the other hand, a word processor might be relatively unimportant to a manager, a graphics package would be unimportant to an executive, and an electronic mail system might be unimportant to an engineer. In the former examples, users might be willing to invest a considerable amount of time in training and learning, whereas in the latter examples they probably would not. Accordingly, the ease of learning of the systems would be more or less important, relative to other design goals such as power, ease of use, and functionality.

Note that *task importance* and *frequency of use* are not necessarily the same thing. The task may have a high importance but be executed with a low frequency. For example, a sales executive might use a market modeling and forecasting system as the basis for strategic planning. The system might be used only once or twice a year (low frequency of use), but it is an extremely important tool to this user. Thus, in spite of low frequency of use, this user might be very willing to expend a considerable amount of time in training and learning to get the benefits of increased power and flexibility.

Another important aspect of the task being automated is its inherent **task structure** (repetitiveness and predictability of operations). Tasks with a great deal of internal structure are more amenable to automation in the first place, but they also suggest different types of user interfaces. In general, the flexibility of the interface should match the degree of structure inherent in the task.

Primary mode of interaction is related to task structure. There are six categories (Miller and Thomas, 1977):

> **Input Mode:**
> Input only (for example, data entry system)
> Input to get output (for example, tax package)
> **Output Mode:**
> Receive structured outputs (for example, management report systems)
> Obtain desired output by selection (for example, database query system)
> **Processing Mode:**
> Limited data manipulation (for example, statistical packages)
> Extensive data manipulation (for example, programming environments)

Roughly, the *tasks in input and output modes tend to be more highly structured,* whereas the *tasks in processing mode tend to be less structured.*

User interfaces may also be thought of in terms of two binary dimensions: **control** and **choice type.** The two kinds of control are **system controlled** and **user controlled** (the system guides and prompts the user through a sequence of steps versus the user chooses a sequence of steps through commands to the system), and the two kinds of choice are **free choice** and **forced choice** (roughly corresponding to fill in the blanks versus multiple-choice selection). There are thus four kinds of interfaces along these dimensions:

> System controlled–forced choice
> System controlled–free choice
> User controlled–forced choice
> User controlled–free choice

Generally, *system-controlled interactions are most appropriate for highly struc-tured tasks* (for example, input and output modes), while *user-controlled interac-tions are most appropriate for unstructured tasks* (for example, processing mode). *Forced-choice interactions are appropriate for very structured tasks* (for example, input and output modes), while *free-choice interactions may be more appropriate for relatively unstructured tasks* (for example, processing mode).

Finally, users may be described in terms of their **job category.** Is the user a manager, a clerk, an engineer, or a secretary? Although this determinant does not have any direct implications for user interface design, it is often correlated with other determinants discussed here. For instance, secretaries usually have higher typing skills and higher turnover rates than executives. Clerks are usually mandatory users, while managers are often discretionary users. Thus, if these other determinants are not directly known, knowing the job categories of users provides the designer with at least some data from which to infer other determinants.

The User's Job and Tasks: Implications for User Interface Design

Job and task characteristics should drive user interface design in many ways. For example, the flexibility of the interface must be compatible with the degree of structure inherent in the tasks being automated. Menus (system controlled–forced choice) and question and answer dialogs (system controlled–free choice) are highly structured interface styles and so should only be used in tasks that are themselves highly structured (input and output modes). Command languages (user controlled–free choice) are highly flexible, unstructured dialog styles and so are appropriate for unstructured tasks (processing mode).

Ease of learning should be compatible with the turnover rate and primary training. In general, the ease of use–ease of learning trade-off should be guided by frequency of use, task importance, and system usage, as follows:

Frequency of use
    High: Ease of use
    Low: Ease of learning and remembering

Task importance
    High: Ease of use
    Low: Ease of learning and remembering

System use
    Mandatory: Ease of use
    Discretionary: Ease of learning and remembering

Low-frequency users will not be able to learn and remember an interface unless it is designed for ease of learning. They will not care so much about ease of use. High-frequency users will learn in spite of a more difficult to learn interface, and they are more concerned with ease of use.

When the task is important, motivation is high and ease of use is a higher priority than ease of learning. When task importance is low, motivation is low and users will not tolerate a high cost in learning time and effort.

When system usage is mandatory, users usually get training, and ease of use will provide them with a sense of power and control, thus keeping up their motivation. When system usage is discretionary, first impressions are more important to create motivation, so ease of learning is a higher priority.

THE USER'S PHYSICAL CHARACTERISTICS

Certain physical characteristics of users affect performance with interactive systems. Figure 2-8 lists some of these. For instance, **handedness** (right or left) may affect the ease of use of keyboards and other input devices, depending on whether they were optimized for one hand or the other. **Color-blindness** will certainly affect performance with color screens if color is used in task-related ways and no other redundant coding techniques are used (see the section on color in Chapter 14).

Gender may have an impact on both motor and cognitive performance. A monitor that must be lifted in order to orient it either horizontally ("landscape") or vertically ("portrait") will not be used by many women if it is too heavy. Women tend to have smaller hands than men, and keyboards and other pointing devices designed for the average male hand will result in poorer performance by women. Fewer women are color-blind than men, so a population of women might perform better on a color-based interface than a population of men. There is also evidence (although it is quite controversial) that women and men tend to have different cognitive styles and thus may perform better or worse on different kinds of interfaces (for example, direct manipulation versus command language).

Finally, certain **physical handicaps,** such as blindness or defective vision, deafness, and motor handicaps, will affect performance on systems not designed with these handicaps in mind.

The User's Physical Characteristics: Implications for User Interface Design

Some simple design goals result from a consideration of the physical characteristics of users. The placement of keys and the design of alternate input devices should accommodate left-handed users. Color (especially red and green) should not be used as the only cue or code for important information on the screen. The range of physical characteristics of both men and women should be considered in designing hardware and controls. And any anticipated physical handicaps, such as deficiencies in sight in older people, should be considered in the design (for example, the use of larger type).

THE USER'S PHYSICAL ENVIRONMENT

Certain aspects of the user's physical environment also affect performance with interactive systems. For instance, the **noise level** in a work area will affect the user's ability to concentrate and avoid making certain kinds of errors. **Privacy** must be considered, not just for security reasons, but also for psychological reasons. A lack of privacy can induce stress in certain situations, and this can affect performance.

Lighting can have significant effects on users. Poor lighting can produce glare and make reading from the screen or finding keys on the keyboard more fatiguing. Fatigue will impede performance and induce errors.

Workspace dimensions and layout are important. Without enough space, users will not be able to arrange materials optimally to support problem solving.

Finally, **furniture and equipment** may have an impact. Poorly designed furniture and workstations may cause stress and fatigue with extended use, and this will degrade performance.

The User's Physical Environment: Implications for User Interface Design

Some simple design goals result from a consideration of the physical environment of users. Avoid voice as an input or output device in open, noisy work areas. It will be disruptive and may cause security problems.

Public versus private use dictates the feasibility of different hardware and input and output device options. For instance, a touch screen may hold up better in public use than a mouse or keyboard.

Glare control is important when lighting is unpredictable. Furniture and workstations should be highly adjustable to accommodate the different physical characteristics and needs of users. And the maximum "footprint" (area of desk space) of a workstation should be derived from an understanding of the type of workspace in which it will be used.

THE USER'S TOOLS

Clearly, performance is affected by the kinds of tools available to the user. A user with a calculator is more effective than one who must do calculations by hand. A secretary with a word processor is more productive than one with a typewriter. But, more importantly, operator performance on word processors may differ according to the effectiveness of the user interfaces of the different systems.

In general, although we cannot alter the user's information processing system or physical characteristics, if we wish to affect performance, we can manipulate any of the other five performance determinants identified and discussed previously (psychological characteristics, knowledge and experience, job and tasks, physical environment, and tools). For instance, we can increase the user's knowledge through education, change the user's job to be wider or narrower in scope, provide performance incentives to motivate the user, redesign the user's work area, or give the user better tools.

As system developers, however, the only determinant we are in a position to affect is the user's tools. *But, if we know the user's level on all other performance determinants, we will be better able to design the tool to more effectively fit the user.* A system must take into consideration the user's job and tasks, knowledge levels, motivation and attitude, physical characteristics, and information processing capabilities.

Subsequent chapters in this book provide specific guidelines for taking these performance determinants into consideration in the design of interactive systems. Before turning to these specific guidelines, however, some final notes on the user profile are in order.

The preceding profile of the user is rather crude for two reasons. First, the purpose of this chapter is not to be an exhaustive treatment of human information processing and psychology, but rather to briefly summarize some relevant determinants of user performance and sensitize system designers to human factors considerations. Second, little is known at this point about user behavior with interactive systems, and to some extent this crude profile represents the state of the art of the science of user psychology. Even less is understood about how the various identifiable characteristics of users relate to optimal interactive system characteristics (Potosnak, 1986). To produce a complete and reliable set of guidelines for systems designers, we need a much more complete and applicable theory of user performance. This will simply have to await more extensive research.

Although we have been able to generically describe some determinants of user behavior and make some very general and largely intuitive statements about how to design systems to address and accommodate these determinants, in fact we have only a rudimentary understanding of how to reliably measure the determinants of user performance and relate them to system design alternatives. For instance, it seems reasonable to suggest that for high-frequency, expert users a precise, parametric command language is often best, whereas for infrequent novice users a menu system is usually best. But how do we define and measure ''frequency'' and ''novice''? And what about the fact that a single system might be used by both types of users? What do we know about the learning process that might help us design an interface that allows for a graceful transition from novice to expert user?

In addition, design goals often conflict with one another. Suppose the task is relatively unstructured, requiring a highly flexible processing mode, which implies a user-controlled, free-choice interaction; but frequency of use is very low and task importance is only moderately high, which implies a simple system-controlled and forced-choice interaction. This would be the case, for instance, in many management information and forecasting systems. Although we all might have intuitions on how to deal with this situation, there is very little well controlled and relevant research to guide us in resolving these design conflicts.

If there is one single important principle to guide systems designers in good human factors design, it would be *never to generalize from oneself and one's peers and never to assume that users will respond to systems the way one expects them to*. When it comes to higher-level mental processes such as problem solving, reasoning, decision making, and psychological variables such as knowledge base, attitude, and motivation, people differ more than they are the same. Technologists are particularly ill-equipped to predict the reactions of nontechnologists to system design features. One pitfall of expertise in an area is an inability to communicate with and identify with nonexperts in the field. The classic communication gap between software and other professionals is further propagated in the design of interactive system interfaces.

Answers to such design issues as the choice of command words for system functions, command language syntax, default values, and keyboard layout should be answered by studying a representative sample of target users, rather than by intuition and introspection or solely on the basis of technical efficiency. The process of design by informal opinion is slowly being replaced by design based on objective, experimental data, but interactive systems design is far behind other design disciplines in human factors research and application.

The best attitude for today's designer to adopt is to think of the user as a different species that one knows nothing about; the user must be investigated scientifically to determine the optimal design features to facilitate the use of interactive systems. Although some intuitive assumptions about user behavior may prove correct, many may not, and only controlled research will provide us with a complete and reliable theory of user behavior from which we can formulate complete and reliable design guidelines.

In the meantime, designers should use the simple checklist provided in Figures 2-7 and 2-8 and adapt it as necessary to describe the users in their intended user population. Irrelevant determinants can be omitted and other determinants added as appropriate for different applications. More specific categories for each determinant should be formulated as appropriate to an application (for example, for frequency of use: less than 1 hour per day, 1 to 4 hours per day, more than 4 hours per day). A questionnaire can be developed based on this adapted checklist and distributed to a representative sample of users. User responses can be collated on a summary sheet and a profile thus obtained. For instance, it might be found that 20% of users use (or will use) a system less than 1 hour per day, 20% will use it 1 to 4 hours per day, and 60% will use it more than 4 hours per day.

If data such as these are obtained for each determinant, they can be used to drive design decisions. For instance, if an ease of use–ease of learning trade-off must be made on a system, knowing that 60% of users will use the system more than 4 hours per day might suggest that the decision should be biased toward ease of use. On the other hand, if it was also known that the majority of users were not computer literate, and that turnover was high, motivation low, and attitude poor, then, in spite of the expected frequency of use, the trade-off might be better made in the direction of ease of learning.

Consider the examples in Figure 2-10. On the left are listed some general characteristics of the expected users of a park information or videotex system. On the right is a user profile of professional users of an airline reservation or phone order system. Notice how different the user profiles are. These profiles would lead us to very different design decisions, as indicated in the bottom of the figure. Users with low computer literacy, low frequency of use, and no training cannot be expected to know or learn about complex keyboards or pointing devices such as

Applying The User Profile

Sample Systems

Park information   Airline reservations
       or   or
Videotex system   Phone order system

User Definitions

All job types	Clerical
All education levels	High School to BA/BS
Male and female	Mostly female
English, Spanish, and others	English
Low computer literacy	Moderate computer literacy
Low frequency of use	High frequency of use
No training, no manual	Mandatory formal training
Discretionary use	Mandatory use

Design Choices

Touch screen	Keyboard
Menus, icons	Command language
Easy to learn (heavy prompting, highly structured)	Easy to use (hidden help, highly flexible)

Figure 2–10   Applying user profiles.

mice, which require some practice to get used to. A touch screen is an intuitive device that requires no learning. On the other hand, users with at least moderate computer literacy, formal training, and high frequency of use will quickly become proficient with a keyboard.

    Menus are good for users low in all kinds of relevant knowledge and experience. Icons may help communicate choices to nonnative speakers. In general, the user profile on the left calls for extreme ease of learning. Ease of use is not an issue at all. This means lots of instructions and prompting and a very simple, structured interaction.

Command languages, on the other hand, are better for high-frequency, expert users because of their efficiency. Efficiency is important in the airline reservation or phone order system because good customer service depends on it. In general, users will learn this system due to their high frequency of use and mandatory training program, and it is more important that the system be easy to use. This means fast and flexible, with hidden help available upon request.

Without this information about the nature of users, there is no rational, intelligent basis for making these kinds of design decisions. One of the most important principles of good user interface design is thus:

☞ **Know the user.**

A user classification strategy such as that described above is a very useful tool for "knowing the user." The designer should keep in mind, however, that "Classification is a cheap solution. Classification arises, not out of inherent characteristics of those things which are classified, but rather out of the need of the classifiers to classify . . . classification acts to increase the distance between designer and client, not decrease it" (Whiteside in Potosnak, 1986).

Classifying users along the dimensions described in this chapter should be considered *a* tool, not *the* tool, for knowing the user. Equally, if not more important, is "Rich, detailed, multifaceted, empathetic awareness for the user in his or her context" (Whiteside in Potosnak, 1986). This can only be obtained through participation with and observation of users performing their jobs.

SUMMARY

This chapter has set the stage for a presentation and discussion of specific principles and guidelines in user interface design by providing the following:

1. An overview of the theories of human information processing that drive many of the principles and guidelines, and
2. A discussion of the user variables that should guide the application of the principles and guidelines.

In our discussion, many examples were offered that pointed to the implications of human cognition and user variables for user interface design. However, in many cases these examples were broad and conceptual, that is, not in an easily accessible and applicable form.

The remaining chapters in the book (with the exception of Chapter 18) offer concise, specific, and well-illustrated principles and guidelines, organized into topics designed to provide easy access to relevant information for designers engaged in a development project. The organization also reflects a top-down approach to design, in that topics covered in earlier chapters relate to design decisions that should be made earlier in the design process, while later chapters discuss issues appropriately considered in later stages of design. Thus, the chapters are presented in an appropriate order for teaching the principles and guidelines in a course.

Chapters 3 through 17 cover:

Conceptual models
Dialog styles:
   Menus
   Fill-in forms
   Question and answer
   Command languages
   Function keys
   Direct manipulation
   Natural language
   Dialog-style summary
Input and output devices
Organization of functionality
Screen layout and design
Response time
Error handling
User documentation

The general format of each chapter is first to discuss the relevant research literature pertaining to the topic, to further motivate the principles and guidelines, and then to present, in list format, the available principles and guidelines related to the topic, many of which are drawn directly from the research presented and discussed. Principles and guidelines consist of a *highlighted, concise statement* of the principle or guideline for easy *access* to relevant information, followed by a *detailed explanation* of the principle or guideline, *including illustrated examples,* for easy *application* of guidelines.

This organization across and within chapters was specifically designed to support both *learning* and *using* the principles and guidelines. The student will wish to read the book cover to cover. The practitioner may want to do this initially, but then will be able to use the book like a handbook during design by looking up the principles and guidelines for specific topics as they are considered in the design process and using them as a checklist to guide design.

REFERENCES

AMBARDAR, ANITA KAK, "Human–Computer Interaction and Individual Differences," *Advances in Human Factors/Ergonomics: Human Computer Interaction,* Gavriel Salvendy, ed. (Amsterdam, Holland: Elsevier, 1984), pp. 207–14.

BAECKER, RONALD M., and WILLIAM A. S. BUXTON, "Cognition and Human Information Processing," *Readings in Human–Computer Interaction,* Ronald M. Baecker and William A. S. Buxton, eds. (Los Altos, Calif.: Morgan Kaufmann Publishers, Inc., 1987), pp. 207–18.

BAILEY, R. W., *Human Performance Engineering: A Guide for System Designers"* (Englewood Cliffs, N.J.: Prentice Hall, 1982).

CARD, STUART K., "The Model Human Processor: A Model for Making Engineering Calculations of Human Performance," *Proceedings of the Human Factors Society 25th Annual Meeting,* 1981, pp. 301–305.

———, THOMAS P. MORAN, and ALLEN NEWELL, *The Psychology of Human-Computer Interaction* (Hillsdale, N.J.: Lawrence Erlbaum Associates, 1983).

———, ———, and ———, "The Keystroke-Level Model for User Performance Time with Interactive Systems," *Readings in Human–Computer Interaction,* Ronald M. Baecker and William A. S. Buxton, eds. (Los Altos, Calif.: Morgan Kaufmann Publishers, Inc., 1987a), pp. 192–206.

———, ———, and ———, "Computer Text-Editing: An Information Processing Analysis of a Routine Cognitive Skill," *Readings in Human–Computer Interaction,* Ronald M. Baecker and William A. S. Buxton, eds. (Los Altos, Calif.: Morgan Kaufmann Publishers, Inc., 1987b), pp. 219–40.

CARROLL, JOHN M., ed., *Interfacing Thought: Cognitive Aspects of Human–Computer Interaction,* (Cambridge, Mass.: The MIT Press, 1987).

CARROLL, JOHN M., and MARY BETH ROSSON, "Paradox of the Active User," *Interfacing Thought: Cognitive Aspects of Human–Computer Interaction,* John M. Carroll, ed. (Cambridge, Mass.: MIT Press, 1987), pp. 80–111.

GARDINER, MARGARET M., "Principles from the Psychology of Memory: Part 2—Working Memory," *Applying Cognitive Psychology to User-Interface Design,* Margaret M. Gardiner and Bruce Christie, eds. (New York: John Wiley & Sons, Inc., 1987), pp. 135–63.

———, and BRUCE CHRISTIE, *Applying Cognitive Psychology to User-Interface Design,* (New York: John Wiley & Sons, Inc., 1987).

HAMPTON, JAMES A., "Principles from the Psychology of Language," *Applying Cognitive Psychology to User-Interface Design,* Margaret M. Gardiner and Bruce Christie, eds. (New York: John Wiley & Sons, Inc., 1987), pp. 189–218.

HITCH, GRAHAM J., "Principles from the Psychology of Memory: Part 1—Episodic and Semantic Memory," *Applying Cognitive Psychology to User-Interface Design,* Margaret M. Gardiner and Bruce Christie, eds. (New York: John Wiley & Sons, Inc., 1987), pp. 119–34.

JOHN, BONNIE E., and ALLEN NEWELL, "Cumulating the Science of HCI: From S-R Compatibility to Transcription Typing," *CHI '89 Proceedings,* May 1989, pp. 109–14, ACM.

LANDAUER, THOMAS K., "Relations between Cognitive Psychology and Computer System

Design,'' *Interfacing Thought: Cognitive Aspects of Human–Computer Interaction,* John M. Carroll, ed. (Cambridge, Mass.: MIT Press, 1987), pp. 1–25.

LINDSAY, PETER, and DONALD A. NORMAN, *Human Information Processing* (New York: Academic Press, 1977).

MILLER L. A., and J. C. THOMAS, JR., ''Behavioral Issues in the Use of Interactive Systems,'' *International Journal of Man–Machine Studies, 1977,* vol. 9, pp. 509–36.

OLSON, JUDITH REITMAN, ''Cognitive Analysis of People's Use of Software,'' *Interfacing Thought: Cognitive Aspects of Human–Computer Interaction,* John M. Carroll, ed. (Cambridge, Mass.: MIT Press, 1987), pp. 260–93.

POTOSNAK, KATHLEEN (moderator), ''Classifying Users: A Hard Look at Some Controversial Issues,'' *CHI '86 Proceedings,* April 1986, pp. 84–88, ACM.

———, and others, ''Classifying Users: A Hard Look at Some Controversial Issues,'' *CHI '86 Proceedings,* April 1986, pp. 84–88, ACM.

SHNEIDERMAN, BEN, *Software Psychology: Human Factors in Computer and Information Systems* (Cambridge, Mass.: Winthrop Publishers, Inc., 1980).

YOUNG, RICHARD M., and ALLAN MacLEAN, ''Choosing between Methods: Analyzing the User's Decision Space in Terms of Schemas and Linear Models,'' *CHI '88 Proceedings,* May 1988, pp. 139–44, ACM.

ZACHARY, WAYNE W., ''A Context-Based Model of Attention Switching in Computer–Human Interaction Domains,'' *Proceedings of the Human Factors Society 33rd Annual Meeting,* 1989, pp. 286–90.

ZUBRITZKY, MONICA, WAYNE W. ZACHARY, and JOAN M. RYDER, ''Constructing and Applying Cognitive Models to Mission Management Problems in Air Anti-Submarine Warfare,'' *Proceedings of the Human Factors Society 33rd Annual Meeting,* 1989, pp. 129–33.

CHAPTER 3

Conceptual Models

The highest level in the design of a software user interface is the conceptual model. The **conceptual** model is the *general conceptual framework through which the functionality is presented*. To understand how to design a good conceptual model, we must first understand the general concept of a mental model. A **mental model** is an *internal representation of a user's current conceptualization and understanding of a system*. A *conceptual model* is a designer's attempt, through aspects of the system's user interface, to facilitate the development of a useful *mental model* of the system by users.

The remainder of this chapter addresses the following questions:

What is a mental model?

What do we know about users' mental models?

Why do people form mental models?

How can conceptual models be designed into an interface?

What are some examples of conceptual models?

What are some specific guidelines for designing conceptual models?

WHAT IS A MENTAL MODEL?

Users do not respond passively to a system. They are actively involved in the interaction. That is, they form goals, intentions, and expectations, draw inferences, and make and test predictions. They make errors that are too systematic to be accounted for by the limitations of short-term memory or attention. Errors often seem best accounted for by positing an *inappropriate mental model* from which users are drawing inappropriate inferences and thus making inappropriate predictions.

Any system can be thought of as comprised of *parts* and *processes*. Whenever people learn to use some new system, device, or mechanism in which some parts or processes are *invisible,* they must form a mental model (Rouse and Morris, 1986), a mental representation (Barnard, MacLean, and Hammond, 1984) or a mental map of the total system. A mental model thus includes some hypotheses or a theory about the *invisible* parts and processes of a system and how they relate to the *visible* parts and processes of the system. Novice users may have very primitive, incomplete, and perhaps even erroneous mental models of a system. As they become more experienced, their mental models evolve to become more accurate and complete.

Several examples of mental models come to mind. For instance, the average automobile owner probably has a very simple model of how an automobile engine works. This model might include simple components (parts) such as a gas tank, a battery, an ignition key, gears, an oil tank, and spark plugs. This basic model might also include knowledge of some simple relationships between these components and the behavior of the automobile (processes). For instance, the user might know that, if nothing happens when the ignition key is turned, the battery is probably dead, and if the engine runs rough, there may be water in the gas tank. This simple, incomplete model allows the user to operate the car in normal conditions and diagnose simple, common problems. However, sometimes when the car will not start, it is not due to a dead battery, and sometimes water in the gas tank is not the cause of hesitation and bucking. Thus, when any new and unfamiliar symptom or behavior occurs, the model is not complete enough to allow the user to diagnose and fix the problem.

On the other hand, an experienced mechanic has a very different, much more complete and accurate mental model of the same system, which includes many more parts and processes. This allows the mechanic to predict system behavior and diagnose problems much more accurately and effectively.

As another example, young children first develop a very simple model of language. In language the parts and processes of the system are not, strictly speaking, invisible, but they are too rich and complex for a child to analyze and memorize all at once. The child first learns a few parts (a basic vocabulary of simple nouns and verbs) and a few processes (simple rules such as adding ''s'' to form plurals and adding ''ed'' to form the past tense). With this simple model the child makes errors in the use of the system, such as saying ''gooses'' for ''geese'' and "goed" for "went," but is able in fact to communicate quite effectively. With time and practice the child's model of language becomes complete and much more accurate.

Similarly, when users first learn to use a new interactive computer system, they have an incomplete, primitive, and inaccurate model of what is going on inside the "black box" as they issue commands and observe and manipulate visible objects on the screen. If they are at least computer literate, they will bring a general model of how computers work with them to a new system. This might include a set of expectations about the use of special keys, such as RETURN, TAB, BACK-SPACE, and cursor keys, and a rudimentary understanding of computer storage, filing, and retrieval processes. If they are computer novices, they have even less of a model to start with. As they become experienced in the use of a particular system, they modify their mental model based on feedback from their experience, and the model becomes more complete and accurate.

MENTAL MODELS: EXPERIMENTAL RESULTS

Research on formal logic problems from the field of cognitive psychology can be brought to bear on the theory of mental models. This research is summarized in Manktelow and Jones (1987) and paraphrased here.

Consider the following problem in formal logic: you are shown four cards and told that each has a letter on one side and a number on the other. The cards are laid out for you as follows:

E   D   4   7

You are given the following rule: If there is a vowel on one side of a card, then there is an even number on the other side. The problem for you to solve is: Which cards would you need to turn over to confirm whether the rule is true or false?

Now consider the following perfectly analogous problem. You are a cashier in a department store, and you have been given the following rule regarding receipts: If a purchase exceeds $20, then the receipt must be signed on the back by the manager. There are four receipts laid out on a table in front of you. Two show the front, with amounts of $30 and $10. The other two show the back, with one signed and one unsigned. Now your problem is to decide which receipts must be turned over to confirm whether or not the rule has been adhered to.

A great deal of research has been conducted on this type of problem, devised by P. C. Wason in the early 1960s. The rule can be abstractly stated as the following conditional statement: "If P then Q" (for example P = a purchase exceeds $20, Q = the receipt must be signed on the back), and the four instances displayed in the problem are stated as P, not-P, Q and not-Q (for example, $30, $15, signed, not signed, respectively). The correct answer to the question "which instances must be tested to confirm or disconfirm the rule" is *P* (for example, $30) and not-*Q* (for example, not signed). A *P* ($30) with a not-*Q* (not signed) on the other side, or a not-*Q* (not signed) with a *P* ($30) on the other side would violate the rule. A not-*P* ($15) or a *Q* (signed), however, has no bearing, since the rule says nothing about what must be on the other side in these cases. In general, only a combination of *P* and not-*Q* would violate the rule, so we must test instances where this might be the case, that is, the *P* and not-*Q* instances.

What is interesting about this little problem is that whether or not people, as a rule, solve it correctly seems to depend on how it is stated, even though the answer is the same regardless of the form the problem is presented in. In general, if the problem is stated in the abstract, such as *P*s and *Q*s, or letters and numbers, people often answer incorrectly (only about 9% get it right). If it is stated in terms of a familiar problem domain, however, such as receipts in a department store, many more people answer correctly (as many as 60%).

One thing early researchers noted was that when people do make errors on this problem they are *systematic,* rather than *random.* That is, most people tend to give the same wrong answer: *P* alone (for example, $30), or *P* and *Q* (for example, $30, and signed). The history of research on this problem is a history of trying to explain what leads people to this *consistently incorrect* answer.

The earliest explanation was that people were not applying logic at all to the problem and instead simply responding to the cues stated in the problem itself: *P* and *Q.* Further research with abstractly stated problems seemed to verify this explanation. However, it remained to explain why people made less errors when the problem was stated in terms of a familiar problem domain.

One theory to explain this phenomenon stated that direct experience with the content of the problem allowed people to solve the problem from memory, without recourse to logical reasoning at all. Many experiments seemed to support this. For instance, when the problem was stated in terms of a postal rule, postal employees familiar with the rule by and large solved the problem correctly, while people unfamiliar with postal regulations did not. However, in some experiments, people did well who could not be said to have had direct experience with the problem content. For instance, people who are not cashiers generally are able to correctly solve the problem of the cashier in the department store.

To explain this, current theory holds that people do indeed rely on experience and memory rather than abstract logic to solve these problems, but they rely on *general* rather than *specific* memories and experiences. For instance, although you might never have been a cashier, you might be able to imagine or remember other experiences in which authorization was required under some circumstances but not others. People are thus able to reason *analogically,* conjuring up analogous situations and drawing conclusions from them. Indeed, when people are given a problem that has real content but is not analogous to any real experience on their part (for example, "If he has milk at dinner, then he has potatoes"), they do not do so well and in fact often protest that the problem is nonsensical. On the other hand, when they are given an acceptable context for such a problem (for example, dietary restrictions dictated by a doctor for health reasons), performance improves considerably.

This seems to be evidence for the theory that to solve a given problem, people rely on already constructed general *schemas* or *mental models* of similar, analogous problems, rather than on direct memories of the exact content of the given problem or on abstract logic. It also suggests that even when people have relevant, applicable models they will not always apply them. They must be able to perceive that the specific problem is an instance of a general problem for which they have a mental model in order for the facilitation of problem solving to occur.

In sum:

> The theory of mental models predicts that sophisticated performance depends on having a highly developed mental model of the world and accessing the right model at the right time. Information which is integrated and elaborated with material held in memory makes it possible for a user to access a model of a system and, assuming it is more or less correct, to draw inferences and predictions accordingly about the actual system. This is true even if the user has never encountered before all the relevant functions of the system first hand. (Manktelow and Jones, 1987)

This research might be taken to suggest that a user interface that *draws maximally upon real-world knowledge and minimally on abstract, logical thinking* will be easier to learn and use. In fact, this is probably why the techniques of metaphor and direct manipulation in user interfaces are so powerful.

The "If P then Q" problem is a relatively simple one, compared to the problem of learning and using a computer system. And the research on this problem does not shed any light on the process of *acquiring* or selecting appropriate mental models, a key process in the successful use of computer systems. A study of *learning* in a more complex problem (Mayhew, 1977) gives additional insights into this process.

In this study, subjects were presented with six problems. The problems each involved a unique solution, but they were related so that the possible problem-solving *strategies* for finding a solution to any given problem were the same. Discovering a general, efficient solution strategy could be considered a matter of constructing a good mental model of the problem domain.

The problem forced overt moves, which allowed a detailed analysis of the solution strategies used. The change in solution strategies within and across problems (that is, with practice) could thus be observed directly, allowing some insight into the nature of the learning process, that is, into the process of acquiring a general mental model of the problem domain.

The problems were basically a set of on-line jigsaw puzzles. Subjects were presented with a list of 16 "pieces" in random order. Their job was to "fit" them together into a 4 by 4 matrix.

Each puzzle, when assembled, resembled a square matrix, and each individual puzzle piece represented one cell of the matrix. Alphanumeric characters defined each piece. Characters were drawn from several "dimensions," each with several "attributes." That is, each piece included various dimensions (specifically letters, numbers, arithmetic signs, and punctuation marks) that varied in the form of specific attributes (such as A and D, 1 and 2, + and −, and : and ;). Each piece of the puzzle matrix consisted of one attribute from each dimension. Thus one piece might consist of A2+? while another consisted of B2*;.

In a real jigsaw puzzle, which pieces fit together is determined by their shape. In these on-line puzzles, which pieces fit together was determined by which attributes pieces had in common. In any given puzzle, two of the four dimensions were *relevant* and two were *irrelevant*. Specifically, one dimension served as a matrix *row* identifier and another served as a matrix *column* identifier. The following example of a completed puzzle shows a puzzle where letters and numbers are the two relevant attributes, while arithmetic signs and punctuation marks are irrelevant.

3W/?	3X+;	3Y*:	3Z−,
5W+,	5X/;	5Y*:	5Z−?
7W/;	7X*:	7Y+?	7Z−,
9W−,	9X+?	9Y*:	9Z/;

In another puzzle, letters and numbers might again be relevant, although used as different identifiers (that is, letters for rows, numbers for columns) and with attributes in a different order (for example, Z, X, W, Y and 9, 7, 5, 3). Still another puzzle in the set might have completely different relevant dimensions, for instance, arithmetic signs and punctuation marks. Thus information contained in the puzzle pieces could be used to put them together and, if used, facilitated the solution to a significant degree.

During the course of assembling a number of such puzzles, which are built on the same principle of relevant and irrelevant dimensions, but differ in which dimensions are relevant and how the attributes in a relevant dimension are ordered, to become maximally efficient at putting the puzzles together, subjects must learn two things: (1) they must learn what properties are common to all the puzzles (that is, the general principle of matrix identifiers in alphanumeric form), and (2) they must learn how to use this commonality to develop an efficient strategy for determining what these identifiers (relevant dimensions) are in a particular puzzle and in what order the attributes appear. The sooner the relevant identifiers are known, the faster the puzzle can be completed, since once they are known all remaining pieces can be fitted without error. For instance, in the preceding example, once one row and one column are complete, all other pieces can be fit without error.

Figures 3-1 through 3-3 show a sequence of three screens during one user's interaction with a particular puzzle. Here it can be seen how the user designated an attempted fit, how feedback was provided, and how the state of the puzzle evolved. Note that each piece is assigned a letter (which is never the same as any of the letter attributes on the pieces themselves) so that the user can refer to it in the dialog. For

```
                                  TEST PIECES

A. 5Y*:                    B. 5Z-?  N. 7W/;                               M. 7Y+?
P. 3W/?       G. 5W+,      D. 3Z-,                          H. 3Y*:  J. 7Z-,  K. 3X+;


                                 TARGET PIECES


                           F. 5X/;
                           L. 7X*:
              E. 9W-,      C. 9X+?  I. 9Y*:    O. 9Z/;

TYPE IN LETTER OF TEST PIECE: K
TYPE IN LETTER OF TARGET PIECE: C
TYPE IN SIDE OF TARGET TO BE TESTED:
      1 = TOP  2 = RIGHT  3 = BOTTOM  4 = LEFT: 3
```

Figure 3–1 An experiment in learning to solve. From Mayhew, "Learning to Solve: An Exploratory Study," unpublished master's thesis, 1977, University of Denver.

```
      *** NO FIT ***
                                  TEST PIECES

A. 5Y*:                    B. 5Z-?  N. 7W/;                      M. 7Y+?
P. 3W/?       G. 5W+,      D. 3Z-,                     H. 3Y*:  J. 7Z-,  K. 3X+;


                                 TARGET PIECES


                           F. 5X/;
                           L. 7X*:
              E. 9W-,      C. 9X+?  I. 9Y*:    O. 9Z/;

TYPE IN LETTER OF TEST PIECE: K
TYPE IN LETTER OF TARGET PIECE: F
TYPE IN SIDE OF TARGET TO BE TESTED:
      1 = TOP  2 = RIGHT  3 = BOTTOM  4 = LEFT: 1
```

Figure 3–2 An experiment in learning to solve. From Mayhew, "Learning to Solve: An Exploratory Study," unpublished master's thesis, 1977, University of Denver.

```
*** CORRECT FIT ***
                         TEST PIECES

A. 5Y*:              B. 5Z-?  N. 7W/;                          M. 7Y+?
P. 3W/?    G. 5W+,   D. 3Z-,              H. 3Y*:  J. 7Z-,

                       TARGET PIECES

                     K. 3X+;
                     F. 5X/;
                     L. 7X*:
           E. 9W-,   C. 9X+?  I. 9Y*:    O. 9Z/;

TYPE IN LETTER OF TEST PIECE:
```

Figure 3–3 An experiment in learning to solve. From Mayhew, "Learning to Solve: An Exploratory Study," unpublished master's thesis, 1977, University of Denver.

each move, the user must specify (1) which piece is to be fitted to (2) which side of (3) which other piece already fitted into the puzzle. In the figures, user input is denoted in bold.

In the data generated from this study of 20 undergraduate students solving six puzzles each, a clear learning curve across the six puzzles emerged. An analysis of the actual sequence of moves made by each subject on each puzzle, plus their running commentary, yielded some insight into the nature of this learning process. Of particular interest in this discussion were the processes of discovering the general principle behind all the puzzles (the two relevant dimensions as row and column identifiers and of discovering more efficient strategies for determining the two relevant dimensions on any new puzzle once this basic principle was understood).

First, the subjects were *very active problem solvers*. Many formed hypotheses about what made the puzzle pieces fit *even before their first move on their first puzzle*. Almost all their moves were driven by a current theory about what made the pieces fit together. This theory was constantly revised as they received feedback. Sometimes feedback coincidentally reinforced an incorrect theory, and this was particularly hard to recover from. For instance, users might say out loud that they thought that perhaps numbers appeared in order in rows. They would try to fit a piece with a 5 to the right of a piece with a 3. It might so happen that both pieces had an X on them, and this was the real reason they fit together. But, because a hypothesis had been confirmed, users would continue to try to apply this model to fit additional pieces. Eventually, it would become clear that this model was incorrect, and the user would survey the pieces currently fit together to try to form a new hypothesis. Then specific moves would be made to test this new hypothesis. Thus it could be observed that *subjects formed, tested, and rejected a variety of different models* before discovering the principle of two relevant dimensions. By the end of the first puzzle, a simple model was thus formed.

The second puzzle created new problems, however. Many subjects assumed that the same two dimensions would be relevant and that attributes would appear in the same order; that is, they assumed maximum similarity across puzzles. This was incorrect, however. Which two dimensions were relevant changed on each subsequent puzzle. *Subjects would apply the simple, incorrect model, receive negative feedback, and revise their model accordingly to be more general.*

Second, as subjects continued through additional puzzles, they were observed to *refine their strategies* for determining which two dimensions were relevant on a new puzzle. There are many different strategies for doing this. For instance, on the first move of a new puzzle, subjects might choose an initial target piece and then systematically and exhaustively try out each other piece, in the order that they appeared in the display, against all four sides of the initial piece. The idea behind this strategy is that once a first fit is made one dimension has been discovered. This systematic, exhaustive (algorithmic) approach helps the user to keep track of what pieces have been tried to ensure that no pieces need to be tried more than once.

An alternative and more efficient strategy is to systematically test dimensions, that is, to hypothesize one dimension at a time and exhaustively test it with the appropriate pieces. For instance, one might first test the dimension of letters by testing all pieces with the letter W against all four sides of a target piece with the letter W on it. The advantage of this strategy is that, even if you do not happen to hit upon a relevant dimension until the third try (the worst case), you automatically know what the second relevant dimension is because there is only one left. Thus, none of the moves made in this strategy are wasted. This is not the case with the piece-by-piece strategy described previously. It could take a long time to discover the first dimension, and then you must start all over again trying to discover the second. In general, there are several points in the puzzles where, as in this example, many strategies exist, but generally, over the long run, one strategy is the most efficient.

Whether or not subjects discovered the most efficient strategy at different points in the puzzle had a lot to do with the nature of the feedback they received. For instance, if subjects chose a relatively inefficient strategy, but were lucky and by chance made a fit in only a few moves, they tended to stick to this strategy. If they eventually had a bad experience with their strategy, and it suddenly took many many moves to get a fit, then they would rethink it, trying to come up with a better strategy. Some subjects seemed to consider the problem quite abstractly, calculating the probability of success of a strategy before actually trying it. However, most subjects seemed to try whatever occurred to them first and only modified their behavior in response to negative feedback. The models they formed thus seemed to be *driven primarily by the nature of their experience with the puzzles, rather than by an abstract analysis of the general principles behind the puzzles*. This, it might be noted, is consistent with the findings on the "If P then Q" problem discussed previously.

Finally, related to this last point, different parts of the puzzle provided varying degrees of consistent, clear feedback. When an inefficient strategy consistently resulted in a high number of errors before a fit, subjects learned better strategies relatively quickly. In other parts of the puzzle where probability played a greater role, strategies less efficient in the long run were not so consistently experienced (and thus so readily perceived) as inefficient, and so learning better strategies (that is, acquiring more accurate models) occurred much less consistently and more slowly.

In sum, the general picture that emerges from the analysis of subjects' strategies in these puzzles is one of *very active problem solvers who always have a current general model in mind that drives their behavior in a very systematic way, but who are also constantly refining and revising this model in response to feedback*. Their models consist of sets of general principles, rules, and strategies. Models are formed and then constantly rejected or broadened to accommodate new experiences and feedback. Individual moves at any time can easily be explained or accounted for in terms of the current model, which is inferred from previous sequences of moves and from subjects' running commentary. Thus, errors, as well as correct moves, can be explained in terms of reasoning logically from a(n incorrect) model. How quickly a subject acquires a complete, correct model seems highly related to the quality of the feedback provided.

Several interesting ideas about how to facilitate the development of a correct mental model emerge from these data. First is the importance of *making departures from any applicable metaphor or analogy clear*. Subjects seemed to assume maximum similarity when they encountered the second puzzle and had to learn that the important analogy across puzzles was a general principle rather than the exact form.

Second is *minimizing irrelevant, misleading information*. Subjects were active problem solvers, always testing out some hypothesis or other. Often their hypotheses concerned irrelevant dimensions. When they were coincidentally confirmed in an incorrect hypothesis, it took them awhile to give it up and move on. It is likely that the puzzles would have been vastly simpler for these subjects if the irrelevant dimensions had been eliminated.

Third is the *importance of clear feedback* in assisting users to form correct, useful mental models. In these puzzles, feedback could be misleading because of the probabalistic nature of the task. As stated previously, the user could choose an incorrect dimension or inefficient strategy and temporarily get positive feedback on it. Subjects did not often seem to analyze the puzzles abstractly. They simply revised their models in response to feedback. Thus, unclear or misleading feedback led to incorrect or inefficient models, which in turn led to errors.

Interaction with a computer system may also involve departures from metaphors, irrelevant and misleading information, and inadequate feedback. It seems clear that *consistent, unambiguous, concrete, informative feedback is the key to facilitating the formation of the complete, correct, and useful models that people naturally seek.* Examples of useful feedback are given in later sections of this chapter.

Other relevant research focuses more directly on the users' mental models of software systems. Some studies are concerned simply with documenting the existence of mental models in users of software systems. For instance, two studies (Young and MacLean, 1988; Masson, Hill, and Conner, 1988) propose likely user mental models of an interface to account for patterns in user errors. Here the idea is that, as observed in Mayhew (1977), users *always* have *some* active mental model that drives their behavior. The model may be faulty (inaccurate or incomplete), but the observed behavior (for example, errors) is rational in that it is rule based and driven by the current mental model. In these studies, a good match between the predictions of behavior following from the hypothesized mental model and the patterns of errors made by users is taken as evidence of the existence of mental models and of their relationship to patterns of behavior in computer–human interaction.

Another study (Casner and Lewis, 1987) specifically addresses the idea that a mental model is a theory or hypothesis about how the *invisible* parts and processes of a software system relate to the *visible* parts and processes. The authors were concerned with investigating how users interpret actions that have *no immediate, visible effect* to take into account *surrounding visible* events.

As an illustration of the phenomenon under study, the authors offer an example from Unix. In the Unix command language, the command "Cat," followed by a file name, generally displays the file. The command "Chmod," when followed by a file name, makes the file inaccessible (that is, undisplayable) to all users. However, there is no feedback (no immediate, visible effect) when the "Chmod" command is issued. The system simply returns the usual system prompt. Later, however, if the user asks to display the file through the "Cat" command, the file is *not* displayed, and an error message is issued.

In this example, a single command, the "Cat" command, has two different results in two different instances: in one, it displays a file; in the other, it does not display the file and issues an error message instead. In the terminology of the authors, this inconsistency is a *paradox* that users must resolve in their mental model of the system. To resolve it, they must *hypothesize* what went on in the "black box" when the "Chmod" command was issued, since they received no immediate, visual feedback from that action.

Casner and Lewis propose a general, simple model that describes how users resolve this and other types of paradoxes that occur in their interaction with software user interfaces due to invisible processes, that is, how users form a mental model. They tested their model by comparing it with users' self-reported explanations of such paradoxes. In some cases their model is supported by the data from users, and in others the model seems too simple to account for the full range of hypotheses users develop as part of their mental models of a system. However, as the authors conclude:

> It is clear that people adjust their interpretation of actions which have no immediate, visible effect to take into account surrounding events. If the surrounding events include a violation of expectation, learners assign a role to these actions in such a way as to resolve the violations. In simple cases this interpretation may be derived by identifying a dialogue as belonging to a stereotyped class, involving a particular kind of hidden event, as in the model. But it appears that the simple machinery in the present model, in which a dialogue can be assigned only one interpretation, is inadequate in general.

Thus, although the details of the proposed mental model "machinery" are not completely supported by the data, the data, as in the studies cited previously, do provide evidence that users do indeed form mental models that relate *invisible* parts and processes of a system to *visible* parts and processes of the system.

Other studies are concerned with variations in mental models across users. Hanisch and co-workers (1988) explicitly measured the mental models of the system *designers* of a system and the *users* of the same system and found important differences between them. This highlights the *need to study user expectations and test the effectiveness of the models they form, rather than assume that users will form the models intended by the designers.*

This study also found evidence that users rely heavily on names and terminology in the interface to start forming mental models of the system. For instance, users expected operations to act similarly if their names implied an analogy, even when the operations were not actually analogous. This points out the *importance of naming and terminology in promoting accurate mental models.*

Another study (Snyder and co-workers, 1985) found *expert* and *novice* mental models of an operating system to be significantly different, suggesting the dynamic nature of mental models with practice. Here mental models were inferred from a sorting task in which users were asked to categorize the total set of operating system commands. Novice and expert users had very different ideas about what commands were related to one another, implying very different ways of conceptualizing the whole system. This suggests that *an interface must promote both effective novice mental models and effective expert mental models and make the transition from novice to expert as smooth as possible.*

McDonald and co-workers (1986) used similar techniques to infer user models from a sorting task of operating system commands. Here the goal was to use expert and intermediate user mental models as the basis for organizing the user interface to an on-line help system for the operating system. This was expected to facilitate the process of forming an effective mental model among novices. In the words of these authors:

> Our motivation is that on-line documentation offers an excellent medium for conveying to users effective system models. This is particularly true of modeless systems,

such as UNIX where little structural information is overtly available to users. In addition to learning details of syntax and semantics, users of documentation systems should develop mental models which allow them to integrate knowledge in order to deal effectively with the problem-solving tasks characteristic of the computing environment.

The following summary of what we know about mental models draws on the preceding and other sources:

1. A mental model includes hypotheses or a theory about the *invisible* parts and processes of a system and how they relate to the *visible* parts and processes of the system.

2. People tend to solve new problems by referring to existing mental models of the real world, rather than by applying abstract logic. They make more errors when references to existing models are not possible or obvious.

3. People are *active* problem solvers whose behavior when learning about new problems or systems can be described as hypothesis-driven or theory-testing behavior. Hypotheses or theories are drawn from existing mental models.

4. People will initially assume maximum similarity between a new problem and an existing model.

5. People tend to rely on direct feedback, rather than on abstract logic, to evaluate the correctness and efficiency of their current mental models.

6. People change their mental models and problem-solving strategies only in response to clearly negative feedback. Thus, they do not always discover complete and optimal models and strategies.

7. Many errors in system use or problem solving can be accounted for by positing rational inferences drawn from erroneous or inappropriate mental models.

Finally, Norman (1987) makes additional general observations about mental models from his extensive study of people's interactions with a wide variety of technological devices, from calculators to computers to watches to VCRs:

1. Mental models are incomplete.

2. People's ability to "run" their models are severely limited.

3. Mental models are unstable: People forget the details of the system they are using, especially when those details (or the whole system) have not been used for some period.

4. Mental models do not have firm boundaries: similar devices and operations get confused with one another.

5. Mental models are "unscientific": People maintain "superstitious" behavior patterns even when they know they are unneeded because they cost little in physical effort and save mental effort.

6. Mental models are parsimonious: Often people do extra physical operations rather than the mental planning that would allow them to avoid these actions; they are willing to trade off extra physical action for reduced mental complexity. This is especially true where the extra actions allow one simplified rule to apply to a variety of devices, thus minimizing the chances for confusions.

In addition, Norman observes that:

> most people's understanding of the devices they interact with is surprisingly meager, imprecisely specified, and full of inconsistencies, gaps and idiosyncratic quirks. The models . . . contain only partial descriptions of operations and huge areas of uncertainties. Moreover, people often feel uncertain of their own knowledge - even when it is in fact complete and correct - and their mental models include statements about the degree of certainty they feel for different aspects of their knowledge. Thus, a person's mental model can include knowledge or beliefs that are thought to be of doubtful validity. Some of this is characterized as ''superstitious'' - rules that ''seem to work'' even if they make no sense. These doubts and superstitions govern behavior and enforce extra caution when performing operations. This is especially apt to be the case when a person has experience with a number of different systems, all very similar, but each with some slightly different set of operating principles.

He concludes that ''we must . . . discard our hopes of finding neat, elegant mental models, but instead learn to understand the messy, sloppy, incomplete, and indistinct structures that people actually have.''

It should be added that one goal of a user interface should be to promote and facilitate the development of neater, more elegant, more stable, more complete, more distinct, and more confident mental models in users. This is the motivation behind the notion of a *conceptual model,* discussed in later sections of this chapter.

WHY DO PEOPLE FORM MENTAL MODELS?

The formation of a mental model of a system, as opposed to simple rote memory of relationships between states and events, allows the users of a system to perform more effectively in a number of ways (Rouse and Morris, 1986). First, it enables them *to predict future (or infer invisible) events.* For instance, the automobile owner knows that if the lights are left on when the car is not running the battery will eventually go dead. The child who learns a new noun knows without being told how to make it plural. The puzzle solver (Mayhew, 1977) learns to predict the correct position of puzzle pieces. And the computer user learns that if the power goes down certain data (in memory) will be lost, but other data (on disk) will not.

Second, mental models allow users *to find causes for observed events.* For example, the automobile owner can determine from the lack of response that the battery is probably dead. Children can usually understand what an adult is telling or asking them even if it includes utterances (or even words) they have never heard before. The puzzle solver can interpret the fit of two pieces as the operation of a simple rule. The computer user can figure out why the contents of a disk disappeared.

Third, a mental model allows users *to determine appropriate actions to cause desired changes*. For instance, the automobile owner can figure out how to get the car started again, children can figure out how to express something they have never said or heard before, and the puzzle solver can apply strategies to most efficiently determine the relevant dimensions in a new puzzle. The computer user can (hopefully!) restore erased files.

Fourth, mental models *serve as mnemonic devices for remembering relations and events*. Recall from long-term memory for dynamically interacting information is better than for independent, isolated information (see Chapter 2). Knowing the connections between the components of an engine and understanding the interaction of processes make it much easier to remember which symptoms are indications of which problems than if we simply were to rote memorize these relationships. Understanding the grammatical rules of language greatly simplifies the job of learning the correct forms of all words and expressions. Simple rules for fitting pieces together allow for much more efficient puzzle solving than random attempts at fitting pieces together. And a software user interface that is consistent and standardized will be much easier to learn and use than an interface with arbitrary differences in the expression of similar commands.

Fifth, a mental model is a natural *means of understanding an analogous device*. Understanding one kind of automobile engine makes it much easier to learn about another. It is easier for people to learn languages that are more similar to their own. For instance, it is easier for a native speaker of English to learn Spanish than Russian. Once subjects have determined what the puzzles do and do not have in common, they solve new puzzles faster. And people bring their knowledge of typewriters to their word processors, their knowledge of conventional mail systems to their electronic mail systems, and their knowledge of the manual way of doing things to any new automated application. Perhaps even more important, they bring their general knowledge of other computer systems to the problem of learning a new system.

Finally, mental models are often oversimplifications of a complex problem space that allow users to apply heuristic problem-solving strategies *designed to overcome information processing limitations*.

The problem of storing, retrieving, and applying knowledge is greatly facilitated if many data can be reduced to a few simple rules (see Chapter 2). For instance, Young and MacLean (1988) hypothesized a simplifying mental model of an interface to account for suboptimal choices between two methods of data entry observed among users. The authors suggest that users find it too cognitively taxing to accurately assess the efficacy of each method in different situations; instead, they adopt a simplified model that allows the application of simple heuristic rules to make the choice. Often the choice will be correct and sometimes it will not, but the strategy for making the choice is manageable. In this view, the strategy of forming mental models is an adaptation to the constraints and bottlenecks of the human information processing system (see Chapter 2).

DESIGNING CONCEPTUAL MODELS

Simply put, the term "mental model" refers to the user's current state of knowledge, both factual and procedural, about a complex system that may have invisible parts and processes. *Users always have mental models and will always develop and modify them, regardless of the particular design of a system.* Our goal as user interface designers is to *design so as to facilitate the process of developing an effective mental model.*

An *effective* mental model is complete and accurate and supports the purposes discussed previously. To facilitate the development of an effective mental model, we can *explicitly design a conceptual model* (Halasz and Moran, 1982; Rubinstein and Hersh, 1984) or conceptual design (Foley and Van Dam, 1982) *into the user interface.* A conceptual model can be projected in a number of ways. These include:

☞ **Making invisible parts and processes visible to the user.**

For example, in a traditional electronic mail system, users may never be aware of how or where mail is stored. To see their incoming mail, they may be required to issue a command such as "View Mail." The filing unit for mail (a *part*) is invisible to them.

An alternative interface might present an icon of an in-box that can be directly accessed (opened) to view mail. This communicates to the user that there is in fact a filing unit that stores incoming mail. Now that the user is aware of such a filing unit, operations (processes) available on other filing units (folders, trashcans, disks, and so on) can also be made available for the in-box through analogous interactions. That is, the same operation (a mouse click or key press) can accomplish the same effect (such as open, move, or close) regardless of the type of filing unit being operated on. This is easier to understand and learn than if there is no visual cue that filing units exist, and there are arbitrary commands for viewing them, such as "View Mail," "List File," and "Directory."

Processes can also be made visible. For example, in a traditional command language interface to a filing system (see Figure 3-4), the user may issue a command such as "Move/DJM:Report/DTH:Report" to move a file from one directory to another. The command is issued and the result is achieved, but it is all invisible to the user. Only the absence of an error message assures the user that the desired action has been correctly executed.

Alternatively, in a direct manipulation interface (see Figure 3-4), the user literally "picks up" a file in one open folder and "drags" it to another folder. Not only are both folders visible, but the user can see the process of movement as it is being executed (a blinking outline of the file icon follows the cursor), as well as the final result (the file is visible in the new folder and no longer visible in the old one).

Users' mental models of the filing structures and processes of a system are developed much more quickly in a system that makes these parts and processes visible. In turn, having a good mental model improves performance on the system.

Poor: **Improved:**

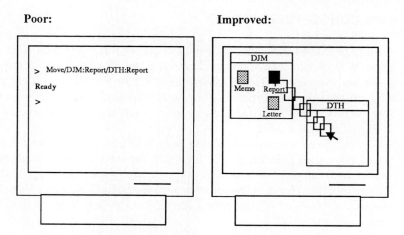

Figure 3–4 Making invisible parts and processes visible.

☞ **Providing feedback.**

In many systems, when a complex command is executed, the user just sits and waits while completely invisible processing occurs. Users are only notified when the process is complete. In such a system, where no feedback is given about or during processing, users cannot easily develop models that allow them to predict how long certain procedures will take and to diagnose problem situations. In some systems, if the system crashes in the midst of a lengthy process, users never even know it until they finally become suspicious and try to cancel out of the process. Such utter lack of feedback (of external system behavior to analyze) makes it difficult indeed to form an understanding of internal processes.

Alternatively, some interfaces provide continuous feedback. In a lengthy process, the system might issue intermediate status messages such as "Loading application . . . ," "Opening file . . . ," and "Searching . . . ." These messages not only teach the user that different subprocesses are being executed to achieve the user's goal, but also reassure the user that the system is in fact working and has not crashed. In addition, such feedback enables the user to form expectations of the average duration of these subprocesses, to estimate the time left to completion, and to quickly assess whether or not a problem has developed. And, when the system does crash or an error occurs, users know which subprocess failed, making it easier to diagnose the problem.

Other examples of useful kinds of feedback include indications of current location in a complex search or transaction process (for example, "Now on Page: 345"), indications of system load on a time-sharing system so that users can anticipate general response time ("Number of users on-line: 25" or "System response time on a scale of 1[slow] to 10[fast] is : 8"), and notification of the successful delivery of mail in an electronic mail system. These types of messages give users feedback on invisible processes that help them to form a general model of those processes. Clear and useful error messages are just as important as status feedback. See Chapter 16 for guidelines on error message design.

☞ **Building in consistency.**

People live in a world where there are rules, patterns, order, and organization. Human information processing is designed to take advantage of this (see Chapter 2). Perceiving or imposing rules and organization on data and information make them easier to learn and remember. Thus, people naturally look for rules and patterns when they are learning a new system. To the extent that they find rules, patterns, and organization, that is, consistency, these will facilitate the learning process.

Consistency can be built into a software user interface in many ways, including:

Consistent location of certain types of information on screens,
Consistent syntax of commands in a command language,
Similar execution of analogous operations in different applications,
Consistent design of command names and abbreviations,
Consistent grammatical form of error messages and instructions,
Consistent design of captions and fields on forms and displays,
Consistent dialog style for different functions, and
Terminology consistent with the users' existing vocabulary.

If there is consistency in the user interface, users may detect this quickly. This will allow them not only to remember things more easily (because there is less to remember), but also to correctly predict how to do things they have not done before. That is, consistency in the conceptual model facilitates the formation of a mental model.

☞ **Presenting functionality through a familiar metaphor.**

Making parts and processes visible, providing feedback, and building in consistency will make even a very novel and unfamiliar environment easier to learn and remember. However, if the conceptual model designed into the user interface is based on an analogous system that the user is already familiar with, this will facilitate learning even more. Two examples of metaphors as conceptual models are given in the next section.

EXAMPLES OF CONCEPTUAL MODELS

To those familiar with the Apple Macintosh user interface and its many look alikes, the best example of the use of a familiar metaphor as a conceptual model is the desktop–office metaphor (see Figure 3-5). The screen looks like an office or desktop, with familiar objects such as folders, documents, an in-box and out-box

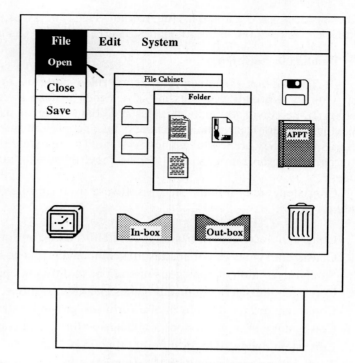

Figure 3–5 Desktop metaphor.

for mail, a trashcan, a clock, an appointment book, and so on. These familiar objects also behave in familiar ways. Documents can be stacked and shuffled, objects can be deposited in and retrieved from the trashcan, documents can be stored in and retrieved from folders, and the "pages" in the appointment book are laid out just as in a hardcopy appointment book.

The use of the mouse and other pointing devices also draws on an already familiar model: the manipulation of physical objects in space. Rather than issue an indirect command or press a function key and answer prompts to move an object from one location to another, we simply "pick up" the object with the pointer and literally "drag" it to the desired location. This is something we already know how to do, and this is exploited in the user interface to a system in which we are not actually manipulating physical objects in space at all.

There are, of course, new things to learn, such as how to scroll a document in its window and exactly how to use the mouse to select and drag objects. But much is analogous to a world that is already familiar to the user.

As another example, in designing an on-line card catalog for a library, we could exploit the existing manual card catalog as a conceptual model. Users could be first presented with three banks of drawers in iconic form: by author, by title, and by subject (see Figure 3-6). After selection, the display would zoom in on the selected bank of drawers and the user would be required to select a letter or range of letters of the alphabet (Figure 3-7). Then a particular "drawer" would be "opened," and the user could scroll through entries in alphabetic order or make quick jumps to sections in the drawer by entering in alpha strings. Entries would be on "cards" or windows, which could be stacked in an overlapping manner to reveal the top line of each (see Figure 3-8). Finally, the layout of information on each card, when selected from the drawer, would be exactly as it currently appears in the manual card catalog.

In yet another example, designing a personal accounting system, the familiar conceptual model of the checkbook could be exploited. A display that looked like a check could be presented for filling in expenditures, and a display that looked like a deposit slip could be presented for recording deposits and transfers of money between accounts. A transaction history that looked like a bank statement or checkbook register could be used to display a history of financial activity.

In all these examples, by presenting already familiar objects, relationships between objects, and operations on objects, we greatly facilitate the process of learning to use the system because we exploit a mental model and a set of expectations that the user already has. The user only has to add some refinements and

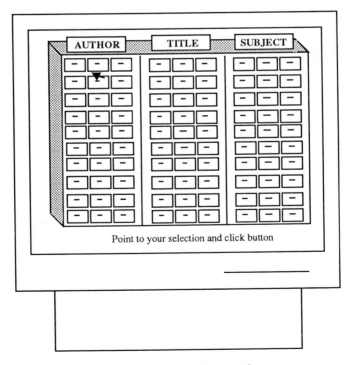

Figure 3–6 Card catalog metaphor.

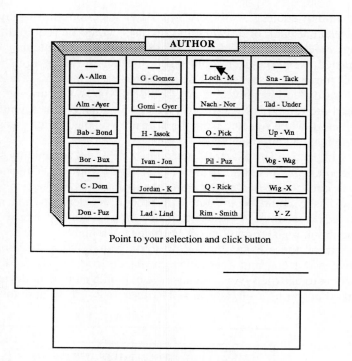

Figure 3–7   Card catalog metaphor.

perhaps some new actions to learn to use the system. It is always easier to build on current models than to develop totally new models.

Note, however, that a designer can do a good job of *presenting a conceptual model without necessarily exploiting an already existing mental model.* And icons are not necessary to the design of a good conceptual model. The other three attributes of good conceptual models, consistency, feedback, and visible parts and processes, can alone facilitate the process of learning a system. For instance, a command language that is consistent in its syntax, provides detailed feedback during and after command execution, and provides context information about the current mode, subsystem, or state will still do a better job facilitating the development of the user's model of the system than a language that does not include these characteristics. The user may have to learn about a new environment with unfamiliar objects, relationships between objects, and processes, but this learning can still be facilitated through more careful design.

Designers should also keep in mind that *exploiting familiar mental models* from the manual world *has two potential problems:*

1. Underutilization of the potential power of computers, and
2. Incomplete metaphors that mislead the user.

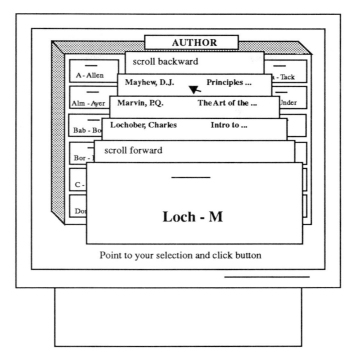

Figure 3–8 Card catalog metaphor.

If we try too hard to mimic the manual world for the sake of familiarity, we may fail to offer some desirable power that the computer affords. For instance, many windowed systems require the user to point to and select the window they wish to work in. This is very direct and analogous to manipulating papers on a desktop. However, one problem we have in managing paper on our desktops is quickly finding what we want in a large stack. This problem is often carried forward in the automated desktop: if the window we want is not visible, we must literally move and shuffle other windows until we can see and point to the window we want. In fact, it is often harder to manipulate windows on a computer screen than papers on a desktop, because the screen is smaller than a desktop and manipulating windows is more indirect than shuffling papers. In an attempt to be complete in the metaphor, designers have often failed to exploit the power of the computer to search quickly through volumes of information.

On the other hand, some windowing systems depart from the literal desktop metaphor and provide operations for quickly finding an obscured window. This is accomplished by (1) simple mouse clicks or key presses that cycle through opened windows, (2) selection from menus of window names, or (3) direct entry of window names.

As another example, in the card catalog metaphor illustrated in Figures 3-6 through 3-8, to be true to the metaphor, drawers were labeled with the exact type of alphabetic ranges that occur in real card catalogs. However, it would probably be easier for users to search for the appropriate drawer if the drawers were simply labeled A to Z, one letter per drawer. This is not done in the manual card catalog simply due to physical constraints. There is no reason not to do it for the on-line card catalog, however, and it would probably increase ease of use. In this case, departing from the metaphor has clear advantages and probably is not dangerous in any way.

The whole point of computers is to make things faster and easier than in the manual world, and, although conceptual models based on familiar metaphors facilitate learning, the designer must be careful not to lose sight of the desire for power and ease of use and thus overlook opportunities to provide these characteristics.

The second potential problem with familiar metaphors as conceptual models is related to the preceding point: incomplete metaphors may actually mislead the user. It may not be possible to construct a complete metaphor, because there simply is not a one-to-one correspondence between manual and automated functions. Or adding additional power that is not available in the manual world (recommended previously) may require departing from the metaphor. Where the metaphor breaks down, users may be misled.

For instance, if we present an automated filing system through the office file cabinet metaphor, we must depart from the metaphor to provide file-based password protection, since there is no way to lock individual documents in a real file cabinet (Halasz and Moran, 1982). In a more serious example, we might want to offer the capability to cross-reference a single document in multiple folders in order to facilitate searching and retrieval. However, the only way to file a document in two folders in a real file cabinet is to make an independent duplicate. In the real file cabinet, making changes to the document in one folder will not affect the duplicate in the other folder, while in the automated filing system, editing the document in one folder automatically edits the document in the other folder since they are in fact the same document, but accessible from two different pathways in the computer filing structure. Reasoning from the file cabinet metaphor, which usually yields correct predictions of system behavior, the user may erroneously assume that editing the file in one folder leaves a duplicate in original form in the other folder. Because the explicitly designed metaphor allows users to successfully draw on knowledge of another system in many cases, they may be misled in parts of the system where the metaphor breaks down.

An important distinction must be made between departures from a familiar metaphor that simply cannot be explained by the metaphor (adding file-based password protection or giving drawers different labels as in the card catalog metaphor) and departures that *violate particular expectations induced by the metaphor* (as in the example of cross-referencing files). The former are probably harmless (and may even increase usability), and where the metaphor is adhered to, this will still facilitate overall learning. The latter, however, are dangerous, and designers must avoid them or provide ample cues and feedback to users so that they clearly understand the unexpected consequence of their actions.

This tension between exploiting metaphors to facilitate learning but violating them to increase power is nicely summed up in an article by Smith (1987). Smith terms interface features that adhere to a single metaphor as **literal** and features that violate the metaphor specifically in order to enhance power as **magical.** Smith also notes that some features are neither literal nor magical in that they depart from the metaphor but do not enhance functionality in any way. These features are termed **external** because they are usually due to constraints imposed by external factors. The three types of features are illustrated through an example system known as ARK, or the Alternate Reality Kit. ARK is a system for creating interactive animated simulations. In Smith's words:

> The interface is quite faithful to a physical-world metaphor: all objects have a visual image, a position, a velocity, and can experience forces. One of the objects is a hand, which the user controls with a mouse. With the hand, the user can carry objects, throw them, press buttons and operate slider controls . . . . The intent is to have the user conclude very quickly that the screen depicts a physical world, and that the user is directly manipulating physical objects. This is the advantage of *literalism*—interfaces strongly based on a well-known metaphor require very little explanation to users . . . .
>
> However, sticking completely to a metaphor can cripple a system's functionality. For example, an ARK user may wish to connect a simulated pushbutton to some ARK device, perhaps for turning the device on and off . . . . Should the user be required to connect the button by drilling a hole in the device and cutting into metaphorical electrical work? . . . In the design of ARK, I considered perfectly literal ways of connection to be too tedious . . . . Instead, the ARK user connects the button simply by dropping it onto the device . . . . Features like these are called *magical* because they enable the user to do powerful things that are outside of the possibilities of the metaphor.

From observations of 52 users learning and using ARK, Smith concludes:

> In ARK, the time to explain the basics is actually measured in seconds. Every piece of added magic is relatively "expensive" because it requires its own explanation: it does not "come for free" as it does when the user realizes that there is a physical metaphor. In designing ARK, I am therefore faced with a tension between the *limitations* imposed by literalism and the *obscurity* of magic. Or, in positive terms, between the *power* of magic and the *learnability* of literalism.

Smith makes some other interesting observations. He notes that some sophisticated computer users took slightly more time to learn the *literal* features of the interface. He suggests they expect more magic than is available. On the other hand, very naive users, such as young children, often seemed to expect the interface to be more literal than it is, that is, they expected *less* magic. The balance between literalism and magic seemed about right for computer novices over 10 years old.

The lessons to draw from Smith's experience and observations seem to be that a little bit of magic (that is, powerful departures from a metaphor) is a good thing because, in combination with a good dose of literalism, ease of learning is still kept at an optimal level, while ease of use (power) is increased. Users seem to adapt easily to a moderate amount of magic. External features (unpowerful departures from the metaphor), on the other hand, while often unavoidable, should be kept to the minimum level possible.

GUIDELINES FOR DESIGNING CONCEPTUAL MODELS

Little research has been conducted to directly assess the influence of different conceptual models in software user interfaces in facilitating learning and use. However, some simple, general guidelines can be summarized from the foregoing discussion.

☞ **Design so as to facilitate the process of developing an effective and efficient mental model of the system.**

Novices learn to use a new system effectively by developing a *mental model*. By applying what we know about mental models and how people acquire them, we can design systems that make it easier to do so. This is accomplished by designing a good *conceptual model* into the interface. The following guidelines suggest how the interface can be designed to facilitate the development by users of useful, efficient mental models.

☞ **Take into account the mental models users will bring with them to the new system.**

Consider how people currently operate in their manual world and what other tools they are familiar with, including other computer systems. Look for opportunities to design a user interface to a new system that builds on models, knowledge, habits, routines, and expectations people already have.

For instance, even if an explicit metaphor is not employed in an interface, it is still important to cast the interface in terms of familiar **objects, relationships between objects, object attributes,** and **actions** from the manual world. New objects to learn about, violations of expected relationships between objects, missing or new object attributes, and unfamiliar actions will all make it harder for a new user to relate the new system to any existing knowledge, thus increasing the time it takes to develop an appropriate and effective mental model of the new system.

For example, it will be harder for computer novices to learn about computer filing objects presented as "Volumes," "Directories," and "Files," where a file is accessed by specifying a ''Pathname,'' than it will be to learn about computer filing objects presented as ''Diskettes,'' ''Folders,'' and ''Documents,'' where a document is accessed by ''opening'' diskettes, folders, and documents. The former case involves unfamiliar objects and actions, while the latter matches well with already familiar objects and actions.

Familiar objects, relationships, attributes, and actions cannot be exploited in an interface unless the designer has a good picture of what these things are in the user's current world. This knowledge can only be gained by conducting a thorough **task analysis** of the user's job and tasks. Task analysis is a design *methodology,* and as such is beyond the scope of this book, which deals only with design *principles and guidelines*. It is important to note here, however, that an effective conceptual model cannot be designed without employing this methodology. Unfortunately, although many human factors engineers are capable of conducting a task analysis, no single source yet exists in the literature for the lay reader.

☞ **A conceptual model should be explicitly designed and effectively presented through the user interface.**

A conceptual model should be designed as the first step in user interface design. It provides a framework for all other design decisions and results in consistency and coherence in the interface. Consistency and coherence facilitate the development of mental models by users.

The characteristics of visible parts and processes, feedback, and consistency (described in later principles) will assist the user in detecting the conceptual model and making effective use of it in developing a useful mental model of the system. The conceptual model can be based on a familiar metaphor, and this is desirable but not necessary. All types of dialog styles (menu systems, command language systems), not just icon-based, direct manipulation interfaces, can and should be based on coherent, consistent conceptual models.

☞ **The intended conceptual model should anticipate *users'* expectations rather than reflect *designers'* knowledge and mental models.**

A conceptual model that is consistent with the *designer's* expectations, but not the *user's,* is not a good conceptual model in that it will not facilitate the development of the user's mental model. For example, a designer familiar with computer architecture and processes might decide to have a single command called ''send'' for both printing files and sending mail to other users. This would make sense to the designer, who has a mental model of computers in which the internal process for these two functions is actually the same: in both cases a file is simply being sent to a different device, either to a printer or to another terminal. Thus, a single command with a device argument that can specify either a terminal or a printer is consistent with the designer's mental model and meets his or her expectations.

However, a nontechnical user unfamiliar with computer architecture and processes has two very different mental models for printing documents and sending documents, and using the same command for both would violate this user's expectations. Finding consistency where important differences are perceived is, as in this case, just as much of a problem as not finding consistency where similarities are perceived. The conceptual model designed into the system must be consistent with users', not designers', expectations.

☞ **Make invisible parts and processes of the system visible.**

A command such as "Open Mailbox" makes objects (that is, *parts*) more visible, as compared to a command such as "View Mail," which does not clearly communicate that a filing object exists that may have properties similar to other filing objects.

Detailed status messages are one way to make *processes* more visible. Messages such as "Now opening application . . . Now searching for file . . . Now loading file . . . " are much more informative than simply a blinking cursor in response to a user request.

There are even more direct ways to make processes more visible. For example, in a traditional command language interface to a filing system, the user may issue a command such as "Move/DJM:Report/DTH:Report" to move a file from one directory to another. The command is issued and the result is achieved, but it is all invisible to the user. Only the absence of an error message assures the user that the desired action has been correctly executed.

Alternatively, in a direct manipulation interface, the user "picks up" a file in one open folder and "drags" it to another folder. Not only are both folders visible, but one can see the process of movement as it is being executed (a blinking outline of the file icon follows the cursor), as well as the final result (the file is visible in the new folder and no longer visible in the old one).

☞ **Build in consistency.**

Consistency is a fundamental feature of a conceptual model that facilitates the development of mental models by users. There are any number of ways to build consistency into an interface. Just a few are reiterated here:

Consistent location of certain types of information on screens,
Consistent syntax of commands in a command language,
Similar execution of analogous operations in different applications,
Consistent design of command names and abbreviations,
Consistent grammatical form of error messages and instructions,
Consistent design of captions and fields on forms and displays,
Consistent dialog style for different functions, and
Terminology consistent with the users' existing vocabulary.

☞ **Design a conceptual model that draws maximally on real-world knowledge and experience and minimally on abstract, logical thinking.**

Using familiar terminology rather than computer terminology is one way to draw on real-world knowledge. The idea behind a "query-by-example" user interface to a database system is another. Instead of requiring users to express queries through some abstract query language, they express queries through a concrete example.

A command language with a syntax as close to English as possible will be easier to learn than one with an arbitrary syntax. Users will be able to draw on their familiarity with English, rather than being required to express syntax in an abstract format. Direct manipulation rather than a command language interface similarly is easier to learn when functionality includes the manipulation of objects in space, because it allows users to draw on existing spatial and motor skills, rather than having to develop new, abstract ways of interacting with objects in space.

In general, it is wise to avoid any requirement to use formal logic (for example, construct or interpret complex relationships and/or draw inferences) in an interface, because it is well documented that people consistently make errors when they must rely on formal logic alone to solve problems.

☞ **Provide consistent, unambiguous, concrete, informative feedback to reinforce the conceptual model.**

Feedback can be provided in many forms (messages, highlighting and other visual cues, sound, and so on). It is important to provide consistency in choosing feedback for various functions within a system. In addition, consider the following:

1. Be generous in providing status messages.
2. Design clear, constructive error messages.
3. Provide visible results of actions (for example, highlight a selected object or display the new location of a moved object).
4. Display actions in progress when possible (for example, show objects moving from one location to another, rather than just showing the end result of a move).
5. Provide as much context information as possible. Examples are maintaining as much history on the screen as possible during command language use, labeling menu screens with the titles of previous menu picks leading to the current screen, and displaying the query criteria on a screen presenting query results.
6. In general, strive for WYSIWYG (what you see is what you get) as much as possible in an interface.

All these types of feedback will project the underlying conceptual model of a system more clearly to users and enable them to more quickly develop appropriate and useful mental models of the system.

☞ **Avoid irrelevant and misleading feedback that will distract from the conceptual model and impede the development of optimal mental models.**

Avoid misleading messages. For instance, a system that issues the error message "File not found" in response to a file name that was correct except that it was missing the required suffix or extension (for example, "Mayhew" entered for "Mayhew.TXT") is very misleading and may violate the user's current mental model of the stability or structure of the filing system. Thinking the file truly cannot be found, the user may try to determine how it got erased or look for it in different directories. In the underlying conceptual model, file names include a suffix, but the feedback in this example does not reinforce the conceptual model. Instead, the message should read something like "Can't recognize filename without extension. Please enter whole file name or just extension now." This message presents the underlying conceptual model more clearly and will prevent users from developing erroneous mental models.

Also avoid irrelevant information on the screen that users may try to interpret and integrate into their mental models. For instance, do not use color if it does not convey any important meaning or have any useful function (see Chapter 14). It will distract users and may even cause them to make erroneous inferences in their attempt to interpret it. Do not display irrelevant information, such as system state codes and terminal numbers meant for system engineers. Again, users may try to interpret it and be misled as they try to form a mental model of the system.

When potentially misleading information cannot be avoided, be careful to point this out to users. For example, if for some good reason the command syntax for a particular command is inconsistent with the syntax for other related commands, the error message issued when the command is incorrectly specified should point this out so that novices do not erroneously conclude that the syntactic rule they thought was operating is in fact simply incorrect in general.

☞ **Choose names, labels, and terminology consistent with the conceptual model.**

For example, if the conceptual model is that of an office filing system, where objects in the interface are analogous to file cabinets, folders, and documents, do not use the word "File" to refer to a document. Although this is a common word for documents in the computer world, if the intention is to project a conceptual model of the office filing system, the term file would be inconsistent with this conceptual model. It would most likely be interpreted as referring to the folder object, since this is the more common use of the word file in office terminology.

Similarly, things that are related should have related names. For instance, the terms "Move" (move within a document), "SuperMove" (move across documents), "Copy" (copy within a document), and "SuperCopy" (copy across documents) do a good job of conveying the relationships between these commands. In fact, they are executed through highly analogous operations. Terms such as "Move," "Lift," "Copy," and "Excerpt," do not communicate the important relationships among them well even though when each is taken alone, it is not bad at conveying the intended meaning. Given that in fact the functions operate very analogously, the former terms do a better job of communicating the underlying conceptual model.

By the same token, names and labels should not mislead by implying relationships that do not actually exist. For example, a menu choice on an electronic calendar that allows some aspects of the calendar to be edited but not others (for example, appointments may be rescheduled but not canceled) should not be assigned a label such as "Edit Calendar," which users might misinterpret as allowing *any* kind of editing, including canceling. Again, the terminology is not consistent with the underlying conceptual model. An improvement in this example might be to assign a clearer label, such as "Edit Appointment Details," or to use the original label, but in fact allow all kinds of editing, including canceling, as users are likely to expect.

☞ **A conceptual model that is based on a familiar metaphor should consistently adhere to that metaphor as much as possible *without sacrificing power*, but should at least not be misleading.**

As discussed in the section called "Examples of Conceptual Models," starting with a familiar metaphor as a base and adding features and functions that do not have counterparts in the preexisting mental model (that is, "magic") is fine, as long as the system does not mislead the user into incorrect uses of the new features and functions by violating expectations set up by the basic metaphor. Generally, if the metaphor does *not* apply in predicting system behavior as often or more often than it *does* apply, then it is probably an inappropriate conceptual model. A little bit of magic, however, is usually a good thing, as it can enhance functionality and power beyond the limits of the metaphor.

☞ **Through the conceptual model, promote the development of both novice and expert mental models.**

Interfaces that provide alternative modes of interaction implicitly recognize that novices and experts are likely to have very different mental models to bring to bear on system use. For instance, Microsoft Word, a menu-driven word processor has "Short Menus" and "Full Menus" choices available. The "Short Menus" version hides advanced functions from the novice. The idea is that it will be easier for novices to begin to form an initial mental model if they are protected from the full complexity of the system. When experienced users are ready to expand their mental models to include more advanced functions, they have easy access to "Full Menus."

Apple's HyperCard user interface includes a similar technique. Several "user levels" of functionality are available, each offering successively richer and more powerful functionality. Again the idea is that a novice can choose to deal with only basic functions. When a simple mental model has been developed, moving through successive levels of the interface allows the more experienced user to add gradually to and build up their mental model in a controlled and systematic fashion. This systematic approach is intended to help users structure their learning experience, thus facilitating the learning of a full, complete mental model.

In both these examples, part of the conceptual model designed into the interface is the partition of functionality into layers or levels in such a way that each layer builds consistently and smoothly on the simpler mental model formed from previous layers.

Another example of building both novice- and expert-oriented conceptual models into a single interface is the notion of menu *bypass*. Many menu interfaces oriented toward novices have a command language bypass. Here the idea is that the mental models of novices are tentative and incomplete, and they need the structure and prompting offered by a menu system. However, as their mental model becomes more complete and accurate, they do not need such assistance and can move on to a more flexible and efficient interface.

The menu structure makes the conceptual model of the system more visible and discernable to novice users, promoting the development of a mental model. Once the mental model is formed, however, presenting the conceptual model overtly is no longer important, and an interface style, such as a command language, that does not overtly present the conceptual model is no problem, and in fact adds power and flexibility to the interface that are not available in the menu interface.

☞ **Provide an active, "intelligent" help system that will reinforce the conceptual model and encourage the development of optimal mental models.**

As reported in a variety of studies (see the preceding discussions of Manktelow and Jones, 1987; Mayhew, 1977; Young and MacLean, 1988; Masson, Hill, and Conner, 1988; Norman, 1987), people do not always form optimal mental models. There is evidence (Mayhew, 1977) that in fact people may only be motivated to improve on less than optimal models in the face of clearly negative feedback.

The idea behind an active *suggestions* system, in contrast to a traditional passive on-line help system, is that the system would record and analyze a given user's interaction. Whenever it detected inefficient usage (such as scrolling when the "Search" command could be used or using "Delete" and "Insert" when the "Replace" command could be used), it would make suggestions to the user, offering instruction on more powerful commands. In effect, the system would look for evidence of incomplete or suboptimal mental models and offer advice aimed at improving mental models.

Of course, the suggestions system would have to be under user control. Some users may not like the idea of the system observing and passing judgment on their performance. If a suggestion system could be turned off at the user's discretion, however, it probably would not be perceived as offensive.

☞ **Documentation should explicitly present the intended conceptual model.**

If consistencies, that is, a conceptual model, have been purposefully built into the user interface, these should be explicitly pointed out in the user documentation. For instance, instead of listing in separate sections on different file types (text, graphics, spreadsheet, and so on) the way to select data from a file, if there is consistency across file types in selection mechanisms, this should be pointed out by having a single section in the manual (or on-line help system) that discusses selection. If a familiar metaphor has been exploited in the conceptual model, then this should be explicitly pointed out: "Your screen is just like a desktop. You will notice familiar objects on it, such as a folder, a trashcan . . . ." Point out rules and consistencies (as well as deliberate inconsistencies, for example, "magic") in the system explicitly, rather than assume that users will detect it on their own. Evidence exists that this assists the user in learning to use the system (Halasz and Moran, 1982; Foss, Rosson, and Smith, 1982; Mayer, 1980).

REFERENCES

BARNARD, P. J., A. MACLEAN and N. V. HAMMOND, "User Representations of Ordered Sequences of Command Operations," *Proceedings, Interact '84,* September 1984, Volume 1, pp. 434–38, IFIP

CASNER, STEPHEN, and CLAYTON LEWIS, "Learning about Hidden Events in System Interactions," *CHI '87 Proceedings,* May 1987, pp. 197–204, ACM.

FOLEY, JAMES, and ANDRIES VAN DAM, *Fundamentals of Interactive Computer Graphics* (Reading, Mass.: Addison-Wesley Publishing Co., 1982), Chapter 6.

FOSS, D. J., M. B. ROSSON, and P. L. SMITH, "Reducing Manual Labor: An Experimental Analysis of Learning Aids for a Text Editor," *Proceedings, Human Factors in Computer Systems,* 1982, pp. 332–36.

HALASZ, FRANK, and THOMAS P. MORAN, "Analogy Considered Harmful," *Proceedings, Human Factors in Computer Systems,* March, 1982, pp. 383–86.

HANISCH, KATHY A., and others, "Novice–Expert Differences in the Cognitive Representation of System Features: Mental Models and Verbalizable Knowledge," *Proceedings of the Human Factors Society 32rd Annual Meeting,* 1988, pp. 219–23.

MANKTELOW, KEN, and JULIAN JONES, "Principles Form the Psychology of Thinking and Mental Models," *Applying Cognitive Psychology to User-Interface Design,* Margaret M. Gardiner and Bruce Christie, eds. (John Wiley & Sons, Inc., 1987), pp. 83–117.

MASSON, MICHAEL E. J., WILLIAM C. HILL, and JOYCE CONNER, "Misconceived Misconceptions?" *CHI '88 Proceedings,* May 1988, pp. 151–56, ACM.

MAYER, R. E., "Elaboration Techniques for Technical Text: An Experimental Test of the Learning Strategy Hypothesis," *Journal of Educational Psychology,* 67, (1980), pp. 725–34.

MAYHEW, DEBORAH J., "Learning to Solve: An Exploratory Study," unpublished master's thesis, University of Denver, 1977.

McDonald, J. E., and others, "A Formal Interface Design Methodology Based on User Knowledge," *CHI '86 Proceedings,* April 1986, pp. 285–90, ACM.

Norman, Donald A., "Some Observations of Mental Models," *Readings in Human–Computer Interaction,* Ronald M. Baecker and William A. S. Buxton, eds. (Los Altos, Calif.: Morgan Kaufmann Publishers, Inc., 1987), pp. 241–44.

Rouse, William B., and Nancy M. Morris, "On Looking into the Black Box: Prospects and Limits in the Search for Mental Models," *Psychological Bulletin,* 100, no. 3 (1986), pp. 349–63.

Rubinstein, Richard, and Harry Hersh, *The Human Factor: Designing Computer Systems for People* (Burlington, Mass.: Digital Press, 1984), pp. 42–58.

Smith, Randall B., "Experiences with the Alternative Reality Kit: An Example of the Tension between Literalism and Magic," *CHI '87 Proceedings,* May 1987, pp. 61–68, ACM.

Snyder, Kathleen M., and others, "Using Cognitive Models to Create Menus," *Proceedings of the Human Factors Society 29th Annual Meeting,* 1985, pp. 655–58.

Young, Richard M., and Allan MacLean, "Choosing between Methods: Analyzing the User's Decision Space in Terms of Schemas and Linear Models," *CHI '88 Proceedings,* May 1988, pp. 139–44, ACM.

CHAPTER 4

Dialog Styles: Menus

Chapters 4 through 11 offer design principles and guidelines relating to particular **dialog styles.** A dialog style is an overall style of interaction. At least seven distinct dialog styles exist and are addressed here and in the following chapters as follows:

Menus
Fill-in forms
Question and answer
Command languages
Function keys
Direct manipulation
Natural language

It is not always possible to draw clear, unambiguous borders between these dialog styles. Most user interfaces employ more than one dialog style, and each may not appear in its most pure form. However, it is convenient and useful to draw distinctions between them for the purposes of presenting research findings and design principles and guidelines.

In each chapter, a given dialog style is addressed in several sections as follows:

A definition of the dialog style

When to use the dialog style

Research results relevant to the dialog style

Principles and guidelines for designing the dialog style

This chapter addresses the dialog style called menus.

WHAT IS A MENU INTERFACE?

A **menu** is a list of options from which the user selects the desired choice. In menu-driven user interfaces, the primary form of interaction is a sequence in which the user is repetitively presented with sets of choices and asked to select one or more from among them. There are many variations of the menu dialog style, and some of these are presented in Figure 4-1. Choices may be *presented* as words in a

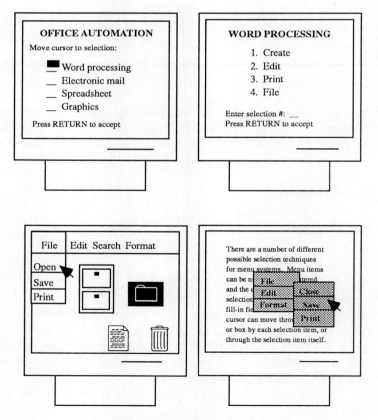

Figure 4-1   Examples of menus.

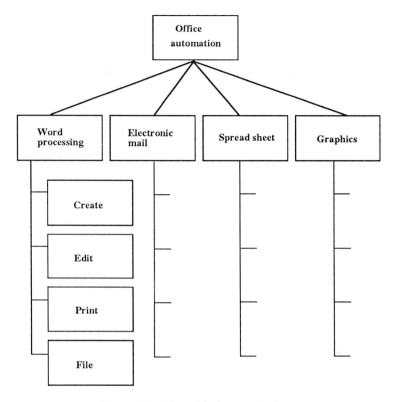

Figure 4–2 Hierarchical menu structure.

list or as collections of icons. Choices may be *selected* by moving a cursor with the keyboard or an alternative input device such as a mouse, or by entering a selection code such as a number, letter, or name from the keyboard.

Perhaps the most common *structure* of menu interfaces is **hierarchical,** as illustrated in Figure 4-2. In this example of an office automation system, the top-level menu presents four choices: word processing, electronic mail, spreadsheet, or graphics. If the user chooses word processing, the next-level menu offers four choices: create, edit, print, or file. If the user had chosen electronic mail or graphics off the main menu, then different sets of choices would be presented. In such a tree structure, each choice made determines which choices will be offered next, and the user might proceed along a number of different pathways.

Alternatively, menus can be structured linearly. In a **linear** menu structure, *alternative* pathways do not exist (see Figure 4-3). There is only one pathway, but at each point the user must still make a selection from among a set of options. For instance, within a print request, the user may be asked a series of questions to define the print job, such as the page size, the printer to be used, alternative paper

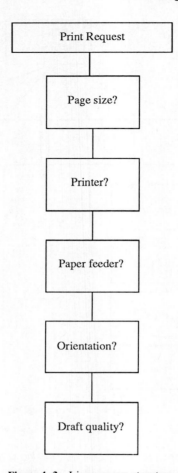

Figure 4–3   Linear menu structure.

feeders, paper orientation, and draft or final quality. Each question presents a menu of valid options to choose from, but all questions are always posed regardless of how any individual question is answered.

Finally, menus can also be **networked.** A networked menu provides an option known as *menu bypass* that allows the user to jump directly from one *leaf* or *node* in a hierarchical menu to another without backing up along the pathway to one leaf and then proceeding down the pathway to another leaf, as would be necessary in a strictly hierarchical menu (see Figure 4-4). For example, common functions such as ''Help,'' ''Quit,'' or ''Print'' might be made available directly on many different levels and menu screens to avoid tedious navigation to these high-frequency options.

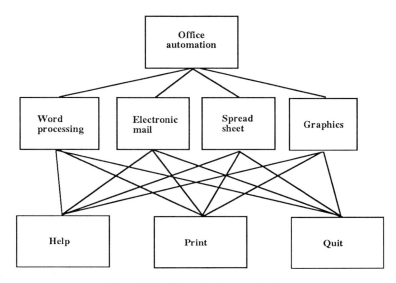

Figure 4–4   Networked menu structure.

WHEN IS A MENU DIALOG STYLE APPROPRIATE?

Menus have particular advantages and disadvantages relative to other dialog styles. The *advantages* include the following:

    Self-explanatory.   Well-designed menus make a system easy to learn because they make both the *semantics* and the *syntax* of the system explicit. That is, they make clear both *what* can be done (semantics) and *how* to do it (syntax). Clear menu choice labels and good instructions on how to select from the menu mean that at any time the user knows everything necessary to take the next step in the dialog, because the interface is relatively self-explanatory. The learning burden is decreased and the need for manuals and training programs is reduced. This might be contrasted with a command language interface, which gives no semantic or syntactic prompting and requires that the user simply know what can be done and how to do it.

    Requires little human memory.   For the same reason that menus are easy to learn, they are also easy to remember. Casual users who may not use a system frequently run the risk of forgetting how to use it between uses. Because a menu interface is potentially self-explanatory, it is not necessary to memorize and retain semantic or syntactic knowledge. Menus rely on **recognition memory** rather than **recall memory.** The user need only recognize the menu choice labels and instructions and does not have to recall (without cues) what actions are possible or how to execute them. Recognition memory is faster and more accurate than recall memory, and menus exploit this fact.

Few keystrokes.   Most menus require only that the user type in a one- or two-character code, or move a cursor with the cursor control keys, or point to a menu choice with an alternative input device (such as a mouse) and press a button. Generally, this requires fewer keystrokes than other dialog styles, such as typing in command names or natural language phrases or entering data in fill-in fields. Fewer keystrokes mean both less time and less opportunity for user error.

Easy error handling.   Because there is such a limited set of valid inputs at any one time, it is relatively easy to do error checking and to design good error reporting.

Enhancements are visible.   Because a menu interface always presents all valid options at any one time, whenever new functions are added to a system they will appear directly in the interface, that is, on a menu screen. Thus users will always notice when new functions are added. This might be contrasted with a command language interface, in which no evidence of enhancements actually appears through the interface, or with a function key interface in which new functions are added by combining labeled function keys in ways not reflected on the labels. In these interfaces, users simply need to know when functions have been added because the interface has not actually changed in any visible way.

In summary, the main advantages of menu interfaces are ease of learning and remembering and simplicity of input. There are serious trade-offs, however. *Disadvantages* of menu systems include:

Inefficient.   It may be simple and fast to make a selection from an individual menu screen. However, in a complex menu system with many choices on each screen and many levels in the hierarchy, it can actually be quite tedious and inefficient to navigate to the desired function. Contrast such a tedious sequence of choices with, for example, simply entering the desired function by name in a command language interface or pressing a single key in a function key interface. These latter interfaces avoid the need to scan through busy screens looking for the desired option, trying to determine down which pathway the desired function might be found, and waiting for the screen to refresh after each choice. Menus may be easy to learn and remember, but except for very simple menu structures, they may not be as easy to use as some alternative dialog styles.

Inflexible.   Menus also force a user through set sequences of steps. The dialog is *system* rather than *user* controlled to a greater extent than some other dialog styles. Unless the menu structure is highly networked, only set sequences of steps are allowed, and these sequences may or may not correspond to the sequence of steps that would best support a given user goal. Thus, unless the user goal or task is inherently highly structured itself, a menu interface may not support it very well.

Impractical for numerous choices. Menus are appropriate when there is a limited number of valid inputs at any given time. If numerous options are available at any one time, this may make a menu dialog style at best cumbersome and at worst impossible. For example, it may be difficult to read and respond to a menu of files or documents if 20 or more files exist. Perhaps they will not even all fit on one screen, requiring scrolling to view all the options. Input codes become harder to design and require more keystrokes when there are many options. Some inputs simply cannot be expressed as menus because of the effectively unlimited values possible, such as names, addresses, numerical values, and the like.

Take up screen "real estate." Menus, especially ones with numerous options, take up space on the screen, potentially competing with other aspects of a display. Dedicated function keys and command languages, for instance, take up considerably less space. Function keys require no screen space, and a command language may require only one line. Where space is at a premium, menus may thus be at a serious disadvantage relative to other possible dialog styles.

Given these relative advantages and disadvantages, we can draw some conclusions about the kinds of tasks and users for which the menu might be appropriate as a primary dialog style. Figure 4-5 lists the user characteristics (see Chapter 2) for which a menu-driven user interface would be a good choice. Generally, because menu interfaces are (potentially) easy to learn, they are good for

Menus are most appropriate for:

☞ User psychology

Negative attitude
Low motivation

☞ Knowledge and experience

Low typing skill
Little system experience
Low task experience
Low application experience
Frequent use of other systems
Low computer literacy

☞ Job and task characteristics

Low frequency of use
Little or no training
Discretionary use
High turnover rate
Low task importance
High task structure

Figure 4-5 When to use menus.

users who are averse to learning, that is, who might have a negative attitude toward the system or low motivation to use it, for whatever reason. This is especially true of discretionary users who make a personal choice whether to buy and use a given system or not, rather than mandatory users.

Users lacking in the applicable types of knowledge and experience will also perform better on a menu system because it is relatively easy to learn both the semantics of the system and the syntax of the interface. And, if a user frequently uses other systems with different user interfaces or uses one system very infrequently, it will be relatively easy to remember how to do something on a particular system if it is menu driven, again because menu interfaces are easy to learn and remember.

Finally, because menus are such a rigid, structured dialog style, they are best suited to tasks that are themselves highly structured, that is, in which a set sequence of steps is always or usually followed. Tasks that are highly unstructured, in which any sequence of individual steps or functions is possible and desirable, do not lend themselves well to a menu-driven interface, which forces the user into set sequences of steps.

DESIGNING MENU SYSTEMS: EXPERIMENTAL RESULTS

The potential advantages and benefits of menus systems as just discussed are not simply inherent in menus as a dialog style. Care must be taken in the design of any menu-driven interface in order to realize those potential advantages. A great deal of research has been conducted to investigate the effects of different design alternatives on the performance of menu users. In this section, the results of some of these studies are presented and discussed. In the subsequent section, general guidelines for menu design are drawn in summary form from these and other studies.

Design issues in menu systems can be divided into five areas:

Menu structure
Menu choice ordering
Menu choice selection
Menu invocation
Menu navigation

Discussion of research studies and general guidelines drawn from them are organized around these issues. Research is not available on all topics.

Menu structure.   One issue regarding menu design is known as the *depth–breadth trade-off* (Miller, 1981). One design alternative is to have only a few choices on any individual menu screen and, therefore, many or at least more levels in the menu hierarchy (depth). The other alternative would be to have more choices on an individual menu screen, thereby reducing the number of levels in the hierarchy. The question is which alternative is optimal in terms of user performance when navigating through a menu system to a target item at the lowest level.

In the abstract, rational arguments could be made to support both alternatives. In a deep menu structure, in spite of the number of levels to navigate through, it might take less time to scan and locate the appropriate choice at each level, because there are so few choices on a screen. On the other hand, in a broad menu structure, there are fewer overt responses to make and less levels to navigate through, even though an individual screen might be quite busy and take longer to scan and read through. The question comes down to a trade-off between search times in long lists versus time for multiple selections and responses.

Miller (1981) first investigated this depth–breadth trade-off by presenting 24 college students with one of four menu structures, all of which had the same 64 target items at the lowest level. The four menu structures were as follows:

Two choices per screen, six levels (2^6)

Four choices per screen, three levels (4^3)

Eight choices per screen, two levels (8^2)

Sixty-four choices all on one screen, one level (64^1)

The 64 target items at the lowest level were the same in all four menu structures and consisted of simple nouns such as "Horse," "Lizard," "Dog," and "Snake." The choices at other levels were categories such as "Animal" for the above target items. These differed across the menu structures and were designed to present logical categories for the target items within the constraints of the menu structure.

The task posed to the users in this study was to find a target item. They were first presented with a target item on the screen and then the top-level menu appeared. They navigated through the menu structure until they located and selected the target item correctly. Each user was given two blocks of trials, for a total of four complete runs through the hierarchy. The time it took to reach the target word and errors were recorded for analysis. Only *user* response time was included in the timing measure; *system* response time, delays, and target-word display time were factored out.

Figure 4-6 summarizes the data from this study. Data are averaged across trials and users within a menu structure. The horizontal axis represents the four menu structures being compared. The left vertical axis represents the average *time* in seconds to navigate to and select a target item (acquisition time or AT), and striped bars in the chart present the timing data for each menu structure. The right vertical axis represents the percentage of trials on which an *error* was made (incorrect menu choices at any level in the hierarchy), and the white bars in the chart present the error data for each menu structure.

In Figure 4-6, it can be seen that the menu structure that provided the best performance in terms of both fastest time and fewest errors was the one with two

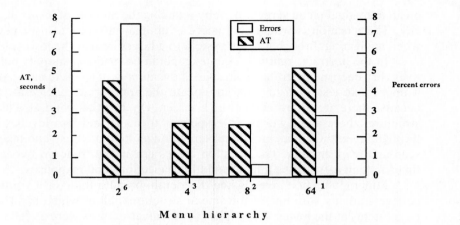

Figure 4–6 A study of menu depth versus breadth. From Miller, "The Depth/ Breadth Tradeoff in Hierarchical Computer Menus," *Proceedings of the Human Factors Society 25th Annual Meeting,* 2, 1981, 296–300. © 1981, by the Human Factors Society, Inc. Reprinted with permission. All rights reserved.

levels and eight choices per level. Making the menu structure deeper (three or six levels) degraded performance. Note, however, that making the menu broad in the extreme (all 64 choices on one level) also degraded performance. The author concluded that, in general, for *well-learned* systems of moderate size, depth should be minimized at the cost of breadth, except if this results in overcrowding of choices on a screen, as in the latter structure. It is interesting to note that the optimal number of items per screen in this study was 8, which corresponds closely to the capacity of short-term memory: 7 ± 2. However, there is a big difference between 8 items on a screen and 64, and we cannot conclude from this study alone how users would have performed with say 10, 20, 30, or 40 items on a screen.

Other studies have since further investigated the depth versus breadth trade-off. Wallace, Anderson, and Shneiderman (1987) compared two structures: three levels with four items per level and six levels with two items per level. They also found the shallower structure (three levels with four items per level) to provide faster search times with fewer errors. They also introduced a time stress variable, asking one group to perform as quickly as possible and the other to take their time and not rush. Users operating under time pressure performed more slowly and with more errors than nonpressured users. Neither structure offered any particular advantage under time pressure conditions; performance on both was degraded about equally. However, the finding does point to the importance of task variables on user performance. Many jobs, such as those of airline reservations clerks, stock brokers, and bank tellers, involve constant time pressure, and this study makes it clear that this will affect performance. Interfaces to systems to be used under such conditions should be tested under comparable conditions, and efforts should be made to find interfaces that support work under such conditions.

Snowberry, Parkinson, and Sisson (1983) evaluated the same depth–breadth conditions as Miller, except they included two variations of the broadest structure: all 64 items on one screen. In the first condition, as in Miller's study, the 64 items were not organized into any particular groups. In the second condition, however, semantically related items were grouped together. The data replicated Miller's in that two levels of eight items per screen were found to be optimal *when* the items in the broadest condition were *not* grouped. However, when the single-level menu of 64 items was *well organized,* performance was *slightly better* than the two-level, eight items per level structure. This suggests the importance of organization *within* menu screens, discussed in the next section, and also that, with proper organization, a single-level menu with as many as 64 items on it may be preferable to deeper menu structures *for experienced users.* This study also found that navigational errors increased from 4% to 34% as depth increased from one level to six levels, respectively.

Landauer and Nachbar (1985) studied depth versus breadth using a very different input device (a touch screen) and rather different types of menu choice items (number and letter ranges). Different depth–breadth conditions organized 4096 target items in one of four structures:

2 choices per screen, 12 levels
4 choices per screen, 6 levels
8 choices per screen, 4 levels
16 choices per screen, 3 levels

High-school-aged subjects each performed a total of 50 tasks on all four structures. Each task involved navigating to a designated target item, beginning at the top-level menu screen. Again, the data revealed that broader, shallower menu structures yielded faster performance than deeper, narrower menu structures. There was a difference in search time of roughly 2 to 1 between the deepest and broadest structures in this study.

This study did not include an extremely broad structure (64 items on one screen) as did the Miller (1981) and Snowberry (1983) studies. On the other hand, another intermediately broad structure (16 items on a screen) was included, and this seemed to provide better performance than the next broadest structure (8 items on a screen), indicating that the trend of improved performance with increased breadth versus depth *may* continue consistently between a breadth of 8 items on a screen and a breadth of 64.

Lee and MacGregor (1985) took a different approach to the question of depth versus breadth in menu hierarchies. Instead of *empirically* comparing a small number of alternative depth–breadth structures by collecting performance data from representative users, they developed a math model of performance parameters in order to *predict* performance under different structures. The parameters in the model included user search strategy (exhaustive or self-terminating, defined later), user reading speed (assumed to range from 33 to 454 words per minute), user key press time (assumed to range from 0.5 to 1 second) and system display time (assumed to range from 0.5 to 1.35 seconds). The latter three parameters were drawn from various sources in the literature. The optimal number of items per screen was computed from the model for a wide variety of conditions across these parameter ranges. The authors concluded:

> It can be seen that search time is a U-shaped function of the number of alternatives per page. Search time is minimized for an intermediate number of alternatives and is typically much longer for very few or very many. Just two alternatives per page (that is, a binary search) appears to be particularly costly in terms of search time.

> It can be seen that the optimum number of alternatives per page for a very wide range of conditions is less than 10. Only when extremely fast readers are using a highly overloaded system (and, consequently, the computer response times are slow) does the optimum ever exceed 10. Even then, search times under such conditions are relatively close to optimal if only a maximum of 10 alternatives is displayed per page. For a very wide range of conditions, it appears that from 4 to 8 alternatives per page is optimal. . . .

> It is also shown that the design of the optimal organization (or, equivalently, the optimum number of alternatives per page) does not depend at all on the size of the database. Larger databases increase total search time, but they do not alter the optimum. Nor, under certain conditions, does the number of errors affect the optimum (although it certainly affects search time).

These conclusions seem consistent with Miller's (1981) data but seem to contradict Snowberry, Parkinson's, and Sisson's (1983). The key to this contradiction seems to lie in one of the parameters in Lee and MacGregor's model: search strategy. Lee and MacGregor considered that users would use one of two search strategies: *exhaustive* or *self-terminating*. The exhaustive strategy assumes that users will read all options before choosing one. The self-terminating strategy, assumes that users will stop searching as soon as they locate an acceptable choice. In the self-terminating strategy, it is also assumed that targets appear equally often in the different possible locations in the list of choices and that thus, *on the average,* users will search through half the options before making a selection. Thus, optimal breadth predictions assume that, even in the best case, users will at least *on the average* search through half the options before making a selection.

Paap and Roske-Hofstrand (1986), however, point out that in fact users may search through substantially *less* than half the options on a screen on average, under two conditions. First, highly practiced users may simply learn the locations of menu items and be able to direct their attention directly to the desired choice on any given menu. Second, if items on a given screen are grouped well (as in Snowberry, Parkinson, and Sisson (1983), users may be able to limit their search to a smaller subset of items on a given screen. Paap and Roske-Hofstrand recalculated predicted optimal breadth values assuming an efficient search strategy based on groupings and came to quite different conclusions about optimal breadth that were more consistent with Snowberry, Parkinson, and Sisson's data. They found that, depending on the other parameter assumptions in Lee and MacGregor's model (that is, reading speed, keying speed, and system response time), optimum breadth values ranged from 16 to as high as 78. That is, when menu choice items on a given screen can be ordered into meaningful groups, users will use this cue to restrict their search to a small subset of the presented items. Thus, there is not such a pronounced trade-off between search time per screen and number of screens, and the fewer responses required on broader menu structures provide an overall advantage.

Paap and Hofstrand's modified model predicts that, when user reading and keying rates are low (as they might be for inexperienced users), 18 to 20 items per screen arranged in four meaningful groups is the maximum breadth and best organization for optimal performance, whereas when user reading and keying rates are high (as they might be for highly practiced users), 38 to 63 items per screen arranged in six to eight meaningful groups is the maximum optimal arrangement, depending on computer response time. The slower the computer response time is in this case, the higher the maximum number of items per screen. In other words, generally, the faster the users in searching and keying and the slower the system in responding, the more advantageous it is to place more items at a given level rather than increase the number of levels.

Although neither Lee and MacGregor (1985) nor Paap and Roske-Hofstrand (1986) collected any empirical data to confirm their models, the results of the four empirical studies cited (Miller, 1981; Snowberry, Parkinson, and Sisson, 1983; Landauer and Nachbar, 1985; Wallace, Anderson, and Shneiderman, 1987) generally provide results consistent with the two models' predictions. Although the studies vary in too many ways (for example, menu choice item types, selection mechanism, and number of trials) for any direct comparisons to be possible, a pattern does seem to emerge that indicates that (1) breadth is generally preferable to depth; (2) when no logical grouping is possible within a menu screen, then up to ten choice items per menu provides optimal performance; but (3) when choice items on a screen can be cast into meaningful groups, then greater breadth continues to provide an advantage, especially when users are experienced and system response time is slow.

Still another factor in making the depth–breadth trade-off is suggested in MacGregor, Lee, and Lam (1986): the nature of the menu choice items. They note that in the Lee and MacGregor (1985) model there are four parameters: search strategy or number of choice items examined before a decision, time to read each choice item, keying time, and system response time. Two of these have to do with *decision* time (the former) and two have to do with *execution* time (the latter). Optimal breadth is differentially affected by these two sets of factors, in that it *decreases* as decision time parameters increase, and it *increases* as execution time parameters increase.

MacGregor, Lee, and Lam go on to point out that the two *decision* time parameters may be affected by the *type* of menu choices. For example, search strategies and reading times may be fairly efficient when menus present simple, single-word commands. More costly search strategies and longer reading times may be required, however, with the kind of menus found on videotex systems, where there may be a huge number of target items (as many as 10,000), menu choice items are phrases or lists rather than single words, and choices involve more category judgment and less simple recognition. In addition, logical grouping within a given menu screen is less often possible in videotex systems, and learning is less likely to occur, since there are so many menu screens in the system and users may only encounter each one quite infrequently.

MacGregor, Lee, and Lam suggest that the available empirical studies, which support a maximum breadth of up to 64 items per screen, employed menu choice types more comparable to simple command menus, for which decision-making times would be relatively low. They gathered data from a simulated videotex menu system, plugged parameter values derived from the data into their model (these parameter values varied somewhat from those assumed in their 1985 study), and found predicted and observed results to be consistent: the optimal number of items per menu (when the possibilities considered were 2, 4, 8, or 16) was 4. They conclude that although Paap and Roske-Hofstrand are correct in concluding that when menu choice items are simple words that can easily be categorized, fairly broad menus are often optimal, there are menu choice types, such as those in videotex systems, in which choice items are more complex and less easily categorized. Because of the corresponding effects on decision-making time, less broad menus are optimal in these cases.

Note that this conclusion does not contradict Paap and Roske-Hofstrand. It simply adds another variable to the equation that predicts optimal breadth. Besides user experience, choice organization, and system response time, we must also consider *menu choice type,* as this interacts with user experience and choice organization to determine decision-making time.

Another study supporting the importance of considering menu choice type in making the breadth–depth trade-off (Norman and Chin, 1988) found that, when users were searching for an item that fit a general description (rather than looking for a specific target item), for menus *of fixed depth* it was better to provide *more breadth* at *lower levels* in the hierarchy. In this study the task was quite analogous to the kinds of search tasks users would engage in on a videotex system: they had to select an appropriate gift for a person whose interests and personality were described to them. Gifts fell into categories such as appliances and accessories, kitchenware, and picnic and cookout accessories. Different ways of casting these gifts into categories in a four-level hierarchy resulted in four variations of breadth: decreasing ($8 \times 8 \times 2 \times 2$), increasing ($2 \times 2 \times 8 \times 8$), concave ($8 \times 2 \times 2 \times 8$), and convex ($2 \times 8 \times 8 \times 2$). The results suggested that greater breadth at the bottom of the hierarchy (that is, the concave and increasing structures) facilitates the search process under these task conditions.

There is one additional factor that was not considered either in the empirical or theoretical studies cited. This is how well a designated set of target items lends itself to different categorizations corresponding to different possible menu structures. It is likely that the target items themselves will lend themselves to one structure better than another in terms of what meaningful categories they can be cast into and that this might override simple depth–breadth issues. We do not know how this factor might interact with others to influence performance, but as Paap and Roske-Hofstrand (1986) suggest, probably *naturalness of categorization* should override predictions of optimal breadth and size of groups. Predictions of optimal breadth from their variation on Lee and MacGregor's model should provide an initial goal for an optimal structure, they suggest, but this should probably then be adapted to preserve naturalness in categorization.

Evidence exists that suggests the importance of natural categorization. Hollands and Merikle (1987) compared search and selection time on a menu hierarchy organized by meaningful categories with menu hierarchies organized alphabetically and randomly. The categorical menu was constructed by collecting empirical data from experts in a subject domain (psychology) performing a sorting task and subjecting the data to a statistical technique designed to determine how people categorize information. This technique, known as "multidimensional scaling," produces a categorization of a set of items that is representative of how a group of people view the relationships between those items. In this case, experts (psychology professors) were given 120 psychological terms (for example, "Functional fixedness," "Identity crisis," "Visual cliff") and asked to sort them into related groups. The multidimensional scaling technique revealed that experts considered the terms to belong to five distinct categories, which could be interpreted as the subfields of psychology: biopsychology, cognition, perception, personality, and social psychology. Thus, the top-level menu in the categorical menu system consisted of these five items, and the 120 terms were distributed in the second-level menu as indicated by the data. Because it represents how experts organize the problem domain, this organization might be considered a natural way to categorize target items in a menu system.

The top-level menu of the alphabetic menu system in this study consisted of alphabetic ranges as follows: A to C, D to F, G to MOT, MOV to SEL, and SHO to Z. The top-level menu in the random menu system consisted of the meaningless group names Group 1, Group 2, and so on. The second-level menus in these two systems included the same 120 terms as in the categorical system, but grouped under the top-level choices alphabetically or randomly, respectively. The alphabetic menu system might be considered less natural as an organization compared to the categorical menu system, while the random system represents a control to establish whether or not meaningful categorization of any sort provides any advantage over no categorization.

Three groups of subjects performed two types of tasks on the three types of menu hierarchies. Subjects varied in level of expertise in the problem domain; that is, they had low, medium and high levels of expertise in psychology. In one type of task, term-matching, subjects were given the exact term to find (for example,

"Functional fixedness"). In the other type of task, definition-matching, they were given a definition of the term to be found (for example, "The minimum stimulus energy necessary for an observer to detect the stimulus") as the definition for the target item "absolute threshold." These two tasks simulate usage by expert and novice users, respectively, in that experts generally have learned the exact menu choice labels that correspond to their desired choice at any point, while novices have not yet learned labels and have in mind only vague definitions of what they are looking for.

Search and select time data from this study revealed some interesting effects. First, both categorical and alphabetic organizations provided an advantage over random organization. Second, when the task was term-matching, alphabetic organization proved advantageous, but when the task was definition-matching, categorical organization was superior. In addition, the subject's level of relevant expertise made a difference. In the term-matching task, low-expertise users performed substantially better with the alphabetic organization, whereas high-expertise subjects performed only slightly better with the alphabetic as compared to the categorical organizations. High-expertise users also performed better than low-expertise users in the definition-matching task, and expertise had a more dramatic positive effect when the menu was categorically organized than when it was alphabetic. The data thus suggest that a more natural organization of items in a menu hierarchy (that is, corresponding to the user's natural categorization of information) will improve the performance of *system* novices and still provide comparable performance by *system* experts, as compared to a less natural although meaningful organization, such as simple alphabetic. The benefit to *system* novices is even more pronounced if they are also *task* experts.

In conclusion, a good guideline for making the depth–breadth trade-off in a menu hierarchy might be stated as follows. Choose a maximum breadth of 4 to 10 items per screen if no useful organization can be imposed on the target items on a given screen and/or if menu choice items are complex (for example, as in an information retrieval system such as videotex). Choose a breadth of up to 20 if an organization can be imposed to effectively group items on a screen and choice items are not complex, but users are inexperienced (infrequent or casual users). Present one-level menus regardless of breadth (constrained only by menu area size and maintaining clear choice item labels) if menu choice items are simple and lend themselves well to categorization, if most users can be expected to be experienced and if system response time is fast. Within these guidelines, naturalness of categorization should always take precedence, and categorization should be based on *empirical* investigation of *user's* natural categorizations when possible.

Another study (Chin, 1989) looked at the issue of menu *structure type*. Users were asked to use a *linear* menu system and were then allowed to create their own new links between items. Then they were asked to use the new menu structures they had created to see if in fact they would use the newly created links.

The initial linear menu system presented a restaurant menu. The menu was organized into four types of cuisine: American, Italian, Mexican, and Chinese.

Within each type of cuisine were eight categories of food: drinks, soups, appetizers, beef, fowl, seafood, vegetables, and desserts. Each category within each cuisine type included eight items.

The menu was organized linearly in that each screen presented all eight items within two categories for one cuisine type (for example, all *American* drinks and soups on the first page, all American appetizers and beef on the second page, all American fowl and seafood on the third page, all American vegetables and desserts on the fourth page, all *Italian* drinks and soups on the fifth page, and so on). Thus, the only way for the user to get to the screen with Chinese desserts, for instance, was to page through all 15 screens that came before it in the linear sequence.

Users were asked to make selections from this linear menu system. For instance, they might be asked to select four beers, one from each cuisine type (that is, one American drink, one Italian drink, and so on). Or they might be asked to select a full-course meal from one cuisine type (that is, one Italian drink, one Italian soup, one Italian appetizer, and so on). They had to navigate through the linear structure to make these selections.

After they had completed a number of such selection tasks, they were instructed on how to create new links in the menu structure. For instance, they could create a new link that would allow them to go directly from the page with American drinks and soups to the pages with Italian, Mexican, or Chinese drinks and soups. Similarly, they could create links to go directly from the page with American drinks and soups to the pages with American fowl and seafood or American vegetables and desserts. These types of links transformed the *linear* menu structure into a *hierarchical* menu structure.

Users could also create *networked* menu structures by creating different kinds of links. For instance, they could create links that would allow them to go directly from American vegetables and desserts to Chinese vegetables and desserts. That is, they could navigate *horizontally* in the hierarchical structure, thus bypassing returning *vertically* to higher-level categories in order to get to the same intermediate category in a different higher-level category.

In fact, users could create any kind of links imaginable, including diagonal links across levels in the hierarchy. It was found that users did indeed create and use new links to facilitate navigation. In addition, it was found that users created *networked* menu structures (a hierarchical structure with links allowing horizontal navigation) and created and used horizontal links more often than diagonal links (90% and 10%, respectively). The types of links users created and used seem to depend on the demands of the type of tasks they were given in their initial use of the linear menu structure.

Two interesting points are suggested by this study. First, given the opportunity, users will tailor menu structures to better support their tasks. Second, different users may have different tasks at different times. One hierarchical organization may best support one type of task, but not another. Allowing users to tailor menu structures allows them to set up optimal structures for the type of tasks they tend to do at any given time. For instance, if most tasks involved selecting from the same food category across different cuisine types, having food category as the highest level in the hierarchy would be optimal. However, if most tasks involved selecting whole meals from within one cuisine type, then having cuisine type as the highest level in the hierarchy would be preferable. One structure will not optimally support all tasks, so tailorability of the structure can improve the usability of the system.

Another aspect of menu structure is *orientation*. Traditional full-screen menu systems presented menu choices in a *vertical* list. Some more recent interfaces present at least some menu choices *horizontally* (for example, Apple's Macintosh and Lotus 1-2-3). One study (Backs, Walrath, and Hancock, 1987) investigated the effects on search time of vertical versus horizontal orientation on full-screen menus.

Menus with 4, 8, or 12 choice items were presented either vertically (one column of 4, 8, or 12 items) or horizontally (1, 2, or 3 rows of 4 items each). The time it took users to locate target items was measured. Users of vertical menus performed faster, regardless of the number of choices in the menu. The difference, although statistically significant, was only a fraction of a second (150 milliseconds). Users did report, however, that vertical menus seemed easier, suggesting that the difference was perceptible to users.

The authors note that these results should not necessarily be generalized to interfaces in which menus are not full screen (for example, Macintosh and Lotus 1-2-3), as it is unclear how other aspects of a display would interact with menu orientation. Even for full-screen menus, however, the advantage of vertical menus is not large enough to make a strong case for avoiding horizontal menus. Other considerations (for example, compatibility with other interfaces used by users) should probably drive a decision on how to orient menus. Also, this study addressed the orientation of *text* menus, and the results may or may not generalize to other menu types, such as icon menus or menus of numerical values.

Yet another menu orientation, the pie menu, was investigated by Callahan and others (1988). A **pie menu** is one in which the menu items at a given level are presented in a pie or circular format (see Figure 4-7), rather than a linear (horizontal or vertical list) format. Callahan and co-workers reasoned from Fitts's law (see Card, Moran, and Newell, 1983) that, since targets in a pie menu are *on the average* larger and closer to the pointer start position (which is always the center of the pie or circle) than are targets in a linear menu, selection times ought to be faster. On the other hand, it was reasoned that some tasks might lend themselves better to pie menus, and other tasks might lend themselves better to linear menus. For instance, compass directions, time, and sets of antonyms (for example, ''Open'' and ''Close,'' ''Up'' and ''Down'') might be better presented in pie menus, whereas numbers, letters, and ordinals might best be presented in linear menus.

The study compared performance on the two types of menus with the two types of tasks. The menu selection mechanism was the mouse, and subjects who participated had little or no mouse experience. On each trial, the target menu item was displayed in the upper-right corner of the screen. Subjects invoked the menu with a mouse button press, dragged the cursor to their selection, and released the

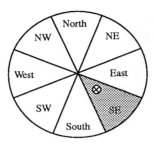

Pop-up pie menu

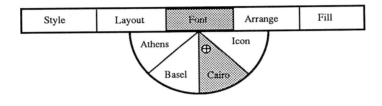

Pull-down pie menu

Figure 4–7 Pie menus.

mouse button to complete selection. Time and error data were collected over 60 trials per subject.

The data were consistent with the predictions of Fitts's law, showing a time advantage for pie menus, regardless of task type. The advantage was slightly less than half a second. This suggests that the pie menu is a promising orientation to consider. However, some important qualifications must be considered.

First, this study only included menus with eight items. It is not clear that the advantage of pie menus would hold up on menus with many more items. Indeed, with a great many menu choices, a pie menu quickly becomes quite impractical. Second, although pie menus can be incorporated into a menu hierarchy by presenting half-circle pie menus as pull-downs from a linear menu bar (see Figure 4-7), it is harder to imagine how pie menus could effectively be presented in deeper menu hierarchies. Third, pie menus require a pointing device and bit-mapped screen with graphics capabilities, which are not always available. More research is required, but it seems worthwhile to consider pie menus for shallow (that is, one- or two-level) menu hierarchies in which a small number of choices appear at each level and for tasks that lend themselves well to a circular arrangement of menu choices.

Another aspect of menu structure concerns the presentation of temporarily unselectable items. Many menu systems today are not full screen, but rather are pop-up or pull-down menus displayed as a part of application screens (for example, Macintosh applications). When major changes in mode occur (for example, a change in application), menu items change substantially. When minor changes in state within a mode occur, however (for example an object is or is not currently selected), some menu items rendered temporarily irrelevant become currently inactive, or unselectable. In most such systems, temporarily inactive items are displayed, but are *grayed out* and cannot be selected. An alternative design would have been to *delete* the unselectable items from the menu.

The potential pros and cons of deletion versus graying out can be summarized as follows. Deletion could potentially decrease search time, as it is well established that search time is a linear function of list length. Depending on the selection mechanism, deletion might also decrease navigation time if selection required moving a cursor through items in order. On the other hand, deletion results in the absolute location of individual menu items changing arbitrarily. This may in fact make searching more difficult, and it may impede learning (see, for instance, Somberg, 1987, discussed later).

Graying out might be expected to facilitate performance by allowing users to maintain learned patterns of searching and navigating. That is, if users can always predict the location of desired menu items, they may both find and navigate to them faster. Its also possible that graying out assists in learning because users can always see where every menu item in a hierarchy is located, even when not all are selectable. On the other hand, graying out means that menus are always at their maximum length, which in turn means more items to search and navigate through. This could potentially impede performance relative to deletion.

Francik and Kane (1987) designed an experiment to compare deletion and graying out of temporarily inactive menu items. *Expert* users of *keyboard-driven* menus were tested under the two conditions. Users performed slightly faster when inactive items were deleted as opposed to grayed out (2.21 versus 2.77 seconds per selection). The difference was significant, but it is not clear whether the result would generalize to *novice* learners and to *mouse* or other input-device-driven menus. In fact, it seems likely that grayed out items would provide an advantage under these conditions. It could be expected that novices would benefit from being able to browse through all items, currently selectable or not, and that being able to see inactive items might contribute to the development of a mental model by making "invisible parts visible" (see Chapter 3). And it is clear from informal experience that predictable item positions can be exploited by rapid learned mouse movements. Until research confirms these expectations, it seems reasonable to conclude that deletion may provide an advantage for expert users of keyboard-driven menus, whereas graying out may prove advantageous for novice users and for users of pointer-driven menus.

Guidelines drawn from this research on menu structure are summarized on pages 144–154.

Menu choice ordering. Once a menu hierarchy or structure is decided on and the choice items that will actually appear on each menu screen have been determined, then one is faced with the question of how to order those items. Which should be at the top of the list? Which at the bottom? Is there any organizing principle that is superior to another in terms of optimizing user search and select time?

This question was addressed in a study (McDonald, Stone, and Liebelt, 1983) that compared two possible organizing principles: (1) logical semantic groups of menu choices, or (2) alphabetical ordering according to the menu choice labels. These two possibilities were compared against a third ordering that was random, that is, no organizing principle was used as a control condition.

In fact, five separate orderings were compared. In three, the high-level organizing principle was logical semantic groups (the authors call this ordering scheme by *category*). Examples of categories were foods, cities, minerals and animals. Within these groups was a secondary organizing principle, and this might again be organized by logical semantic groups or be alphabetical or random.

For instance, within the group foods, actual food items might be ordered by subcategory (for example, breads, meats, and vegetables), alphabetically (for example, broccoli, lamb, and muffins), or randomly (for example, lamb, carrots, and beef). Thus, these first three orderings were as follows:

Category-category (CC)
Category-alphabetic (CA)
Category-random (CR)

The last two orderings were simple alphabetic and simple random:

Alphabetic (A)
Random (R)

One hundred users took part in this study, 20 in each of the five different ordering conditions. They were all secretaries from a temporary employment agency. They were presented with a target item on the screen, followed by one menu screen on which 64 menu choices appeared, including the target item. Each menu choice had a randomly assigned one-character selection code associated with it. The task was to find the target item and enter its code on the keyboard. Each user had to find each of the 64 target items five times.

One other variable was considered in this study. It concerned the way the task was presented. Half the users in each ordering condition received as target items the menu choices as they actually appeared on the menu screen. This was called the *explicit target* condition. The other half received instead a dictionary definition of the actual menu choice. This was called the *definitions* condition. For instance, if a menu item was "Beef," users in the explicit targets condition were asked to find and select "Beef," while those in the definitions condition might be asked to find and select something like "the meat of a cow."

This is an interesting variation on the task. The explicit target users represent *expert* users who have learned the exact menu choice labels of a menu system, while the definitions users represent *novice* users who have general goals in mind, but have not yet learned the actual menu choice labels in a given menu system.

Figure 4-8 summarizes the results from this study. First, it can be observed that, regardless of the organizing principle, users located the targets faster when they were given explicit targets as compared to when they were given only definitions. This suggests that expert users will outperform novice users in locating desired choices on menus, a not too surprising conclusion.

The next finding of interest is that the categorical–categorical grouping provided the best performance, and, with one exception, all three categorical groupings provided better performance than either alphabetic or random orderings. The exception was the alphabetic grouping when users were given explicit targets. This condition provided performance comparable to the categorical–categorical grouping with explicit targets. This is not too surprising, as one would expect a person to be able to locate a particular word in an alphabetically ordered list quite quickly. Note, however, that when users are given definitions rather than explicit targets an alphabetic grouping provides one of the worst search times, second only to no grouping at all.

A conclusion that might be drawn from this study is that for expert, high-frequency users an alphabetic ordering might be as usable as a categorical ordering, while for novice, casual users, a categorical or logical semantic grouping is clearly

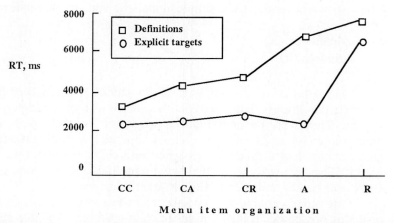

Figure 4-8 A study of ordering on menu screens. From McDonald, Stone, and Liebelt, "Searching for Items in Menus: The Effects of Organization and Type of Target," *Proceedings of the Human Factors Society* 27*th Annual Meeting,* 2, 1983, 834–37. © 1983, by the Human Factors Society, Inc. Reprinted with permission. All rights reserved.

superior. It seems that when users know the exact menu label that they are looking for they are as fast searching for items based on alphabetic cues as on semantic cues. However, when they have only a general goal or definition in mind but are unsure of the exact menu label for the function they want, then a logical semantic grouping facilitates their search more than an alphabetical ordering. Given that menu systems are generally chosen to support novice, casual users, these data suggest that ordering by logical semantic groups is a good organizing principle to employ.

These data, while addressing organization *within* levels, are consistent with the findings of Hollands and Merikle (1987), which looked at organization of items *across* levels. However, this study did *not* include other possible ordering schemes, such as *order of use* or *frequency of use,* and thus we do not know how these ordering schemes might compare with the two that were investigated. Designers often order menu items by expected frequency of use. The idea is to minimize the search time for the most frequently used options by putting them at the top of the list.

Hollands and Merikle (1987) also focused on relative *search* time by holding the *selection method* constant across conditions. If the selection mechanism involves moving a cursor with cursor keys through the list, a frequency of use ordering scheme might also serve to minimize selection time. With a cursor selection scheme, ordering by semantic groupings might result in placing some frequently used options at the bottom of the list, thus increasing selection time even if search time is reduced. That is, it might be easy to locate a desired item at the bottom of a screen because the user is familiar with the semantic group the item appears in, but moving the cursor from the first to last choice with arrow keys would take many keystrokes. These and other potentially interacting variables were not addressed in this study, limiting the generalizability of the results.

However, it is probably reasonable to conclude that with a selection mechanism that is not affected by choice position, such as entering a letter or number code, the conclusions drawn from this study (Hollands and Merikle, 1987) regarding categorical versus alphabetic ordering schemes are valid.

Another study (McDonald, Molander, and Noel 1988) contrasted the performance on menus organized by item similarity (as in the categorical organizations discussed previously) with performance on menus organized by frequency of cooccurrence, that is, on which items often selected in sequence were grouped together. In this study, users had to select multiple food items from a simulated fast-food register. The simulated register consisted of a flat (that is, horizontal rather then vertical) touch screen with a 4 by 6 matrix of soft keys, each labeled with the name of one food item. Menu items consisted of such choices as hamburger, cheeseburger, Coke, root beer, eggs, and pancakes.

Two menu layouts were tested. On one, items were grouped according to similarity (Coke with root beer, hamburger with cheeseburger), and on the other layout, items were grouped according to expected frequency of cooccurrence (Coke with hamburger and fries, eggs with bacon and orange juice). Unlike in the previous study, these groupings were not derived from the experimenters' intuitions, but from a statistical technique applied to subjects' ratings of item similarity and item complementarity. And, unlike the previous study, menu items were grouped in a two-dimensional matrix layout rather than in linear columns.

Subjects were given two groups of food order tasks, one in which the food items to be selected were similar (Coke and root beer) and one in which the food items to be selected were complementary (Coke and hamburger). Subjects of varying levels of computer experience each processed 240 food orders, including both kinds of tasks. Each subject used only one of the two menu layouts. Time and error data were collected.

The main finding was that each menu layout best supported a different task type, as expected. That is, the menu on which items were grouped by similarity provided better performance when the task involved selecting similar items (Coke and root beer), while the menu on which items were grouped by frequency of cooccurrence resulted in faster performance when the task involved selecting complementary items (Coke and hamburger).

This study suggests two important ideas: (1) the way menu items should be grouped depends on the type of tasks people will most likely or most often be doing, and (2) formal methods can be brought to bear to determine exactly what groupings will best support a given task. (These methods are beyond the scope of this book, which is about design *principles and guidelines* rather than design *methods,* but are a part of the skills of many human factors professionals who may be available in-house or as external consultants.)

Note that the selection technique in this study, touch screen, was different than that in the previous study. It is possible that selection technique may interact with choice order in some way not revealed by either study because there are two parts to menu selection: searching for the desired choice, and selecting it. In a touch screen menu, items selected in sequence benefit from being close to one another in two ways: during searching and during selection. When the selection technique is via the keyboard, however, items in a group may be found faster, but it is not necessarily true that they will be selected faster. This will depend on the selection technique (for example, letter codes, number codes, or cursor selection). Thus both menu order and selection technique must be considered in order to design a menu that facilitates both searching and selecting items likely to be chosen in sequence.

Other menu ordering schemes were considered in another study (Somberg, 1987). This study included an alphabetic ordering and a random ordering, as in the McDonald, Stone, and Liebelt (1983) study. It also included two other orderings: *frequency of use* and *positional constancy.* In the frequency of use order, target items most often appeared nearer the top of the list, regardless of semantic relationships or alphabetic order. In the positional constancy order, a given item always appeared in the exact same location in a list, regardless of whether other items that appeared with it involved semantic relationships between items or alphabetic order.

Subjects with varying degrees of computer experience performed 492 selection tasks each in which 40 different target items were randomly assigned to tasks. This allowed an analysis of how efficiently subjects would learn the location of the 40 target items with practice and whether performance over time would depend on menu ordering. Very few errors were made, but the timing data revealed that, as expected, *any* ordering provided better performance than *no* (random) ordering. Alphabetic and frequency-of-use orderings provided roughly comparable performance. Most interesting, positional constancy resulted in *poorer* performance than alphabetic or frequency-of-use orderings *initially,* but with practice resulted in *better* performance than any other ordering. That is, it seemed that some rule-based ordering (for example, alphabetic or frequency of use) provided an advantage to inexperienced users, whereas positional constancy provided better performance among experienced users. Or, put another way, if item position was constant, once the position of items was learned, items could be found and selected faster than if items were located according to some rule, but in fact appeared in different absolute locations across menus.

These data (interpreted in the light of the data from other studies) suggest that the optimal ordering scheme might depend on whether inexperienced or experienced users are of higher priority. If ease of *learning* is most important (for example, if most users are casual, infrequent users), a rule-based ordering such as semantic category might be best.

If ease of *use* is more important, however (for example, if most users will be high-frequency users), positional constancy should probably take precedence. In fact, in a real system it might be possible to achieve a choice ordering in which both semantic categories and positional constancy were present. This might provide optimal performance for both novices and experts.

An ordering scheme based on frequency of cooccurrence or frequency of use should probably override a categorical or positional constancy ordering if task demands make ordering on the basis of these criteria useful.

Guidelines drawn from this research on menu choice ordering are summarized on pages 154–157.

Menu choice selection. In the previous discussions, we several times brought up the issue of menu selection mechanisms. A variety of selection mechanisms are available. Perhaps the most common are single-character letter or number selection codes, which are entered in a fill-in field followed by some terminator key such as "Execute" or "Return." Alternatives include moving a cursor (for example, a reverse video bar or block cursor to the left of the choice items) through the list of choices with the cursor control keys and pressing a terminator key when the cursor is located on the desired choice, or pointing directly to the choice with an alternative input device such as a mouse, joystick, or touch screen (see Figure 4-1).

One study (Perlman, 1984) compared letter and number selection codes to see if one or the other resulted in faster selection. The rule of assignment of particular

letters or numbers to menu choices was also investigated. A simple single menu of
eight choices was designed with four different selection codes, as follows:

Compatible letters
A. Assembler
B. Buffer
C. Compile
D. Debug
And so on.

Compatible numbers
1. Assembler
2. Buffer
3. Compile
4. Debug
And so on.

Incompatible letters
A. Buffer
B. Debug
C. Assembler
D. Compile
And so on.

Incompatible numbers
1. Buffer
2. Debug
3. Assembler
4. Compile
And so on.

As shown, in a *compatible letters* selection code the selection code corresponds to the first letter of the menu choice label. In an *incompatible letters*
selection code, the selection letters do *not* correspond to the first letters of the
menu choice labels. In a *compatible numbers* selection code the number code
corresponds to the ordinal alphabetical position of the first letter of the menu
choice label. In an *incompatible numbers* selection code the number code does *not*
correspond to the ordinal alphabetical position of the first letter of the menu choice
label.

Sixteen computer-naive undergraduate students participated in this study.
They each performed the selection task with all four selection codes presented in
different order to different users. In a given selection code condition, the menu was
constantly displayed in the upper-left corner of the screen. One of the eight menu
choices would appear in the lower-right corner of the screen, and users were timed
as they located and entered the correct selection code from the menu for each
target.

Figure 4-9 summarizes the timing data from this study, averaged across users
and across trials within each selection code condition. The bars in the graph
represent the average selection time in seconds for each of the four selection codes.
Here it can be seen that both compatible codes resulted in faster selection time than
either incompatible code. Compatible letters provided the best performance, but it
is not true that letters are always better than numbers. Incompatible letters resulted
in the worst performance.

This makes sense, as we can imagine a user discovering quickly that letter
codes correspond to menu choice labels. Once this is discovered, the user need not
even look at the menu to enter the correct selection code. It is less likely that users
will notice that number codes correspond to the ordinal alphabetical position of the
menu choice labels, and so they still may look at the menu to determine the correct
code. When incompatible letters are used, it appears that some sort of *interference*

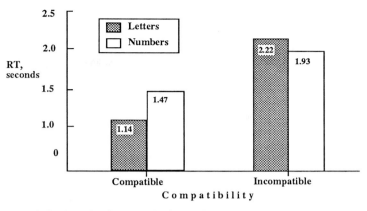

Figure 4–9 A study of menu selection codes. From Perlman, "Making the Right Choices with Menus," *Proceedings, Interact '84,* 1, 1984, 291–95. With permission.

is going on due to the fact that the selection codes in fact correspond to the first letter of choices other than the target in the list. This is not such a problem with number codes, as there is not as natural an association between words and the ordinal alphabetical position of their first letters as there is between words and their first letters.

We might conclude from this study that letters are superior to numbers as selection codes, but only if the letters correspond to the menu choice labels. Compatible letters will be easy to design for some menu systems that have only a few, static items on each screen and good labels that do not share the same first letter. Compatible letters will be harder to achieve with more complex menu systems with many, dynamic choices on a screen that have labels that share the same first letter. An example might be file name menus. Sometimes the labels can be redesigned to have different first letters, but this may mean sacrificing the clarity of the labels, which may not be desirable.

Finally, this study did not directly compare other alternative selection codes, such as cursor positioning, or other variables, such as number of choices on the screen. Thus the results are limited in their generalizability. However, it can probably be concluded that, for simple menu systems in which single-character codes are to be used as a selection mechanism, compatible letters are better than numbers if clear labels can be designed with mutually exclusive first letters.

A later study (Shinar and others, 1985) compared letter and number codes directly to cursor positioning as an alternative choice selection mechanism and varied the number of menu choices to see if this might interact with the selection mechanism in any important way. The three selection mechanisms compared included numbers, compatible letters (that is, the first letter of the menu choice label), and cursor positioning with arrow keys. The number of choices per menu ranged from two to nine. Subjects were all computer naive, with no keyboard experience as well. They were presented first with a simple question and then with a menu that presented a set of multiple-choice answers to the questions. Each subject answered a set of eight questions 55 times spread over several sessions. Within each selection mechanism group, users were further divided into two groups: one had the eight questions and multiple-choice answers presented in a consistent order and the other had them presented in random order. Thus, for users of the number selection codes and the cursor selection mechanism, the changing order of menu choices meant different keystrokes to select the correct answer across presentations of a particular question. For users of the letter selection codes, however, although the position of the correct answer changed, the keystrokes to select it did not. Time and error data were collected.

The findings were as follows. The different groups did not perform differently in the number of errors made, but there were significant differences in the time to select choices. Generally, subjects who received menu choices in a consistent order across presentations of a given menu performed faster, regardless of the selection mechanism. The cursor selection mechanism showed a slight advantage in early trials when the number of choices was small (four or less). However, with some practice and on menus with many choices (five to nine), letter codes emerged as the optimal selection mechanism, with number codes coming in second and cursor selection last. Whereas increasing the number of menu choices increased the selection time with the cursor selection mechanism, selection times did not increase significantly when the number of menu choices increased with letter codes, except when menu choice order was random.

Thus, after a modest amount of practice (440 trials), first-letter codes provided significantly (statistically) faster selection times as compared to number codes or cursor selection. Thus, again, if unambiguous first-letter codes can be designed consistently across all menu screens in a system, this seems desirable. Cursor selection did not compare favorably with the number or letter codes except for first-time users (that is, on the first 80 trials) on menu screens with a small number of options.

These results should be interpreted carefully, with some qualifications. First, cursor selection was accomplished via the keyboard with the arrow keys. A cursor selection mechanism where the input device is a pointing device, such as a mouse, was not included. Thus, this study does not offer data that suggest that letter code selection is *always* faster than cursor selection; the data only suggest that letter codes are superior to *keyboard* cursor selection. Second, it is not always possible to assign unambiguous first-letter codes to all menu choices in a complex menu system without sacrificing menu choice label clarity. Probably it would be better to opt for number codes (or possibly cursor selection by pointer) rather than sacrifice menu choice label clarity in order to provide letter codes. And, third, one advantage of cursor selection is the more *direct* nature of selection. Users can more easily confirm their choices before executing them when a cursor is pointing directly to the selected choice than when they must compare a code in a fill-in field to the code by a choice. It is possible that *casual* users, who may never gain the experience level of the subjects in this study, would *prefer* cursor selection for this reason.

Guidelines drawn from this research on menu choice selection are summarized on pages 157–162.

Menu navigation. Navigating through a menu system is facilitated by a number of design techniques, including good screen layout and design, the presence of context information to remind users where they are, menu bypass, and efficient selection mechanisms. One study (Teitelbaum and Granda, 1983) looked at the impact of consistent screen design conventions on information search performance while navigating through a menu interface. In particular, the effect of consistent location of screen parts on search time was measured.

Forty users recruited from a temporary employment agency participated in this study. All had little or no experience with computers. Two menu systems were designed, each with four levels and two to five choices at each level. Menu choices were constructed from simple categories. An example of one pathway down the menu system might be Sports, Football, Superbowl Winners, and Cowboys.

Both menu systems contained the same menu choices in the same structure. They differed only in the *location* of five different parts of the menu screens: title, topic heading, page number, entries, and instructions. In the *constant* menu system, these screen parts always appeared in the same location across all screens. For instance, the title might always appear centered on the top line and the instructions might always appear left justified on the last three lines. In the *random* menu system, these parts appeared in different locations across screens. For instance, on one screen the instructions might appear on the bottom of the screen and on another screen they might appear at the top.

Users were given target words from the lowest level of the menu hierarchy (for example, ''Cowboys'') and asked to navigate from the top level through the system and select that item. While navigating through the levels of the menu system, they were periodically interrupted and asked a question such as ''What is the page number on the next list?'' or ''Where is PF3 defined on the next list?'' Then the next screen would appear, and users were timed until they made a verbal response to the question. Answering the question required searching the menu screen to find the information that contained the answer. Each user answered 20 such questions. The average time to answer the questions was computed across users and across each consecutive pair of trials for each of the two menu systems, and the two systems were compared.

Figure 4-10 presents the data from this study. Reaction time (RT) was measured in milliseconds, or thousands of a second, and is represented by the vertical axis. The horizontal axis represents the ten blocks of trial pairs. That is, block 1 is trials 1 and 2 averaged together across users, block 2 is trials 3 and 4 averaged together across users, and so on. The curve with round data points represents users

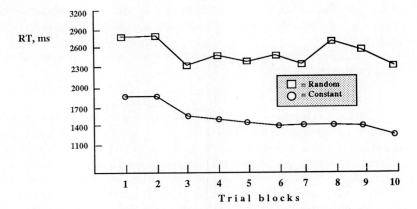

Figure 4–10 A study of consistency in menu design. From Teitelbaum and Granada, ''The Effects of Positional Constancy on Searching Menus for Instructions,'' *CHI '83 Proceedings,* 1983, 150–53. With permission.

of the constant menu system, and the curve with square data points represents users of the random menu system.

The first thing to note is that users of the *constant* menu system performed significantly better on the search task than users of the *random* menu system right from the start and all through the experiment. That is, random menu users did not catch up with practice. If the data are collapsed across all ten trial blocks, it can be seen that constant menu users overall performed 73% faster (about 1 second) than random menu users.

The second interesting observation that can be made from these data is that while the across-blocks curve for the constant menu users is statistically significant, the curve for random menu users is not. That is, constant menu users learned and improved with practice, while random menu users did not. Most of the learning that occurred in constant menu users took place in the first three blocks, or six trials.

While naming the page number or where PF keys are defined are not actual tasks that users of menu systems might perform, they do search menu screens for these kinds of information for many reasons, one of which is to navigate through the system. Although this study measured screen search time, rather than navigation time per se, the data *suggest* that if information is consistently located across menus in a system, users will be able to navigate through it faster (because they can process each screen in the pathway faster), especially after some amount of practice. Although not directly addressed in this study, it is probably true that others types of consistency, such as the use of different fonts and visual cues (for example, boldface or reverse video) for certain types of information, will also enhance user performance navigating through menu systems by decreasing search times on individual screens.

In fact, another study (Foltz and others, 1988) found that, while making simple changes in menu structure (for example, adding or deleting levels) after users had learned a menu system did *not* degrade performance, making changes in terminology (that is, menu choice labels) did. Thus, different labels for the same function represent another kind of inconsistency that can affect ease of navigation.

Another study (Lee and Chao, 1989) considered the possibility of a menu bypass technique in which users could navigate immediately to deeper levels in a menu hierarchy (as deep as the second to lowest level) by typing in keywords corresponding to menu screen titles (as an alternative to navigating step-wise through successive levels). The experimental menu system they used in their study was adapted from a videotex system in which 401 menu screens arranged hierarchically provided access to 1381 documents. The hierarchy depth ranged from three to seven levels, and the number of choices per screen (the breadth) ranged from two to nine. The videotex system represented contained documents relating to a wide variety of subjects, including sales and rentals, travel and transportation, and government.

Subjects had never used a videotex system before. They were given typical kinds of videotex search goals, such as "What is showing tonight at the Towne Cinema?" Starting at the top-level menu, they had to navigate to the document that would provide an answer to such questions. They had a choice of navigating stepwise through all levels or employing keywords to jump directly to menu screens at any level. Keywords corresponded to menu screen titles and thus could be observed and remembered while navigating through the hierarchy in stepwise fashion. Over a number of trials, certain questions were repeated a number of times so that keywords could be learned.

The data revealed that, over time, subjects increasingly used the keyword navigation method and jumped to deeper and deeper levels in the hierarchy for repeated questions. As a result, average search time decreased by almost 50% over seven trials, from 61 seconds to 27 seconds. On the other hand, for novel or nonrepeated questions, subjects continued to use the traditional stepwise navigation method. When they used the stepwise method, although they improved somewhat with practice, they did not reach the level of performance reached when using the keyword method. In a posttest questionnaire, 90% of the subjects expressed a preference for a system that offered both stepwise and keyword navigation as compared to systems that offered a stepwise method only or a keyword method only. These data generally support the notion of offering a menu bypass mechanism for experienced users.

Guidelines drawn from this research on menu navigation are summarized on pages 163–170.

A final note on this survey of research findings on menu system design is in order. It might be argued that *statistically* significant results in such studies may not be *practically* significant. That is, a 0.5- to 1-second difference in screen processing time may or may not be important to users. One way to look at this is to consider how often users process screens and how many users there are. Small differences add up very quickly when there is a high volume of transactions and a large population of system users. A 0.5- to 1-second improvement in screen processing time can be significant indeed if there are hundreds or thousands of users and screens are processed many times a day by each user. On the other hand, if only a small number of users use the system infrequently, a difference of 1 second probably will have no significant impact on *overall* user productivity. Then, again, even a small number of infrequent users may find an inconsistent and unpredictable user interface to be frustrating to use. As the Teitelbaum and Granda (1983) study found, inconsistencies in menu design may degrade performance even for first-time users before extensive practice. Users may find even a small performance degradation frustrating if they also perceive the system as unpredictable and poorly designed.

DESIGNING MENU SYSTEMS: PRINCIPLES AND GUIDELINES

The results of the studies discussed and other studies of performance using menu systems can be summarized in a set of general principles and guidelines for good menu design, which are presented in this section. These principles and guidelines can be organized around the five different design issues, as follows:

Menu structure
Menu choice ordering
Menu choice selection
Menu invocation
Menu navigation

Menu structure.   Issues in the design of menu structure include breadth versus depth (the number of levels and the number of choices at a given level), the categorization of lowest-level choices into higher-level choices, menu choice orientation, display of unselectable items, and menu choice labels. Research supporting the following guidelines for designing menu structure is reviewed and discussed on pages 120–132.

☞ **Match menu structure to task structure.**

Figure 4-11 shows two possible ways to structure a three-level menu in an office automation product. In the "Poor" version, the user first picks word processing (WP) from a top-level menu, then chooses an action such as Print or Send, and finally chooses a document from a directory menu on which to perform the action previously selected. Note what happens if a user wishes to edit, print, and then send a particular document, say the one called DocA.

First the user must select WP from the top-level menu. Then the user selects

Poor:

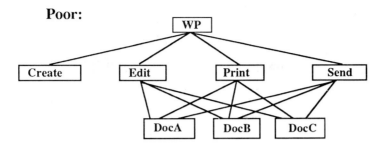

Improved:

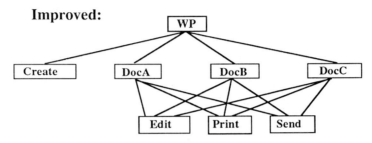

Figure 4–11   Matching menu structure to task structure.

Edit, followed by DocA. After editing the document, the user must then close DocA in order to get back to the second-level menu and select Print. After choosing Print, the user is again presented with the directory menu and must choose DocA again. The user now returns to the second-level menu and picks Send. The directory menu is presented yet again, and the user selects DocA for the third time. In this structure, the user must select DocA from a menu every time he or she wants to perform some individual action on it. This is not very efficient, given that users are likely to want to perform consecutive actions on a single document.

Alternatively, consider the "Improved" menu structure. In this structure, the user selects DocA first and is then presented with a menu of actions. When one action is complete, the user is returned to the action menu and can select another. DocA is still open, and need not be selected again. To change documents, the user would have to back up one more level in the menu. However, given that users will probably most often perform consecutive actions on a single document, this structure supports the user's task better by structuring the menu organization to reflect this goal.

Generally, menu organization should reflect the most efficient *sequence* of steps to accomplish the most likely or most frequent user goal. Note that the two structures in Figure 4-11 offer the exact same functionality. One simply supports the task better than the other.

☞ **Provide users with an easy way to tailor menu structure to task structure.**

Given that all users will not always be doing a single type of task, even the best default menu structure will not be optimal in all cases. Allowing users to tailor a menu structure to support the type of task they do most often and to change this structure when the nature of their tasks changes builds in flexibility and usability not found in simple, traditional menu systems.

For instance, in the previous example, some users may most often perform a variety of actions on a single document, while others may tend to perform a single action across a number of documents. If users could set up *either* structure illustrated in Figure 4-11, overall productivity across users would be enhanced even more than if a good but inflexible default structure were provided.

☞ **Minimize menu hierarchy depth at the expense of breadth.**

Figure 4-12 shows two different menu structures: the deep structure has many levels (three), but few choices at each level (two). The broad structure has fewer levels (two), but more choices at each level (five or more).

Generally, two factors affect whether a menu hierarchy should be deep or broad: user *decision-making time* and user *execution* time. In general, when user

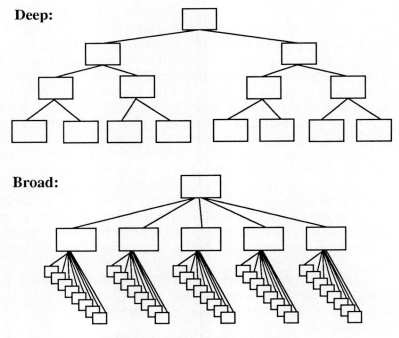

Figure 4–12   Menu breadth versus depth.

User/Task Variables	Maximum Optimal Breadth
Choice items *are* complex and/or Choice items *cannot* be grouped	Up to 10 choice items per screen
Choice items *are not* complex and Choice items *can* be grouped but Users are infrequent/casual users	11 to 20 choice items per screen
Choice items *are not* complex and Choice items *can* be grouped and Users are frequent/expert users	21 or more choice items per screen

Figure 4–13 Optimal maximum menu breadth.

decision-making times are long, less breadth is desirable, but when user execution times are long, more breadth is desirable.

These factors are in turn influenced by several variables. Decision-making times are longer when (1) users are inexperienced as opposed to experienced, (2) choice items are complex and require categorical judgments (as in a videotex system) as opposed to simple (as in a simple command menu), and (3) choice items lend themselves well to categorization, as opposed to when they do not.

Execution times are longer when system response times are longer and when the selection mechanism takes more time (for example, keyboard versus mouse pointing).

Figure 4-13 presents in chart form the maximum optimal number of choices per screen under different conditions. For instance, up to but no more than 20 choices per screen is optimal when users are casual, infrequent users of the system, choice items are simple, and choice items can be arranged in some meaningful organization. The chart should be used as a starting point for making depth–breadth decisions. Then, within the range of optimal breadth recommended by the chart, the actual breadth and depth should be determined by the most natural categorization of items into a hierarchy. The most natural categorization should be determined empirically, through statistical analyses applied to data collected from representative users of the system being designed. When breadth is to be variable at different levels, keep in mind that greater breadth at deeper levels may facilitate searching for inexperienced users, although this consideration should not override natural categorization.

There is one condition under which depth may be preferable to breadth even when the preceding guidelines would suggest otherwise. This is when groups of users will consistently be using only a subset of the total functionality. Allowing users to navigate down a pathway to the desired functionality means they will never have to encounter and scan through low-level options that they never use. This is called *insulation,* and there is some evidence that it may be advantageous in some circumstances (Paap and Roske-Hofstrand, 1988).

☞ **On full-screen text menus, present menu choice lists vertically.**

There is evidence that on full-screen text menus a vertical list of menu choices is slightly easier to search than a horizontal list (see Figure 4-14). This guideline does not necessarily apply, however, for menus that share the screen with application displays (for example, Lotus 1-2-3 and Macintosh), for menus of nontext items (for example, icons), or when other goals such as consistency within and across applications need to be considered.

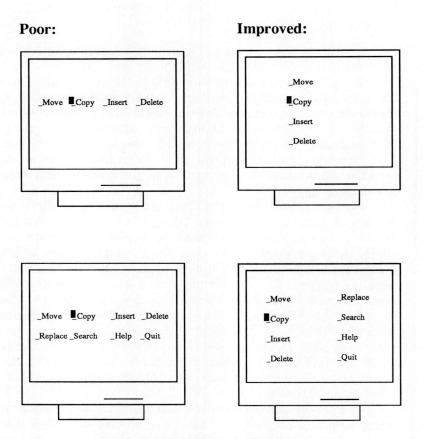

Figure 4–14 Vertical versus horizontal menus.

Acceptable:

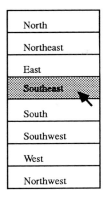

Improved:

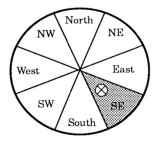

Figure 4–15 Vertical versus pie menus.

☞ **Consider pie menus for one- or two-level mouse-driven menu hierarchies with short menu choice lists, especially when the choices lend themselves well to a circular, pie format.**

Figure 4-15 illustrates a pie menu as an alternative to simple pull-down or pop-up vertical menus. There is evidence that pie menus allow faster selection times as compared to vertical menus when a mouse is used for selection, particularly when the menu choice items lend themselves well to a circular, pie format (for example, time, compass points, and sets of antonyms). However, pie menus are probably not practical for hierarchical menu structures with more than two levels or for menu lists with many choices. And they may not provide performance advantages if choice selection is by the keyboard.

☞ **Choosing graying out or deletion of inactive menu items depends on user experience and input device.**

Deletion refers to the deletion of currently inactive menu items due to temporary and minor changes in system state, while *graying out* refers to displaying

Grayed out:

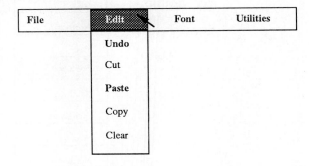

Deleted:

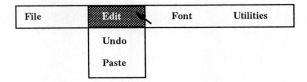

Figure 4–16 Grayed out versus deleted inactive menu items.

currently inactive menu items in a lighter font and making them unselectable (see Figure 4-16). Deletion seems to provide an advantage to *expert* users of *keyboard*-driven menus. It seems likely, however that *novices* and users of *pointer*-driven menus might benefit more from graying out. Therefore, the choice should be made partly based on the input device and partly on whether novice or expert users are given a higher priority. Since menus as a dialog style are intended for novice, casual users in general, in the absence of any specifically agreed upon priority, it would seem sensible to choose graying out.

One possibility is to provide graying out as a default and offer users the option of switching to deletion. Experts, at least of keyboard-driven menus, might in fact choose to take advantage of this option.

☞ **Create logical, distinctive, and mutually exclusive semantic categories with clear meanings.**

Figure 4-17 shows pull-down menus from a university student on-line course registration system. Labels in the "Poor" version such as "General information" and "Special functions" are too vague and do not communicate to the user what might be found at the next level below. Evidence has been found that vague labels such as these significantly degrade navigating correctly through the menu hierarchy (Dumais and Landauer, 1983; Paap and Roske-Hofstrand, 1988). Labels such as "View Course Requirements" and "View Transcript" provide more informa-

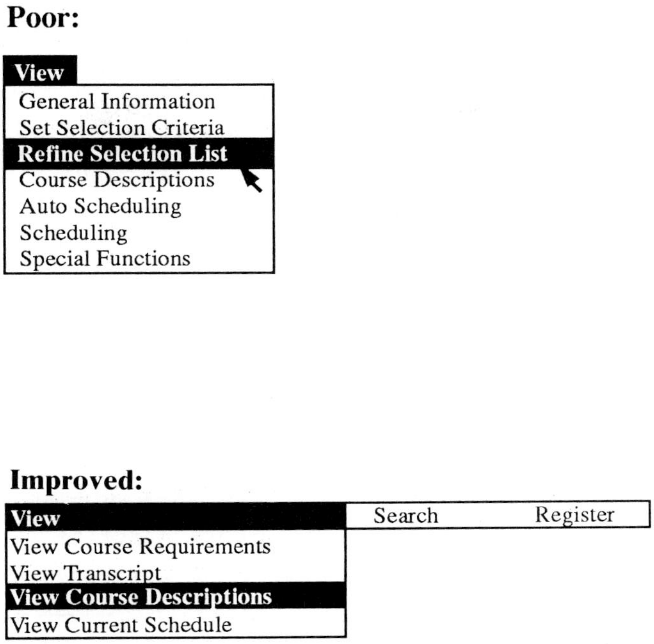

Poor:

View
General Information
Set Selection Criteria
Refine Selection List
Course Descriptions
Auto Scheduling
Scheduling
Special Functions

Improved:

View	Search	Register
View Course Requirements		
View Transcript		
View Course Descriptions		
View Current Schedule		

Figure 4–17 Logical, distinctive, mutually exclusive, clear semantic categories.

tion about the choices. They reflect a more logical way of categorizing functions and have more distinctive labels. In general, categorize and label items in a hierarchy in such a way as to *maximize* the similarity of items *within* a category and *minimize* the similarity of items *across* categories (Paap and Roske-Hofstrand, 1988).

Labels such as ''Set Selection Criteria'' and ''Refine Selection List'' are also problematic because they assume the user knows something about how the system works (that is, that the user will select courses from a database of courses by specifying search criteria in successive refinements). Grouping these functions under a category called ''Search'' reflects a better way to both group functions and label them because it refers to user goals, rather than to particulars of the way the system operates. Menu choice labels should always be phrased in terms of user goals, rather than in terms of system architecture or particular user interface conventions.

☞ **Menu choice labels should be brief, consistent in grammatical style and placement, and matched with corresponding menu titles.**

Figure 4-18 shows two sets of menu labels across two screens. In the ''Poor'' version, labels such as ''List all requirements for possible majors and minors'' and

Poor: **Improved:**

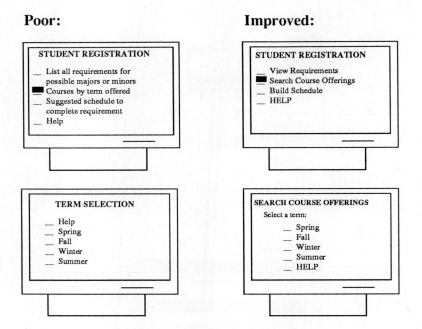

Figure 4–18   Brief, consistent menu choice labels.

"Suggested schedule to complete requirements" are simple too wordy. "View requirements" and "Build schedule" are more concise and thus easier to read, without sacrificing important meaning.

Note the first word in each label on the first screen of the "Poor" version. "List" is a verb, "Courses" is a noun, "Suggested" is an adjective, and "Help" could be either a verb or a noun; it is not clear since there is no grammatical consistency in the other labels. Inconsistent grammatical form adds complexity to the menu labels and makes it more difficult to read and interpret them. Alternatively, the first screen of the "Improved" version consistently uses verbs as the first word of the menu choice. This makes the labels easier to read and understand.

When menu items appear on more than one screen, it is a good idea to have them always appear in the same location. Note the position of the "Help" choice in the two screens of the two systems. The fact that it is consistently located in the "Improved" version will make it easier to find.

In the "Poor" version, the cursor is placed on a choice labeled "Courses by term offered." When this choice is selected, the user is taken to a screen that is titled "Term selection." This is not a bad label for this screen, but it does not correspond to the label the user chose to get there. This may leave novice users wondering if they indeed went to the screen they wanted or have made a mistake. It creates unnecessary confusion. If menu screen titles always match the menu choice labels that lead to them, as in the "Improved" version, users will be reassured that they are where they meant to be.

☞ **Consider menu choice descriptors if choice labels may not be clear and unambiguous.**

Some evidence (Lee and others, 1984; Dumais and Landauer, 1983; Snowberry, Parkinson, and Sisson, 1985; Paap and Roske-Hofstrand, 1988) suggests that including menu choice descriptors in addition to simple labels increases satisfaction and decreases errors, although search times may also be increased.

Figure 4-19 illustrates two techniques for providing menu choice descriptors: "Look-ahead" and "MicroHelp." "Look-ahead" is illustrated at the top of the

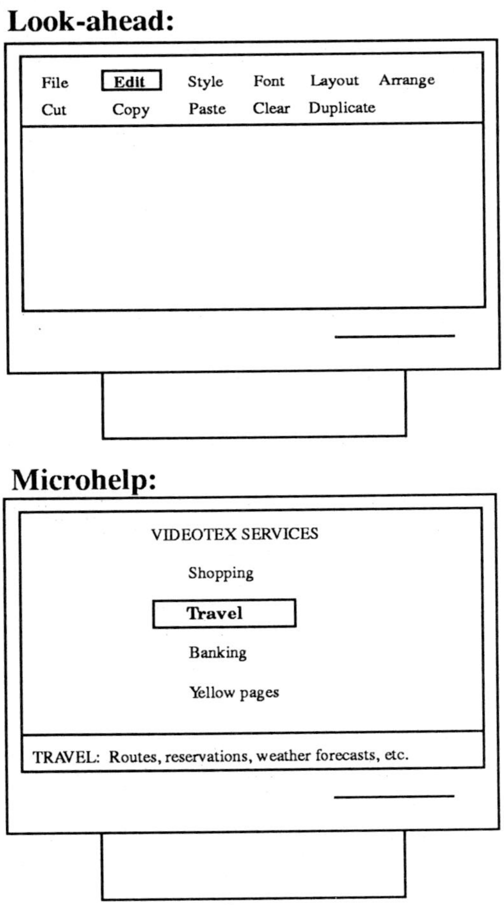

Look-ahead:

File	Edit	Style	Font	Layout	Arrange
Cut	Copy	Paste	Clear	Duplicate	

Microhelp:

VIDEOTEX SERVICES

Shopping

Travel

Banking

Yellow pages

TRAVEL: Routes, reservations, weather forecasts, etc.

Figure 4–19 Menu choice descriptors.

figure. In this technique, all choices at the next level are displayed when the cursor is resting on a choice on the current level. In the example, all "Edit" choices are displayed because the cursor is on "Edit." If the user steps the cursor ahead to the "Style" choice, then the second line would change to display all the "Style" choices. If the user selects "Edit" instead, the "Edit" submenu pops up to the top line, and appropriate submenus are displayed below as the cursor moves from choice to choice.

"MicroHelp" is illustrated at the bottom of the figure. Here, as the cursor steps through the choices of a menu, a message line at the bottom of the screen presents a description of what will be found down this pathway. This description can be a list of actual choice labels or a more general prose description of the types of choices available.

Which technique is used depends on the format of the menus (for example, full-screen or bar menus) and the number of choices at submenu levels.

Choice descriptors take up space on the screen, and this must be traded off against other goals for the display area. Descriptors are especially useful when users are casual and infrequent and choice labels are broad, general, vague, and potentially ambiguous.

Menu choice ordering.   Once a menu hierarchy or structure is decided on, and the choice items that will actually appear on each menu screen have been determined and labeled, we are faced with the question of how to order these choice items. Which should be at the top of the list? Which at the bottom? Is there any organizing principle that is superior to another in terms of optimizing user search time?

The following guidelines are drawn from the research findings on menu choice ordering reviewed and discussed on pages 133–137.

☞ **Order menu choice labels according to convention, frequency of use, order of use, categorical or functional groups, and/or alphabetical order, depending on the user and task variables.**

Figure 4-20 shows five possible ways to group the choices within a given menu. In the "Conventional" organization, items are ordered according to some common conventional order. Items such as months of the year, days of the week, numbers, sizes, and primary colors all have a standard, conventional order.

In the "Frequency of Use" organization, choices are listed in order of expected frequency of use. Thus, for example, Help users are expected to most often consult the general Help index, and next often ask for Keyboard Help, and so on.

In the "Order of Use" organization, choices are listed in the order users are expected to use them in sequence. That is, it is anticipated that users in an electronic mail system will typically first read a piece of mail, then forward it, then print it, and so on.

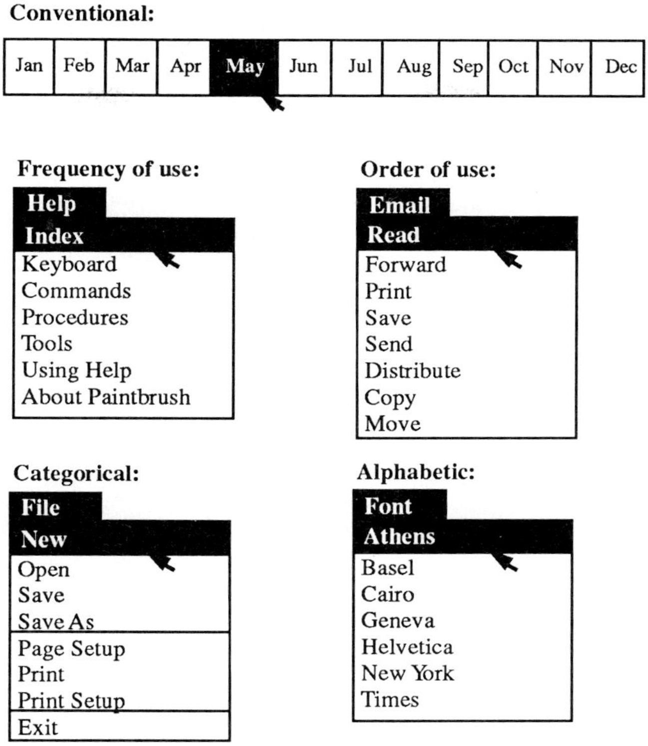

Conventional:

Jan	Feb	Mar	Apr	May	Jun	Jul	Aug	Sep	Oct	Nov	Dec

Frequency of use:

Help
Index
Keyboard
Commands
Procedures
Tools
Using Help
About Paintbrush

Order of use:

Email
Read
Forward
Print
Save
Send
Distribute
Copy
Move

Categorical:

File
New
Open
Save
Save As
Page Setup
Print
Print Setup
Exit

Alphabetic:

Font
Athens
Basel
Cairo
Geneva
Helvetica
New York
Times

Figure 4–20   Menu choice ordering schemes.

In the "Categorical" organization, choices are grouped according to semantic categories. For example, file manipulation commands are in the first group, print commands in the second, and so on.

Finally, in the "Alphabetic" organization, the choices are simply listed in alphabetic order.

Figure 4-21 offers a guideline to follow to choose an appropriate organization for menu items on a given screen. If any conventional order applies, it ought to take priority over any other possible ordering scheme. If there is no conventional order to follow and if there are more than five or six choices on a menu, it is a good idea to group them in some way to facilitate scanning and searching. If there is a clear difference in the anticipated frequency of use of the menu choices, and especially if selection is by keyboard cursor movement, then ordering items by frequency of use will minimize both search time and selection time for both novice and expert users.

If there is in fact an anticipated, natural, and likely order of use inherent in the menu choices, then an order of use organization might be appropriate. For novice,

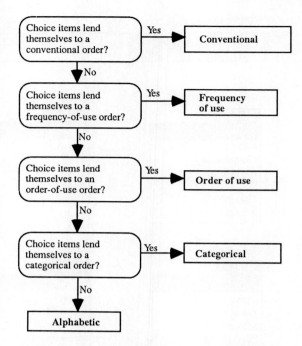

Figure 4–21 Choosing menu choice ordering schemes.

casual, or infrequent users, if there is a natural way to group choice items by functional or semantic categories, this is desirable. These users will not know the exact label of the choice they want, and so an alphabetical ordering will not help them.

If no other ordering scheme lends itself well to the menu choices, then alphabetic is better than random ordering, especially for high-frequency, expert users.

High-frequency, expert, "power" users will also benefit more from positional constancy (that is, if a given item appears on more than one menu, it appears in the same ordinal position on all menus), even if achieving positional constancy means sacrificing consistency in one of the preceding ordering schemes.

Note that ordering schemes can also be *nested* when there are a large number of choices on a screen and this seems appropriate. For instance, choice items might be ordered in logical semantic categories, but groups could be listed in order of expected frequency of use, and items within groups could also be ordered by expected frequency of use or alphabetically.

When logical semantic categories are used as an ordering scheme, it is a good idea to label category groups to facilitate searching. Category labels should be visually distinct from choices. Separate categories by blank lines. For very long lists within categories, insert a blank line between each group of five items (Galitz, 1989). Figure 4-22 provides some examples.

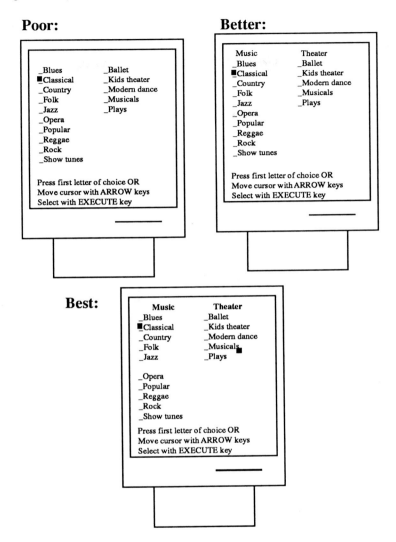

Figure 4–22 Formatting menu choice categories.

Menu choice selection.   A variety of selection mechanisms is available. Perhaps the most common are single letter or number selection codes, which are entered in a fill-in field followed by some terminator key such as "Execute" or "Return." Alternatives include moving a cursor (for example, a reverse video bar or block cursor to the left of the choice items) through the list of choices with the cursor control keys and pressing a terminator key when the cursor is located on the desired choice, or pointing directly to the choice with an alternative input device such as a mouse, joystick, or touch screen. The following guidelines are drawn from the research findings on menu choice selection reviewed and summarized on pages 137–141.

☞ **On keyboard-driven menu systems, cursor selection is acceptable for shorter menus, especially if use is expected to be casual. For longer menus and/or for high-frequency users, mnemonically lettered selection codes are preferred if practical. On pointer (for example, a mouse) driven interfaces, providing a pointer cursor selection mechanism is recommended.**

Figure 4-23 shows four alternative keyboard-driven menu selection mechanisms. If menus are short, say less than eight items, then moving a cursor through the selections is an attractive selection mechanism because it is more direct than reading and entering a code. Cursor selection is especially attractive when use is expected to be casual, since ease of learning and comfort level are more important than ease of use in this case. One drawback to cursor selection, however, is that it is harder for the user to take advantage of type-ahead or to make an easy transition to a command language bypass.

If menus have many items on them, simple cursor movement results in many keystrokes to get to some items, and entering in a one-character code is faster. It

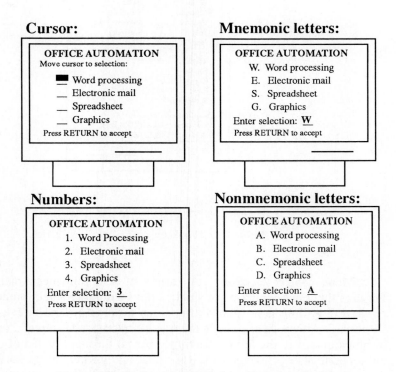

Figure 4–23 Keyboard menu choice selection mechanisms.

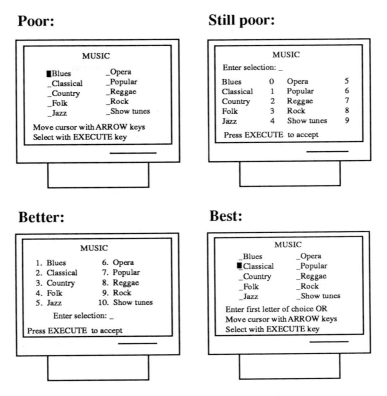

Figure 4–24   Formatting menu selection.

has also been empirically demonstrated (Shinar and others, 1985) that with frequent use a one-character code quickly shows a performance advantage over cursor selection even on menus with few items.

If a one-character code is to be the selection mechanism, then mnemonic letters (that is, letter codes derived from the first letter of the menu choice label) are optimal, if this can be accomplished without resulting in unclear menu choice labels in order to avoid duplicating first letters. If this is not possible, then numbers are the next best choice. It is recommended that nonmnemonic letters be avoided, as this seems to slow down selection time and may induce errors as well.

Besides the advantage of being easier to learn, mnemonic letters also have the advantage of not changing as new items are added to a menu. If numbers are used, and a designer wants to add items but preserve some ordering scheme such as categorical or by frequency or order of use, the numbers assigned options would have to change. Letters would not have to change in this case as long as unambiguous first letter codes could be designed for the new items.

A few guidelines for formatting menu screens that use keyboard selection codes are described next, and illustrated in Figure 4-24.

If numbers are used, it is recommended to always start with the number 1, never with 0 (Galitz, 1989). As Galitz points out, "Only computers begin counting with zero, people never do."

When character codes are used, either letters or numbers, it is recommended that choices be left justified in columns, with the codes aligned in a column to the *left* of the choices. When codes are aligned in a column to the right of the choices, this too often results in a wide separation between at least some choices and their codes. This makes it hard for the eye to track from choice to code and may result in errors of selection.

When selection codes are used, a well-labeled selection field (for example, "Selection" or "Enter selection code") should appear *below* the choices. This is where the eye will be after searching through the list of choices and also provides a shorter scanning distance between the selection field and the keyboard (Galitz, 1989).

One possibility (illustrated as the "Best" option in Figure 4-24) is to combine cursor movement with mnemonic letter codes. That is, the user can move the cursor one choice at a time with the cursor keys, but can also simply type in the first letter of a choice and the cursor will automatically jump to the first choice with that first letter. Pressing the letter again would jump to the next choice with that first letter, and so on (thus unique first letters are not required). When the cursor is positioned on the desired choice, pressing a key such as "Return" or "Execute" would accept the choice. This has the advantage of directness, but also provides a shortcut for moving the cursor on lengthy menus.

If the system has an alternative input device, such as a mouse or touch screen, and if many other tasks can be or must be accomplished using this alternative device, then it can also be used for menu selection. Although one study (Karat, McDonald, Anderson, 1984) found entering keyboard selection codes to be faster than pointing with a mouse, if users' hands are already on the mouse, this may be the preferred and faster selection mechanism. On the other hand, if such a device is available but the user's hands are most often on the keyboard, then both a keyboard and an alternative input device menu selection mechanism are recommended so that users are not forced to go back and forth between the keyboard and alternative device too frequently.

☞ **Provide menu selection defaults when possible.**

Menus should come up with a default selection to save keystrokes. In selection code mechanisms, the default code would appear in the fill-in field, so the user need only press the acceptance key (for example, "Execute" or "Return"). In cursor selection mechanisms, the cursor would be positioned on the default choice, and, again, the user need only press the acceptance key.

Several alternatives for defaults are possible. Defaults might be the last item selected from the menu or the most frequently used item, if these are appropriate given the expected use of the menu choices. If no logical default can be determined, then simply having the first choice in the list be the default is reasonable (this may or may not be the most frequently used, depending on the organizing principle used to order the choices).

Menus with pointing device selection mechanisms cannot provide defaults if the selection mechanism is a one-step process, such as touching the choice with the finger or pressing a mouse button once. However, defaults would provide no advantage in these mechanisms because input operations are already at a minimum.

☞ **Distinguish between "Choose one" and "Choose many" menus.**

Some menus present mutually exclusive choices, and the user can only select one at a time. Others present a list of options that may be selected in combination simultaneously. Examples are given in Figure 4-25.

In the "Choose one" menu, after having chosen an object, the user can only select one action at a time to operate on that object. The user can select many actions in sequence by accessing the menu repetitively, but at any one pass through the menu, only one action can be chosen.

In the "Choose many" menu, a menu of text attributes is presented. The user may wish a given text string to be both bold *and* italic, and so it makes sense to allow the user to select these two attributes simultaneously in one pass through the menu.

There are many different ways to design the input to a "Choose many" menu. One common way is to present the user with a menu that looks identical to a "Choose one" menu and operates like one as the default and then provide a way to go into "Choose many mode." This is often accomplished by pressing a special key, but often there is no prompting on the screen regarding the use of this special

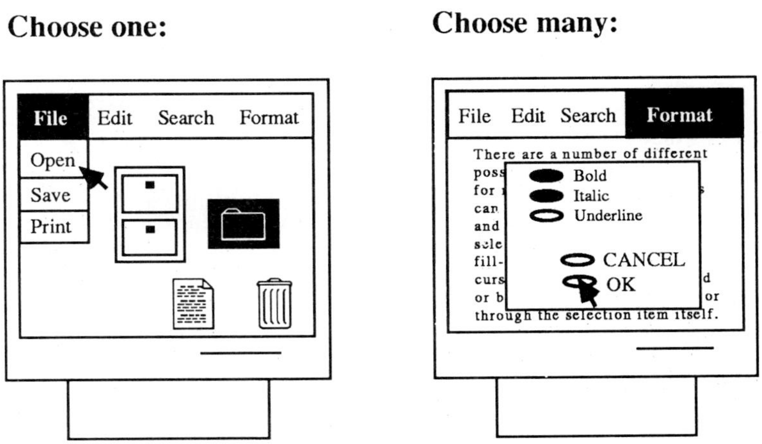

Choose one: **Choose many:**

Figure 4–25   Choose one versus choose many menus.

key. The rationale given for this approach is that keystrokes are minimized in the default "Choose one" mode.

The problem with this approach is that many users never discover the "Choose many" mode. If, however, "Choose many" menus look distinctively different from "Choose one" menus and have a well-prompted selection mechanism, as in the examples in Figure 4-25, then users will quickly perceive the difference and understand how to use "Choose many" menus without having to discover, learn, and remember special mode keys.

It is often appropriate to *hide* infrequently used or advanced functions to protect novice and casual users from complexity, but this is not an appropriate situation for this approach. Using the "Choose many" capability of menus is most likely a basic, high-frequency function in most systems.

☞ **Provide menu selection feedback.**

Provide users with visual feedback indicating which options are selectable, which option the pointer or cursor is currently pointing to, and which options are currently selected (Paap and Roske-Hofstrand, 1988). For example, in Figure 4-26, nonselectable options are presented in dim or grayed out text, the option the cursor is currently pointing to is in reverse video, and currently selected options have a check mark by them.

Menu invocation.   In most menu systems, the user is always presented with a menu at the appropriate time, or the top-level menu is permanently visible in some reserved area of the screen. Some newer menu systems, however, have *pop-up* menus, in which the user must take some action in order to bring up a menu. The following guideline for using these two approaches to menu invocation should be followed:

☞ **Reserve pop-up or user-invoked menus for high-frequency users and situations where screen real estate is scarce. Permanent menus are preferred.**

Figure 4-27 shows examples of "Permanent" and "User invoked" menus. In the "Permanent" menu system, the top-level menu is permanently displayed

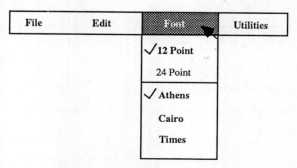

Figure 4–26   Menu selection feedback.

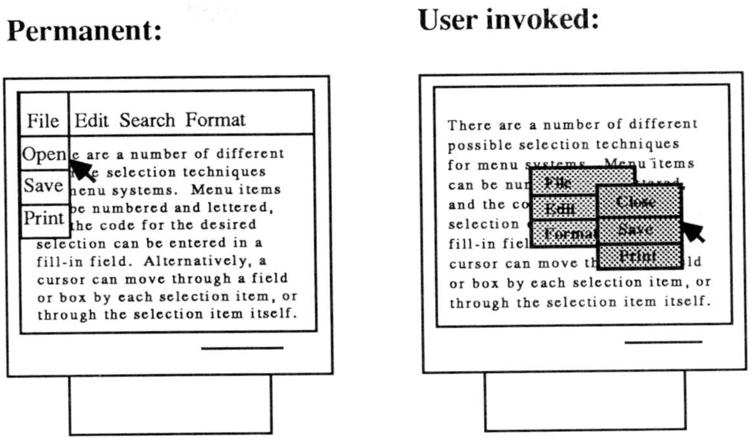

Permanent: **User invoked:**

Figure 4–27   Menu invocation.

across the top of the screen. The second-level pull-down menu only appears when a selection from the top-level menu is made.

In the user-invoked menu, on the other hand, the normal state of affairs is the display screen with no menus visible. The user must press a key on the keyboard or alternative input device (for example, a mouse button) to bring up the top-level menu that is appropriate given the current state of the dialog.

This approach has the advantage of not taking up space on the screen, but it also has the disadvantage of requiring that users know what functions are available through menus, and remembering how to invoke them. Given that menus are intended to support novice and casual users in the first place, it should be kept in mind that user-invoked menus detract from the potential benefit of menus of making semantics and syntax obvious in the interface. Thus it is recommended that user-invoked menus should only be used when screen real estate is at a premium and when most users can be expected to use the system fairly frequently.

Menu navigation.   Navigating through a menu system is facilitated by a number of design considerations, including good screen layout and design, the presence of context information to remind the user where they are, menu bypass, and efficient selection mechanisms. The following guidelines are drawn from the research findings reviewed and discussed on pages 141–143.

☞ **Establish conventions for menu design and apply them consistently on all menu screens within a system.**

Figure 4-28 shows examples of two screens from two versions of a system. In the "Poor" version, there is no consistency between the two screens in title location and format, pushbutton location, and menu option layout and design. As

Poor:

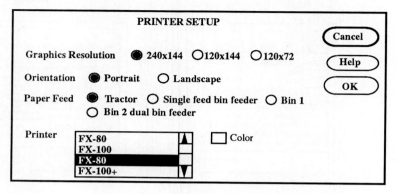

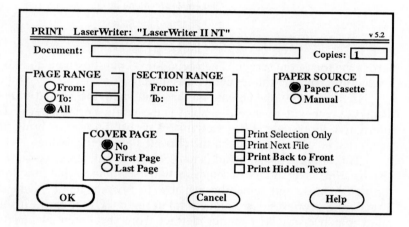

Figure 4–28 Consistency in menu design.

suggested in one study (Teitelbaum and Granda, 1983), this kind of inconsistency can increase search time while navigating through a menu system.

In the "Improved" version, on the other hand, conventions for title location and format, button location and options layout and design have been consistently followed.

Generally, it is a good idea to design and document a set of screen design standards, guidelines, and conventions and then require that these be adhered to by all designers of screens for a given system. Within-application consistency is always important, and often it is important to also achieve across-application or across-product consistency if users are expected to use several or many applications and products. This consistency will facilitate learning and also result in an easier to use system.

Improved:

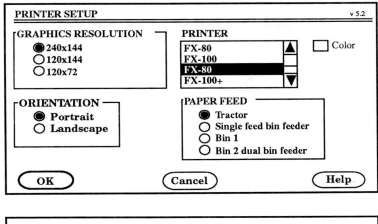

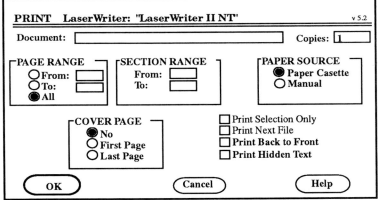

Figure 4–28 *(Continued)*

☞ **Consider the use of context labels, menu maps, and place markers as navigational aids in complex menu systems.**

When menu systems are very deep and complex, novice and casual users can easily get lost and have difficulty remembering how to get somewhere from their current location or what they have and have not already done. One way to assist users in navigating in complex menu systems is to provide plenty of context information on each screen, including clear titles and reminders of choices made in previous menus.

For example, in a videotex system that allows users to shop by catalog, perform banking and bill paying activities, and make travel reservations, a user may be on a screen on which they are to confirm the amount to be paid and date of payment in order to make payment on one of their charge cards. They might have arrived at this screen through a fairly long sequence of screens on which they made menu choices and entered information in fill-in fields. On the confirmation screen, it would be helpful to include **context labels** something like the following:

> SERVICE: **Pay Bills**
> CHARGE ACCOUNT: **Master Card**
> PAYMENT AMOUNT: **Minimum payment ($32.00)**
> PAYMENT DATE: **Due date (3/15/90)**

It is true that such a header takes up a significant number of lines on the screen. However, for infrequent users, reminders such as this are often more important than minimizing the number of screens to pass through. They minimize the amount of information users must carry in short-term memory as they complete a task that requires many screens, and they help users keep track of where they are and determine how to navigate to other desired locations in the system.

One study (Apperley and Field, 1984) described a system that used a similar technique for displaying navigational history on menu screens. In addition to just providing context, however, the history was itself also a navigational aid, as users could select an item in the history as a way of navigating back to arbitrary points in the hierarchy. Selecting the choice from a particular level brought the user back to that level.

Other navigational aids include menu maps and place markers, as illustrated in Figure 4-29. A **menu map** is simply an overview of the menu hierarchy, perhaps with a "You Are Here" marker, that users can access at any time from their current location in the menu structure. Billingsley (1982) found evidence that previewing a menu map can facilitate navigation. Average search times were cut in half if users were allowed to study a menu map first before navigating through the system. While it may not be possible to present a complete menu map for a very complex hierarchy on the screen, some investigators have been investigating other maplike aids with some success (see Paap and Roske-Hofstrand, 1988).

Other kinds of **place markers** can also give users information about their current location. In Figure 4-29, the sample place marker is a symbol in the upper-right corner of the screen made up of a number sign (#) and dashes (-). The position of the # indicates the level in the menu hierarchy. Thus, in the first screen the user is at the top level, and in the second screen he or she is at the second level. Dashes to the right of the # indicate how many levels lie below the current screen if the pathway indicated by the current location of the cursor is taken. Other representations of current location could also be designed.

☞ **Consider the use of direct access through type-ahead, menu screen names, and user-created macros to facilitate navigation for expert users.**

Menu maps: **Place markers:**

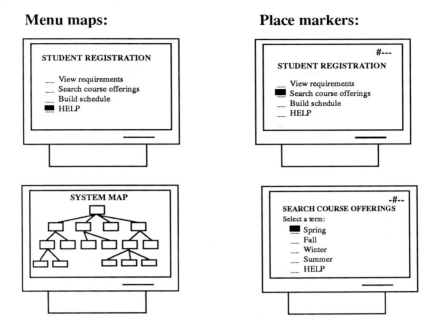

Figure 4–29 Menu navigation aids.

High-frequency, expert users will become frustrated by tedious navigation through complex menu hierarchies. It is desirable to provide a *menu bypass* for these users, and several possible mechanisms are available.

Type ahead allows a user to enter all choices from all menus down the desired pathway without viewing each screen successively. In the example in Figure 4-30, the user could enter W on the first menu to get into Word Processing. On the second menu they might enter F to choose the Filing option, and on a third menu they might enter C to select the Copy command. Alternatively, on the first-level menu they might enter WFC followed by the return key, and this would take them directly to the Copy screen, without viewing the middle two menus. Once users learn the selection codes for frequently used choices, they can easily begin to use a bypass mechanism such as this.

Alternatively, each screen could have a short, mnemonic name that could be typed in the selection code fill-in field of any screen. In the example in Figure 4-30, the name of the Copy screen is COP, and if the user enters this instead of a single-letter code on the top-level menu, the system will bypass intervening screens and go directly to the Copy screen.

A third alternative would allow users to create *macros* or small files containing the keystrokes used to navigate through the menu system to a particular screen.

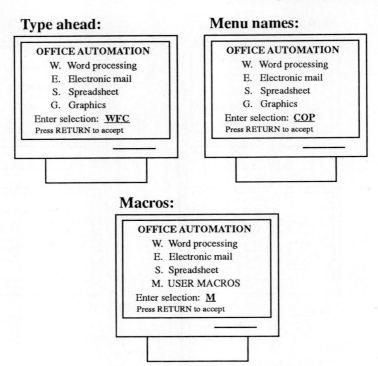

Figure 4–30 Menu bypass mechanisms.

These files could be assigned short names and directly executed from a macro screen or through a special sequence of keys.

Type ahead has the advantage of being based on the same semantic and motor knowledge as normal navigation through the menu hierarchy. Frequent users of the system will learn the selection codes from each menu and find this bypass mechanism easy to learn and remember. However, the resulting codes for screens (for example, WFC) are not particularly mnemonic and therefore will be more difficult to learn for infrequent users. Also, they generally only work for navigating forward through a menu system; so if the user wants to go from one leaf or node in the hierarchy to another, backing up to a common higher level must be accomplished before typing ahead down the new pathway.

Infrequent users may find it easier to learn and remember mnemonic *menu names* such as COP, and they are more efficient for leaping directly form leaf to leaf. *Macros* are simply more powerful than either type ahead or menu names, because users can build very complex navigation and data entry tasks including decision processing and then execute them with a single keystroke. This power comes with some added complexity, however as an interface to the macro capabilities must be learned.

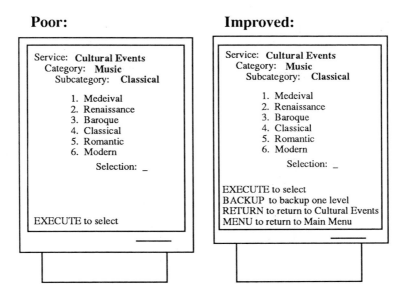

Figure 4–31 Backward navigation.

☞ **Facilitate backward navigation.**

The "Improved" screen in Figure 4-31 illustrates a way to facilitate backward navigation. The user has navigated down several levels in a videotex system for city tourists, first selecting "Cultural Events" from a main menu also offering such categories as "Shopping," "Accommodations," and "Transportation." Under "Cultural Events" a second-level menu offered such choices as "Museums," "Art Galleries," "Theater," and "Music." The user chose "Music" from this second-level menu and then chose "Classical" from a third-level menu of music categories such as "Jazz," "Country and Western," "Rock," and "Popular." Now the user is choosing from a fourth-level menu offering types of classical music.

It seems likely that, besides wanting to back up a single level or return to the main menu in this system, users might also want to return to the top level of the category of service they are currently in, in this case "Cultural Events." The user is likely to want to peruse through different entertainment options awhile before switching to some completely different service area, such as "Accommodations." Adding a shortcut to return to this intermediate-level menu will facilitate a high-frequency pathway in the menu hierarchy.

As this example illustrates, it should always be possible to escape quickly from any point in a menu hierarchy back to the main menu, as well as to back up one level at a time. In a deep menu hierarchy, it is also desirable to be able to navigate directly back to certain intermediate-level menus that have a high probability of being accessed from certain lower-level menus. Single keystrokes for these navigational options should be available and should be prompted for on the screen.

REFERENCES

APPERLEY, M. D., and G. E. FIELD, "A Comparative Evaluation of Menu-based Interactive Human–Computer Dialogue Techniques," *Interact '84 Proceedings,* 1984, pp. 103–107, IFIP.

BACKS, RICHARD W., LARRY C. WALRATH, and GLENN A. HANCOCK, "Comparison of Horizontal and Vertical Menu Formats," *Proceedings of the Human Factors Society 31st Annual Meeting,* 1987, pp. 715–17.

BILLINGSLEY, P. A., "Navigation through Hierarchical Menu Structures: Does It Help to Have a Map?" *Proceedings of the Human Factors Society 26th Annual Meeting,* 1982, pp. 103–107.

CALLAHAN, JACK, and others, "An Empirical Comparison of Pie vs. Linear Menus," *CHI '88 Proceedings,* May 1988, pp. 95–100, ACM.

CARD, STUART K., THOMAS P. MORAN, and ALLEN NEWELL, *The Psychology of Human-Computer Interaction* (Hillsdale, N.J.: Lawrence Erlbaum Associates, 1983).

CHIN, JOHN P., "A Dynamic User-adaptable Menu System: Linking It All Together," *Proceedings of the Human Factors Society 33rd Annual Meeting,* 1989, pp. 413–17.

DUMAIS, S. T., and T. K. LANDAUER, "Using Examples to Describe Categories," *CHI '83 Proceedings,* December 1983, pp. 112–15, ACM.

FOLTZ, PETER W., "Transfer between Menu Systems," *CHI '88 Proceedings,* May 1988, pp. 107–112, ACM.

FRANCIK, ELLEN P., and RICHARD M. KANE, "Optimizing Visual Search and Cursor Movement in Pull-down Menus," *Proceedings of the Human Factors Society 31st Annual Meeting,* 1987, pp. 722–26.

GALITZ, WILBERT O., *Handbook of Screen Format Design,* 3rd ed. (Wellesley, Mass.: QED Information Sciences, Inc., 1989), pp. 177–202.

HOLLANDS, J. G., and PHILIP M. MERIKLE, "Menu Organization and User Expertise in Information Search Tasks," *Human Factors,* 29, no. 5 (October 1987), pp. 577–86.

KARAT, J., J. E. MCDONALD, and M. ANDERSON, "A Comparison of Selection Techniques: Touch Panel, Mouse and Keyboard," *Interact '84 Proceedings,* 1984, pp. 149–53, IFIP.

LANDAUER, THOMAS K., and D. W. NACHBAR, "Selection from Alphabetic and Numeric Menu Trees Using a Touch Screen: Breadth, Depth and Width," *CHI '85 Proceedings,* April 1985, pp. 73–78, ACM.

LEE, E., and G. CHAO, "The Increasing Utility of Incorporating Keywords in Menu Systems as Users Increase Experience," *Behavior & Information Technology,* 8, no. 4 (July–August 1989), pp. 301–308.

———, and JAMES MACGREGOR, "Minimizing User Search Time in Menu-retrieval Systems," *Human Factors,* 27, no. 2 (April 1985), pp. 157–62.

———, and others, "Optimizing the Design of Menu Pages for Information Retrieval," *Ergonomics,* 27 (1984), pp. 1051–69.

MacGregor, James, Eric Lee, and Newman Lam, "Optimizing the Structure of Database Menu Indexes: A Decision Model of Menu Search," *Human Factors,* 28, no. 4 (August 1986), 387–400.

McDonald, James E., Mark E. Molander, and Ronald W. Noel, "Color-coding Categories in Menus," *CHI '88 Proceedings,* May 1988, pp. 101–106, ACM.

———, Jim D. Stone, and Linda S. Liebelt, "Searching for Items in Menus: The Effects of Organization and Type of Target," *Proceedings of the Human Factors Society 27th Annual Meeting,* 2, 1983, pp. 834–37.

Miller, Dwight P., "The Depth/Breadth Tradeoff in Hierarchical Computer Menus," *Proceedings of the Human Factors Society 25th Annual Meeting,* 1981, pp. 296–300.

Norman, K. L., and J. P. Chin, "The Effect of Tree Structure on Search in a Hierarchical Menu Selection System," *Behavior & Information Technology,* 7, no. 1 (January–March 1988), pp. 51–66.

Paap, Kenneth R., and Renate J. Roske-Hofstrand, "The Optimal Number of Menu Options per Panel," *Human Factors,* 28, no. 4 (August 1986), pp. 377–86.

———, and ———, "Design of Menus," *Handbook of Human–Computer Interaction,* Martin Helander, ed., (Amsterdam: North-Holland, 1988), pp. 205–35.

Perlman, Gary, "Making the Right Choices with Menus," *Proceedings, Interact '84,* 1, 1984, pp. 291–295.

Shinar, David, and Helman I. Stern, "Alternative Option Selection Methods in Menu-driven Computer Programs," *Human Factors,* 29, no. 4 (August 1987), pp. 453–60.

———, and others, "The Relative Effectiveness of Alternative Selection Strategies in Menu Driven Computer Programs," *Proceedings of the Human Factors Society 29th Annual Meeting,* 1985, pp. 645–49.

Snowberry, K., S. R. Parkinson, and N. Sisson, "Computer Display Menus," *Ergonomics,* 26 (1983), pp. 699–712.

———, S. R. Parkinson, and N. Sisson, "Effects of Help Fields on Navigating through Hierarchical Menu Structures," *International Journal of Man–Machine Studies,* 22 (1985), pp. 479–91.

Somberg, Benjamin L., "A Comparison of Rule-based and Positionally Constant Arrangements of Computer Menu Items," *CHI '87 Proceedings,* May 1987, pp. 255–260, ACM.

Teitelbaum, Richard C., and Richard E. Granda, "The Effects of Positional Constancy on Searching Menus for Instructions," *CHI '83 Proceedings,* 1983, pp. 150–53, ACM.

Wallace, Daniel F., Nancy S. Anderson, and Ben Shneiderman, "Time Stress Effects on Two Menu Selection Systems," *Proceedings of the Human Factors 31st Annual Meeting,* 1987, pp. 727–31.

CHAPTER 5

Dialog Styles: Fill-in Forms

WHAT IS A FILL-IN FORM INTERFACE?

A **fill-in form** interface is similar to a paper fill-in form; it is simply presented on a computer screen rather than on paper. It is a structured, formatted form containing a number of **fields** in which the user is expected to type in data. Usually, each field has a label or **caption** that indicates the type of data to be entered in that field.

Figure 5-1 shows two examples of fill-in form interfaces. They differ in general layout, format of fields, and the amount and location of prompting and instructions included on the form.

WHEN IS A FILL-IN FORM DIALOG STYLE APPROPRIATE?

Fill-in forms have particular advantages and disadvantages, relative to other dialog styles. *Advantages* include the following.

Self-explanatory. Well-designed fill-in forms make a system relatively easy to learn because they make both the *semantics* and the *syntax* of the system explicit. That is, they make clear both *what* can be done (semantics) and *how* to do it (syntax). Clear captions and good prompts regarding valid inputs and their proper format can provide users with everything they need to know to correctly fill in the

```
┌──────────────────────────────────────────────────────┐
│ ▬          International - Currency Format             │
│                                                        │
│ Symbol Placement: │ $1              │ ▼ │   ╭────────╮ │
│                                             │   OK   │ │
│ Negative:         │ ($123.22)       │ ▼ │   ╰────────╯ │
│                                             ╭────────╮ │
│ Symbol:           │ $         │             │ Cancel │ │
│                                             ╰────────╯ │
│ Decimal Digits:   │ 2  │                               │
│                                                        │
└──────────────────────────────────────────────────────┘
```

```
┌──────────────────────────────────────────────────────┐
│ ▬                  LOAN APPLICATION                    │
│ Name:    │ Dr. Deborah J. Mayhew        │  ╭────────╮ │
│                                             │   OK   │ │
│ Address: │ Box 248, W. Tisbury, MA  02575│ ╰────────╯ │
│                                             ╭────────╮ │
│                                             │ Cancel │ │
│ Date: ▐ 4/8/91 ▌        Amount: │         │ ╰────────╯ │
│ Rate: │         │       # Months: │       │           │
│──────────────────────────────────────────────────────│
│ HINT: Date:  mm/dd/yy format - no leading zeroes       │
└──────────────────────────────────────────────────────┘
```

Figure 5–1 Examples of fill-in forms.

form. Because the interface is relatively self-explanatory, the learning burden is decreased and the need for manuals and training programs is reduced. This might be contrasted with a command language interface, which gives no semantic or syntactic prompting and requires the user to know what can be done and how to do it.

Requires little memory. For the same reason that fill-in forms are easy to learn, they are also easy to remember. Casual users who may not use a system frequently run the risk of forgetting how to use it between uses. Because a fill-in form interface is potentially self-explanatory, it is not necessary to memorize and retain semantic or syntactic knowledge. Fill-in forms rely mostly on *recognition memory* rather than *recall memory*. The user need only *recognize* the captions, prompts, and instructions and does not have to *recall* (without cues) what input is required and how to format it. Recognition memory is faster and more accurate than recall memory, and fill-in forms exploit this fact.

Efficient use of screen real estate. As compared to a menu system, fill-in forms make efficient use of space on the screen. A traditional menu system asks only one question per screen so that several or even many screens are necessary to complete a given task, whereas many input fields might appear on a single fill-in form screen. For expert, high-frequency users, minimal prompting and instructions mean even more space available for user input on a single screen. Of course, fill-in forms take up much more screen space than, say, a command language or function key interface would, but they are more space efficient than, for instance, menus or icon-based direct manipulation interfaces.

Accommodates parameters with many possible input values.   Fill-in fields lend themselves well when input is required from the user that may take on any of a large number of values. For instance, if the system requires that the user specify a name, an address, a numerical value, an identification number, and so on, it would not be practical or possible to present the possibilities in a menu. A well-labeled and prompted fill-in field is usually the best input format for this type of data. When users are high-frequency, expert users, sometimes fill-in fields are preferable to menus of options even when the number of valid inputs is limited, because of the relative space efficiency of fill-in forms as compared to menus.

Provides context.   Because there are usually several or many fill-in fields on a single screen, users get broader context information than they would on, say, a menu or question and answer interface. In these latter two dialog styles, the user cannot see what is going to be asked next. For instance, suppose the system requires that the user enter in his or her name and address. In a fill-in form, there might be several captions and fields on a single screen such as "Name," "Address," "City," "State," and "Zip Code." If, on the other hand, the dialog style was question and answer, the user would be asked for these parameters one at a time. When the question "Address" came up, because the user could not see future questions, it might be unclear whether this meant just street address, or full address, including city, state, and zip code. Seeing all required inputs on the fill-in form provides this kind of context, which helps users respond correctly to each input field.

Enhancements are visible.   Because a fill-in form interface always presents all the required input fields, whenever new functions are added to a system they will appear directly in the interface, that is, on a fill-in screen. Thus users will always notice when new functions are added.

For instance, suppose a multiple-user system had only one printer. The print request fill-in form would not have a field for specifying the desired printer, because only one is available. If more printers were later added to the system, a new field might appear on the screen asking for a printer name. Thus all users would discover that multiple printers are now available. A good fill-in form would now also provide some way besides the manual (for example, prompts or on-line help) for users to find out the valid printer names. Contrast this with a command language interface, in which no evidence of the newly available printers would actually appear through the interface. In such an interface, users may never know that features or functions have been added because the interface has not changed in any visible way.

In summary, the main advantages of fill-in form interfaces are ease of learning and remembering and efficiency of input. There are serious trade-offs, however. *Disadvantages* of fill-in form systems include the following.

Assumes knowledge of valid inputs.   Although good captions and simple brief prompts help users to know what type of input is required and how to format it, for many fields, users may not know what the valid inputs are. For instance, although it is easy to prompt the user for the valid inputs to a yes or no field such as

"Married: __ (Y or N)",

there may not be enough room on a screen to prompt for the valid inputs to fields such as "Size," "Part Number," or "Department." This will not be a problem for high-frequency, expert users with substantial semantic knowledge of the problem domain, but may be for other types of users. To offset this disadvantage, on-line help systems can, and often should, provide menus of valid input options, although this will require an extra step or two. The fact remains that a fill-in form itself often does not afford room for good prompting, and this is a drawback to keep in mind.

Assumes typing skill.   Entering data into fill-in fields requires typing. If users are not touch typists, then this dialog style may be slow relative to others such as function keys, menus, or direct manipulation, which require less typing.

Error prone.   Even if users are touch typists, typing presents opportunities for user input errors, and so fill-in forms may be more error prone than dialog styles that require less typing, such as menus, direct manipulation, and function keys.

Assumes knowledge of special keys.   Fill-in forms also require knowledge of special keys for form navigation (for example, screen to screen, field to field, and field group to field group navigation, as well as acceptance or cancellation of a filled in form). Keys such as "Tab," "Return," and "Backspace" are often used for these functions. Unless screen space is taken to instruct users on the use of these keys, users will be required to remember their correct use. Very computer naive users are particularly unfamiliar with and confused by these navigation keys.

Inflexible.   Most fill-in forms make it difficult to fill in fields in any order other than the order in which the fields appear. The dialog is *system* rather than *user* controlled to a greater extent than some other dialog styles (for example, command languages, natural language, and direct manipulation). Unless a complex form provides easy ways to jump from field group to field group or other ways of moving the cursor, such as a mouse or touch screen, the user is more or less forced to fill in the fields in a particular order. Thus, unless the user goal or task is inherently highly structured itself, a fill-in form interface may not support it very well.

In sum, the main drawbacks of fill-in forms as compared to some other dialog

Fill-in forms are most appropriate for users with:

☞ User psychology

Negative or neutral attitude
Low to moderate motivation

☞ Knowledge and experience

Moderate to high typing skill
Little to moderate system experience
Moderate to high task experience
Low to moderate application experience
Moderate to frequent use of other systems
Moderate to high computer literacy

☞ Job and task characteristics

Moderate to high frequency of use
Little or no training
Discretionary use
Low to moderate turnover rate
Other systems = paper forms
Moderate task importance
High task structure

Figure 5–2   When to use fill-in forms.

styles are the assumption of certain types of semantic and syntactic knowledge, the need for typing skill, and inflexibility.

Given these relative advantages and disadvantages, we can draw some conclusions about the kinds of tasks and users for which the fill-in form as a primary dialog style might be appropriate. Figure 5-2 lists the user characteristics (see Chapter 2) for which a fill-in form user interface would be a good choice.

Generally, because fill-in form interfaces are (potentially) easy to learn, they are good for users who are averse to learning, that is, those who might have a negative attitude toward the system or low motivation to use it for whatever reason. This is especially true of discretionary users, who make a personal choice whether to buy and use a given system, compared to mandatory users.

Users lacking in certain types of knowledge and experience will also perform better on a well-prompted fill-in form interface relative to some other dialog styles because it is relatively easy to learn both the semantics (to some extent) of the system and the syntax of the interface.

One important qualification to this is that users with low typing skill, low computer literacy, and/or low task experience (semantic knowledge of the problem domain) will be slowed down on a fill-in form interface relative to a menu or question and answer interface. Very computer naive users who will use a system only infrequently (for example, videotex users) find even a fill-in form too complex and confusing. They are not familiar with the concept of a cursor, and having to learn how to navigate backward and forward across fields and how to edit within fields distracts them considerably from the task at hand. They make many errors, take many minutes to fill out even the simplest of fill-in forms, and get very frustrated (Mayhew, 1989, unpublished study of a videotex system). Although a fill-in form may still be better for this type of user than, say, a command language interface, resorting to a simple question and answer or menu interface will probably be better for casual and infrequent users who will never become expert and are not concerned with efficiency of use so much as ease of learning and remembering.

If users are used to working with paper forms, then on-line fill-in forms that have been designed to be compatible with paper forms will be relatively easy to learn and use. The user will already be familiar with valid input values and proper formats and need only learn how to navigate in the on-line form.

Finally, because fill-in forms are a relatively rigid, structured dialog style, they are best suited to tasks that are themselves highly structured, that is, tasks in which a set sequence of steps is always or usually followed. Tasks that are highly flexible, in which any sequence of individual steps or functions is possible and desirable, do not lend themselves well to a fill-in form interface, which usually forces the user into set sequences of steps.

DESIGNING FILL-IN FORMS: EXPERIMENTAL RESULTS

The potential advantages and benefits of fill-in form interfaces as just discussed are not inherent in fill-in forms as a dialog style. Care must be taken in the design of any fill-in form to realize the potential advantages. Unfortunately, relatively little research has been conducted to investigate the effects of different design alternatives on the performance of users of fill-in form interfaces. In this section, some study results are presented and discussed. In the following section, general guidelines for fill-in form design are drawn from these studies and from our knowledge of human information processing and are presented in summary form.

The design of fill-in form systems can be divided into six separate issues:

Fill-in form organization and layout
Fill-in form caption and field design
Fill-in form input formats
Fill-in form prompts and instructions
Fill-in form navigation
Fill-in form error handling

Research studies and general guidelines are organized around these issues. Research studies are not currently available on all issues, so only some topics are covered in this section.

Fill-in form caption and field design.   Many variations on caption and field design are possible. We must consider the alignment or justification of captions and fields in lists, the visual distinctiveness of captions versus fields, the clarity of captions, and the form of input fields and cursors. The latter issue was investigated in a study (Savage, Habinek, and Blackstad, 1982) that compared four field indicators in combination with several cursor types.

These authors point out that there are at least three major goals in designing input field indicators: (1) to draw the user's attention to the need for user input, (2) to give some indication of the nature of the required input, and (3) to avoid detracting from the legibility of the filled in field. They compared performance on four different field indicators with three different measures of ease of use.

The four different field indicators compared were:

Dot column separators:	. . . . . .
Reverse image:	███████
Broken underline:	– – – – –
Brackets:	< >

The three performance measures were: (1) estimating field length (time and errors), (2) finding the cursor (time and errors), and (3) readability (correct transcription of data from filled in fields). Forty-eight users participated in this study, each performing the three tasks 25 to 35 times with each of the four field indicator types. The users came from a broad range of job types, including programmers, designers, engineers, and clerks.

Figure 5-3 summarizes some of the results of this study. Data were averaged across trials and users within each field indicator type. Significant differences in performance across field indicator types were found on all measures of performance. When a block cursor was used, users performed consistently better with a broken underline field indicator than with any of the other three types. That is, it was faster and easier to estimate the field length, find the cursor, and read data in the fields when a broken underline was used as the field indicator.

The data presented in Figure 5-3 are from users who used a block cursor (a solid block in one character position). Some of them had a blinking block cursor and some a nonblinking block cursor. The data are collapsed across these latter two variations.

Other data from this study indicated that, generally, a nonblinking line cursor (a short line just under one character position) was inferior to both a blinking line cursor and a block cursor, either blinking or not. The nonblinking line cursor resulted in the poorest performance when in combination with an underscore (unbroken straight line) as a field indicator type. Also, a line cursor or block cursor

Performance Measure	Field Indicator			
	Dot column separators	Reverse image	Broken underline	Brackets
Field length est. (errors)	4.47	36.50	1.84	59.53
Field length est. (seconds)	3.90	3.16	3.02	3.43
Finding block cursor (errors)	0.25	0.19	0.06	0.19
Finding block cursor (seconds)	2.35	3.18	2.34	2.43
Readability (errors)	1.78	2.72	1.69	1.69

Figure 5–3 A study of field indicators. From Savage, Habinek, and Blackstad, "An Experimental Evaluation of Input Field and Cursor Combinations," *Proceedings of the Human Factors Society 26th Annual Meeting,* 1982, 629–33. © 1982, by the Human Factors Society Inc. Reprinted with permission. All rights reserved.

in combination with a reverse-image field indicator produced poor performance on these tasks.

A conclusion that can be drawn from this study is that a blinking block cursor in combination with a broken underline field indicator is an optimal way to design input fields on a fill-in form. Note, however, that the performance measures in this study did not include the actual speed or correctness of input. Knowing how many positions are available in an input field, finding the cursor, and reading fill-in data are certainly important aspects of performance with on-line fill-in forms, but they are not the only important ones.

It is interesting to note that two commonly used field indicators in on-line fill-in forms are: (1) reverse image and (2) no indicator at all (that is, simply a colon and white space following the caption). In fact, Savage, Habinek, and Blackstad report that users in a pilot study expressed a preference for reverse-image field indicators as compared with an underscore or no indicator. The fact that users performed most poorly with reverse-image field indicators is an interesting example of the independence of measures of *preference* and measures of *performance*. That is, users will often express a preference for an interface technique that in fact results in poorer performance when performance is objectively measured.

Fill-in form input formats. One interesting design issue in fill-in forms is whether or not to require users to enter a terminator key after each field (such as "Return," "Tab," or cursor keys) to move the cursor to the next field. The alternative is to provide **auto tab.** Auto tab automatically moves the cursor to the next field after the user has entered a character in the last position of an input field. The purpose of auto tab is to save keystrokes by eliminating the need for a terminator key.

Auto tab may be a good idea for high-frequency data entry clerks when all fields on a screen or system have fixed-length fields, so users must always enter a character in the last position of each input field. The elimination of an extra keystroke for each field will probably allow these users to work faster.

However, if users are not high-frequency and if fields are variable length, that is, if users will not always be entering a character in the last position of every field, then auto tab may actually interfere with performance. This is because a user will have to stop and look at the screen after filling in each field to determine if a terminator key is necessary or if the cursor has automatically jumped to the next field. By contrast, if the user simply *always* has to press a terminator key, it is not necessary to stop and look at the screen after each field.

A study of the use of auto tab (Galitz, 1972) in fact revealed that manual tabbing produced faster data entry and fewer keying errors when compared with auto tabbing. Unpublished data from more recent studies also confirm that auto tab slows performance and produces errors for novice users of variable-length fill-in fields. These data are an interesting example of the point made in Chapter 1 that reducing keystrokes may decrease *response* time, but at the same time increase *think* time, so that the overall time of the interaction or task is in fact increased.

Another study (Gould and others, 1988) compared seven different input methods for entering dates. These methods included three variations of a traditional fill-in field and four variations of direct manipulation selection and may be summarized as follows:

1. *Entry by requested completion:* The user entered abbreviations or codes in each part (month, day, and year) of the entry field (for example, "s" or "9" for September). When the user pressed "Tab" or "Enter," the system filled in the entry and moved the cursor to the next part of the entry field.

2. *Entry by auto completion:* The user entered abbreviations or codes in each part of the entry field. The system *automatically* filled in the field part (for example, month) and moved the cursor to the next part of the field *as soon as* unambiguous entry was made.

3. *Entry by modification:* The user edited a displayed example date.

4. *Selection by one field:* The user incremented or decremented a *complete* date (month, day, and year) *one day at a time* via the arrow keys.

5. *Selection by multiple fields:* The user incremented or decremented each date *part* (month, day, and year) separately via the arrow keys. They moved the cursor from one part to the next.

6. *Selection by analogue representation:* The user incremented or decremented the *complete* date (month, day, and year) *one day at a time* via a slider bar operated with arrow keys.

7. *Selection from a graphic representation:* The user selected the month, day, and year successively from graphic representations via arrow keys.

Twenty-eight subjects participated, half with prior computer experience and half without. They were asked to enter complete dates in response to such prompts as "Halloween 1989." All subjects used all seven methods in different orders. Overall, the three fill-in field methods produced better performance (that is, less time and errors) and were preferred as compared to the four selection techniques, even for the inexperienced computer users. There was little difference in performance between the three fill-in field methods, although most subjects expressed a positive attitude toward the autocompletion method.

These data seem to suggest that for simple entry of data even inexperienced users will perform better with simple entry in a fill-in field as compared to direct manipulation selection. However, these data should be interpreted cautiously. The task required only simple entry of a known date, and all methods were keyboard driven. When entry tasks require mostly *motor* processing (as in this task) and very little *perceptual* or *cognitive* processing, then it is logical that an entry technique that requires the fewest keystrokes (as the entry techniques generally do compared to the selection techniques) would provide fastest performance. However, it is possible that direct manipulation selection would provide better performance, especially for novice and casual users, when valid entry values are not known or when entry values depend on context, and thus when perceptual and cognitive processing plays a larger role in the interaction. And it is possible that selection would provide an advantage when the selection mechanism involved a pointing device rather than the keyboard.

For instance, if the user entered a date that had to be exactly 1 week later than an already entered date, then it seems likely that pointing to the date on a calendar display in which the first date was already selected would be simpler and faster than calculating the date that was 7 days later than the first date and then entering it. Similarly, selecting a date from a pop-up menu of currently unscheduled dates might be simpler and faster than reviewing a list of dates already scheduled, determining what dates were unscheduled, and then typing one in. In these tasks, pointing might be faster even if the selection mechanism involved the keyboard. A pointing device might provide even more of an advantage.

Some evidence that direct manipulation selection may be superior to fill-in field entry when tasks are more complex is provided by another study (Greene and others, 1988). In an experiment very similar to that in the Gould and others (1988) study, it was found that, when entry items were drawn from a large pool of possible entry values and/or were difficult to spell, then computer-inexperienced subjects performed better with a selection method than with an unaided (no autocompletion) entry method. Entry of difficult to spell items from a large pool of possible inputs requires more cognitive processing than does entry of known dates. This added complexity in the task seems to have produced the anticipated result; that is, selection provides some advantage over fill-in field entry, even when selection is via the keyboard. It was also found, however, that autocompletion entry fields produced better performance than selection techniques even for computer-inexperienced subjects.

Another study (Gould and others, 1989) provides some evidence that when selection is via a pointing device it might be faster than field entry via the keyboard. Date entry tasks similar to those in the Gould and others (1988) study were performed by users using a touch screen. They performed as fast or faster than the computer-inexperienced subjects using entry techniques in the 1988 study.

Taken together, these data suggest that, for simple known inputs, direct keyboard entry in fill-in fields will allow faster input than direct manipulation selection methods via the keyboard. When the task requires complex perceptual and cognitive processing or when a pointing device is available, however, it is advisable to provide direct manipulation selection as an *alternative* (not as a substitute) dialog style. The data also suggest that system completion of unambiguous partial input may be desirable.

Fill-in forms have been empirically demonstrated to provide advantages over other dialog styles under other circumstances as well. Ogden and Boyle (1982) found that computer-naive subjects performed faster and expressed higher preference for a form interface as compared to a command language interface in a simple report formatting task. While viewing a report on a computer screen including four columns of data with column headings, subjects could make formatting changes such as changes to the column heading name, the width of columns, the margins between columns, the format of data in columns, and whether or not data in a given column would be displayed. In the command language interface, subjects could type in a simple command line such as "Change Head = Student For 2" (change the heading of the second column to "Student") without losing the view of the report on the screen and instantly see the results of their edit. In the forms interface, subjects had to first type in the command "SHOW FORMAT," then edit a form presenting all current report formatting parameters, and then type in the command "SHOW REPORT" to review their edits. Despite the apparent simplicity of the command input, however, the lesser demands on memory inherent in the form interface resulted in faster performance for this class of users.

Forms can also be used in novel ways to enhance usability. Jeffries and Rosenberg (1987) compared a forms-based interface to a programming language-like interface for the task of allowing users to write procedures for managing their electronic mail messages. Users could write procedures such as "Notify me when new mail about a meeting or appointment arrives" or "Delete messages from Bob and messages more than 300 lines long." Eighteen programmers and nonprogrammers participated in this study. Nonprogrammers and half the programmers used a forms-based interface. In this interface they filled in values in a template rule form. An example is given next in which a user sets up a procedure to check his mail every day at 5 A.M. and refile any mail that is over two days old, read, and not tagged. User input is expressed in bold.

```
IF
    When: Every day at 5:00 A.M.
    Header contains:
    Msg body contains: <string>
    Folder name is: In-Tray
    Msg length is:
    Msg is: Read AND NOT tagged
    Date sent is: More than 2 days ago
THEN
    Move-to: Old-Mail
```

The other half of the programmers used a language-based interface. An example of user input in this interface follows:

WHEN daily (5:00 A.M.)
   FOREACH msg IN "In-Tray"
     IF read (msg) AND
       NOT tagged (msg) AND
       date-sent (msg) > 2 days ago
     THEN move-to-folder (msg, "Old-Mail")

Programmers using the form performed 50% faster than programmers using the language and 24% faster than nonprogrammers using the form. Nonprogrammers using the form performed as fast as programmers using the language. Other data cited suggested that nonprogrammers using the form were two to three times faster than they would have been using the language. Thus a forms alternative to a procedural language allowed nonprogrammers to perform faster than they would using a programming language and as fast as programmers using a programming language, and even improved the performance of programmers. What is interesting about this study is that it suggests the use of forms in an area where forms have not traditionally been applied: the definition of rule-based procedures. Guidelines drawn from this research or input format design are summarized on pages 195–204.

DESIGNING FILL-IN FORMS: PRINCIPLES AND GUIDELINES

Design issues in fill-in form interfaces are divided into six separate issues:

Fill-in form organization and layout
Fill-in form caption and field design
Fill-in form input formats
Fill-in form prompts and instructions
Fill-in form navigation
Fill-in form error handling

Principles and guidelines presented are organized around these issues.

Fill-in form organization and layout.   The following guidelines address general issues regarding within- and across-screen organization and the layout of fill-in fields.

☞ **Design and organize the form to support the task.**

It is important to consider the way a user will be using an on-line fill-in form. For instance, if users will be filling in the on-line form directly from a paper form, then the on-line form should be similar in organization, format, and wording to the paper forms. Simple navigation from field to adjacent field in the list is probably sufficient, as users are probably simply copying data from the paper form in the order it is listed on the form. If the paper and on-line form match, the order of presentation on the on-line form will match the order in which users will be entering data.

On the other hand, suppose a fill-in form were to be designed to support phone orders of catalog merchandise or a customer service inquiry system. In these examples it might be important to provide very flexible cursor movement as customers may provide input information in any possible order. Forcing the operator to go through input fields in a prescribed order would not support this task well.

☞ **Organize groups of items related semantically, by sequence of use, by frequency of use, and/or by relative importance.**

Figure 5-4 shows two alternative layouts of a print request fill-in screen. In the "Poor" version, input items are simply presented in a vertical list, in no particular order, and with no spacing to separate the long list into groups. This form is hard to scan through, and it will take awhile even for frequent users to learn the location of particular items. This may not be a problem if the user always fills in every field, but it is likely that many fields will hold defaults, and the user will only want to change one or two fields on any given print request. Then it will be hard to scan for the desired fields and learn their location.

In the "Improved" version, on the other hand, input items have been divided into four semantic categories: document title, scope of print request, print parameters, and miscellaneous. These semantic groups have been visually grouped by the use of white space and borders. This screen will be easier to scan and learn.

Probably, grouping by semantic categories should be the overriding organizing principle for most fill-in form screens. Alternative ordering schemes that can be applied within or across semantic groups or that may override semantic grouping as the primary ordering scheme include *sequence of use, frequency of use,* and *importance.*

Sequence of use as an order is appropriate if users are working from a paper form or from information provided by a customer (for example, phone order or customer service inquiry). In these cases, fields ought to be ordered according to

Poor:

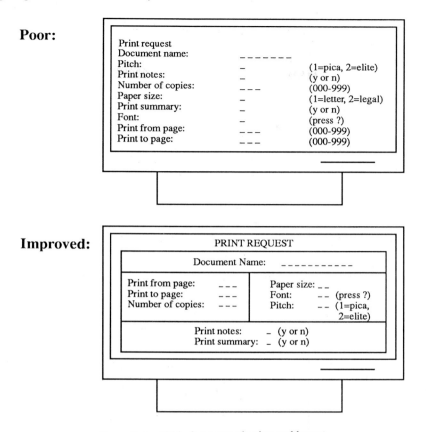

Improved:

Figure 5-4   Fill-in form organization and layout.

the paper form order or the order likely to be used by the customer. For instance, the best order for name and address fields is the most familiar order, as follows:

First: _____ M.: _____ Last: _____
Street: _____
City: _____ State: _____ Zip: _____

Avoid presenting name and address fields in an unfamiliar order, such as

Last Name: _____
Zip: _____
State: _____
City: _____
First name: _____
Middle name: _____
Street: _____

Even the following order, although the cursor moves through the items in a more or less familiar order, does not provide a familiar *spatial* order of the items:

Last name: _____
First name: _____
Middle name: _____
Street: _____
City: _____
State: _____
Zip: _____

Frequency of use is an appropriate grouping principle when only some fields will be edited each time the form is used. In this case, the fields most often used should be grouped and located at the top of groups. For instance, in Figure 5-4, the document name is most likely to be entered, so it is located at the top of the form. The next most frequently edited fields are those in the print scope group, so this group is next in order, and so on.

Importance may be an appropriate ordering principle in some forms. For instance, required fields should appear at the top of groups, while optional fields should appear at the bottom. However, semantic groupings should almost always take precedence over importance.

☞ **Keep the number of groups to a minimum while limiting the size of groups to 12 to 14 characters wide and 6 to 7 lines high.**

Data suggest (Tullis, 1988) that two of the best predictors of search time to find a single data item on a computer screen are *group size* and *number of groups*. It appears that keeping group size within the 5-degree visual angle to which the eye is most sensitive enhances searching behavior, because the whole group can be taken in in a single eye fixation. This visual angle corresponds roughly to 12 to 14 characters wide and 6 to 7 lines high on a text-based computer screen.

The number of groups also affects search time, with increasing numbers of groups resulting in increasing search times, even when group size is small. Thus, minimizing the number of groups without exceeding the maximum recommended group size is suggested to facilitate searching.

☞ **Use white space to create balance and symmetry and lead the eye in the appropriate direction.**

In the "Poor" version of the print request screen in Figure 5-4, white space has not been strategically used to guide the user's eye. First, it has not been used to create groups to facilitate scanning as just discussed. Second, it actually works against the logical organization of the screen. The input fields are laid out horizontally in rows: caption, input field, prompt. However, substantial white space separates the three parts of each field, and no white space separates fields vertically. The result is that the screen looks as if it is made up of columns and the eye is drawn up and down, while the fields are actually oriented horizontally and the eye should be reading left to right.

In the "Improved" version, on the other hand, white space is used both to visually support the grouping of semantically related fields and to draw the eye horizontally within groups, as appropriate.

☞ **Separate logical groups by spaces, lines, color, or other visual cues.**

Besides white space, logical groups can be visually reinforced by lines or borders, as in Figure 5-4, or even color. The advantage of color for separating groups of information is that, unlike white space and borders, it does not take up any additional screen space. Thus, on very busy screens where we might not want to sacrifice whole columns or rows to white space or borders, color can distinguish groups without taking up screen real estate.

☞ **Minimize the number of screens for high-frequency users and slow system response time. Maximize screen clarity for infrequent users and fast system response time**

High-frequency users will soon learn the locations of fields on a busy input screen and are usually most concerned with efficiency. Thus, making the most efficient use of screen space is recommended for these users. Also, if system response time is slow, users may be frustrated by idle wait time between screens and prefer busier, but less screens, even if they are harder to scan. If the decision is made to include many fields on each screen, then the other principles of good layout become even more important.

On the other hand, infrequent users are less likely to learn field locations and may actually work faster with more screens if each screen is simple and clear, especially if system response time is reasonably fast.

☞ **Keep related and interdependent items on the same screen**

Do not require users to retain information in memory from one fill-in screen to another. For instance, giving instructions on how to access functions on a *main* screen, but not on the screens from which the function is likely to be accessed, is poor design. Similarly, separating interdependent fields such as "Amount Owed" and "Amount Paid" from "Amount Due" will unnecessarily tax human short-term memory. Keeping fields that provide context for other fields all on the same screen will minimize screen flipping and input errors.

Fill-in form caption and field design.   A number of guidelines regarding the design of captions and fields can be offered to facilitate the scanning and reading of fill-in forms. Research supporting the following guidelines is reviewed and discussed on pages 178–179.

Poor:

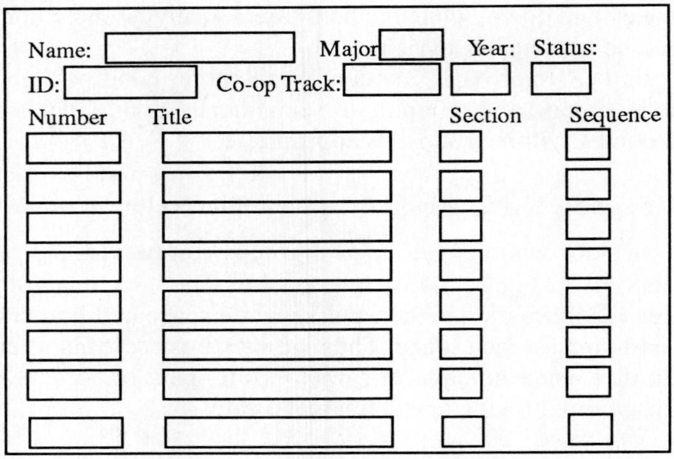

Improved:

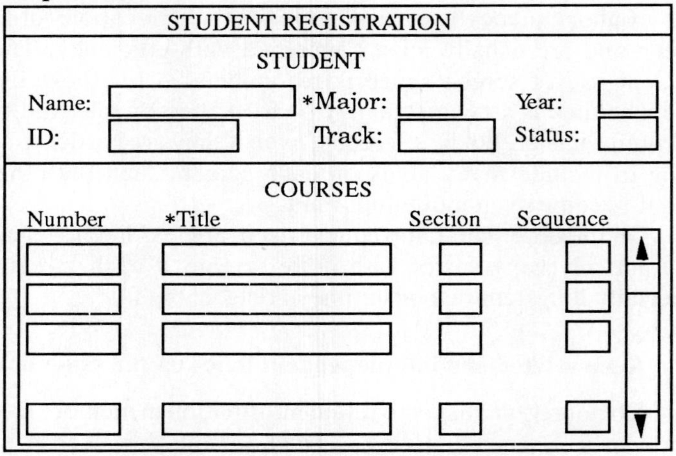

Figure 5-5   Fill-in form caption and field design.

☞ **In western cultures, for single fields, place the caption to the left. For list fields, place the caption above, left justified above alpha lists, right justified above numeric lists.**

Note in Figure 5-5 on the "Poor" screen that, while the "Name" and "Major" fields have the caption to the left and the input field to the right, the fields

"Year" and "Status" have input fields below their captions. Not only is this an inconsistency that will leave users wondering where to look for input fields, but it simply is not as natural (in western cultures) to read up and down as it is to read left to right. Thus, for items with a single input field, it is a good idea to consistently locate fields to the right of captions, as in the "Improved" version.

On the other hand, some fill-in items are lists, as in the "Number," "Title," "Section," and "Sequence" fields in Figure 5-5. In these input items, one caption is followed by a list of fields. In this case it is most appropriate to place fields in a column below the caption, rather than in a horizontal list separated by commas.

☞ **Justify captions and fields according to user, task, and data type, respectively.**

The following guidelines for aligning captions and fields are based on reasoning from principles rather than on research. Research comparing performance on forms using different justification rules is not yet available.

Consider the following four examples aligning *captions* in a list:

```
Name:        _____
Title:       _____
Rank:        _____


Name:            _____
Title:           _____
Rank:            _____
Telephone number: _____


Name:........... _____
Title:.......... _____
Rank:........... _____
Telephone number: _____


            Name: _____
            Title: _____
            Rank: _____
Telephone number: _____
```

The first three left justify the captions. This is desirable, especially when users are not working from a source document, because they are likely to be scanning down the list of captions, and this is easier to do if the captions are left rather than right justified. Left justification of captions works well *if,* as in the first example, captions are all roughly the same length.

However, if the caption lengths vary considerably, as in the second and third examples, then to keep *fields* left justified, some captions will be separated from their fields by a large distance. This may make it hard for the eye to connect captions and fields. Tying the caption and field together by a line of dots, as in the third example, makes it easier to associate the proper field with its caption, but it still does not eliminate lengthy eye movements, and it adds considerable "noise" to the screen.

Perhaps the best strategy is to try to make captions within a group close to the same length. If this can be done without sacrificing caption clarity, it will allow both captions and fields to be left justified without separating any captions from their fields by too much space. For instance, in the second, third, and fourth examples, if the caption "Telephone number" was abbreviated to "Phone," captions would be closer in length and could be laid out as follows:

```
Name:  _____
Title:  _____
Rank:  _____
Phone:  _____
```

Abbreviated caption names are recommended only if they are easily recognizable or if the user is working from a source document so that the caption on the screen is easily related to a caption on the source document through relative position as well as through caption name.

If users are *not* working from source documents, captions *cannot* be abbreviated without sacrificing clarity, use is fairly infrequent or turnover is high (so that unclear captions may not be learned and remembered easily), then right justification of variable-length captions (as in the fourth example) is recommended in favor of using a line of dots. High-frequency users, on the other hand, will quickly learn unclear abbreviations and benefit from the greater readability of left-justified captions. Figure 5-6 summarizes these guidelines.

Fields in lists should also be justified. Always *left* justify **alpha fields.** Notice in the following that the second example is easier to scan and read than the first.

```
Name: John D. Smith
Title: Senior Vice President
Organization: Research and Development

Name:          John D. Smith
Title:          Senior Vice President
Organization:  Research and Development
```

Also note the lack of field justification in the top section of the "Poor" fill-in screen in Figure 5-5 and the alignment of fields in the "Improved" version.

Left justify **numeric input fields,** but *right* justify or decimal-align numeric input upon *display,* as follows:

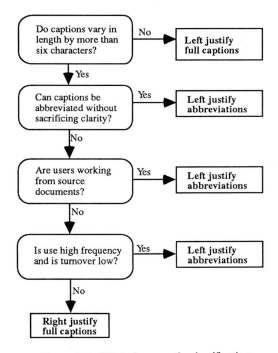

Figure 5-6   Fill-in form caption justification.

Input: Display:

Monthly rate: 1.5 _____   Monthly rate: _____   1.5
Annual rate: ´18.0 _____   Annual rate: _____ 18.0

Data that have been entered left justified (for example, in the "Input" example) can be redisplayed right justified or decimal aligned (for example, in the "Display" example) as soon as the cursor is moved out of the field. Thus users do not need to enter leading zeros, minimizing keystrokes, but the data are also easy to scan and read once entered.

☞ **Separate the (longest) caption (in a left-justified group) from its field by no more than one or two spaces (following the delimiter, for example, a colon). Separate one caption field group from another by three or more spaces horizontally or by one or more lines vertically.**

Note the examples in Figure 5-5. In the "Poor" version, captions run into fields without any spatial separation. In combination with the lack of justification, this makes it difficult to distinguish captions, fields, and caption–field pairs from one another. In the "Improved" version, spatial separation make this distinction easier.

☞ **Break up long columnar fields or long columns of single-field items into groups of five separated by a blank line.**

In the "Poor" fill-in screen in Figure 5-5, a set of data (Number, Title, and so on) is presented in list form, with many rows to be displayed. When long lists occur on input or display screens, it is a good idea to separate every three to five rows by a blank line, especially if input is from paper forms or data are being transcribed from the screen to paper. Breaking the data into groups, as in the "Improved" version, facilitates place keeping, thus minimizing place searching and the transcription errors of duplication or omission. Even though adding blank lines means we can fit less data on the screen, scrolling time is probably less than the perceptual and cognitive processing time involved in place keeping during reading and transcribing.

☞ **Provide distinctive field group and section headings in complex forms.**

When there are many fill-in fields on a form and there is a logical way to organize them in semantic groups, it is a good idea not only to use white space and perhaps borders to distinguish groups, but also to give group names or titles to field groups. Note that the "Improved" example in Figure 5-5 has two field groups with titles: "Student" and "Courses." The user can get a quick idea of where to search for a given field before reading any field captions by scanning the field group names. This is not possible in the "Poor" version.

On very complex forms, sometimes several levels of group headings are useful. Make them distinctive from one another. The use of capital letters, font size, and indentation can accomplish this (Galitz, 1989). For example:

AUTO INSURANCE APPLICATION

OWNER   AUTOMOBILES
    Name: _____   AUTO 1
    Street: _____   Make: _____
    City: _____   Model: _____
    State: _____ Zip: _____   ID: _____
                                                  AUTO 2
DRIVERS   Make: _____
    Name: _____   Model: _____
    Name: _____   ID: _____
    Name: _____

☞ **Distinguish captions from fields.**

Distinguish captions from fields with a visual cue, such as bold versus plain, uppercase versus lowercase, or different colors, and (for single field items) with a delimiter, such as a colon. Use the more salient cue (for example, boldface or a

Poor:

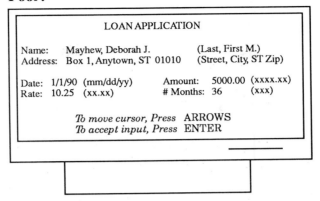

Improved:

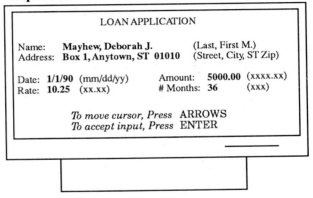

Figure 5–7 Distinguishing captions and fields.

brighter color) to highlight fields rather than captions, since fields are the more important focus of attention.

Note the examples in Figure 5-7. In the "Poor" version, both captions and fields are in plain text. When data are filled in, it is very hard to scan and search as everything looks the same. In the "Improved" version, the fields are in bold. When fields are filled in, it is much easier to scan and search because the use of plain and bold text will make it easier to tune out either captions or fields.

☞ **Captions should be brief, familiar, and descriptive.**

Avoid wordy captions such as
    First line of street address:

when more concise captions, such as
    Address Line 1:
will suffice.

   Use abbreviations and contractions when data entry is from a source document, as users will be able to relate abbreviations on the screen to full captions on
the source document. It is also acceptable to use abbreviated captions if the
abbreviations are standard and recognized in the user community. When data entry
is not from a source document, and abbreviations are not standard in the user
community, however, only use abbreviations when frequency of use is high and
turnover low. Spell out captions in full whenever space permits.

   Avoid computer jargon, but exploit user jargon. Use consistent terminology.
For instance, do not use
    SSN:
as the caption for a social security number on one screen, and
    Social Security Number:
as the caption for the same piece of data on another screen. Users may
assume there is some important difference and become confused.

☞ **Indicate the number of character spaces available in a field.**

   Before starting to fill in a field, it is often useful for users to know the
maximum number of characters. When entering a name, street address, or document title into a database, for instance, users will be able to come up with more
mnemonic and less ambiguous input if they know how many characters are
available.

   One good way to indicate input fields is with broken underlines (versus
column separators, unbroken underscore, brackets, or reverse video) that are
overstruck when data are entered. If a broken underline is used, a block cursor will
be more noticeable than an underline cursor.

☞ **Indicate when fields are optional.**

   Some fields on a fill-in form must be filled in, while others are optional. In the
screens in Figure 5-5, for instance, the two fields "Major" and (Course) "Title"
can be, but need not be, filled in. If the user fills them in, they will be verified. If not,
the system will look them up. Other fields, however, must be filled in.

   It is a good idea to indicate to users which fields, if any, are optional so that
they do not unnecessarily waste keystrokes. This is not done in the "Poor" screen
of Figure 5-5, but an asterisk is used to indicate optional fields in the "Improved"
version. Other ways to indicate optional fields are to include the word "Optional"
in the prompt or MicroHelp line or to use a different color or other visual attribute
such as shading in the fill-in area. For example, on a black screen, required fields
could be displayed in white dashed underlines and text and optional fields in
yellow. Or, where fill-in fields are indicated by boxes, required fields could be
white boxes and optional fields could be gray boxes.

Fill-in form input formats.   The following design guidelines are aimed at both speeding up user input and reducing input errors. Research supporting the following guidelines is reviewed and discussed on pages 187–194. The first set of guidelines refers to *formatting input fields*.

☞ **Consider providing system completion of unambiguous partial input.**

For instance, allow users to enter "Ja" or "1" for "January" and "Jun" or "6" for "June." When the user moves the cursor to the next field, fill in the complete entry. This technique allows both ease of entry and ease of reading of fill-in fields.

☞ **Consider providing pop-up or pull-down menus for fill-in fields with many but well-defined entry options.**

When use is casual, users are inexperienced, the number of valid inputs is large, and/or inputs are difficult to spell or remember, consider providing the option of pop-up or pull-down menus within fields to present entry options. Even if selection is via the keyboard, it can be faster than entry under these circumstances. Distinguish with some visual cue the fields with entry menus from those without. An example is given in Figure 5-8.

☞ **Avoid complex rules for entering data in the various fields of a form.**

If, for instance, entry in some fields depends on values entered in other fields, at the very least, make this relationship clear on the screen. Better yet, provide pop-up entry fields that do not appear unless and until they become relevant (see Figure 5-9).

In general, avoid requiring that users make such decisions as the following:

- Should these data always be keyed?
- If that field is keyed, should this one be keyed?
- If the data is X, then should I be keyed in the field?
- If a 4 goes here, where should other figures be keyed?   (Galitz, 1989)

☞ **Provide meaningful groupings to break up long input formats.**

Many alphanumeric data that are commonly used and fairly lengthy are broken up into small groups of characters to facilitate reading and transcribing. Examples are telephone numbers, social security numbers, dates, time, and credit card numbers.

Other lengthy input data that designers have any control over should similarly be broken up into groups of three to four characters separated by spaces, dashes, or some other symbol. This will make it easier to transcribe these data from paper to screen, or vice versa, and easier to read. For instance, if the interface designer is designing a code to identify records in a data base, something like:

Acceptable:

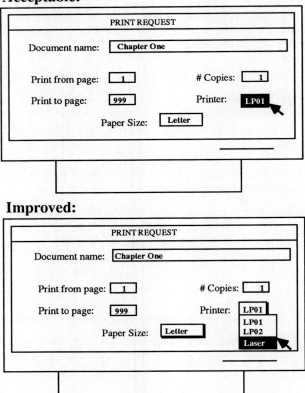

Improved:

Figure 5–8   Fill-in form pull-down entry menus.

EMP-SAL-235

will be easier to read and transcribe than

EMPSAL235.

Similarly, a part number such as

386 6547 231

will be easier to read and transcribe than

3866547231.

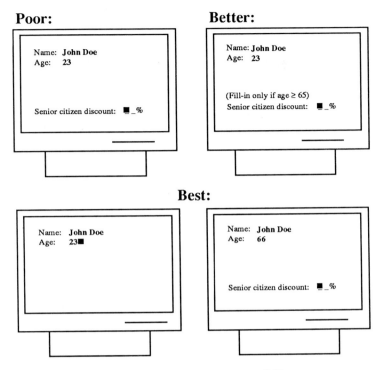

Figure 5–9   Fill-in form pop-up entry fields.

Designers should maintain these conventions when displaying data, but not require users to enter separator characters if possible. For instance, designers should always display times as, for example,

11:32:07 pm,

and not as

113207p.

However, users should be able to *enter* a time in the latter format and not be required to enter colons and spaces. The user will have to enter either leading zeros, spaces, or cursor movement keys to format some times correctly, but this will still be faster than typing colons (which require the shift key), and the space between the numeric and alpha characters will not be necessary. The input field can have the colons and space built in, providing syntactic prompting (with auto tab in effect across parts of the field), or the field can be reformatted when the cursor leaves the field.

The following are examples of poor and improved input formats with example user inputs:

Poor: **Improved:**

DATE: _____   DATE: ____/____/____
   (e.g. 1/12/90)   (e.g. 011290)
DATE: _____
   (e.g. 011290)

TIME: _____   TIME: ____:____ **pm**
   (e.g. 8:15AM)   (e.g. 0815a)
TIME: _____
   (e.g. 0815am)

PHONE: _____   PHONE: (____)____-_____
   (e.g. (508) 693-7149)   (e.g. 5086937149)
PHONE: _____
   (e.g. 5086937149)

CARD #: _____   CARD #: ____-____-____-____
   (e.g. 1234567890123456)   (e.g. 1234567890123456)
CARD #: _____
   (e.g. 1234-5678-9012-3456)

In all the improved versions, the formatting characters (for example, parentheses and hyphens) are protected positions, and auto tab is in effect. That is, when the user types a character into the position prior to a protected formatting character, the cursor automatically jumps to the next editable position in the field.

Note that, while the improved versions do not in *all* cases minimize the total number of keystrokes for all possible inputs, they do minimize the *total input time*, which includes not only keying time but also time spent in *perceptual* processing (for example, reading input as or after it is entered for verification of correctness or keeping track of the input as it is transcribed from a source) and *cognitive* processing (for example, understanding what format is expected or recovering from input errors). Although requiring leading zeros and auto tab are not *generally* recommended, they *are* advised in this special case.

Flexible input and/or good syntactic prompting can be used if auto tab and embedded formatting characters are not possible. One study (Mayhew 1989, unpublished) found that computer-naive, first-time users of a videotex system faced with a phone number input field like the previous "Improved" example, *except that formatting characters were not protected and auto tab was not in effect,* made numerous errors and had great difficulty recovering from them. They typed over formatting characters by mistake and then spent time and more errors trying to restore them. The software platform supporting the application did not, however, support auto tab and embedded protected formatting characters. In this case, switching to a phone number input field like the first ''Poor'' phone example, allowing *any* form of input (for example, the user could enter or not enter hyphens and parentheses) and adding detailed prompting, reduced entry time and errors considerably.

☞ **Provide defaults whenever possible. Allow simple (single key) acceptance of defaults.**

Whenever there is a most likely or most commonly entered value for an input field, prefill the field with this value as the default to minimize keystrokes and typing errors. A single key (for example, ''Tab'') should both accept the default value and move the cursor out of the field.

Decide whether system, session, file, or screen defaults are appropriate. A **system default** is one that is constant across the system and, if changed, is restored every time the system is powered down and back up again. For example, a printer may be set as a system default. It will always appear as the default on any screen that asks the user to specify a printer. It may be altered on one pass through a screen, but will always appear whenever that screen is accessed again.

A **session default** is one that the user sets upon log in or at any other point and remains in effect until it is changed again or until the user logs off. For instance, the paper orientation for printing (vertical or horizontal) may be set during one particular print request. It will then appear as the default in any other print request screen that is accessed during the current session, even if the user has changed documents.

A **file default** is one that is relevant only to a specific document. For instance, a user may set up a format line in a text document and specify margins and tab stops. This format line remains in effect for all parts of the document except where it is specifically changed. The default format line for one document is unrelated, however, to the format line of other documents.

A **screen default** is one that pertains only to a particular screen. For instance, there may be several screens in a system that require input of a document or file name. On any given screen, the default document name will be whatever was filled in the last time that screen was accessed. Thus, the print request screen and the archive screen may have different document names as the current default, depending on what the last value entered in them was.

Sometimes a single screen will contain input fields for which the best defaults are not all of one type. For instance, one screen might have some fields that contain a session default, some that contain a file default, and some that contain a screen default. If this is the case, it is important to make clear which is which so that users can learn which fields to scan for to change and which will not need to be modified, given their current goal.

For instance, suppose a document formatting screen contained input fields for paper orientation and margins, and paper orientation contained a session default, while margins contained a file default. If these fields were grouped together and formatted identically, the user might have trouble remembering which values would remain constant when changing documents and which would change. This means that the user must carefully scan and read the screen each time it is accessed to confirm that the defaults are as desired. On the other hand, if some visual cue such as grouping or formatting were used to tag session versus file defaults, then users would more quickly learn which values had to be checked and modified upon changing documents and which did not. The less actual reading and scanning the user has to do, the more useful the defaults are in the first place. Thus, distinguishing different kinds of defaults, especially when they appear on the same screen, is recommended to increase throughput with fill-in forms.

The following guidelines refer to *designing input data*.

☞ **Make high-frequency inputs easy to express (for example, y/n, 00, defaults)**

In general, minimize the number of keystrokes for high-frequency users and/or high-frequency inputs, but maximize memorability and ease of learning for less frequent users and/or low-frequency inputs. For instance, if there are many yes/no questions on a form, a lowercase ''y'' or ''n'' will be faster to enter than uppercase letters or whole words. Similarly, on systems with many numeric input fields and high-frequency users, a double zero key (''00'') will speed up input. Also, providing defaults for common, high-frequency inputs such as ''y'' or ''n'' will minimize data entry keystrokes. For high-frequency, expert users, less keystrokes per input field means not only faster input but less opportunity for input errors.

☞ **Let the user specify the unit of measurement. Do not require transformations or calculations.**

If, for instance, length is an input field, let the user both enter the length and specify whether it is in inches or centimeters. Do not require one or the other, as this may force some users to translate from one measurement unit to another, something they may not know how to do or that will at least slow them down and introduce errors. Its simple enough to have the system do the translation based on the user's specification of the measurement unit.

It is of course true that allowing users to specify the unit of measurement of an input field may require additional keystrokes, thus potentially slowing down their keying speed. However, if users are expected to vary in which measurement units they are familiar with or tend to use, then overall it is probably more efficient to let them specify measurement units. This can be handled by having one measurement unit be the default, requiring no specification for whichever unit is expected to be more frequently used, or by having the user specify measurement unit preferences at the beginning of a session and setting that unit as the session default. This keeps additional keystrokes to a minimum while still allowing users to select a measurement unit to minimize translations.

☞ **Design meaningful input data whenever possible.**

Data or codes based on common English usage will be easier to learn and remember than arbitrary codes (Galitz, 1989). For instance, identifiers for employees or users of an electronic mail system that consist of their initials (for example, "DJM") or some contraction of their name (for example, "DJMAYHEW"), rather than an arbitrary number (for example, "41967"), will be easier to learn and remember. Codes such as "M" and "S" for "Married" and "Single" will be easier to learn and remember than codes such as "1" and "2."

☞ **Allow abbreviated input when it can be unambiguously interpreted (for example, "yes" or "ye" or "y").**

Do not require users to spell out whole words or numbers if they can be distinguished from other valid inputs in abbreviated form. This is not to say that users should be forced to abbreviate. Often novice users are more comfortable spelling out inputs in full, or experienced users will know that full words will result in better system response time because the search can be conducted more efficiently. It is therefore often desirable to allow either full inputs or unambiguous abbreviations to accommodate both novices and experts.

It is also helpful to respond to ambiguous inputs by presenting a menu of possible matches to select from, rather than just an error message. For instance, in an on-line phone book, it would be desirable to allow users to type in full names and addresses when they know them to provide optimal response time, but also partial names and/or addresses when they are unsure. They can then be presented with all entries in the database that match the partial input and can browse through them until they recognize the one they want.

☞ **A system should be "case blind" when it really does not matter (for example, "YES" or "Yes" or "yes").**

In some input fields, case (upper or lower) is important, and the data have a different meaning depending on which is entered. For instance, in the input field for a "search" command, the user may in fact only want to search for instances of a word that starts with a capital letter, such as "Rose" versus "rose" (one is a name, the other a flower). In such a case, obviously the case matters.

When it does not, however, as in entering "Y" or "N" in a yes–no fill-in field, then the system should correctly recognize either case and not require the user to enter one or the other. In particular, users should not be required to enter upper-case letters when this is unrelated to the meaning of the input, as the use of the shift key is not only an extra keystroke but also an opportunity for error. But even requiring lowercase only can be a problem, as users may make the error, and unless the error message is clear, not understand that the problem is simply case rather than some other aspect of the input.

☞ **Keep input fields short if possible.**

When designers are designing the valid inputs to input fields (as opposed to designing fields to accommodate data that already are in use in the user community), minimizing the length of the input data is recommended. Figure 5-10 presents some error rate data for fields of different length. Here it can be seen that the rate of input errors increases as the length of input data required in the field is increased. Thus, keeping input keystrokes to a minimum will generally not only decrease input time but also input errors.

The exception to this guideline is the case of casual, infrequent users. Sometimes, longer input is more mnemonic and thus easier to remember, even if it takes more time to enter and might induce typos. For these users, easy to remember input data may be more important than efficient input formats.

Error Percentages for Varying Field Lengths

Average number of characters per field	Percent of fields in error
3	1.4
5	2.0
7	2.6
9	3.1
11	3.6

Frequency of Character Substitutions

Character pairs	Cumulative frequency
I - 1	25%
O - 0	50%
B - 8	60%
Z - 2	70%

Figure 5–10 Sources of fill-in form input errors. From Galitz, *Handbook of Screen Design* (QED Information Sciences, Inc., 1985, 170 Linden Street, Wellesley, MA 02181) pp. 74–75. With permission.

☞ **Do not combine letters and numbers in a single field.**

When designing input data, such as part numbers and other types of identification codes, it is important to try to avoid mixing alpha and numeric characters in the same code string. There are two reasons for this.

First, if people are transcribing from handwritten paper forms, certain numbers and letters are easily mistaken for each other. Figure 5-10 presents some data regarding the frequency with which certain number-letter pairs are confused. This confusion arises especially in reading handwritten data, but also in reading typed data displayed on a CRT depending on the resolution of the screen. A good example of what *not* to do is the British and Canadian zip code system. These zip codes combine letters and numbers, such as

M2B-0I8.

In handwritten form, this could easily be mistaken for

MZ8-O1B,

and entered this way on a system.

Second, the alpha and numeric keypads on most keyboards are in different locations. It is easy to rest the hands in a *home* position on one or the other and touch type, but it slows input down considerably to have to alternate between them, and this can also induce keying errors. Thus mixed letters and numbers in an input field slow down input and produce keypunch and transcription errors and so should be avoided.

☞ **Avoid frequent shifts between upper- and lowercase characters.**

The shift key is simply an extra keystroke and will slow down input and perhaps even induce errors, especially for nontouch typists. Unless upper- and lowercase letters carry important meaning, to require uppercase, and particularly to require frequent shifts between upper- and lowercase, will only slow down users and so should be avoided.

☞ **Avoid uncommon letter sequences.**

Some letter sequences, such as "an" or "th," are quite common in the English language. The QWERTY keyboard, used on most computer systems, positions letters that commonly appear in sequence in locations that will be relatively easy to hit in succession. Note, for instance, that "a" and "n" are pressed by different hands, as are "t" and "h." It is easier and faster to hit two keys with alternate hands than with two fingers of the same hand.

By contrast, many infrequent letter pairs, such as "fg" or "xz," because they are infrequently pressed in sequence, are positioned in places more difficult to hit in succession. For instance, not only are "x" and "z" hit by the same hand, but they are not on the home row, and are hit by the fourth and fifth fingers, respectively, a particularly difficult transition for the left hand to make.

Often, when designing input data such as identification codes, we use random letter combinations or vowel deletion abbreviations, and this may result in input data that will slow down data entry because of the positions of the alpha keys on the keyboard and the relative difficulty of hitting certain letters in succession. Thus it is recommended that uncommon letter sequences be avoided when designing input data.

☞ **Do not require leading zeros.**

Requiring leading zeros in input data such as integers and dates may make programming a little easier, but it makes user input more difficult by adding keystrokes. A little extra effort on the part of the programmer could result in a large reduction of keystrokes and errors if many users use the system quite frequently.

Leading zeros should be required only if they are standard in the culture (for example, in the minute and second parts of a time field) or sometimes if leading zeros have been standard and are familiar in the user population (that is, if a datum has always contained leading zeros in the manual, paper system before the implementation of an on-line system). One other case in which a leading zero is acceptable is if it eliminates the need to enter other more difficult to key characters, such as in a formatted date or time field where otherwise a slash or colon must be entered.

Fill-in form prompts and instructions.   Some fill-in forms have **prompts,** or brief syntactic or semantic instructions associated with individual fields. Some also have **instructions** that apply to the whole screen, such as instructions for cursor movement, the use of special function keys, or screen acceptance and cancellation. The following guidelines apply.

☞ **Provide prompts when use will be relatively infrequent, inputs must be formatted, and users are not working from a source document.**

Only high-frequency users can be expected to remember the syntactic requirements of formatted input fields. Other users will benefit from prompts instructing them and reminding them of the proper input syntax. Users working from source documents have exact inputs in front of them, so they will not require prompting in most cases.

☞ **Prompts should be brief and unambiguous.**

Note the "Poor" screen in Figure 5-11. Prompts such as

(Put last name first, then first, then middle)

Poor:

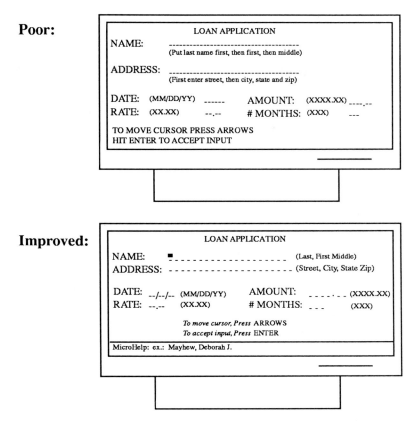

Improved:

Figure 5–11 Fill-in forms prompts and instructions.

and

(First enter street, then city, state, and zip)

are simply too wordy and hard to read. The alternative prompts in the ''Improved'' version,

(Last, First Middle)

and

(Street, City, State Zip)

respectively, are brief and concise without sacrificing any important information.

Examples of correct input, such as the one in the MicroHelp line at the bottom of the "Improved" screen in Figure 5-11, are also useful in prompting input. Here an example is presented of correct input to whatever field the cursor is currently in, taking up less screen space than would including an example next to every field. Often users find it easier to understand a simple example than to understand an abstract formalism for syntactic structure.

Another useful thing to provide in prompts, when appropriate and possible, is ranges of possible values. For instance, in an insurance form, if there are maximum and minimum policy amounts that can be sold, then it might be useful to prompt the user with this information. A prompt such as

(Min. $5,000, Max. $100,000)

might be displayed next to the policy amount field or in a MicroHelp line when the cursor is in the policy amount field.

Make sure, however, that any such prompts are not misleading. For instance, if the input field did not accept dollar signs or commas, then the prompt should read

(Min. 5000, Max. 100000),

so as not to mislead the user into incorrectly entering dollar signs and commas in the field.

☞ **Place prompts to the right of fields or in a MicroHelp line at the bottom of the screen.**

Note that the prompts in the "Poor" screen in Figure 5-11 are placed either under the field or between the caption and field. This can be problematic. When prompts are placed under fields on a busy screen without a lot of white space, it can be unclear as to whether the prompt applies to the field *above* it or the field *below* it. Probably, most of us have had the experience of filling in a name and address form and realizing partway through it that we are one field off in our input. When fields are in a column and prompts are above or below them, it is simply often hard to tell at a glance which prompt applies to which field.

The problem with placing prompts in between captions and fields is that the users who no longer need the prompts must still read through them while scanning from captions to fields. It is hard to ignore a prompt that is in between two things that must be scanned or read.

Placing prompts to the right of fields, as in the "Improved" screen in Figure 5-11, avoids both these problems. It is clear which field the prompt is associated with, and it is easy to ignore the prompts when they are no longer needed.

If possible, and if screen real estate is scarce, placing prompts in a MicroHelp line at the bottom of the screen can be very useful (see Figure 5-12). The prompt that appears in the MicroHelp line is tied to the field that currently contains the

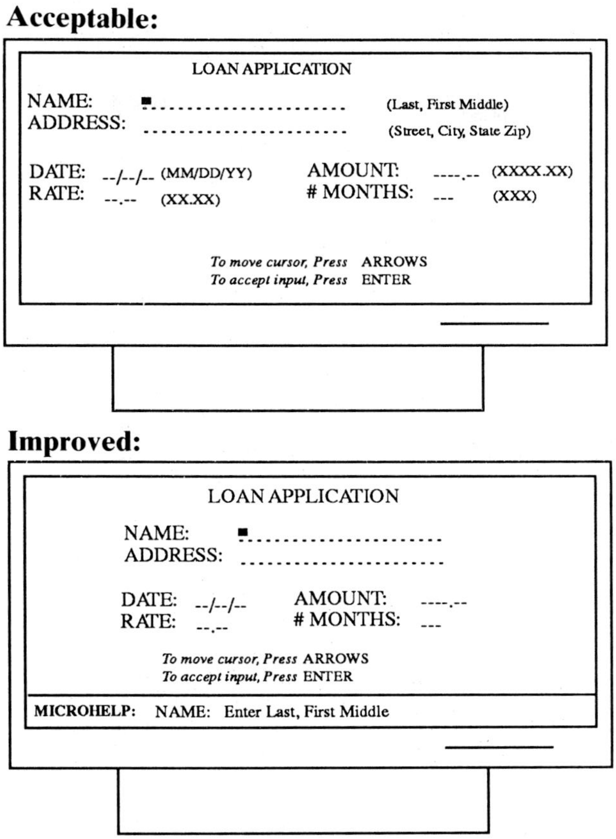

Acceptable:

LOAN APPLICATION

NAME: ■...................... (Last, First Middle)
ADDRESS: .... (Street, City, State Zip)

DATE: __/__/__ (MM/DD/YY)   AMOUNT: ____.__ (XXXX.XX)
RATE: __.__ (XX.XX)   # MONTHS: ___ (XXX)

To move cursor, Press ARROWS
To accept input, Press ENTER

Improved:

LOAN APPLICATION

NAME: ■......................
ADDRESS: ....

DATE: __/__/__   AMOUNT: ____.__
RATE: __.__   # MONTHS: ___

To move cursor, Press ARROWS
To accept input, Press ENTER

MICROHELP: NAME: Enter Last, First Middle

Figure 5–12   Fill-in form prompts in a MicroHelp line.

cursor. The advantages to this approach to prompting are that relatively little space is taken up by prompting, experts are not required to read through prompts, and the screen is less cluttered. The disadvantage is that prompts are somewhat removed spatially from their fields, requiring more eye movement.

Embedding a prompt in an input field is not advisable because entering data in the field overwrites the prompt. For instance, consider the following embedded prompt:

DATE: **mm/dd/yy**

When the user enters data, the field now looks like this:

DATE: **10/10/91**

If the user returns later to the field to reconsider the input, the prompt is now gone and cannot be retrieved. Now it may not be clear whether the day or month should be expressed first.

☞ **Provide instructions for navigation and completion on the screen or through on-line help.**

Every fill-in form should include a minimal set of general instructions on how to navigate between fields, cancel out of the screen, and accept the filled in screen. Expert, high-frequency users may quickly learn these functions and have no further need of the instructions; but every system will always have some novice and casual users, and it is very frustrating for these users to need to consult a manual for this very basic information. Usually, only one or two lines are necessary for this information, and this can usually be made available even on complex, busy form screens. If there are strong reasons for not including these instructions on every screen, they should at least be easily accessible through an on-line help system.

☞ **Place instructions in a consistent location across screens and make them visually distinctive.**

Although capital letters have been used for the instructions on the "Poor" screen in Figure 5-11, this attribute has also been used for all captions on the screen, so the instructions do not stand out as much as they might. The "Improved" screen uses italics and a different font for instructions, and they are more easily distinguished on this screen.

Pick one location for instructions on screens and place them there consistently across all screens in the system.

☞ **Use consistent terminology and consistent grammatical form and style in instructions.**

Note the different grammatical form of the instructions in the "Poor" screen in Figure 5-11. One instruction uses the term "Press" and is stated in result-action form, while the other uses the term "Hit" and is stated in action-result form. Users of this screen may wonder what the difference is between "Hit" and "Press" and will find these instructions more difficult to read than those in the "Improved" screen, which use consistent terminology ("Press") and grammatical form (result-action). In addition, the instructions in the "Improved" screen use italics for most of the instruction, but nonitalic capital letters for key labels. This makes it easier for users to scan for and recognize key labels, instead of reading through every instruction completely.

Fill-in form navigation.   Mechanisms must be designed on fill-in forms to allow users to move from field to field, to accept a filled in screen, to cancel a screen, and to move forward and backward between screens. The following guidelines apply.

☞ **When a form is first entered, position the cursor in the most likely default position.**

On forms where most or all fields will always be entered or edited, position the cursor in the top-left field. On forms where only a few fields are generally edited (for example, when commonly used defaults are prefilled in most fields), position the cursor in the first of the likely to be edited fields or, if appropriate, in the last edited field from the last transaction.

☞ **Arrange field groups consistently with default cursor movement. Vertical groups are preferable to horizontal if cursor movement can be vertical.**

Some systems only allow (or have as a default) cursor movement from left to right. That is, keys such as "Tab" and "BackTab" move the cursor by field right or left, respectively, and no alternative, or a relatively awkward alternative (for example, "Shift/Tab" and "Shift/BackTab"), exists for moving the cursor directly down or up by field.

If the cursor movement default is left and right, groups of related items should be arranged *horizontally* rather than *vertically* (Galitz, 1989). For instance, the following example would be *inappropriate* in this case, because the logical order of the fields is inconsistent with the default movement of the cursor:

BENEFICIARIES

First: _____   Fourth: _____
Second: _____   Fifth: _____
Third: _____   Sixth: _____

A grouping more consistent with cursor movement for this case would be

BENEFICIARIES

First: _____   Second: _____

Third: _____   Fourth: _____

Fifth: _____   Sixth: _____

When cursor movement by fields can be programmed to default to up and down, it is preferable to do so and to arrange groups accordingly, as in the first example. There is some evidence that vertical groups are easier to search than horizontal groups (Tullis, 1988).

Be sure that the use of white space reinforces the arrangement of groups and movement of the cursor, as in the preceding examples. In the first example, when the cursor moves vertically, the display gives the impression of columns as appropriate. Similarly, in the second example, when the cursor moves horizontally, the display gives the impression of rows.

In sum, three aspects of group orientation must be consistent: the default direction of cursor movement (left and right or up and down), the logical order of fields within groups (left and right or up and down), and the spatial arrangement of groups (as rows or columns). Any inconsistency among these factors will confuse users and slow them down.

☞ **Allow forward and backward movement by field and within fields.**

In keyboard-driven fill-in forms, users should be allowed to move the cursor forward and backward within each field by character to facilitate editing, rather than having to retype an entire field. Users should also be able to move both forward and backward by fields, rather than only forward with screen "wrap-around."

It is important in complex forms to provide a hierarchy of navigation techniques (for example, next character, next field, next field group, next section, next form) to facilitate navigation, rather than requiring all movement be one field at a time, which could become quite tedious.

When we increase the flexibility of navigation, we also increase complexity, because there are now more commands or keys to learn and remember and prompting for them takes more space on the screen. Note the instructions on the "Improved" screen in Figure 5-13. "Tab" is the key for moving forward by field, the most basic navigation command. To prompt for all other navigation functions (next and previous character, previous field, next and previous field group, next and previous section, next and previous form) on the screen would take up too much space, so these are hidden but easily accessible through an on-line help facility. How to get into help is prompted on the screen.

☞ **Make protected areas on the screen completely inaccessible. Allow the cursor to rest only on user-editable areas.**

No keys on the keyboard should move the cursor into noneditable areas. On some systems, the "Tab" key moves from field to field, while the arrow keys move from column to column or row to row on the screen. On these systems, the arrow keys can move the cursor into noneditable areas, such as white space or captions. This can be very confusing to users, and some users have even been observed to use only arrow keys, never discovering the tab key, resulting in extremely inefficient navigation through the form. Do not ever allow the cursor to be moved into a noneditable area. This will eliminate errors and inefficient navigation.

☞ **Do not use auto tab unless fields have fixed lengths and users are high frequency and experienced.**

Poor:

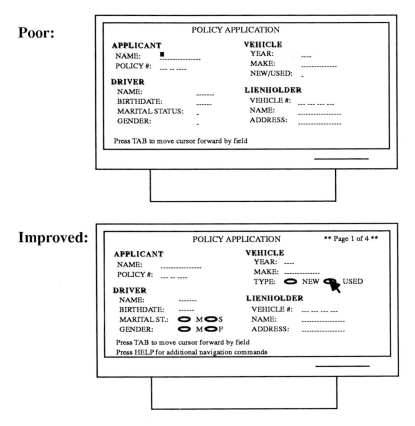

Improved:

Figure 5–13 Fill-in form navigation.

If fields are of variable length (for example, name and address fields) rather than fixed length (for example, zip code or part number), then input will probably be slowed down rather than facilitated by *auto tab* (automatic movement of the cursor to the next field when the last position in a field is filled in), because users will have to stop and look up at the screen after each field to determine where the cursor is. Similarly, if users are low-frequency, novice users, then even if fields are fixed length, auto tab should be avoided. This is because these users may not have learned or remembered the lengths of fields, and auto tab may be confusing. Users may try to enter longer than allowed data in fields, and because they are looking at the keyboard rather than the screen, they will not notice that the cursor has moved on to another field. They may wipe out defaults in later fields inadvertently and not know how to recover. These users are also not as concerned with efficiency, so auto tab provides no important advantage to them.

Thus, auto tab should be reserved for high-frequency, expert users of forms where all fields are of fixed length. Mixing auto tab and manual tab on a single form or throughout a single system will create problems even for these users, so unless all fields are fixed length, auto tab should still be avoided.

One other case in which auto tab is acceptable is within the parts of a formatted field, such as in a formatted date or time field.

☞ **Provide titles and page numbers or place markers on screens in a multiscreen form.**

Sometimes all the related fill-in fields for a task will not fit on one screen, and the form must be broken into separate screens. In this case, it is a good idea to notify the user of this and provide information regarding the user's current location in the form. Note that in the "Poor" version of Figure 5-13 there is nothing on the screen to indicate to the user that more fields must be filled in than are currently visible. By contrast, the "Improved" screen has a field in the upper-right corner of the screen, highlighted by asterisks, that tells users which page they are currently viewing in a multipage form.

☞ **Direct manipulation increases flexibility, speed, and ease of learning for navigation through fields.**

If a system includes an alternative input device such as a mouse or touch screen, this device can be used to facilitate fill-in form navigation. Being able to point directly to an input field (rather than step to it using cursor keys) allows faster, more flexible form navigation. This may be important if there is no constant order for entering data in fields, such as in a customer service inquiry system. It is also easier to remember how to point with a mouse or touch screen than to remember which keys on the keyboard move the cursor forward and backward by field or by field group. The "Poor" screen in Figure 5-13 requires stepping through fields one at a time, and there are quite a few fields on the screen, so that many keystrokes may be required to move to a desired field. Alternatively, the "Improved" screen allows direct manipulation with a mouse. The user simply points to the desired field to navigate to it.

Using a touch screen or mouse with a fill-in form requires that the user move the hands back and forth between the keyboard and the alternative device. For simple forms, direct manipulation navigation may provide no advantage, as time saved moving the cursor is lost moving the hands to the device. On complex forms, however, a pointing device may result in more efficient navigation in spite of the need to move the hands back and forth. Still, probably a system that allows navigation by direct manipulation should also allow the user to use cursor keys, because this will still be faster when moving from one field to an adjacent or very close by field.

Fill-in form error handling.   Users will inevitably make errors entering data on fill-in forms, and the following guidelines concern error handling in forms.

Poor:

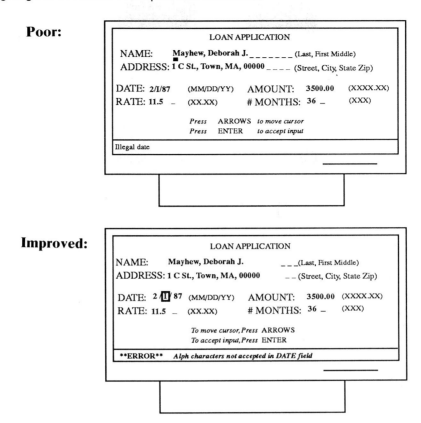

Improved:

Figure 5–14   Fill-in form error handling.

☞ **Allow character edits in fields.**

When users make simple typos in fields, they should be able to edit character by character, rather than having to erase and retype the entire field. Thus the user must be able to move the cursor forward and backward by character within fields, and overstrike or insertion and deletion must be allowed.

☞ **Place the cursor in the error field after error detection. Highlight the error field if possible.**

In the "Poor" screen in Figure 5-14, when an input error has been detected, the cursor returns to the default position of the first field in the upper-left corner, and no marker of any sort draws attention to the erroneous field. Only the error message at the bottom of the screen provides information regarding the location of the error field. In the "Improved" version, on the other hand, the cursor is relocated on the field that is in error, in fact, on the particular character in the field that is in error. This will facilitate error detection and correction.

☞ **For independent fields, withhold error reporting until user request.**

If fields are unrelated to one another, that is, if correct input to one does not depend on the input in another, then the user should control when error checking will occur. Data entry clerks usually prefer to enter all data in a form before error checking occurs, as field by field error checking will slow them down. On the other hand, when correct input to fields depends on the input in other fields, then error checking should occur on a field by field basis so that users do not enter a great deal of erroneous data that will have to be corrected.

☞ **Provide semantic and syntactic information in error messages depending on user knowledge.**

Some users will know a lot about the *semantics* of the application they are using, that is, a lot about the problem domain. Others will not. Some will have a great deal of *syntactic* knowledge, that is, how to accomplish particular things on a given system, and others will not. Error messages should be designed to provide the kind of information users need, but not the kind of information that they do not need. The designer needs to know how much semantic and syntactic knowledge most users can be expected to have in order to design effective error messages.

In the "Poor" screen in Figure 5-14, the message

Illegal Date

provides very little information of any kind. This might be acceptable or even appropriate for users with a lot of semantic and syntactic knowledge, but most likely many users will not have one or both of these kinds of knowledge. The term "Illegal" is also unnecessarily negative and dramatic.

The alternative message in the "Improved" version assumes that users will have *semantic* information (they will know what dates are valid), but may not have *syntactic* information (they will not know exactly how to format dates), and so this latter type of information is presented in the error message. The *syntactic* message

Alpha characters not accepted in DATE field

is particularly good here because, depending on the resolution of the screen, users may not detect that an "I" rather than a "1" has been entered. A *semantic* error message such as

February dates range from 1 to 29

may not have helped here.

REFERENCES

GALITZ, WILBERT O., "IBM 3270 On-line Evaluation," *INA Technical Report, E5320-A02/ M72-0001,* January 20, 1972, referenced in Wilbert O. Galitz, *Handbook of Screen Format Design* (Wellesley Hills, Mass.: QED Information Sciences, Inc., 1985), p. 70.

————, *Handbook of Screen Design* (Wellesley Hills, Mass.: QED Information Sciences, Inc., 1985), pp. 74–75.

————, *Handbook of Screen Format Design,* 3rd ed. (Wellesley, Mass.: QED Information Sciences, Inc., 1989), pp. 103–54.

GOULD, JOHN D., and others, "Empirical Evaluation of Entry and Selection Methods for Specifying Dates," *Proceedings of the Human Factors Society 32nd Annual Meeting,* 1988, pp. 279–83.

————, and others, "Entry and Selection Methods for Specifying Dates," *Human Factors,* 31, no. 2 (April 1989), pp. 199–214.

GREENE, SHARON L., and others, "Entry-based versus Selection-based Interaction Methods," *Proceedings of the Human Factors Society 32rd Annual Meeting,* 1988, pp. 284–87.

JEFFRIES, ROBIN, and JARRETT ROSENBERG, "Comparing a Form-based and a Language-based User Interface for Instructing a Mail Program," *CHI '87 Proceedings,* May 1987, pp. 261–66, ACM.

MAYHEW, DEBORAH J., "A Usability Test of a Videotex Prototype," Unpublished Study, 1989.

OGDEN, WILLIAM C., and JAMES M. BOYLE, "Evaluating Human–Computer Dialog Styles: Command vs. Fill-in for Report Modifications," *Proceedings of the Human Factors Society 26th Annual Meeting,* 1982, pp. 542–45.

SAVAGE, RICKY E., JAMES K. HABINEK, and NANCY J. BLACKSTAD, "An Experimental Evaluation of Input Field and Cursor Combinations," *Proceedings of the Human Factors Society 26th Annual Meeting,* 1982, pp. 629–33.

TULLIS, THOMAS S., "Screen Design," *Handbook of Human-Computer Interaction.* Martin Helander, ed. (Amsterdam: North-Holland, 1988), pp. 377–411.

CHAPTER 6

Dialog Styles: Question and Answer

WHAT IS A QUESTION AND ANSWER INTERFACE?

A **question and answer** interface combines some of the features of both menus and fill-in form interfaces in a unique dialog style. As with a menu system, the user is posed with a single question at a time. Like a fill-in form interface, however, the user is expected to type in an answer, rather than select one from a list, and *syntactic* and *semantic* prompting may or may not be included with the question. Sometimes the questions and answers scroll up the screen and a certain portion of the history of the dialog is always in view, and sometimes each new question refreshes the screen, erasing any previous questions and answers.

Figure 6-1 shows a question and answer dialog for an on-line tax form. Note here that the answers to some questions ("Enter your marital status" and "Are you filing jointly or separately?") determine which question will be presented next ("Are you filing jointly or separately?" and " Enter your spouse's name," respectively). That is, while some question and answer dialogs might be *linear,* there may be a *hierarchical* or *networked* structure to the dialog, just as with some menu systems. This is an advantage over a fill-in form approach when not all questions need be answered by all users. The user need only see those questions that are pertinent, making the interface simpler and cleaner than would simply implementing manual tax forms as fill-in forms.

Figure 6-2 shows another example of a question and answer dialog. In this

216

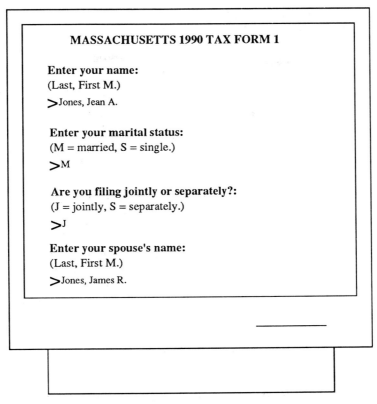

Figure 6–1 An example of a question and answer interface.

case the question and answer interface is an alternative dialog style to the traditional command language interface to an operating system. Users may simply type in commands if they know them. If they do not, they can get assistance in the form of a prompted question and answer dialog to express their requests.

In the example, the user remembers the name of the copy command, but not the proper syntax for expressing the parameters or arguments. Typing in "Copy" followed by the "Return" key takes the user into the question and answer mode. The user is first prompted for the first argument, the source file. The user does not remember the proper way to express a file name, however, and another press of the "Return" key produces even more detailed prompting. At any point the user could type in the remainder of the correct command string, followed by the "Return" key, and the system would accept the input. The user could, however, enter the whole command string through a question and answer dialog that prompted the user for each element in the string in its proper order and form.

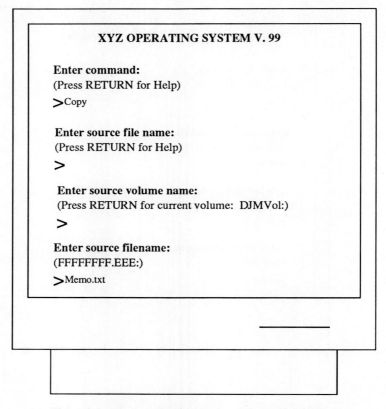

Figure 6–2   An example of a question and answer interface.

WHEN IS A QUESTION AND ANSWER DIALOG STYLE APPROPRIATE?

Question and answer interfaces have particular advantages and disadvantages relative to other dialog styles. *Advantages* include the following:

Self-explanatory.   Well-designed question and answer interfaces make a system easy to learn because they make both the *semantics* and the *syntax* of the system explicit. That is, they make clear both *what* can be done (semantics) and *how* to do it (syntax). Clearly phrased questions and good prompts regarding valid answers and their proper format can provide users with everything they need to know to correctly step through the dialog. Because the interface is relatively self-explanatory, the learning burden is decreased and the need for manuals and training programs is reduced. Contrast this with a command language interface, which gives no semantic or syntactic prompting and requires that the user simply know what can be done and how to do it.

Requires little human memory. For the same reason that question and answer interfaces are easy to learn, they are also easy to remember. Casual users who may not use a system frequently run the risk of forgetting how to use it between uses. Because a question and answer interface is potentially self-explanatory, it is not necessary to memorize and retain semantic or syntactic knowledge. Question and answer interfaces rely mostly on *recognition memory,* rather than *recall memory.* The user need only *recognize* the questions and prompts and does not have to *recall* (without cues) what input is required or how to format answers. Recognition memory is faster and more accurate than recall memory, and question and answer interfaces exploit this fact.

Simple and nonintimidating. As compared to a complex fill-in form or a command language, a question and answer dialog is simple and easy to understand and use, because the user need only see and respond to one well-prompted question at a time. Complex fill-in forms, even though they are self-explanatory, can be intimidating by their very complexity and density of information. Command languages are intimidating in that they require so much knowledge to operate. Question and answer dialogs can be very appropriate when users are both inexperienced and unmotivated because such dialogs are both simple and supportive.

Accommodates parameters with many possible input values. Question and answer interfaces lend themselves well when the input required from the user may take on any of a large number of values. For instance, if the system requires that the user specify a name, an address, a numerical value, an identification number, and so on, it would not be practical or possible to present the possibilities in a menu. Clearly phrased questions with ample syntactic and semantic prompts are the best input format for this type of data when users are casual, inexperienced, low frequency, and computer phobic.

Accommodates tasks with a hierarchical structure. The nature of some computer-user dialogs is such that user input at one point determines what additional data will and will not be required. Question and answer dialogs support this type of task structure well since only one question is posed at a time. Questions can be arranged in an order that allows all questions that are not relevant to a given user to be bypassed altogether.

Figure 6-1 provides an example of this type of task structure. In an automated tax form implemented as a question and answer dialog (as opposed to a fill-in form), if a user indicates that he or she is married, then and only then will it be necessary to provide data regarding filing status and spouse. Users who indicate that they are single need never see these questions.

Accommodates complete and clear prompting. Because a question and answer dialog presents only one question at a time on the screen, there is no shortage of space in which to provide clear, complete prompting on valid inputs and their correct format. This is in contrast to some menus, on which options are so numerous that little space is left over for instructions, and fill-in forms, in which more space for prompts and instructions means less fields can be fit on a single screen. Thus, it is easier to design a question and answer interface that is truly completely self-explanatory than it is for some other dialog styles.

Enhancements are visible. Because a question and answer interface always prompts all required input, whenever new functions are added to a system they will appear directly in the interface, that is, on a question screen. Thus users will always notice when new functions are added.

For instance, suppose tax laws change and new deductions are allowed. A new question would appear in the on-line tax form dialog to ask users if they qualify for this new deduction. Contrast this with a command language interface, in which no evidence of the newly available functions or features would actually appear through the interface. In such an interface, users would have to know when features or functions have been added because the interface has not actually changed in any visible way.

In summary, the main advantages of question and answer interfaces are that they are simple, nonintimidating, and self-explanatory. There are serious trade-offs, however. *Disadvantages* of question and answer systems include the following:

Inefficient. It may be simple and self-explanatory to answer each individual question in a question and answer dialog. However, in a system that is complex, requiring a great deal of user input that is very interrelated, a question and answer dialog could be tedious indeed. Contrast such a lengthy sequence of inputs with, for example, simply entering the desired input in a command language interface or even presenting many questions all on one fill-in screen. These latter interfaces avoid the need to step through many screens (fill-in forms and command languages) and scan through lengthy questions and prompts (command languages). Question and answer interfaces may be easy to learn and remember, but except for very simple task structures, they may not be as easy to use as some alternative dialog styles. This is especially true if system response time is slow.

Assumes typing skill. Answering questions in a question and answer format requires typing. If users are not touch typists, then this dialog style may be slow relative to others, such as function keys or menus, that require less typing.

Error prone. Even if users are touch typists, typing presents opportunities for user input errors, and so question and answer interfaces may be more error prone than dialog styles that require less typing, such as menus, direct manipulation, and function keys.

Inflexible. Most question and answer interfaces make it difficult to answer questions in any order other than the order in which the questions are posed. The dialog is system rather than user controlled to a greater extent than some other dialog styles. Unless a question and answer interface provides efficient and powerful ways to navigate back and forth between questions, the user is forced to answer questions in a particular order. Thus, unless the user goal or task is inherently highly structured itself, a question and answer interface may not support it very well.

No forward context. Because questions are generally asked one at a time, the user cannot (as they can on a fill-in form) see what questions will be asked next, when this may be important context information. For instance, suppose the user is asked to enter an address. Without knowing what the next question is, the user may not know whether just a street address is expected (and the city, state, and zip code will be posed as separate questions) or whether a full address is expected. Or, on an automated expense form, the user may be unsure of which expenses to include in an answer to the question "How much was spent on transportation?" Does this mean all types of transportation or just ground transportation? Will airfare be asked for in a separate question or not? Without being able to see future questions, it may not be clear what is required in answering a current question.

In sum, the main drawbacks of question and answer interfaces as compared to some other dialog styles are that they are inefficient for experienced users, inflexible, and error prone due to the need for typing skill.

Given these relative advantages and disadvantages, we can draw some conclusions about the kinds of tasks and users for which the question and answer interface as a primary dialog style might be appropriate. Figure 6-3 lists the user characteristics (see Chapter 2) for which a question and answer dialog style would be a good choice.

Generally, because question and answer interfaces are (potentially) simple, nonintimidating, and easy to learn, they are good for users who are averse to learning, that is, those who might have a negative attitude toward the system or low motivation to use it, for whatever reason. This is especially true of discretionary users, who make a personal choice whether to buy and use a given system or not, rather than mandatory users.

Users lacking in certain types of knowledge and experience will also perform better on a well-prompted question and answer interface relative to some other dialog styles because it is relatively easy to learn both the semantics of the system and the syntax of the interface due to the extensive prompting that is possible. Thus, when users are infrequent or turnover is high, it may be an appropriate dialog style. One important disadvantage to question and answer interfaces is that users with low typing skill will be slowed down relative to a menu interface, although a question and answer interface may still be better for this type of user than, say, a command language interface. And high-frequency, expert users will find them tedious and inflexible, especially when system response time is slow.

Question and answer interfaces are
most appropriate for users with:

☞   **User psychology:**

Negative attitude
Low motivation

☞   **Knowledge and experience**

Moderate to high typing skill
Little to moderate system experience
Low task experience
Low application experience
Moderate to frequent use of other systems
Low computer literacy

☞   **Job and task characteristics**

Low frequency of use
Little or no training
Discretionary use
High turnover rate
Low task importance
High task structure

Figure 6–3   When to use question and answer interfaces.

Finally, because question and answer interfaces are a relatively rigid, structured dialog style, they are best suited to tasks that are themselves highly structured, that is, in which a set sequence of steps is always or usually followed. Tasks that are highly flexible, in which any sequence of individual steps or functions is possible and desirable, do not lend themselves well to a question and answer interface, which usually forces the user into set sequences of steps. Thus, the example in Figure 6-1 of a tax form is a good task for a question and answer dialog, because computing taxes is quite structured in that later fields or values are very often dependent on earlier ones. On the other hand, in the example in Figure 6-2, an operating system, a question and answer dialog is only advised as an alternative interface, not a replacement for the command language interface. The tasks that users do with an operating system are highly unstructured, and to force high-frequency, expert users into a question and answer dialog would be inappropriate.

DESIGNING QUESTION AND ANSWER DIALOGS: PRINCIPLES AND GUIDELINES

Little, if any, research has been conducted to date specifically aimed at understanding question and answer interfaces. The guidelines that follow are thus based on basic research in cognition and aspects of design that are analogous to other dialog styles that have been studied.

☞ **Always maintain a system title on the screen. Provide subtitles for context if appropriate.**

In Figure 6-4, note the title at the top of the "Improved" screen. This title should always remain visible, even as questions scroll off the screen as the dialog progresses. It should not scroll off the screen, as in the "Poor" version.

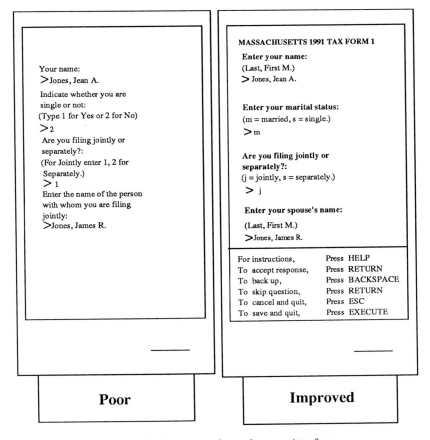

Figure 6-4 Designing question and answer interfaces.

Sometimes subtitles are also appropriate to help the user maintain context. For instance, a state tax form contains many sections or categories of questions. Subtitles to identify these categories or sections, such as "Filing status," "Deductions," "Exemptions," and "Schedule C: Business profit or loss," would be helpful.

Titles and subtitles should remain at the top of the screen, should be displayed in distinctive text (for example, all caps, centered, and indented), and should be hierarchically ordered. Examples are

MASSACHUSETTS 1991 TAX FORM 1
Adjustments to Tax
Tax after Credits

MASSACHUSETTS 1991 TAX FORM 1
   Adjustments to Tax
      Tax after Credits

MASSACHUSETTS 1991 TAX FORM 1: Adjustments to Tax: Tax after Credits

Subtitles would change as the user navigated through different sections of the tax form question by question.

☞ **State questions in clear, simple language.**

Questions should not be unnecessarily wordy, such as "Enter the name of the person with whom you are filing jointly" on the "Poor" screen in Figure 6-4. "Enter your spouse's name" on the "Improved" screen says the same thing much more simply and will be easier to read and understand.

Questions should be phrased in consistent grammatical form. In Figure 6-4 note that there are two questions asking for a name. In the "Poor" version, however, they are phrased in very different grammatical forms:

"Your name"
"Enter the name of the person with whom you are filing jointly"

By contrast, the two questions in the "Improved" screen use the same form when asking for the same type of data:

"Enter your name"
"Enter your spouse's name"

These are both less wordy and consistent in grammatical form, making them easier to read and understand.

Avoid negatives, such as "Check here if you do not smoke." Negatives are a more complex grammatical form and harder for people to read and understand. It is also possible that users who are scanning such a question quickly will note the key words "Check" and "smoke" and not see the word "not." Thus, negatives may also induce errors. Therefore, always phrase questions in the positive voice, such as "Check here if you smoke."

☞ **Provide brief prompts and instructions.**

Prompts associated with individual questions describing valid inputs (semantics) and proper syntax for responses should be clear, but also brief and concise. Wordy prompting is both more difficult to read and adds clutter to the screen, making it hard to scan.

In the "Poor" version of Figure 6-4, some questions have no prompts ("Your name"), and some have complex wordy prompts ("For Jointly enter 1, 2 for Separately." The "Improved" screen consistently includes prompts, and they are brief and concise ("Last, First M." and "J = jointly, S = separately," respectively).

If some users need more information than can be provided in a brief prompt of five to seven words, then provide more detailed input information on request through an on-line help system (note the reference to "Help" in the "Improved" screen).

☞ **Use visual cues and white space to distinguish questions, prompts, instructions, and user input.**

In the "Poor" version of Figure 6-4, note that everything, questions, answers, and prompts, is in plain text, without even white space to separate parts of the dialog. This makes it hard to scan back through the dialog history and search for particular questions or answers and also gives a cluttered, disorganized look to the screen.

By contrast, the "Improved" version has separated each group of question, prompt, and answer by white space. Questions are presented in bold text and prompts in plain text of the same size. Answers are distinguished by an arrow prompt and a smaller font. Instructions are presented in the bottom portion of the screen, separated from the dialog by a border, and formatted in a unique fashion.

Any visual cues could have been used to identify these dialog parts. Other cues include capital versus lowercase letters, indentation, and spatial location (Galitz, 1989). Examples are

OWNER'S LAST NAME:
Mayhew

Owner's Last Name:
Mayhew

Owner's Last Name: Mayhew

The idea is to use different cues and to use them consistently. This makes the dialog history easier to scan and read, and gives a more organized, less cluttered look to the screen. Even if no history is maintained, and there is never more than one question group on the screen at a time, consistent formatting will make the questions and answers easier to read.

☞ **Do not require unnecessary transformations or translations.**

In the "Poor" version in Figure 6-4, note the question "Indicate whether you are single or not." The format for answering this question is a "1" or a "2." "1" means "yes" and "yes" means "single." Thus the user needs to perform a number of translations in order to correctly answer the question. It requires fewer translations to simply ask "Enter your marital status," as in the "Improved" version, and have the user indicate married or single through a simple mnemonic code.

Similarly, the question "Are you filing jointly or separately" in the "Poor" version requires the user to translate "jointly" into "1," whereas in the "Improved" version, although a translation is required ("jointly" into "j"), it is an easier, less error prone translation to make because of the mnemonic association between "jointly" and "j."

☞ **Avoid yes/no responses to questions involving binary answers. Provide mnemonic codes for alternatives.**

In Figure 6-4, the two questions "Indicate whether you are single or not" and "Are you filing jointly or separately" are binary. That is, there are only two possible answers. When questions involve binary answers, there is a temptation to format the response as "Yes" or "No." For instance,

> "Are you married? (Y or N)"
> "Are you filing jointly? (Y or N)"

But this requires a translation, as described previously. Instead, it is easier to read and respond to such a question if the two choices are coded in some mnemonic way, such as "s" for "single" and "m" for "married." This type of answer will result in faster responses with less errors.

☞ **Minimize typing requirements.**

Design the answer input to minimize typing. When answers can be abbreviated rather than spelled out ("m" for "married," "y" for "yes"), always allow this. State valid abbreviations or abbreviation rules in prompts. Do not require capital letters where this is not necessary (for example, do not require "M" for "married" or "Y" for "yes").

☞ **Provide flexible navigation.**

Many question and answer interfaces present one question at a time on the screen and do not provide a way to scan backward through the dialog history. Usually, you also cannot scan forward to future questions without answering current questions. Question and answer dialogs can be improved by providing a way to return to and edit previous questions, a way to scan forward through future questions, and a way to quit the session before completion of the dialog and enter again later where you left off. The instructions at the bottom of the "Improved" screen in Figure 6-4 illustrate ways to provide these capabilities. It is important to provide instructions for these capabilities or users may never discover and make use of them.

REFERENCES

GALITZ, WILBERT O., *Handbook of Screen Format Design, 3rd ed.* (Wellesley, Mass.: QED Information Sciences, Inc., 1989), pp. 173–77.

CHAPTER 7

Dialog Styles:
Command Languages

WHAT IS A COMMAND LANGUAGE INTERFACE?

Command languages are the original, traditional style of computer–human interaction. The user types in requests through an artificial (that is, nonnatural) language with its own unique semantics, vocabulary, and syntax. In a traditional command language interface, the only prompting and instructions provided by the computer are a simple "ready" prompt, such as an arrow, asterisk, or other special symbol, and brief, coded error messages when an unrecognizable command string is entered. Users can more or less enter any command at any time and can often string many commands together in a single request. However, users must remember the proper names and syntax for commands (or look them up), because there is no on-screen prompting or instructions through the interface.

Figure 7-1 shows a hypothetical command language dialog between a user and an operating system. System prompts and output are in plain text, and user inputs are prompted with an arrow and displayed in bold. In this example, the user starts out at the highest level of the operating system (indicated by the READY prompt) and then enters the text editor (indicated by the EDIT prompt). Once in the editor, the user asks for a listing of *all* files in the library DJM that were authored by MAYHEW (the * is a "wildcard"). On the final command line, the user asks for a printout of the document DOCY, pages 1 through 10, one copy, to be spooled to printer q01.

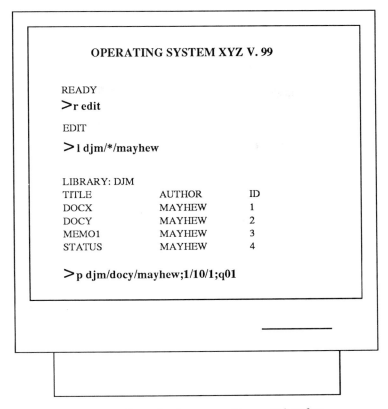

Figure 7–1   Example of a command language interface.

Note that the user can accomplish on a single screen what might take many screens through, say, a menu interface. However, the user must have memorized the commands and syntax for expressing requests. The interface provides minimal prompting. Even the EDIT prompt, which reminds users that they are in the editor, will soon scroll off the screen, and users must simply remember where they are.

Figure 7-2 provides another example of a command language dialog, this one from an older Digital Equipment Corporation operating system. Here, system output is in plain text, and user input is in bold capital letters (although in the actual system, all text is displayed in plain lowercase text). Here it is even more apparent that the burden of the interaction is on the user. On the other hand, the user can accomplish a great deal in very little space without having to wait for screen refreshes and without scanning through screens of menus or fill-in fields.

In this example, the user logs in and enters Teco, the text editor. Note that the prompt changes from an arrow to an asterisk to indicate which level the user is currently at. The user command inside the editor opens a document, searches for

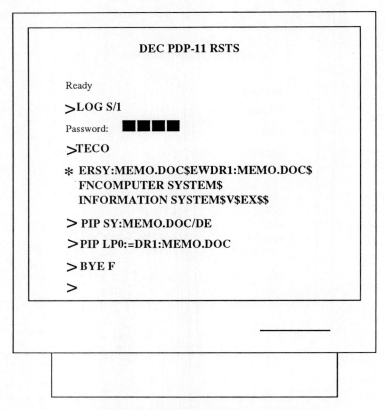

Figure 7–2   Example of a command language interface.

the string COMPUTER SYSTEM and replaces it with the string INFORMATION SYSTEM, prints out the line containing the string for verification (this is not shown in the example), and then saves the edited text to a new file and exits from the editor. Then the user enters the file transfer utility PIP, the original file is deleted, and the new file is printed. Finally, the user logs off.

Again, the language is very powerful and relatively few keystrokes are required to express complex commands, but the user must remember cryptic and arbitrary command abbreviations and syntax and must avoid making typing errors when entering command strings.

WHEN IS A COMMAND LANGUAGE DIALOG STYLE APPROPRIATE?

Command languages have particular advantages and disadvantages, relative to other dialog styles. *Advantages* include the following:

Powerful.   Command languages can be a very powerful form of interaction. Often there are many ways to accomplish the same thing, some more efficient than others. Simple commands can often be strung together so that in a single entry the user can accomplish what might take 20 or 30 menu screens or fill-in fields in those dialog styles. Entering one complex command language string frees the user to do other things while the system carries out the command, whereas the menu or fill-in form demands a continuous give-and-take interaction: the user must repeatedly wait for screens to refresh, and scan and read through menu options or field captions, prompts, and instructions.

Additional power and efficiency are afforded by languages that provide the ability to construct complex procedures, save them as files, scripts, or macros, and reexecute them repetitively with a simple name. This reduces keystrokes and memory load and allows highly specialized, tailored routines to be automated.

Flexible, user controlled.   Generally, the user can do anything in any order through a command language interface. Unlike menus, fill-in forms, and question and answer dialogs, which force the user through a set sequence of steps to get to a desired utility or function, command languages allow the user to specify a request directly, without navigation through forms and screens. The user is more in control of the interaction and can leap directly from one function to another without intervening steps.

Fast, efficient.   Although a command language interface requires more typing than some other dialog styles, it is probably the fastest, most efficient of all dialog styles. Expert, high-frequency users who are also good typists can correctly enter even lengthy, complex commands faster than they can step through multiple screens, scanning for menu options or navigating between and filling in fields. Thus, when speed of interaction is important and users can be expected to be frequent users and good typists, command language interfaces provide a distinct advantage over other dialog styles.

Uses minimal screen "real estate."   A traditional command language interface requires only one line on the screen for command entry. This leaves most of the screen available for whatever else should or must be displayed. This is in contrast to menus or fill-in forms, which take up considerable space on the screen. Thus, when screen "real estate" is at a premium, command languages provide an important advantage over some other dialog styles. In sum, the main advantages of command languages are speed, power, and space efficiency. There are serious trade-offs, however. *Disadvantages* of command languages include the following:

Difficult to learn.   Space efficiency is achieved by eliminating prompting and instructions from the screen. Speed of input is achieved by short command names, simplified parameter specifications, and single keystroke syntactic delimiters. The result is cryptic command names and arbitrary syntactic delimiters that must be rote memorized due to the lack of prompting and instructions.

Command language interfaces rely totally on *recall,* as opposed to *recognition,* memory. This makes a command language much more difficult to learn than most other dialog styles. In effect, ease of use is achieved at the price of ease of learning. This will be the right trade-off to make in the case of some users and tasks, but not others.

Difficult to remember.   For the same reason that a command language is difficult to learn initially, it is also difficult to remember if there are long periods between uses. Infrequent users, especially those that also use other systems with different user interfaces, will find it difficult to remember the vocabulary and syntax of a command language that was designed for speed of use, given the demands on recall (versus recognition) memory.

Assumes typing skill.   Typing is maximized in a command language interface as compared to other dialog styles, such as menus, function keys, or direct manipulation. Thus, unless users are touch typists, they may actually be slowed down on a command language interface relative to other dialog styles that may require more screens, but less typing, to accomplish a task.

Error prone.   Even touch typists are presented with more opportunity to make keying errors in a command language interface as compared to other dialog styles that require minimal typing. Thus, the heavy typing required in a command language not only potentially slows down input but may also increase errors, which in turn decreases overall throughput.

Enhancements are invisible.   Because there is little or no prompting of any sort in a command language interface, the user has no way of knowing (through the interface) when changes and enhancements have been made to the system. A whole new subsystem may have been added, but this will not in any way be visible to the user. Only memos and manuals will bring this to the user's attention. This is in contrast to some other dialog styles, such as menus and fill-in forms, in which new functions appear as new menu options or fill-in fields, thus notifying the user of their presence.

In sum, the main drawbacks of command language interfaces are that they are difficult to learn and remember and more error prone than some other dialog styles.

Given these relative advantages and disadvantages, we can draw some conclusions about the kinds of tasks and users for which a command language as a primary dialog style might be appropriate. Figure 7-3 lists the user characteristics (see Chapter 2) for which a command language interface would be a good choice.

Because command languages impose a significant learning burden on users, they are best suited for users who are very motivated and have a positive attitude towards computer in general. If not motivated, then they at least should be mandatory (that is, required to use the system) and required to take a formal training program. Unmotivated discretionary users will probably simply not make the

Command language interfaces are most appropriate for users with:

☞ User psychology

Positive attitude
High motivation

☞ Knowledge and experience

Moderate to high typing skill
High system experience
High task experience
High application experience
Infrequent use of other systems
High computer literacy

☞ Job and task characteristics

High frequency of use
Formal training
Mandatory use
Low turnover rate
High task importance
Low task structure

Figure 7–3   When to use command language interfaces.

investment in learning and will not use or will underuse a command language-driven system.

Also, due to the lack of prompting and instructions and the general learning burden, users who are high in all types of relevant knowledge and experience are best suited for command language interfaces. Users low in *task* (problem domain) experience will find the lack of *semantic* prompting a problem, and users low in *system* (syntactic) experience will similarly find the lack of *syntactic* prompting a problem.

Computer-literate, highly motivated touch typists who use the system very frequently (several hours every day) and for whom speed of interaction is of primary concern are the best candidates for a command language interface. In fact, for these users a command language is probably the best choice of dialog style.

DESIGNING COMMAND LANGUAGES: EXPERIMENTAL RESULTS

Some studies (Whiteside and others, 1985; Antin, 1988) have demonstrated the potential advantages and benefits of command languages over other dialog styles. However, these potential advantages and benefits are not inherent in command languages as a dialog style. Care must be taken in the design of any command language in order to realize the potential benefits. Similarly, the potential drawbacks to command languages can be minimized through careful design.

Probably because they are the oldest and most common dialog style, command languages have been more extensively studied and are thus better understood than most other dialog styles. In this section, some research results are presented and discussed. In the following section, general guidelines for command language design are drawn from these studies and from our knowledge of human information processing and are presented in summary form.

The design of command languages can be divided into four separate design issues, as follows:

Command language semantics
Command language syntax
Command language lexicon
Command language interaction

Research studies and general guidelines are organized around these issues. By far, most research has addressed the lexical issues of command naming. However, some studies are available that investigate other aspects of command language design.

Command language semantics. The semantics of a command language is the set of functionality that it provides and how that functionality is broken down into language elements. A *system* may be rich or minimal in *functionality,* meaning that there are many or few functions available, respectively. In turn, a *command language interface* to a system may be *rich* or *minimal.* A **rich** language has many commands, some of which provide redundant, more efficient and powerful ways of doing things that could be done (although less efficiently) with more basic commands. A **minimal** language, by contrast, has a smaller set of core commands, which must be combined to achieve more complex functions.

For instance, a *minimal* text editor language might include two commands, "delete" and "insert." Three functions are available through these two commands: "delete," "insert," and "replace." "Replace" is achieved by using the "delete" and "insert" commands in sequence.

A *rich* language to the same editor, on the other hand, might include three commands: "insert," "delete," and "replace." The "replace" command provides a more efficient (less keystrokes) way of accomplishing what could be done with the "insert" and "delete" commands.

Note that both languages provide the same functionality: three functions. However, one language (the minimal one) does so with fewer commands, so there are less commands for the designer to design and the user to learn. The other language (the rich one) provides a separate command for each function, so there are more commands to learn, but the language is also more efficient to use.

Designers must decide both how much functionality to build into a system and which functions to assign to separate commands and which to make available only through sequences of basic commands.

One study (Kraut, Hanson, and Farber, 1983) looked indirectly at the issue of how much *richness* to provide by studying the usage of a particular system. Actual usage data were collected by a software monitor from 170 expert, frequent users of the UNIX operating system over a 9-day period. These users varied in their job descriptions and included office workers, programmers, managers, and technical staff. Their use of the system was monitored as they conducted their normal daily work. The tasks they used the system for were primarily document preparation and electronic mail. Three measures were tabulated from the raw data, including the frequency of use of individual commands, the sequencing of commands, and the error rates for individual commands.

One of the most interesting results of this study was that of the more than 400 commands available in UNIX a mere 5% (approximately 20) of the most frequently used commands accounted for about 70% of the total use. Among these users, the full set of available functionality was grossly underused.

As the authors of this study point out, there are a number of possible reasons for underused commands. In some cases, commands may not be used due to redundancy (richness). That is, if there are several ways to do the same thing, some ways may not get used. This is fine if the underused ways are the less efficient ones, but if they are the more efficient ones, then this suggests poor design.

In other cases, for individual users some commands may have been underused due to a lack of need given the task requirements. This is not a reflection on the design of the command language interface so much as on the design of the functionality itself. But for at least some commands, it is likely that the low use was due to difficulty of learning and use, that is, to poor design of the command language.

Another interesting result from this study involved error rates. Users can make three kinds of errors while using a command language: *lexical, syntactic,* and *semantic*. A **lexical error** is an error in entering command names and abbreviations or parameter specification. A **syntactic error** is an error in the expression of a command, such as a missing parenthesis or incorrect use of delimiters. Lexical and syntactic errors cannot be parsed by the command processor and result in error messages. **Semantic errors** are valid (lexically and syntactically) commands that do not accomplish what the user actually intended. For instance, a user may wish to copy File A to File B, but copy File B to File A instead, by entering the command parameters in the wrong order. The system will accept and carry out the command because it is syntactically and lexically correct, but it is still a serious error from the user's point of view. Semantic errors do not result in error messages.

In this study, only lexical and syntactic errors were tallied. Error rates for individual commands ranged from as little as 3% to as high as 50%. A 50% error rate is high indeed, and this does not even include semantic errors, which were not tallied. And error rates were often higher after an initial error. That is, it was more likely that users would make another error after the initial incorrect use of a command than before the initial error. This is a sad commentary on the quality of error handling.

Besides poor error handling, the authors identified three additional primary sources of errors: (1) deviations from syntactic rules, (2) the need for nonvisible status information (for example, filename), and (3) commands requiring large amounts of planning ahead without intermediate feedback.

The underutilization of commands, the high error rates, and the sources of errors found in this study all indicate that the design of the command language was not optimal from the point of view of ease of learning and ease of use. UNIX is a very rich, powerful operating system, and the command language interface to it is very rich and redundant. This study seems to suggest, however, that its very richness was achieved at the price of overwhelming complexity, and that even frequent, expert users underutilized the system and made many errors. As the authors of this study suggest, changes in design, such as more consistency in syntactic rules, easy access to status information, a more interactive style, better error feedback, and even alternative interfaces to more and less frequently used commands, could all improve user performance without necessarily reducing the richness of functionality of the system.

Another study (Good, 1985) employed the same technique of analyzing usage data to guide the design of the command language and keypad interface to a new system. One main issue was the decision on how rich or minimal the command language should be. Command frequency of use data had previously been collected by other researchers from five existing text editors, and these data were used to help decide which functions should be assigned individual commands in a new text editor. The editors varied in the richness of their command sets. The editors studied and the number of individual commands they each included were as follows:

CCA Emacs:	206 commands	
Yale's Z:	74 commands	
Digital's EDT:	49 commands	(Keypad only)
Digital's WPS:	64 commands	(Keyboard only)
EPT:	29 commands	

Usage data for these editors was collected over periods ranging from 10 days to 2 months. The number of tallied command invocations for each editor ranged from 400,000 to 22,000,000. Users included programmers, technicians, students, managers, faculty, researchers, and secretaries.

Based on this extensive usage data, the command set for a new editor was designed to include approximately 70 commands. These were selected as follows: High-frequency commands (those ranked in the top 20% by frequency of use) from the five editors studied were included. Examples were an erase character and an erase line command. The most frequently used of these commands were assigned to dedicated function keys, and the rest were made available through the command language.

Low-frequency but high-power commands were also included. An example was the "global replace" command. The function of replacing all instances of a text string with another text string could be accomplished through multiple executions of the "search" and "replace" commands. But the "global replace" command was vastly more efficient, and so even though it was not as frequently used as other commands, it was included because of the power it afforded when it was needed.

Low-frequency and low-power commands were specifically excluded. An example of such a command was a cursor motion by sentence command. Not only was it infrequently invoked, but moving the cursor to the end of the sentence with arrow keys was not really much more difficult than using the cursor motion by sentence command. Therefore, to keep the command set simple without sacrificing power, commands such as this, included in some of the editors studied, were excluded from the new editor.

This paper provides a particularly nice example of using objective data to help make the richness–minimality trade-off in designing a new command language system.

Guidelines drawn from these and other studies relating to the design of command language semantics are summarized on pages 251–253.

Command language syntax.   Once the command set (*semantics*) is decided on, then a *lexicon* (command names and/or abbreviations) and a *syntax* must be designed. The syntax of a command language involves both the format for specifying command parameters and punctuation in multiple command strings. This section addresses studies of syntactic design.

One study (Ledgard and others, 1980) compared a traditional, notational command language syntax to a more natural English-like syntax. Two text editors identical in functionality but differing in their command language design were used in this study. Examples from the two languages follows:

Notational:	English-like:
FIND:/TOOTH/;-1	BACKWARD TO "TOOTH"
LIST:10	LIST 10 LINES
RS:/KO/,/OK/;*	CHANGE ALL "KO" TO "OK"
LIST:/KO/;*	LIST ALL LINES WITH "KO"
or	or
L:/KO/;*	LALW "KO"

Whereas the notational language used various punctuation marks as parameter delimiters, special codes such as "*" for "all", and an un-English-like parameter order (for example, "LIST:/KO/;*" = list with "KO" all lines), the English-like language, without being English, was much closer to it, using words instead of special codes, spaces and words as parameter delimiters, and an English-like parameter order. To equalize the number of keystrokes required for a command in the two languages, abbreviations were allowed in the English-like language. Examples of abbreviated commands for the English-like language are given in the last two lines of the command strings for this language.

Twenty-four users, eight at each of three different experience levels, each learned and used 15 commands in both editors to accomplish simple editing tasks. Two measures of performance were taken: (1) the percentage of the total tasks presented that were completed in a fixed time period, and (2) the percentage of commands that were not correctly executed, that is, on which errors were made.

Figure 7-4 presents the data from this study. Here it can be seen that, for this simple set of functionality, users at all levels of experience performed better on the English-like command language on both measures of usability. They accomplished more in the given time period and made fewer errors. In fact, the differences were more dramatic in novice users than in expert users (novice users performed almost twice as fast and made a little more than half the errors on the English-like language as compared to the notational language); but even expert users performed more efficiently and correctly on the English-like editor.

This study suggests that a more natural, English-like syntax might be easier to learn and use than the traditional, notational type of syntax found in most commercial command language interfaces. One caution here is that, although it may be easy to design an English-like syntax with unambiguous, short abbreviations for a set of 15 commands, it may be less easy to do so for a more typical command set of 40 to 400 commands.

Another study (Barnard and others, 1981) provides an interesting contradiction to the general suggestion that an English-like syntax is desirable in a command language. The English language, like all natural languages, is not perfectly consistent in syntactic design. There are many exceptions to general syn-

User Experience Level	% Tasks Completed		% Erroneous Commands	
	Notational	English-like	Notational	English-like
Novice	28	42	19	11
Familiar	43	62	18	6.4
Expert	74	84	9.9	5.6

Figure 7–4 A study of command language syntax. From Ledgard, Whiteside, Singer, and Seymour, "The Natural Language of Interactive Systems," *Communications of the ACM,* 23, 1980, 556–63. With permission.

tactic rules. This study asked the following question: should a command language be consistent with English (which is not always internally consistent) or internally consistent, even when this means being inconsistent with comparable English expressions?

Argument order was the syntactic rule investigated. Four languages were designed and studied. Two are discussed here, one with internally consistent argument order rules, and one with argument order rules consistent with English, but internally inconsistent. Examples follow:

Consistent:	English:
SEARCH **MsgID,** File#	SEARCH (for) File# (in) **MsgID**
SAVE **MsgID,** Ref#	SAVE **MsgID** (as) Ref#
DELETE **MsgID,** Digit	DELETE Digit (from) **MsgID**

Note that in the *consistent* language the recurring argument (MsgID) always appears in the first position in the argument list. By contrast, in the *English* language, the recurring argument appears in whatever position it would in an English expression of the command, even though this means it appears in a different position in the argument string for different commands. For instance, note the "Save" command. It would be very awkward to say, in English, "Save as reference number 2, message XYZ." It is much more natural to say "Save message XYZ as reference number 2."

Forty-eight users participated in the full study of four languages. Twelve used the consistent language and 12 the English language described above. Users were trained on a set of six commands. They then were presented with command names and asked to generate correct argument strings. Each user was tested on all six commands eight times. A number of performance measures were taken.

Task time, number of errors, and number of help requests were significantly less with the consistent (non-English) syntax as compared to the English syntax. This advantage of the non-English syntax was evident from the initial trials and persisted even with practice. Thus, while the Ledgard and others (1980) study suggested that, in general, a more English-like syntax seems to improve ease of learning, this study seems to suggest that internally consistent syntactic rules are better than English-like syntactic constructs when English-like constructs would result in syntactic inconsistencies.

It is interesting to note that a performance difference occurred even with this very small command set (only six commands). It is very likely that the advantage of consistent rules would be even more dramatic in more typical command sets of 40 or more commands.

Perhaps the overall conclusion to be drawn from these two studies is that dominant English syntactic forms should be adapted but then applied consistently, even in commands where analogous English phrases would depart from dominant rules.

As a final note, it should be obvious that a command language being designed for users with a primary language other than English (for example, Chinese or Arabic) should follow the syntactic rules of that language, rather than English. However, the same general principal applies: Use dominant natural language constructs when possible, but depart from them when necessary to achieve internal consistency in syntactic rules.

Guidelines drawn from these and other studies concerning the design of command language syntax are summarized on pages 253–256.

Command language lexicon. The lexicon of a language is its vocabulary. In the case of a command language, this mainly means command names and/or abbreviations. A number of studies have investigated the effect of command names and abbreviations on user performance.

Several studies (see Barnard and Grudin, 1988, for a review) have investigated the naming behavior of both users and designers. These studies have consistently reported interesting results. There is a very low probability that any two users or designers will suggest the same name for a given function. There is little consistency in the *form* of names generated by different or even the same designer. And even when designers and users have the opportunity to review and use their own name sets and can observe the inconsistencies in them and experience the difficulties in remembering or using them, they do not attempt or seem to know how to make constructive changes. Thus it is clear that neither designer nor user intuition provides a sound basis for command name and abbreviation design. Accordingly, studies have sought to discover what properties of a command name set will provide optimal performance.

One study (Carroll, 1982) investigated the effects of two command name characteristics, *congruence* and *hierarchicalness,* on ease of learning. In this study, subjects were taught a set of 16 commands to a hypothetical toy robot system. Commands corresponded to movements of the robot's body and arms through three-dimensional space. In paper and pencil tests, subjects were tested on their memory for correct command names on a battery of tests that required both simple recall of command names and meanings and solving robot movement problems that involved the use of the commands.

Four different command languages were designed and tested based on the two characteristics of congruence and hierarchicalness. These languages are presented in Figure 7-5. **Congruence,** as defined by Carroll, means that "commands with a contrary function. . .are assigned names that are semantic contraries in English." For example, commands to raise and lower the robot arm are semantic opposites. Therefore, congruent commands would be ones whose names were considered opposites in the English language, for example, "Up" and "Down" or "Raise" and "Lower." Name pairs such as "Up"and "Lower" or "Raise" and "Down" would be considered noncongruent.

Hierarchicalness, in Carroll's definition, means that "lexical elements of a command are repeated and form a basis for organizing the command language."

Congruent		Noncongruent	
Hierarchical	Nonhierarchical	Hierarchical	Nonhierarchical
Move robot forward	Advance	Move robot forward	Go
Move robot backward	Retreat	Change robot backward	Back
Move robot right	Right	Change robot right	Turn
Move robot left	Left	Move robot left	Left
Move robot up	Straighten	Change robot up	Up
Move robot down	Bend	Move robot down	Bend
Move arm forward	Push	Change arm forward	Poke
Move arm backward	Pull	Move arm backward	Pull
Move arm right	Swing out	Change arm right	Pivot
Move arm left	Swing in	Move arm left	Sweep
Move arm up	Raise	Move arm up	Reach
Move arm down	Lower	Change arm down	Down
Change arm open	Release	Change arm open	Unhook
Change arm closed	Take	Move arm close	Grab
Change arm right	Screw	Move arm right	Screw
Change arm left	Unscrew	Change arm left	Twist

Rating:	1.86	**1.63**	1.81	2.73
Errors #1	**0.50**	2.13	4.25	1.63
Errors #2	**0.75**	1.25	4.63	2.38

Figure 7–5 A study of command name design. From Carroll, "Learning, Using and Designing Filenames and Command Paradigms," *Behavior and Information Technology,* 1, no. 4 (1982), 327–46. With permission.

Commands such as "Move arm forward" and "Move arm backward" have a consistent structure (operator, operand, and specifier) that forms the basis of the command names. Separately identified command parameters are actually folded into the command name. By contrast, the command names "Advance" and "Retreat," assigned to the same functions, illustrate nonhierarchical names. They are independent words, not formed by common operator names and differing operands and specifiers.

Preference ratings and error scores from two of the various performance tests administered are presented in Figure 7-5. Generally, users performed better on congruent as opposed to noncongruent commands. They also expressed a general preference for congruent commands (a lower number indicates a higher preference).

The hierarchical, congruent language produced the best performance on the two objective performance measures, indicating that both naming characteristics are indeed important in facilitating the learning of a command language. Interestingly enough, however, the *nonhierarchical noncongruent* language was *not* the worst; it resulted in *fewer* errors than the *hierarchical noncongruent* language, which produced the worst performance of all. The author speculates that, while the total lack of naming rules was obvious in the nonhierarchical noncongruent language, the partially rule based nature of the hierarchical noncongruent language may have seduced users into applying rules where they did not exist. This is consistent with the finding by Barnard and others (1981) that perfect internal consistency in syntactic rules is important to the learnability of a command language.

Note that the most *preferred* language (congruent nonhierarchical) was *not* the language that produced the best *performance* (congruent hierarchical). Perhaps users imagined that the shorter command names in the congruent nonhierarchical language would be easier to remember and use. This study, however, indicated that the longer but more rule-based names were easier to *remember*.

We do not know, however, how the languages would compare on an *ease of use* measure (for example, speed of input) because one was not taken in this study. Certainly, the greater number of keystrokes in the hierarchical languages would be expected to result in longer keying times, but it is not clear whether or not this would be canceled out by less time spent consulting manuals and on-line help and recovering from errors. Even so, keystrokes in hierarchical languages could probably be reduced by allowing abbreviations, thus achieving ease of learning without sacrificing ease of use.

Thus, this study provides an interesting case of user preferences not necessarily corresponding to objective measures of usability. Although it is always extremely important to consult users during design and to take into consideration their preferences and opinions, it is also important to realize that they are not always able to analyze design options from the point of view of optimizing cognitive, perceptual, and motor performance. Thus, applying well-established guidelines and conducting objective performance testing is always necessary.

Another study (Barnard and others, 1982) investigated another characteristic of command names: specificity. Command names may be *general* or *specific*. The authors define these characteristics as follows:

> The semantics underlying **generic** words like "change" or "move" represent information covering a whole class of potential actions or operations. More **specific** terms such as "substitute" or "advance" invoke additional semantic information concerning the precise nature of the change or movement. For example, "substitute" presupposes "change" and also conveys additional information such as "replace with an entity of a similar type"; while "advance" presupposes "move" with the addition of directional information (Bold is mine).

In this study, 48 computer-naive users used a word processor to edit misspelled proverbs. They were first exposed to a set of 12 commands available on the word processor. Then they were presented with strings such as "stitch in a time xpqy aves nine'' and asked to correct them using the command set and an on-line help facility. Each proverb required a minimum of six commands to correct.

One-half of the users used a system with *general* command names for 10 of the 12 functions, and the other half used a system with more *specific* command names for the same functions (the Help and Cancel commands had the same name on both systems). Examples from these two sets of command names follow:

Specific	General
Fetch	Transfer
Send	Put
Front	Move
Insert	Add
Rubout	Edit
Split	Open

The study compared both learning and remembering specific versus general command names. In an initial learning session, users corrected eight proverbs. Several weeks later, users returned for a session to test their memory of the commands and corrected four more proverbs. The average time (across users within command sets) to complete each proverb was computed, as was the average frequency of reference to the Help system. The latter data are summarized in Figure 7-6.

Generally, users of the *specific* command names performed the editing tasks with significantly less references to Help than users of the *general* command names. All users became more proficient (faster) with practice (across trials), and this was largely due to significantly less commands used and on-line help refer-

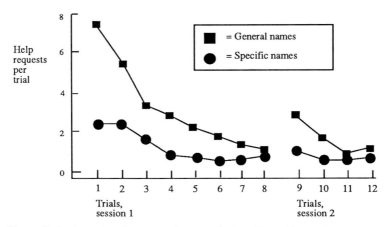

Figure 7-6 A study of command name design. From Barnard, Hammond, MacLean, and Morton, ''Learning and Remembering Interactive Commands,'' *Proceedings, Human Factors in Computer Systems,* March 1982, 2–7. With permission.

ences made per proverb in later trials. All users regressed slightly between the initial learning session and the follow-up memory session, but users of the *specific* names maintained a consistent performance advantage across all trials. Further analysis revealed that, while users of *general* names spent more time accessing and viewing on-line help, they made quick decisions to do so. And users of *specific* names spent less time using on-line help, but when they did, they first spent longer periods of time thinking about it before deciding to access help.

Thus it would seem that specific command names are easier to learn and remember than general command names, in that less reference to on-line help was necessary. Again, it is interesting that a significant effect was found on performance with such a small command set (only ten). It is not clear from this data how specific versus general command names would affect performance on systems with more typical sets of 40 or more commands, but it seems not unlikely that specific command names might afford an even greater advantage when there are many more commands to discriminate among. It also seems likely that it will be easier for designers to come up with specific rather than general command names for a large command set.

At least one study (Grudin and Barnard, 1984b) has provided evidence that command names whose common usage corresponds well to their associated functions (for example, "Delete") led to better performance than semantically unrelated words, pseudowords, and consonant strings (for example, "cat," "nrof," "pip"). Semantic relatedness may be another level of specificity.

On the other hand, Barnard and Grudin (1988) reviewed subsequent studies on specific versus general command names with contradictory results and concluded that "specificity per se is perhaps less crucial than the overall level of ambiguity in mapping from names to operations." That is, in some cases (although not all), more specific names make it easier to discriminate between command names in a set, while general names make the differences between command names less clear. They go on to point out that, certainly in some cases, more general command names would be desirable. For instance, when one general name could be used for similar operations in different contexts, it might be better to have a single, general name for all analogous operations rather than separate specific names for variations on an operation. In these cases, *context* may serve to make the details of command usage less ambiguous, while a common, general command name will serve to highlight useful analogies and reduce the learning burden by reducing the total number of command names. For example, single "cut" and "paste" commands that apply across all contexts (for example, text, graphics, spreadsheet, and electronic mail) are probably more useful than specific terms for these operations in different contexts.

Still another aspect of command names is **familiarity.** The command names chosen by designers may or may not be the ones users would anticipate. Furnas (1985) points out that users can correctly guess the name chosen by designers for a function or object only about 10% to 15% of the time. However, if the system allows the two most common synonyms to access the same object or function, then the "hit rate" goes up to 80% to 90%, a dramatic improvement. Furnas describes an *adaptive* system that, when users type in an incorrect name, allows them to add that name to the system's vocabulary as a synonym, which from then on will be recognized. For instance, if users type in "Hardcopy" in an attempt to invoke the "Print" command, after the "Print" command has successfully been invoked, the system will ask the user if "Hardcopy" should be added to the vocabulary as a synonym for "Print." If the user responds "yes," then the system will thereafter recognize the command "Hardcopy" as "Print."

Furnas points out that such an adaptive system is a relatively inexpensive and effective way to design a set of command names. Both data collection and system redesign are cheap and efficient as they are built right into the system software, and both users and usage are real, as opposed to laboratory simulations. In one implementation of such an adaptive system, he reports an initial hit rate of 47%. After the system had been in use for a short while, 23% of user inputs would have been missed in the original system, but were correctly handled by the adapted system.

Another approach to designing familiar command names is reported in Wixon and others (1983). In this study, users were allowed to use any terms they wanted for commands in a simulated natural language interface to an electronic mail system. As more users used the system, the command language parser was continuously edited to be able to correctly recognize the terms that each new user used. The hit rate of the parser increased from 3% to 80% over the course of testing 67 users. This hit rate was accounted for to a significant degree by simply allowing the three most common terms for a function or object. That is, simply allowing three synonyms and determining which synonyms to allow by gathering data from representative users resulted in a command set that the majority of users would anticipate.

The previous studies investigated full command names. However, many command languages allow or even require abbreviations, and other studies have looked at how various possible abbreviation rules affect performance. One of these studies (Benbasat and Wand, 1984) observed the user's natural tendency to abbreviate command names.

Twenty-four computer-literate, nonprogrammer students in an MBA program were taught a set of 14 full command names in an on-line inventory control simulation model. They were told only that they could abbreviate names, but were not told how. The system actually only accepted unambiguous truncation of command names as valid abbreviations (for example, "Sea" for "Search" and "Sen" for "Send"). If users entered ambiguous truncations (for example, "Se"), they were presented with a menu of options to choose from ("Search" and "Send"). Other abbreviation schemes, such as vowel deletion ("Srch" for "Search"), produced error messages.

The users were presented with a problem to solve that required use of the 14 commands, and their abbreviation behavior was observed. Findings were as follows:

Only 15 of 24 users (62.5%) chose to abbreviate with any consistency, and they abbreviated only about 60% of the time. Six users never used abbreviations at all, and three did once or twice and then never again.

Thirteen of the 15 users who abbreviated used the correct truncation rule consistently. That is, only two ever attempted any other abbreviation scheme. Put another way, out of a total of 1525 command invocations (across all users), only 3 involved the use of an abbreviation that was not a simple truncation of the command name. Only 1.8% of all attempted abbreviations were in error, and almost all of these were ambiguous truncations.

The occurrence of abbreviations was correlated with both command length and command frequency of use. That is, users tended to abbreviate the longer commands and the commands they used most frequently more than short and infrequently used commands. Abbreviations tended to be between three and five letters, somewhat correlated with the length of the original full command name.

This study seems to indicate that users have a natural tendency to choose truncation as an abbreviation rule. However, these users had past experience with computer systems and may have encountered the truncation rule elsewhere. Another study (Grudin and Barnard, 1984a) found evidence that the use of truncation is in fact related to experience, and less experienced users do not naturally assume truncation to the extent that more experienced users do. Other studies reviewed in Ehrenreich (1985) have also found that inexperienced computer users do not usually or consistently choose truncation as a preferred abbreviation rule.

The Wand and Benbasat study also did not *directly* compare performance in learning truncated abbreviations with other abbreviation rules such as vowel deletion. We know from other studies that users do not always perform best on interfaces that they express a preference for. Thus we cannot conclude from this study that truncation as an abbreviation rule is easier to learn or use than alternative abbreviation rules, only that it may be more natural in that *experienced* computer users expect it.

It is interesting that not all users chose to abbreviate when it was an option, and even those that did abbreviate did not do so always. They tended to abbreviate long and frequently used command names, but not short and infrequently used names. This suggests that allowing users to use both full names and abbreviations might be desirable. Many command languages in fact allow *only* abbreviations, and give error messages in response to full command names.

It is also important to distinguish the task of translating a full command name into its proper abbreviation (an **encoding** task) from the task of recognizing the command name from its abbreviation (a **decoding** task). There is suggestive (though not conclusive) evidence from other studies (Streeter, Ackroff, and Taylor, 1983; Grudin and Barnard, 1984a; Ehrenreich, 1985) that names are more recognizable from abbreviations derived from phonetic and vowel deletion rules than abbreviations derived from truncation. For instance, although it may be easier to *generate* "Sea" from "Search" and "Ret" from "Return," it may in fact be easier to *recognize* "Search" from "Srch" and "Return" from "Rtrn." Other studies (see Ehrenreich, 1985 for a review) have consistently found that the rank ordering of (the relative performance on) different abbreviation rules is different for an *encoding* task as compared to a *decoding* task. Thus one abbreviation rule may be best when *entering* commands and another when *reading* commands or *recognizing,* for example, function key labels. A designer must consider how a command language is going to be used in order to choose the best abbreviation rule.

Another study of abbreviations (Grudin and Barnard, 1985) found that when subjects learned and used abbreviations right away, rather than learning and using full command names first, even when they had a consistent abbreviation rule they tended to forget the abbreviations more often (twice as often) than subjects who first learned and used full command names. The authors speculate that abbreviations may become directly associated with functions and lose their association with command names unless users learn and use full command names first. When users forget abbreviations and do not have the command name in memory to reconstruct the abbreviation from, they make errors in which the command name is wrong but the abbreviation rule is correct (for example, "DEL" for the "erase" command). If the command name has been well learned, on the other hand, reconstructing a forgotten abbreviation is easy.

This study also found that subjects using abbreviations of their own creation tended to create inconsistent abbreviations (for example, varying number of letters and varying abbreviation rules) and made many more errors in using them (five times as many) than subjects who learned and used a consistent abbreviation rule devised by the authors (that is, two-letter truncation). This is another example of the independence of *preference* versus *performance* measures. Subjects performed more poorly on their own design than on the design of human factors experts.

Even more interesting, after their bad experience using their own abbreviations, subjects were given an opportunity to redesign them. Most chose to keep their abbreviations in spite of the problems they had experienced, noting that they could not think of any better set of abbreviations. This again illustrates the importance of applying principles and testing in the design process, rather than relying only on designer or user intuitions.

The preceding studies represent a small sample of the many studies that have investigated abbreviations. Many more are reviewed and discussed in Ehrenreich (1985). Abbreviation rules investigated in the studies reviewed included:

1. Truncation:	append =	APPE	
	execute =	EXEC	
2. Vowel deletion:	append =	APPND	
	execute =	EXCT	
3. Contraction:	append =	APND	
	execute =	EXTE	
4. Minimum to distinguish:	translate =	TRANS	
	transfer =	TRANF	

5. Phonetic: append =   APND
                                execute =   XQT
6. First syllable: append =   APPN
                                execute =   EXEC
7. User created: (by individuals)

Ehrenreich concludes in this review that:

1. Naturally produced. . . abbreviations [that is, user created] have generally been inferior to rule-generated abbreviations when the task is encoding.
2. In all encoding tests involving truncation, these abbreviations have consistently been found to be as good as or better than other abbreviations.
3. If all studies are considered, there are no consistent differences among abbreviation techniques on decoding performance.
4. When comparing two or more abbreviation techniques under the same conditions, there may be one ranking of the abbreviation techniques for encoding and a different ranking for decoding performance.
5. Encoding performance on rule-generated abbreviations can be enhanced by using a simple rule and teaching that rule to the user. No similar advantage has been found for decoding performance. (Brackets mine)

In addition, Ehrenreich points out that

> when working with the rules presented in this paper, a single abbreviation can often be decoded into more than one word (whereas the rule will always produce only one abbreviation when used for encoding). Thus, *the finding that rules do not help in decoding may be the result of testing inappropriate rules*. (Italics mine)

A phonetic rule, in which abbreviations are formed by choosing letters that when pronounced sound most like the word, has been suggested in some studies as a rule to facilitate decoding. Further research is necessary to determine if a phonetic rule, or indeed other as yet unstudied rules, may provide an advantage over other rules during decoding. Ehrenreich suggests that if, in fact, some other rule than truncation proves to be advantageous in decoding, then designers must either decide which task is more important to their users, encoding or decoding, or allow two abbreviation rules to be valid so that both encoding and decoding are facilitated.

In another recent review of the preceding studies, plus the many others that have addressed the issues of command names and abbreviations, Barnard and Grudin (1988) point out the difficulty of drawing simple guidelines for command naming from the research literature due to the many varying factors during actual usage of a command language that have not been systematically controlled for within or across studies. They refer to a number of such factors that may influence the selection of an optimal name set.

1. Size of the command set
2. Semantic interrelationships among commands
3. Typical use of commands in random versus structured sequence
4. Relative and absolute frequency of use of individual commands
5. Users' past experience with other command sets
6. Users' past experience with chosen names in other contexts
7. Age, reasoning ability, and spatial memory ability of users
8. Relative importance of ease of learning and remembering versus ease of use
9. Relative importance of encoding (generating) versus decoding (recognizing) command names

Barnard and Grudin point out that variations in these factors will most likely result in different command name and abbreviation characteristics providing optimal performance, but since we do not know exactly how these factors interact with name characteristics, this limits the generalizability of simple guidelines. They emphasize the need for a thorough task and user analysis to identify these factors and thorough and rigorous user interface testing to confirm the usability of the chosen name set.

These observations are in fact generally true of any of the design issues discussed in this book. Guidelines drawn from research studies that measure behavior in specific, limited contexts are offered only as *one* tool for making design decisions. *All* guidelines should *always* be *carefully and intelligently interpreted* and applied in the context of a thorough user and task analysis, and a design based on carefully applied guidelines should still always be *tested* in the actual context in which it will be used.

Barnard and Grudin go on to make the following suggestions regarding the design *process,* which also apply equally well to other design issues beyond command naming:

1. The full command set should be defined before name design commences.
2. The command name designer should *not* be someone who is familiar with the internal aspects of the system.
3. The designer should have access to the results of a thorough task and user analysis.
4. Iterative testing and redesign should always be conducted.
5. The name set should be tested and evaluated by someone other then the designer.

Within this context, it is also recommended that the guidelines offered later in this chapter be taken as a starting point for design between steps 3 and 4.

Guidelines drawn from these and other studies concerning the design of command language lexicon are summarized on pages 256–261.

Command language interaction.   Besides the structure of the command language itself, the *structure of the interactive dialog* is an important aspect of command language interface design. This would include such issues as the location of the command line and the quality of feedback, error handling, and on-line assistance.

One study (Granda, Teitelbaum, and Dunlap, 1982) investigated the effect of command line location. Locating the command line at the top of the screen (line 2) was compared to locating it at the bottom of the screen (line 23). Locating the command line at the top resulted in more and larger head movements and longer input time relative to locating it at the bottom. The time difference per single command input was over 3 seconds, a significant difference indeed for high-frequency users. The greater time seemed to be accountable for by the greater number and magnitude of head movements made as the user repetitively reviewed the required input (which was located directly above the command line in both cases) and looked down at the keyboard for entry. More than one head movement from screen to keyboard was most likely required, because the input specification exceeded the limits of human short-term memory and because users looked back from the keyboard to the screen to verify the correctness of their input.

When input to be entered on a command line is located next to the command line on the screen (as was the case in the task employed), this study suggests that locating the command line at the bottom rather than the top of the screen provides significant advantages. However, many command language interfaces require that users recall required input from memory, rather than read it from the screen. It is not clear that these findings would generalize to such systems. On the other hand, many command language interfaces display a history of past commands immediately above the command line, and users are likely to be studying feedback from previous commands to determine what input to enter next. This situation is more analogous to the task used in this study. Thus it might seem that, in such systems, locating the input line at the bottom of the screen and scrolling history up from the bottom line might be advisable. Most command language interfaces do not work this way. The command line starts out at the top of the screen, moves down to the bottom as successive command lines are entered, and then remains at the bottom until the screen is cleared.

It is also not clear from this study where systems that display not only a command line but other data on the screen should present the command input line. This will probably depend on how the user scans and reads other data on the screen in order to decide on input to be entered in the command line. That is, eye and head movement between data and command line, as well as between command line and keyboard, must be considered.

In the absence of research relevant to this type of task scenario, designers are advised to locate the command line at the bottom of the screen unless it seems clear that the users eyes will be elsewhere just prior to command input. If this is the case, designers should test other command line locations against the bottom of the screen to determine the optimal location.

Guidelines regarding the design of command language interaction drawn from this study and from experience are summarized on pages 261–264.

DESIGNING COMMAND LANGUAGES: PRINCIPLES AND GUIDELINES

As previously stated, the design of command languages can be divided into four separate design issues, as follows:

Command language semantics
Command language syntax
Command language lexicon
Command language interaction

Principles and guidelines presented are drawn from the research literature discussed previously and are organized around these issues.

Command language semantics.   The complete set of functionality that a system provides and how that functionality is broken down into language elements is referred to as the *semantics* of the command language. A system may be rich, including a great deal of functionality, or minimal, meaning there are few functions available. In turn, a command language interface to the system may be rich or minimal. A *rich* language (as opposed to system) is one that has many commands, some of which provide redundant, but more efficient and powerful ways of doing things that could be done (although less efficiently) through combinations of more basic commands. A language with a smaller set of core commands that must be combined to achieve more complex functions is referred to as *minimal*.

The following guideline applies. It is based on the research discussed on pages 234–237.

☞ **Balance power and simplicity (richness and minimality, respectively) according to user needs.**

Note the three sets of functions in Figure 7-7. In the left column, for each set of functions, is a set of command names from rich languages. On the right are sets of commands from minimal languages for the same three sets of functions. For instance, a *rich* command language interface to a text editor might include three commands: "Insert," "Delete," and "Replace." The "Replace" command provides a more efficient (less keystrokes) way of accomplishing what could be done with the "Insert" and "Delete" commands.

Alternatively, a *minimal* language to the same editor might include only the two commands "Delete" and "Insert." However, the same three functions, "delete," "insert," and "replace," are available through these two commands. The

Rich:	Minimal:
Delete Insert Replace	Delete Insert
Copy Move Rename Delete	Copy Delete
Tally checks Subtract checks tally Subtract single check Tally charges Subtract charges tally Subtract single charge Tally deposits Add deposits tally Add single deposit Tally transfers Add transfers tally Add single transfer Compute current balance	Subtract debit amount Add credit amount

Figure 7–7 Rich versus minimal command sets.

"replace" *function* is achieved by using the "Delete" and "Insert" *commands* in sequence.

Note that, for all three sets of functions, *both languages provide the same functionality:* three, four, or thirteen functions, respectively. For each command set, one language (the minimal one), however, does so with fewer commands, so there are less commands for the designer to design and the user to learn. The other language (the rich one) provides a separate command for each function, so there are more commands to learn, but the language is more efficient to use.

The designer must find a happy medium between richness (which provides power and ease of use, but also complexity) and minimality (which provides simplicity and ease of learning, but less power). Whether ease of learning or ease of use is of higher priority will always depend on the characteristics of the users and the task domain. A good rule of thumb is to *build in richness for high-frequency, powerful functions, but opt for minimality when providing for low-frequency, low power functions.* Usage studies of related applications can provide valuable input to this design issue (see, for example, Good, 1985).

Poor:	**Improved:**
VolB!FileA!D$$	search (for) filea (in) volb.
FileA!VolB!ER$L!:KO:!*$$	open filea (in) volb. list all lines with "KO".
	OR
	s filea volb.
	o filea volb. lal "KO".

Figure 7–8   Command language syntax.

Command language syntax.   Once the command set (semantics) is designed, then a syntax (structure) and lexicon (command names and/or abbreviations) must be designed. The syntax of a command language specifies both the format for entering command parameters and punctuation in multiple command strings.

The following guidelines are drawn from the research literature summarized and discussed on pages 237–240.

☞ **Provide consistency in syntax.**

Note the "Poor" examples of command language strings in Figure 7-8. In this language, parameters are expressed first, followed by commands. Both commands in the example require two parameters: volume name and file name. However, the "Delete" ("D") command expects the volume name first, while the "Read" ("ER") command expects the file name first. This arbitrary inconsistency in the syntactic rule governing parameter position will lead to user errors. One consistent rule, such as "file name always follows volume name," will be easier to remember and result in fewer syntactic errors. Note that the "Improved" version is consistent in the position of the two parameters.

Other aspects of syntax (besides parameter order or position) that should be governed by consistent rules include the use of upper- and lowercase letters, use of punctuation symbols, "wildcard" capabilities, and specification formats.

☞ **Use an action–object syntax.**

When designing an English-based command language, the syntax should reflect an action–object grammar. That is, all commands should start with a command name that is a verb (an action), followed by parameters, or objects. This is because English is largely an action–object grammar. In the imperative voice, we say, for example, ''get the file,'' ''send the file,'' and ''print the file,'' rather than ''the file get,'' ''the file send,'' and ''the file print,'' respectively. Thus, if command languages have an action–object grammar, they will seem more familiar, and more natural.

Note the two command sets in Figure 7-8. In the ''Poor'' version, parameters (file name and volume name) are expressed first, followed by command names (''D'' for ''Delete,'' and ''ER'' for ''Edit read''). Alternatively, in the ''Improved'' version, command names (''Search'' and ''Open'') come first, followed by parameters.

Of course, command languages designed to support users with native languages other than English should have a grammar that is based on the predominant grammatical rules of the native language. Some natural languages in fact have object–action grammars.

The reader might have noted that many graphical, direct manipulation interfaces have an object–action grammar. First the user selects an object (a folder, file, or object from a palette) and then a command or action. This may seem to contradict the guideline here. In fact, it does not. This guideline applies only to language-based interfaces, not to direct manipulation interfaces.

In the English language, we do generally express first the action and then the object for imperatives, so it is appropriate that a language-based interface should reflect this. However, in a direct manipulation interface, we are not speaking a language, but rather are manipulating objects in space. When we manipulate objects in space in the manual world, we usually pick up the object first and then perform some action on it or with it. Thus, an object–action grammar is consistent with our experience when *doing,* while an action–object grammar is consistent with our experience when *speaking.*

☞ **Avoid arbitrary use of punctuation.**

The ''Poor'' example in Figure 7-8 shows a command language that has arbitrarily assigned certain symbols to perform as punctuation in the command language. In particular, exclamation points delimit commands and parameters within a simple command, colons act as quotation marks delimiting literal strings, a single dollar sign separates individual commands, and a double dollar sign terminates a command string, requesting execution. Asterisks represent wildcards. These symbols are unmnemonic and unfamiliar (and may even be used for different purposes across command languages), which makes them difficult to learn and remember.

In the ''Improved'' version, familiar punctuation from the native language, English, has been adopted in the command language. Spaces delimit commands and parameters (words), periods separate individual commands (sentences), quotation marks delimit literal strings, and carriage returns terminate command strings (paragraphs), requesting execution. Wildcards are expressed through familiar words such as "all." Because they are drawn from the familiar native language, these punctuation conventions will be easier to learn and remember.

☞ **Avoid positional grammars.**

In a positional grammar in a command language, the parameters are identified (by the command parser) exclusively by their relative position in the parameter list. That is, in a command such as "Copy/FileA/FileB," the system always takes the first parameter (FileA in this case) to be the source file and the second parameter (FileB) to be the destination file. Thus, the result of this command is to copy FileA to FileB. If the command is expressed as "Copy/FileB/FileA," then the result will be to copy FileB to FileA. The system knows which parameter is which by its relative position.

This is easy for the parser, but it may be a problem for the user, who must remember the correct position for different parameters. In this example of the copy command, misremembering the proper order can have fairly serious consequences, destroying the file one actually wanted to preserve and replacing it with the one intended to be destroyed.

An alternative to positional grammars is keyword grammars, where keywords, rather than position, identify parameters in a list. For example, in the "Improved" version of Figure 7-8, keywords such as "for" and "in" serve to specify parameters. The user has the choice or entering "Search for FileA in VolB" or "Search in VolB for FileA," and either will be correctly understood. The burden of remembering which position corresponds to which parameter is removed, and the user need not fear that a command will be misinterpreted.

Keywords add keystrokes to a command language. However, a command language could have a positional grammar as the default for expert, high-frequency users, with the option of using keywords available for novice and less frequent users. If no keywords appear, then parameters would be interpreted by position. If keywords do appear, they would override position in the parser's interpretation of the command string.

☞ **A command language syntax should be natural and mnemonic.**

A language based on the dominant grammatical rules of the native language, such as that in the "Improved" example in Figure 7-8, will be easier to learn and remember than a language that has an arbitrary and unfamiliar syntax, such as the "Poor" version in Figure 7-8. However, it is more important that syntactic constructs be internally consistent than that they be like the users' native language. Natural languages have many inconsistencies and exceptions to rules, and this should not be mimicked in command languages. It is exactly these inconsistencies and exceptions that little children stumble on when learning language. Analogously, users learning a command language will make errors where dominant rules are violated. This has been demonstrated in studies of this issue (Barnard and others, 1981; Kraut, Hanson, and Farber, 1983).

☞ **Allow defaulting of optional parameters.**

Make the simplest, most common form of a command easy, and then allow users to add options to the simple form. For example (Smith and Mosier, 1986), in an electronic mail system the simplest command for searching through messages might be "READ NEXT." Optional parameters could then be added to allow more specific searches, for example, "READ NEXT 3/28/90." In the absence of parameters specifying date, sender, and the like, these parameters would default to "All." This layered approach will allow users to learn the language in an incremental fashion. Because they do not need to always enter a value for every optional parameter, they also do not need to learn about these optional parameters initially. Defaulting not only facilitates learning, but actually saves keystrokes as well.

☞ **Avoid frequent use of shift or control keys.**

Shifted characters are more error prone than nonshifted characters. Functions requiring multiple keystrokes in sequence (for example, the use of "control" or "command" keys) are also more error prone than single keystroke functions. Thus, the use of shift and control keys should be minimized to minimize both errors and keystrokes in a command language.

Note the heavy use of shifted characters in the "Poor" example in Figure 7-8 (!, $, :, *, and capital letters for command abbreviations). Alternatively, shifted characters have been minimized in the "Improved" language. Only the quotation marks require the use of the shift key, and this is a reasonable trade-off, given that quotes to delimit literal strings will be easier to learn and remember than other symbols.

Command language lexicon.   The lexicon of a language is its vocabulary. In the case of a command language, this mainly means command names and/or abbreviations. The following guidelines apply. They are drawn from the research summarized and discussed on pages 240–249.

☞ **Design command names to be hierarchical, congruent, specific, familiar, consistent in grammatical form, and discriminable.**

Hierarchicalness (Carroll, 1982) means that "lexical elements of a command are repeated and form a basis for organizing the command language." Commands such as "Move forward" and "Move backward" (see Figure 7-9) have a structure built on common and specific elements that forms the basis of the command names. Examples of nonhierarchical names would be the command names "Go" and "Back" assigned to the same functions. They are independent words, not formed by combinations of common and specific elements. Hierarchical command names will be easier to learn and remember, although not necessarily easier to use, as they clearly require more keystrokes. Good abbreviations can solve this problem, however, without sacrificing the advantage of hierarchical names.

	Poor:	**Improved:**
Hierarchicalness	Go	Move forward
	Back	Move backward
Congruence	Add	Insert
	Kill	Delete
Specificity	Change	Replace
	Directory	Search
Familiarity	Extract	Delete
	Transmit	Send
Grammatical consistency	Print	Print
	Directory	Search
Distinctiveness	Sen(d)	Send
	Sea(rch)	Find
	Sel(ect)	Choose

Figure 7–9 Command language lexicon: names.

Figure 7-10 shows two sets of command names for a bibliographic search system. Note that the ''Poor'' name set is partly hierarchical and partly nonhierarchical. This is particularly problematic, because it has been suggested (Carroll, 1982) that languages that are partially rule based may be even harder to learn than languages that are not at all rule based. This may be because, if rules are inconsistently adhered to, users are seduced into applying the rules where they do not apply. Thus, the ''Improved'' command set is consistently hierarchical. The set of abbreviations available reduces the increased keystrokes inherent in a hierarchical command name. The very fact that the names are hierarchical makes it easier to generate a set of abbreviations that are also formed by one simple rule: the first letters of each word in the hierarchical command names. Since all commands have two words (unlike in the ''Poor'' name set), all abbreviations will also have two letters, making them easier to remember.

Congruence means that ''commands with a contrary function . . . are assigned names that are semantic contraries in English'' (Carroll, 1982). For example, the functions of entering and removing text are semantic opposites. Command names considered to be antonyms in the English language, for example, ''Insert/ Delete'' in the ''Improved'' column in Figure 7-9, would be considered congruent. By contrast, name pairs such as ''Add/Kill'' in the ''Poor'' column would be considered noncongruent. Congruent command names will be easier to learn and remember.

| **Poor:** | | **Improved:** | |
Names	Abbreviations	Names	Abbreviations
Next page	NP	Next page	NP
Previous page	PP	Previous page	PP
Home	H	First page	FP
Next document	ND	Next document	ND
Previous document	PD	Previous document	PD
First document	FD	First document	FD
Screen print	SP	Print screen	PS
Print document	PR	Print document	??
Mail it	MI	Print result	PR
Request	R	Display request	DR
Help	H	Display help	DH
Time	T	Display time	DT
Full	FL	Format full	FF
Short	SH	Format short	FS
Location	LO	Format location	FL
Select services	SS	Select services	SS
Exit	EX	Exit services	ES
Modify	M	Modify request	MR
New search	NS	Change request	CR
Change drawer	CD	Change drawer	CD
Change cabinet	CC	Change cabinet	CC

Figure 7–10   Command language lexicon: names and abbreviations.

In Figure 7-9, the third pair of commands illustrate *specific* versus *general* command names. "Change" and "Directory in the "Poor" column are general names that could cover many possible meanings. By contrast, "Replace" and "Search" are examples of submeanings of "Change" and "Directory." That is, they are more specific. Specific command names will be easier to learn and remember.

The exception to this is when a single, more general term can be applied to variations in a function across contexts. In this case, a single more general name will highlight the important semantic relationships between a given function across contexts, and the context will serve to make any subtle variations in command usage less ambiguous. For example, the commands "Move," "Copy," "Cut," and "Paste" should have these general names regardless of the context in which they are applied (text, graphics, spreadsheets, electronic mail, and so on), rather than different, more specific names in each context. However, the most specific term that makes sense across all contexts is advised. That is, "Move" is still more specific than "Reorganize" or "Change," but it applies equally well across contexts.

Another aspect of specificity is semantic distinctiveness. Avoid words with highly similar semantic connotations to denote different functions. For example, avoid name pairs such as "Sum" and "Count," "Erase" and "Delete," "Quit" and "Exit," "Display" and "View," and "Compose" and "Create" (Smith and Mosier, 1986). The semantic similarity in these names will make it difficult for users to remember the semantic differences in their usage.

Names such as "Extract" and "Transmit" (see Figure 7-9) are relatively infrequently used in the English language and are therefore less *familiar* than names such as "Delete" and "Send." Familiar command names will be easier to learn and remember than unfamiliar ones.

Command names should also be *grammatically consistent*. For instance, note the command names "Print" and "Directory" in Figure 7-9. "Print" is a verb, while "Directory" is a noun. By contrast, both "Print" and "Search" are verbs. Assigning the same grammatical form to all commands names will make them easier to learn and remember. Making them all verbs will at the same time satisfy the guideline of an action–object grammar.

Many words in the English language serve as both verbs and nouns, depending on the context. Examples are "a list" and "to list," "a change" and "to change," and "a file" and "to file." As long as all command names that have only one reasonable interpretation (at least within the domain of the system) are verbs (for example, "Print" and "Move"), then other ambiguous names will be interpreted as verbs, and the whole name set will be perceived by users as consistent in grammatical form.

Note the last set of command names in Figure 7-9. They all start with "Se." This makes them all look similar and requires similar keystroke sequences, especially in their abbreviated form. Words that look similar will be harder to read. Words that are spelled similarly will induce typing errors, because users will develop motor habits for the most frequently used ones that will be hard to break when typing a less frequently used but very similar word. *Distinctive* command names, such as "Send," "Find," and "Choose" for the same functions, will increase reading rate and decrease errors.

☞ Use user jargon and avoid computer jargon.

Every industry has its own set of jargon. This is as true for the computer industry as for other industries such as banking, insurance, medicine, and manufacturing. Individual companies and departments, besides adopting the industry jargon, also develop their own unique jargon.

When designing systems for users in industries other than the computer industry, it is important to avoid the use of computer science jargon in all aspects of the user interface, including command names. Words like "directory," "pathway," "node," "block," "transmit," and "volume" are all jargon from the computer industry that will be unfamiliar and convey little meaning to users from other industries. They should thus be avoided.

On the other hand, designers should make the effort to discover what the relevant industry, company, and department jargon is for the set of users of a system and should use these terms throughout the interface as appropriate. These

| | **Abbreviations** | |
Name	Poor:	Improved:
Move forward	MovF	MovF
Move backward	Mvb	MovB
Insert	I	Ins
Delete	Dl	Del
Replace	Repl	Rep
Search	Srch	Sea
Delete	X	Del
Send	Sn	Sen
Print	Prt	Pri
Search	Srch	Sea
Send	Sn	Sen
Find	Fi	Fin
Choose	Ch	Cho

Figure 7–11   Command language lexicon: abbreviations.

terms will be more familiar and convey more meaning than will more general terms from the English language. For instance, if a university uses the word "term" instead of "semester" and "sequence," instead of "time slot," then these terms should be used in system user interfaces.

☞   **Use a simple, consistent rule for command name abbreviations.**

Figure 7-11 presents a "Poor" and "Improved" set of abbreviations for the command names listed in the "Improved" column of Figure 7-9. Note that no particular rule is consistently followed in generating the "Poor" abbreviations. Some are formed by all the consonants in the word, or vowel deletion ("Srch"), some by some of the consonants ("Dl"), some by four-character truncation ("Repl"), some by two-character truncation ("Ch"), and some by arbitrary symbols ("X"). As there is no consistent rule by which to generate a correct abbreviation from a known command name, users must simply rote memorize correct abbreviations, a formidable task in very large command sets.

By contrast, the set of "Improved" abbreviations follows a simple abbreviation rule: single word commands truncate to the first three letters; multiple word commands add the first letter of the second word. Once command names are known, the users need never even see a correct abbreviation. If they know the simple rule, they will be able to correctly generate an abbreviation for any known command name. The learning and memory burden will be greatly reduced.

Figure 7-10 also gives examples of "Poor" and "Improved" command abbreviations. The "Poor" set have different lengths (partly due to the different lengths of the command names) and are generated by several different rules. Users will undoubtedly make errors applying the wrong rule to generate a given abbreviation, and this set will be hard to learn and remember. The one simple consistent rule from which all abbreviations are generated in the "Improved" set will make it much easier to learn and remember these command abbreviations.

Note the "??" in the "Improved" column. Here the abbreviation for the "print document" command following from the rule (that is, the first letter of each word) would result in an ambiguous abbreviation, because "PD" is already taken as an abbreviation for the "Previous document" command. Renaming the command would violate the hierarchical rules behind the design of the command names. Sometimes, as in this case, it is not possible to be perfectly consistent. The idea however, is to *minimize* inconsistency, even if it cannot be eliminated entirely. In this case, an abbreviation such as "PRD" for "Print document" is advisable. Changing the command name might make it hard to remember the name, and at least this abbreviation is somewhat mnemonic. It will cause some errors, but the whole command set will still produce less errors overall than the "Poor" version.

☞ **Allow full command names and emphasize them in training, even if abbreviations are allowed.**

Evidence suggests that some users will prefer to spell out full command names, at least initially, and especially for shorter and less frequently used commands (Benbasat and Wand, 1984). Other evidence suggests that users who first learn full command names find it easier to remember abbreviations later than users who learn abbreviations immediately (Grudin and Barnard, 1985). For these two reasons, it seems advisable to allow full command names *and* abbreviations and to emphasize full command names in training (for example, in the manual and on-line tutorial and help systems).

Command language interaction.   Besides the structure of the command language itself (that is, semantics, syntax, and lexicon), the structure of the dialog or interaction can be designed to enhance the usability of a command language system. The following principles apply. They are drawn from the study reported on page 250 and from experience.

☞ **Locate the command line at the bottom of the screen or window, unless it is clear that the user's eyes will be elsewhere at input time.**

Some evidence (Granda, Teitelbaum, and Dunlap, 1982) suggests that locating the command line at the bottom, rather than at the top, of the screen results in faster input times. However, studies that vary the task type to see how this affects optimal command line location have not been conducted. Designers are thus advised to locate the command line at the bottom of the screen unless it seems clear that the users eyes will be elsewhere just prior to command input. If this is the case, designers should test other command line locations against the bottom of the screen to determine the optimal location.

☞ **Provide interactive support through defaults, command editing, intelligent interpretation, type-ahead, and feedback.**

Defaults, such as the current library as the default in specifying a file name, reduce keystrokes, making a command language easier to use. Defaults can be dangerous, however. If, for instance, a parser assumes the last used parameter value in a command with a missing parameter, this may be useful and save keystrokes. A user might name a file in an ''open'' command and then issue a series of commands such as ''print,'' ''send,'' ''edit,'' ''save,'' and ''close,'' without having to type in the filename repetitively.

However, if a user enters a command to save all files on disk, and then goes on to delete a particular file and forgets what the last used file name was, the results of relying on the default will be disastrous. The user might inadvertently delete all files on disk, because the parser will note the missing parameter and default to the last used file name, which was ''All.''

Thus, defaults are very useful, but they make certain kinds of errors more likely. The user should always be asked for a confirmation on any command that has drastic, irreversible consequences.

Many older command languages required a user to retype an entire command string when a simple error such as a one-character typo was made. This is particularly frustrating when the command string entered is very long, requiring many keystrokes. *Command editing* is simply allowing the user to move the cursor into the erroneous command string, overstrike, delete, and insert characters, and reexecute. Allowing command editing will save many keystrokes and much frustration for both novice and expert command language users.

Command language parsers that make *intelligent interpretations* of erroneous input will also be easier to use. For instance, simple typos and spelling errors could be processed as follows:

''delate'': Did you mean ''delete''? Y or N

Type-ahead refers to the capability to enter multiple commands in a string, without waiting for each to execute before entering the next. Usually, two delimiters are available, one to separate commands entered in a multiple-command string and one to request execution of the whole command string. When later commands in the string depend on the success of earlier commands, and earlier commands fail, users should have the option of canceling all later commands or making a correction and reexecuting later commands without having to reenter them.

Most traditional command language systems provide minimal *feedback.* The only way the user knows that a command was *syntactically* correct is by the absence of an error message. There is often no way to know whether the command was *semantically* correct without actually going in to inspect the data that the command operated on. Confirmation messages such as "All files moved from Library A to Library B" following completion of a move command can be very useful feedback, especially for novice or infrequent users. Periodic feedback during command execution, such as case by case verification of global replace commands, interactive listings of file names as they are moved, and the like, can also be very useful. Expert, high-frequency users, however, should have the option of turning off all confirmation messages and interactive feedback.

☞ **Provide memory aids such as on-line quick reference and prompting.**

A good on-line *quick reference* for correct command names, abbreviations, and syntax will be very useful, not only for novices, but also for expert users who use some commands only occasionally or have been away from the system for awhile.

Another useful technique is to allow the user to omit parameters for which they cannot remember the correct syntax and to prompt them in response. Figure 7-12 gives an example of this prompting technique.

☞ **Provide function keys for high-frequency commands.**

If certain commands are very frequently used and a system is supported by a dedicated (versus generic) keyboard, then these commands are candidates for dedicated function keys. For instance, "print" and "save" commands might be very frequently used by all users of a command language system. A single keystroke for very frequent commands such as these will minimize keystrokes, thus reducing both time and errors.

Programmable function keys on a generic keyboard can also be used for this purpose, but they will not be as easy to remember. An on-line quick reference system just discussed should provide reminders of function key assignments in this case.

☞ **Make the language user tailorable.**

There are a number of ways to allow users to tailor a command language interface to fit their needs. *User-defined abbreviations* allow the user to define, through some sort of simple interaction, abbreviations for commands that will then be recognized by the system.

User-defined synonyms allow the user to define one or more alternative command names to the system commands names, which will then be recognized by the system. For instance, the user might define a synonym "Quit" to the "Log off" command, because two other systems that he or she uses have "Quit" as the command to leave the system. It will no longer be a problem to remember which command is correct on which system.

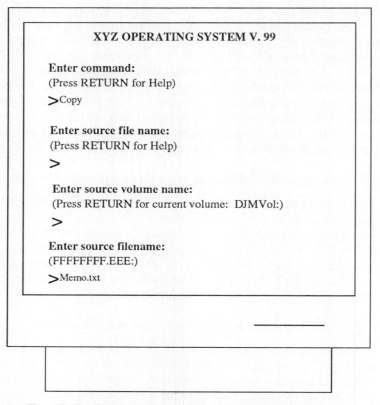

Figure 7–12   Command language interaction: interactive prompting.

User-defined and named macros with variables and decision logic allow users to automate very frequently used command strings, even when some parameters vary with use.

Allowing users great flexibility in tailoring a command language interface is desirable and useful, but it does not excuse the designer from designing an optimal default command language. Many users will never use the tailoring capability, and these users still need a well-designed system. In addition, as demonstrated in a number of studies (for example, Grudin and Barnard, 1985), users cannot always predict which design alternatives will improve their own performance, and often their preferences do not correspond to good design choices from the point of view of objective measures of throughput and errors. Thus, although a tailorable command language is more powerful, it must be well designed, according to all the preceding principles and guidelines, in its default form. When possible, documentation and training materials should provide sound advice on good naming and abbreviation rules.

REFERENCES

ANTIN, J. F., "An Empirical Comparison of Menu Selection, Command Entry and Combined Modes of Computer Control," *Behavior & Information Technology,* 7, no. 2 (April–June 1988), pp. 173–82.

BARNARD, PHIL J., and JONATHAN GRUDIN, "Command Names," *Handbook of Human–Computer Interaction,* Martin Helander, ed., (Amsterdam: North-Holland, 1988), pp. 237–55.

————, and others, "Consistency and Compatibility in Human–Computer Dialogue," *International Journal of Man–Machine Studies,* 15 (1981), pp. 87–134.

————, and others, "Learning and Remembering Interactive Commands," *Proceedings, Human Factors in Computer Systems,* March 1982, pp. 2–7.

BENBASAT, IZAK, and YAIR WAND, "Command Abbreviation Behavior in Human–Computer Interaction," *Communications of the ACM,* 27, no. 4 (April 1984), pp. 376–83.

CARROLL, JOHN M., "Learning, Using and Designing Filenames and Command Paradigms," *Behavior and Information Technology,* 1, no. 4 (1982), pp. 327–46.

EHRENREICH, S. L., "Computer Abbreviations: Evidence and Synthesis," *Human Factors,* 27, no. 2 (April 1985), pp. 143–56.

FURNAS, GEORGE W., "Experience with an Adaptive Indexing Scheme," *CHI '85 Proceedings,* April 1985, pp. 131–36, ACM.

GOOD, MICHAEL, "The Use of Logging Data in the Design of a New Text Editor," *Proceedings, CHI '85,* 1985, pp. 93–113, ACM.

GRANDA, RICHARD E., RICHARD C. TEITELBAUM, and GREGORY L. DUNLAP, "The Effect of VDT Command Line Location on Data Entry Behavior," *Proceedings of the Human Factors Society 26th Annual Meeting,* 1982, pp. 621–24.

GRUDIN, JONATHAN, and PHIL BARNARD, "The Cognitive Demands of Learning and Representing Command Names for Text-Editing," *Human Factors,* 26, no. 4 (August, 1984b), pp. 407–22.

————, and ————, "The Role of Prior Task Experience in Command Name Abbreviation," *Proceedings, Interact '84,* 1, (September, 1984a), pp. 439–43.

————, and ————, "When Does an Abbreviation Become a Word? And Related Questions," *CHI '85 Proceedings,* April 1985, pp. 121–26, ACM.

KRAUT, ROBERT E., STEPHEN J. HANSON, and JAMES M. FARBER, "Command Use and Interface Design," *Proceedings, CHI '83,* 1983, pp. 120–24, ACM.

LEDGARD, H. F., and others, "The Natural Language of Interactive Systems," *Communications of the ACM,* 23 (1980), pp. 556–63.

SMITH, S. L., and J. N. MOSIER, "Design Guidelines for User–System Interface Software," *Technical Report ESD-TR-84-190* Mass.: Mitre Corp., (Bedford, Mass.: September 1986).

STREETER, L. A., J. M. ACKROFF, and G. A. TAYLOR, "On Abbreviating Command Names," *Bell System Technical Journal,* 62, no. 6, Part 3, (1983), pp. 1807–28, ACM.

WHITESIDE, JOHN, and others, "User Performance with Command, Menu, and Iconic Interfaces," *Proceedings, CHI'85,* 1985, pp. 185–91, ACM.

WIXON, DENNIS, and others, "Building a User-Defined Interface," *CHI '83 Proceedings,* December 1983, pp. 24–27, ACM.

CHAPTER 8 _____

Dialog Styles:
Function Keys

WHAT IS A FUNCTION KEY INTERFACE?

In a **function key** interface, commands and sometimes objects are specified by pressing special keys on the keyboard, rather than by typing them in (as in command language or natural language interfaces) or by selecting them from a menu (as in menu or direct manipulation interfaces). Note the example in Figure 8-1. In a function key-driven word processor, the screen is dedicated to the display of a document, and the keyboard includes **dedicated function keys** for the different word processing commands such as "Insert," "Delete," "Indent," "Center," "Move," and "Copy."

To execute a command, the user presses a function key and indicates parameters by selecting areas of text to operate on or by answering questions in a dialog on the screen. In this example, function keys are *dedicated* to particular commands. That is, labels are etched on the key surface, and keys do not take on different labels or meanings in different contexts. Sometimes, however, keys are pressed in combination to change their meaning.

For instance, the shift key in combination with function keys might change their meaning. Perhaps the "Copy" key is used to copy text *within* a document, and the "Shift/Copy" keys are used to copy text *across* documents. Or, worse, but just as common, perhaps the control or command keys are used in combination with arbitrary function keys to make additional commands accessible. For exam-

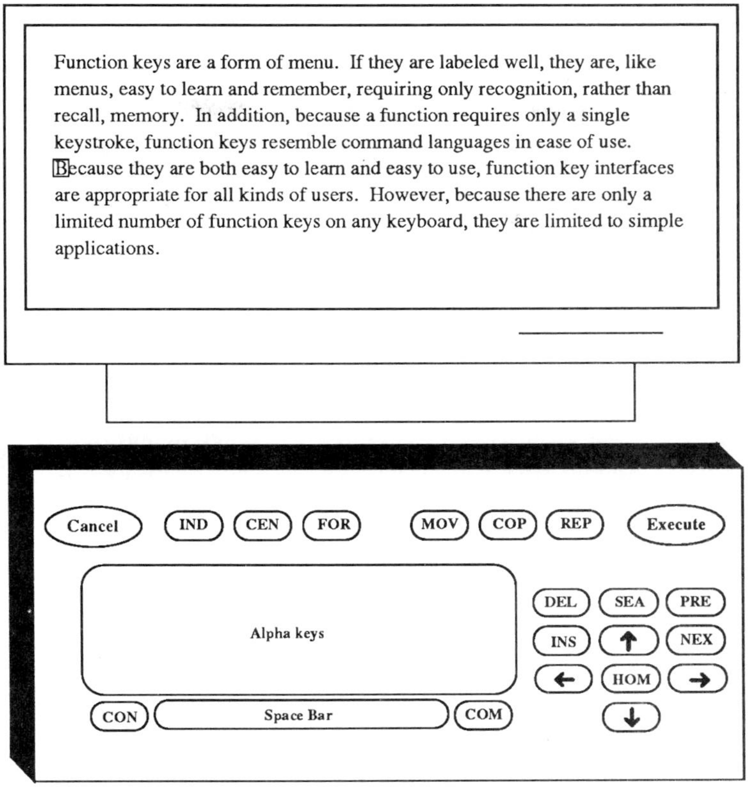
Function keys are a form of menu. If they are labeled well, they are, like menus, easy to learn and remember, requiring only recognition, rather than recall, memory. In addition, because a function requires only a single keystroke, function keys resemble command languages in ease of use. Because they are both easy to learn and easy to use, function key interfaces are appropriate for all kinds of users. However, because there are only a limited number of function keys on any keyboard, they are limited to simple applications.
Cancel
IND
CEN
FOR
MOV
COP
REP
Execute
Alpha keys
DEL
SEA
PRE
INS
NEX
HOM
CON
Space Bar
COM

Figure 8–1 Example of a dedicated function key interface.

ple, the control–format keys might be used to enter a page break, because there is no dedicated key for page break.

An alternative approach to a function key interface is illustrated in Figure 8-2. Here function keys on the keyboard are labeled with generic identifiers, usually numbers. **Soft function key** labels are presented on the screen, giving the command names for the function keys. The screen labels and function key labels may be related simply by spatial location, as in Figure 8-2, or the screen labels might include the function key number or label as well as the command name. For instance, on the screen the label "PF1: UNDO" might appear, instead of just "UNDO."

The advantage of soft keys on the screen is that the labels can change. That is, the function keys can take on different meanings depending on the current context on the screen, but appropriate, recognizable labels will always appear. Thus many more commands can be made easily available than with dedicated function keys.

This works well as long as enough keys are available to provide all possible

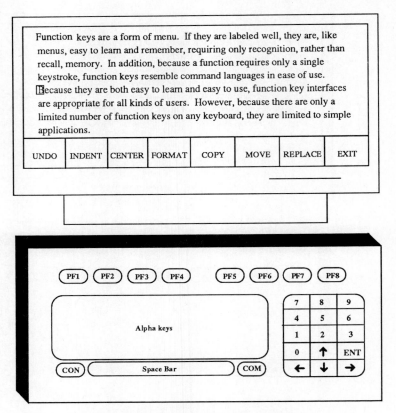

Figure 8–2 Example of a soft function key interface.

commands at any given point in the dialog. However, if more commands must be made accessible than can be fit on the number of available function keys and their soft labels, two solutions are possible: (1) function keys can be doubled up using qualifier keys such as "Shift," "Control," and "Command," or (2) a menu structure can be imposed on the soft keys on the screen, requiring the user to step through a few menu levels to get to the desired command. At this point we have **soft function key menus,** a kind of hybrid dialog style: part function key interface and part menu interface.

WHEN IS A FUNCTION KEY DIALOG STYLE APPROPRIATE?

Function key interfaces have particular advantages and disadvantages, relative to other dialog styles. *Advantages* include the following:

Self-explanatory. Well-designed function key interfaces make a system easy to learn because they make both the semantics and the syntax of the system explicit. That is, they make clear both *what* can be done (semantics) and *how* to do it (syntax).

Clear key labels (on the key or on the screen) are like a menu of commands. Good prompting for parameters helps users know what parameters are possible and how to express them. A well-designed function key interface can thus provide users with most of what they need to know to correctly accomplish their goals. Because the interface is relatively self-explanatory, the learning burden is decreased and the need for manuals and training programs is reduced. Contrast this with a command language interface, which gives no semantic or syntactic prompting and requires the user to know what can be done and how to do it.

Some ease of learning is sacrificed in a *dedicated function key* approach when doubling up of keys is required to provide all necessary functions, especially if the key combinations are not mnemonic or rule based.

Requires little human memory. For the same reason that function key interfaces are easy to learn, they are also easy to remember. Casual users who may not use a system frequently run the risk of forgetting how to use it between uses. Because a function key interface is potentially self-explanatory, it is not necessary to memorize and retain semantic or syntactic knowledge. Function key interfaces rely mostly on *recognition memory* rather than *recall memory*. The user need only recognize the function key labels and prompts and does not have to recall (without cues) what commands are possible, what parameters are valid, or how to format them. Recognition memory is faster and more accurate than recall memory, and function key interfaces exploit this fact.

Again, some ease of remembering is sacrificed in a *dedicated function key* approach when doubling up of keys is required to provide all necessary functions, especially if the key combinations are not mnemonic or rule based.

Easy to use. *Dedicated function keys* and nonmenued *soft function keys* provide the ultimate in ease of use. A single keystroke issues a command. This is certainly faster than typing in a command name (as in a command language or natural language interface) and is even faster than keyboard-driven menu selection, which might involve several keystrokes for cursor movement or two keystrokes to enter a code and a terminator key. Some ease of use is sacrificed in a *soft function key menus* approach because some commands require multiple keystrokes. And a certain amount of mental translation is required in *soft function key* interfaces to determine what physical key is appropriate based on soft labels on the screen. This is much more direct with *dedicated functions keys,* where the meaningful labels are directly on the keys themselves.

Flexible. Function keys do not impose any particular sequence of use on users. They can be used in any order. Thus, they support unstructured tasks relatively well. The flip side of this advantage, however, is that they do not provide structure for users low in task and system knowledge in the way that a menu or fill-in form interface would.

Requires little or no screen "real estate". A *dedicated function key* interface requires no screen space at all, except possibly part of one line for parameter prompting. A *soft function key* or *soft function key menus* approach requires only one or a few lines on the screen for label display. This leaves most of the screen available for whatever else should or must be displayed. This is in contrast to full screen menus or fill-in forms, which take up considerable space on the screen. Thus, when screen "real estate" is at a premium, function keys provide an important advantage over some other dialog styles.

Low typing requirements. Pressing a single key to issue a command is not only faster than typing in a command name, even for touch typists, it also presents less opportunity for user error. Less keystrokes generally mean less errors.

In summary, the main advantages of function key interfaces are that, unlike most other dialog styles, they are both easy to learn *and* easy to use. All function key interfaces do involve trade-offs, however. *Disadvantages* of function key interfaces include the following:

Limited number of keys available. A *dedicated function key* approach is ideal in that it does not take up much or any screen space and is both easy to learn and use. However, only a certain number of function keys can exist on a keyboard before it becomes unwieldy and difficult to use. Thus, the *dedicated function key* approach is appropriate *only* if functionality is very limited. When functionality is rich, two alternatives are possible: (1) doubling up keys to provide additional functions, or (2) going to a *soft function key* approach. The former sacrifices ease of learning and ease of use, and the latter takes up screen space. If functionality is so rich that a *soft function key menus* approach is necessary to provide all functions, then ease of use is sacrificed. Thus, the limited number of available keys forces the designer to make certain trade-offs on any system that is at all rich in functionality.

Hardware approaches to expansion are expensive. When *dedicated function key* systems are enhanced with additional functionality, then two alternatives are possible: doubling up keys or redesigning the keyboard with more keys or new labels. The former solution usually results in an interface that is less easy to learn and use. However, the latter solution, designing and manufacturing new keyboards, can be very expensive, especially considering that many systems may need to be upgraded more than once during the life of the product.

Software approaches to expansion sacrifice screen space efficiency and ease of use. Soft function key interfaces accommodate the expansion of functionality without requiring hardware changes. However, they take up more screen space than dedicated function keys. *Soft function key menus* sacrifice ease of use, as some functions will require multiple keystrokes.

       Makes keyboard system or application specific. *Dedicated function key* interfaces mean that a keyboard is designed to optimally support a specific application or system. If users wish to run other software on a workstation, the function key labels on the keyboard will no longer be meaningful; so ease of learning and remembering is sacrificed on other applications or systems that employ the function keys. A *soft function key* approach avoids this problem, but has disadvantages of its own, as discussed previously.

       In sum, the variations to a function key approach differ slightly in how well they achieve the potential benefits and suffer from the potential drawbacks. The *dedicated function key* approach is both easy to learn and use, but only if functionality is simple enough so that doubling up of keys is not required. Doubling up of keys reduces both ease of learning and ease of use. This approach has the added advantage, however, of requiring minimal screen space.

       The *soft function keys* approach accommodates somewhat richer functionality without sacrificing ease of learning or use, but it takes up more screen space than a dedicated function key approach. If all functions can be presented in a nonmenued soft function key interface (but cannot be accommodated by dedicated function keys) and screen space is not at a premium, then this approach is ideal.

       Finally, the *soft function key menus* approach accommodates very rich functionality while maintaining ease of learning, but does so at the expense of ease of use and screen real estate relative to *dedicated function keys*.

       Given these relative advantages and disadvantages, we can draw some conclusions about the kinds of tasks and users for which function key interfaces might be appropriate as a primary dialog style. Figure 8-3 lists the user characteristics (see Chapter 2) for which a function key dialog style would be a good choice.

       Because function key interfaces are potentially both easy to learn and easy to use, they support a wide variety of users. The ease of learning means that function keys are appropriate for discretionary users with negative attitudes, low motivation, moderate levels of semantic and syntactic knowledge, low frequency of use, and little or no training. However, because function key interfaces are easy to use, they are also appropriate for mandatory users with positive attitudes, high motivation, high levels of semantic and syntactic knowledge, and high frequency of use. Function keys provide little structure to the dialog, so a moderate amount of task, application, and computer experience is prerequisite.

       Because of the limited number of available function keys on a keyboard, function key interfaces can only provide both ease of learning and ease of use for systems with a very limited task domain, that is, limited functionality. *Soft function keys* maintain ease of learning and ease of use for systems with moderate functionality, but screen real estate is required, and enhancements will inevitably drive

Function key interfaces are most appropriate for users with:

☞ **User psychology**

> Negative to positive attitude
> Low to high motivation

☞ **Knowledge and experience**

> Low typing skill
> Low to high system experience
> Moderate to high task experience
> Moderate application experience
> Low to high use of other systems
> Moderate to high computer literacy

☞ **Job and task characteristics**

> Low to high frequency of use
> Little or no training
> Discretionary use
> Low to high turnover rate
> Low to high task importance
> Low task structure
> Limited task domain

Figure 8–3   When to use function key interfaces.

the system to a *soft function key menus* approach. To accommodate rich functionality, a function key interface must sacrifice either ease of use (*soft function key menus*) or ease of learning and ease of use (doubling up keys).

DESIGNING FUNCTION KEY INTERFACES: EXPERIMENTAL RESULTS

Little, if any, research has been conducted to date that directly studies user performance with function key interfaces. The available guidelines are thus based on basic research in cognition and human factors and aspects of the design that are analogous to those of other dialog styles that have been studied. For instance, research findings on grouping menu options from the menu literature can be applied to the placement of function keys. Studies documenting the value of consistency in menu and command language design probably can be applied to certain aspects of designing function key interfaces.

The reader is refered to the Experimental Results sections of Chapters 4 through 7 for a review of relevant although indirect literature. Some of the few available studies more directly relevant to function key design are discussed next.

One important issue in function key design is label design. Studies from the literature on abbreviations (see Ehrenreich, 1985, for a review) have consistently found that the rank ordering of (that is, the relative performance on) different abbreviation rules differs depending on whether the test task is an *encoding* task (abbreviations must be generated from full names) or a *decoding* task (full names must be recognized from abbreviations). Thus it appears that one abbreviation rule may be best when *recalling* and entering commands and another when *recognizing*, for example, function key labels.

There is suggestive (though not conclusive) evidence (Streeter, Acknoff, and Taylor, 1983; Grudin and Barnard, 1984; Hirsch-Pasek, Nudelman, and Schneider, 1982) that names are more recognizable from abbreviations that are derived from phonetic and vowel deletion rules than from abbreviations derived from truncation rules. For instance, although it may be easier to *recall* "Sea" from "Search" and "Ret" from "Return," it may in fact be easier to *recognize* "Search" from "Srch" and "Return" from "Rtrn." One of these studies is reported next.

Hirsch-Pasek, Nudelman, and Schneider (1982) compared abbreviations based on five different rules: (1) truncation with consistent number of letters, (2) truncation with minimum letters to distinguish, (3) phonetic, (4) vowel deletion, and (5) user generated. Subjects first studied a set of name–abbreviation pairs and then were given an *encoding* task. If they could not correctly recall at least 85% of the abbreviations, they were given another study–test cycle. The study–test cycle was repeated as many times for each subject as was necessary to get performance above 85% correct recall. It was found that it took singificantly less study–test cycles to learn consistent truncation rule abbreviations to criterion than any other type of abbreviation.

Following this *encoding* task, subjects were given a *decoding* test with the same set of names and abbreviations. Here they had to recognize the name from the abbreviation. In this test, the vowel deletion and phonetic abbreviation rules produced the best performance. It is possible that this finding was due to the fact that subjects using these rules performed better simply because they had more study trials on the name–abbreviation pairs during the *encoding* task. Thus the study is not conclusive, but it does suggest that vowel deletion and phonetic rules may facilitate decoding relative to other rules.

An important issue in the design of *soft function key* interfaces is the spatial layout of soft key labels on the screen. One study (Bayerl, Millen, and Lewis, 1988) looked at the spatial layout of soft key labels as a function of the keyboard layout of corresponding function keys. Six conditions were compared, as follows:

1. Screen labels (F1 to F8 plus function names) horizontal at the bottom of screen; keys (labeled F1 to F8) horizontal at the top of the keyboard.
2. Screen labels in a matrix (2 by 4) at the left and bottom of the screen; keys in a matrix at the left and bottom of the keyboard.

3. Screen labels horizontal at the bottom of the screen; keys in a matrix at the left and bottom of the keyboard.

4. Screen labels in a matrix at the left and bottom of the screen; keys horizontal at the top of the keyboard.

5. Screen labels in a column at the center and bottom of the screen; keys in a matrix at the left and bottom of the keyboard.

6. Screen labels in a column at the center and bottom of the screen; keys horizontal at the top of the keyboard.

The two key layouts (horizontal row and matrix) are the two found most commonly on current keyboards. Note that in the first two conditions the spatial layout of soft labels is *consistent* with the layout of keys on the keyboard, whereas in the last four conditions the spatial layout of labels is *inconsistent* with the layout of keys on the keyboard.

Thirty-six subjects with varying levels and types of computer and keyboard experience participated in the study. Each subject used all six label–key combinations in different orders. Their task was to press three function keys appropriately in response to prompting by their soft labels. In each condition, subjects performed 40 such tasks. Time, error, and preference data were collected.

The different conditions did not produce reliable differences in error rates, but did produce significant effects in the time and preference data. Significant results were as follows.

Overall, the horizontal layout of function keys on the keyboard produced faster performance than the matrix layout. Overall, the centered column of soft key labels produced worse performance than did the horizontal or matrix layouts of soft key labels, but these latter did not differ significantly from each other in speed of input.

The two conditions in which the soft label layout was *consistent* with key layout (conditions 1 and 2) produced faster performance (by about one-quarter of a second per keystroke) than any of the conditions with *inconsistent* layouts (conditions 3 to 6). The fastest condition of all was the horizontal layout of both labels and keys (about one-twentieth of a second faster than the consistent matrix layout, and about one-quarter to one-third of a second faster than any of the inconsistent layouts).

Fifty-six percent of the subjects expressed a preference for the horizontal layout of keys, and 80% preferred a consistent layout of keys and labels to an inconsistent layout.

Although the performance differences are small, they could add up quickly with frequent use, and the preference data suggest that the difference is perceivable by users. Thus, it seems safe to conclude that, when designers have the option, horizontal layouts of keys and labels should be designed, but at least an attempt to match screen layout of labels to keyboard layout of keys is desirable.

Findings from another study (Walker and Olson, 1988) suggest the importance of consistency in another context. The authors redesigned the assignment of qualifier keys (for example, "Cntrl," "Esc," and "Alt") to alpha keys in a system that allowed such key pairs as a shortcut to menu selection of functions. Key combinations for 56 of 90 functions were redesigned. In the original system, key combinations were formed from arbitrary assignments of the three qualifier keys to a fairly arbitrary assignment of alpha keys. In the redesigned system, rules for assigning both qualifier and alpha keys were consistently followed.

The rules for assigning qualifier keys in this multimedia editor were as follows:

> The Esc key was used for all *system* related commands, e.g., **Esc S** for *lsave file:*

> The Alt key was used for all *deletions,* e.g., **Alt BW** for *delete backword a word;*

> The Control key was used for all *other* types of actions.

The rule for assigning alpha keys was to use two letters, each the first letter of words that described the specifics of the function in an adverb–object order. Thus, the whole command string had a consistent syntax of verb–adverb–object. Verbs were indicated by qualifier keys, and adverbs and objects were indicated by first letter abbreviations. For example, the function "delete back a word" would be expressed as "Alt BW." A comparison of some of the delete commands in the original and redesigned systems will illustrate the lack of a rule-based syntax in the former and the presence of such a syntax in the latter:

Function	Original	Redesigned
Delete forward a character	Cnt D	Alt FC
Delete forward a word	Esc D	Alt FW
Delete forward a line	Cnt K	Alt FL
Delete forward a paragraph	Esc K	Alt FP

Subjects were given a list of function and key assignment pairs for one design or the other. Unlike in the example, function *descriptions* were carefully designed to *obscure* the mnemonic, rule-based nature of the redesigned assignments. However, the functions were *organized* as in the preceding to reveal the semantic relationships among commands. After a number of study–test trials, subjects were presented with functions in a *random* order and were asked to recall key assignments. Forty subjects participated. Most had at least some computer experience but none were familiar with the original system.

Subjects correctly recalled over *twice* as many key assignments in the redesigned system as compared to the original. The authors concluded that in spite of the extra keystrokes involved in the redesigned system (two alpha keys rather than one for every function), the time saved referring back to manuals and making errors would probably heavily outweigh the extra keying time. It was the rule-based nature of the redesigned key assignments, they argued, that resulted in improved learning and recall.

Although in this study alpha keys rather than function keys were used in combination with qualifier keys, it seems likely that these results will generalize somewhat to a system in which qualifier keys are used in conjunction with function keys to provide increased functions. However, it is not clear from this study how much the rules for qualifier keys and the rules for mnemonic alpha keys respectively contributed to the ease of learning. Function assignment based on qualifier keys plus function keys labeled with *numbers or unrelated names* may not contribute *as much* to the overall mnemonic nature of key combinations as did mnemonic alpha keys. But *some* systematic assignment of qualifier keys and function keys will undoubtedly provide a performance advantage over arbitrary assignments. Examples of rule-based assignments of both qualifier and function keys are given in the following section.

DESIGNING FUNCTION KEY INTERFACES: PRINCIPLES AND GUIDELINES

☞ **Provide enough function keys to support functionality, but not so many that scanning and finding are difficult.**

Figure 8-4 presents two examples of a keyboard with *dedicated function keys*. The "Poor" version has too many, all crowded together. This keyboard will be difficult to learn and use. By contrast, the "Improved" version has a moderate number of function keys. This makes it possible to use grouping and white space to facilitate scanning and finding function keys. This keyboard will be much easier to use.

When designing a keyboard with *dedicated function keys,* the designer must strike a balance between providing a dedicated function key for every major, frequently used command available on the system and avoiding an overcrowded keyboard that will be difficult to use. Doubling up function keys for some commands (for example, "Shift/Copy") is one way to keep function keys to a minimum, but usually this results in unmnemonic key sequences that are difficult to learn and remember.

One approach to facilitating learning and memory on a *dedicated function key* system that adds qualifier keys to increase functions is to provide *color coded multiple labels* on each key. Qualifier key labels are color coded correspondingly. For example, the "Shift," "Alt," and "Control" keys might be labeled in red,

Poor:

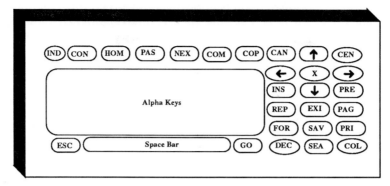

Improved:

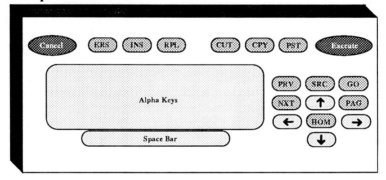

Figure 8–4   Poor and improved function key design.

blue, and green. Each dedicated function key would have three labels, one each in red, blue, and green. This would notify the user that "Shift" in combination with the key would provide the red function, "Alt" in combination with the key would provide the blue function, and so on. Although users have to do a little visual searching to figure out the appropriate key combination for a given function, recall memory is kept at a minimum.

Soft function keys are another approach. They allow more commands to be made available through a few function keys without sacrificing ease of learning, as the key labels appear on the screen and change with context.

☞ **Reserve the use of function keys for generic, high-frequency, important functions.**

Even in systems that have other primary dialog styles (for example, command languages, fill-in forms, and even direct manipulation), function keys can provide added ease of use for universal functions that are likely to be frequently used across a range of applications and functions whose importance merits additional ease of use. In systems very rich in functionality, the limited number of available function keys should be reserved for functions with these characteristics.

When functions are expected to be generic and universal across applications, then *dedicated function keys,* with permanent labels etched on keytops, are appropriate. Candidates are "Page forward," "Page backward," "Print," "Help," "Escape," "Cancel," "Undo," "Execute," "Enter," and the like (Brown, 1988).

Soft function keys should be employed even in systems with other primary dialog styles for functions that (1) are generic across screens and subsystems, (2) will be frequently used, or (3) are of particular importance (for example, for safety or security functions). These three characteristics suggest a need for ease of use, which function keys provide.

☞ **Arrange in groups of three or four based on semantic relationships.**

Note in the "Poor" keyboard in Figure 8-4 that not only are there too many keys, but they are not organized into any kind of meaningful groups. This contributes to the difficulty of finding a desired key.

In contrast, the "Improved" keyboard organizes keys into logical, meaningful groups. *Navigation* keys all appear in a cluster in the lower right. *Editing* keys appear in two groups across the top of the keyboard: basic editing commands ("Erase," "Insert," and "Replace") and more powerful editing commands ("Cut," "Copy," and "Paste"). The two *control* keys "Execute" and "Cancel" stand out due to their location at opposite ends of the keyboard. Arranging function keys in semantic groups like these will greatly facilitate learning and remembering the position of desired keys.

☞ **Base groupings on flow of use *rather* than on semantic relationships for high frequency of use.**

Sometimes two or three function keys are commonly used *in sequence*. For instance, perhaps the way to navigate to a particular page in a document in a word processing application requires two function keys and a number key. The sequence might be (1) "Go" key, (2) number key indicating page, (3) "Execute" key. This is likely to be a very commonly executed sequence. Designers need to consider how to facilitate high-frequency key sequences such as this.

Keeping in mind that alternating hands is easier than alternating fingers on the same hand, and certain finger sequences (for example, index finger to middle finger and vice versa) are easier than others (for example, little finger to index finger and vice versa), keys should be placed to facilitate transitions between command keys pressed in sequence.

In this example, it would be best to place the "Go" and "Execute" keys close together and on the same side of the keyboard so that they can be struck by the same hand without much movement, whereas the number key is struck by the other hand. The arrangement of these keys in the ''Improved'' keyboard in Figure 8-4 accomplishes this.

If certain function keys are used in sequence with very high frequency, then placing them according to flow of use should override the goal of placing them in semantically related groups.

☞ **Distinguish groupings by space, size, and color.**

Having organized function keys into logical, semantic groups, these groupings can then be made more distinctive by the use of space, size, and color. Note that in the ''Poor'' keyboard in Figure 8-4, all keys, including alpha and function keys, are the same size and color: white. In addition, no space separates groups of keys.

In contrast, the ''Improved'' keyboard separates key groups by space, size, and color (indicated by shading). For instance, a cluster of keys in the lower right of the keyboard includes only navigation keys. Within this group, the most basic and most frequently used navigation keys, the arrow keys, stand out from other navigation keys due to their different color. The two sets of editing keys, and the two control keys all reside in the top row of the keyboard, but are separated by space, size, and color.

Generally, use neutral colors (like beige or gray) for alpha keys and black, white, and colors for function keys. Use colors with cultural connotations to help communicate key meanings, such as green for the ''Execute'' key and red for the ''Cancel'' key. Use larger keys for more frequently used keys, more generic keys, or keys with serious consequences.

Reinforcing logical, semantic groups of function keys with the cues of space, size, and color will make a keyboard easier to learn and use.

☞ **Label keys clearly and distinctively. Recognizability takes precedence over consistency.**

Key labels should clearly communicate key meanings. Whether key labels appear on the keys themselves or on the screen, there is usually limited space for key labels. Thus, we are often forced to use abbreviations.

Whereas we recommended a simple, consistent rule such as three-letter truncation for command abbreviations in a command language interface, this is clearly *not* the best approach in a function key interface. This is because entering commands in a command language involves generating an abbreviation from a known word, which is an *encoding* task. Finding function keys appropriate to a goal, by contrast, involves recognizing a word from its abbreviation. This is a *decoding* task. Encoding and decoding are different kinds of mental processes. The former involves *recall* memory, while the latter involves *recognition* memory. When tapping recognition memory, the emphasis should be on recognizability. An abbreviation that is easy to recall is not necessarily easy to recognize.

For example, consider the two commands ''Search'' and ''Delete.'' A simple, consistent truncation rule for abbreviations would produce "Sea" and "Del." A simple, consistent vowel deletion rule would produce "Srch" and "Dlt." However, consider which would be more recognizable on a function key. "Srch" is probably more recognizable than "Sea." But "Del" is probably more recognizable that "Dlt." Thus it is recommended that the two function keys be labeled "Srch" and "Del" even though these two abbreviations are inconsistent in length and abbreviation rule. This is because recognizability is more important than recall in a function key interface.

Note in the "Poor" keyboard in Figure 8-4 that a simple truncation abbreviation rule is consistently applied to generate abbreviations for all keys. This results in some difficult to recognize commands, such as "Pas" for "Paste," "Con" for "Control," "Rep" for "Replace,"and "Can" for "Cancel." In the "Improved" keyboard, some abbreviations were formed by truncation and some by vowel deletion ("Pst" for "Paste" and "Rpl" for "Replace"). These abbreviations are easier to recognize.

Other examples can be seen in Figure 8-5. Assume that *dedicated function keys* for the functions from a bibliographic search system can fit two lines of four characters each for labels. In the "Poor" set of labels, a consistent, simple four-letter truncation rule is used to generate labels. However, this results in some difficult to recognize abbreviations, such as "Prin Resu," "Disp Requ," and

Function name	Dedicated F-Key Label Poor:	Improved:	Soft F-Key Assignment Poor:	Improved:
Next page	Next Page	Next Page	F1	F1
Previous page	Prev Page	Prev Page	F2	Shift F1
First page	Firs Page	Frst Page	Shift F4	Control F1
Next document	Nex Docu	Nex Doc	F3	F2
Previous document	Prev Docu	Prev Doc	F4	Shift F2
First document	Firs Docu	Frst Doc	Shift F5	Control F2
Print screen	Prin Scre	Prnt Scrn	Shift F8	F3
Print document	Prin Docu	Prnt Doc	Control F1	Shift F3
Print result	Prin Resu	Prnt Rslt	Control F2	Control F3
Display request	Disp Requ	Disp Rqst	Control R	F4
Display help	Disp Help	Disp Help	Control H	Shift F4
Display time	Disp Time	Disp Time	Control T	Control F4
Format full	Form Full	Form Full	F6	F5
Format short	Form Shor	Form Shrt	F5	Shift F5
Format location	Form Loca	Form Locn	Control F3	Control F5
Select services	Sele Serv	Slct Serv	Shift F6	F6
Exit services	Exit Serv	Exit Serv	Shift F7	Shift F6
Modify request	Edit Requ	Edit Rqst	Control M	F7
Change request	Chan Requ	Chng Rqst	Shift F1	F8
Change drawer	Chan Draw	Chng Drwr	Shift F3	Shift F8
Change cabinet	Chan Cabi	Chng Cbnt	Shift F2	Control F8

Figure 8–5   Poor and improved function key labels.

"Chan Requ." In the "Improved" set of labels, different abbreviation rules are used: sometimes four-character truncation, sometimes three-character truncation, sometimes simple vowel deletion, and sometimes partial vowel deletion. The governing principle in choosing these abbreviations was recognizability, not rule consistency. Whatever abbreviation scheme produced the most recognizable abbreviation was chosen. Thus, for example, "Prnt Rslt," "Disp Rqst," and "Chng Rqst" were chosen as alternatives for the above abbreviations based on their improved recognizability. Recognizability seems to be enhanced by applying a *phonetic* rule: the abbreviation that *sounds* closest to the full name when pronounced is the most recognizable.

Another aspect of recognizability is *distinctiveness*. Labels should be easy to discriminate from one another. For instance, "ON" and "DN" could easily be confused (Smith and Mosier, 1986), as might "ENT" and "END" or even "EXIT" and "EXEC." It is desirable to design command names with distinctive abbreviations. However, when the only way to do so would be to choose less familair command names, this might not be advisable. When distinctiveness must be sacrificed for other aspects of recognizability such as familiarity, confusions between labels that look alike can be minimized by locating them in different areas of the screen and keyboard.

☞ **Place high-use keys within easy reach of home row.**

To facilitate overall throughput and minimize errors, function keys that are frequently used should be easy to reach and easy to return from. Locating them near to the home row of the alpha keys will accomplish this.

For instance, on the "Poor" keyboard in Figure 8-4, the cursor keys are located at the top of the screen. This is a long reach from the home row. There is likely to be a lot of movement between the alpha keys and the cursor control keys, and this keyboard does not support this transition well.

In contrast, the cursor keys on the "Improved" keyboard are located directly to the right of the home row. If there are indicators, such as raised dots or deeper key surfaces on the home row of the alpha keyboard and on the middle row of the cursor keys, a high-frequency user will soon be able to move from alpha keys to cursor keys and back without looking at the keyboard. This will greatly facilitate throughput.

☞ **Place the most frequently used keys *within* function key groups in the most accessible positions.**

Some function keys are laid out in a single row, usually at the top of the keyboard. Others are arranged in a matrix of rows and columns, often to the left of the keyboard. The most accessible (easiest to find) keys *within* these configurations are the end keys in a row of keys and the corner keys in a matrix of keys. Locate higher-frequency functions on these more accessible keys (Brown, 1988).

☞ **Place keys with serious consequences in hard to reach positions.**

An exception to the preceding two guidelines is that even high-use keys should *not* be located near the home row or in other easily accessed locations *if* they have serious destructive consequences. In general, any function key with serious consequences should be located in a relatively difficult to reach position, even if it is frequently used. The rationale for this is that keys that are easy to reach will more often be pressed in error. If the error is easy to recover from, this is not so important. If the error is disastrous, then it is.

For example, keys such as "Cancel" and "Delete" are likely to be frequently used. However, their consequences can be serious, and so they should not be located in a spot where they will be easy to hit by mistake. Notice on the "Poor" keyboard in Figure 8-4 that the "Delete" function, labeled "X", is located right in the center of the cursor control keys. The "Cancel" function, labeled "Can," is also located between two cursor control keys. This would undoubtedly result in frequent errors, many of which might be very difficult to recover from. By contrast, the "Delete" function, labeled as "Ers" (for "Erase"), and the "Cancel" function, labeled as "Cancel" on the "Improved" keyboard, are both positioned in the upper-left corner, where they are much less likely to be hit by accident.

Whenever the previous guidelines (making high-use keys easy to reach) come in conflict with this guideline (making keys with serious consequences hard to reach), this guideline should take precedence.

☞ **Minimize the use of *qualifier* keys (for example, Shift, Alt, Command, Control). Use them consistently when they are necessary.**

When *dedicated function keys* are used, and even sometimes when *soft function keys* are used, it often becomes necessary to double up keys to provide all functions. The *qualifier* keys most commonly used to expand the function key interface to include additional functionality are "Shift," "Control," "Alt," and "Command." The use of these keys should be minimized, because it is often difficult to come up with any scheme for assigning qualifier keys that is at all mnemonic, and so the resulting key sequences are usually difficult to learn and remember. Because they involve multiple keystrokes, they are also less efficient and more error prone than single keystroke commands.

If the qualifier key approach is taken, however, then care should be taken to ensure that only the less frequently used commands are assigned to multiple key sequences and to try to employ some rule or pattern in assigning key combinations to functions so that they are easier to learn and remember.

For example, if an application includes commands to move, copy, and replace data *within* a file, these might be accessed through dedicated function keys labeled "Move," "Copy," and "Replace." Commands that allow the user to move, copy, and replace data *across* files could then be made available through the key sequences "Shift/Move," "Shift/Copy," and "Shift/Replace." Thus a rule has been designed into the key sequences: the "Shift" key *increases the scope* of the command. The "Command" and "Control" keys could be used in other rule-based ways. This will make it easier to remember when to use "Shift," "Control," and "Command."

Figure 8-5 also gives examples of a *soft function key* approach that doubles up keys to provide 21 functions through eight function keys. On the keyboard, keys are labeled F1 through F8. In the "Poor" set of function keys, no particular pattern or governing principle has been employed to assign qualifier keys and function keys to commands. The user must simply rote memorize them or constantly refer to the soft labels on the screen. It will be very difficult to learn them. In the "Improved" set of keys, however, an attempt has been made to associate keys with commands. Each numbered function key is associated with a semantically related set of commands. For instance, all paging commands are accessed through F1, and all print commands through F3.

The use of "Shift" and "Control" is governed by two principles: either relative frequency of use or command scope. For example, it is expected that within paging commands, "Next page" will be *most frequently used,* followed by "previous page," followed by "First page." Thus, "Next page" is simply F1 with no qualifier, "Previous page" takes the "Shift" qualifier, and "First page" takes the "Control" qualifier. Similarly, because "Display request" is expected to be more frequently used than "Display help," which is in turn more frequently used than "Display time," these are assigned F4, "Shift F4," and "Control F4," respectively.

Command scope governs other assignments of qualifier keys. A "request" is made within a "drawer," and a "drawer" is a subset of a "cabinet." Thus, "Change request" is simply F8 with no qualifier, "Change drawer" takes the "Shift" qualifier, and "Change cabinet" takes the "Control" qualifier. Similarly, a "screen" is a subset of a "document," which is a subset of a "result." Thus, printing these three units of data is assigned to "F3," "Shift F3," and "Control F3," respectively.

Although these rules are not intuitively obvious and there is in fact more than one simple rule, once the user perceives them (or reads about them in a manual), it will be easier to memorize correct function key sequences in this "Improved" set than in the "Poor" set. And care has been taken to ensure that the most frequently used commands are single keystroke functions (no qualifier keys) and that the next most frequently used commands take the "shift" rather than the "control" qualifier key, because it is more familiar. This will help keep keystrokes and errors to a minimum.

Note that the sample rules in the preceding examples for consistently combining qualifier keys with function keys follow the principle of *hierarchicalness* (Carroll, 1982) discussed in Chapter 7.

☞ **Preserve spatial relationships between soft function key labels on the screen and generic function keys on the keyboard. A horizontal layout is preferred.**

If function keys on the keyboard are laid out in a horizontal row, lay out soft labels on the screen in a horizontal row. If, on the other hand, function keys on the keyboard are laid out in a matrix to the right or left of the keyboard, lay out soft labels in a matrix to the right or left of the screen, respectively. *Consistent* spatial layout of keys and labels is most important. Whenever possible, a horizontal layout of both keys and labels is preferable. Evidence suggests faster performance on a horizontal layout (Bayerl, Millen, and Lewis, 1988).

Observe the layout of horizontal *soft function key* labels in Figure 8-6. Even though the horizontal layout is consistent with the horizontal layout of the keys on the keyboard, the *order* of key numbers on the screen bears no relationship to the *order* of key numbers on the keyboard. In addition, shifted functions are indicated on the screen by an up arrow before the key number and take up a space in the key

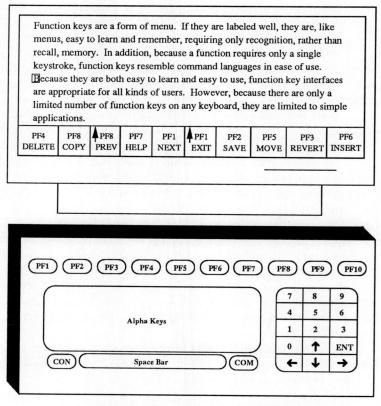

Figure 8–6   Poor soft function key assignments.

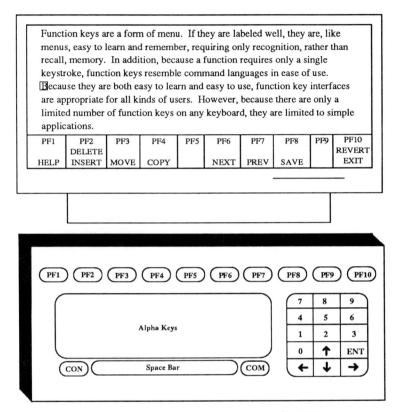

Function keys are a form of menu. If they are labeled well, they are, like menus, easy to learn and remember, requiring only recognition, rather than recall, memory. In addition, because a function requires only a single keystroke, function keys resemble command languages in ease of use. Because they are both easy to learn and easy to use, function key interfaces are appropriate for all kinds of users. However, because there are only a limited number of function keys on any keyboard, they are limited to simple applications.

PF1	PF2 DELETE	PF3	PF4	PF5	PF6	PF7	PF8	PF9	PF10 REVERT
HELP	INSERT	MOVE	COPY		NEXT	PREV	SAVE		EXIT

Figure 8–7 Improved soft function key assignments.

layout just as nonshifted functions do. This will make it hard to find the key on the keyboard after reading the number of the key from the screen.

By contrast, note how *soft function key* labels are organized in Figure 8-7. They appear in the same order as function keys on the keyboard. Thus, the relative location of labels on the screen corresponds perfectly to the relative location of corresponding keys on the keyboard.

In addition, shifted function labels appear above nonshifted function labels within a given soft label, just as they do on most keyboards. They do not take up a unique spot on the label layout. This preserves the spatial relationship between keys and labels and taps an already familiar convention for indicating shifted functions (that is, labels for shifted characters on the number and punctuation keys are located above unshifted labels). It will be much easier to match labels on the screen with keys on the keyboard with this design. Less searching and eye movement between the screen and the keyboard are required, and key assignments will be learned more quickly.

Also note that shifted keys have been used for some functions even though unshifted keys are available. This was purposefully done to make dangerous functions ("Delete" and "Revert") a little harder to access by mistake. Finally, note that there is some semantic grouping of key labels in this layout. The generic commands "Help" and "Exit," which are always present, always appear at the ends of the function key row. Edit commands are clustered together ("Insert," "Delete," "Move," and "Copy"), as are navigation commands ("Next" and "Prev"). "Save" is near to "Exit" because they are related, but not immediately adjacent so that "Exit" will not be accidentally hit when "Save" is intended.

☞ **Be consistent in function key assignments across screens, subsystems, and related products.**

In *soft function key* systems, where soft labels may change from screen to screen, it is very important to consistently locate common, recurring functions. For instance, functions like "quit" and "help" should always be assigned to the same key, regardless of what other labels vary from screen to screen. Inconsistent location of common functions will introduce errors.

Similarly, on both *soft function key* and *dedicated function key* interfaces, changing key locations of common functions across related products used by the same users will cause persistent errors and should be avoided if at all possible. Several unpublished studies have documented the occurrence of errors when such inconsistencies are introduced.

On *soft function key* systems, *related* functions on different screens should be assigned to the same key (Smith and Mosier, 1986). For example, if one screen has an "Undo" function that reverses simple edits, another screen has a "Revert" function that reverts to the last saved version, and a third screen has a "Clear" function that clears fill-in fields, these three related functions should be assigned to the same key on the different screens. Even though function names are specific to the context, users will learn to associate the *generic* meaning with the physical key, and this will speed learning and finding.

Conversely, *avoid* assigning functions with highly *dissimilar* functions to the *same* key when possible. For example, do not have the same key provide a "Clear" function on one screen and a "Fill" function on another. This will produce persistent errors in use.

☞ **Provide feedback when function keys are pressed.**

Often, pressing a function key naturally results in some change in system state with corresponding changes to the screen. For instance, when the "Delete" key is pressed, things disappear, when the "GoTo" key is pressed, the display changes, and when "Help" is pressed, a new window appears.

In other cases, pressing a function key does not cause any clear, visible result. For instance, the "Save" key may not cause any activity or change on the screen. Pressing a "Repaginate" or "Copy to Clipboard" key may also not provide any inherent feedback.

There should *always* be some feedback in response to a function key press, so when feedback does not occur as a *natural* result of the function invoked, the interface should provide it somehow. For instance, if the "Save" key is a dedicated function key, a message should appear on the screen providing a confirmation of the save, such as "DOCA saved in FOLDERXYZ." Pressing the "Copy to Clipboard" key could result in an indication on the screen that the clipboard currently contains a clipping. Pressing the "Repaginate" key could result in a counter that is updated as each new page break is created during the process.

When function keys have soft labels on the screen, pressing the key on the keyboard could result in the soft label highlighting or going into reverse video until the operation is complete.

☞ **Gray out or delete labels of currently inactive keys.**

In a *soft function key* system, key labels on the screen may change as context changes. Sometimes most labels stay the same, but some change or become temporarily inactive. Temporarily inactive keys should have their soft labels either grayed out (preferred) or deleted (if graying out is not possible) to indicate that they are currently inactive. Displaying them normally may lead users to assume that they are active, and induce errors. For example, when no data have been entered in a fill-in form, the "Clear" function key label should be grayed out or deleted. Similarly, when the screen contents are not printable, the "Print" key label should be disabled.

Conversely, *all* currently active function keys should *always* have their labels displayed. However, in a system that uses *both dedicated* and *soft function keys,* dedicated function key labels (for example, "Enter," "Tab") do not need to be redundantly displayed on the screen.

☞ **Provide a status indicator on mode keys.**

Some keyboards have mode keys such as "Caps Lock," "Auto Underline," and "Num Lock." The problem with modes is that users must remember which mode they are in. If they are looking at the screen as they enter data, this may not be a problem. If they are looking at a source document or the keyboard, however, they may erroneously enter a great deal of data without noticing that they are in the wrong mode. Thus it is useful to provide mode indicators in other locations besides the screen. One way to do this is to provide an indicator on the mode key itself, such as a little red light that goes on in one mode and off in the other.

REFERENCES

BAYERL, JEANNE P., DAVID R. MILLEN, and STEVEN H. LEWIS, "Consistent Layout of Function Keys and Screen Labels Speeds User Responses," *Proceedings of the Human Factors Society 32nd Annual Meeting,* 1988, pp. 344–46.

BROWN, C. MARLIN, *Human–Computer Interface Design Guidelines* (Norwood, N.J.: Ablex Publishing Corporation, 1988), pp. 79–92.

CARROLL, JOHN M., "Learning, Using and Designing Filenames and Command Paradigms," *Behavior & Information Technology,* 1, no. 4 (1982), pp. 327–46.

GRUDIN, JONATHAN, and PHIL BARNARD, "The Role of Prior Task Experience in Command Name Abbreviation," *Proceedings, Interact '84,* 1, (September 1984), pp. 439–43.

EHRENREICH, S. L., "Computer Abbreviations: Evidence and Synthesis," *Human Factors,* 27, no. 2 (April 1985), pp. 143–56.

HIRSCH-PASEK, K., S. NUDELMAN, and M. L. SCHNEIDER, "An Experimental Evaluation of Abbreviation Schemes in Limited Lexicons," *Behavior & Information Technology,* 1 (1982), pp. 359–69.

SMITH, S. L., and J. N. MOSIER, "Design Guidelines for User–System Interface Software," *Technical Report ESD-TR-84-190,* (Bedford, Mass.: Mitre Corp., September 1986).

STREETER, L. A., J. M. ACKROFF, and G. A. TAYLOR, "On Abbreviating Command Names," *Bell System Technical Journal,* 62, no. 6, Part 3 (1983), pp. 1807–28, ACM.

WALKER, NEFF, and JUDITH REITMAN OLSON, "Designing Keybindings to Be Easy to Learn and Resistant to Forgetting Even When the Set of Commands Is Large," *CHI '88 Proceedings,* May 1988, pp. 201–206, ACM.

CHAPTER 9

Dialog Styles: Direct Manipulation

WHAT IS A DIRECT MANIPULATION INTERFACE?

Generally, a direct manipulation interface is one in which users *perform actions directly on visible objects*. This is in contrast to interfaces in which users *indirectly specify actions, parameters, and objects* through language (for example, command language or menu interfaces). The term direct manipulation was first coined by Shneiderman (1982, 1983) to describe new interfaces having the following characteristics:

1. Continuous representation of objects
2. Physical actions or labeled button presses in place of command language
3. Rapid incremental reversible operations with immediately visible results

Sometimes called "point-and-select" interfaces, direct manipulation interfaces often include a pointing device such as a mouse, trackball, or touch screen and often make heavy use of graphics in displaying objects and actions.

Some direct manipulation interfaces, however, do not involve graphics and pointing devices. For example, contrast old-fashioned text editors with modern word processors. In a text editor, text is moved in a very indirect way through a command language. For instance, the user might enter a command string invoking the "move" command, specifying the text to be moved by a line number and a character string and specifying the destination by some number of characters or lines, forward or backward, to move the text to. Then the user can ask for verification by asking to see a listing of the lines from which the text has been taken and the lines to which the text has been moved. Both action and verification are indirect, accomplished through language.

By contrast, many modern word processors allow the user to "point" (using the traditional cursor keys) to the text to be moved in context, select a "move" command from a menu or function key, and "point" directly to the character position, in context, where the text should be inserted. The user watches as the text from which the string was removed closes up and is reformatted and the text in which the string is inserted opens up and is reformatted. Verification is automatic and occurs during operation. This is a much more direct procedure. Many modern word processors are properly called direct manipulation word processors, even though they do not involve graphics, windows, or pointing devices, because they have this quality of point-and-select interaction.

Figure 9-1 gives an example of a direct manipulation interface to a filing application. In a command language interface, a *nondirect manipulation* interface, a user would open a file by, for example, invoking an "open" command and specifying a "volume," "library," and file by name. A file might be deleted by

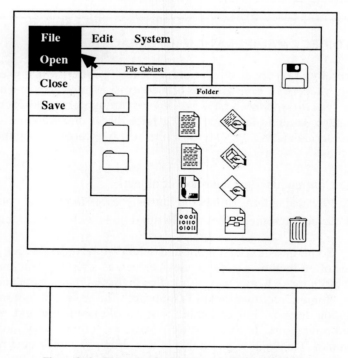

Figure 9–1 Example of a direct manipulation interface.

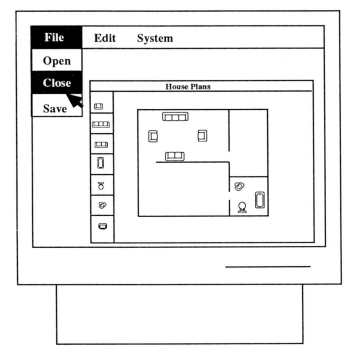

Figure 9–2   Example of a direct manipulation interface.

invoking a "delete" command, again followed by a full specification of the file name.

Figure 9-1, on the other hand, shows a direct manipulation interface to filing. Users open "file cabinets" (disks) by pointing to the desired one with a pointing device (for example, a mouse) and then pointing to the "open" command in the menu. A file cabinet window opens up, displaying the contents of the file cabinet: several folders. The desired folder is opened in the same way, displaying its contents: several documents. The desired document can be opened in the same way, or it can be literally "dragged" (using the pointing device) to the trash can to delete it. Users *directly manipulate* the objects displayed on the screen in ways analogous to the way they manipulate similar objects in space in the manual world to accomplish their goals.

Another example is provided in Figure 9-2. This is an interior design application. A layout or floor plan for one floor of a building is displayed on the screen in a window. On the side of the window is a "palette" of furnishings, including chairs, couches, bathroom fixtures, and so on. The user can select these objects, deposit them in a room on the floor plan, and then move them around at will by dragging them with a pointing device. This will clearly be much more direct and natural, and more efficient and error free, than typing in the names of furnishing objects and specifying room names and x and y coordinates for their destination. In a way, direct manipulation means that, instead of "saying it," users simply "do it."

Notice in the preceding examples that some aspects seem more "direct" than others. For instance, moving an object by dragging it across the screen seems more direct than opening an object by selecting an "open" command from a menu. In fact, there is probably no such thing as a *pure* direct manipulation interface. Instead, direct manipulation might better be thought of as a *quality* that is present to different degrees in different interfaces.

Various descriptions and definitions of direct manipulation have been put forth. Perhaps the most comprehensive definition and discussion of direct manipulation is offered in Hutchins, Hollan, and Norman (1986). This definition may be summarized as follows.

There are two aspects of directness, *distance* and *engagement*. Hutchins and coauthors suggest first that "The systems that best exemplify Direct Manipulation all give us the qualitative feeling that we are directly *engaged* with control of the objects—not with the programs, not with the computer, but with the semantic objects of our goals and intentions" (italics mine). They then go on to state that "Direct Engagement occurs when a user experiences direct interactions with the objects in a domain. Here, there is a feeling of involvement directly with a world of objects rather than of communications with an intermediary." They point out that interfaces generally fall into two categories based on directness of engagement: *interfaces as conversation* (for example, command language, natural language, and fill-in forms) and *interfaces as model worlds* (direct manipulation). The latter provide more of a feeling of direct engagement than the former.

The second aspect of directness is *distance*. Hutchins and coauthors distinguish two types of directness: semantic distance and articulatory distance. **Semantic distance** refers to the subjective distance between the user's intentions and the semantic objects and operations provided by the interface. If objects and operations provided are neither too low level nor too high level and map to users intentions well, then an interface is semantically direct. (The reader is referred to Chapter 7 in which semantic distance in that context is discussed as *richness* versus *minimality*.)

Minimizing semantic distance in **execution,** according to Hutchins and coauthors, "requires matching the level of description required by the interface language to the level at which the person thinks of the task." Semantic distance in **evaluation** refers to "the amount of processing structure that is required for the user to determine whether the goal has been achieved. If the terms of the output are not those of the user's intention, the user will be required to translate the output into terms that are compatible with the intention in order to make the evaluation." Semantic distance in execution and evaluation requires more cognitive effort. Minimizing semantic distance relieves the user of cognitive effort.

Articulatory distance, according to Hutchins and coauthors, refers to the relationships between *meanings* of expressions and their *physical form*. During **execution,** articulatory distance refers to the directness of the relationship between the meanings behind desired *actions* and the form in which actions are actually performed. If the user cannot easily carry out a path of action due to an inflexible and inappropriate structure in the interface, then it will be perceived as articulatorily distant. Being able to *easily* select any object of interest and then *immediately* perform any operation on it provides articulatory directness. Entering a command name and object name is more distant in this sense than performing an action directly on an object. During **evaluation,** articulatory distance is a matter of the distance between the form and meaning of system *output*. The visible results of an action reflected in the object itself are more direct (less distant) than a status message.

Direct manipulation is thus seen by Hutchins, Hollan, and Norman (1986) as a quality that may be present to different degrees, rather than a well-defined dialog style per se. Direct manipulation as a quality is most present in interfaces that present a model world and that minimize semantic and articulatory distance.

Note that it is possible to provide a model world interface in which semantic and articulatory distances are large (and thus the interface might be called direct manipulation but there would be minimal directness). Abstract, unfamiliar, nondistinct icons; semantic elements too low or too high to support user tasks well; articulatory distance in evaluation, such as numbers when graphs would be more effective, or the use of color to indicate status when shape would be more meaningful; all these design aspects would decrease the directness of the interface, increasing cognitive load. *Designers need to understand that employing icons and pulldown menus of actions does not necessarily in and of itself make a usable interface.* Care must be taken to build in both semantic and articulatory directness in order to fully achieve the potential benefits of direct manipulation interfaces. This is an extremely important point.

Hutchins, Hollan, and Norman (1986) also point out that there are some inherent *disadvantages* to direct manipulation interfaces. For example, it can be tedious and inefficient to perform some types of tasks through direct manipulation techniques. Examples are highly repetitive actions, and searches based on screening criteria. Other interaction techniques should be provided for these types of tasks. Second, there is a high need for precision and accuracy in directly manipulating objects. Sometimes this is better left to the system, which can more easily be precise and accurate. Third, direct manipulation interfaces may make some types of tasks easier, but they do not teach the user about the task domain. Manipulating elements in a direct manipulation CAD system may be direct and easy, but you have to know how to design before the system is useful. The interface does not teach you about good design.

Shneiderman (1982) claims that experts can work rapidly to carry out a wide range of tasks on direct manipulation interfaces. Hutchins, Hollan, and Norman (1986) contest this claim and suggest that expert users would probably be faster with a command language interface. In fact, the appropriateness of direct manipulation interfaces for novices and experts most likely depends on the tasks they are doing. For instance, consider the interior design application illustrated in Figure

9-2. Surely even expert users will perform more efficiently on this interface as opposed to a command language interface to the same functionality. This is because the task is inherently spatial and visual. On the other hand, it does seem likely, as suggested previously, that experts would perform repetitive tasks and search tasks more quickly through other interface techniques, such as languages, and that for some data entry tasks experts will perform more quickly through direct data entry than through direct manipulation selection (see, for example, the discussion of Gould and others, 1988, and Greene and others, 1988, on pages 180–182.)

Other authors offer useful discussions of direct manipulation. Ziegler and Fahnrich (1988) define directness and manipulation as separate characteristics. **Manipulation** is defined as allowing reference to objects and operations by pointing at visible representations of these referents and involving a high degree of interactivity and feedback. This notion is similar to Hutchins and coauthor's (1986) description of *engagement.*

Directness is defined at three levels (corresponding to Hutchins and coauthor's notions of semantic distance, articulatory distance in execution, and articulatory distance in evaluation). Directness is subjective, that is, in the mind of the user. What feels direct to a novice may not feel direct to an expert. Perceived directness will also depend on the different tasks different users need to do and how well the interface supports a particular task. For example, for many programmers, assembler language feels *semantically* very *indirect,* because objects and operations are at a level much lower than users' intentions. Many objects and actions must be manipulated to obtain simple goals. On the other hand, for some users a higher-level language would be perceived as semantically indirect, because they would want to manipulate objects in ways not provided by the language and could not, due to the loss of low-level objects and actions of interest.

Wolf and Rhyne (1987) offer a clarifying taxonomy that is useful in thinking about direct manipulation. They note that there are two main parts of any user interaction: specifying an object and specifying an action. Various techniques are available for both, and they vary in their feeling of directness. To summarize:

Techniques for specifying objects:

1. *Name generation:* for example, type in an object name
2. *Visual correlation:* for example, select a visual object by pointing to it
3. *Gesture generation:* for example, draw a symbol that refers to an object

Techniques for specifying actions:

1. *Name generation:* for example, type in an action name
2. *Visual correlation:* for example, select an icon or word representing an action by pointing to it
3. *Analogous actions:* for example, drag an object to a new location
4. *Gesture generation:* for example, draw a symbol that refers to an action, such as draw an X on an object to delete it

5. *Coded selection:* indicate the action by a shorthand code such as a function key press or double mouse click

Wolf and Rhyne suggest that *all* direct manipulation interfaces are characterized by specifying *objects* through *visual correlation.* That is, objects are selected by visually indicating a visual representation of the object. The visual representation of the object may be text or graphical. Visual indication may be by pointing or through some other visual technique, such as drawing a circle around an object. This is similar to Hutchins, Hollan, and Norman's (1986) notion of *direct engagement* and Ziegler and Fahnrich's (1988) definition of *manipulation.*

Object specification technique thus *defines* direct manipulation. Then, action specification techniques determine *the degree to which* an interface is direct manipulation. Analogous actions (for example, dragging an object to the trashcan to delete it) feel most direct, followed closely by gesture generation. Hutchins and coauthors (1986) might say here that analogous actions are more *articulatorally* direct than is gesture generation.

Wolf and Rhyne point out that a given direct manipulation interface (for example, Apple's Macintosh or Lotus' Lotus 1-2-3) usually employs a variety of action specification techniques. For example, on the Macintosh, some actions are performed through analogous actions ("move," "copy," "delete," "resize"), but most are performed through visual correlation ("cut," "paste"), and a few are performed through coded selection ("open," "close"). Thus different parts of the interface feel more direct than others.

Synthesizing the preceding discussions, we could summarize the definition of direct manipulation with the following points:

1. All direct manipulation interfaces allow users to interact directly with (for example, select by pointing to) objects of interest.

2. Direct manipulation interfaces vary in *semantic distance* and in *articulatory distance,* and these two types of distance can be present in the design of *execution* (input) or *evaluation* (output).

3. *Semantic distance in execution* occurs when manipulable objects and actions are at too low or too high a level, given users' intentions and goals. For example, allowing only straight lines in a graphics program makes it unnecessarily tedious to draw rectangles.

4. *Semantic distance in evaluation* occurs when users must interpret, calculate, or translate output before they can determine if their goals and intentions have been met. For example, providing only raw numbers when users are interested in sums or other derived numbers requires mental calculations and creates a feeling of semantic distance.

5. *Articulatory distance in execution* occurs when the physical form of actions does not map directly to their meaning. For instance, moving by dragging with a mouse is much more direct than moving by typing in a command name and object name.

6. *Articulatory distance in evaluation* occurs when the physical form of output does not map directly to its meaning. For instance, a matrix of numbers may be less direct than a line graph when the user is looking for trends in data.

7. Semantic and articulatory distance may be present in different degrees across different objects and actions in a given interface. Thus direct manipulation is a continuous quality, rather than a characteristic that is present or absent. That is, interfaces are not either direct manipulation or not direct manipulation; they are simply more or less direct as compared to other interfaces.

8. Semantic and articulatory distance are subjective, that is, in the mind of the user. What feels direct to one user doing one task might feel indirect to another user doing another task. Thus the perception of direct manipulation depends somewhat on user and task characteristics.

Many applications with more traditional dialog styles, such as command languages, menus, or fill-in forms, could, with a little creativity and the necessary hardware support, be converted to direct manipulation interfaces. For example, observe the screen in Figure 9-3. This is a fill-in form screen included in an office automation package that supports the management of meetings. Users can send meeting invitations to colleagues and also request reservations for meeting rooms and audiovisual equipment. Figures 9-4, 9-5, and 9-6 illustrate how more direct manipulation could be built into the interface to this function.

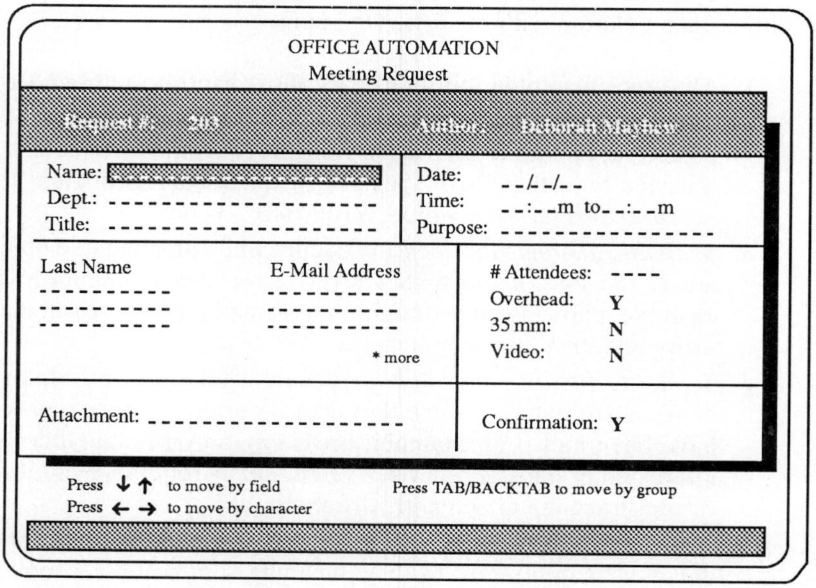

OFFICE AUTOMATION
Meeting Request

Request #:   203   Author: Deborah Mayhew

Name: ▓▓▓▓▓▓▓▓▓▓▓▓▓▓	Date: _ _/_ _/_ _
Dept.: _ _ _ _ _ _ _ _ _ _ _ _ _ _ _ _ _ _	Time: _ _:_ _m to_ _:_ _m
Title: _ _ _ _ _ _ _ _ _ _ _ _ _ _ _ _ _ _	Purpose: _ _ _ _ _ _ _ _ _ _ _ _ _ _ _ _ _ _

Last Name	E-Mail Address	# Attendees: _ _ _ _
_ _ _ _ _ _ _ _ _ _	_ _ _ _ _ _ _ _ _ _	Overhead: Y
_ _ _ _ _ _ _ _ _ _	_ _ _ _ _ _ _ _ _ _	35 mm: N
_ _ _ _ _ _ _ _ _		Video: N
	* more	

Attachment: _ _ _ _ _ _ _ _ _ _ _ _ _ _ _ _ _ _	Confirmation: Y

Press ↓ ↑ to move by field   Press TAB/BACKTAB to move by group
Press ← → to move by character

Figure 9-3 Example of a traditional fill-in form interface.

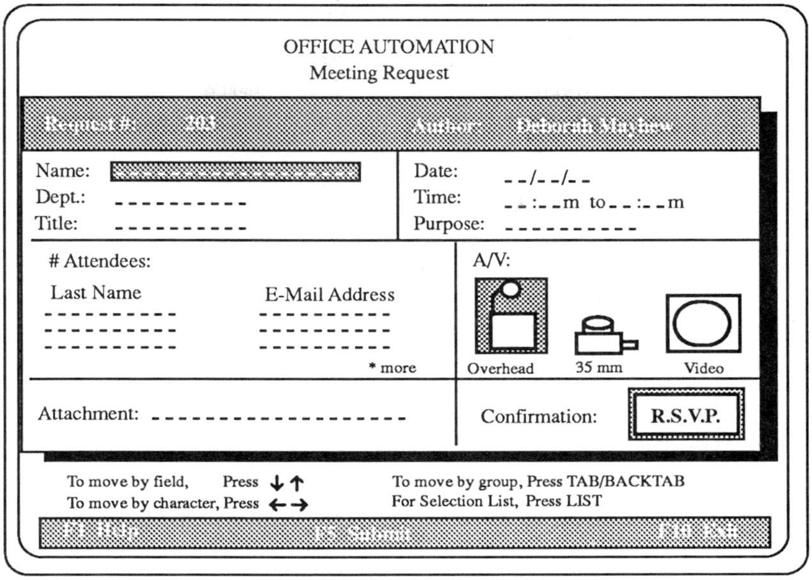

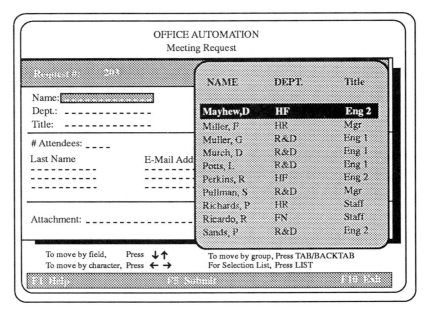

Figure 9–4 Example of a traditional fill-in form interface redesigned as a direct manipulation interface.

Figure 9–5 Example of a traditional fill-in form interface redesigned as a direct manipulation interface.

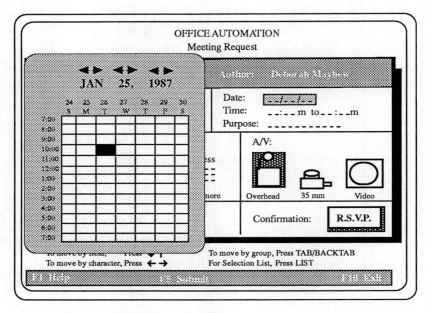

Figure 9–6 Example of a traditional fill-in form interface redesigned as a direct manipulation interface.

In Figure 9-4, the requests for audiovisual equipment and attendee confirmations have been converted from fill-in fields to direct manipulation icons. Instead of entering "Y" or "N" in fill-in fields, the user points to the equipment desired to select it. Selected equipment icons are highlighted. The "R.S.V.P." form can be selected in the same way. Selected icons can be deselected by pointing to them again, and deselected items are dehighlighted.

In Figure 9-5, the user has moved the cursor to the fields where the name, department, and title of the meeting caller are to be specified (this might not be the same person as the user entering the request on the system). The user has two options: the information can simply be typed in the fill-in fields or a function key labeled "LIST" can be pressed, bringing up a window that presents employees from the appropriate organizations. Now the user can directly point to and select the appropriate name, the window will disappear, and the name, department, and title selected will pop up in the fill-in fields.

Other fill-in fields provide the same option. In Figure 9-6, the user has moved the cursor to the "Date" field and is preparing to enter the date and time of the proposed meeting. This can be done by typing information in the field or, again, by pressing the "LIST" key to get a window of time and date options. In this case, a time grid is presented. The user could change the date by clicking on the arrows above the month, day, or year or by selecting a different day of the week. When the desired date is displayed, time slots can be selected by pointing to the cells in the grid that correspond to the desired day and start and end times of the meeting. Selected time cells are highlighted and can be deselected. When a time and date have been selected, the user presses "F5" ("submit"), the window disappears, and the time and date pop up in the appropriate fill-in fields. It is possible that the date and time window could even somehow (for example, by graying out time cells) indicate which times are free on the calendar of the meeting caller or even the calendars of all invitees combined. This would require the system to have access to electronic calendars of all the users and that users keep these calendars up to date. It is technically possible, however, and would make this a very powerful and useful application.

The main point, however, is that users are given a direct manipulation alternative to typing data in fill-in fields. Fill-in forms require typing, which is slow and error prone. They also require that the user knows, remembers, or finds out such things as names, electronic mail addresses, and free time slots. The direct manipulation interface, especially in combination with some powerful functionality, both reduces the time and errors of typing and removes the burden of memory and mental calculation.

The example in Figures 9-4, 9-5, and 9-6 made use of icons, windows, and a pointing device. None of these things were necessary, however, in converting the fill-in form to a direct manipulation interface. Audiovisual equipment could have been selected in a similar fashion as names and times, without displaying icons. Names in the list and times on the grid could have been "pointed to" by moving a cursor with cursor keys, instead of with a pointing device. And lists could have been presented on a refreshed screen, rather than in a window, with control returned to the master form after a selection had been made. Such an interface would still be considered to be direct manipulation. It is the point-and-select nature of an interface that makes it direct manipulation, not the use of icons, pointing devices, and windows. These latter techniques can enhance a direct manipulation interface, but do not define it.

Shneiderman (1986) gives many examples of applications that could potentially be converted to direct manipulation interfaces, some of which he describes and discusses in some detail. Many of these applications are listed in Figure 9-7. For example, as Shneiderman points out, in a personnel records system:

> A building floor plan showing departments might be shown, and when a department is chosen, individual offices become visible. On moving the cursor into a room, details about its occupant appear on the screen. If you choose the wrong room, merely back out and try another.

Alternatively, an organization chart with titles could be presented. Selecting a title box would bring up a window of information on the current "occupant" of that title and position in the organization.

In another example,

Sample applications for which a direct manipulation interface could be designed:

Flight simulator
Display-based text editors
Battleship management
Personnel system
Database query by example
Video games
CAD
Manufacturing and process control
Programming of industrial robots
Office automation systems
Windowing systems
Visual programming
Rolodex
Checkbook maintenance
Bibliographic search
Airline reservations
Warehouse inventory
Operating systems

Figure 9–7   Sample applications for which a direct manipulation interface could be designed. From Shneiderman, *Designing the User Interface: Strategies for Effective Human-Computer Interaction,* © 1986, Addison-Wesley Publishing Co., Inc. Reading, MA. Reprinted with permission.

Why not do airline reservations by showing the user a map and prompting for cursor motion to the departing and arriving cities? Then, use a calendar to select the date and a clock to indicate the time. Seat selection is done by showing the seating plan of the plane on the screen, with a diagonal line to indicate an already reserved seat.

Shneiderman provides many other interesting descriptions, some brief and some extensive, of applying the notion of direct manipulation interfaces to the wide variety of application types listed in Figure 9-7. Direct manipulation will not always be appropriate, however. This will depend on aspects of the users and the tasks they are doing.

WHEN IS A DIRECT MANIPULATION DIALOG STYLE APPROPRIATE?

Direct manipulation interfaces have particular advantages and disadvantages, relative to other dialog styles. *Advantages* include the following:

Easy to learn and remember. Because direct manipulation interfaces tap user models that people already have (that is, manipulating objects in two-dimensional space), they are relatively easy to learn and remember. They are not completely self-explanatory, however, as is, say, a well-designed menu system, because there is usually little or no prompting on the screen. However, once the user grasps a few key concepts and becomes aware of the analogies to manipulating objects in space and fluent in the use of the pointing device, then even applications fairly rich in functionality become relatively easy to learn. Once interactions have been learned, because they are quite natural, they are also relatively easy to remember across sessions.

Direct, WYSIWYG. Because direct manipulation interfaces are direct and usually have a "what you see is what you get" quality, they allow users to focus on *task semantics* (that is, what they are trying to do, or *functional* tasks), rather than on *system semantics* and *syntax* (that is, how to do it, or *operational* tasks). This makes the interaction much more natural, more efficient, and less error-prone than in some alternative dialog styles, such as command languages or even natural language interfaces. It is often simply easier to "do it" than to "say it."

Flexible, easily reversible actions. If you did not mean to select an item, one quick motion deselects it. This is easier than retyping a command string. If you did not mean to throw a file in the trash can, simply open the trash can and retrieve the file. This is much easier than remembering and executing a complex command for data restoration. Actions in a direct manipulation interface are usually very easy to reverse or undo.

Provides context and instant, visual feedback. In Figures 9-5 and 9-6, presenting lists of valid inputs to fill-in fields provides rich context for users, and this helps them accomplish their tasks more efficiently and more effectively. The highlighting of selected objects provides feedback and confirmation before final acceptance and execution and while context is still available.

When the application involves moving objects around in space, as in Figure 9-2, users get direct, visual feedback while the object is being moved, with the context of the current position of all other objects always visible. This is in contrast to, say, a command language interface, which would require the specification of *x* and *y* coordinates to move objects and in which feedback would be delayed until after the execution of the command. Fine adjustments would be very tedious and inefficient.

Exploits human use of visual–spatial cues. People rely heavily on visual and spatial information and are usually faster in processing this type of information than in processing language. As the saying goes, "a picture is worth a thousand words." Direct manipulation interfaces exploit this natural human ability.

Less error prone.   The low typing requirements and the visual feedback in direct manipulation interfaces mean less opportunity for user input errors. This in turn means there is less need for complex error handling and error messages.

In summary, the main advantages of direct manipulation interfaces are ease of learning and remembering and feedback, context, and flexibility. There are serious trade-offs however. *Disadvantages* of direct manipulation interfaces include the following:

Not self-explanatory.   Although direct manipulation interfaces are relatively easy to learn, they are not necessarily intuitive or obvious to the first-time user. They are not self-explanatory in the way that a menu, question and answer, and some fill-in form interfaces can be. There usually is little or no prompting in a direct manipulation interface. Once the user learns a few key concepts and conventions, these tend to apply in many situations and are easy to remember. But they are not always obvious from looking at a screen in a direct manipulation interface for the first time.

Imagine a completely computer naive user sitting down at an Apple Macintosh application for the first time. They have not read the manual and have never used any computer system, let alone this one. On the screen are some words across the top and perhaps a window or two. On the window edges are a number of funny-looking little shapes. In the windows are some other little shapes with names or maybe some text. Now, the user wants to edit the document in one of the windows, but that window is partially obscured by the other window. There is a mouse, but the user has never used one before. Without reading the manual, how would this user have any idea what to do?

Contrast this with a simple menu screen that lists five options, clearly labeled, and has a message instructing the user how to select the desired option. This user can probably step through a simple task without any reference to a manual; everything the user needs to know at any time is prompted on the screen. The menu is self-explanatory. But the direct manipulation user must know many things because they are not prompted on the screen: how to bring a window to the top, how to use the scroll buttons, how to select text, how to use the pull-down menus, and so on. Although it is not difficult to learn and remember these operations, they are not immediately obvious from the interface alone.

Can be inefficient.   Direct manipulation interfaces often mimic actions taken in the manual world. If users want to manipulate an object, they point to it. If they want to move an object, they drag it with a pointing device. Although this analogy to manual actions makes the interface easy to learn, it also mimics inefficiencies in the manual world. Thus, for high-frequency expert users, especially touch typists and especially when there are more actions and objects than can all be made visible on one screen, direct manipulation interfaces can be inefficient when compared to some other dialog styles, such as command languages.

For instance, it may be simple and fast to select an icon or window that is at least partially visible. However, on a very busy screen with many more icons in each window than can be seen simultaneously and with many open windows, some of which are completely obscured under other windows, it can actually be very tedious and inefficient to navigate to the desired icon or window. Just as in the manual world, where if you have a stack of papers on the desk you must shuffle through them until you see the desired paper, icons must be scrolled within windows, and windows must be moved about to bring the desired one into view. If the user does not know exactly where the desired window or icon is, this can take some time.

Contrast such a tedious manual searching operation with, for example, simply entering the desired window or object by name in a command language interface or pressing a single key in a function key interface. These latter interfaces avoid the need to scan through busy screens, manipulating objects, looking for the desired object, and waiting for the screen to refresh while scrolling or moving windows. Direct manipulation may be *easy to learn and remember,* but under some task conditions, it may not be as *easy to use* as some alternative dialog styles.

May be difficult to design recognizable icons. Many direct manipulation interfaces are icon based. Although using pictures instead of words may seem appealing for many reasons, it may be difficult to design recognizable icons for many objects and actions. It is usually particularly hard to design good icons for actions. For instance, try to imagine a good icon (that is, one recognizable by most people without any accompanying name) for the commands "save," "quit," "change," "undo," or "calculate."

Icons take more screen "real estate" than words. An icon for a command or object is usually bigger than a name. And it is often necessary to accompany icons with names because of the problem described previously. Thus, icons may take up more than twice the space that words alone do. When screen "real estate" is scarce, this can be a serious drawback to icon-based direct manipulation interfaces, as compared with other dialog styles.

In sum, the main disadvantages of direct manipulation interfaces are that they can be more difficult to use for some task types, especially for high-frequency expert users, and that icons are difficult to design and expensive in terms of screen "real estate."

Given these relative advantages and disadvantages, we can draw some conclusions about the kinds of tasks and users for which direct manipulation as a primary dialog style might be appropriate. Figure 9-8 lists the user characteristics (see Chapter 2) for which a direct manipulation user interface would be a good choice.

Generally, because direct manipulation interfaces are (potentially) easy to learn, they are good for users who are averse to learning, that is, those who might have a negative attitude toward the system or low motivation to use it for whatever reason. This is especially true of discretionary rather than users who make a

Direct manipulation interfaces are most appropriate for users with:

☞ User Psychology

> Negative attitude
> Low motivation

☞ Knowledge and experience

> Low typing skill
> Moderate system experience
> Moderate to high task experience
> Moderate application experience
> High frequency of use of other systems
> Low computer literacy

☞ Job and task characteristics

> Low frequency of use
> Moderate training
> Discretionary use
> High turnover rate
> Low task importance
> Low task structure

Figure 9–8 When to use direct manipulation interfaces.

personal choice whether to buy and use a given system or not, rather than mandatory users. For the same reason, they are good for users low in frequency of use and with high turnover rates.

Because they minimize typing, direct manipulation interfaces are good for users with low typing skill. Because they are *not* self-explanatory, they are *not* good when little or no training and/or no good manuals are available and when users are low in task experience. Although direct manipulation interfaces are appropriate for users low in frequency of use and system and application experience, they are also good for users high in frequency of use and experience when user tasks are appropriate. Inherently, spatial tasks and tasks requiring significant perceptual and cognitive resources lend themselves well to direct manipulation. Highly repetitive tasks (which involve more motor and less perceptual and cognitive resources), for example, do not.

DESIGNING DIRECT MANIPULATION INTERFACES: EXPERIMENTAL RESULTS

The potential advantages and benefits of direct manipulation interfaces as just discussed are not inherent in direct manipulation as a dialog style. Care must be taken in the design of any direct manipulation interface in order to realize the potential advantages. Some research has been conducted to investigate the effects of direct manipulation interfaces on the performance of users. In this section, the results of some of these studies are presented and discussed. In the following section, general guidelines for direct manipulation design are drawn from these and other studies in summary form.

A number of studies have tried to directly compare direct manipulation interfaces to nondirect manipulation interfaces to empirically determine the relative advantages and disadvantages of the different dialog styles. One study (Roberts and Moran, 1982) produced data comparing command language interfaces (on text editors) with direct manipulation interfaces (on text editors and word processors). Actually, the purpose of the study was not to directly compare direct and nondirect manipulation interfaces, but to establish a methodology for measuring the usability of editors and to generate some benchmark data from eight existing editors. However, since the eight existing editors measured included two command language editors (Teco and Wylbur) and six direct manipulation editors, we can look at the data and compare editors with the two alternative dialog styles.

Roberts and Moran generated 32 core tasks from a possible set of 212 typical operations available on editors and assessed the usability of the eight editors through four measures: (1) the average time for *experts* to complete a core task, (2) the percentage of task time *experts* spent making and correcting errors, (3) the average time it took *novices* to learn a core task, and (4) the percentage of the 212 possible operations available on a given editor.

As can be seen in Figure 9-9, the two nondirect manipulation editors, Teco and Wylbur, generally produced worse usability scores than the six direct manipulation editors on almost all measures. On Teco and Wylbur, experts took an average of 49 and 42 seconds, respectively, to complete core tasks. Experts on all the direct manipulation editors took 37 seconds or less.

On Teco and Wylbur, experts spent 15% and 18% of the task time making and correcting errors. In contrast, on all direct manipulation editors except one, experts spent only 11% or less of the time making and correcting errors.

Novices took 19.5 and 8.2 minutes on average to learn each core task on Teco and Wylbur, respectively, while on the direct manipulation editors they took 7.7 minutes or less.

And these advantages of direct manipulation editors cannot be accounted for by simpler functionality. While Teco and Wylbur included only 39% and 42% of the 212 possible functions, respectively, the direct manipulation editors included from 37% up to 77%.

Thus, these data would seem to suggest that direct manipulation interfaces to editors are easier to use (for experts) and easier to learn (for novices) than nondirect manipulation interfaces to editors, even when the former are richer in functionality.

Another study (Whiteside and others, 1985) set out to directly compare several different dialog styles (command languages, menus, and icon-based, direct manipulation interfaces) and came up with contradictory results. Seven different

	Time (expert) Sec/Task	Errors (expert) % Time	Learning (novice) Min/Task	Functionality % Tasks
Teco	49	15	19.5	39
Wylbur	42	18	8.2	42
Emacs	37	6	6.6	49
NLS	29	22	7.7	77
Bravox	29	8	5.4	70
Wang	26	11	6.2	50
Bravo	26	8	7.3	59
Gypsy	19	4	4.3	37

Figure 9–9   A study of direct manipulation and non direct manipulation editors. From Roberts and Moran, "Evaluation of Text Editors," *Proceedings, Human Factors in Computer-Systems,* March 1982, 136–41. With permission.

existing systems were tested: four with command language interfaces, two with icon-based direct manipulation interfaces, and one with a menu interface. The systems were not identified by name or vendor.

Seventy-six users participated in this study. They were divided into three categories based on experience: (1) "System" users were expert users of the system they were tested on, (2) "new" users had no computer experience at all, and were first-time users of the system they were tested on, and (3) "transfer" users had some computer experience, but were first-time users of the system they were tested on.

Users were presented with a simple introduction to a system and provided with documentation and on-line help. They were then asked to perform a set of simple file manipulation tasks, such as displaying, merging, and sending files. They were timed while doing these tasks, and a simple completion rate measure was computed, giving the average percentage of a task completed in a 5-minute period.

Since 5 minutes was determined to be the fastest possible time in which a practiced expert user might finish these tasks, the score computed represents how actual performance on the different systems compared with ideal, expert performance. A higher score is a better score.

The average completion rate scores for users at each of the experience levels on five of the tested systems are presented in Figure 9-10. Some very interesting and unexpected results were obtained. Striped bars represent the average score for "new" users, that is, computer novices. Here it can be seen that users performed equally poorly on all systems. No particular advantage of one dialog style over another is evident in the data. This is surprising, because we would have predicted that menus and iconic interfaces would be easier to *learn* than command languages. However, although the difference is not significant, there seems to be a slight advantage of the command language interface over other interfaces in the data. This is contrary to expectation, but perhaps the task was too limited and simple for any significant differences in ease of learning to emerge. The task was in fact of relatively short duration, so the effects of practice on these various dialog styles are not addressed in this study.

Solid bars represent the performance of "transfer" users. These users had used other systems before and were familiar with computers, but were novices on the system they were tested on. Here we see a large and significant advantage of command language interfaces over menu or iconic interfaces. This again is quite surprising. We have stated that command languages will be harder to learn than either menu or direct manipulation interfaces, and this seems to be directly contradicted by these data. One possible reason for this surprising result is that perhaps the other systems that these users had experience with were command language

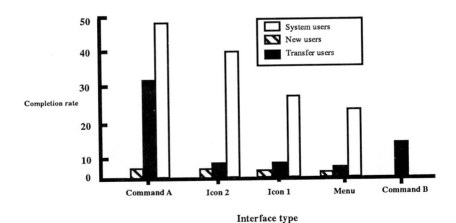

Figure 9–10 A comparison of dialog styles. From Whiteside, Jones, Levy, and Wixon, "User Performance with Command, Menu, and Iconic Interfaces," *Proceedings, CHI* '85, 1985, 185–91. With permission.

systems, and it was easier for them to learn a new but similar type of interface than to learn a very different type of interface. But we cannot conclude this from the data presented in this study. This is only a speculation.

Finally, the scores of "system" users are represented by white bars. These users are expert users of the system they were tested on. These data make sense. As we would have predicted, command language interfaces were easier to use than iconic interfaces, which in turn were slightly easier to use than the menu system.

What are we to make of these data? One clue comes from comparing data within an interface type. Notice the large difference in performance between the two command languages for "transfer" users, and the large difference in performance between iconic interfaces for "system" users. Clearly, there is something else going on here besides dialog style alone that is affecting the ease of use and ease of learning of these systems. All command languages are not equal. All direct manipulation interfaces or all menu systems are not equal.

Whiteside and co-workers went back and analyzed the interfaces measured in this study to try and explain their data. They observed that there are many other design issues besides the simple choice of dialog style in an interface, and they concluded that these other design issues overshadowed the choice of dialog style in determining usability. They identify several of these design issues and give examples. For instance, all interfaces contained inconsistencies that interfered with user performance. In the command language interfaces, inconsistencies in syntax occurred. In the iconic interfaces, inconsistencies in the grammar of mouse button use occurred. In the menu system there were inconsistencies in the use of function keys.

Another lower-level design issue was the amount of feedback provided. In the command language systems, cryptic wording in error messages was a problem. In the iconic interfaces, often the shape of the cursor was meant to communicate important information to the user, but users did not understand this. In all interfaces, confirmation messages often simply did not occur or appeared somewhere outside the user's current focus of attention and were not noticed.

As Whiteside and coworkers conclude, choice of dialog style alone may not be the overriding determinant of usability. Poor (or careful) design at lower levels may cancel out the potential benefits (or drawbacks) of a dialog style.

This does not necessarily mean, however, that choice of dialog style is not important. We cannot conclude this from the data in this study, because the quality of design at lower levels was not held constant across the systems studied. Thus the study is a test of particular interfaces, not of general dialog style types. This is in fact the case with *all* the studies reviewed here that attempt to compare direct to nondirect manipulation interfaces.

Another study (Karat, 1987) compared the performance of novice users on command language and direct manipulation interfaces to a simple filing and retrieval system and found a clear advantage for the direct manipulation system. Twenty subjects were instructed on a small set of filing functions ("list directory," "change directory," "copy file," "delete file," and "list file"). One-half the subjects performed tasks requiring these functions on a command language system where functions had names and directory and file names had a specific syntax. The other half performed the same tasks on a direct manipulation system in which all operations were performed by pointing to and selecting objects displayed with simple character graphics. An extensive hierarchical filing structure with 207 different directories was used to make the tasks nontrivial.

The results showed a clear performance advantage for the direct manipulation interface. Twice as many subjects completed the tasks with the direct manipulation interface. They also completed the tasks faster and with less time making and recovering from errors. The relative advantage of direct manipulation also increased as a function of the depth of the files manipulated in the hierarchy. Thus it seemed that the spatial nature of the direct manipulation interface was easier to understand and use than the path specification for files employed in the command language interface.

There was, however, a single task in which the command language provided better performance. This was the case of a task involving copying a file within the highest-level directory and renaming it. This involved extensive scrolling in the direct manipulation interface, and in this case command language users were faster. This supports the idea that *task type* as well as *user type* may play an important role in determining the appropriateness of alternative dialog styles. The spatial nature of direct manipulation interfaces may make it easier to understand and carry out an inherently *spatial task,* such as filing. However, even when the task is inherently spatial, when the task space becomes too large, a direct manipulation dialog may simply become too unwieldy.

These results are inconsistent with the Whiteside and others (1985) study. Given the simpler systems and tasks in this study, it is possible that variations in low-level details were minimized, allowing the simple effects of dialog style to emerge. However, the two studies vary in too many ways to draw any strong conclusions to account for the conflicting results.

Card, Moran, and Newell (1983) report a study comparing different text editors. Two were direct manipulation and three were not, as in the Roberts and Moran (1982) study. All subjects were expert users of the system they were tested on. The two direct manipulation editors showed clear efficiency advantages, as much as 50% to 200% faster as compared to the nondirect manipulation editors.

Shneiderman and Margono (1987) also found that on simple file manipulation tasks (for example, "open document," "copy document," and "delete document") inexperienced subjects learned more quickly and preferred a direct manipulation interface to a command language interface.

Ziegler and Fahnrich (1988) review several other studies producing evidence of an advantage of direct manipulation interfaces for text editing and file manipulation tasks.

All these studies compared the performance on tasks within a fairly limited task domain: file manipulation and editing. Thus it is not possible from these studies to generalize about the relative advantages and disadvantages of direct manipulation across different task domains.

One study (Bailey, Knox, and Lynch, 1988) compared a direct manipulation interface to a nondirect manipulation interface on a system from a very different task domain. Two oscilloscopes were compared, one with a physical "knobs and dials" interface and one with a software-based direct manipulation interface including icons, pop-up menus, and a tool panel. In the knobs and dials interface, all low-level functions were available at a single level through individual controls. The direct manipulation interface, besides being a software versus hardware interface, also presented functions through a multilevel menu hierarchy.

The performance of eight expert users of both systems doing typical measurement tasks was compared to determine if the newer direct manipulation interface increased or decreased productivity compared to the older knobs and dials interface. The tasks users were asked to perform varied in type and complexity.

Several measures of performance were taken and analyzed. Accuracy in measurement was equal for both interfaces. However, overall, users of the direct manipulation interface performed tasks 77% faster than users of the knobs and dials interface. The greatest advantage of the direct manipulation interface occurred in the more complex tasks. In addition, more detailed analyses suggested that the direct manipulation interface encouraged simpler, more efficient problem-solving strategies and reduced memory load.

The authors interpret the data to mean that, in spite of the increased *motor* steps in the direct manipulation interface due the greater menu depth, apparently the *cognitive* complexity of the task was considerably reduced in the direct manipulation interface, thus reducing the overall task time.

Although direct manipulation provided an advantage for *all* tasks in this study, some tasks showed more of an advantage than others. Three other studies already reviewed in Chapter 5 (Gould and others, 1988; Greene and others, 1988; Gould and others, 1989) also provide some evidence that the advantage of direct manipulation over other possible dialog styles depends on task characteristics. These three studies looked at simple data entry tasks and compared several field fill-in techniques to several direct manipulation (point and select) techniques. When the task was simple entry (for example, enter a known date), the fill-in field techniques were faster than direct manipulation even for inexperienced users. When the task was more complex, however, and involved entering difficult to spell entry items from a large pool of possible items, then direct manipulation entry was faster than simple fill-in field entry. Thus it seems that, when the task involves complex cognitive and perceptual processing, direct manipulation may provide an advantage over simple data entry in fill-in fields, even though more keystrokes (or other motor movements, for example, with a mouse) are required.

What are we to conclude from these comparative studies? Taken as a whole, they seem to provide some evidence of the superiority of direct manipulation interfaces. However, the systems compared in each study were different in a variety of ways beyond dialog style, so strong conclusions about dialog style superiority are not possible from these studies alone. Also, as discussed in the introductory section to this chapter, direct manipulation is a *quality present to varying degrees* in interfaces, rather than a dialog style per se. This means that no one interface can definitively represent the concept of direct manipulation in comparative studies such as these.

These studies do suggest, however, that building the quality of direct manipulation into interfaces can *in particular cases,* for particular users doing particular tasks, provide advantages compared to other particular interfaces. Whether or not direct manipulation will provide a performance advantage will probably depend, however, on how well the direct manipulation interface maps to users' goals, intentions, and tasks and what alternative interface it is being compared to. Designers are advised always to premise a design on a good user and task analysis and always to test their design objectively with representative tasks and users. A simple-minded approach of adding icons, windows, pointing devices, and pull-down menus to a system interface will not necessarily contribute to usability.

In spite of the somewhat inconclusive data presented, however, it still seems probable that interfaces that differ in their primary dialog style, but are equally well (or poorly) designed at lower levels, will differ in the ways described in the "Advantages" and "Disadvantages" discussion in this and previous chapters on dialog styles. Thus it is recommended that designers make dialog style choices based on user characteristics, as suggested in these chapters, but also carefully follow the design guidelines offered for each dialog style.

Other studies have investigated particular aspects of direct manipulation interfaces to try to determine what aspects contribute to usability within this overall dialog style. All direct manipulation interfaces allow users to employ spatial location as a retrieval cue, and this is commonly suggested to be a powerful cue. Dumais and Wright (1986) empirically measured the usefulness of spatial location as a retrieval cue. Subjects read and filed news articles and then were asked to retrieve them. In one condition, the "Location" condition, articles were filed and retrieved based on location (in a two-dimensional space) alone. Users selected locations as they filed each article. In a "Name" condition, articles were represented by names in two columnar lists on the screen. Subjects did not control the location of articles in the lists, only their names. Names were limited to two characters. In a "Name–Location" condition, subjects filed articles both by name and location. In a "Two Name" condition, subjects were allowed to assign two 2-letter names per article, but did not control location. Seventy computer-naive subjects filed 30 articles each and were asked to retrieve them by description after each block of 10 had been filed. The primary measure of performance was how many erroneous retrievals were made before correct retrieval of a given article.

The "Location" condition produced the worst performance. The two naming conditions produced the best performance, though they did not differ significantly from one another. Adding locational cues to name cues (the Name–Location condition) did not seem to improve performance over names alone.

This study seems to suggest that spatial cues such as location do not add to the ease of retrieving objects. However, these data should be interpreted carefully. In fact, the naming conditions both included locational cues. Each named object had a specific location in a list. Presumably, they were filed in the list in the order the subject read them. Perhaps arbitrary location on the screen could not be meaningfully associated with article content, but users remembered the order in which they had encountered and filed articles and were using this in association with location as a retrieval cue. If this is in fact what they were doing, then this data could actually be interpreted as *supporting* the importance of locational cues, rather than discounting it. In general, it seems likely that if location (or any other visual cue such as color and shape for that matter) can be *meaningfully* associated with object attributes, then location will be a useful retrieval cue; but if it cannot, then it will not be useful.

Lansdale (1988) reports two experiments in which the power of three visual characteristics of icons (shape, color, and location) in facilitating retrieval was tested. Subjects either assigned or were assigned icons varying on these three dimensions to 18 files whose contents they read. Later they were presented with brief file descriptions and were asked to recall the exact dimensions of the icons.

While a positive advantage for user-defined versus system-defined icons was observed, color and location seemed to contribute very little to recall and meaningfulness of shape only slightly. The authors speculate that visual attributes alone do not facilitate memory *if the user cannot find meaningful ways to associate these attributes to object attributes.*

We note here that Hutchins, Hollan, and Norman (1986) might argue that color and location in this task were *articulatorally distant* cues for object attributes, reducing the *directness* of the association. Perhaps this also accounts for Dumais and Wright's (1986) lack of an effect of location on recall. Location in their task might also have been articulatorally distant for the object attributes users were expected to associate with this visual cue.

Thus it seems likely that the usefulness of the spatial and visual characteristics of icons may depend primarily on the *articulatory closeness* of object attributes and icon attributes. When there is too much articulatory distance, perhaps the task of association becomes reduced to simple rote memory, not unlike learning to associate nonsense syllables with meaningful words or concepts. An important point for designers is that *simply providing an icon does the user no particular favor. Icons must be carefully designed to allow natural and meaningful associations to be drawn between icon attributes and important object attributes.*

The foregoing discussion of the Lansdale study begins to suggest the importance of good icon design as an aspect of the overall design of direct manipulation interfaces. Some studies directly investigate icon design. One study (Nolan, 1989) reported on the development of an icon set for a commercial system. System objects for which icons were to be designed included documents, spreadsheets, a clock, illustrations, a dictionary, mail, folders, databases, a phonebook, and the like.

First, 72 subjects were presented with object definitions, followed by a set of two to six alternative icons per object, and were asked to rank order the alternative icons for "appropriateness." In this test, subjects consistently preferred *concrete, familiar* icons to *abstract, unfamiliar* ones (for examples of concrete and abstract icons, see Figure 9-15). Then a draft set of icons was designed based on this feedback.

In a second test, 294 subjects were asked to select the correct icon from *the total set,* given an object definition. Fourteen subjects were tested for each of 21 object definitions. This revealed which icons were easily distinguished and which were commonly confused with other icons.

Sometimes confusions seemed accountable for by simple *visual* similarity. Other times the confusions seemed to be more *conceptual;* that is, although two icons were visually very dissimilar, they both seemed like a good match to the object definition. For example, the dictionary and document icons were confused. The former looked like a book and the latter like a page. Although they were not very similar looking, *conceptually* both a book and a page could be considered representative of either a dictionary or a document. This suggests that icons in a set should both be visually distinct from one another and represent unique conceptual features of an object. Another study (Remington and Williams, 1986) also found evidence that visual similarity in icons degraded search times and introduced errors in identification.

Icon *labels* were not included in either of these studies and would undoubtedly reduce the conceptual confusions. They would probably also reduce errors due to visual confusions. However, maximal visual and conceptual distinctiveness in icon design will probably still speed search times, even when icons are accompanied by labels.

Another study sheds some light on the issue of icon labels. Brems and Whitten (1987) presented seven icons from an interactive videodisc application to subjects and asked them to identify the functions represented by the icons. In contrast to the Nolan (1989) study, icons represented actions rather than objects. Actions included "Main menu," "Previous menu," Menu map," "Previous page," "Next page," "Play," and "Pause." The icons had no labels.

In the first of two tests, subjects were not given function definitions. Based on a simple description of the application, they were simply asked to identify what function was represented by each icon. Performance was quite poor. For all but one of the icons, less than 50% of the subjects were able to identify the function represented. Subjects did considerably better when they were given a matching test like that in the Nolan study. However, the identification test is more analogous to what users with little task and system knowledge actually do on their first encounter with a system. They see a collection of icons and must imagine what each might represent.

In a *preference* test, subjects were asked to choose between three interface variations: icons alone, icons with labels, or labels alone. Only one subject preferred icons alone, and the other 23 were split between icons with labels and labels only. Although no *performance* data were taken to compare these three alternatives, taken together, both the identification and preference data suggest the importance of icon labels.

Another study (Egido and Patterson, 1988) specifically looked at icon labeling. Twelve subjects navigated through a menu hierarchy to retrieve target items from a database. Three databases were presented: the *Audubon Guide to North American Marine Creatures,* the *Audubon Guide to North American Birds,* and a commercial flowering bulb catalog. Each contained over 250 target items. Items were arranged in a hierarchy of categories. For example, the top-level menu for the marine creatures database presented two choices: invertebrates and vertebrates.

Subjects searched for target items under three conditions: names only, pictures (examples) only, and names and pictures. They were presented with a target item followed by a top-level menu and asked to navigate to and select the target item using a joystick for menu item selection. Several measures of performance were taken, including the number of menu selections made during a search (both forward and backward) and the "think time" per selection and across selections.

On the measure of number of selections, there was a clear advantage in the "pictures and labels" condition, with "pictures only" coming in second and "labels only" third. On the other hand, think time per selection was faster for "labels only" and equally slower for both picture conditions. That is, users spent more time per selection decision but less time and less selections *overall* when they had both pictures *and* labels to guide their choices, as compared to pictures or labels alone.

This seems to support the importance of labeling icons. However, some important points must be considered when interpreting these data. First, the pictures employed in this study were photographs on videodisc, not abstract icons. It is not clear that these results would generalize to iconic representations. Second, pictures represented *examples* of categories from the same level as the target item. For instance, the picture representing vertebrates was a whale, and the picture representing invertebrates was a jellyfish. Such *examples* could have been presented with *words* rather than *pictures,* and it is not clear whether it is the *picture* or the specific, concrete *example* that facilitated searching. Third, items searched for were simple nouns (for example, whale), and it is not clear if pictures would facilitate the search for verbs or adjectives as well.

Nevertheless, this study offers suggestive evidence that icons or words alone are not optimal and that combining them may offer some important advantages, at least in some cases.

Nolan's (1989) study focused on the *confusability* of icons *within a set.* Another paper (Rogers, 1989) discusses the importance of designing icons *within a set* to facilitate learning and use. First, Rogers notes that icons may be used to identify a variety of referent types:

Objects (for example, a document)
Actions (for example, the cut command)

    System states (for example, busy, ready)

    Message type identifier (for example, warning, error)

    Object attribute (for example, line style, fill pattern)

She then notes that different possible *design schemes* can form the basis of icon design. These include the following:

Resemblance: the icon resembles its referent through visual resemblance (a book to represent a dictionary)

Symbolic: the icon represents its referent through an abstract image (a cracked glass to represent the attribute ''fragile'')

Exemplar: the icon represents a typical example or characteristic of a class of objects (a fork and knife to represent restaurants)

Arbitrary: the icon is an arbitrary image whose association with its referent must be learned

Analogy: the icon represents physical or semantic associations with the referent (a wheelbarrow full of bricks for the ''move'' command)

Rogers describes experiments shedding light on the relative effectiveness of these different design schemes. First, it was found that while subjects found *arbitrary* icons to be meaningful in *small* sets (for example, two), the icons lost much of their potency when embedded in large sets where users had to discriminate between many icons.

    Second, icons for actions based on the depiction of the *action and the object* were quite effective (for example, a page and an arrow to depict the ''go to the top of the page'' action). Third, icons based on *analogy* were relatively ineffective. Fourth, while command names produced equivalent performance as compared to icons (based on a depiction of both action and object) in an initial learning task, when memory for name and icon meaning was tested a week later, icons produced better recall.

    It is important to point out in this and other studies of icon design that particular sets of icons are tested and authors define the important differences between them through subjective interpretation. That is, what is considered ''arbitrary'' or ''resemblance'' or ''analogy'' is somewhat subjective, and any two experts may disagree as to whether an icon has good ''resemblance'' (for example) or not. And there may be other differences between icons besides those that the experimenters focus on that account for the performance differences between them. Thus, it will take many studies by different researchers to establish clear definitions of the qualities that make good icons. In the meantime, however, some tentative conclusions can be drawn by careful interpretation of available results.

    Rogers concludes that icons with *the most direct mapping to their referent,* that is the least *articulatory distance* (see Hutchins, Hollan, and Norman, 1986) will produce the best performance. She also suggests that when designing a set of icons it is necessary not only to design in unique visual characteristics so that icons can be discriminated, but also to design in a "grammar" to the whole set so that the icons also highlight important *similarities* between icons and present a coherent whole.

One way to do this is by choosing a single mapping scheme (for example, analogy, or action and object) and basing all icons on that scheme. Another way is to build *both similar and discriminating* visual characteristics into icons representing *instances of a class* of referents. For example, on the Apple Macintosh, all applications are shaped like a diamond. This distinguishes them from other object types, such as folders and files. However, each application icon also has a unique detailed design within the diamond shape that helps to distinguish it from other application icons. The common shape helps users to see the important relationships between objects, while the detail helps them to find a particular application of interest.

DESIGNING DIRECT MANIPULATION INTERFACE: PRINCIPLES AND GUIDELINES

The results of the studies discussed previously and other studies of performance using direct manipulation systems can be summarized in the set of general principles and guidelines for good direct manipulation design presented in this section. There are not many guidelines to offer at this time, because this dialog style is relatively new, and we have relatively little experience with it and little research available on it.

☞ **Minimize semantic and articulatory distance in dialog design.**

Semantic distance is the *psychological* distance between the user's intentions and goals and the manipulable objects and actions of the interface. An example of semantic distance in *execution* (input) would be having actions at too low a level, given the user's intentions. Examples are given in Figure 9-11(a). For instance, having only *line* drawing available in a draw application when users will want to draw *rectangles* and other *geometric shapes* will result in a perception of semantic distance. Or, providing only two elementary commands, "Add" and "Subtract," might be perceived as semantic distance in a check balancing application where the user might wish to perform certain kinds of addition and subtraction operations routinely.

Examples of semantic distance in *evaluation* (output) are offered in Figure 9-11(b). For instance, presenting low level data items in a matrix but not calculating and presenting row and column totals when that is the user's main interest would be perceived as semantically distant. Similarly, requiring users to pick out past due accounts in an Accounts Receivable display by reading each due date and then scanning over to see if payment had been received would also be experienced as

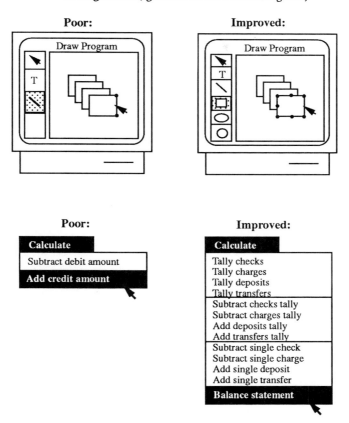

SEMANTIC DISTANCE
EXECUTION
(When manipulable objects and actions are at too low or
too high a level, given users' intentions and goals.)

Figure 9–11(a)   Semantic distance in execution.

semantically distant. Instead, users could be allowed to request a display of past due amounts only.

"Articulatory distance" refers to the relationship between the desired action or result and the *form* of the input or output in the interface. Examples of articulatory distance in *execution* (i.e., input) are offered in Figure 9-12(a). In the first, selecting a command to move an object, instead of simply moving it by "dragging," would seem more articulatorily distant to users. Similarly, "dragging" via cursor keys would feel more distant than "dragging" via a mouse. Examples of operations which lend themselves well to true direct manipulation in the sense of minimal articulatory distance in execution are given at the bottom of the figure.

SEMANTIC DISTANCE
EVALUATION

(When users must interpret, calculate or translate output
before they can determine if their goals and intentions
have been met.)

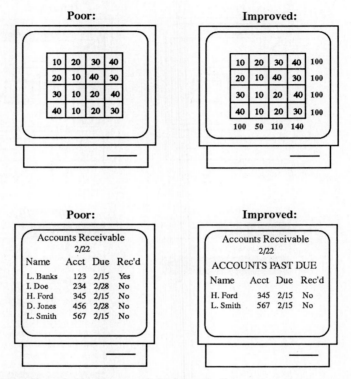

Poor: **Improved:**

Poor: **Improved:**

Figure 9–11   *(Continued)* (b) Semantic distance in evaluation.

Examples of articulatory distance in *evaluation* (output), given in Figure 9-12(b), would be, first, presenting data in spreadsheet form when a graphical display of trends would more directly support the user's evaluation task. Second, presenting a status update by *stating* the percent done, as opposed to *visually representing* the percent done, would also seem more articulatorly distant. Representing a container object such as a folder would be less distant than representing it by an abstract shape.

Other examples might be presenting a status message in response to the "move" command, rather than displaying the object in its new location, and representing an object attribute such as status (for example "planned," "in progress," "completed") by color rather than by graphic representation (see Figure 9-20).

Semantic and articulatory distance are continuous variables. Increasing dis-

ARTICULATORY DISTANCE
EXECUTION

(When the physical form of actions do not map directly
to their meanings)

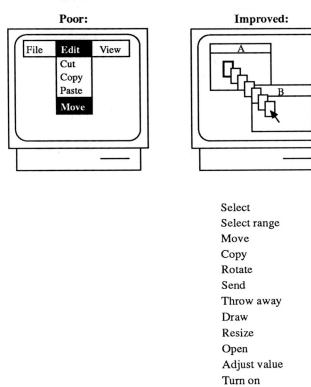

Select
Select range
Move
Copy
Rotate
Send
Throw away
Draw
Resize
Open
Adjust value
Turn on

Figure 9–12(a)   Articulatory distance in execution.

tance increases relative cognitive load, that is, requires more cognitive and perceptual processing on the part of the user. Decreasing distance decreases cognitive load, thus making a user interface easier to use. Within the limitations of the hardware and software platform of an application, every attempt should be made to *minimize semantic and articulatory distance.* A thorough understanding of users' intentions, tasks, and goals is necessary to achieve this.

☞ **Provide visual feedback for position, selection and movement, and physical feedback for modes.**

Note the arrow pointer or cursor on the "Poor" screen in Figure 9-13. It is pointing to the "Project" icon. However, there is no feedback to inform the user

ARTICULATORY DISTANCE
EVALUATION

(When the physical form of output does not map directly
to its meaning.)

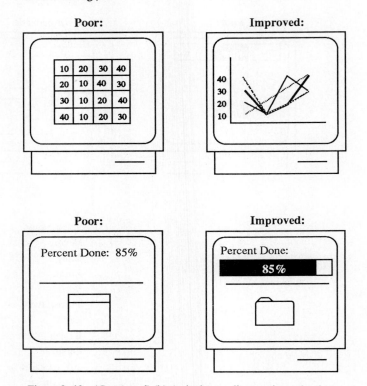

Figure 9–12 (*Continued*) (b) Articulatory distance in evaluation.

that the pointer is indeed pointing to the icon and that if the selection button is pressed the icon will be selected. There is some area within, and perhaps around the icon that is active; that is, that will respond to selection. But this active area is invisible to the user, and no *feedback* is provided to let the user know the active area has been entered.

By contrast, on the "Improved" screen, icons are highlighted when the pointer enters the active area. This is important feedback to help users develop efficient and appropriate motor habits for selecting icons. A change in cursor shape is another technique used to inform users that they are currently pointing to some active area.

Highlighting can also be used to indicate that an object has been selected. It is important to confirm selection with some sort of visual cue, and visual cues can also be useful feedback if users are distracted or interrupted and need to remember

Poor:

Improved:

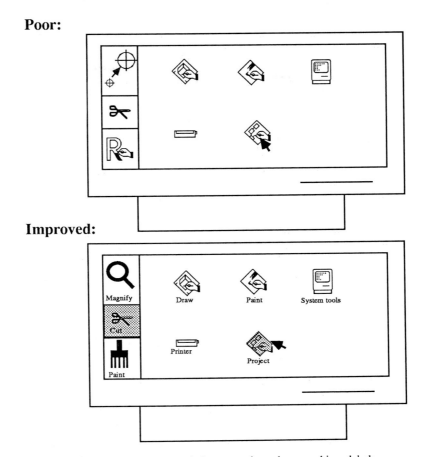

Figure 9–13   Consistency in icon mapping scheme and icon labels.

what objects they have selected. For example, note in the "Improved" screen in Figure 9-13 that the "cut" command is highlighted to indicate it has been selected. It would stay highlighted until the cut command was complete.

Other kinds of feedback are also important. If the user can watch the smooth movement of an icon or window as they move it, rather than simply point to a location and ask for an icon or window to be moved there, they will be able to be much more accurate, and movement will require less trial and error. It is not necessary to provide smooth movement of the entire icon or window, however. A simple outline will do, so that users can see the moved icon or window in relation to other objects on the screen as they position it. This is illustrated in the top-right screen in Figure 9-12(a).

Keeping the mouse button pressed down while moving an object is another kind of useful feedback. Users have a physical reminder that they are in "move mode." If, instead, the user pressed once to pick up an object and pressed a second time to put down the object, then there would be no feedback about the current mode if the user stopped moving for a moment. Thus physical, as well as visual, feedback can also be useful.

☞ **Follow all general guidelines for good interface design given elsewhere in this book.**

Direct manipulation interfaces should follow all other general guidelines for good interface design, including the following:

Consistency
Good conceptual model (see Chapter 3)
Good feedback
Good organization of functionality (see Chapter 13)
Good screen layout and design (see Chapter 14)
Effective use of color (see Chapter 14)
Good error handling (see Chapter 16)

☞ **Provide an alternative interface for high-frequency, expert users.**

Direct manipulation interfaces mimic actions taken in the manual world. If users want to manipulate an object, they point to it. If they want to move an object, they "drag" it with a pointing device. Although this analogy to manual actions makes the interface easy to learn, it also mimics inefficiencies in the manual world. Thus, for high-frequency expert users, especially touch typists (and when there are more actions and objects than can all be made visible on one screen), direct manipulation interfaces can be inefficient when compared to some other dialog styles, such as command languages.

For instance, it may be simple and fast to select an icon or window that is at least partially visible. However, on a very busy screen with many more icons in each window than can be seen simultaneously, and with many open windows, some of which are completely obscured under other windows, it can actually be tedious and inefficient to navigate to the desired icon or window. As in the manual world, where if you have a stack of papers on the desk, you must shuffle through them until you see the desired paper, so must icons be scrolled within windows, and other windows must be moved about to bring the desired one into view. If the user does not know exactly where the desired window or icon is, this can take some time.

Contrast such a tedious manual searching operation with, for example, simply entering the desired window or object by name in a command language interface or pressing a single key in a function key interface. These latter interfaces avoid the need to scan through busy screens, manipulating objects, looking for the desired object, and waiting for the screen to refresh while scrolling or moving windows. Direct manipulation may be *easy to learn and remember,* but except when dealing with a small number of objects on the screen, it may not be as *easy to use* as some alternative dialog styles.

Thus, it is recommended that if some users are expected to be high-frequency, expert users, even if direct manipulation is appropriate as a primary dialog style, alternative interfaces should be made available. For instance, recent applications for the Apple Macintosh contain many keyboard shortcuts for commands that are otherwise executed by direct manipulation or by selecting command names from a hierarchical menu system. It is also possible to select non-visible windows by pointing to their name in a menu, rather than by actually locating them on the screen. These shortcuts have been added to accommodate expert, high-frequency users.

In particular, provide nondirect manipulation alternatives for highly repetitive actions and for powerful searching capabilities.

The following guidelines refer to icon design.

☞ **Choose a consistent icon design scheme.**

There are many ways to design icons for actions or commands. Three different design schemes are represented on the command "palette" on the left side of the "Poor" screen of Figure 9-13. The top icon in the palette represents the command "magnify." This icon is designed by *depicting a before and after representation* of the command. The middle icon represents the "cut" command. It is designed by *depicting the tool* that would accomplish this operation in the manual world. Finally, the bottom icon represents the "paint" or "fill-in" command. It is designed by *depicting the action* itself.

Each icon is, by itself, not a bad representation of the command (although there is some agreement among researchers and some evidence as well that *less direct* mappings, such as depicting the tool, will not be as effective; see for example Hemenway, 1982, and Rogers, 1989). However, *inconsistency* in the mapping scheme chosen to generate the icons will make it harder for users to learn their meanings and find the right icon when looking for a particular command.

In the "Improved" version of Figure 9-13, on the other hand, all command icons in the palette have been designed by *depicting the tool* that would be used to accomplish the operation in the manual world. This consistency in the icon mapping scheme will facilitate learning and using the icons.

Another important aspect of consistency in icon design is to use visual attributes of icons to identify important relationships between icons. Sometimes there are several classes of related objects in an interface. Objects within a class could take on the same shape but vary in their details. This would allow them to be distinguished from one another, but also be identified with their class. For example, on the Apple Macintosh, all application icons are diamond shaped. Other classes of objects, such as folders and files, take other shapes. Application icons

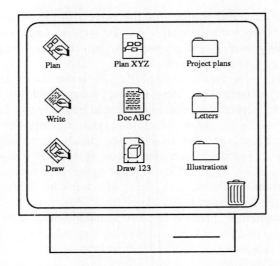

Figure 9–14   Similarities in icons to express relationships.

are distinguished from one another not only by their labels, but also by detail within the shape. This makes it easy to search for and identify any particular application icon. Figure 9-14 provides an example.

☞ **Design icons to be concrete and familiar.**

There is evidence (Nolan, 1989) to suggest that users prefer and are better able to recognize *concrete, familiar* icons as compared to *abstract, unfamiliar* ones. Examples are given in Figure 9-15.

Although it is often true that more concrete icons are also more familiar icons, this is not always the case. For example, a telephone icon is familiar, but would be a fairly abstract way to represent a phone*book*. Similarly, some icons may be familiar although they are abstract. For instance, a red bar passing over an object such as a cigarette is an abstract but very familiar way of expressing "No Smoking."

If a referent cannot be represented by an icon that is either familiar or concrete, then it is not a good candidate for iconic representation. A verbal label may simply be more effective in this case.

☞ **Minimize articulatory distance in icon design.**

The more directly the icon maps to its referent, the better. When the referent is an object, this is relatively straightforward. Concrete and familiar icons, as in Figure 9-15, map more directly to their referents than do abstract or unfamiliar icons, thus minimizing *articulatory distance*. In the case of actions or attributes, it

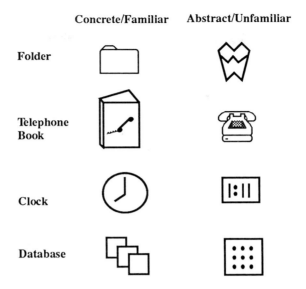

Concrete/Familiar   Abstract/Unfamiliar

Folder

Telephone
Book

Clock

Database

Figure 9–15   Concrete, familiar versus abstract, unfamiliar icon design.

is more difficult to achieve articulatory directness. For actions, there is some evidence (Rogers, 1989) that icons representing the *action and object* (for example, an X over text on a page for the cut command) are more direct than icons based on *analogy* (for example, scissors), or on the *object* of the action (for example, text on a page), or on *abstract symbols* (for example, an X). Examples are shown in Figure 9-16.

☞ **Design icons in a set to be visually and conceptually distinct.**

Icons should look *visually* distinct from one another. This will speed the search process. They should also be *conceptually* distinct. That is, the icons should represent features of objects that are relatively unique within the set of objects. This will reduce confusions between icons.

Consider the examples in Figure 9-17. Different icon pairs for a dictionary and phonebook are illustrated. The pair labeled ''Conceptual similarity,'' although visually dissimilar, are conceptually similar in that each looks like a book. Both a dictionary and a phonebook are in fact books, and so the icons represent non-unique features of the two objects. This will produce confusion in selecting icons. The icon pair labeled ''Conceptual distinctiveness,'' on the other hand, includes detail that capitalizes on the unique features of the two types of books: words versus numbers. The phone represented on the phonebook icon also helps to reinforce the conceptual differences between the two objects.

However, these two icons are also visually similar. Each has the exact same

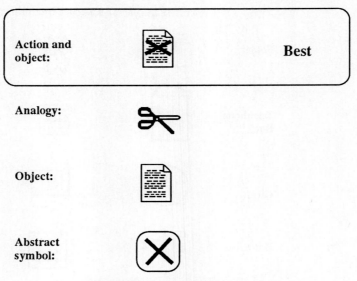

Action and
object:

Best

Analogy:

Object:

Abstract
symbol:

Figure 9–16   Icon mapping schemes.

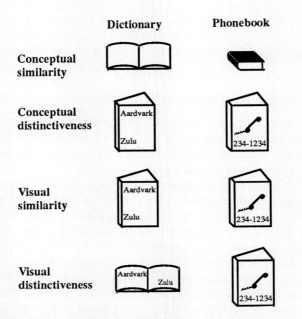

Dictionary   Phonebook

Conceptual
similarity

Conceptual
distinctiveness

Visual
similarity

Visual
distinctiveness

Figure 9–17   Conceptual and visual distinctiveness in icon design.

Poor:

Improved:

Figure 9–18   Borders detract from visual distinctiveness of icons.

shape, even though the detail within the shape varies. This will slow down search times.

Many icons designers provide good detail in icons, but then surround each icon with a rectangular border. This detracts from the visual distinctiveness of each icon and should be avoided. Figure 9-18 illustrates this.

Finally, the icon pair in Figure 9-17 labeled "Visual distinctiveness" is optimal, because not only are the two icons dissimilar in overall shape, but they also include detail that makes them conceptually discriminable as well. Icons that are *both* visually and conceptually distinct will provide the best performance (the least confusions and the fastest search times).

☞ **Avoid excessive detail in icon design.**

Include only enough detail to make icons distinctive. Excessive detail is distracting and does not add discriminability or recognizability. Examples are given in Figure 9-19.

☞ **Design icons to communicate object relations and attributes whenever possible.**

Design in similarities, such as overall shape or color, for icons that belong to a related set (see, for example, Figure 9-14). When icons can take on important

Poor: **Improved:**

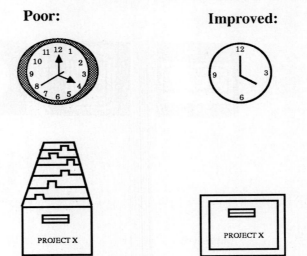

Figure 9–19   Avoid excessive detail in icon design.

Poor: **Improved:**

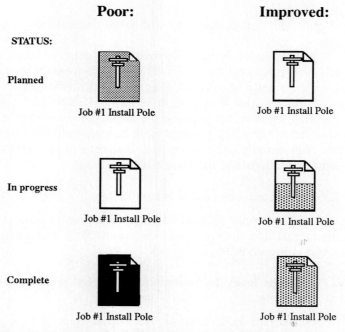

Figure 9–20   Expressing object attributes through icon design.

attributes, design aspects of the icons to communicate these attributes in a meaningful way. Figure 9-20 shows two ways to indicate job status (that is, "planned," "in progress," or "complete"). Using different colors will not be as effective as using a fill pattern because the proportion of the icon filled with the fill pattern is *articulatorally less distant* (see the first guideline on pages 316–320) from the object attribute of status than is an arbitrary assignment of color.

☞ **Accompany icons with names.**

The value of icons as compared to words is that it can be easier to *discriminate* between *familiar* pictures than between familiar words when searching for a particular item. Consider, for instance, scanning down the palette of command icons in the "Improved" version of Figure 9-13. It would take much less time to locate the magnifying glass or paintbrush icon than to find the words "Magnify" or "Paint" in a list of words.

However, it is not necessarily true that icons are more *recognizable* on first encounter than are words. Look at the five icons on the screen in the "Poor" version of Figure 9-13. Would you know the meaning of any of these icons if you had never seen them before? Probably not. On the other hand, if you saw the list of words "Draw, Paint, System Tools, Printer, Project," it would be much easier to imagine what these represented.

Because icons are easy to *discriminate,* but not necessarily easy to *recognize* on first encounter, it is recommended that icons always be accompanied by names, as in the "Improved" screen in Figure 9-13. The names will allow users to *learn* the meanings of icons. Once the meanings are known, the icons will allow users to *search* for and find desired objects faster than would words alone. Thus, both words and icons are better than either words or icons alone, because they support two different mental processes, both of which are important.

☞ **Limit the number of icon types to 12 if possible, but at most to 20.**

It may be difficult for users to learn and remember the difference between icon types if the number exceeds 20 (Galitz, 1989). As the number of icon types increases, aspects contributing to good icon design such as concreteness, familiarity, visual and conceptual distinctiveness, consistent design scheme and constrained detail (see the preceding guidelines) become more and more important.

Each icon type (for example, application, folder, or file) can have many instances, however, as long as they are distinguished at least by labels. Visual distinctions between instances of an icon type are also recommended when possible.

☞ **Allow users to choose between iconic and text display of objects and actions.**

For some users and some tasks, text labels may at times be more effective than icons. Thus, even when an interface is primarily iconic, it is desirable to give users the option of displaying objects and actions as simple text labels on a case by case basis.

REFERENCES

BAILEY, WAYNE A., STEPHEN T. KNOX, and EUGENE F. LYNCH, "Effects of Interface Design upon User Productivity," *CHI '88 Proceedings,* May 1988, pp. 207–12, ACM.

BREMS, DOUGLAS J., and WILLIAM B. WHITTEN II, "Learning and Preference for Icon-Based Interface," *Proceedings of the Human Factors Society 31st Annual Meeting,* 1987, pp. 125–29.

CARD, STUART K., THOMAS P. MORAN, and ALLEN NEWELL, The Psychology of Human–Computer Interaction (Hillsdale, N.J.: Lawrence Erlbaum Associates, 1983).

DUMAIS, SUSAN T., and WILLIAM P. JONES, "A Comparison of Symbolic and Spatial Filing," *CHI '85 Proceedings,* April 1985, pp. 127–30, ACM.

————, and ANNETTE L. WRIGHT, "Reference by Name vs. Location in a Computer Filing System," *Proceedings of the Human Factors Society 30th Annual Meeting,* 1986, pp. 824–28.

EGIDO, CARMEN, and JOHN PATTERSON, "Pictures and Category Labels as Navigational Aids for Catalog Browsing," *CHI '88 Proceedings,* May 1988, pp. 127–32, ACM.

GALITZ, WILBERT O., *Handbook of Screen Format Design,* 3rd ed. (Wellesley, Mass.: QED Information Sciences, Inc., 1989), pp. 173–77.

GOULD, JOHN D., and others, "Empirical Evaluation of Entry and Selection Methods for Specifying Dates," *Proceedings of the Human Factors Society 32d Annual Meeting,* 1988, pp. 279–83.

————, and others, "Entry and Selection Methods for Specifying Dates," *Human Factors,* 31, no. 2 (April 1989), pp. 199–214.

GREENE, SHARON L., and others, "Entry-based versus Selection-based Interaction Methods," *Proceedings of the Human Factors Society 32d Annual Meeting,* 1988, pp. 284–87.

HEMENWAY, K., "Psychological Issues in the Use of Icons in Command Menus," *Proceedings, Human Factors in Computer Systems,* March 1982, pp. 20–24.

HUTCHINS, EDWIN L., JAMES D. HOLLAN, and DONALD A. NORMAN, "Direct Manipulation Interfaces," *User Centered System Design,* D. A. Norman and S. W. Draper, eds. (Hillsdale, N.J.: Lawrence Erlbaum Associates, 1986), pp. 87–124.

KARAT, JOHN, "Evaluating User Interface Complexity," *Proceedings of the Human Factors Society 31st Annual Meeting,* 1987, pp. 566–70.

LANSDALE, M. W., "On the Memorability of Icons in an Information Retrieval Task," *Behavior & Information Technology,* 7, no. 2 (April–June 1988), pp. 131–52.

NOLAN, PETER R., "Designing Screen Icons: Ranking and Matching Studies," *Proceedings of the Human Factors Society 33rd Annual Meeting,* 1989, pp. 380–84.

REMINGTON, R., and D. WILLIAMS, "On the Selection and Evaluation of Visual Display Symbology: Factors Influencing Search and Identification Times," *Human Factors,* 28, no. 4 (1986), pp. 407–20.

ROBERTS, TERESA L., and THOMAS P. MORAN, "Evaluation of Text Editors," *Proceedings, Human Factors in Computer-Systems,* March 1982, pp. 136–41.

ROGERS, Y., "Icons at the Interface: Their Usefulness," *Interacting with Computers: The Interdisciplinary Journal of Human–Computer Interaction,* 1, no. 1 (April 1989), pp. 105–17.

SHNEIDERMAN, BEN, "The Future of Interactive Systems and the Emergence of Direct Manipulation," *Behavior & Information Technology,* 1 (1982), pp. 237–56.

———, "Direct Manipulation: A Step beyond Programming Languages," *IEEE Computer,* 16 (1983), pp. 57–69.

———, Designing the User Interface: Strategies for Effective Human-Computer Interaction (Reading, Mass.: Addison-Wesley Publishing Co., 1986), pp. 179–223.

———, and S. MARGONO, "A Study of File Manipulation by Novices Using Commands vs. Direct Manipulation," *Proceedings of 26th Annual Technical Symposium of the Washington D.C. Chapter of the ACM* (Gaithersburg, Md.: National Bureau of Standards 1987).

WHITESIDE, JOHN, and others, "User Performance with Command, Menu, and Iconic Interfaces," *Proceedings, CHI'85,* 1985, pp. 185–91, ACM.

WOLF, CATHERINE G., and JAMES R. RHYNE, "A Taxonomic Approach to Understanding Direct Manipulation," *Proceedings of Human Factors Society 31st Annual Meeting,* 1987, pp. 576–80.

ZIEGLER, J. E., and K. P. FAHNRICH, "Direct Manipulation," *Handbook of Human–Computer Interaction,* Martin Helander, ed. (Amsterdam: North-Holland, 1988), pp. 123–33.

CHAPTER 10

Dialog Styles: Natural Language

WHAT IS A NATURAL LANGUAGE INTERFACE?

A lot of research has been conducted to develop on-line processing of *natural language,* that is, human languages such as English, French, Arabic, or Chinese. Different lines of investigation include natural language **translation** (that is, translating text stored in one language, such as English, into another language, such as French), natural language **understanding** (for example, natural language as a programming language or command language interface to applications), and natural language **generation** (for example, replies to database queries in natural language).

Natural language as a dialog style involves mostly natural language *understanding:* allowing users to express requests to a software application in their native language. Often it also involves natural language *generation:* reporting results of operations in the user's native language. Examples of natural language dialogs are given in Figures 10-1 and 10-2.

For the purposes of this discussion, a keyboard as an input device and a screen as an output device are assumed. That is, it is assumed that users will enter natural language requests by typing sentences or phrases on a standard QWERTY keyboard and will read outputs on the screen. Another possibility, of course, is to provide voice input and output, so that the user speaks a request, rather than types it, and gets a spoken response, rather than one typed on the screen. This section does not address this type of natural language interface. Voice input and output are discussed in Chapter 12.

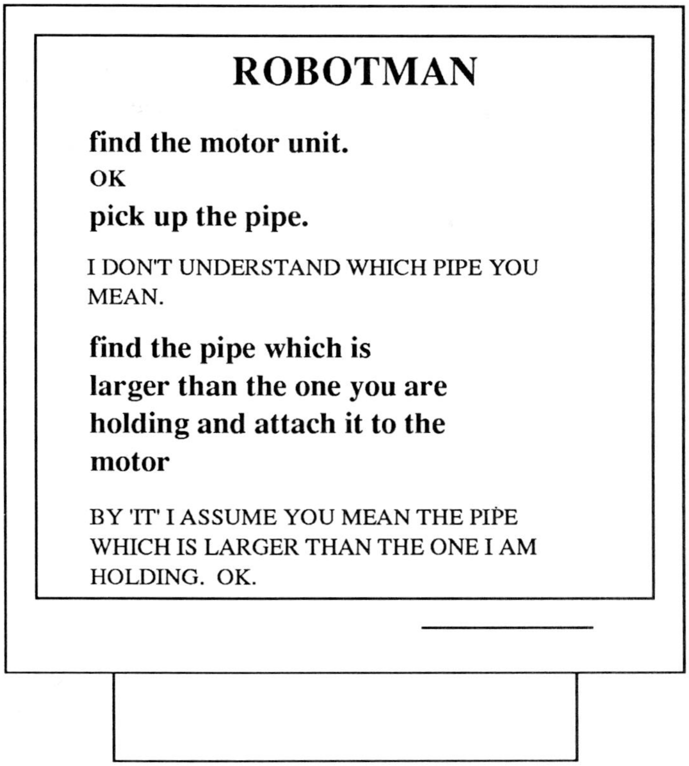

ROBOTMAN

find the motor unit.
OK
pick up the pipe.

I DON'T UNDERSTAND WHICH PIPE YOU MEAN.

find the pipe which is larger than the one you are holding and attach it to the motor

BY 'IT' I ASSUME YOU MEAN THE PIPE WHICH IS LARGER THAN THE ONE I AM HOLDING. OK.

Figure 10–1 An example of a natural language interface.

Although some applications with natural language interfaces are currently commercially available, natural language as a dialog style is not yet in widespread use. This is primarily because the current technology is limited, and natural language parsers are somewhat expensive to develop and run.

The commercial systems that *are* currently available are not *true,* full-blown natural language parsers in that they are not able to understand any and all dialog that would be understood by another person. Instead, they understand a limited subset of natural language; as such, they are more accurately referred to as *restricted* natural language systems. For simplicity, from hereon we will use the terms *natural language* or **restricted natural language** interface or system to refer to a restricted natural language interface or system, and the terms *true* or *full-blown* to refer to the *theoretical* idea of a **true natural language** interface or system.

The notion of a *restricted natural language* interface is important to understand. A good overview of the limitations of restricted natural language interfaces is offered in Ogden (1988) and is paraphrased here.

Natural language interfaces differ in their degree of *habitability*. **Habitability**

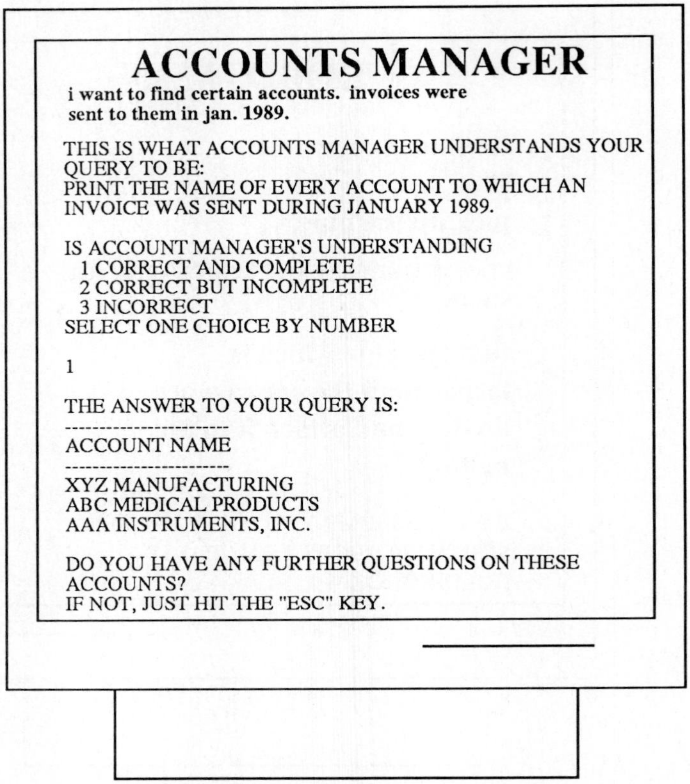

ACCOUNTS MANAGER

i want to find certain accounts. invoices were
sent to them in jan. 1989.

THIS IS WHAT ACCOUNTS MANAGER UNDERSTANDS YOUR
QUERY TO BE:
PRINT THE NAME OF EVERY ACCOUNT TO WHICH AN
INVOICE WAS SENT DURING JANUARY 1989.

IS ACCOUNT MANAGER'S UNDERSTANDING
    1 CORRECT AND COMPLETE
    2 CORRECT BUT INCOMPLETE
    3 INCORRECT
SELECT ONE CHOICE BY NUMBER

1

THE ANSWER TO YOUR QUERY IS:

ACCOUNT NAME

XYZ MANUFACTURING
ABC MEDICAL PRODUCTS
AAA INSTRUMENTS, INC.

DO YOU HAVE ANY FURTHER QUESTIONS ON THESE
ACCOUNTS?
IF NOT, JUST HIT THE "ESC" KEY.

Figure 10–2   An example of a natural language interface.

is a term used to express the degree to which users can *easily and naturally* use the language to express everything required for their tasks using only sentences allowed by the system. Four domains of a natural language interface determine its overall habitability: the conceptual, functional, syntactic, and lexical domains.

The **conceptual domain** of a language refers to the *total set of objects and actions* it provides. For example, if a database system does not have information about managers, then the request "What is the salary of John Smith's manager" is outside the conceptual domain of the interface.

Note that the conceptual domain of the *language* is not necessarily the same as the conceptual domain of the *application*. For example, if the system's reply to the preceding request was "The database does not contain information identifying employee's managers," then the request could be said to be covered by the *language's* conceptual domain, but not by the *application's* conceptual domain. That is, the language *understood* the request, even though the application did not *support* it.

The **functional domain** of a language is defined by what can be expressed directly through the language without elaboration or details. It is similar to the notion of *semantic distance* discussed in Chapter 9 and the notion of *richness versus minimality* discussed in Chapter 7. For example, the request "What is the salary of John Smith's manager" may be out of the functional range of the language because it requires two retrievals from two different tables in the database and these are not explicitly referred to in the request. However, the user might be able to get at the desired information by first asking "Who is John Smith's manager" and then asking "What is Mary Jones salary" (given that the answer to the first question is "Mary Jones"). Note that the problem in the first request is not *conceptual,* as the information necessary to answer the question in fact exists in the database. The problem here is also not *syntactic,* because the system might accept a request such as "What is the name of John Smith's manager," which has the same syntactic form as the first request, but is functionally different in that it only requires one retrieval from a single table.

The **syntactic domain** of a language refers to the variety of syntactic forms in which a request can be paraphrased and still be understood. For example, a system might not accept "What is the salary of John Smith's manager," but might in fact accept "What is the salary of the manager of John Smith." Not accepting possessives is an example of a syntactic restriction.

The **lexical domain** of a language refers to the vocabulary words it understands. For example, the system might not understand the request "What is the salary of John Smith's manager" but it might understand "What are the earnings of John Smith's manager." Here the system understands the word "earnings" but not the word "salary."

Current natural language interfaces vary in overall habitability. More importantly, they vary in how they restrict usage in each domain: conceptual, functional, syntactic, and lexical. All natural language interfaces are extremely limited *conceptually,* in that the interface only understands requests regarding the limited domain of the specific application. That is, users cannot ask personnel databases questions about the financial status of the company. And they cannot even ask about details of personnel unless these details are stored in the personnel database. However, as long as users have a good understanding of the task domain of the system, this is not a problem.

Restrictions in *functionality, syntax,* and *lexicon* are more problematic because it may be hard for users to detect whether a request was rejected due to one or another of these factors. For example, if the user knows that a database contains information about managers and salaries, but the request "What is the salary of John Smith's manager" is rejected, it may be difficult for them to determine if the problem was functional, syntactic, or lexical and, therefore, to determine which of the alternative requests given in the previous examples would be accepted. Thus, unless natural language interfaces are highly habitable in that they accept and correctly interpret most functional, syntactic, and lexical forms naturally used by users, they may in fact not be as easy to learn as we would expect a natural language system to be.

The concepts of conceptual, functional, syntactic, and lexical habitability become important in discussing the pros and cons of natural language interfaces and in interpreting the available research data on natural language interfaces, which are reviewed in later sections.

WHEN IS A NATURAL LANGUAGE DIALOG STYLE APPROPRIATE?

Natural language interfaces have particular advantages and disadvantages, relative to other dialog styles. *Advantages* include the following:

Easy to learn.   In thinking about the possible syntactic forms of command languages, natural language itself arises as a possibility. The idea is that humans already know their own natural language, and the use of computers would be greatly facilitated if users did not have to invest in learning to translate their thoughts into some arbitrary artificial language. It would seem that natural language interfaces would provide the ultimate in ease of learning: no learning would be required since the computer would understand the user's language.

This is true to some extent, but there are two important qualifications. The first is that although the user need not learn the *language* (that is, syntax and lexicon) of the system (because they already know it), they may still need to learn the *capabilities* of the system *and the characteristics of the problem domain* (the system semantics). And, in fact, although a natural language interface may make it simple to learn the former, it may at the same time make it more difficult to learn the latter (see disadvantages, discussed later).

The second qualification is that, given the state of the art in natural language understanding, it is not quite true that systems truly understand natural language the way another person would. The user must learn the *restrictions* of *particular* natural language interfaces, such as how they interpret ambiguous input, and what kinds of phrasing and terminology they actually understand correctly. Thus, there is always some learning required of the particulars of a given restricted natural language interface.

Taking into account these two important qualifications, however, it is true that a big part of the appeal of natural language as a dialog style is its potential ease of learning as compared to other dialog styles.

Easy to remember.   Obviously, the same characteristics that make a natural language interface easy to learn make it relatively easy to remember when use of a system is infrequent. At the same time, the two qualifications discussed previously apply here. It may be easy to remember the syntax and lexicon of the interface, but not necessarily easy to remember the semantics of the system. And, depending on the relative habitability of the interface, it may or not be easy to remember the syntax and lexicon.

Less transfer problems to other natural language systems.   When people use several systems on a regular basis, they often experience *transfer* problems. That is, because each system has a unique user interface, users may have trouble remembering the correct way to accomplish a task on a given system. Users of several command language systems, for instance, may have trouble remembering whether the "log-off" command on a particular system is "Logoff," "Quit," "Bye," "Exit," or "Kill," because different command languages use different command names for this function.

In theory, if all natural language interfaces were *true full-blown* natural language processors, then users would experience *minimal* transfer problems, since all systems would share a common interface (some transfer problems would still occur due to the natural ambiguity inherent in natural language). In current *restricted natural language* systems, however, transfer problems are not minimized. Parsers tend to accept only one or at most several terms for a given object or function and are restricted to certain syntactic structures. Thus, to some extent, each natural language processor is a different subset of a given natural language, and learning in one may or may not transfer to another.

However, there is certainly more compatibility across natural language systems than there typically is, say, across command languages, function key systems, or even direct manipulation interfaces. Thus, there will most likely be less transfer problems for users who use multiple restricted natural language systems on a regular basis than for users who use multiple systems with other dialog styles.

Powerful.   Like any command language, natural language can be a very powerful form of interaction. Often there are many ways to accomplish the same thing, some more efficient than others. Simple commands can often be strung together so that in a single entry the user can accomplish what might take 20 or 30 menu screens or fill-in fields. Entering one complex natural language string frees the user to do other things while the system carries out the command, whereas the menu or fill-in form demands a continuous give-and-take interaction. In contrast to natural language users, the user of these latter dialog styles must repeatedly wait for screens to refresh, and scan and read through menu options or field captions, prompts, and instructions. The power of a natural language interface depends, however, on its functional habitability. Not all natural language interfaces are as powerful as they might be.

Flexible, user controlled.   Generally, the user can do anything possible in any logical order through a natural language interface. Unlike menus, fill-in forms, and question and answer dialogs, which force the user through a set sequence of steps to get to a desired utility or function, natural language allows the user to specify a request directly, without navigation through forms and screens. The user is more in control of the interaction and can move from one function to another directly without intervening steps.

Fast, efficient.   Although a natural language interface requires more typing than some other dialog styles, it is probably, for certain types of users, one of the fastest, most efficient of all dialog styles, perhaps second only to command languages. Expert, high-frequency users who are also good typists may be able to correctly enter even lengthy, complex commands faster than they could step through multiple screens, scanning for menu options or navigating between and filling in fields. Thus, when speed of interaction is important and users can be expected to be frequent users and good typists, natural language interfaces may provide a distinct advantage over other dialog styles.

Uses moderate screen "real estate."   A natural language interface requires only a few lines on the screen for command entry. The clarification dialog required in a natural language interface (see Disadvantages, discussed next) demands a bit more screen space than would, say, a command language interface, but still not as much as some other dialog styles, such as menus or fill-in forms, which take up considerable space on the screen. This leaves most of the screen available for whatever else should or must be displayed. Thus, when screen "real estate" is at a premium, natural language provides an important advantage over some other dialog styles.

In sum, the main advantages of natural language interfaces are that they may be relatively easy to learn and remember and are also powerful, flexible, and efficient. There are serious trade-offs, however. *Disadvantages* of natural language interfaces include the following:

Assumes knowledge of the problem domain.   At first blush, it may seem that a natural language interface would provide the ultimate in ease of learning. But a distinction between learning the *syntactic and lexical domains* of an *interface* and the *conceptual domain* of an *application* must be made. Consider the following analogy between person–person communication and person–computer communication.

It would seem difficult to argue with the observation that it would be easier for an English-speaking American to communicate with a Russian if the Russian could speak English than if the American had to learn Russian. Therefore, doesn't it follow by analogy that it would be easier for a user to communicate with a computer if the computer could understand that user's natural language than if the user had to learn a specialized command language or other type of interface? Not necessarily.

Suppose the Russian is a geneticist, and the American has never studied either biology or genetics. To communicate with the Russian geneticist about his or her area of expertise, the American layperson must first learn the jargon of the discipline and some basics about the field. The fact that the Russian knows English certainly makes a dialog easier than if he or she did not, but, in fact, geneticists and other specialists really have a language of their own. And that language is based on many unspoken assumptions and known facts.

It is not just the natural language of communication that is the problem for the

American layperson and Russian geneticist. The inability to communicate stems as much from the fact that the American lacks a body of knowledge that the Russian assumes in his or her attempts to communicate about genetics. This situation is analogous to a user's attempts to communicate with a computer.

If users are familiar with a system's *body of knowledge,* say the structure and contents of a database, then a well-designed command language for making queries may not be very hard to learn and use. By contrast, if users are utterly unfamiliar with the internal structure of a database and the meaning of the data it contains, then knowing they can query the database in natural language may not really help at all, just as the fact that a Russian geneticist speaks English does not entirely solve the problem of discussing genetics with a lay English-speaking American.

In fact, forcing *conceptual* novices (users unfamiliar with the problem domain) to learn a structured, concise, notational language may actually help them to learn about the system's *conceptual domain,* and structure the problem they are trying to solve. For instance, if database queries that are *functionally* similar must be phrased in a *syntactically* similar manner (which is not the case in natural language, but is in a command language), then users may begin to understand the relationships between them and begin to form a better model of the underlying structure of the database.

The point is that the *language* of communication is only one aspect of successful communication. The two parties involved in a dialog must also have a common *base of knowledge* and *assumptions* about the subject under discussion for a successful interaction to occur. Unqualified enthusiasm about the use of natural language for computer–human interaction fails to take this distinction into account.

While a menu, fill-in form, or question and answer interface teaches the user about the conceptual or problem domain of a system through heavy prompting and instructions, a natural language interface, like a command language interface, provides no conceptual prompting and therefore assumes conceptual knowledge on the part of the user. A natural language interface, like a command language interface, will not (in and of itself) help the user learn the conceptual domain of the application, while a menu, fill-in form, or question and answer interface would. In the words of one natural language researcher (Zoltan-Ford, 1984), ''Just because people know how to drive a car does not mean that they can drive cross-country without a map.''

Requires lengthy confirmation and clarification dialogs. Because natural language is so rich, redundant, and context dependent, a lot of **clarification dialog** must go on between parties in a dialog. If you listen to your own conversations with people, especially on technical topics, you will observe that much of your half of the conversation involves *repeating, paraphrasing,* and *clarifying* what your partner has said. You do this automatically and unconsciously. And, because speaking and listening are fast and easy, it does not seem to impede the conversation.

When natural language is employed as a dialog style on a keyboard- and screen-based application, the same kind of clarification dialog must often occur. However, typing and reading are not as efficient as speaking and listening. Thus, for expert, high-frequency users, natural language interfaces can become very tedious when compared to a concise, limited command language. Figures 10-1 and 10-2 provide examples of the sort of clarification dialog that usually must occur in the use of a natural language interface, but that would not need to occur in a traditional command language interface because of its lack of ambiguity.

Concise, specialized, notational languages have been around for centuries, long before the advent of computers. Notational language systems for the problem domains of mathematics, music, and chemistry, for instance, have been refined over human history and enjoy a high degree of acceptance. It would never occur to an expert mathematician or musician that natural language might be a superior way to communicate with other experts on their subject. In fact, natural language would probably be considered a very awkward and confusing way for experts to communicate about ideas within these domains.

Notational languages differ from natural languages in a number of interesting and important ways. First, they have a *one-to-one correspondence between symbols and meanings,* whereas natural languages include many words with the same meanings and multiple meanings for the same word.

Second, *nothing is assumed except when explicitly stated,* whereas in natural language communication there are always innumerable unstated assumptions that determine correct interpretation.

Third, *deductions are made from an invariant frame of reference,* whereas in natural language conversation, the meaning of the exact same utterance in two different situations may differ strongly based on context.

These characteristics of formal languages are exactly what eliminate the need for the clarification dialogs that must occur in a natural language communication. Communicating with a computer about a structured database of information is probably more like talking to a mathematician about math than it is like talking to a neighbor about politics. Once learned (and/or if the user has a fairly deep understanding of the problem domain), a precise, notational (but well designed) language may, in fact, be a far more efficient and effective means of communication than would natural language.

Assumes typing skill.   Typing is maximized in a natural language interface, as compared with a menu, function key, or direct manipulation interface. Thus, unless users are touch typists, they may actually be slowed down on a natural language interface relative to other dialog styles that may require more screens, but less typing, to accomplish a task.

Error prone.   Even touch typists are presented with more opportunity to make keying errors in a natural language interface, as compared to other dialog styles that require minimal typing. Thus, the heavy typing required in a natural language interface not only potentially slows down input, but may also increase errors, which, in turn, decreases overall throughput.

Enhancements are invisible.   Because there is little or no prompting in a natural language interface, the user has no way of knowing (through the interface) when changes and enhancements have been made to the system. Whole new subsystems or database tables may have been added, but this will not in any way be visible to the user. Only memos and manuals will bring this to the users' attention. This is in contrast to some other dialog styles, such as menus and fill-in forms, in which new functions naturally appear as menu options or fill-in fields, notifying the user of their presence.

May create unrealistic expectations, encourage users to relinquish responsibility, and generate negative reactions.   Shneiderman (1980a,b) points out that natural language interfaces, because they seem so humanlike and intelligent, may encourage naive users to form unrealistic expectations concerning a system's capabilities. Users may try asking unrealistic questions, such as asking a simulation model how to improve profits, rather than asking for forecasts of profits based on particular input parameters.

Related to this point, natural language interfaces may also encourage naive users to relinquish responsibility. Because the system understands natural language, it seems intelligent, and naive users may be less likely to question data or information they receive from a system. However, the quality of output always depends on the quality of input, as well as the correctness and accuracy of the application software.

Shneiderman also notes that some users may be offended by ''cute'' or ''salesy'' messages from a system that has been designed to seem ''conversational'' on both sides of the dialog. And a system that seems to be intelligent (because it speaks a natural language) but that generates erroneous output (due to correctly parsed but semantically misinterpreted natural language queries) may generate mistrust, anger, fear, and anxiety in users.

Expensive to implement.   Last but not least, a *true natural language* interface is probably the most expensive type of dialog style to implement, in terms of both coding effort and computer resources required for execution (although *restricted natural language* interfaces, as discussed in the next section, are not unreasonably expensive). This expense simply may not be justified in many applications, even those for which natural language may otherwise appear to be an appropriate dialog style.

In sum, the main drawbacks of natural language interfaces are that they provide little or no conceptual assistance, are error prone and tedious for the expert, high-frequency user, and are expensive to implement.

Given these relative advantages and disadvantages, we can draw some conclusions about the kinds of tasks and users for which natural language as a primary

Natural language interfaces are most appropriate for users with:

☞ User psychology

Negative attitude
Low motivation

☞ Knowledge and experience

High typing skill
Low system experience
High task experience
Low application experience
High frequency of use of other systems
Low computer literacy

☞ Job and task characteristics

Low frequency of use
Little or no training
Discretionary use
High turnover rate
Low task importance
Low task structure

Figure 10–3   When to use natural language interfaces.

dialog style might be appropriate. Figure 10-3 lists the user characteristics (see Chapter 2) for which a natural language interface would be a good choice.

In the preceding discussions, it was pointed out that, for any dialog to be successful, both parties must share not only a common language but also a common knowledge base and common assumptions. This suggests a division of users' knowledge into two domains: conceptual or *semantic* (knowledge of the problem domain) and *syntactic* (knowledge of the language of the dialog) (see Shneiderman, 1980b, 1986). Each dimension is a continuum. Shneiderman suggests that where users fall on these two dimensions of knowledge determines the appropriateness of natural language as a choice of dialog style.

A user who is inexperienced both in the problem domain and on the new system (*low semantic, low syntactic knowledge*) is an unlikely candidate for natural language interfaces. Without an understanding of how the data in the problem domain are structured and interrelated, the user will be unable to phrase appropriate requests without a great deal of prompting and hand holding. Teaching this user about the problem domain would be facilitated by a menu or fill-in form interface, and probably even through a precise command language. But the lack of prompting, as well as the ambiguities, richness and redundancies of natural language, will not assist the user in coming to understand the precise relationships between data.

At the other extreme, users who are both well versed in the problem domain and experienced in the use of a particular system, say with a concise command language interface (*high semantic, high syntactic knowledge*), would probably find natural language, with its extensive typing and lengthy clarification dialog, to be cumbersome, tedious, and inefficient by comparison.

Users such as data entry operators have much more syntactic than semantic knowledge (*low semantic, high syntactic knowledge*), and, like the complete novice, the free form of natural language will not help them to structure and understand a problem domain that is unfamiliar to them. It will be more tedious to use than the command language or fill-in forms they are familiar with.

This leaves the user who is sophisticated about the problem domain but unfamiliar with the interface of a new system (*high semantic, low syntactic knowledge*). For this type of user, natural language may be perceived as very user friendly. These users already understand the data they are dealing with and how to structure the problems they are trying to solve. A natural language interface would relieve them of the task of learning a new computer language to get access to the data they need. An example might be an expert lunar geologist seeking information from a database of data on lunar rocks (see the example in the discussion of experimental results on pages 344–345).

However, with frequent use even this type of user eventually would learn a command language (that is, acquire high syntactic knowledge), and, once learned, a precise, concise language might be easier to use and more efficient than natural language. *Thus, the type of user most likely to benefit from a natural language interface is one who is sophisticated about the problem domain, but an infrequent user or a user of many different systems.* This kind of user would have trouble learning and remembering the particulars of artificial command languages and may not use any one system enough to achieve the potential efficiencies of such languages.

Examples of application domains with this type of user might include library card catalogs, airline schedule databases, and automatic teller machines (ATMs). Even so, alternative dialog styles such as menu systems may be just as appropriate for this kind of user, and they are certainly less expensive to build and run. In sum, when deciding whether or not the expense and complexity of a natural language interface is justified, an analysis of the intended user population and alternative dialog styles is in order.

There is little debate that existing command language interfaces are often difficult to learn, frustrating, and intimidating for novice, nontechnical users. However, this does not necessarily lead to the conclusion that natural languages are superior as a dialog style. It merely suggests that currently available command languages are not well designed for ease of learning. They can be greatly improved by following the design guidelines offered in Chapter 7 and may always be the best choice of dialog style for certain types of users and applications.

Natural language does offer some of the benefits (for example, ease of learning and remembering) of other dialog styles, such as menus, fill-in forms, and question and answer dialogs, that command languages do not offer. However, unlike those dialog styles, natural language, like command languages, also offers power, flexibility, and user control. How important this combination of characteristics is for an intended user population will determine whether the considerable expense of implementing a natural language interface is justified.

DESIGNING NATURAL LANGUAGE INTERFACES: EXPERIMENTAL RESULTS

The relative advantages and benefits of natural language interfaces have been tested in a variety of studies. Shneiderman (1980a) reports an interesting set of data about the use of a natural language system:

> An appealing system without clarification dialog is LUNAR (Woods et al., 1972, Woods, 1973) which responds to lunar geologists' questions about the rocks brought back by the Apollo 11 moon flight. At the Second Annual Lunar Science Conference, in 1971, LUNAR was presented with 111 actual requests: 10 percent could not be parsed or interpreted, 12 percent "failed due to trivial clerical errors" (which were corrected immediately after the conference) and 78% were handled satisfactorily. Successfully handled queries included:
>
> Give me the average SM analysis of Type A rocks
> Give me the oxygen analysis in S10084
> What samples contain chromite
> Give me the EU determinations in samples which contain ILM
>
> Woods reports that "a class of graduate students in information retrieval given an appropriate introduction spent an hour and a half asking it questions and found only two that failed." A psychology graduate student had to pose six questions before constructing one with which the system could cope. These different experiences underline the impact of user background in using natural language systems.

This informal study provides support for some of the discussion in the previous section. The lunar geologists represented users with *high semantic* but *low syntactic* knowledge. Their 10% miss rate probably reflects both the limits of the natural language parser and the users' lack of syntactic knowledge.

The information retrieval students represent users with *low semantic* but *high syntactic* knowledge. Their low miss rate reflects their understanding of databases and traditional database query languages in general and the brief instruction they were given in lunar geology data (that is, system semantics). The psychology student, on the other hand, represents the user with *low syntactic* and *low semantic* knowledge. As predicted in an earlier discussion, a natural language interface did not really help a user low in *semantic and syntactic* knowledge to learn to use the system effectively and efficiently. Although the sample sizes in this study are small and the methodology somewhat informal, the data do support the caution recommended previously in the use of natural language interfaces.

Shneiderman (1980a) also reports a study of his own comparing the performance of users accessing information from a database using a natural language interface and a more traditional database query language called SQL. Users (22 programming students) were told about a department store employee database and were asked to pose questions to it to help them decide which department to work for. All subjects used both the SQL and the natural language interfaces, half using one first and half using the other first. SQL users were instructed in its use. Natural language users were told to phrase questions in English. Each query was scored according to its *validity* (that is, if it was answerable from the database) and its relevance to the problem of deciding in which department to work.

More *invalid* queries were posed by natural language users than by SQL users (1.91 versus 0.23 per user, respectively), especially if they used natural language before using SQL. Invalid queries posed by natural language users were often relevant to the problem at hand, just not answerable from the database. There was no difference in the number of valid queries posed by the two groups of users. This result reflects on the *conceptual habitability* of the natural language interface. Data regarding the types of errors (for example, syntactic, lexical) and efficiency of input are not reported.

This study seems to indicate that there were no clear advantages of the natural language interface when compared with a concise query language and that, in fact, these natural language users were misled into posing invalid questions. However, it is not really that clear-cut.

The necessary instruction that SQL users received (not given to natural language users) about the particulars of SQL undoubtedly educated them on the nature of the database contents as well, giving them an advantage over natural language users in distinguishing valid from invalid though relevant queries. What this study does suggest, however, is that learning a more concise, precise query language may help users to structure their problems. That is, it may implicitly teach them about the *conceptual domain* of the system. This is implied by the finding that SQL users made less invalid queries.

Another study (Small and Weldon, 1983) also compared the performance on systems with natural language and SQL interfaces to database query applications using a more controlled (and perhaps less naturalistic) task. Twenty users were shown printouts of complete database tables marked up with special notation to indicate specific desired query results. They were then asked to pose the query that would have produced the result. As in the Shneiderman study, all users used both interfaces, but in different orders. The performance measures taken included the time between viewing the result and initiating a query (*think time*) and the total time to express a valid query (*response time*).

SQL	ENGLISH
Select Doctor from Staff where Specialty = Select Specialty from Services where Department = "Family Services"	Find all doctors listed on staff whose specialty falls within the department of family services in the services table.

QUERY	TIME TO FIRST RESPONSE in seconds	TIME TO VALID in seconds
SQL	69.8	84.6
ENGLISH	78.0	92.5

Figure 10–4 A comparison of a natural language versus an artificial language interface. From Small and Weldon, ''An Experimental Comparison of Natural and Structured Query Language,'' *Human Factors,* 25, no. 3, 1983, 253–63. © 1983 by the Human Factors Society, Inc. Reprinted with permission. All rights reserved.

Figure 10-4 presents an example of a query and its valid expression in both natural language and in SQL and the data from this study. Here we see that SQL produced faster performance than did natural language (English) on both measures of efficiency.

Again, these data seem to cast doubt on the benefits of natural language interfaces. However, it is actually not too surprising, when users are working *backward* from a query result expressed by marked up database tables, that it might be more direct for them to express the query in terms of the tables (as SQL requires) than to paraphrase it in natural language. The study does not necessarily prove that users working *forward* from general requirements in their mind, rather than *backward* from database tables, will work faster in SQL than in natural language. That is, it is not clear that the task in this study really reflects the mental processes users are executing when they actually query databases.

It is also important to note that even in the natural language system the users were required to make explicit reference to the database tables (see Figure 10-4). A request such as ''Who are the doctors in family services'' would be invalid in this system, because two tables must be consulted in this problem (''Staff'' and ''Services'') and neither is explicitly referred to. This is an example of *functional inhabitability*. Had the natural language system been more habitable functionally (for example, if it had allowed requests such as ''Who are the doctors in family services''), the natural language system might have showed an advantage.

Thus, in both these latter studies, the advantages exhibited by SQL may have been due to the *poor conceptual and functional design* of the natural language system, rather than to any inherent disadvantage in natural language interfaces in general.

Finally, it should be kept in mind that in both these studies only a small subset of SQL was used, and it is unclear just how complex the queries in the tasks were. Perhaps in very complex queries, requiring a much more extensive knowledge of SQL, natural language would have started to show an advantage. And neither of these latter two studies makes a distinction in user experience, which the first study and the discussion in the previous section suggest will determine the appropriateness of natural language as a dialog style.

In sum, studies that try to directly compare natural language interfaces with alternative dialog styles really only compare a *particular* natural language interface to a *particular* alternative. Natural language interfaces vary in the degree to which they are conceptually, functionally, syntactically, and lexically habitable. These characteristics will undoubtedly determine the usability of the natural language interface under investigation, but they are not measured or controlled for in these studies. No one natural language system can represent the realm of possible natural language systems, so no strong conclusions regarding the relative usability of natural language versus other dialog styles can be drawn from the studies of the sort that have been conducted.

Whereas the preceding discussion reviewed laboratory studies of experimental systems, Ogden (1988) reviewed a number of studies that sought to evaluate the usability of prototype or commercial natural language systems. The results consistently indicated a fairly high rate of conceptual, functional, syntactic, and lexical errors among users. This was particularly the case when users were untrained in the task domain and language restrictions and when they were performing tasks of their own choice, rather than experimenter-defined tasks. However, since the whole point of natural language interfaces is to minimize the learning burden, these results reflect more on the design of the restricted natural language interface than on the users. By the same token, these results reflect on the inadequate conceptual, functional, syntactic, and lexical habitability of the *particular* restricted natural language interfaces evaluated, rather than on the potential usability of natural language interfaces.

Other studies have investigated different ways to design a natural language system to see if certain design variables would have any effect on performance. Given the complexity and expense of building *true, full-blown natural language* parsers, a number of studies have investigated the potential usefulness of *restricted* natural language interfaces, that is, systems that understand only a subset of a *natural language*. In fact, *all* natural language systems are restricted, in that they only cover certain conceptual, functional, syntactic, and lexical domains. These studies attempt to determine what restrictions are in effect *not* restrictive, in that they still cover the range of most likely input forms from users.

One study (Zoltan-Ford, 1984) investigated the utility of restricted natural language interfaces through three main variables in the design of a natural language dialog: (1) the *vocabulary* used *by the system* in providing feedback, (2) the *conversational style* used *by the system* in providing feedback, and (3) the *flexibility* allowed in *user input*.

Two sets of system *vocabularies* were tested: familiar and unfamiliar. The *familiar* vocabulary consisted of common words such as "Enter," "Product," and "Change," while the *unfamiliar* vocabulary consisted of less frequently used words such as "Input," "Item," and "Alter." Note that this variable represents *lexical* restrictions.

Two types of system *style* that differed in length and similarity to natural language conversation were tested: conversational and terse. The *conversational* style consisted of longer, complete, grammatical sentences, such as "You can tell me that you want to enter a new product . . .," while the *terse* style was shorter, using only verbs and nouns, such as "You can enter new product . . . ." This variable represents *syntactic* restrictions.

Two levels of *flexibility* in user input were tested: restricted and unrestricted. In the *restricted* version, the computer only responded to user requests that contained the vocabulary and style of communication used by the program's outputs. When restricted users entered requests that did not mimic the program's output, they received an error message. The error message told them in the program's output vocabulary and style that the computer could not understand their message and asked them to rephrase their request. This cycle of nonconforming input and error message output was repeated until the user entered a request in the appropriate form, that is, when the input conformed to the program's vocabulary and style of communication.

In the *unrestricted* version, user input was not restricted to the style and vocabulary employed in the system output. The computer responded to all user requests, regardless of the vocabulary or phrase structure used.

The authors were interested in finding out whether users would naturally mimic the style and vocabulary of the system output in their input and, if not, if they could be "shaped" to use the system style and vocabulary by restricting valid inputs to the style and vocabulary of system outputs and by providing helpful feedback to this effect.

A command language-driven inventory control system was used as the basis for this study. A natural language *front end* was superimposed on this system using the "Wizard-of-Oz" technique. That is, user inputs entered on one terminal were intercepted on another terminal by an experimenter or "wizard" who was out of sight of the user. The wizard translated this user input into the command language of the system and entered it on her terminal. The system then sent output back to the user's terminal. Thus, users assumed they were communicating with software, when in fact there was another person in the loop, translating user input into command language input.

Forty-eight computer-naive users participated in this study and were given inventory control problems to solve, which involved creating, manipulating, and retrieving inventory files through natural language requests. They used "systems" with different combinations of the three variables described: vocabulary, style, and flexibility. The language they used in their input requests was quantified by four measures: (1) *messages,* or the number of unprompted inputs users entered into the system, (2) *mean message length,* or the average number of words in a given input, (3) *words,* or the total number of unique words used by a user, and (4) *output-conforming messages,* or the number of messages that conformed to the system output style and vocabulary. The following results were observed.

People seemed naturally to model the conversational style of the system they were using. That is, among people using an *unrestricted* system, those using a system with a conversational style used 60.39% more words in their requests than did people using a system with a terse style.

People could also be *shaped* to use a particular conversational style by restricting valid inputs. People using restricted systems generated 2.5 times as many output-conforming messages than did people using unrestricted systems. And the number of output-conforming messages increased across tasks, that is, with practice with the system. People did conform more consistently when they used a restricted terse system than when they used a restricted conversational system. But even among users of the unrestricted systems, 78% entered messages that at least contained the verbs found in the program's outputs, indicating some degree of shaping.

People tended to use a relatively small set of vocabulary in their natural language session, regardless of whether they used a restricted or unrestricted system and what kind of style and vocabulary it used. Seventy-seven percent of all unique words used were introduced in the first third of users' sessions.

In general, unrestricted users tended to take more control of the interaction, whereas restricted users tended to allow the computer to prompt them for details of their requests and thus pace the interaction.

Finally, an attitude measure indicated that most users' attitudes toward computers became more positive after use of a natural language system, and this was most true of users who used the more flexible, unrestricted systems.

The author draws a number of design recommendations from these data, as follows:

1. Provide a consistently worded program output: users will model it;
2. Design the program to communicate with tersely phrased outputs of the form "verb–noun": users will model this more so than they will conversational outputs of the form "pronoun–modal auxiliary–verb–determiner–noun;
3. Include nonthreatening error messages that reiterate those vocabulary and/or phrases that the processor can understand: if the program cannot understand their initial requests, users will alter their vocabulary and phrase structures to be like those provided in the error messages.

The author suggests that these guidelines, plus flexibility in the sense of accepting spelling errors and personal word preferences and phrase structure, will result in systems that increase user satisfaction with and attraction to computers.

The data that indicate that users will mimic and can be shaped by system output language and style also suggest that a natural language interface that really only accepts a small subset of natural language words and phrases may still be a successful dialog style, because users will easily and naturally conform to these *syntactical* and *lexical* restrictions and still find the system easy to learn and satisfying. Restricted natural language systems are clearly much less expensive to build, and so this is a significant finding.

Another study (Ringle and Halstead-Nussloch, 1989) also compared restricted and unrestricted natural language interfaces. In this case the natural language interface was to a tutoring system for a word processor. As users performed editing tasks on an unfamiliar word processor, they were allowed to pose questions in natural language to the tutor. The tutor was actually a human (sitting at another terminal in another room), but in this case, unlike in the previous study, the subjects were aware of this.

In one condition, the tutor responded in a *natural* fashion, interpreting any user input as best he could and responding in a natural conversational manner. In the other condition, the tutor responded in a *restricted* (that is, syntactically and lexically) fashion. In this case, slower response times (rather than error messages) indicated to users that they had entered difficult to parse inputs, and status messages gave some indication of the source of the difficulty.

Nine subjects used both tutors, in different orders. It was found that subjects using the restricted system entered more syntactically well formed, less complex inputs than subjects using the natural system. That is, they adapted to the system's constraints easily. Subjective measures indicated that they did not perceive the restricted system as being less natural or helpful than the natural system. As in the Zoltan-Ford (1984) study, then, this study suggests that, through effective feedback, users can be shaped to enter easily parsable inputs without losing a sense of interacting with a true natural language system.

Still another study investigated the idea of shaping users to adapt to a restricted natural language interface (Leiser, 1989). Leiser points out that *convergence* (the term used for the phenomenon of adopting the language form of a dialog partner) is a phenomenon that occurs naturally during dialogs between people. Leiser reviews literature that indicates that people demonstrate convergence in a wide range of aspects of language, including utterance length, speech rate, frequency of interruption, level of self-disclosure, and use of syntactic structures and features. He suggests that, since convergence is a natural phenomenon in person–person dialog, it might occur naturally in person–computer dialog; if so, it could be exploited to shape user input to the constraints of a restricted natural language system without sacrificing the perception of naturalness.

As in the Zoltan-Ford (1984) study, different language forms were used in the system output to see if users would naturally adopt these forms. The task was to retrieve information from a database of information regarding students in a university. Four language forms were used. Whereas in the Zoltan-Ford (1984) study, system language form was presented in prompts and error messages, here system language form was presented in clarification statements following user input. Language forms varied in lexical and syntactic details. Thus, for example, in response to the input "How many students did French in 1982" the system might respond in one condition, "Did you mean to say: Give the number of people who took French in 1982," and in another condition, "Did you mean to say: How many students did French in 1982." Using the Wizard-of-Oz technique, all user inputs were accepted and responded to, and the main measure of interest was whether or not users would naturally adopt the language form of the clarification statements *when there was no penalty for not doing so.*

Strong evidence was found that convergence indeed occurred. That is, over time, subjects adopted the lexical and syntactic forms of the system output more and more in their input statements. This occurred even though there was no penalty (for example, slower response time or error messages) for not doing so. This again suggests that if system output is carefully phrased to match optimal (that is, the most easily parsable) forms of input, users will naturally adopt these forms, even in the absence of explicit reinforcement.

Another interesting example of the tendency of users to mimic system language is cited in Damerau (1981). In the natural language system under study, users were observed to make *errors* because the system presented clarification statements in a form *not* valid for input, and users mimicked them. Thus, it seems that it is not only helpful to phrase system output in valid input forms, but it is in fact misleading not to do so.

Although these four studies vary somewhat in the variations on language form that they employed and how those forms were communicated to users, taken together they seem to indicate that users will naturally tend to mimic a consistent language form if they can perceive one in system output, and that even when the system is intolerant of deviations from this form (for example, gives error messages), users will still perceive the interface to be a natural language interface. This supports the utility of restricted natural language interfaces, which are considerably less complex and less expensive to implement compared to unrestricted, full-blown natural language interfaces.

The key to designing successful restricted natural language interfaces thus seems to be in selecting a set of conceptual, functional, syntactic, and lexical restrictions that do not render the system unhabitable, and in providing consistent feedback to users so that they can directly observe and thus easily learn the restrictions. A methodology for designing a good restricted natural language interface is suggested by another study (Wixon and others, 1983). In this study, as in others discussed previously, the Wizard-of-Oz technique was again employed, but in a slightly different way and for a different purpose.

Sixty-seven computer-naive users participated in this study over a 7-month period. They were presented with an electronic mail task on a command language system that provided no menus, no on-line help, no documentation and no instruction. None had ever used an electronic mail system before. They were simply told to do whatever they thought might work to accomplish their task.

Unknown to users, a "wizard" or experimenter was intercepting their input and translating it into system-recognizable commands whenever their input was unrecognizable by the current command parser. Thus, users were allowed to create their own *lexicon* and *syntax*. The experimenter defined the tasks, that is, the *functions* that users were to invoke. The software kept a log of user input, and after several users had been tested, the system would be redesigned to accept new input forms generated by recent users. The system was thus continuously redesigned and retested in an iterative fashion, based on novice user expectations and preferences.

The initial system could recognize only 7% of users' input, and novice users accomplished almost no useful work in an hour. Using this design methodology, the experimenters produced a final version of the system that could recognize 76% of users' commands and on which novices could successfully accomplish the entire task within an hour with no instructions or prompting at all.

Over the many iterations of system design, the hit rate of the parser was strongly correlated with its complexity, that is, the number of rules and words it included. The addition of some rules and words made large differences in the hit rate of the parser, while the addition of others made only small differences. An example of a high-impact change was allowing the three most commonly used synonyms for vocabulary words (increasing *lexical* habitability). Examples of low-impact changes included making the system "space-blind" in interpreting sequences of words and numbers, such as "memo3" = "memo 3" (increasing *syntactic* habitability), and allowing the fourth and fifth most common synonyms for words. To be successfully parsed, most user commands observed early on in the experiment required multiple changes in the parser. That is, it was rules in combination, rather than any individual rule, that had a significant impact on parser hit rate.

This study suggests a methodology for creating the kind of restricted natural language interface recommended by Zoltan-Ford (1984) and others. A natural language system that is restricted will be more practical to implement, but if the restrictions are based on user expectations and preferences, the system may seem unrestricted.

Note that in this study the "hit rate" or number of parsable inputs is used as a measure of usability. It is important to realize that the number of parsable inputs may be a good measure of *syntactic* and *lexical* habitability, but may or may *not* be a good measure of *functional* habitability. This is because users may find a small number of simple input forms that are successful and use them consistently, even though they are functionally inefficient. This would result in a high rate of parsable inputs, but would not reveal the functional power (or lack thereof) of the system.

For example, a user entering 12 requests of the form "Find all invoices for jan (feb, mar, and so on) 1989" would enter 12 parsable inputs, but a user entering several inputs of the form "Find all invoices for each month in 1989" might get several error messages, because the system could not handle the functionality inherent in this request. If most users exhibit the former behavior, as seems likely given the studies that show how quickly and naturally users adapt to restrictions, then simple hit rate will not provide a complete measure of the ultimate habitability of a given natural language system. In the Wixon and others (1983) study, some but not many of the changes made to the parser in response to user input were functional. Most were lexical and syntactic. Having defined the users' tasks in this study may have limited the extent to which unhabitable restrictions in functionality were revealed.

Another example of building an empirically derived, restricted natural language interface is offered in Whalen and Patrick (1989). Here the basic system was a hypertext database of information regarding the organization in which the researchers worked. Instead of the usual method of navigating through hypertext, which involves selecting highlighted words embedded in hypertext paragraphs, users could phrase requests for information by typing in natural language input. In fact, not even a restricted natural language parser was involved. Instead, the parser compared user inputs to special template strings containing keywords that were associated with each hypertext paragraph and transition between paragraphs. Following a particular search algorithm, the system took the user to the paragraph that best matched their input.

Initially, a small database containing a few paragraphs of information was implemented. People were then asked to search for information. Paragraphs and transition pathways were created to accommodate new requests. That is, in this study, *functional habitability* was also empirically determined by not restricting users' tasks to predefined tasks.

In the end, the system contained 68 paragraphs and 108 transitions. At that point, 10 subjects were asked to search the database for anything of interest to them for as long as they found it useful and interesting. These subjects entered an average of about 20 queries each. The database was able to respond correctly to 59% of these natural language queries. Subjects were not under the impression that the system actually understood natural language; they seemed to understand that the system was searching for keywords extracted from their input. However, they expressed a positive attitude toward the interface, saying they would use such a database again if it contained useful information.

One of the applications natural language interfaces are most commonly applied to is database query. It has been well established in the cognitive psychology literature that people have difficulty with formal logic relations (for example, conditionals, such as "If . . . then" relations, and rules involving union, "or," and intersection, "and," relations). Querying databases often involves applying such logic relations. Formal database query languages involve precise ways to phrase such relations, but natural language potentially allows users to phrase queries in a variety of ways. Given that people typically have trouble with formal logic relations, the question arises as to whether natural language interfaces will facilitate or compound this problem. One study has addressed this question empirically (Ogden and Kaplan, 1986).

Using the Wizard-of-Oz technique, these researchers presented query problems to subjects by presenting database tables on paper with elements missing from them and asking them to enter queries to the system in natural language that would retrieve the missing elements. The database contained information about students in a university, including name, home state, grades, and major. For example, subjects might be given a table in which student names were missing for all students whose home state was Texas and who also were majoring in physics. A correct response here would be something like "Get all students who are from Texas *and* who major in Physics." Thirty-six subjects with some computer but no database experience participated. The only logical relations required in the query problems were *intersection* ("and") and *union* ("or") relations.

When the problem involved an intersection ("and") relation, subjects consistently used "and." When they used "or," it was *almost always* to refer to a union ("or") relation. However, when the problem involved a union ("or") relation, subjects used "and" 30% of the time and "or" 60% of the time. The implication of this is that in a natural language interface, while "or" can be safely interpreted to mean union ("or"), "and" is used ambiguously, sometimes to mean intersection ("and") and sometimes to mean union ("or"). That is, if "and" and "or" are interpreted strictly by their formal logic meanings, the system will sometimes misinterpret users' intended requests.

A more detailed inspection of subjects' input revealed that other parts of their requests (besides the words "and" and "or") could be used to correctly interpret their intentions. In particular, it was observed that "and" was used *between two relative clauses* when the intent was to express a union ("or") relation, but not when the intent was to express an intersection ("and") relationship. For example, to express a union ("or") relation, subjects might enter "Which students live in Idaho *and which* major in psychology?" To express an intersection ("and") problem instead, they would enter "Which students live in Idaho *and* major in psychology?" Applying this simple interpretation rule increased the system's correct interpretation of user input for union ("or") problems from 63% to 76%.

This study illustrates some of the difficulties in interpreting natural language input and, like the Wixon and others (1983) and Whalen and Patrick (1989) studies, emphasizes the need to study the way users use natural language in specific contexts as input to the design of restricted natural language parsers.

A paper by Guindon (1988) reviews literature that summarizes the kinds of language constructs people use under various conditions of real-time constraints. Language in these situations (for example, informal spoken language and typed natural language input to computer systems) differs markedly from formal written speech. It is characterized by short, simple sentences or incomplete phrases, the active voice, and various nongrammatical constructs, such as lack of agreement between constituents (for example, "What is the ten most expensive car?"). In addition, in Guindon's own research, he has noted that when users are interacting with a computer through natural language they also show evidence of a lack of "belief in a shared context," which is typical in person to person dialog. An example of this is a low use of pronouns (for example, "it" and "them") to refer to referents identified earlier in the conversation. These observations on the way language differs according to context (for example, written, person to person, person to computer) again points to the importance of the empirical determination of commonly used language constructs as input into the design of a natural language interface and to the viability of the notion of a *restricted* natural language parser.

None of the preceding studies concerned with restricted subsets of natural language compares performance on a natural language interface to performance on other possible interface types (for example, command languages). None of the studies that *does* attempt to directly compare natural language interfaces to alternative interface styles effectively controls important user variables, such as frequency of use and task experience, or interface variables, such as conceptual, functional, syntactic, and lexical habitability.

However, taken together, the studies reviewed here suggest that a *restricted* natural language system, if designed to offer *conceptual, functional, syntactic, and lexical habitability* based on *empirical data,* might provide a reasonable hit rate without requiring special training. This in turn suggests that a restricted natural language interface *may* be a useful and practical interface style for *casual, infrequent* users performing tasks from a *familiar task domain.* Comparative studies still need to be carried out, however, to determine whether empirically derived restricted natural language interfaces are in fact superior to other possible types of interfaces in these cases.

As a final note, the preceding studies and other studies reviewed by Ogden (1988) seem to suggest that users can adapt more easily to conceptual, syntactic, and lexical restrictions than to functional restrictions. Thus, the potential advantages of natural languages over other dialog styles may lie in providing functional habitability. Designers may be well advised to focus primarily on determining what language forms would provide functional habitability in a restricted natural language interface and providing feedback consistent in form with the syntactic and lexical restrictions of the system.

In sum, although it has not been empirically determined, it would appear that restricted natural language is a promising dialog style for certain classes of users and tasks. However, all the studies reviewed that consider restricted natural language interfaces assume that a *single set of restrictions* can be found that will be habitable by the *majority of users.*

A different approach is taken in a new product called SQLearn, developed by ProLab Software, Inc. (Van Praag, 1990). SQLearn allows *each user* to tailor the language to fit *his or her own functional, syntactic, and lexical requirements.* SQLearn allows database users using SQL, a common database query language, to create their own restricted natural language interfaces as an alternative to using SQL. Users have free rein to create any kind of language they choose, including non-English forms and ranging from verbose, natural-language-like variations to terse, cryptic command-language-like forms. Users simply "teach" the system, through examples, how to recognize their preferred language forms. Teaching

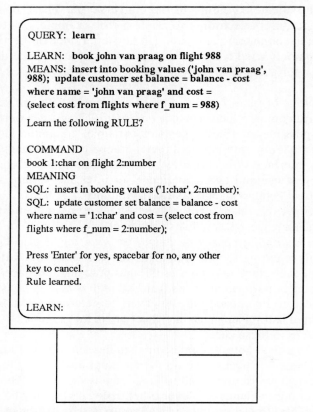

QUERY: **learn**

LEARN: **book john van praag on flight 988**
MEANS: **insert into booking values ('john van praag', 988); update customer set balance = balance - cost where name = 'john van praag' and cost = (select cost from flights where f_num = 988)**

Learn the following RULE?

COMMAND
book 1:char on flight 2:number
MEANING
SQL: insert in booking values ('1:char', 2:number);
SQL: update customer set balance = balance - cost
where name = '1:char' and cost = (select cost from
flights where f_num = 2:number);

Press 'Enter' for yes, spacebar for no, any other
key to cancel.
Rule learned.

LEARN:

Figure 10–5   SQLearn. From ProLab Software, Inc., 120 East 86th Street, NY, NY 10028. With permission.

examples are phrased in the form "THIS means THAT," where "THIS" is a language form of the user's choice and "THAT" is the SQL equivalent of the desired meaning.

Figures 10-5 through 10-8 illustrate the development and use of restricted natural language interfaces using SQLearn. User inputs are displayed in bold and system output in regular text. The application might be used by a travel agency to make travel bookings for customers and keep track of billing information.

Figure 10-5 illustrates how the user would teach the system *syntactic* rules. Users enter the "learn" mode from normal query mode by entering the word "learn." The prompt "Learn" notifies them that they are in learn mode. Then users enter a phrase they would like to teach the system to understand, followed by the equivalent SQL statement, which they would like the system to understand their phrase to mean. The system repeats their example back to them, substituting

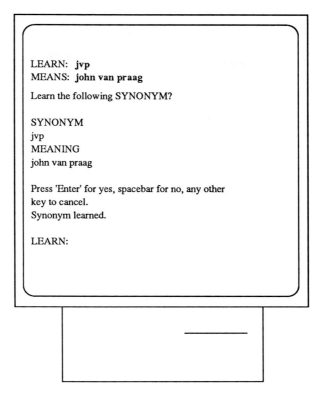

Figure 10–6 SQLearn. From ProLab Software, Inc., 120 East 86th Street, NY, NY 10028. With permission.

variable names for what it recognizes as potential input variables. Thus, the system creates a *general rule* from a *specific example*.

Also note that the user is creating a more *functionally,* as well as *syntactically,* habitable language in this example. What in SQL requires several separate statements referring to several separate tables in the database has been reduced to one simple statement that makes no explicit reference to any tables or fields.

Figure 10-6 illustrates how users can teach the system lexical rules. Any number of synonyms can be defined for field names, field values, and table names.

Figures 10-7 and 10-8 illustrate how users can minimize the keystrokes required in their tailored input language, but still receive clarification dialog in a more usable output language. As shown in Figure 10-7, users can create abbreviated forms of previously created rules. The system will now accept their abbreviated input, but (as shown in Figure 10-8) will provide clarification in the form they initially defined, rather than in SQL. By thus creating rules and synonyms in a layered approach, users can completely shield themselves from SQL and tailor

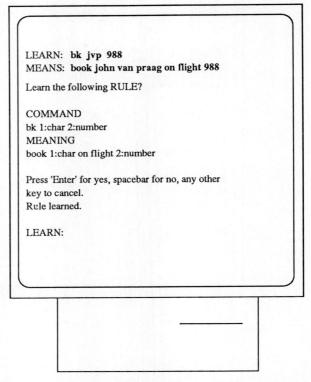

LEARN: **bk jvp 988**
MEANS: **book john van praag on flight 988**

Learn the following RULE?

COMMAND
bk 1:char 2:number
MEANING
book 1:char on flight 2:number

Press 'Enter' for yes, spacebar for no, any other
key to cancel.
Rule learned.

LEARN:

Figure 10–7   SQLearn. From ProLab Software, Inc., 120 East 86th Street, NY,
NY 10028. With permission.

both the inputs and outputs of the system to their own personal functional, syntactic, and lexical preferences.

Users familiar with SQL should be able to create tailored, restricted natural language interfaces for themselves quite easily. Database administrators could use SQLearn to create restricted natural interfaces for users unfamiliar with SQL. While these users would initially learn a restricted natural language tailored to a group, rather than to them personally, the languages would probably still be easier for them to learn than SQL. And they can then modify and tailor the language initially provided to them using the same SQLearn capabilities used by the administrator.

Although SQLearn was still in beta testing at the time of this writing and has not been empirically evaluated and compared against other interface types, it seems to represent a very promising vehicle for maximizing the functional, syntactic, and lexical habitability of restricted natural language interfaces so that the potential benefits of natural language interfaces can be realized at a reasonable cost.

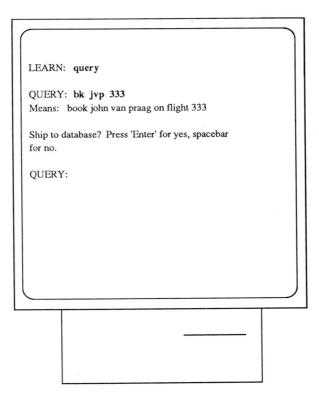

LEARN: **query**

QUERY: **bk jvp 333**
Means: book john van praag on flight 333

Ship to database? Press 'Enter' for yes, spacebar
for no.

QUERY:

Figure 10–8 SQLearn. From ProLab Software, Inc., 120 East 86th Street, NY,
NY 10028. With permission.

DESIGNING NATURAL LANGUAGE INTERFACES:
PRINCIPLES AND GUIDELINES

Like direct manipulation, commercially viable and available natural language interfaces are relatively new, so we have little experience with them and little
research to draw upon. However, the preceding studies and others can be summarized in a few design guidelines for natural language interfaces.

☞ **Provide a restricted natural language interface that is conceptually, functionally, syntactically, and lexically habitable. Determine the subset of true natural
language to include empirically using the Wizard-of-Oz technique.**

In a restricted natural language interface, conceptual, functional, syntactic,
and lexical restrictions should be tailored to users' expectations and preferences.
These can be determined through iterative testing and redesign with the Wizard-of-

Oz technique, using representative users performing tasks of their choice (see the discussion of habitability on pages 333–336 and 345–359 and the discussion of the Wizard-of-Oz technique on pages 348–349 and 351–354).

☞ **Phrase all system output in conceptually, functionally, syntactically, and lexically valid input forms.**

It has been found that users will naturally mimic the language form of system outputs in their own inputs. Thus, users can be *shaped* to provide valid and easy to parse inputs by stating all system prompts, clarification statements, and error messages in valid input forms.

☞ **Prompt and clarify in terse but clear language. Use consistent familiar terminology and simple, brief grammatical form.**

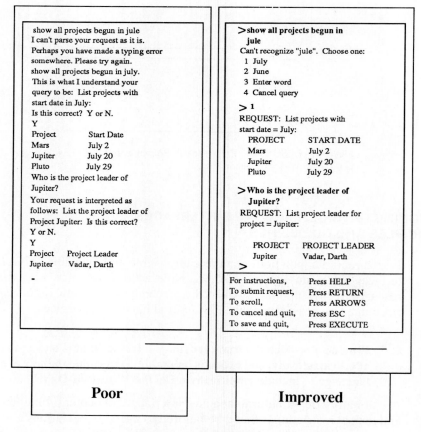

Figure 10–9   Natural language design guidelines.

Note the verbose and wordy prompting in the "Poor" version of Figure 10-9. This is not only difficult to read and clutters up the screen without adding any real value, but it will also encourage users to phrase inputs in the same verbose style (see Zoltan-Ford, 1984). This increases their typing time and probably their syntactic and semantic errors as well. The inconsistent grammatical style of the two clarification dialogs ("This is what I understand your query to be" versus "Your request is interpreted as follows") will also require more attention from the user than is necessary.

Note, by contrast, the system output in the "Improved" version. Simple captions and short phrases are used. This is easier to read and will encourage users to enter input in the same terse style, which will be faster and less error prone. The consistent style for clarification dialog ("REQUEST:") will also make it easier for users to find (or ignore) this output.

☞ Provide cooperative responses.

Handle ambiguities and simple errors cooperatively. Instead of simply noting an error and asking for reentry, as on the "Poor" screen in Figure 10-9, present users with likely interpretations and let them make choices with one or two keystroke responses, as in the "Improved" screen.

Also, make reasonable interpretations of requests. For instance, suppose a user makes the following request to a personnel database: "list the addresses of all employees in department xyz." A literal interpretation of this request would result in a listing of addresses, with no names! The user has not explicitly asked for names, only addresses. However, a *cooperative* system would assume that the user wanted the data in the name field of each record as well as the data in the address fields.

☞ Provide an optional clarification dialog.

Note in both the "Improved" and "Poor" versions of Figure 10-9 that users' questions are paraphrased in a form of *clarification dialog* before answers are displayed. However, while the "Poor" version requires user input in response to the clarification dialog, in the "Improved" version no confirmation is required before the answer is displayed.

Some systems have no clarification dialog. This can be dangerous because users may often enter *syntactically* correct requests that are not interpreted as they were intended (that is, *semantically*) and thus receive data that they then use incorrectly. For instance, suppose a user of a personnel records system enters the following three requests in this order:

"Get all employees who have been with the company less than 2 years"
"Take all employees with salaries greater than $30,000"
"List them"

It is not clear what the user wants to list. If the user wants all employees of less than two years *and* with salaries greater than $30,000, but the system assumes the "get" and "take" requests to be independent, then the user will get a list of *all* employees whose salaries are greater than $30,000. Without a clarification dialog that paraphrases the second request in a way that makes the system's assumptions clear, users might never realize that they did not get what they wanted. If they then use system output to make business decisions, this can be a serious kind of error indeed. Thus, clarification dialogs are an important part of a natural language interface.

On the other hand, clarification dialogs are tedious and can get in the way of users who are very familiar with a system and have learned its restrictions and vocabulary. Thus, it is a good idea to provide clarification dialog as a default, but give users a way to turn the clarification dialog off and on, according to their needs.

One way to make a clarification dialog a little less intrusive is to restate the user's request (for verification) but not require any input to confirm the request, as in the "Improved" screen in Figure 10-9. This way users can review the clarification if they wish, but it does not slow down the presentation of output or require any user interaction, as does the "Poor" version. Or you might require only a carriage return for confirmation.

☞ **Distinguish between user input and system output with white space and visual cues.**

When a dialog history is visible, it is important to make it easy to scan through past questions and pick out pertinent information. This can be done by using visual cues of various sorts. Note in the "Poor" version of Figure 10-9 that all text is plain and no white space separates segments of the dialog. The dialog history all seems to run together, and it is difficult to find particular pieces of it without simply reading through the whole thing.

In contrast, the "Improved" version uses bold text and an arrow to separate user input from system output, capital letters to tag clarification dialog and to separate captions from fields in output data, and white space to separate each question and answer pair and to separate clarification dialog from output data. This screen is much easier to scan and read.

☞ **Provide a way to view and edit dialog history.**

One potential advantage of a natural language interface is that, like a command language, it takes up minimal screen real estate. One to four lines at the bottom or top of the screen should usually be enough to display one user input request and one system response.

However, it can be very useful to keep as much dialog history visible on the screen as possible as context to help users remember where they are and what they have done to date. This is particularly important because natural language interfaces make heavy use of context (that is, past input) in interpreting user requests.

Viewing a dialog history will help users review and verify the assumptions the system will be using in parsing new input. Note in both examples in Figure 10-9 that the whole screen is used for the natural language dialog, and so answers to previous questions are visible when users phrase new requests.

It is also useful to allow users to edit and reexecute input, rather then reenter long input strings.

☞ **Provide instructions for navigation.**

Users will need navigation commands to enter requests, scroll forward and backward through the dialog history, and exit the dialog. These should be prompted on the screen, as in the "Improved" version of Figure 10-9. No prompting, as in the "Poor" screen, means that users will have to remember these conventions. Since natural language interfaces are best for casual users with low syntactic knowledge because such interfaces require little learning and memory, it is counterproductive then to require users to learn and remember these other aspects of interaction.

REFERENCES

DAMERAU, F. J., "Operating Statistics for the Transformational Question Answering System," *American Journal of Computational Linquistics,* 7 (1981), pp. 30–42.

GUINDON, RAYMOND, "How to Interface to Advisory Systems? User Request Help with a Very Simple Language," *CHI '88 Proceedings,* May 1988, pp. 191–96, ACM.

HAUPTMANN, ALEXANDER G., and BERT F. GREEN, "A Comparison of Command, Menu-Selection and Natural Language Computer Programs," *Behavior & Information Technology,* 2, no. 2 (1983), pp. 163–78.

LEISER, R. G., "Exploiting Convergence to Improve Natural Language Understanding," *Interacting with Computers: The Interdisciplinary Journal of Human–Computer Interaction,* 1, no. 3 (December 1989), pp. 284–98.

OGDEN, WILLIAM C. "Using Natural Language Interfaces," *Handbook of Human–Computer Interaction,* Martin Helander, ed. (Amsterdam: North-Holland, 1988), pp. 281–99.

———, and CRAIG KAPLAN, "The Use of *And* and *Or* in a Natural Language Computer Interface," *Proceedings of the Human Factors Society 30th Annual Meeting,* 1986, pp. 829–33.

RINGLE, M. D., and R. HALSTEAD-NUSSLOCH, "Shaping User Input: A Strategy for Natural Language Dialogue Design," *Interacting with Computers: The Interdisciplinary Journal of Human–Computer Interaction,* 1, no. 3 (December 1989), pp. 227–44.

SHNEIDERMAN, BEN, *Designing the User Interface: Strategies for Effective Human–Computer Interaction* (Reading, MA: Addison-Wesley, Inc., 1986)

———, *Software Psychology: Human Factors in Computer and Information Systems* (Cambridge, Mass.: Winthrop Publishers, Inc., 1980b).

———, "Natural vs. Precise Concise Languages for Human Operation of Computers,"

Proceedings, 18th Annual Meeting of the Association for Computational Linguistics and Parasession on Topics in Interactive Discourse, June 19–22, 1980a, University of Pennsylvania, pp. 139–41.

SMALL, DUANE W., and LINDA J. WELDON, "An Experimental Comparison of Natural and Structured Query Language," *Human Factors,* 25, no. 3 (1983), pp. 253–63.

TENNANT, HARRY R., KENNETH M. ROSS, and CRAIG W. THOMPSON, "Usable Natural Language Interfaces through Menu-based Natural Language Understanding," *CHI '83 Proceedings,* 1983, pp. 154–60, ACM.

VAN PRAAG, JOHN, Personal communication, April 1990, ProLab Software, Inc., 120 86th Street, NY, NY 10028, 212-831-0700.

WHALEN, THOMAS, and ANDREW PATRICK, "Conversational Hypertext: Information Access through Natural Language Dialogues with Computers," *CHI '89 Proceedings,* May 1989, pp. 289–92, ACM.

WIXON, DENNIS, and others, "Building a User-defined Interface," *CHI '83 Proceedings,* 1983, pp. 24–27, ACM.

WOODS, W. A., "Progress in Natural Language Understanding—An Application to Lunar Geology," *Proceedings of the National Computer Conference,* 42, (1973), pp. 441–50, referenced in Ben Shneiderman, ed., *Software Psychology: Human Factors in Computer and Information Systems* (Cambridge, Mass.: Winthrop Publishers, Inc., 1980), pp. 202–203.

ZOLTAN-FORD, ELIZABETH, "Reducing Variability in Natural-language Interactions with Computers," *Proceedings of the Human Factors Society 28th Annual Meeting,* 1984, pp. 768–72.

CHAPTER 11

Dialog Styles: Summary

In the preceding chapters, dialog styles are discussed in their *pure* form. That is, the advantages and disadvantages of each and their associated guidelines are discussed without considering the possibilities or the effects of combining them within a given system interface. In fact, however, most interfaces consist of a combination of dialog styles. And, if we look too closely, it is often difficult to rigorously identify and define the dividing line between dialog styles.

For example, many interfaces commonly referred to as direct manipulation interfaces are really menu interfaces in which menu choices are presented as icons rather than words. Many fill-in forms have pull-down menus associated with individual fields. And most natural languages are not really true natural languages, and so the dividing line between what should be called a restricted natural language and what should be called a command language is hard to pinpoint.

Some authors (Wixon and Good, 1987; Whiteside in Potosnak and others, 1986) have argued that, when it comes to interface design, categorization of dialog styles or of users is an unproductive and even seriously misleading exercise. They suggest that if designers rely on simple categorizations such as those presented in this book, *rather* than on studying *real* users doing *real* work and developing designs through iterative testing, this will blind them to other important aspects and details of the design problem.

There is a great deal of truth in this point of view. If designers do rely *exclusively* on categorizations such as these, they will undoubtedly generate unusable designs. However, the purpose here of categorizing users and dialogs styles is *not* to provide a *substitute* for observing users first hand and iteratively testing designs. Nor is it meant to imply that user types and dialog styles should be considered independently. It is offered as a *context or organizing structure through which designers can begin to sort out the important variables in their design issues*.

The design guidelines offered in this book had to be organized in some way or another, and organizing them according to their relative relevance to individual dialog styles seems as reasonable and useful as any other organization. The reader will have noticed that some guidelines apply to more than one dialog style, but in general these are not repeated across chapters. No organization would have allowed sets of completely mutually exclusive guidelines. Because dialog styles are not perfectly mutually exclusive categories with mutually exclusive sets of guidelines, and because a given interface will usually employ more than one dialog style, when designing a given interface, designers will want to refer back to *all* the preceding chapters on dialog style design.

Rather than blinding designers, however, considering the advantages and disadvantages of each dialog style in its *pure* form *should begin to suggest to designers productive ways to combine them*. For example, some of the disadvantages cited for fill-in forms are that memory is required for valid fill-in field values, and typing errors are common. Some of the advantages of menus, on the other hand, are low memory and typing requirements. This suggests that combining fill-in forms and menus in some way may offer the best of both worlds. One possibility is to have optional pull-down menus accessible from those fill-in fields that lend themselves to menu presentation of valid inputs.

Other examples of creative and potentially powerful combinations of dialog styles are reported in the literature. Tennant, Ross, and Thompson (1983) and Hendrickson (1989) describe systems in which menus and natural language are combined. They suggest that prompting sentence construction through menus can communicate the coverage and limitations of the system, cut down on typing time and errors, and minimize development costs, thus eliminating the main disadvantages of natural language while retaining its ease of learning, flexibility, and power. As an example, users of such a system might construct the request "Find color and name of parts whose color is green or blue" through the following steps:

1. Select "Find" from a command menu.
2. Select "color" from an attributes menu.
3. Select "and" from a connectors menu.
4. Select "name" from an attributes menu.
5. Select "of" from a connectors menu.
6. Select "parts" from a nouns menu.
7. Select "whose color is" from a modifiers menu.
8. Select "green" and "blue" from a colors menu.

Each menu appears in a different window, and users select menu options with a mouse. Menus and menu options appear or become active only when they are relevant and valid. The request is displayed in a separate window as it is being built.

Cohen and others (1989) describe systems combining natural language and direct manipulation. Users can point to graphical representations of objects and then refer to them in natural language input. For example, a user could enter a request such as "How many boards were processed at these (point) (point) stations?" Or they could point to the "Move" command on a menu and then enter "each board at a down machine here (point)." In each case, ("point") indicates a selection of a graphical object with a pointing device, and this object is incorporated into the interpretation of the sentence.

In these examples, one major limitation of direct manipulation, inefficiency in repetitive operations and search operations, is bypassed by the natural language component. At the same time, some of the drawbacks of natural language, such as indirectness, and heavy typing requirements, are alleviated by the direct manipu-

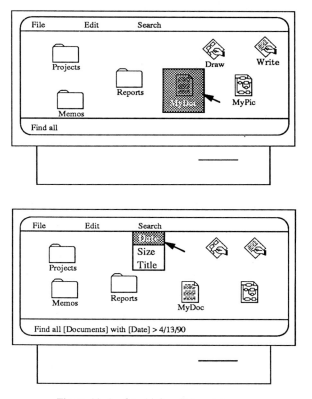

Figure 11-1   Combining dialog styles.

lation component. An example of an interface combining restricted natural language and direct manipulation is given in Figure 11-1. *Multimodal* interfaces such as these have yet to be empirically evaluated. However, they seem to hold promise. And it is the analysis of the relative strengths and weaknesses of *each dialog in its pure form* for *different types of users* that leads a designer to consider particular combinations such as these.

Thus, the categorizations of users and dialog styles presented in this book are offered as a way of organizing what we currently know about user interface design and of structuring the problem of studying users and making initial interface design decisions, which can then be subjected to testing.

IDENTIFYING APPROPRIATE DIALOG STYLES

The first step in dialog design is *identifying potentially appropriate dialog styles,* given user and task characteristics. The second step is *deciding how to integrate them in a single interface* to maximize overall usability. The third step is to *design the details of each dialog style well.* The first step is discussed in this section, and

User profile	Dialog style						
	Menu	Fill-in forms	Question and answers	Command language	Function keys	Direct manipulation	Natural language
User psychology							
Attitude	Negative	Negative Neutral	Negative	Positive	Negative	Negative	Negative
Motivation	Low	Low Moderate	Low	High	Low	Low	Low
Knowledge and experience:							
Typing skill	Low	Moderate High	Moderate High	Moderate High	Low	Low	High
System experience	Low	Low Moderate	Low Moderate	High	Low	Low	Low
Task experience	Low	Moderate High	Low	High	Moderate High	Low	High
Application experience	Low	Low Moderate	Moderate	High	Moderate	Low	Low
Use of other systems	Frequent	Moderate Frequent	Moderate Frequent	Infrequent	Infrequent	Frequent	Frequent
Computer literacy	Low	Moderate High	Low	High	Moderate High	Low	Low

Figure 11–2 Dialog styles summary.

User profile

Dialog style

Job and task characteristics	Menu	Fill-in forms	Question and answers	Command language	Function keys	Direct manipulation	Natural language
Frequency of use	Low	Moderate High	Low	High	Low	Low	Low
Primary training	Little or none	Some	Little or none	Formal	Little or none	Little or none	Little or none
System use	Discretionary	Discretionary	Discretionary	Mandatory	Discretionary	Discretionary	Discretionary
Turnover rate	High	Low Moderate	High	Low	Moderate	High	High
Other systems		Paper forms					
Task importance	Low	Moderate	Low	High	Moderate	Low	Low
Task structure	High	High	High	Low	Low Moderate	Moderate	Low

Figure 11–3 Dialog styles summary.

the second step is discussed in the next section of this chapter. The third step is described in Chapters 4 through 10, according to dialog style.

In Chapters 4 through 10, the advantages and disadvantages of each dialog style are discussed, and a summary of the user characteristics (described in Chapter 2) that each dialog style would support well is given. This section presents a summary of these analyses of each dialog style and a strategy for selecting an appropriate set of dialog styles for an application. Figures 11-2 and 11-3 list user characteristics by name down the left column and dialog styles by name across the top row in a matrix format. Figure 11-2 presents half the user characteristics and all dialog styles, and Figure 11-3 presents the remaining user characteristics and all dialog styles.

Each cell in the matrices holds the particular *value* of the *user characteristic* in that row, for which the *dialog style* in that column would be appropriate. For example, in Figure 11-2, reading down the column under "Menu," it can be seen that menus might be appropriate for users with *negative attitude, low motivation, low typing skill, low system experience, low task experience,* and so on. This is a summary of the discussion on when to use menu systems presented in Chapter 4.

In contrast, reading down the column under command languages, it can be seen that command languages might be an appropriate dialog style for users with *positive attitude, high motivation, moderate to high typing skill, high system*

User profile

Dialog style

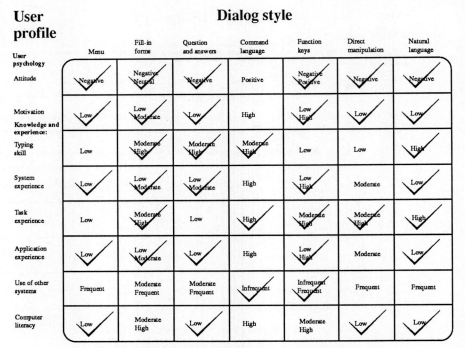

Figure 11–4   Sample use of dialog styles summary: first pass.

experience, high task experience, and so on. This is a summary of the discussion on when to use command languages presented in Chapter 7.

☞ **Select appropriate dialog styles according to user and task characteristics.**

Although these matrices do not provide a "cookbook" or algorithmic approach to choosing a dialog style based on user characteristics, they can provide a useful structure for analysis. After determining where the intended users fall on each user characteristic (see Chapter 2), we first read across each row (user characteristic) in the four matrices, checking every cell that matches the user characteristics (or *priority* user characteristics; see Chapter 2).

For instance, suppose the *high-priority* users in a user population had the following characteristics:

Attitude	Negative
Motivation	Low
Typing skill	High
System experience	Low
Task experience	High

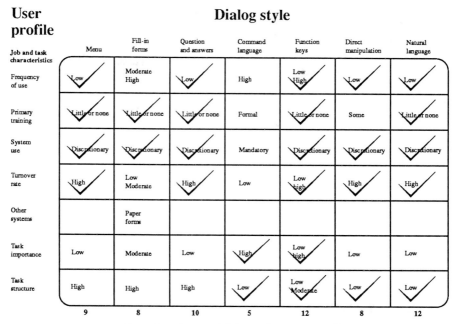

User profile / Dialog style

Job and task characteristics	Menu	Fill-in forms	Question and answers	Command language	Function keys	Direct manipulation	Natural language
Frequency of use	Low ✓	Moderate High	Low ✓	High	Low High ✓	Low ✓	Low ✓
Primary training	Little or none ✓	Little or none ✓	Little or none ✓	Formal	Little or none ✓	Some	Little or none ✓
System use	Discretionary ✓	Discretionary ✓	Discretionary ✓	Mandatory	Discretionary ✓	Discretionary ✓	Discretionary ✓
Turnover rate	High ✓	Low Moderate	High ✓	Low	Low high ✓	High ✓	High ✓
Other systems		Paper forms					
Task importance	Low	Moderate	Low	High ✓	Low high ✓	Low	Low
Task structure	High	High	High	Low ✓	Low Moderate	Low ✓	Low ✓
	9	8	10	5	12	8	12

Figure 11–5 Sample use of dialog styles summary: first pass.

Application experience	Low
Use of other systems	Infrequent
Computer literacy	Low
Frequency of use	Low
Primary training	None
System use	Discretionary
Turnover rate	High
Task importance	High
Task structure	Low

This might be a description of, say, university students using an automated card catalog system in the university library.

These values can be matched to the values identified for each user characteristic for the dialog styles in the matrices, checking every cell where a simple match is found. For instance, since users in our example are *negative* in *attitude* and low in *motivation,* then all dialog styles except command languages would be checked in the two rows for these two characteristics. Since they are *high* in *task experience,* fill-in forms, command languages, function keys, direct manipulation, and natural language would be checked in the task experience row. Figures 11-4 and 11-5 show an initial marked up set of matrices for the users just described.

User profile

Dialog style

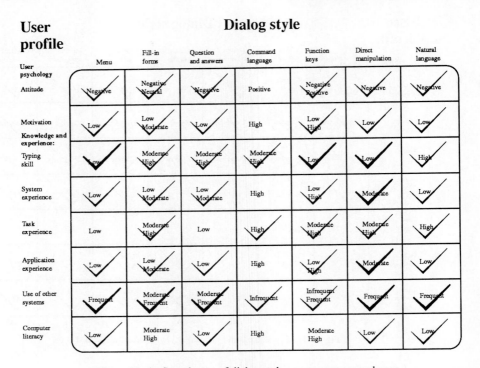

User psychology	Menu	Fill-in forms	Question and answers	Command language	Function keys	Direct manipulation	Natural language
Attitude	~~Negative~~ ✓	~~Negative~~ Neutral ✓	~~Negative~~ ✓	Positive	~~Negative~~ Positive ✓	~~Negative~~ ✓	~~Negative~~ ✓
Motivation	Low ✓	Low Moderate ✓	Low ✓	High	Low High ✓	Low ✓	Low ✓
Knowledge and experience:							
Typing skill	~~Low~~ ✓	Moderate ~~High~~ ✓	Moderate ~~High~~ ✓	Moderate ~~High~~ ✓	Low ✓	Low ✓	High ✓
System experience	Low ✓	Low Moderate ✓	Low Moderate ✓	High	Low High ✓	Moderate ✓	Low ✓
Task experience	Low	Moderate ~~High~~ ✓	Low	High ✓	Moderate ~~High~~ ✓	Moderate ~~High~~ ✓	High ✓
Application experience	Low ✓	Low Moderate ✓	Low ✓	High	Low High ✓	Moderate ✓	Low ✓
Use of other systems	Frequent ✓	Moderate Frequent ✓	Moderate Frequent ✓	Infrequent ✓	Infrequent Frequent ✓	Frequent ✓	Frequent ✓
Computer literacy	Low ✓	Moderate High	Low ✓	High	Moderate High	Low ✓	Low ✓

Figure 11–6   Sample use of dialog styles summary: second pass.

Next, each *unchecked* cell should be further inspected against two criteria. First, does the dialog style have any *serious disadvantages* for users other than those indicated in the cell for each row or user characteristic? If not, then it should be checked. For example, the users described above have high typing skill. Menus are particularly good for users with low typing skill, so this cell has not been checked. However, they do not carry any penalty for good typists. Thus, menus should get a check on the typing skill characteristic because, even though they provide no special advantage for high-skill typists, they do not introduce any particular disadvantage for this user type.

Similarly, while question and answer dialogs offer a particular advantage to users who frequently use other systems, they pose no significant disadvantage for users who infrequently use other systems. Thus, question and answer should get a check on the use of other systems characteristic because, even though they provide no special advantage for infrequent users of other systems, they do not introduce any particular disadvantage for this user type. In sum, when the user characteristics noted in each cell do *not* match the user characteristics in the user profile, they should *still* be checked if the dialog style *does not pose any particular disadvantage for the user characteristics* in the user profile.

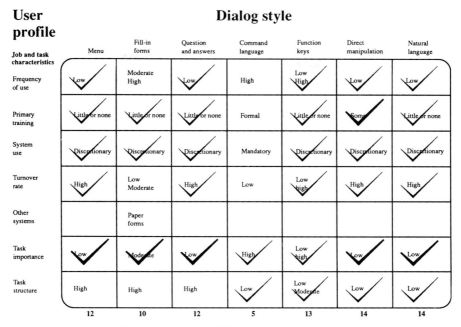

Figure 11–7 Sample use of dialog styles summary: second pass.

Second, the remaining unchecked cells should be considered in the light of *task* characteristics that may interact with *user* characteristics. For example, direct manipulation is said to be best for users with some primary training and some system and application experience. This is because when functionality is at all complex there can be a learning curve with direct manipulation interfaces. Even though our sample users are lacking in training and experience, however, the functionality of the system and task is so simple that it would be possible to build a prompted direct manipulation interface that required no training and experience. Thus, direct manipulation would be appropriate for these *user* characteristics in the light of these interacting *task* characteristics. Thus, direct manipulation should get a check on the primary training, system experience, and application experience characteristic because task characteristics override user characteristics in these cases.

Figures 11-6 and 11-7 show a final analysis. Heavier check marks indicate checks that have been *added* to those in the initial pass through, according to the two criteria described previously.

Next, we sum the number of checks for each dialog style across user characteristics, and note which dialog style columns contain the most ''hits,'' that is, for which there are the most matches between actual user and task characteristics and user characteristics for which that dialog style is considered appropriate. The number of matches for each dialog style is tallied at the bottom of each column in Figure 11-7.

Here we see that the dialog styles that best match the user characteristics of our sample user population are natural language and direct manipulation. The closest competitor is function keys. The characteristics that make natural language particularly appropriate are the *high task experience, low task structure, low frequency of use,* and *high typing skill.* The characteristics that give direct manipulation a particular advantage are *high task experience, low task structure,* and *low frequency of use.*

Other dialog styles are not flexible enough to support a low task structure (for example, question and answer and menus), carry too great a learning and memory burden for low-frequency users (for example, command languages and fill-in forms), or require too much familiarity with computer systems (for example, function keys) to be appealing to novice users.

The high typing skill of these users meets the requirements of a natural language interface. The high task experience of these users also meets the requirements of natural language and direct manipulation interfaces and suggests that the support that menus, fill-in forms, and question and answer dialogs afford to semantic novices is not necessary. Thus, the flexibility of natural language and direct manipulation interfaces turns out to be the key factor making them more appropriate to this set of users than other competing styles.

Thus, the matrices suggest natural language or direct manipulation as the best dialog style for these users. However, this initial suggestion must be integrated with other factors. Maybe the cost of a natural language interface cannot be justified. Perhaps the available hardware will not accommodate a good direct manipulation interface. Or perhaps there are other additional user characteristics not listed in this matrix of sample user characteristics that will point more strongly to one or another of these dialog styles. Because the list of characteristics in these matrices is incomplete, that is, not an exhaustive list of all factors that will ever be relevant in any development project, it cannot provide a reliable final conclusion in all cases. However, the designer can modify the matrices to include other user characteristics that are relevant to a particular project.

Another factor that is not taken into account in the simple use of the matrices described is the *relative importance* of the different user characteristics. For instance, frequency of use may be a more important factor than, say, turnover rate. The simple check-off scoring strategy outlined gives all user characteristics equal weight in the scoring. But the designer may actually end up choosing a dialog style with a lower check-off score because some user characteristics are more important than others and should carry more weight. The characteristics could be prioritized and a weighting factor included in the scoring technique. Or we could simply compute the simple scores and then "eyeball" the highest-scoring dialog styles with these relative priorities in mind to make a final decision.

In any case, even the conclusion arrived at from a modified and weighted matrix should be tested against other relevant factors, such as cost, hardware constraints, and issues of compatibility with other products. That is, the matrices provide a *framework for analysis,* rather than an algorithmic, cookbook strategy to help select an appropriate primary dialog style for a given set of users and tasks.

Most systems incorporate more than one dialog style. Secondary dialog styles should also be evaluated against user and task characteristics, as described previously. Guidelines for combining dialog styles are given in the next section.

After dialog styles are thus chosen, the appropriate chapters can be referred to for guidelines for designing each dialog style. Later chapters provide further guidelines relevant to all dialog styles.

INTEGRATING MULTIPLE DIALOG STYLES

Although it might be seen as a form of inconsistency, there is nothing inherently wrong with incorporating multiple dialog styles within a single interface. In fact, since different dialog styles lend themselves better to different tasks and users and most systems are used by different users performing a variety of tasks, there are inherent advantages to incorporating multiple dialog styles. For example, while some user inputs are best solicited through menus, others cannot be and are best solicited through fill-in fields. The key to the usability of an interface incorporating multiple dialog styles, however, is *smooth integration.*

☞ **Assign dialog styles consistently.**

When multiple dialog styles are employed, they should be *consistently* assigned to functions and other referents in a manner perceivable by users. For example, a system may be primarily menu driven, but present fill-in forms whenever user inputs cannot be solicited by menus (for example, name and address). However, the system should not, for example, *arbitrarily* present fill-in forms for some of these inputs and question and answer dialogs for others.

Similarly, if function keys are used in conjunction with pull-down menus, there should be some rule to determine which referents will be assigned to menus and which to keys. One reasonable rule would be that *actions* will always be assigned to keys and *objects* to menus. Or, as in the "Improved" screen in Figure 11-8, only *generic actions* (which operate on a whole object rather than on data, for example, "Help," "Quit," "Save," and "Cancel") will be assigned to keys; *data actions* and *only data actions* will be assigned to menus. It would be poor design to have some generic actions, data actions, and objects arbitrarily assigned some to function keys and some to menus, as in the "Poor" screen in Figure 11-8. A consistent rule linking referents to dialog styles will facilitate learning and using an interface. Such rules are a part of the conceptual model of the interface (see Chapter 3).

An example of a set of consistent rules for assigning dialog styles to referents in a primarily direct manipulation interface is given next. The application is equipment management for a utility company. Here *objects, object attributes,* and

Poor:

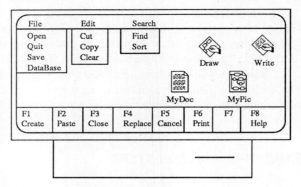

Improved:

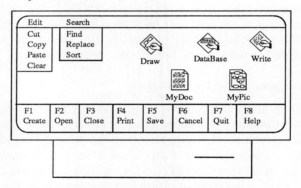

Figure 11–8 Consistent use of dialog styles.

actions are consistently assigned to either a variety of *menu* types, a *command language,* true *direct manipulation,* or *fill-in forms*.

1. *Object instances* (for example, an existing electrical line) are always represented in *icon menus* (a set of icons in the editable area of a window).
2. *Object templates* (an electrical line type) are always represented in *palettes* or *tool boxes* (a set of icons in a noneditable area of a window).
3. All *actions* ("Install," "Remove") are always presented in *text pull-down menus* from a main *menu bar*.
4. Most *actions* are also available through *command language* shortcuts ("CNTL I" for "Install"), which are always displayed beside their menu labels in the pull-down menus.

5. Some *actions* ("Move") are also available through *direct manipulation.*

6. *Object attributes* (line type, line age, line status) are always displayed and modified through *fill-in forms.*

7. *Object attribute* forms are always accessed from a "View Attributes" pick in a *pull-down menu* from the main *menu bar.*

8. Alternative *object attribute* values are offered in *text or icon pull-down menus* activated from *fill-in fields* in the object attribute form.

If rules such as these are consistently followed, users will experience the interface as coherent and predictable and will find it easier to learn and easier to use, in spite of, and in fact because of, the need to learn to use multiple dialog styles. That is, consistent rules in the use of dialog styles will help users form a useful *user model* of the system more easily and quickly. Consistent rules are the key to smooth integration of multiple dialog styles in a multimodal interface.

☞ **Provide alternative dialog styles for different user types.**

Sometimes alternative dialog styles are offered to accommodate users at different experience levels. For example, applications for Apple's Macintosh provide almost all commands through pull-down menus appropriate for novice and casual users. However, a command language bypass for many commands is available to high-frequency users and experts. Commands are invoked with two keystrokes: a special qualifier key called the option key and a single alpha key. There are two ways in which this approach to alternative dialog styles for users at different experience levels illustrates smooth integration.

First, the command language bypass and the menu interface are easily available on a *function by function* basis. That is, users do not have to be in one mode or the other for the duration of a session. At any time they can choose which method they want to use to invoke a function. This is important because users are not simply novices or experts or low- or high-frequency users of *the system.* They are novices or experts or low- or high-frequency users of *individual functions.* A user who uses one function frequently but another only rarely can thus easily use the command language form for the former and the menus for the latter.

The second way that this approach illustrates smooth integration of these two dialog styles is that all commands are listed by their menu labels in the menus. Thus, while novice users are using the menus, they can begin to learn the commands for the functions they invoke most frequently. This allows a smooth transition between novice and expert dialog styles. Using the former facilitates the learning of the latter.

In sum, the designer should consider all possible dialog styles against user and task characteristics. They can often be effectively combined to tap the advantages and alleviate the disadvantages of individual dialog styles. The key to *multimodal* interfaces, however, is smooth integration. This is achieved by building in consistent rules for the assignment of interface components to dialog styles.

REFERENCES

COHEN, PHILIP, and others, "Synergistic Use of Direct Manipulation and Natural Language," *CHI '89 Proceedings,* May 1989, pp. 227–34, ACM.

POTOSNAK, K., and others, "Classifying Users: A Hard Look at Some Controversial Issues," *CHI '86 Proceedings,* April 1986, pp. 84–88, ACM.

TENNANT, H. R., K. M. ROSS, and C. W. THOMPSON, "Usable Natural Language Interfaces through Menu-based Natural Language Understanding," *CHI '83 Proceedings,* Dec. 1983, pp. 154–60, ACM.

WIXON, DENNIS, and MICHAEL GOOD, "Interface Style and Eclecticism: Moving beyond Categorical Approaches," *Proceedings of the Human Factors Society 31st Annual Meeting,* 1987, pp. 571–75.

CHAPTER 12

Input and Output Devices

Although this book is primarily focused on software user interface design, all software is mediated through hardware, and the hardware forms part of the overall system user interface. Thus, some discussion of input and output devices is presented in this chapter.

Input and output devices are the channels through which users and software communicate. Both people and computers have input and output devices, and they must interface with one another, in much the same way that human thought processes and computer software must interface with one another.

Human input devices include the sensory organs of sight, hearing, smell, taste, and touch. From the point of view of computer–human interaction, the key **human input devices** are the **eyes** and **ears** and the sensory organs of **touch.** Users *see* screens, *hear* beeps, clicks, and voice output, and *feel* hardware devices.

The key **human output devices** are the **hands** and, in more recent technologies, the **voice** and **eyes.** Users operate keyboards and other computer input devices, such as touch screens, mice, and joysticks with their hands. Some systems accept voice input, and some even incorporate eye-tracking technology so that where the eyes are directed is actually detected and interpreted by the computer.

Computer input devices (for example, keyboards) interact with human output devices (hands), and computer output devices (screens) interact with human input devices (eyes). We cannot alter or improve *human* input and output devices, but we *can* design *computer* input and output devices to be as compatible as possible with human input and output devices. To do this, we need to know the **operating characteristics** of the human input and output devices, that is, the capabilities and limitations of human vision, audition, tactile sensation, and motor coordination.

The field known as **hardware human factors** or **ergonomics** has made a study of drawing on what is known about these human operating characteristics, and applying them to the design of computer input and output devices. This chapter gives an overview of our current understanding regarding the optimal design of computer input and output devices.

Computer input devices considered in this chapter include the following:

Keyboards
Pointing devices
Voice-synthesis systems
Other input devices

Computer output devices discussed include the following:

VDT screens
Voice-recognition systems
Other output devices

These are not necessarily complete and exhaustive lists of possible computer input and output devices. They are representative of the devices most readers are expected to be familiar with in their use of or design of computer systems.

INPUT DEVICES

The traditional input device is a **keyboard.** More recently, various **pointing devices** such as mice, touch screens, and trackballs have become popular. **Voice-recognition** systems are just beginning to find their way into significant numbers of commercial products. Other less common devices are also in experimental use. These four types of input devices are discussed here in terms of their usability, given the operating characteristics of the human output devices that must operate them.

Keyboards

Keyboard design issues include hardware **operating characteristics,** such as the shape of keys and the force required to depress them, and **key layout.** Several standard groups of keys are considered here in terms of layout: alpha keys, cursor keys, and numeric keypads. Issues regarding the layout of function keys are discussed in Chapter 8.

Keyboard Operating Characteristics

Ergonomists have studied how to design the general operating characteristics of keyboards to optimize usability. Figure 12-1 presents some currently accepted and recommended values for these operating characteristics (Cakir, Hart, and Stewart, 1980; Galitz, 1980).

Keyboard thickness refers to the distance between the base and home row of the keys.

Keyboard angle refers to the angle at which the top surface of the keyboard unit slopes upward from the horizontal edge nearest the body to the horizontal edge farthest from the body. This will affect the angle at which the user must hold the wrists while typing. On some keyboards this slope is adjustable.

The **palm rest area** refers to the amount of keyboard surface below the bottom row of keys (usually the space bar and some other keys) available for resting the palm of the hand during pauses between typing.

Keytop size refers to the breadth, width, or diameter of the top surface of a key. If it is too small, it will be difficult to control with the fingertip. If it is too large, it will be harder to press keys in rapid sequence. Given that peoples' hands and fingertips vary in size, the value given here represents an optimal average.

Key center spacing refers to the distance between the centers of vertically or horizontally adjacent keys. This will affect how easy it is to press keys in rapid sequence.

Key force range refers to the amount of physical force necessary to depress a key to the point where a key press is registered. Keys may be more or less resistant, requiring more or less pressure to depress. Too little force means it will be too easy to depress keys by mistake. Too much force will result in unnecessary fatigue.

Characteristic	Optimal Value
Keyboard thickness	30–50 millimeters (mm) (2 inches)
Keyboard angle	5–15 degrees
Palm rest area	50 mm (2 inches)
Keytop size	12 –15 mm (0.6 inch)
Key center spacing	18–20 mm (0.75 inch)
Key force range	15–125 grams (0.5–4.5 oz)
Key displacement range	3–5 mm (0.2 inch)
Keytop surface	Square, concave
Activation feedback	Tactile and audible
Keytop surface finish	Matte, low glare
Home row indicators	Raised dot, deeper dish

Figure 12–1 Keyboard operating characteristics. From Cakir, Hart, and Stewart, *The VDT Manual* (New York: John Wiley and Sons, 1980) and Galitz, *Human Factors in Office Automation* (Atlanta, GA: Life Office Management Association, Inc., 1980). With permission.

Key displacement range refers to the distance that the key must be pressed downward before a key press is registered. This will affect how easy it is to register a keystroke and how easy it is to press keys in rapid sequence.

Keytop surface refers to the shape of the top of the key. Square keys have been found to be easier to use than round ones, and concave key surfaces have been found to be easier to use than flat key surfaces.

Activation feedback refers to the possible cues the user might receive to indicate that the key press has registered. Keyboards whose only feedback is character displays on the screen are difficult to use. Adding tactile feedback (feeling the resistance when the key is pressed to the bottom of its displacement distance) improves performance. Adding audible feedback (a ''click'') improves performance. Providing both audible and tactile feedback seems to be optimal.

Keytop surface finish refers to both the feel and look of the key top surfaces. A textured or matted finish (as opposed to a glossy, smooth finish) minimizes slipping and also reflection and glare from the keyboard.

Home row indicators refer to the tactile characteristics of home row keys, which makes them distinguishable from other keys. They make it easier to tell by feel alone that the fingers are resting on the home row. Having home row indicators can increase touch typing speed by reducing the need to look away from the source document or screen to the keyboard. Tiny raised dots in the center of the home row keys work well, and a deeper dish to the concave surface than for other keys also works.

Keyboard Layout

Most keyboards can be thought of as containing one or more major groups of keys. These include **alpha keys, cursor keys, numeric keypads,** and function keys. The former three are discussed here. (Function keys are discussed in Chapter 8.)

Alpha keys.   Most computer keyboards follow the standard layout for alpha keys used on mechanical and electric typewriters for over a century. This layout is known as the **QWERTY** layout for the arrangement of letters on the left side of the row above the home row. Figure 12-2 illustrates the QWERTY keyboard layout and an alternative layout known as the **Dvorak** layout, which was proposed in the 1920s.

Given the frequency of use of different letters of the alphabet in the English language, it has been estimated (Cakir, Hart, and Stewart, 1980) that the QWERTY layout results in roughly 57% of all typing being done with the left hand, the least strong and coordinated hand for the majority of people (see Figure 12-2). In addition, only two of the most frequently used letters of the alphabet (a and s) appear in the home row, which means that most frequently used letters are not located in the easiest to reach positions. And only 20% of the most frequently used ''digrams'' (that is, letters appearing in sequence) in English, Spanish, and German

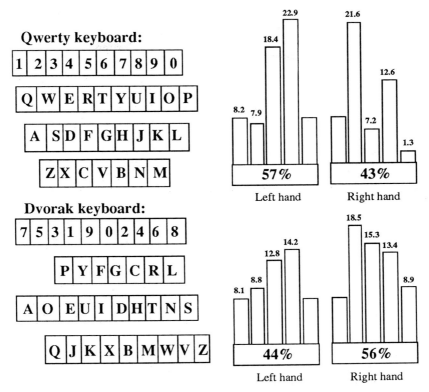

Figure 12-2　Alpha key layouts: QWERTY and Dvorak. From Cakir, Hart, and Stewart, *The VDT Manual* (New York: John Wiley and Sons, 1980). With permission.

can be keyed using alternate hands. It has been shown that keying two keys in sequence with alternate hands is easier than keying them with the same hand.

In fact, the design of the QWERTY keyboard was intentional and based on an understanding of human operating characteristics. The old-fashioned mechanical typewriter of the 1870s could not keep up with the speed of expert touch typists when keys were laid out in a manner more compatible with these human operating characteristics. Typists would type too fast, and keys would jam, ultimately cutting into overall productivity, not to mention user satisfaction. Thus, the QWERTY keyboard was carefully designed to slow typists down *just enough* to accommodate the limitations of the mechanical keyboard, while optimizing overall throughput.

Electronic keyboards, of course, are not as limited as mechanical keyboards. In the 1930s a new keyboard layout was perfected by and named after August Dvorak, based on improving human performance. This layout was designed so that only 44% of the typing load is carried by the left hand (see Figure 12-2), 70% of the typing load is from the home row, and 40% of the most frequent digrams can be keyed using alternate hands (Cakir, Hart, and Stewart, 1980). By one estimate (Galitz, 1980), the Dvorak keyboard, as compared to the QWERTY keyboard, reduces the total distance the hands of a typist must move in an 8-hour work day from 10 miles to 1 mile. Some studies (for example, Kroemer, 1972) show that more words per minute can be achieved on the Dvorak as compared to the QWERTY keyboard.

In spite of the apparent superiority of the Dvorak keyboard, the QWERTY keyboard has remained the standard layout even for the electronic keyboards of computers. There are two probable explanations for this. First, both vendors and users probably perceive the cost of retraining users already familiar with the QWERTY keyboard as too high. Second, many computer users are not highly skilled touch typists, and so the productivity gains made possible by the Dvorak keyboard are not really relevant to them. They will never even approach the maximum typing speeds allowed by either keyboard, so the fact that the Dvorak keyboard may allow faster typing speeds is a nonissue. For them, the cost of retraining is simply not justified.

However, there is some movement toward greater use of the Dvorak keyboard on computers. In 1983, the American National Standards Institute accepted the Dvorak keyboard as an alternative standard to the QWERTY keyboard. Vendors such as Apple, Digital Equipment Corporation, and IBM now build Dvorak options into their hardware and software. Meanwhile, however, QWERTY remains the industry standard and seems likely to continue to do so until the Dvorak keyboard starts penetrating schools where typing is taught.

Besides the QWERTY and Dvorak alpha key layouts, other lesser used layouts exist. The **alphabetic** keyboard, which simply lays out alpha keys in alphabetic order from left to right and top to bottom, appears on some commercial products such as hand-held calculators, remote-control devices, and children's computer toys and games. Anyone who is a touch typist familiar with either the QWERTY or Dvorak keyboard, will find an alphabetic keyboard startlingly difficult to use, despite their familiarity with the alphabet. Card (1987) predicts from a human information processing model (see Chapter 2) that typing on the alphabetic keyboard should be about 8% slower than on the QWERTY keyboard. Some empirical evidence for a performance difference between a QWERTY and an alphabetic keyboard is reported in Mahach (1989). Difficulty using an alphabetic keyboard may be less severe for nontouch typists who have not been trained on standard keyboards (for example, children).

Still another type of computer keyboard has been researched but not yet adopted by any segment of the industry. A **chorded** keyboard is one in which there are only ten or less keys so that the fingers never travel from one key to another. The 26 letters of the alphabet and other characters are available by pressing *combinations of keys simultaneously,* like playing a chord on the piano.

Gopher, Hilsernath, and Raij (1985), report performance data from such a keyboard. The keyboard consists of five keys per hand, each set mounted on an upright panel on which the hand rests in a vertical position so that the palms face one another and the thumb and fingers line up in a vertical column. Combinations of one to five keys produce 31 possible chords, enough for the full alphabet on each hand. Thus, typing can be accomplished with a single hand or by alternating hands. Chords are assigned to keys according to letter frequency of use and chord difficulty.

Initial testing with 100 subjects suggests that the chords can be learned in about 45 minutes, and that proficiency reaches about 35 words per minute after about 20 hours of practice and approaches 60 wpm after about 60 hours. Error rates at these speeds are low, only 1% to 2%. Control data suggests that novice QWERTY users reach only half this typing speed in the same amount of time. Thus, the chorded keyboard would appear to be *easier* (faster) *to learn*. Data are not yet available to determine the maximum typing speed afforded by the chorded keyboard for experts, so it is not yet possible to compare it to the QWERTY keyboard on *ease of use*.

One other interesting observation made by these researchers is that the subjects who learned the chorded keyboard were all experienced QWERTY users, yet they experienced no *interference* in learning the chorded keyboard. That is, the highly automated motor skills they had for using the QWERTY keyboard did not interfere with their learning of the chorded keyboard, nor did learning the chorded keyboard interfere with their QWERTY keyboard skill. Since one source of resistance to alternative keyboards might be that users in transition will use both kinds and experience frustrating interference using both, this is an important point. It may be that this is one reason the Dvorak keyboard has not been widely accepted. It is too similar to the QWERTY keyboard, and QWERTY users would probably experience significant interference in learning the Dvorak layout. Making the transition from the QWERTY keyboard might be considerably easier with a chorded keyboard because the two sets of typing skills are so different that they will not interfere with one another. However, chorded keyboards have yet to receive any serious attention in the computer industry, probably for the same reasons that the Dvorak keyboard has not. On the other hand, Kirschenbaum, Friedman, and Melnik (1986) report that a single-handed chorded keyboard allows disabled users who cannot operate a standard QWERTY or similar keyboard to gain access to computers.

Cursor keys.   Most computer keyboards have four special **cursor keys** for moving the cursor up, down, left, and right through text, menu options, fill-in fields, or other display objects. These keys are typically labeled with arrows, and are sometimes called *arrow keys*.

☞ **Lay out cursor keys in an inverted-T layout.**

There are a number of alternative ways of laying out these keys in relationship to one another. Five possibilities are shown in Figure 12-3. The three ''Poor''

Poor:

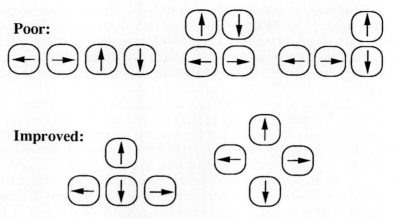

Improved:

Figure 12–3 Cursor key layouts.

arrangements in the top row of Figure 12-3 are considered nonoptimal because the relative positions of the four keys do not correspond as much as they might to the relative directions they represent. For instance, in the first and second arrangements, the up and down keys are oriented left and right with respect to one another. In the third arrangement, the down key is to the right of (rather than below) the right key. Thus, users must perform a mental translation to remember the relative position of the keys if they are not looking at them.

The two "Improved" layouts in Figure 12-3 are considered to be superior because the relative positions of the keys correspond better to the relative directions they represent. The "cross" layout is optimal in this respect, as the relative position of the four keys corresponds perfectly with the relative directions they represent.

Some people prefer the inverted-T layout, however, because it offers a home row for the fingers to rest on while doing a fairly good job of preserving the relationship between position and direction. One study (Good, 1985) found that, across five different editors with various cursor key layouts, the most frequent cursor key transition by far was *down* to *left*. The inverted-T cursor key layout accommodates this high-frequency transition by locating both the down and left keys in this home row, where the two fingers that it is easiest to alternate between (index and middle) can rest on them.

☞ **Locate the cursor keys to the right of and in line with the alpha home row.**

Besides the layout of cursor keys in relation to one another, another important issue in cursor key layout is their location relative to other major key groups on the keyboard. It is recommended that the cursor keys be located out of the alpha area, to the right of alpha area, and in line with the home row of the alpha area. This will make it easiest to find and move to them during typing, while minimizing the striking of cursor keys by mistake.

Numeric keypad.   Two numeric keypad layouts are common: the **telephone** layout, starting with 1 in the upper-left corner, and the adding machine or **calculator** layout, starting with 7 in the upper-left corner. These layouts are illustrated in Figure 12-4.

☞ **Use the telephone layout for the numeric keypad.**

Either layout is superior to the arrangement of numbers across the top row in the alpha key area if a great deal of exclusively numeric input is expected. The available studies (Lutz and Chapanis, 1955; Deininger, 1960) suggest that the telephone layout may yield superior performance. Since more computer users are likely to be familiar with and used to the telephone layout than the calculator layout, this would seem to be the preferable choice.

☞ **Locate the numeric keypad to the right of the alpha key area.**

Most numeric keypads are located to the right of the alpha key area. This seems appropriate since usually the majority of users will be right handed. A choice of left or right handed keyboards would be even better.

Preferred: **Acceptable:**

1	2	3
4	5	6
7	8	9
	0	

7	8	9
4	5	6
1	2	3
	0	

Telephone   Calculator

Figure 12–4   Numeric keypad layouts.

☞ **Make the numeric keypad stand out.**

Sometimes other keys are grouped with the numeric keys, such as arithmetic operators, an "Enter" key, and a "Clear" key. This makes it a little bit more difficult to orient the hand quickly on the numeric keypad. Distinguishing the numeric keys from others in the keypad by color or size or including a home row indicator such as a raised dot on the center row of keys can reduce this problem.

Pointing Devices

Traditional computer systems employed only cursor keys as a mechanism for locating the input area and pointing to desired display objects. More recently, alternative pointing devices have become popular. These pointing devices are used for a number of different types of operations (Foley, Wallace, and Chan, 1984). They include **point**ing to a target, **select**ing a target, free form **draw**ing, **position**ing an object, rotating or **orient**ing an object, defining a **path** between points, **quantify**ing input (for example, by scrolling through a menu of numeric values), and **manipulat**ing text.

Alternative pointing devices vary in how effectively they perform these different operations. For instance, continuous-motion pointing devices, such as the mouse, trackball, and some joysticks, are better for *drawing* than noncontinuous-motion devices, such as cursor keys, touch screens, and some joysticks. Cursor keys can be more accurate, although slower, for *pointing* than some continuous-motion devices such as trackballs.

Pointing Devices: Advantages and Disadvantages

The advantages and disadvantages of a representative set of currently available pointing devices are discussed next. They are summarized in Figure 12-5, presented on page 393 in this section.

Cursor keys.   There are a number of *advantages* of cursor keys. First, they are *particularly convenient for working with text* at the character level and with other displays of discrete objects. This is because the cursor keys can be coordinated with some meaningful unit of the display such as characters and lines in a text display or fields in a fill-in form. Greater accuracy can be achieved than with a device that allows movement anywhere on the screen and requires the user to position the pointer accurately on a small target. It is true that the greater accuracy of cursor keys trades off against speed, so the importance of this advantage depends on the task at hand.

A second advantage of cursor keys is that they can be located a short distance from the alpha key area of the keyboard, making them *easy to reach from the home row*. A third advantage is that because they are embedded in the standard keyboard they *do not take up any additional desk space*.

One *disadvantage* of cursor keys is that they allow *no diagonal or continuous movement.* Related to this, it may require *many distinct operations or steps to point* to a target. Most allow *no speed control,* although some keyboards include a "fast" key; when held down in conjunction with a cursor key, it offers it a second, faster speed. Others provide ways to jump directly across display units, such as a "home" key that takes the cursor to the upper-left corner of the screen or special keys that jump the cursor by word, sentence, paragraph, or page.

Compared to other pointing devices, perhaps the major disadvantage of cursor keys is that there is *no direct relationship* between finger or hand movements on the keys and cursor movement on the screen on the dimensions of *speed, distance, and, in some cursor key layouts, direction.*

That is, the *distance* the cursor moves on the screen is not related to the *distance* the fingers or hands move on the cursor keys (distance is instead related to *number* of key presses or the *time* a key is held down). The *speed* of the cursor movement on the screen is unrelated to the *speed* of finger or hand movements on the keys (in most cases, only one speed is available, which is achieved when a key is held down). And, although on some cursor key layouts (the inverted-T and cross layouts) there is some relationship between the *direction* the fingers and hand move on the keys and the *direction* the cursor moves on the screen, on other layouts there is no such direct relationship (see Figure 12-3).

Contrast this lack of a direct relationship between hand movement and cursor movement with another pointing device: the mouse. If the mouse is moved more quickly or slowly, the cursor is moved more quickly or slowly. If the mouse is moved up, down, or diagonally, the cursor will move up, down, or diagonally. If the mouse is moved far or near, the cursor will move far or near, in direct proportion to the hand movement. There is a very direct relationship between hand and cursor movement on all three dimensions: speed, direction, and distance. This is why the mouse is a more natural device to use once the user has achieved some initial level of eye–hand coordination.

Joystick. There are a number of different kinds of joysticks. Some are *small* and grasped between the thumb and index finger. They require fine motor coordination. Others are *larger* and are grasped by the whole hand. They require more gross motor coordination.

Some joysticks, called **force** joysticks, are stationary and respond to pressure. Continuous pressure in a particular direction achieves distance. Variations in the amount of pressure result in different speeds of cursor movement. Other joysticks are **movable** within a dish-shaped area, and the distance of movement of the cursor corresponds to the distance of movement of the joystick.

Some joysticks are like cursor keys in that they allow no diagonal movement, only horizontal or vertical. Others allow *diagonal movement,* and still others allow *continuous motion* in any direction.

Thus, individual joysticks vary in the advantages and disadvantages they offer. One *advantage* that all joysticks offer is a *direct relationship* between hand and cursor movement on the dimension of *direction.* Some *allow diagonal or continuous movement.* Some can be mounted right on a keyboard and thus *do not require any additional desk space,* a consideration important to many users.

On the other hand, many joysticks suffer from a number of *disadvantages.* Those not mounted on the keyboard *require that the hand be removed from the keyboard,* thus slowing down users doing a significant amount of typing. These also *require additional desk space* beyond the keyboard itself. With most, there is an *indirect relationship* between hand and cursor movement on the dimensions of *speed and distance. Speed* may correspond to amount of *pressure,* and *distance* may correspond to the amount of *time* the joystick is pressed. Joysticks can be more *fatiguing to use* over long periods of time, as compared to, for instance, mice or cursor keys, which allow the hand to rest on the device. Some joysticks allow *no continuous or even diagonal movement,* some afford *no speed control,* and some are simply *slow and inaccurate.* It should be pointed out that most of these disadvantages are not necessarily inherent in the idea or general concept of a joystick, but are realized in actual implementations.

Mouse.   Two kinds of mice are in common use: mechanical and optical. **Mechanical mice** house a rubber ball that rolls along on the desk or mouse pad surface as the user moves the mouse. A device inside the mouse detects the motion of the ball in two dimensions. **Optical mice** have no moving parts. They include a light detector that responds to vertical and horizontal stripes on a special pad. Both mechanical and optical mice vary in their accuracy and durability. Mice also vary in size, shape (for example, rectangular or dome shaped), and number of buttons (from one to three).

One *advantage* that all mice offer is a *direct relationship* between hand and cursor movement on all three dimensions of *direction, distance, and speed.* This makes them one of the more natural devices to use. They also all allow *diagonal and continuous movement and speed control.*

On the other hand, mice suffer from some *disadvantages.* They all *require that the hand be removed from the keyboard,* perhaps slowing down users who do a significant amount of typing. They also *require additional desk space* beyond the keyboard itself, even more so than a trackball or joystick, which are stationary. *Traveling long distances* (for example, on large screens) *may be difficult,* although this can be somewhat controlled by setting the ratio of mouse distance to cursor distance. Some are simply *slow and inaccurate.*

Perhaps the main disadvantage, though, is that mice *require a certain amount of learned eye–hand coordination* and can seem awkward and difficult to use to first-time users. Many experienced mouse users find this difficult to believe until they watch a representative set of first-time users.

First-time users become confused if the pointer or an object they are moving disappears off the screen. They often lift the mouse slightly off the surface of the desk without realizing it and then cannot understand why the cursor is not responding to their hand movements. If they reach the edge of the desk but the cursor is still in the middle of the screen, they cannot figure out how to move the cursor further. They orient the mouse incorrectly and then do not understand why the cursor does not move straight up when they move the mouse straight up. They make many unnecessary, jerky movements and find it difficult to home in on targets.

It takes some time to get used to a mouse, which depends to a certain extent on the natural level of eye–hand coordination of the individual user. Users with less coordination than the average often find their first experience with a mouse to be quite frustrating.

On the other hand, most regular mouse users find a good mouse very easy to use and often prefer it to other devices, including cursor keys, even for text manipulation.

Trackball. A trackball is a spherical object, a ball, that rotates freely in all directions in a socket. Users move the trackball with the tips of their fingers, and its direction and speed are *tracked* by the device and translated into cursor movement.

One *advantage* of trackballs is the *direct relationship* between hand and cursor movement on the two dimensions of *direction and speed*. They also all allow *diagonal and continuous movement* and *speed control*. Some can be mounted right on a keyboard and thus *do not require any additional desk space,* a consideration important to many users.

On the other hand, trackballs suffer from several *disadvantages*. Those not mounted on a keyboard *require that the hand be removed from the keyboard,* perhaps slowing down users who do a significant amount of typing. They also *require additional desk space* beyond the keyboard itself. Some are simply *difficult to control,* making accuracy a problem. All have an *indirect relationship* between hand and cursor movement on the dimension of *distance*. The ball simply goes round and round in its socket, so there is no clear, visible relationship between the distance the ball has traveled in its socket and the distance the cursor has moved across the screen. Using a trackball involves both fine motor control of the fingers (for accurate pointing) and gross motor movements of the hand (for moving long distances) and so can be *fatiguing to use* for prolonged periods of time.

Touch screen. A touch screen is a special surface mounted right on the computer screen. There are several kinds of touch screens, including pressure sensitive, resistive, infrared, and capacitive. **Pressure-sensitive** touch screens respond to pressure. **Resistive** touch screens respond to the meeting of two surfaces, brought together under pressure. The surfaces have conductive coatings, and their meeting causes a drop in resistance, which generates an electronic signal. **Infrared** or LED touch screens project vertical and horizontal light beams across the surface and respond to a break in the light beams due to the presence of the finger or stylus. **Capacitive** touch screens detect the capacitance of the human body. Touch screens can be operated with the fingers or in some cases with any object, such as a stylus or pencil. Users point to and touch objects right on the screen to select them or directly indicate a pathway of motion for a cursor or object to follow. They vary in how sensitive and thus how accurate or error prone they are.

The major *advantage* of a touch screen is that not only is there a *direct relationship* between hand and cursor movement along all three dimensions of *speed, distance, and direction,* but this relationship is even more direct than it is with other devices, because the surface the hand or stylus is moving on is the same surface that the cursor is moving on. Using a touch screen is like directly manipulating the objects on the screen, just as we would directly manipulate them in the manual world. Using a stylus with a touch screen affords a *high degree of accuracy.* Touch screens allow *continuous motion* in all directions, and require *no additional desk space.* Finally, touch screens *stand up well in high-use environments* (Shneiderman, 1986). Resistive touch screens offer the greatest resolution (at the pixel level), while other types offer resolution at 1/4 to 1/2 inch. Capacitive and resistive touch screens are less susceptible to inadvertent activation than other types.

Although the touch screen might seem to be the most natural and intuitive device of all, it does suffer from some serious *disadvantages.* The *finger or stylus may obscure parts of the screen* that the user needs to see to complete some operation. The *finger may be too large for accurate pointing* with small objects (text, for instance) and *requires that the user move the hand rather far away from the keyboard.* A **stylus** is more accurate, but still requires movement of the hand away from the keyboard and *up and down* between typing and pointing. Either the finger or the stylus will be *very fatiguing to use* for extended periods of time, as the arm must be held up in the air. Finally, the *screen can get soiled* from the fingers, causing distracting glare and patterns on the screen surface. This may be considered a particularly serious problem in some environments, such as hospitals, where a high degree of cleanliness is expected. Different types of touch screens are more or less susceptible to other problems, such as parallax (infrared), dirt and scratches (pressure), temperature and humidity (capacitive), and misalignment (resistive) (Brown, 1988).

Touch tablet.　　Touch tablets, like touch screens, are pressure, heat, light, or light blockage sensitive surfaces, but they lie on the desktop, as opposed to being mounted right on the computer screen. Touch tablets can also be operated with the fingers, a light pen or any object such as a stylus or pencil. There is a one-to-one or proportional relationship between any position on the touch tablet and a corresponding position on the screen. If the user touches the upper-left corner of the touch tablet, the cursor on the screen will jump to the upper-left corner on the screen. If the user traces a path across the touch tablet, the cursor on the screen will follow the same path.

A major *advantage* of a touch tablet is that there is a *direct relationship* between hand and cursor movement along all three dimensions of *speed, distance, and direction,* but this relationship is not as direct as with a touch screen. It is more analogous to a mouse. Using a stylus with a touch tablet affords a *high degree of precision,* but less accuracy than a touch screen for obvious reasons. Touch tablets allow *continuous motion* in all directions and, unlike touch screens, *do not obscure the users view of the screen* and *do not result in soiling of the screen.*

Disadvantages of touch tablets are that they *require additional desk space* beyond the keyboard, and they *require that the user move the hand from the keyboard.* Again, the *finger may be too large for accuracy* with small objects, and the *stylus must be picked up and put down* between typing and pointing.

Figure 12-5 summarizes the relative advantages and disadvantages of the pointing devices just discussed.

	Cursor keys	Mouse	Joy stick	Track ball	Touch screen	Touch tablet
Speed	Slow	Fast	Medium	Medium	Fast	Medium
Accuracy	High	Medium	Medium	High	Low	Medium
Speed control	Some	Yes	Some	Yes	Yes	Yes
Continuous movement	No	Yes	Some	Yes	Yes	Yes
Fatigue	Low	Medium	Medium	Medium	High	Medium
Directness	Direction	Direction, distance, speed	Direction	Direction, speed	Direction, distance, speed	Direction, distance, speed
Footprint	No	Yes	Some	Some	No	Yes
Best uses	Cursor	Cursor Point Select Draw Drag	Cursor Point Select Track Drag	Cursor Point Select Track	Point Select	Point Select

Figure 12–5 Advantages and disadvantages of alternative pointing devices.

Pointing Devices: Experimental Results

Several studies have attempted to directly compare performance with different types of pointing devices. Two measures are typically taken: speed and accuracy. One study (Card, English, and Burr, 1978) compared three devices: a mouse, a joystick and a set of cursor keys. Four users participated, each using all three devices, in random order. They had little or no computer experience and no experience with any of the devices tested. Their task was to point to and select a highlighted word or phrase on a screen of text. The target size and distance from the starting cursor position were varied, and each subject performed 1200 to 1800 trials over several days.

The mouse tested was a *mechanical* mouse. The joystick was a *force* joystick that allowed diagonal and continuous motion in all directions. The cursor keys were arranged in a cross layout.

The experimenters looked at both ease of learning and ease of use by inspecting performance early and late in the experiment. It was found that there was a steeper learning curve with the mouse and cursor keys than with the joystick, implying that the joystick might have been *easier to learn* than the other two devices.

Figure 12-6 presents the *ease of use* data from the study, that is, the average performance across users across the last 600 trials in the experiment (excluding the first 200 trials of each day, considered to be warm-up). Three measures of time were taken: the time to move the hand from the starting position (the space bar) to the device, the time to move the cursor to the target once the hand was on the device, and the total time, or the sum of the hand-to-device and the cursor-to-target times. The percentages of trials in error (targets missed) for each device are also presented.

	Hand to device time (s)	Cursor to target time (s)	Total time (s)	Error rate (%)
Mouse	0.36	**1.29**	**1.66**	**5**
Joystick	0.26	1.57	1.83	11
Cursor keys	**0.21**	2.31	2.51	13

Figure 12–6 A study of pointing devices. From Card, English, and Burr, "Evaluation of Mouse, Rate-Controlled Isometric Joystick, Step Keys, and Text Keys for Text Selection on a CRT," *Ergonomics,* 21, no. 8 (1978), 601–13. With permission.

It is interesting to note in these data that, although it is quicker to get the hand from the keyboard to the device with cursor keys, it is quicker to get the cursor to the target once the hand is on the device with the mouse and joystick. The latter time tends to cancel out the former, so the *total* time to select a target from the resting position of the hand is fastest for the mouse, nearly as fast with the joystick, and considerably slower with cursor keys.

In addition, no speed–accuracy trade-off is evident in these data. The least errors were made with the mouse, followed by the joystick and cursor keys, respectively.

Another study (Albert, 1982) compared a larger set of pointing devices. A set of cursor keys and a force joystick were again included, but a mouse was not, and eight additional devices were studied, including a touch screen, touch tablet, and trackball.

Eight subjects participated in this study. Their task was to point to and select a 1¼-inch-square green target on a 19-inch black screen with a white cross hair cursor. The target appeared on the screen in a random position. When successfully selected, it would disappear, the terminal would beep, and another target would appear. Subjects spent about 1 hour during which they used each device for 50 trials. They switched back and forth between devices every 10 trials, in random order. They were told to be both as fast and as accurate as possible and that their object was to achieve the highest possible score in the shortest possible time.

Ease of use was measured by summarizing the data across all users and all trials on two measures: speed (number of pixels per second) and accuracy (number of pixels from the target center of the selected point). The data from five of the ten devices tested are presented in Figure 12-7. Here it can be seen that the best and worst devices for *speed* were the touch screen and keyboard, respectively, while the best and worst devices for *accuracy* were the trackball and touch screen, respectively. Some trade-off between speed and accuracy is apparent. In particular, the touch screen provided the best performance as measured by speed, but the worst when measured by accuracy. The trackball, while the most accurate, was only the third fastest. This suggests that the designer might want to carefully consider whether speed or accuracy is more important, given the task and users, when choosing an appropriate pointing device.

Why was a speed–accuracy trade-off apparent in this study, while no such trade-off was apparent in the Card, English, and Burr (1978) study? Are these data contradictory? The answer lies in looking at which devices were compared in the two studies. If we look at the joystick and keyboard cursor keys, the only devices common to both studies, we note that in the Albert study there was also no speed–accuracy trade-off for these two particular devices. Just as in the Card, English, and Burr study, the joystick was both faster *and* more accurate than the cursor keys. Thus it appears that some devices do trade off speed and accuracy (for example, touch screens), while others do not (for example, a mouse).

When applying the conclusions from these studies to the choice of input device, it should be kept in mind that these studies employed a particular *task*

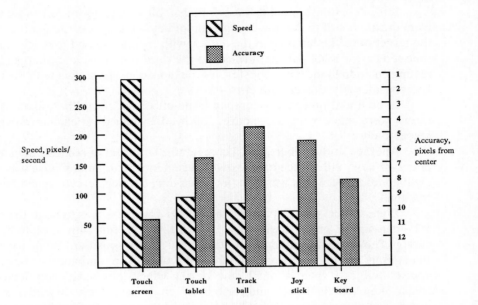

Figure 12–7 A study of pointing devices. From Albert, "The Effect of Graphic Input Devices on Performance in a Cursor Positioning Task," *Proceedings of the Human Factors Society 26th Annual Meeting,* 1982, pp. 54–58. © 1982, by the Human Factors Society, Inc. and reproduced with permission.

(simply pointing to and selecting targets) and particular *targets* (text, and a 1¼-inch square). It is not clear how well these data would generalize to other *task* types (for example, defining regions on drawing pathways) or other *target* types (for example, much smaller or larger targets). Buxton (1987) gives a nice example of the way task type can influence input device performance. He contrasts a continuous joystick to the controls found on the familiar "etch-a-sketch" children's toy: two knobs that can be simultaneously operated to manipulate the horizontal and vertical dimensions. If the task is to draw rectangles, clearly the etch-a-sketch device is superior, as drawing perfectly straight horizontal and vertical lines is very difficult with a continuous joystick. However, if the task is to write your name in script, obviously the joystick would be a much more efficient and effective device, because free form drawing is very difficult with the etch-a-sketch controls. From this simple example it should be clear that results from a test comparing input devices on a particular task cannot be generalized to other tasks unless they are very similar.

It is also important to note in these studies that cursor key movement was by rows and columns on the screen. In many applications, cursor keys are programmed to jump between discrete objects on the screen, such as menu items, fill-in fields, or icons. Other data (Ewing and others, 1986) suggest that, when defined in this way, cursor keys might actually result in faster target selection than continuous motion devices such as mice and trackballs.

These studies also measure *continuous performance on one type of task,* whereas in most applications the user *alternates between many different types of tasks* (for example, typing, selecting small icons, selecting large icons, and defining regions). Thus, it is also not clear from these data which device or combination of devices might optimize *overall* performance in an application that requires many different alternating task types. One study (Karat, McDonald, and Anderson, 1984) found cursor keys to be faster than and preferred over a mouse for tasks that mixed typing and pointing. Another (Greenstein and Baijal, 1989) found that, even when the user's *primary* task involved pointing and selecting with a mouse, *occasional* numeric entry was faster with a numeric keypad than with a variety of mouse techniques for numeric input. Mack and Lang (1989) found a stylus-operated touch screen to be comparable to a mouse on both speed and accuracy measures for performing standard office tasks involving pointing, selecting, and dragging in a direct manipulation, windowed interface. Epps (1987) found a trackball and mouse to be superior to joysticks and touchpads for graphic manipulation tasks such as line drawing and "rubber-banding" (note that this is a different task and different results than those reported in Albert, 1982). Thus it seems clear that one device will not necessarily always be optimal, and that the best device (or best combinations of devices) will depend on both the individual tasks and the particular mix of tasks within an application.

In addition, most of the studies cited focused on *ease of use* for the experienced user. The Card, English, and Burr (1978) study suggests that, while the mouse is easier to *use* than the joystick for certain tasks, it may be more difficult to *learn.* Informal observations of first-time mouse users also support this possibility. Thus, these data should not be generalized to *ease of learning.* If a designer is interested more in ease of learning (for example, for very infrequent users of a system), these data should not be drawn on for direction.

Finally, as pointed out in illuminating detail by Buxton (1987), any study comparing devices compares only *particular instances of a device type,* which may or may not be representative of other devices of the same type. For example, Buxton describes two isometric (force) joysticks that, in spite of all their similarities, differ in size, the muscle groups they employ, and the amount of force they require. Clearly, each might produce very different performance results. Thus, in comparison with another device type, such as a mouse, in one case the joystick might be faster than the mouse, and in the other case the mouse might be faster than the joystick. Just as joysticks vary significantly in their operating characteristics, so do mice, touch screens, and trackballs. Thus it should be clear that conclusions regarding input device types *in general* are not warranted by single studies of *particular* representatives of input device types.

Buxton gives another example in which a particular *spring-loaded* joystick seems to have more ergonomic features in common with a trackball than with another (*isometric*) joystick. Buxton concludes that we need a new classification scheme for input devices that focuses on the "dimension of maximum importance" (for example, the ability to specify absolute versus relative values or the ability to move continuously versus in only vertical or horizontal directions), rather than on the commonalities in appearance and electronics shared by devices of a given type.

While the preceding discussion focused on comparing different types of pointing devices, other studies have focused on optimizing the design of the interaction with a particular device type. Potter, Shneiderman, and Weldon (1988) noted that the many potential benefits of touch screens have not been realized due to high error rates and attempted to find an interaction strategy that would minimize errors. They compared three interaction strategies:

1. *Land on:* the cursor is directly under the finger. Only the position of first contact between finger and screen is interpreted by the system as user input. If there is a target in this position, it is selected.
2. *First contact:* the cursor is directly under the finger. Any and all positions of the finger during contact between finger and screen are interpreted by the system as user input. The target first contacted is selected.
3. *Take off:* the cursor is about 1/2 inch above the finger. Any and all positions of the finger during contact between finger and screen are interpreted by the system as user input. A target is highlighted when contact is made and selected if the finger is released while the cursor is on it.

Many touch screens employ the *land-on* strategy, and errors occur due to parallax between the touch screen surface and the display surface, causing users to misjudge the position they are pointing to by a significant margin. This study sought to determine whether the *first-contact* or *take-off* strategies might eliminate or at least counteract this source of errors.

Targets were two-letter postal state abbreviations embedded in a 10 by 5 matrix of abbreviations in alphabetic order; letters were 1/4 inch square. Twenty-four computer science students served as subjects, and each used all three strategies. Each strategy session was preceded by a short practice session (of five trials).

It was found that the *take-off* strategy significantly reduced errors compared to the commonly employed *land-on* strategy (a difference of 2.25 versus 5.08 errors over 15 trials). However, target selection with the *take-off* strategy took longer than with either of the other two strategies (4.18 seconds, versus 3.55 for land-on and 3.39 for first-contact). Thus, there seemed to be a speed–accuracy trade-off. The authors note that a learning curve for the take-off strategy was observed and had not reached asymptote by the fifteenth trial; so it is possible that with practice the time for the *take-off* strategy might approach that of other strategies. They also note that further refinements in the design of the *take-off* strategy (for example, locating the cursor under the finger, rather than 1/2 inch above it) may further decrease both time and errors. They conclude that with further refinement and investigation the *take-off* strategy may prove to be useful in situations with smaller and more densely packed targets, thus opening the door to touch screens as input devices in applications where they typically have not been accepted due to error rates.

Jackson and Roske-Hofstrand (1989) compared two different techniques for selection with a mouse. In the most commonly used strategy, users selected objects by pointing and clicking. As an alternative, they selected objects by circling them. Jackson and Roske-Hofstrand point out the potential advantages of circling. They argue that it is a natural gesture, it can be easily extended to select not just a single object, but groups of objects or even regions of a display, it does not require the additional operation of clicking, and it liberates a mouse button for other functions.

Results from testing indicated that circling was in fact slower than clicking. However, a clear trend occurred when the objects selected increased from one to two: time *increased* for clicking and *decreased* for circling. Circling time approached clicking time when two objects, as opposed to one, were selected. Jackson and Roske-Hofstrand did not include conditions where subjects had to select more than two objects. Given these trends, however, it seems possible that, with more objects to select, circling might eventually become faster than clicking. Jackson and Roske-Hofstrand conclude that circling may be a desirable selection technique to include as an alternative to clicking.

Input device types themselves (for example, a mouse or trackball) can also be designed in different ways that affect their usability. Hodes and Akagi (1986) report a series of seven experiments that guided the design and development of a new mouse. First, users of existing mice (all rectangular in shape with buttons on the top surface) were observed and problems were identified, including unnatural and fatiguing wrist positions and finger movements and difficulty orienting the hand on the mouse without looking. Then a series of prototypes was constructed and subjected to *preference* tests in comparison with existing mice. Through a series of iterations of prototype development and preference testing, a design was developed that included what had been identified as optimal features. These were a rounded, domelike shape with the peak toward the front, buttons in the front and stiff enough so that fingers could rest on them without activating them, a wide top front surface, a matte texture on top to prevent glare, and a highly textured gripping surface on the sides. Final testing of a working prototype revealed better *performance* and higher *preference* for the new design compared to two competitive mice.

Other studies also indicate that the design of the selectable objects on the screen is just as important as the design of the interaction technique and input device itself. A study by Valk (1985) compared performance on ten different designs of a two state (on–off) touch screen button. The buttons were all designed with ON and OFF labels in white letters on a brown background. A white border designated touchable areas. The current state of each button was indicated by highlighting the background of the appropriate label in orange. The buttons varied primarily in the amount and kind of graphic detail included on the button.

Results from 20 users identifying and changing the state of each of the ten buttons ten times revealed significant performance differences between the buttons. Buttons whose touchable area included the whole button, rather than some designated part of it, produced the best results. Subjects tended to aim their touches directly at the labels, indicating that it is important to center the labels rather than place them at the edge of the touchable area. Subjects also performed better with buttons that included familiar graphics, such as a light switch.

While this study does not necessarily reveal the best design for two-state buttons, it does indicate that the design of the touch button, as well as the interaction technique used to select it, is important and will affect performance in terms of both time and errors.

Pointing Devices: Guidelines

Based on the foregoing general analysis of the advantages and disadvantages of the various alternative pointing devices and the experimental data discussed, some simple guidelines regarding the choice of a pointing device can be drawn. These are presented next.

☞ **Base input device(s) selection on careful task analysis and testing.**

The results of a thorough task analysis should be considered against the relative advantages and disadvantages of the different alternative input devices, as discussed previously and summarized in Figure 12-5. Multiple input devices should be made available when a variety of tasks is integrated within a single application system. Research has not yet revealed clear, complete guidelines for input device selection, and devices within a type (for example, mice or joysticks) vary considerably in different aspects of usability. Thus any choices should be tested prior to final decisions. The following rough guidelines represent a starting point for decision making and should not be considered final.

☞ **Use touch screens when the opportunity for training is low, targets are large, discrete and spread out, frequency of use is low, desk space is at a premium, and the task requires little or no text input.**

Finger-operated touch screens are faster and easier to learn than other devices. Thus, they are appropriate when the opportunity for training and frequency of use is low. They suffer from low accuracy, however, so they are most appropriate when targets are large and spread out on screen. They are also fatiguing to use, another reason to limit them to low-frequency users. They should not be used in systems that require a lot of typing, because the frequent hand motion between the keyboard and screen will be slow and fatiguing. A type of application that meets these criteria might be a typical public information system, such as the sort found in hotels and amusement parks.

When using touch screens, consider the following design guidelines (Brown, 1988):

1. Design touch-sensitive buttons to be a minimum of 3/4 by 3/4 inch and at least 1/8 inch apart.

2. Provide visual feedback (for example, highlighting) in response to button presses. Sometimes auditory feedback is also appropriate.

3. When the consequences are destructive or difficult to undo, minimize inadvertent button selections by requiring confirmation after selection.

☞ **Provide cursor keys for tasks involving heavy text manipulation or movement through structured arrays of discrete objects.**

In spite of the Card, English, and Burr (1978) data, many users prefer cursor keys for text manipulation, which are probably faster than continuous motion pointing devices when there are only a few discrete targets on the screen that are valid cursor positions. It is interesting to note that, while the earlier Apple Macintoshes had no cursor keys on the keyboard, later versions of the Macintosh do. Having both cursor keys and a mouse seems to be the desired configuration for many users.

☞ **Provide an alternative pointing device for graphical tasks.**

Most other pointing devices are faster than cursor keys for many task and target types, especially graphics and drawing applications.

☞ **Mice are faster than trackballs or joysticks.**

Both the Card, English, and Burr (1978) data and the buying behavior of computer users seem to suggest that the mouse is preferred over and superior to other currently available pointing devices for many users and for certain kinds of tasks.

☞ **Minimize hand and eye movement between input devices.**

Often it is appropriate to include two or more input devices in interface, such as a keyboard, cursor keypad, and mouse. When an interface involves multiple input devices, every attempt should be made to minimize the hand and eye motion involved in switching among them by careful design of the dialog to minimize switching. For example, if a fill-in form includes some text entry and some multiple-choice selections, each input type should be grouped together so that only one switch between input devices is necessary.

On the other hand, this principle needs to be balanced against other principles for grouping, such as frequency of use or semantic relationships. Switching should be minimized within these other constraints, depending on their relative importance.

Voice Recognition

Although keyboards and pointing devices are certainly the most common input devices on current commercial and in-house applications, at least one other is starting to appear in commercial systems: **voice recognition.** Instead of typing or pointing, the user *speaks* to the computer.

The basic idea behind voice technology (as both both input and output) is that in many situations the user is already overloaded with *visual* and *manual* tasks. Shifting some of the work load to the *auditory* channel could potentially reduce the competition for the limited available cognitive resources and thus facilitate overall performance.

There are two main challenges in voice technology. The first is technical. The state of the art in both *voice recognition* (input) and *voice synthesis* (output) has a long way to go before it truly simulates human language. The second challenge is in the human factors area. Voice technology is not a panacea. It will only be effective if it is smoothly integrated with other input and output devices, and if the details of the voice interaction are well designed. Only preliminary guidelines are currently available to assist designers in deciding *when, where,* and *how* to apply voice input and output within a given application, and much research is still needed before we will know how to realize the ultimate potential of this promising technology (Simpson and others, 1985).

The first *voice-recognition* (voice input) system was developed by Bell Laboratories in 1952. Voice-recognition systems became commercially available in 1972 (Helander, Moody, and Joost, 1988).

Current commercially available voice-recognition technology is fairly limited. Only *discontinuous speech* can be processed, that is, individual words with intervals of silence between them, as opposed to phrases, sentences, or conversational speech. Due to memory constraints and current methods for storing voice data, most commercially available voice-recognition systems only recognize relatively *small vocabularies* (50 to 350 words). The vocabulary of an average person, by contrast, is closer to around 5000 words. On the other hand, some application domains might only require a vocabulary of 350 or less words, and current voice-recognition technology may thus be practical for these domains (Helander, Moody, and Joost, 1988).

Linguists divide spoken language into five levels of variability: language families, individual languages (for example English or Spanish), dialects, idiolects (that is, the speech of an individual), and variations in individual speech over time (Simpson and others, 1985). Whereas people have no trouble understanding different idiolects, dialects, and even different languages, most currently available voice-recognition systems are *speaker dependent* and *must be "trained"* to understand the specific *idiolect* of individual users. That is, they learn to recognize the particular pitch and accent of a given speaker and cannot generalize that knowledge to understand a speaker with a significantly different pitch and accent, let alone a different dialect.

Systems are trained by having users speak each vocabulary word or utterance to the system several times. From this input, the system forms templates for each word or utterance that capture a set of characteristic features and to which it compares later user input. Recognition occurs by searching for a match between a user-entered word and a template stored in memory.

Speaker-dependent systems can be trained on *multiple users,* but this becomes very memory intensive and thus often *impractical.* Speaker-dependent systems also *limit the size of the vocabulary* simply because users would not tolerate the time necessary to train a system on a large number of words.

Even for speakers on which a system has been trained, there is typically a *10% or greater error rate,* and this *error rate increases* when the user suffers from *colds, stress, or fatigue,* which can change the pitch and pronunciation of words. Errors are due both to natural variations in human speech and to weaknesses in the recognition algorithms. The amount of variation in a given input word during training determines to some extent the amount of variation tolerated during recognition. Thus, normal variations in an individual's speech over time and in noisy environments can result in recognition errors.

Recognition accuracy is also affected by the phonetic distance or discriminability *between* word templates. For example, confusions may occur between "quit" and "pick" but would be less likely between "quit" and "select." Finally, current voice-recognition systems do not perform as well as human listeners because they are unable to make use of the pragmatic and linguistic context of an utterance to help interpret it, the way that humans do.

The possibility of misrecognized words means that very careful confirmation of input and efficient error handling procedures must be built into the system. An error on the part of the computer is also psychologically much more frustrating and disturbing than a user error. Users must speak very carefully and consistently, and this can be perceived as tedious and frustrating for users. Some errors can be minimized by careful selection of maximally discriminable words and by employing only small vocabularies (for example, 30 words), but often the utility of the device is decreased when these measures are taken.

Four types of recognition errors are possible (Helander, Moody, and Joost, 1988). **Substitution** errors occur when one utterance from the vocabulary is mistaken for another. **Rejection** errors occur when an utterance belonging to the vocabulary is detected but not recognized. **Insertion** errors occur when an utterance is detected that was not spoken (for example, due to noise in the environment). **Deletion** errors occur when an utterance that was spoken is not detected.

There is a trade-off between *substitution* and *rejection* errors, because users can select a rejection level. A low rejection level decreases substitution errors at the expense of increasing rejections. A higher rejection level decreases rejections, but at the expense of increasing substitutions. Errors in recognition are often caused by human errors, such as forgetting the valid vocabulary, failing to follow speech patterns used during system training, and conversing with co-workers while the microphone is on.

Given the common rate of errors in voice input, feedback and effective error recovery procedures are particularly important. Some research (Helander, Moody, and Joost, 1988) suggests that screen feedback is more effective than voice feedback via voice synthesis. However, one reason for employing voice input in the first place is that the user's eyes are busy or a workstation is not available. Screen output is obviously not an alternative in these cases. And feedback and error correction may increase the overall recognition rate, but they will also further degrade user response time. Designers thus must trade off between speed and accuracy in designing voice interaction.

Finally, current systems work effectively only in *controlled environments* with minimal background noise. Background noise can increase the error rate to a point where the system seems unusable. The cost of current voice-recognition systems ranges from $200 to $30,000, depending on vocabulary size and typical error rates (Helander, Moody, and Joost, 1988).

Helander, Moody, and Joost (1988) review some of the currently implemented applications of voice recognition. These include applications from industry (for example, warehouse inventory), medical practice (data collection), the military (battle management), consumer products (sewing machines), office (voice mail), and public domains (banking).

There is ongoing research and development in the area of voice-recognition systems, and *future* systems are expected to improve on many of the limitations described here. Future systems may eventually accommodate *continuous speech* (that is, conversational speech) with *large vocabularies* (5000 to 20,000 words). Currently, some speaker-independent systems are available, but they only recognize a small vocabulary of 10 to 20 words (Helander, Moody, and Joost, 1988). The ultimate goal is to achieve systems that are *speaker independent,* recognize *continuous speech,* average as little as *0% to 1% error rates,* and operate in *noisy environments* without an increase in error rates.

Voice Recognition: Advantages and Disadvantages

Regardless of the state of the technology, voice-recognition systems have certain advantages and disadvantages, relative to other input devices. Voice-recognition systems offer particular *advantages* when the user's *hands are otherwise occupied,* when *mobility is required,* or when the user's *eyes are busy* (Shneiderman, 1986). Other input devices, such as keyboards and pointing devices, require the use of the hands and usually the eyes and tie the user to the workstation. Voice input, by contrast, requires neither the hands or eyes to operate, and with a remote, hand-held or head-mounted input microphone, it can be operated at any distance from the workstation or computer itself. In certain environments, these may be very important advantages.

On the other hand, voice input also carries certain significant *disadvantages* relative to other input devices. Voice input is transient. There is *no natural feedback* mechanism allowing users to verify their input, the way there is when typing or pointing on a screen. Adding verification procedures inevitably slows throughput down significantly (Isenberg, Yntena, and Wiesen, 1984).

Voice input in systems operating in public or open office environments can be very *disruptive* to others and suffers from a *lack of privacy and security* as well. Voice input may actually be more *fatiguing to use* over long periods of time than many hand-operated input devices. It might also actually be *slower* than other input devices for many operations. For instance, imagine having to move a cursor by repeating the word down over and over, as opposed to moving the cursor with a mouse (Murray, Van Praag, and Gilfoil, 1983). Discontinuous voice input requires a pause of about 200 milliseconds between utterances. This limits the input rate to about 20 to 40 words per minute, as compared to 50 to 60 words per minute for an experienced typist.

Speech is also a *single-channel mode;* that is, users cannot speak two or more messages simultaneously, and they cannot listen while speaking. By contrast, users can perform multiple motor movements simultaneously (for example, with two hands or with hands and feet), and they can view screen displays while making motor movements.

Finally, the current *error rates* of voice-recognition systems is a significant disadvantage as compared to other devices. Unlike people, voice recognizers are very sensitive to noise in the environment and to variations in speech within and across speakers.

The reader should note that the issue of voice input is separate from the issue of natural language. Given a voice input system, the underlying software of an application can be designed to accept natural language or to accept only a concise, artificial command language. Either natural language or command languages can be input through other input devices besides voice-recognition systems. Issues in the use of natural language and command language are discussed in Chapters 10 and 7, respectively.

Voice-recognition systems (input) are also to be distinguished from voice-synthesis systems (output). Voice synthesis is discussed later in the section on output devices.

Voice Recognition: Experimental Results

The performance of an experimental 20,000-word-vocabulary, speaker-dependent, discontinuous voice recognition system called The Tangora was tested by Brown and Vosburgh (1989). Unlike most commercially available voice recognizers, the system does more than simple template matching. It also uses surrounding words to help recognize a given word. It does this by preestablished conditional probabilities, based upon a quarter-billion-word corpus of words drawn from general office correspondence. Under ideal conditions (that is, practiced, motivated, and knowledgeable users and test materials carefully controlled for content and style), the recognition rate of the Tangora system is 95% or greater.

Brown and Vosburgh tested the system under broader conditions to see how it would hold up in less than ideal, and more realistic, situations. Twelve speakers participated, half male and half female. They read some preselected sentences and also dictated sentences of their own composition. One-half of the preselected sentences were drawn from general office correspondence (similar to the sentences the recognition system was based on) and one-half were drawn from the *New York Times* business section (dissimilar to the sentences the recognition system was based on).

There was a great deal of variability in recognition errors *across* subjects, ranging from 9.2% to 27.4% for user-composed sentences. On the other hand, there was a great deal of consistency *within* subjects. This suggests that the speech of some users will be easier to recognize than others, in spite of the fact that the system is trained to each particular user.

Gender did not seem to be a factor in rate of recognition errors. However, the content and style of input sentences did affect error rate. The system made less errors on sentences similar to, as opposed to dissimilar to, those its conditional probabilities were based on. That is, use of context contributed to recognition only when the specific context rules of the system applied to the content and style of input.

The most common type of error by far (92%) was *substitution* errors (recognizing a spoken word as another word in the vocabulary); 2.5% of the errors were *deletion* errors, and 5.5% were *insertion* errors. Subjects made very few *segmentation* errors (for example, failing to pause between words or inserting a pause in the middle of a word), suggesting that, even when dictating sentences, users may not have a hard time adjusting to a *discontinuous* speech recognizer.

The authors conclude that the system is currently too narrowly focused (in its use of context to facilitate recognition) to support a *general-purpose,* speech-to-text application, although it may be adequate for specialized applications. Even for specialized applications, the relatively high rate of errors (9.2% to 27.4%) implies the need for powerful error identification and correction functions. The authors also point out the need to determine why some speakers are easier to recognize than others so that speech recognizers can be designed to be less sensitive to such individual differences. On the other hand, the authors were encouraged that users made few segmentation errors and interpreted this to mean that discontinuous speech recognition would be acceptable for speech-to-text applications. However, although the authors do not describe the system training procedure, it is hard to imagine most potential users being willing to train a system on 20,000 words.

Halstead-Nussloch (1989) reports that the maximum-size vocabulary for 95% recognition accuracy rates ranges from 15 to 30 words and that environmental noise reduces recognition accuracy from 95% to 80%, even with a noise-canceling microphone. He reviews other literature that also indicates that user's speech patterns change in response to environmental noise, further contributing to the degradation of accuracy under these conditions.

Gardner and others (1985) found that, over a two-month period after training a system to specific speakers, overall accuracy was fairly stable, although there was a trend of change in user speech patterns, resulting in an increase in the phonetic distance between input words and trained templates. They suggest that it is possible that over longer periods of time this distance may increase enough to start degrading accuracy, and that it may thus be necessary to retrain a system periodically to maintain acceptable accuracy rates. They also found that neither general training in public speaking nor experience using a speech-recognition system significantly improved accuracy, indicating that no special training *for users* is necessary to optimize use of a speaker-dependent speech-recognition system.

Helander, Moody, and Joost (1988) review research that bears on vocabulary design. This research suggests a number of things. First, longer utterances (for example, a short phrase, rather than a single word, or multisyllable words rather than single-syllable words) are more discriminable and easier to learn to pronounce consistently. Short words and letters of the alphabet should thus be avoided. Second, words with similar subparts (for example, repair and despair) are easily confused and should be avoided. Third, users can more consistently pronounce familiar words, and so users should have input into the design of vocabularies. More research is required to define more complete guidelines for vocabulary design in order to optimize recognition accuracy, given current voice-recognition technology.

Other studies have sought to empirically compare voice input to other input devices. Isenberg, Yntena, and Wiesen (1984) report the development of a speaker-dependent, discontinuous voice interface to a baggage sorting application for an airline. Destination name confusions were reduced by having the operator first specify "East Coast" or "West Coast" as categories. When confusions still occurred (for example, Boston/Austin), they were routed to a special location for resolution. Destination names were designed as city names rather than flight numbers, as these seemed more natural to users. Speakers trained the system in the environment it was to be used in to minimize the effects of environmental noise on recognition accuracy. Upon implementation, it was found that the speech recognition interface increased throughput from 15 to 35 bags per person per minute, with only about 2 bags per thousand missing their plane.

Gardner-Bonneau, Bonneau, and Martin (1987) compared voice, mouse, and keyboard input in a database query application. They reviewed other such studies in which in some cases the keyboard resulted in faster input, while in other cases voice did. In these studies, the device that provided better performance seemed to depend on the nature of the input. For example, voice input might prove superior for entering information about objects, while the keyboard might be superior when the input was information about spatial relations.

Gardner-Bonneau and co-workers found that voice input resulted in faster input times when users were given *precomposed* queries to enter, but that mouse input was faster when users had to *construct* valid queries from general descriptions of query goals. This is probably because the interaction designed for mouse input was *menu driven* and probably provided *helpful structure* to users, while no such structure is inherent in a voice input interaction. Further supporting this interpretation are data showing that, when errors were excluded from the timing data, voice appeared to be faster than the mouse.

Since the condition in which subjects had to compose their own queries from general goal descriptions more closely matches how users would be using the system in the real world, the data from this condition are the more interesting and important. They suggest that, while the *motor* component of input may be facilitated by voice input, the *cognitive* component will not necessarily be. This in turn points to the importance of designing the *details of interaction techniques,* above and beyond the importance of choosing an appropriate input device.

Simpson and others (1985) conclude from a literature review that voice recognition is not a useful substitute for manual data entry when such tasks are already being performed successfully and is likely to improve performance only in complex tasks that involve high cognitive, perceptual, and motor loading. Theoretical and empirical work by Wickens and co-workers, reviewed in Helander, Moody, and Joost, (1988), suggests that voice recognition might effectively be *combined* with other manual input devices under certain conditions to optimize overall input. Assigning subtasks to voice or manual devices should depend on whether the input is verbal or spatial in nature. For example, pointing to objects or tracking objects could be done with a pointing device, while issuing commands could be done with voice. Different cognitive resources are involved in manual and verbal input, and dividing a given task between them means that noncompeting resources might be drawn on simultaneously, allowing faster completion of a task that requires both types of input. This seems like a promising possibility, but more research is needed to establish guidelines for assigning voice and manual input devices to different subtasks within an overall dialog in order to achieve possible benefits.

Some researchers (Nishida, 1986; Petajan and others, 1988) are developing lip-reading technology to augment voice recognition in noisy environments, such as aircraft and factories. Speakers face a camera, which sends digitized video data to a microcomputer with special-purpose hardware and software for video processing. Lip readers can be used in combination with speech recognizers in two ways. In the simplest of the the two, the lip reader simply determines start and stop points for speech, while the speech recognizer actually recognizes the speech. This is useful in noisy environments where voice recognizers have a difficult time distinguishing speech from nonspeech sounds. In the second method, lip readers actually contribute to the recognition of particular words. In one experiment (Petajan and others, 1988), a speech-recognition system combined with a lip reader reduced recognition errors by half as compared to the speech recognizer alone.

Voice Recognition: Guidelines

The following guidelines are based on the general advantages and disadvantages of voice recognition and the experimental results just discussed.

☞ **Consider voice as an input device only when the constraints of the state of the art in voice input technology are manageable.**

Given current technology, consider the use of voice recognition only under the following circumstances (Halstead-Nussloch, 1989):

1. The system can be trained to understand specific users.
2. The required vocabulary is small (15 to 30 words).
3. The environment is quiet.
4. The cost of a recognition error is low.
5. Identification and correction of errors are easy.

☞ **Consider voice recognition as an input device when the user's hands are occupied, mobility is required, or the user's eyes are busy.**

Given the relative advantages of voice recognition under these conditions, *possible current and future applications* include *speech to text,* such as being able to dictate a memo or report to a word processing application and then edit it in the standard way. The *"10 cent workstation"* concept views the telephone as a remote voice input device to office or home computer systems. Users could call in and ask to hear electronic calendar entries and electronic mail via voice commands through the mouthpiece of a standard telephone. *Factories* currently make use of simple voice-recognition systems when users' eyes and hands are tied up handling and viewing assembly line parts. *Service and repair personnel* might communicate by voice through a hand-held or head-mounted device to computer-aided diagnostic systems located in a central office, as they disassemble and perform tests on equipment. Some factory *robots* are currently operated by voice, allowing the operator to keep his or her eyes on the robot at all times. We can imagine voice operation of *medical* equipment, such as computer databases, diagnostic systems, and automated drug and fluid dispensers by surgeons whose eyes and hands are occupied. Finally, obvious applications for voice input are for those *disabled* in the eyes and hands.

☞ **Avoid voice recognition as an input device in open environments, when privacy is important, when even low error rates are unacceptable, when frequency of use is high, and when speed is important.**

Given the relative disadvantages of voice recognition under these circumstances, *inappropriate applications* for voice input might include *automatic teller machines,* where security and privacy are issues, and *public information systems,* where noise level poses serious disadvantages.

☞ **Provide structure in the output dialog to guide voice input.**

Like command language and natural language interfaces, an *unprompted* voice input interface provides no structure to assist users in accomplishing their goals. This may be appropriate for expert users, but novice and casual users may do better with prompted interfaces, such as menu, question and answer, and forms-based dialogs. Voice input can be combined with these dialog styles to provide structure for these types of users.

☞ **Provide a familiar and distinctive vocabulary.**

Users will be more consistent when pronouncing familiar words. Longer words and phrases will be more discriminable by the recognizer than shorter ones. Thus, letters and digits make poor input. Multisyllable words and short phrases make better input. Words should also be maximally distinct from one another. Avoid easily confused words like "pick" and "quit." "Pick" and "select" will be less likely to be confused. These vocabulary guidelines will help to minimize recognition errors.

Other Input Devices

A number of other input devices have been experimentally developed and tested, but are not yet in wide commercial use. In very specialized application domains, it may be appropriate to consider them.

☞ **Consider alternative output devices when particular user, environment, and task characteristics (and other considerations) seem to require special capabilities.**

One study (Geiser, 1989) tested the usability of employing a *numeric keypad* for *text entry*. The user "writes" characters by tracing block letters on the 3 by 3 matrix of keys in the numeric keypad. On small and portable products that require only occasional entry of text input, Geiser points out that a full alpha keyboard is impractical, and a handwriting tablet also takes up too much space and may be too expensive. "Writing" characters on the numeric keypad may provide an inexpensive, compact, and usable alternative for occasional text input.

Geiser tested 20 subjects by having them write their own surname three times after a brief introductory training session. User error rates decreased from 2% to 0% by the third trial, although system recognition error rates remained at 2%. User input times were about 2 seconds per character, which is better than the input times reported for other input methods using the numeric keypad, such as keychording or multiple key codes.

In another study (Mahach, 1989), a **handwriting recognition device,** which allows users to enter data with a metal- or lead-tipped pen on a glass screen, was compared to typing on a standard QWERTY keyboard and to mouse or cursor key selection of soft keys laid out on the screen for entering letters and words. While the handwriting recognition system was slower and more error prone than standard keyboard entry, it compared favorably on an input time measure to mouse selection of alpha keys displayed on the screen and was superior to cursor key selection of alpha keys displayed on the screen. The author points out that for a different task, such as form and chart fill in, where most data entry is item selection rather than text entry, handwriting recognition as an input device may well prove superior to either the mouse or the keyboard on both speed and accuracy measures and would probably also be easier for novice users to master.

An evaluation of a simulated **gesture-recognition device** is reported by Wolf (1988). Two versions were compared to keyboard input: in one users made marks with a stylus right on the display screen, and in the other users made marks on a tablet that was separate from the display screen. The application was a spreadsheet. In the keyboard-driven system, users moved a cursor to mark a range of cells and typed in a command name. In the gesture-recognition systems, users made hand-drawn marks similar to standard text editing symbols to indicate both cell ranges and commands. For example, a line through a row of cells would select them, and a curlicue like the one used in text editing would delete them. Users of all systems were trained on six spreadsheet commands and then performed multiple tasks using these six commands. Eighteen subjects performed tasks on all three input device types.

Subjects using the gesture-recognition devices performed faster than keyboard subjects. They took 76% of the time per operation taken by keyboard users. Although this is interesting, it is not too surprising, given that more physical movements are required using the keyboard as an input device on these tasks. It would be more interesting to know how the gesture-recognition device compared with other *pointing* devices, such as a mouse or joystick, on this task. The author notes that gesture-recognition systems might be useful for tasks that combine drawing and text operations. If the gesture-recognition device included hand-writing-recognition capabilities, this might be the case. However, this remains to be tested empirically in a study that combines gesture and handwriting recognition in a single input device in a task that requires both drawing and text entry and compares such a device to alternatives, such as a mouse and keyboard combination.

Some researchers have considered the *foot* as a *human* input device and have devised various **foot-operated computer input devices.** Some research has focused on *foot switches* as an alternative to frequently used keys. Pearson and Weiser (1986) describe a class of foot-operated input devices referred to as *moles*. They point out that the potential benefit of a foot-operated pointing device is that, during typing, the hands never have to leave the alpha keyboard for cursor positioning. Pearson and Weiser report performance data for a mole. The right foot rests on a pedal set in a frame that allows it to slide vertically and horizontally.

Time and errors were compared on a target selection task for the mole and a mouse. Mouse time included time moving the hands between the keyboard and mouse (homing time), as well as cursor movement time. Several different sized targets were used. Ten mouse-naive subjects were trained on both devices and then tested.

Overall, even including homing time, the mole was *slower* (by several seconds per target) and *more error prone* (two to four times as many errors) for target selection than the mouse. However, as target size increased to 1/8 inch square and larger, mole and mouse time became essentially equal. Text size on a screen is typically 1/16 by 1/8 to 1/4 by 1/8 inch. Thus, when targets are as large or larger than text and when frequent homing is required, the authors suggest that the mole might be considered when a mouse is impractical for some reason (for example, limited desk space) because it provides more or less equivalent performance in *throughput* for trained users. Since *error rates* for different target sizes are not reported, however, it is not possible to evaluate whether or not error rates for larger targets would be acceptable, even if throughput was. Also, long-term use was not investigated, so it is not clear how fatiguing it would be to use the device. And it should be kept in mind that the device only allows vertical and horizontal movement. Thus, the continuous, nonlinear movement possible with a mouse, which is important in certain tasks such as drawing, is not possible.

Still another alternative input device is an **eye tracker.** A description and evaluation of an eye-tracking device is reported in Ware and Mikaelian (1987). People fixate on visual objects by moving the eye to cause the object to be imaged on the foveal region of the eye, where visual acuity is highest. Normal eye movements are quite fast, suggesting that pointing with the eye might be an efficient method for the selection of objects on a computer screen. It also offers an alternative to hand-operated input devices for disabled users.

The eye tracker tested in this study determined eye position on the screen by means of a television camera that digitized an image of the user's eye, which included a reflected image of the screen. The relative position of the fovea on the screen could be calculated quite accurately from this digitized image. In two different experiments, time and errors to point to and select highlighted menu options were measured for three different selection techniques and varying target sizes. The three different selection techniques were as follows:

1. *Dwell time:* If the user fixated on a menu option more than 0.4 second, it was selected.
2. *Screen button:* Fixating on a select button displayed on the screen selected the last menu option fixated on.
3. *Hardware button:* Pressing a button on a keyboard selected the option currently fixated on.

Each user was given 35 trials with each of the three selection techniques.

When selecting objects larger than a single character (for example, a word), the results indicated that selection times with the eye tracker were faster (under 1 second) than selection times for other pointing devices, such as a mouse, reported elsewhere in the literature (for example, Card, English, and Burr, 1978). Selection was fastest with the hardware button and slowest with the screen button. Under some task conditions, this hardware button selection technique was more error prone than the dwell time technique, but the authors speculate that this error rate may decrease with practice and under different task conditions.

The authors further note that in their task (and in tasks typically used to measure selection times with other devices) visual search time was minimized because targets were highlighted. They point out that in actual applications the advantage of an eye-tracking device over, say, a mouse might be even more pronounced, because, in effect, visual searching and selecting are combined in a single visual movement. When using a hand-operated pointing device, on the other hand, the user must first visually search for the target on the screen, then visually search for the cursor on the screen (and perhaps even for the device on the keyboard or desk), and then visually track the cursor as it is moved to the target. This involves much more eye movement. Thus, when visual search is a component of the selection task, eye-tracking devices may implicitly require much less eye movement than other devices.

The authors conclude that "where speed is of the essence, cost is no object, [target] sizes are moderate, and it is important that the hands be reserved for other activities, the eye tracker may be the input device of choice" (brackets mine).

Another study (Glenn and others, 1986) directly demonstrated the greater efficiency of an eye-tracking device with a dwell time selection technique over mouse selection on simple tasks where some visual search was involved. Several eye-tracking algorithms were compared. There is a great deal of noise in eye movements, and different algorithms vary in how they compute the user's point of attention from samples of eye movements and fixations. Three different feedback conditions were also included: no feedback, discrete feedback (a target was highlighted when fixated on), and continuous feedback (a cursor tracked eye position at all times). The authors were interested in finding the optimal combination of eye-tracking algorithm and feedback form to maximize speed and accuracy. They were also interested in comparing eye tracking as an input device to the mouse.

The task involved searching a random array of 27 dark blue dots on a light blue background to find the target dot, which was black. Six subjects performed on 18 trials in each condition, which varied in device (mouse or one of three eye-tracking algorithms) and feedback (none, discrete, or continuous). In the discrete feedback condition, the target turned green after a dwell time of 0.5 second. In the continuous feedback condition, a cursor followed the user's eye movement continuously, and the target was selected after a dwell time of 0.5 second. In the mouse condition, the target was selected when the mouse button was clicked while the pointer rested on the target.

The results indicated no difference between the two feedback conditions (discrete versus continuous). All three eye-tracking algorithms produced faster performance as compared to the mouse. Selection times were 0.1 to 0.3 second longer per target using the mouse. Accuracy was essentially the same with the mouse and two of the eye-tracking algorithms. However, there was a clear speed–

accuracy trade-off within the three eye-tracking algorithms. The algorithms that sampled eye movement and fixations over time to filter out random eye movements and reduce errors took longer. The algorithm that did not screen out random eye movements was faster but produced more errors. The authors conclude that different algorithms might be employed in different applications, depending on whether speed or accuracy was more important.

It is interesting that the two feedback conditions did not produce different results. It was speculated beforehand that continuous feedback might either *enhance* performance by giving important feedback as users direct their gaze or *degrade* performance by distracting the user's attention from the search and target objects. Apparently it did neither. On the other hand, it is possible that the different types of feedback might enhance or degrade performance on other types of tasks, such as tracking or manipulation tasks.

It is also interesting that the experimental eye-tracking system used in this research is part of a larger system that combines eye-tracking and voice recognition for input. Users control the cursor with eye tracking and issue commands with voice input. This is a potentially powerful combination that requires no manual manipulation at all for input. The benefits of such a system are particularly apparent for handicapped users, for users constrained by g forces (for example, in space), for high-frequency users who would suffer from fatigue in long-duration manual manipulation tasks, and for users whose hands need to be free for other activities.

Two **data gloves** are described in Zimmerman and others (1987). These devices consist of a lightweight cotton glove worn on the hand of the user, which is equipped with a variety of sensors that detect hand, wrist, and finger movements and provide tactile feedback simulating contact, hardness, and surface texture. The user wears the glove and interacts with ''virtual'' objects on a computer screen or objects manipulated by a robotic hand controlled by glove movements. Users can pick up, throw, twist, squeeze, and put down objects or communicate with sign language. Possible applications include transcription of sign language for the handicapped, manipulation of objects in a simulated three-dimensional environment, and control of robotic hands in environments hostile to human life (for example, outer space, undersea, or areas with high radiation).

Weimer and Ganapathy (1989) describe an experimental CAD system that combines data glove and voice input. The user interacts with a simulated three-dimensional world on the screen by talking and gesturing. The hand gesture language is quite simple and is based on the assumption that speech is often more efficient than gesture and that, in normal discourse, people only use gestures to augment speech for those few things that are more easily gestured than spoken. Thus, voice input is used primarily for defining broad actions, such as ''translate,'' ''rotate,'' and ''scale,'' while hand gestures with the data glove select objects to operate on and control the details of the operation. Operations are terminated by saying ''OK'' or naming a new operation. The types of tasks that can be accomplished in this manner include the following:

Operating a virtual control panel

Selecting objects or geometric figures

Translation, rotation, and scaling of objects

Perturbing control points of bicubic patches

Defining space curves and swept surfaces

Weimer and Ganapathy observe from their own experience that adding voice input to the hand gesture interface resulted in a significant improvement in usability. No formal usability testing is reported, but, again, we can imagine the applications in which voice and gesture input would provide a particularly natural and more viable form of input. When more such experimental systems are available, formal testing will be necessary to determine just how to optimize the use of these input devices in specific applications through the design of specific interaction techniques.

One study (Hauptmann, 1989) investigated how people might *naturally* use gesture and speech input by using the Wizard-of-Oz technique (see Chapter 10). Users were placed in front of a screen displaying a three-dimensional object (a cube) that they were told they could manipulate through speech and hand gestures. They were given specific tasks to accomplish, which involved rotating, moving, or scaling (shrinking or expanding) the object. In three different conditions they were told they could use speech only, hand gestures only, or speech and hand gestures together. Video cameras recorded their speech and gestures, and a "wizard" or hidden experimenter actually controlled the object on the screen in response to the speech and gestures. In this way, the speech and gestures that people might *naturally* use for these simple operations could be observed.

The speech and gestures used by 36 subjects were collected and analyzed. A detailed classification scheme was developed for both speech and gesture inputs. The results can be summarized as follows.

Users used a small number of words (223 total, with 141 different words that were actually useful for the task) and simple syntactic structures (93.6% were imperatives). In their hand gestures, they usually used more than a single finger, and they made movements in all three dimensions. Most gestures were not well aligned in space with the object being manipulated In general, there was a great deal of uniformity in the use of both gestures and speech. Users expressed a clear preference for the gesture and speech interface over the speech only and gesture only interfaces.

The authors find this encouraging in that it suggests that a system that recognized a limited speech and gesture vocabulary and syntax would still be perceived as natural and useful. They suggest, based on their data, that a multifinger and three-dimensional gestural language will seem most natural. Since gestures were not well aligned in space with the object being manipulated, they note that clear feedback on the locus of a gesture will be necessary to minimize recognition errors in interfaces with many objects. They also caution that their experimental tasks were quite simple and involved only a single object, so there are limits to the generalizability of their results.

Buxton and Myers (1986) investigated the possibility of the simultaneous use of **two hand-operated input devices.** They point out that people use both hands simultaneously in many routine tasks, such as turning a page while writing and steering a car while switching gears. They performed two experiments to see if users would naturally operate two available input devices simultaneously and if two input devices offered any performance advantages over one. In their first experiment, users had to move an object and resize it. For each operation they were provided with a separate input device, one operated by each hand. They were trained to use each device separately and were not instructed to use them simultaneously. Nevertheless, when asked to perform tasks that required both moving and resizing, all but one of 14 subjects eventually performed the tasks by operating both devices simultaneously. Six did so right from the start. Overall, the 14 subjects engaged in parallel use of the two devices 41% of the time, and their performance was faster when they did so.

In the second experiment, performance on a task requiring both scrolling and selecting was measured using a single device operated by one hand or two devices operated by opposite hands. In this experiment, subjects did not tend to use the two devices simultaneously, but they still performed faster with the two devices when they did use them, as compared to when they used just one.

The authors speculate that in this latter task each operation was too complex to be easily carried out in parallel, but that the increased efficiency in hand motion afforded by the two separate devices still resulted in a performance advantage relative to the single device. They also note that the 2 out of 24 subjects who *did* use both devices simultaneously produced the best performance scores, indicating that perhaps, with more practice, increased benefits due to the parallel use of two input devices might be realized in more complex tasks. Although most user interfaces currently available are designed with a single input device, the authors conclude that using both hands in parallel comes naturally to people and could be exploited in interface design to increase efficiency.

OUTPUT DEVICES

The traditional output device for interactive computer systems is the **screen.** More recently, **voice-synthesis** systems use voice as an alternative output device, and some commercial products currently incorporate voice output. Still other output devices have also been investigated and are discussed here.

Screens

Screen design issues include **hardware operating characteristics** such as resolution, flicker, and glare.

Screen Operating Characteristics

Figure 12-8 lists some important hardware operating characteristics of computer screens and their recommended values (Rouse, 1975; Rupp, 1981).

Symbol brightness refers to the perceived *luminance* of the foreground objects on the screen, such as text, icons, or graphic elements. Luminance is measured in millilamberts (mL) (Rouse, 1975). On most modern workstations, symbol brightness is user controlled.

Symbol–background contrast refers to the *relative luminance* of the foreground objects on the screen (for example, text or icons) compared to the screen background. Contrast is measured as the ratio of the background luminance minus the symbol luminance to the background luminance plus the symbol luminance (Rouse, 1975). On most modern workstations, contrast is also under user control.

Flicker refers to the refresh rate of the display on the screen. At a critical speed the refreshing of the screen becomes imperceptible to the human eye. Below that rate, the screen appears to flicker. The perception of flicker depends somewhat on luminance (Rouse, 1975). Flicker is also more apparent in the peripheral vision, where there are more motion detectors. Thus flicker may be more noticeable on large screens, where a significant proportion of the screen surface is always in peripheral vision. Flicker is distracting and annoying and can be very fatiguing over long periods of viewing.

Screen glare refers to the amount of light reflected from the screen surface. The amount of glare depends partly on the screen surface itself and partly on the angle of the surrounding light sources. Some screen surfaces are more glare resistant than others, and antiglare shields can be attached to many workstation screens.

Characteristic	Optimal value
Symbol brightness	25 – 50 mL
Symbol–background contrast	88% – 94%
Flicker	50 Hz
Screen glare	Glare control
Symbol size	2.6 mm at 50 cm
Resolution	
Character format	5 by 7 pixels
Screen angle	Adjustable
Image polarity	Positive
Color	
Bit mapped versus character based	

Figure 12–8   Screen operating characteristics. From Rouse, "Design of Man-Computer Interfaces for On-Line Interactive Systems," *Proceedings of the IEEE,* 1975 (June), 63 (6), 847–57 and Rupp, "Visual Display Standards: A Review of Issues," *Proceedings of the SID,* 1981, 22(1), 63–72. With permission.

Symbol size is most important when the symbols displayed are text. One European standard (DIN) for text is 2.6 mm at 50-cm viewing distance (1.25 inches at 20 inches). Larger text sizes are recommended, especially for users with vision defects. Many modern workstations have user-controlled text size on the screen.

Resolution refers to the number of pixels, or manipulable points, per unit of screen height and width. It affects the clarity and detail of symbols on the screen. High-resolution screens allow fonts with more discriminable characters, making reading easier. Resolution also affects the quality of graphic displays. Currently, the resolution on standard-size screens ranges from 320 by 200 to 640 by 480.

Character format refers to the number and configuration of pixels per text character. Most international standards specify a minimum of 5 by 7 pixels per character (Rupp, 1981).

Screen angle refers to the angle of the screen surface in relation to the user's line of sight. This affects the comfort of looking at the screen over long periods of time and the ease of reading. Newer workstations allow the user to tilt the screen back and forth to some degree to adjusting the viewing angle to accommodate individual preferences.

Image polarity refers to whether the foreground or background is lighter, that is, contains more white light, for instance, on black and white terminals, whether the display is black text on a white background (positive polarity) or white text on a black background (negative polarity). Positive polarity is more similar to paper documents. It has been suggested that, if the user is working from a paper document, positive polarity is important to minimize eye readjustment (and thus fatigue) as the eye travels back and forth between the paper and screen. This has not, however, actually been substantiated (Rupp, 1981). And flicker is usually more apparent on screens with a white or light background. Many modern workstations allow the user to choose image polarity, and current international standards generally specify positive polarity as preferred (Rupp, 1981).

Many modern workstations offer a palette of **colors** under software control, which can be effectively used in the design of application screens (see Chapter 14). Color monitors can be used as monochrome screens under user control.

Older workstations are **character based,** whereas many modern workstations are **bit mapped.** The latter allow graphics and multiple fonts in displays, which can be effectively used in software interface design.

Voice Synthesis

Although the screen is certainly the most common output device on current commercial and in-house applications, at least one other is beginning to appear in commercial systems: voice output. Instead of displaying output on the screen, the computer *speaks* to the user.

There are two types of voice output, voice synthesis and digitized speech. **Digitized speech** is recorded human speech that is digitized. **Synthesized speech** is speech generated by concatenating basic speech sounds by rule (Simpson and others, 1985). Synthesized speech is necessary for anything but small, well-defined vocabularies. Text to speech applications require voice synthesis.

Current voice-synthesis technology produces speech that is recognizable, but unnatural sounding and tiring to listen to. There is, however, ongoing research and development in the area of voice synthesis, and *future* systems are expected to improve, eventually approaching a quality indistinguishable from human speech.

Speech synthesis requires a great deal of computer memory. A single second of speech (about two words) requires from 80,000 to 160,000 bits of storage. The same two words stored as text would only require about 100 bits (Streeter, 1988). In general, greater intelligibility can only be achieved at the expense of increasing storage requirements.

Streeter (1988) reviews the current state of voice-synthesis technology. This review is summarized and paraphrased here. There are many technical difficulties in implementing voice synthesis due to the nature of human speech. First, there are many rules of pronunciation and many exceptions to these rules. For example, consider the words "tough," "bough," "though," and "through." Although they have many letters in common, they are pronounced very differently. Exceptions such as these make it very difficult to develop letter to sound rules to use in speech generation. One project reported by Streeter documented at least 1100 such exceptions in the English language.

One possible way to get around these exceptions is to include a dictionary of words with pronunciation rules for each word. However, this would take about 5 megabytes alone in storage, and no dictionary could ever contain all the necessary words (for example, proper names and technical jargon); so letter to sound rules would still be necessary. Proper names are a particularly difficult problem in voice synthesis. There are over 1.5 million uniquely spelled surnames in America. Whereas many commercial voice synthesizers typically obtain correct pronunciations for about 90% of ordinary words, correct pronunciation of surnames is much worse, only 70% or less.

Synthesizers vary in their basic unit of storage. The possibilities for basic storage units are as follows:

Words
Syllables
Demisyllables (half-syllables, such as "str" and "ing" in the word string)
Diphones (half of one phoneme plus half of another, such as "st" in "string")
Phonemes (a distinctive sound in the language, such as the "k" sound in "keep" and "cot")

The larger the size unit is the better the speech quality, but the more units to be stored. For example, the numbers of each unit in the English language are roughly as follows:

Words	>100,000 (not including proper names, plurals, and so on)
Syllables	> 10,000
Demisyllables	1,000
Phonemes	40

Words and *syllables* have not been used in text to speech voice synthesis due to the exorbitant storage requirements. Although they have the least storage requirements, using *phonemes* as the basic unit is still problematic because phonemes change significantly in sound depending on surrounding phonemes. For example, the "k" phoneme sounds very different in the two words "keep" and "cot." Thus, complex synthesis rules are necessary that take the context of each phoneme into account, and, even so, many pronunciation errors still occur. Nevertheless, most synthesizers currently on the market are phoneme-based synthesizers, because the storage requirements of other types of synthesizers have been prohibitive. Diphone- and demisyllable-based synthesizers have been developed experimentally and show promising results for the future. As the cost of memory decreases they become more practical, and they do provide more natural sounding speech.

Besides simple word pronunciation, other problems in producing natural sounding speech include varying intonation to correctly convey meaning in sentences, such as for questions versus declarative statements and other aspects of grammatical structure. Variations in intonation also convey affect, such as humor, sadness, emphasis, sarcasm, and even personality traits such as self-confidence. Current synthesizers do not perform well on these dimensions, and this accounts in part for their unnatural sound and the fatigue produced by extended listening. Thus, speech synthesis quality includes much more than simple intelligibility.

Voice Synthesis: Advantages and Disadvantages

Regardless of the state of the technology, voice-synthesis systems have certain advantages and disadvantages relative to other output devices. Voice-synthesis systems offer particular *advantages* when the user's *eyes are busy,* when *mobility is required,* or when *the user has no access to a workstation with a screen.* Output on a screen requires that the eyes be on the screen and ties the user to the workstation. Voice output, by contrast, requires neither the eyes nor proximity to the workstation or computer itself. In certain environments, these may be very important advantages.

On the other hand, voice output carries certain significant *disadvantages* relative to the screen as an output device. Voice output in systems operating in public or open office environments can be very *disruptive* to others and suffers from a *lack of privacy and security* as well. Headphones can eliminate this problem, but may be *uncomfortable to use* over long periods of time. Poor-quality voice synthesis is extremely *fatiguing* to listen to. Perhaps most important, however, is that voice output is *transient,* thus taxing human short-term memory much more heavily than screen output. Users cannot scan and refer back to speech output the way they can with screen output. When output exceeds a few simple bits of information, it may be impractical to expect people to remember them long enough to make decisions.

Speech is also a *single-channel mode;* that is, users cannot listen to two or more messages simultaneously, and they cannot speak while listening. By contrast, users can take in multiple visual messages on a screen more or less simultaneously and perform multiple motor movements simultaneously (for example, with two hands or hands and feet). Finally, comprehending spoken language is *slower* than reading, and this is even more the case when comprehending synthetic speech. A typical speech output rate is 120 to 180 words per minute, while a typical reading rate is 200 to 300 words per minute, and text can be effectively scanned at a rate of 1000 words per minute.

Voice Synthesis: Experimental Results

Some studies have compared different voice-synthesis devices. Speech-synthesis systems vary in the rules they employ to translate letters, words, and phrases into sound. The effectiveness of these rules determines the overall intelligibility of the synthesized speech (see the preceding discussion). Pisoni and Nusbaum (1986) compared four available speech-synthesis systems on two simple speech-recognition tasks. In a *constrained* task, users were presented with six multiple-choice words and asked to identify which one matched a target word. Words were all of the form CVC (consonant, vowel, consonant). In a given multiple-choice set, six words varied by only one letter, either the first or last. For example, the target word might be "cat" and the multiple-choice alternatives "rat," "sat," "pat," "cat," "mat," and "bat," or "car," "cat," "can," "cab," "cad," and "cap."

In an *open-response* task, users were simply asked to write down the word spoken on each trial. The measure of performance was the percent correct. Results were as follows:

System	Task constrained (%)	Task free response (%)
DECtalk (male voice)	96.7%	86.7%
DECtalk (female voice)	94.4	
MITalk-79	93.1	75.4
Prose 200	94.3	
Votrax Type-'n-Talk	67.2	

Here it can be seen that there were considerable differences among systems and also that human performance *within* a given system depends significantly on task dimensions (although the rank order of the systems did not change on the two different tasks).

Streeter (1988) reports the results from another comparison of eight currently available synthesizers and natural speech. This study found an error rate of 0.53 for natural speech and a range in error rate from 3.25 to 35.56 across the eight synthesizers.

The tests in these studies represent simple laboratory tasks, which differ significantly from how speech synthesis might actually be used in real applications. Thus, it seems likely that performance might vary still more on tasks that involve sentences rather than single words and that differ in instructions and training, cognitive load, degree of uncertainty, message set, available context, and other task factors.

A variety of studies has investigated the use of voice synthesis in real applications, comparing it to alternative output devices. One study (Roberts and Engelbeck, 1989) compared voice synthesis to screen output as a primary output device. The application involved advanced phone capabilities, such as call routing, call screening, and message retrieval. Different input and output device combinations were compared, all embedded in a standard phone or phonelike device: (1) standard push-button input, tone output; (2) push-button input, voice-synthesis output; and (3) keyboard and mouse input, screen output. Eight users drawn from the general public used each system to perform a variety of tasks during three sessions across two days.

Timing data generally showed the screen phone to be faster than the standard phone, which in turn was faster than the voice-synthesis phone. Preference data generally correlated with these performance data. Errors were roughly equal in number across the three phones, but took longer to recover from in the voice-synthesis and standard phone interfaces. This in part accounts for the timing differences noted previously.

The timing differences were substantial, a 35- to 50-second difference per task between the fastest (screen based) and slowest (voice synthesis based) phones. The authors express surprise that the timing differences were not larger, however, and that there was no significant difference in error rates, given the very different quality of feedback across the phones: tones are very limited in providing feedback and voice is transient, whereas a screen provides an opportunity for rich and nontransient feedback. The authors had expected significant differences in error rates based on these differences in feedback quality. They observe that the lack of significant differences in error rates and the lack of a larger difference in timing could be due to two factors.

First, perhaps the functionality the subjects were required to learn was too limited to reveal the potential advantages and disadvantages of the different input and output devices. Second, perhaps the details of the accompanying *software* interface components canceled out the expected effects of the *hardware* interface components. The authors note that much of the error behavior observed could have been designed out of the screen- and voice-based interfaces without changing the input and output devices.

Nevertheless, the data do suggest that the transient and linear nature of voice output may carry significant disadvantages when compared to screens as output devices. This in turn suggests that, unless voice also offers significant advantages (such as no access to a workstation or eyes busy) to outweigh these disadvantages, a screen may be superior to voice as a primary output device. In this case, these advantages weigh heavily, because users are not expected to have or buy phones including screens and keyboards in the near future. Thus the authors conclude that efforts must be made to improve the *design* of voice-synthesis-based interfaces to *minimize* the problems arising from the linear and transient nature of voice output. This is an important point. Just as dialog style alone does not determine usability, neither does output device alone. While output devices have inherent potential advantages and disadvantages, these can be canceled out or overcome through the design of the details of the user's interaction with the output devices in combination with the software aspects of the interface.

Simpson and others (1985) review a study of the use of voice output in cockpits. It was found that pilots *preferred* voice output only for warning messages and preferred paper or screen displays for everything else that involved less time critical information and information that had to be remembered or referred to over a period of time.

On the other hand, Robinson and Eberts (1987) found that pilots *responded faster* to screen displays of emergency messages (warning messages) as compared to speech messages when performing the *dual task* of flying a flight simulator through enemy territory and responding to emergencies such as engine fire. They argue that, despite the fact that diagnosing visual displays of emergencies would seem to *compete with the same cognitive resources* being used in the flight task, the *greater compatibility* between the *visual* display, the *spatial* nature of the problem, and the *manual* response outweighed the competition for visual resources, resulting in an overall advantage for the visual output compared to speech. This is an important finding. It suggests that the choice of an appropriate output device for a given task is complex, involving interactions between the *inherent nature of the task* (for example, spatial or verbal), the *competition for cognitive resources* (for example, visual, auditory, or motor) between dual tasks, and the *associated input devices*. Although available research has yet to reveal clear guidelines for when to choose voice as an output device, it is possible that it will be optimal *only* when tasks are inherently verbal in *both* input and output, *and* competing tasks are already placing demands on the visual and motor channels. Even when these criteria are met, careful design of the voice interface to avoid overtaxing human short-term memory and to allow efficient navigation will still be important to achieve the potential benefits of voice output in these situations.

Other studies have focused on voice-synthesis quality. A number of variables in voice synthesis appear to affect *intelligibility*. Herlong and Williges (1988) found that a speech rate of 180 words per minute yielded more accurate transcriptions than a rate of 240 wpm. However, they found no effect of voice type (male versus female) on intelligibility and no advantage of navigational aids based on voice type (that is, coding menu level in a hierarchy by voice type.)

Merva and Williges (1987) systematically varied speech rate and amount of available *context* information and measured their effects on intelligibility. Three context conditions were included. In the *context* condition, a single word provided context prior to the utterance to be transcribed. For example, the word "weather" might precede the utterance "Rain ending later today." In the *no-context* condition, no context preceded each utterance. In the *context-plus* condition, users were first familiarized with all utterances before any were presented with the speech synthesizer, and they also received the same context word prior to each utterance, as did subjects in the *context* condition. Two speech rates were included: 180 and 240 wpm (natural conversational speech is typically at a rate of 180 wpm).

The subjects, 24 students, were untrained and heard and transcribed 30 utterances each. A measure of transcription error rates indicated a clear advantage for the slower speech rate (180 wpm) and for conditions providing context. Subjects also improved with practice in all conditions. A single word of context (the *context condition*) reduced error rates as compared to the *no-context* condition by over 50%. The slower presentation rate also reduced errors by 50% overall.

A second experiment included a different set of speech rates (150, 180, and 210 wpm) and introduced the variable of *utterance repetition* to see if this would improve accuracy. Utterances were repeated one, two, or three times. Context was provided, but not systematically varied. Nineteen untrained students participated in this experiment. They were asked to rate their level of certainty for each transcription.

Error rates in these data were divided into two groups to see if there were any effects of information location on transcription accuracy. Accuracy in transcribing the *first word* of an utterance was compared to accuracy in transcribing the *last word* in the utterance.

All independent variables (speech rate, number of repetitions, and information location) produced significant effects. The optimal speech rate was 180 wpm, with 150 wpm coming in second, although not significantly different. Two or three repetitions reduced errors by about 60% as compared to a single utterance. However, subjects correctly perceived 95% of all utterances repeated only once. Three repetitions did not significantly improve performance over two. Less errors were made on words at the end of utterances than on words at the beginning. Subjects certainty ratings corresponded quite well to their actual error rates.

The authors draw several conclusions from these data. They point out that, while faster speech rates and no repetitions result in faster *system* response time, they may reduce accuracy for novices and thus increase *user* response time by adding error recovery time. Repetitions increase overall accuracy, but also increase system response time and do not seem necessary for most utterances. Users seem able to assess the likelihood that they have made a transcription error. Thus, it might be useful to allow user-controlled repetitions so that users get fast system response time when they are fairly certain of their accuracy, but can improve their accuracy when necessary by requesting repetitions. In addition, speech rate might be increased for experts, depending on observed error rates.

The importance of context and the fact that users are more accurate in transcribing information at the end of utterances suggests that designers might build redundant context information into the *beginning* of messages and place critical information at the *end*. For example, "Today's weather report: Today rain will end" (instead of "Rain ending today"), or "Message from John Smith: Meeting changed to 3 P.M." (instead of "Meeting changed to 3 P.M. by John Smith").

The importance of context in enhancing intelligibility is also discussed in Streeter (1988). She points out that the minimum quality of synthetic speech available in the mid 1970s was adequate for a simple application in which incoming phone calls were announced, for example, "Phone call for Doug." Only about 20 names were included, and people are particularly good at recognizing their own name even in acoustically noisy environments. The high salience of names and the simplicity of the application meant that even poor-quality speech synthesis was acceptably intelligible. On the other hand, Streeter points out that even today's voice-synthesis technology would not be adequate for an application such as a dial-in service for the Associated Press News. The vocabulary here is unlimited and unpredictable, including many unfamiliar and difficult to pronounce words, such as foreign names and acronyms. This means users have very little context to help them interpret less than perfectly intelligible speech. An experimental system of this sort revealed only about a 70% intelligibility rate.

Relative intelligibility may in turn affect other aspects of the human processing of synthetic speech output. Two studies (Waterworth and Thomas, 1985; Thomas and others, 1989) found that people had better recall for information spoken in natural versus synthetic speech. The data suggested that synthetic speech is harder to recall because it requires more cognitive resources to understand or encode, leaving limited resources to maintain encoded items in memory. The study procedures involved memorizing word lists or single-digit number lists, not very natural tasks, and it is unclear whether these results would generalize to real uses of voice output systems. The findings suggest, however, that the general design principle of minimizing the human short-term memory burden may be even more important when output is synthesized speech.

There is more to synthetic speech than simple *intelligibility*. Another important issue in the design of voice output is speech *quality*. Halstead-Nussloch (1988) reports that synthetic speech gets low subjective ratings for intelligibility by users, even when they perform fairly well with it. Both natural and synthesized speech can vary on a number of qualitative dimensions that may not affect intelligibility, but do affect subjective ratings of acceptability and appropriateness. These dimensions include *fullness* (richness, pitch, heaviness) and *clarity* (clearness, roughness, smoothness), among others. Rosson and Cecala (1986) created 36 different synthesized voices varying on these and other dimensions and asked users to rate them on these dimensions and on their appropriateness in different situations. Twenty different situations were created, including weather reports, games, travel directions, catalog ordering, and the like. It was found that users felt that different voice qualities were differentially important in different situations. For example, *richness* seemed to be considered appropriate in information situations (for example, catalog ordering), while *pitch* seemed important in entertainment situations (for example, games). These findings indicate that designers must consider other aspects of voice quality besides intelligibility to ensure user acceptance of voice interfaces, and that different aspects of quality will contribute to acceptance in different application areas. Since research on this aspect of speech quality is scant, at this time only empirical testing will reveal the appropriate qualities of speech for a given application.

The previous studies focused primarily on *synthesized* speech. *Recorded natural speech* can also be used as a primary output device. Regardless of whether voice output is recorded natural speech or synthesized speech, there are many issues in the design of a voice output interface. Voice differs significantly from graphical or text displays in that it is linear and transient. Users cannot scan and review voice output the way they can scan and review a screen. Thus, careful design is necessary to facilitate navigation and avoid overtaxing human memory.

One study (Aucella and Ehrlich, 1986) reported the iterative design and development of the voice prompts for a voice messaging system. This system allowed users to leave recorded messages, record messages for future delivery, review accumulated messages, send immediate responses to messages, and forward messages, among other things. A voice menu interface presented these options. Iterative testing of the design of the menu structure and prompt wording led to a number of design changes. For example, prompts were rephrased so that variable information was up front. For instance, the original prompt "There are three messages in your mailbox" was changed to "Three messages are in your mailbox." This allowed expert users to more quickly extract the necessary information and preempt the end of the phrase to move on to the next desired prompt or action.

Note that this latter point may seem to contradict Merva and Williges's (1987) suggestion to place critical information at the *end* of messages. However, there is an important difference in the two contexts in which these recommendations are made. When *variable* information appears in *predictable* phrases, then Aucella and Ehrlich's recommendation seem appropriate. Users will learn what to expect and will be focused only on the variable information. Putting it first will allow users to more quickly move on in the dialog. When information is quite *unpredictable* in both form and location in the dialog, on the other hand, Merva and Williges's recommendation makes sense. Even frequent users may not be able to predict output forms, and putting critical information at the end of utterances will thus be optimal.

Other changes were also made. Prompts were added when it was discovered to be necessary. For instance, the prompt "The pound key is in the lower right of your telephone key pad" was added because it was observed that novices had difficulty finding the pound key when prompted to use it. Infrequently used options were relocated farther down in a list of options. A help system was added to teach novice users certain input formats, such as dates.

Still other changes were made to better meet novice users' expectations. For example, in an initial design, users were required to press a key to send a message. If they hung up without pressing this key, their message was not sent. It was learned through interviews that many users failed to press this key and their messages were not sent. The system was redesigned so that messages were automatically sent upon hanging up. This case study illustrates some of the issues in designing voice interfaces and emphasizes the importance of iterative testing and redesign.

Voice Synthesis: Guidelines

Based on the inherent advantages and disadvantages of voice as an output device, and on the experimental results just discussed, the following guidelines are offered for using voice synthesis as an output device in user interfaces.

☞ **Consider voice synthesis as an output device when the user's eyes are busy, when mobility is required, or when the user has no access to a workstation or screen.**

Simpson and others (1985) list a number of general situations that suggest the use of voice output.

1. For warning signals, because an auditory signal does not require that the user's attention be oriented in any particular direction or location
2. When there are already too many visual displays
3. When the user's head or body position cannot be predicted
4. When lighting conditions preclude vision
5. In conditions where anoxia is possible, because audition is less sensitive to anoxia than vision

Given the relative advantages of voice output in these situations, *possible current and future applications* include *text to speech,* such as being able to listen to the output of database queries, or mail messages. The *"10 cent workstation"* idea views the telephone as a remote voice output device for office or home computer systems. Users could call in and listen to electronic calendar entries and electronic mail via voice synthesis. We can imagine voice output from *emergency reporting systems.* For instance, a fire alarm system might repeat directions for escape that are determined by the location and severity of the fire. Sight may be obscured by smoke, or people may not be located near posted emergency directions. A calm, humanlike voice giving specific instructions might even reduce panic. Finally, there are obvious applications that voice output might make possible for the *blind.*

☞ **Avoid voice synthesis as an output device in an open environment, when privacy and security are important, when frequency of use is high, when multiple messages must be displayed simultaneously, and when the limits of human memory would be overtaxed.**

Given the relative disadvantages of voice output in these circumstances, *inappropriate applications* for voice output might include *automatic teller machines,* where security and privacy are issues and instructions may be too complex to expect people to remember while listening, and *public information systems,* where noise level is a serious disadvantage and human memory would again be taxed.

☞ **Use an output rate of approximately 180 words per minute.**

Intelligibility is affected by output rate. Research results indicate that 180 wpm is more intelligible than 240 or even 210 wpm for novices, although accuracy increases with practice even for higher speech rates. Thus, it is advisable to provide a rate of 180 wpm as a default speech rate and then provide increased rates for experts depending on observed error rates when speed of overall throughput is critical.

☞ **When output messages are unpredictable, begin any synthesized message with a few noncritical words that provide context to allow the user to pick up the speech cadence and quality and get oriented to the subject matter.**

Some evidence suggests that users are more accurate in transcribing information at the end of utterances, as compared to the beginning. Evidence also suggests that context information just prior to a message increases recognition accuracy. Thus, designers are advised to build redundant context information into the beginning of messages and place critical information at the end, for example, "Today's weather report: Today rain will end" (instead of "Rain ending today"), or "Message from John Smith: Meeting changed to 3 P.M." (instead of "Meeting changed to 3 P.M. by John Smith").

☞ **When there is variable information in output that is otherwise predictable in location and form, place the variable information first.**

For example, in a structured, prompted voice mail interface, a phrase such as "*Three* messages are in your mailbox" might be better than "Your mailbox contains *three* messages." The former allows the expert user to extract the critical (variable) information right away and preempt the latter part of the phrase to move on in the dialog more quickly.

☞ **Structure voice instructional prompts to present the goal first and the action last.**

Leopold and Van Nes (1987) suggest that a voice prompt such as "For scanning through the messages received, please say scan" is preferable to one such as "Please say scan if you want to scan through received messages," because users will not have to remember the command word while they listen to its definition. For this reason, it is a good idea in general to always structure voice prompts in the form of goal first and action last.

☞ **Provide a capability for users to request repetitions of messages.**

Evidence suggests that repetitions increase accuracy *overall,* but they also increase system response time and do not seem necesary for most utterances. In addition, users seem aware of when they have and have not made a transcription error. Thus, it might be useful to allow user-controlled repetitions so that users get fast system response time when they are fairly certain of their accuracy, but can improve their accuracy when necessary by requesting repetitions.

☞ **Structure a voice output dialog according to user and task characteristics.**

Halstead-Nussloch (1989) offers the following guidelines based on research findings. Design a *user-controlled* (for example, command-based) dialog flow when the following apply:

1. Functionality can be divided into five or less distinct modes
2. Each mode contains a large and complex structure of functions
3. The user frequently needs to change modes
4. Frequency of use is high

Design a *system-controlled* (for example, auditory menu-based) dialog when the following apply:

1. Functionality falls into six or more distinct modes
2. Each mode contains moderate complexity and structure of functions
3. The user rarely needs to change modes
4. Frequency of use is low

☞ **Structure auditory menus for ease of comprehension and navigation.**

Halstead-Nussloch (1989) offers the following guidelines for voice menus:

1. Provide an auditory title or heading for each auditory menu
2. Minimize the number of options per menu and the total number of options in the menu hierarchy
3. Provide options in the format "To do function X, enter Y"

4. Order options according to expected frequency of use (most frequent first)
5. Design option labels to be distinct and mutually exclusive
6. Allow interrupts so that the user can enter a choice immediately after recognizing a given option
7. Automatically repeat options if the user has not made a choice after 12 seconds
8. Allow the user to request repeats at any time
9. Do *not* require a terminator after a choice (analogous to the "Return" or "Enter" terminators often associated with keyboard input)
10. When option lists are long, provide a fast-forward option
11. Provide immediate access to Help at any time during the dialog

Leopold and Van Nes (1987) also suggest layering prompts to offer assistance to novices but not impede experts. This is similar to point 6 above. An example is given next.

System	**Novice**	**Expert**
You can now record your message.		
PAUSE		Record!
During recording you can stop, start again, repeat, or erase.		
PAUSE		Record! (only if previous opportunity missed)
When you want to start your message, please say record. When you have finished your message, please say end.	Record!	Record! (only if previous opportunities missed)

In addition, Leopold and Van Nes (1987) suggest confirmation messages, as illustrated in the following example from a railway information system.

System:	Your destination is . . .
User:	Amsterdam
System:	Amsterdam!
	OR
	You want to go to Amsterdam?
	OR
	Amstel Station or Central Station?
	(both are in Amsterdam)

Users should be allowed to turn off such confirmations once they are experts and if the recognition system is fairly reliable, except in cases where the results of commands are destructive (for example, erasing messages).

☞ **Consider voice quality to increase user acceptance of voice output.**

Users express preferences for *different* voice qualities in *different* contexts, such as information systems as opposed to games. Voice qualities include *gender, pitch, fullness, smoothness, clarity, heaviness,* and the like. Voice output will also be considered more natural if intonation can be introduced to convey *affect,* such as sadness, humor, emphasis, and sarcasm, and personality traits such as self-confidence.

Other Output Devices

Some researchers have investigated the use of **sound** as an output device. One author describes a mouse-driven direct manipulation interface to a word processing application in which sound in conjunction with synthesized speech substitutes for the screen as an output device. This experimental system was devised with visually impaired users in mind. Users move a cursor on the screen with a mouse, and different tones provide feedback on cursor position. One set of tones identifies different screen windows, such as menus and documents. Another set of tones identifies components of the currently *active* window, such as menu selection labels. Object names (for example, menu labels or document names) and text contained in documents can also be reviewed through speech synthesis.

Evaluation of this experimental system showed that performance was quite poor. In fact, users performed 15 times slower than a sighted user using the screen, rather than sound, as output. The memory burden of having to *recall* the meaning of sounds and object locations, as compared to having only to *recognize* visual cues and objects, probably accounts for much of this difference.

One interesting observation made by the author is that users in fact seemed to rely on locational cues rather than on tone differences to identify objects. That is, they seemed to locate a desired object by moving the cursor across the screen and *counting* the number of tones preceding the one identifying the desired object, rather than by the tone in and of itself. Only one test subject seemed to associate objects with specific tones, and this subject had a musical background. Thus, even for visually impaired users, arbitrary tones may not provide very effective cues.

Another study (Brown, Newsome, and Glimert, 1989), using a much simpler task, found that nondisabled users performed as quickly using tones as a search cue as when using visual search cues. Prior to the presentation of six columns of five text items on the screen, either a learned tone or a visual cue indicating which column the target item would be in was presented. Only six tones had to be learned, which probably was a reasonable memory load. The motivation behind this study was the idea that since displays are exclusively visual, when they become too complex the substitution of audial cues and codes for some information might enhance performance. Since no performance difference was found between audial and visual cues in their study, the authors suggest that sound may be an equally effective cue. However, it is not at all clear from this study alone whether sound would be a worse, equal, or better cue as compared to visual cues in *real situations presenting much more complex information and tasks* than this simple study.

Six members of a panel (Buxton and others, 1987) described experimental systems in which sounds varying in the dimensions of pitch, volume, duration, timbre (harmonic content), attack (volume rise time), and timing were used to present scientific data. In some cases, sound alone was used for visually impaired users. In other cases, sound was combined with visual displays for nonimpaired users. Those who reported evaluations of the systems indicated some evidence of the value of sound for coding information. Impaired users could interpret learned sounds with a fairly high rate of accuracy, and nonimpaired users demonstrated some improvement when sound was *added* to visual displays.

The preceding studies all considered only simple variations in the dimensions of sound itself, such as *pitch, loudness,* or *duration.* That is, only the physics of the sound waves themselves were considered as cues, and these were associated in an *arbitrary* way with objects or locations in the visual interface. Gaver (1986) points out that an *arbitrary* association between abstract tone qualities and visual interface elements results in *articulatory indirectness in evaluation* (see Chapter 9). He puts forth the idea of "auditory icons." Auditory icons incorporate not only the dimensions of sound itself, but also the dimensions of the sound's *source.* This is important information that is heavily used in interpreting sound in the real world. Gaver offers the following example of an auditory icon:

> One can imagine how a single sound could be used to give information about a file arriving in a message system. The file hits the mailbox, causing it to emit a characteristic sound. Because it is a large message, it makes a rather weighty sound. The crackle of paper indicates a text file—if it had been a compiled program, it would have clanged like metal. The sound comes from the left and is muffled: The mailbox must be in the window behind the one that is currently on the left side of the screen. And the echoes sound like a large empty room, so the load on the system must be fairly low. All this information from one sound!

In this example, it can be seen how properties of the *source* of sound are included in the sound and associated in a *meaningful* way with the information that the sound represents. Gaver points out that auditory icons do not have to be completely realistic. They can be caricatures or cartoons of real-world sounds or even *metaphoric* (for example, changing tones to indicate changing height), just as visual icons are. He suggests, however, that in general the more *articulatorily direct* the relationship between the sound and its referent, the easier it will be to learn and remember sound associations. The exception to this might be certain purely *symbolic* sounds, such as a siren for errors and applause for acceptance, which, although abstract, are so familiar that they will provide a high degree of articulatory directness. The notion of auditory icons seems much more promising than the use of simple physical variations in sound dimensions, but it awaits empirical evaluation and direct comparison with other types of output for communicating different classes of information.

To summarize this chapter on input and output devices, there is a general tendency to enthusiastically and unanalytically adopt new input and output technologies such as pointing devices and voice input and output systems without considering the actual advantages, disadvantages, and "value added" as described in the preceding sections. Regardless of the type or state of the art of input and output devices, it should be clear from the discussions in this chapter that they have different characteristics that influence their relative usability for different tasks, environments, and users. These characteristics should be carefully considered in choosing input and output devices(s) for an application. New technology should not be blindly applied simply because it is new or because it *seems* better. Task analyses and testing are *always* necessary to determine the relative benefits of new input and output devices.

REFERENCES

ALBERT, ALAN E., "The Effect of Graphic Input Devices on Performance in a Cursor Positioning Task," *Proceedings of the Human Factors Society 26th Annual Meeting,* 1982, pp. 54–58.

AUCELLA, A. F., and S. F. EHRLICH, "Voice Messaging Enhancing the User Interface Design Based on Field Performance," *CHI '86 Proceedings,* April 1986, pp. 156–61, ACM.

BROWN, C. MARLIN, *Human–Computer Interface Design Guidelines* (Norwood, N.J.: Ablex Publishing Corporation, 1988), pp. 133–56.

BROWN, MEGAN L., SANDRA L. NEWSOME, and EPHRAIM P. GLINERT, "An Experiment into the Use of Auditory Cues to Reduce Visual Workload," *CHI '89 Proceedings,* May 1989, pp. 339–46, ACM.

BROWN, NORMAN R., and ANN MARIE VOSBURGH, "Evaluating the Accuracy of a Large-vocabulary Speech Recognition System," *Proceedings of the Human Factors Society 33rd Annual Meeting,* 1989, pp. 296–300.

BUXTON, WILLIAM, "There's More to Interaction Than Meets the Eye: Some Issues in Manual Input," *Readings in Human–Computer Interaction,* Ronald M. Baecker and William A. S. Buxton, eds. (Los Altos, Calif.: Morgan Kaufmann Publishers, Inc., 1987), pp. 366–75.

———, and B. MYERS, "A Study in Two-Handed Input," *CHI '86 Proceedings,* April 1986, pp. 321–26, ACM.

———, and others, "Communicating with Sound," *Readings in Human–Computer Interaction,* Ronald M. Baecker and William A. S. Buxton, eds. (Los Altos, Calif.: Morgan Kaufmann Publishers, Inc., 1987), pp. 420–24.

CAKIR, A., D. J. HART, and T. F. M. STEWART, *The VDT Manual* (New York: John Wiley and Sons, Inc., 1980).

CARD, S. K., "Human Limits and the VDT Computer Interface," *Readings in Human–Computer Interaction,* Ronald M. Baecker and William A. S. Buxton, eds. (Los Altos, Calif.: Morgan Kaufmann Publishers, Inc., 1987), pp. 180–91.

CARD, STUART K., WILLIAM K. ENGLISH, and BETTY J. BURR, "Evaluation of Mouse, Rate-controlled Isometric Joystick, Step Keys, and Text Keys for Text Selection on a CRT," *Ergonomics,* 21, no. 8 (1978), pp. 601–13.

DEININGER, R. L., "Human Factors Studies in the Design and Use of Pushbutton Telephone Keysets," *Bell System Technical Journal,* 39 (1960), pp. 995–1012.

EPPS, BRIAN W., "A Comparison of Cursor Control Devices on a Graphic Editing Task," *Proceedings of the Human Factors Society 31st Annual Meeting,* 1987, pp. 442–46.

EWING, JOHN, and others, "An Experimental Comparison of a Mouse and Arrow-jump Keys for an Interactive Encyclopedia," *International Journal of Man–Machine Studies,* 1986, p. 23.

FOLEY, JAMES D., VICTOR L. WALLACE, and PEGGY CHAN, "The Human Factors of Computer Graphics Interaction Techniques," *IEEE Computer Graphics and Applications,* November 1984, pp. 13–48.

GALITZ, WILBERT O., *Human Factors in Office Automation* (Atlanta, Life Office Management Association, Inc., 1980).

GARDNER, DARYLE JEAN, and others, "Automated Speech Recognition as a Function of Format Speech Training and Passage of Time between Template Training and Testing," *Proceedings of the Human Factors Society 29th Annual Meeting,* 1985, pp. 937–41.

GARDNER-BONNEAU, DARYLE JEAN, JOHN ROBERT BONNEAU, and BENGT MARTIN AHLSTROM, "Voice Recognition Technology Potential for a Complex Map Query System," *Proceedings of the Human Factors Society 31st Annual Meeting,* 1987, pp. 956–60.

GAVER, WILLIAM W., "Auditory Icons: Using Sound in Computer Interfaces," *Human–Computer Interaction,* 2, no. 2 (1986), pp. 167–77.

GEISER, GEORG H., "Handprinted Data Entry with a Touch-sensitive Numeric Keypad," *Proceedings of the Human Factors Society 33rd Annual Meeting,* 1989, pp. 305–309.

GLENN, FLOYD A., III, and others, "Eye–Voice-Controlled Interface," *Proceedings of the Human Factors Society 30th Annual Meeting,* 1986, pp. 322–26.

GOOD, MICHAEL, "The Use of Logging Data in the Design of a New Text Editor," *Proceedings, CHI '85,* 1985, pp. 93–113.

GOPHER, DANIEL, HANNA HILSERNATH, and DAVID RAIJ, "Steps in the Development of a New Data Entry Device Based upon Two Hand Chord Keyboard," *Proceedings of the Human Factors Society 29th Annual Meeting,* 1985, pp. 132–36.

GREENSTEIN, JOEL S., and ANISH BAIJAL, "An Investigation of Techniques for Occasional Numeric Data Entry," *Proceedings of the Human Factors Society 33rd Annual Meeting,* 1989, pp. 310–14.

HALSTEAD-NUSSLOCH, RICHARD, "The Design of Phone-based Interfaces for Consumers," *CHI '89 Proceedings,* May 1989, pp. 347–52, ACM.

HAUPTMANN, ALEXANDER G., "Speech and Gestures for Graphic Image Manipulation," *CHI '89 Proceedings,* May 1989, pp. 241–45, ACM.

HELANDER, MARTIN, TARYN S. MOODY, and MICHAEL G. JOOST, "Systems Design for Automated Speech Recognition," *Handbook of Human–Computer Interaction,* Martin Helander, ed. (Amsterdam: North-Holland, 1988), pp. 301–19.

HERLONG, DAVID W., and BEVERLY H. WILLIGES, "Designing Speech Displays for Telephone Information Systems," *Proceedings of the Human Factors Society 32rd Annual Meeting,* 1988, pp. 215–18.

HODES, D. G., and K. AKAGI, "Study, Development and Design of a Mouse," *Proceedings of the Human Factors Society 30th Annual Meeting,* 1986, pp. 900–904.

ISENBERG, DAVID, DOUWE YNTENA, and RAY WIESEN, "Designing Speech Recognition Interfaces for Talkers and Tasks," *Advances in Human Factors/Ergonomics: Human Computer Interaction,* Gavriel Salvendy, ed. (Amsterdam: Elsevier, 1984), pp. 455–58.

JACKSON, JEFFREY C., and RENATE J. ROSKE-HOFSTRAND, "Circling: A Method of Mouse-based Selection without Button Presses," *CHI '89 Proceedings,* May 1989, pp. 161–66, ACM.

KARAT, JOHN, JAMES MCDONALD, and MATT ANDERSON, "A Comparison of Selection Techniques: Tough Panel, Mouse and Keyboard," *INTERACT '84 Proceedings,* 1984, pp. 149–53.

KIRSCHENBAUM, ALAN, ZWI FRIEDMAN, and ARIE MELNIK, "Performance of Disabled Persons on a Chordic Keyboard," *Human Factors,* 28, no. 2 (April 1986), pp. 187–94.

KROEMER, K. H. E., "Human Engineering the Keyboard," *Human Factors,* 14, no. 1 (1972), pp. 51–63.

LEOPOLD, F. F., and F. L. VAN NES, "Control of Data Processing Systems by Voice Commands," *Behavior & Information Technology,* 6, no. 3 (July–September 1987), pp. 323–27.

LUTZ, M. C., and A. CHAPANIS, "Expected Locations of Digits and Letters on 10-Button Keysets," *Journal of Applied Psychology,* 29 (1955), pp. 314–17.

MACK, ROBERT L., and KATHY LANG, "A Benchmark Comparison of Mouse and Touch Interface Techniques for an Intelligent Workstation Windowing Environment," *Proceedings of the Human Factors Society 33rd Annual Meeting,* 1989, pp. 325–29.

MAHACH, KAREN RENEE, "A Comparison of Computer Input Devices: Linus Pen, Mouse, Cursor Keys and Keyboard," *Proceedings of the Human Factors Society 33rd Annual Meeting,* 1989, pp. 330–34.

MERVA, MONICA A., and BEVERLY H. WILLIGES, "Context, Repetition, and Synthesized Speech Intelligibility," *Proceedings of the Human Factors Society 31st Annual Meeting,* 1987, pp. 961–65.

MURRAY, J. THOMAS, JOHN VAN PRAAG, and DAVID GILFOIL, "Voice versus Keyboard Control of Cursor Motion," *Proceedings of the Human Factors Society 27th Annual Meeting,* 1983, p. 103.

NISHIDA, S., "Speech Recognition Enhancement by Lip Information," *CHI '86 Proceedings,* April 1986, pp. 198–204, ACM.

PEARSON, G., and M. WEISER, "Of Moles and Men: The Design of Foot Controls for Workstations," *CHI '86 Proceedings,* April 1986, pp. 333–39, ACM.

PEARSON, GLENN, and MARK WEISER, "Exploratory Evaluation of a Planar Foot-operated Cursor-positioning Device," *CHI '88 Proceedings,* May 1988, pp. 13–18, ACM.

PETAJAN, ERIC, and others, "An Improved Automatic Lipreading System to Enhance Speech Recognition," *CHI '88 Proceedings,* May 1988, pp. 19–26, ACM.

PISONI, DAVID B., and HOWARD C. NUSBAUM, "Developing Methods for Assessing the Performance of Speech Synthesis and Recognition Systems," *Proceedings of the Human Factors Society 30th Annual Meeting,* 1986, pp. 1344–48.

POTTER, RICHARD L., BEN SHNEIDERMAN, and LINDA J. WELDON, "Improving the Accuracy of Touch Screens: An Experimental Evaluation of Three Strategies," *CHI '88 Proceedings,* May 1988, pp. 27–32, ACM.

ROBERTS, TERESA, and GEORGE ENGELBECK, "The Effects of Device Technology on the Usability of Advanced Telephone Functions," *CHI '89 Proceedings,* May 1989, pp. 331–38, ACM.

ROBINSON, CHRISTOPHER P., and RAY E. EBERTS, "Comparison of Speech and Pictorial Displays in a Cockpit Environment," *Human Factors,* 29, no. 1 (February 1987), 31–44.

———, and A. J. CECALA, "Designing a Quality Voice: An Analysis of Listeners' Reactions to Synthetic Voices," *CHI '86 Proceedings,* April 1986, pp. 192–97, ACM.

ROUSE, WILLIAM B., "Design of Man–Computer Interfaces for On-line Interactive Systems," *Proceedings of the IEEE,* 63, no. 6, (June 1975), pp. 847–57.

RUPP, BRUCE A., "Visual Display Standards: A Review of Issues," *Proceedings of the SID,* 22, no. 1, (1981), pp. 63–72.

SHNEIDERMAN, BEN, *Designing the User Interface: Strategies for Effective Human–Computer Interaction* (Reading, MA: Addison-Wesley, Inc., 1986).

SIMPSON, CAROL A., and others, "System Design for Speech Recognition and Generation," *Human Factors,* 27, no. 2 (April 1985), pp. 115–42.

STREETER, LYNN A., "Applying Speech Synthesis to User Interfaces," *Handbook of Human–Computer Interaction,* Martin Helander, ed. (Amsterdam: North-Holland, 1988), pp. 321–43.

THOMAS, MARGARET, and others, "Short Term Memory Demands in Processing Synthetic Speech," *Proceedings of the Human Factors Society 33rd Annual Meeting,* 1989, pp. 239–41.

VALK, MARY ANN, "An Experiment to Study Touchscreen Button Design," *Proceedings of the Human Factors Society 29th Annual Meeting,* 1985, pp. 127–31.

WATERWORTH, JOHN A., and CATHY M. THOMAS, "Why Is Synthetic Speech Harder to Remember Than Natural Speech?" *CHI '85 Proceedings,* April 1985, pp. 201–206, ACM.

WEIMER, DAVID, and S. K. GANAPATHY, "A Synthetic Visual Environment with Hand Gesturing and Voice Input," *CHI '89 Proceedings,* May 1989, pp. 235–40, ACM.

WOLF, CATHERINE G., "A Comparative Study of Gestural and Keyboard Interfaces," *Proceedings of the Human Factors Society 32rd Annual Meeting,* 1988, pp. 273–77.

WARE, COLIN, and HARUTUNE H. MIKAELIAN, "An Evaluation of an Eye Tracker as a Device for Computer Input," *CHI '87 Proceedings,* May 1987, pp. 183–88, ACM.

ZIMMERMAN, THOMAS G., and others, "A Hand Gesture Interface Device," *CHI '87 Proceedings,* May 1987, pp. 189–92, ACM.

CHAPTER 13

Organization
of Functionality

WHAT IS ORGANIZATION OF FUNCTIONALITY?

Organization of functionality refers to where information and functions are located in relation to one another within the possible pathways through screens in the system. The *functionality* of a system provides *what* the user needs. *Screen design* principles (see Chapter 14) help the designer to present information in a useful manner, that is, *how* the user needs it. The way *functionality is organized* determines whether information and functions are presented *when* and *where* users need them. Although the way functionality is organized is absolutely key to the usability of an interactive system, it is commonly ignored in system design and is generally unaddressed in the human factors literature.

The notion of organization of functionality and its importance to usability are best described through some examples. Figure 13-1 shows two possible ways to structure a three-level menu in an office automation product. In the "Poor" version, the user first picks word processing (WP) from a top-level menu, then chooses an action such as "print" or "send," and finally chooses a document from a directory menu on which to perform the action previously selected. Note what happens if a user wishes to edit, print, and then send a particular document, say the one called "DocA." First the user must select "WP" from the top-level menu. Then the user selects "Edit," followed by "DocA." After editing the document, the user must then close DocA in order to get back to the second-level menu and

Poor:

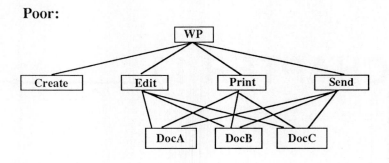

Improved:

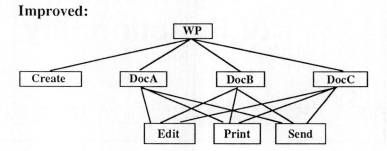

Figure 13–1   Example of organization of functionality.

select "Print." After choosing "Print," the user is again presented with the directory menu and must choose "DocA" again. The user now returns to the second-level menu and picks "Send." The directory menu is presented yet again, and the user selects "DocA" for the third time. In this structure, the user must select "DocA" from a menu everytime he or she wants to perform some individual action on it. This is not very efficient, given that users are often likely to want to perform consecutive actions on a single document.

Alternatively, consider the "Improved" menu structure. In this structure, the user selects "DocA" first and then is presented with a menu of actions. When one action is complete, the user is returned to the action menu and can select another. DocA is still selected and need not be selected again. To change documents, the user would have to back up one more level in the menu. However, given that users will probably most often perform consecutive actions on a single document, this structure supports the user's task better by structuring the menu organization to reflect this goal.

Generally, the *organization of functionality should reflect the most efficient sequence of steps to accomplish the most likely or most frequent user goal.* Note that the two structures in Figure 13-1 offer exactly the same functionality. One simply supports the task better than the other.

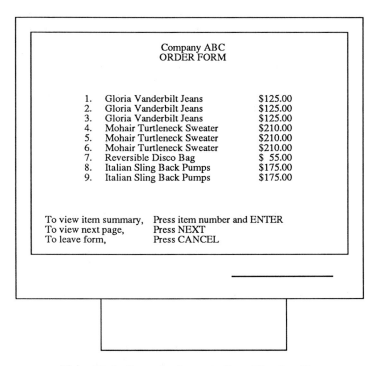

Figure 13-2   Example of organization of functionality.

As another example, consider the screens in Figures 13-2 and 13-3 from an on-line catalog ordering system. In this system, users browse or search through screens describing particular products. They can select products as they go, specifying choices such as size, color, and quantity, and these items will be added to an electronic order form. When they are done, they can review their selections through the screens illustrated in Figures 13-2 and 13-3 and make changes before finalizing their order. Note that the summary screen in Figure 13-2 gives only the full name and price of each item selected. To review more detailed information regarding a selected item, the user specifies the item number and is taken to a screen such as that in Figure 13-3. This screen provides detailed information on that selection, including size, color, and quantity.

Thus, the order summary is organized into two levels, with general information summarized at the top level and more detailed information provided at a second level on an item by item basis. At first, this may seem like a reasonable way to organize this information.

However, consider for a moment what many catalog order customers are likely to do when ordering. When the items being ordered are clothing, as they are in this example, people usually need to try on several sizes to get the right one, and

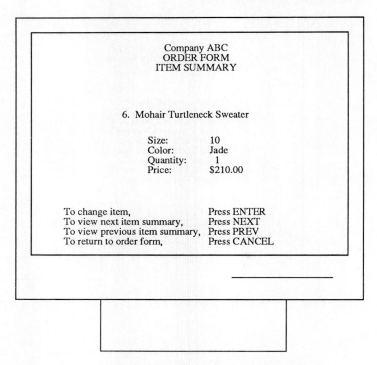

Company ABC
ORDER FORM
ITEM SUMMARY

6. Mohair Turtleneck Sweater

Size: 10
Color: Jade
Quantity: 1
Price: $210.00

To change item,   Press ENTER
To view next item summary,   Press NEXT
To view previous item summary,   Press PREV
To return to order form,   Press CANCEL

Figure 13-3 Example of organization of functionality.

they may wish to see the actual color of items in order to match them with other clothes they may own. Colors reproduced in catalogs (or on computer screens) are not always accurate.

Thus, what people often do is order a single item in several colors or several sizes, intending to keep only one. When they are reviewing their order, they will want to confirm that they have ordered the selection of sizes and colors that they wished. It is instructive to walk through this typical scenario, given the organization of functionality in Figures 13-2 and 13-3.

Note that none of the information that users will often want to confirm (size and color) is available at the top level (Figure 13-2). To get this information, users must go to the second level. But they cannot even get the information they really want at the second level without a great deal of trouble. They must go back and forth between levels, choosing each item at the top level and viewing its detail at the second level. Since they will probably not be able to remember information as they are conducting this tedious navigation, they will end up writing down on paper the detail at each second-level screen so that they can compare items to confirm that all desired colors and sizes have been ordered. Thus, not only a great deal of screen flipping is necessary, but also some fairly extensive note taking. The organization of functionality seriously overtaxes human short-term memory capacity and duration. Clearly, this organization of functionality does not support a common task that many users are likely to want to accomplish in this application: confirming the selection of colors and sizes across items.

An alternative organization of functionality for this system is given in Figure 13-4. Here the information considered most important, size and color, is included in the top-level summary. This makes the confirmation of color and size choices a trivial task. To fit this information on the screen, the item names have been considerably shortened, providing less information to identify the item. This is certainly a trade-off, but it is most likely the appropriate one when considering the task at hand. It will certainly be easier to remember an item by its abbreviated name than to remember all the sizes and colors that have been ordered when no indication of them is displayed. And, if you cannot remember, say, what kind of jeans you ordered, then only one step down to one second-level screen is required to identify three items on the top level. By contrast, to confirm colors and sizes in the original design, all three second-level screens would have to be accessed.

In this alternative design, second-level screens could provide full item names, any other order information not included on the top-level summary, and additional

```
                        Company ABC
                        ORDER FORM

   NO.   ITEM        COLOR    SIZE      PRICE   QUANTITY

   1     Jeans       Black     8       $125.00      1
   2     Jeans       Black    10       $125.00      1
   3     Jeans       Black    12       $125.00      1
   4     Sweater     Red       8       $210.00      1
   5     Sweater     Blue      8       $210.00      1
   6     Sweater     Orange    8       $210.00      1
   7     Disco Bag                     $ 55.00      1
   8     Pumps       Black    81/2M   $175.00       1
   9     Pumps       Black     9M     $175.00       1



   To view item summary,   Press item number and ENTER
   To view next page,      Press NEXT
   To leave form,          Press CANCEL
```

Figure 13–4 Example of organization of functionality.

information such as fabric type, other available color and size choices, and cleaning instructions. The idea is that information that must be compared across items or that is otherwise likely to be important in confirming and finalizing an order (for example, price information) should be easily available with minimal navigation and minimal across-screen memory and mental calculation requirements.

Note that the alternative design in Figure 13-4 does not provide any more information than do the screens in Figures 13-2 and 13-3. The difference is in how that information is organized and made available, that is, not *what* is presented, but *where, when,* and *how* it is presented.

ORGANIZATION OF FUNCTIONALITY: PRINCIPLES AND GUIDELINES

One simple guideline results from these examples.

☞ **Organize the functionality of a system to support common user tasks.**

Poor organization of functionality is a common flaw in user interface design. There are probably several reasons why this is so. Often the way functionality is organized seems to be driven by the need for *ease of implementation,* that is, by what is a logical organization from a technical implementation point of view, rather than by an *analysis of user tasks.* For instance, many office automation systems are divided into separate applications, such as word processing, graphics, spreadsheet, and electronic mail. Data from each application can sometimes be cut from a parent object and pasted into another object of a different type, but usually editing capabilities are then sacrificed.

In fact, users do not think in terms of *applications or data types.* They think in terms of *tasks,* such as sending a document to a colleague or generating a report that might include text and graphics based on spreadsheet data. The way office automation systems are organized by *application* may be logical and efficient from a technical implementation point of view, but it does not support the tasks of users as well as it might.

Sometimes the organization of functionality reflects the *organization of the product development team* that built it. That is, graphics and word processing capabilities may be separated into different applications rather than integrated not so much because of technical implementation concerns, but because different organizational entities were assigned responsibility for these different functions. It is always easier for groups to work independently than to coordinate with one another.

Another reason for poor organization of functionality is a *focus on features and functions,* rather than on overall *tasks.* Systems analysis encourages this focus. Lack of contact with real users is also responsible. In the office automation example, focusing on word processing functions and graphics functions independently would be an example of a typical systems analysis approach to system design. Here it fails to note that users do not build text or graphics; they build *documents*.

Finally, poor organization of functionality is sometimes due to a simple-minded tendency to *mimic the manual world*. Inefficiencies in the manual systems that computers are meant to automate are thus carried forward into the user interface. The power of the computer goes unexploited due to a simple lack of thought and creativity on the part of the designer. Thus, in the manual world, we might cut and paste illustrations drawn by a draftsperson into a document typed by a typist. This approach is mimicked in the office automation product.

The organization of functionality of a system should be explicitly designed based on a clear analysis and understanding of the main tasks of the intended users. Sometimes technical constraints will lead to a less than optimal organization, and this is fine if the trade-off is consciously considered and made. However, less than optimal ways of organizing functionality from a user's point of view should never be designed due to a simple lack of information and consideration or as an artifact of irrelevant circumstances such as project team organization.

WINDOWING

Windowing systems offer some important advantages in organizing functionality to facilitate the user's task. Windowing systems have a variety of uses and come in several types. These are discussed next. The *uses* of windowing systems include the following:

Quick context switching with place saving.   Multiple open windows allow users to move back and forth between activities without losing their place. For instance, in an office automation system, users might have several documents open at once, as well as a calendar and phone book. They could be editing a document and be interrupted by a phone call requiring them to enter an appointment in the calendar and look up a number in the phone book to make another call. In a traditional nonwindowing system, they would have to close down any one activity in order to go into another. When they returned to the first activity, they would have to find where they left off manually, that is, by scrolling or searching. In a windowing system, however, the user can switch from one activity to another simply by switching windows. All activities are always at least partially visible and maintain their current context and state while other activities are being carried out. When the user's work is naturally fragmented, with many activities carried on more or less simultaneously, windowing can help support this work style in a way that traditional nonwindowing systems cannot.

Work in one, monitor another.   Sometimes users set one activity in motion and then must wait for it to be completed. They would like to go on to accomplish other things, but also want to know when the initial activity has been completed so they can take some next step. That is, they want to make progress on one task while monitoring the status of another. Windowing can support this. For instance, a user might want to edit one document while monitoring the print request for another. Or a programmer might want to edit one program file while monitoring the compile request of another. Or a user might want to work on various activities but monitor an in-box to intercept important incoming mail as soon as it arrives.

Cut and paste.   Moving or copying data from one file to another involves selecting it from one file and designating an insertion point in the other. If both files are simultaneously visible, this will be easier and faster than if each file must be separately opened and closed. Windows can make this possible and provide a particular advantage when the user needs to move or copy many fragments of data from one file to another. A traditional system would require repeated openings and closings of files, each time searching for the data or destination location. Windowing allows the user easy movement back and forth between files without losing his or her place in either.

Compare.   Sometimes users need to directly compare data in two or more different files. For instance, if users are using a simulation model, they might want to compare the results of running the model on different sets of parameters. Users might want to compare graphs of sales data from different years. Or users might want to look at old and new versions of programs or documents to determine where changes have been made. In all these cases, being able to see both files simultaneously is crucial. Windows would make this possible.

Show more detail, preserve context.   In some tasks, users need to zoom in on some detail, while preserving the context or big picture the detail is set in. For instance, in a graphics application, users might want to blow up some section of a drawing to edit detail, but they need to see the surrounding area of the drawing to edit accurately. Programmers may want to see a complete flow chart of an algorithm and be able to zoom in on the actual code for some segment of the flow chart, change it, and see the effect on the rest of the program through the flow chart. Multiple windows would support these situations.

Display same object in different forms.   Sometimes users want to view a set of data in different forms. For example, users may want to see a set of data graphed in a pie chart or line chart, but also to see the exact numbers in the spreadsheet from which the graph was built. Or users might want to see a single three-dimensional object rotated in space at different angles. Windows would allow users to see different views of the same data or object simultaneously, which could greatly facilitate problem solving.

Give command, see results.   In any interactive system, there are two main components: user input and system output. In many traditional nonwindowing systems, the display area is dedicated to one thing at a time, either collecting input (for example, through a fill-in form, menu, or question and answer dialog) or displaying output (for example, data from a database, a display of a file, or the results of running a simulation model). This means that the user must wait as the system refreshes the screen between input and output and also that they lose the history or context of their input when output is displayed. Windows would allow users to enter input in one display area and view results in another. The input window could hold a dialog history, allowing users to review the input that resulted in the output and also to review past requests. Transitioning between input and output is faster, since they are always both visible.

Get HELP, preserve context.   Traditional on-line help systems in nonwindowing environments present help screens by completely replacing the problem screen (the point in the dialog where the user requested help) with the help screen. Thus, the context of the problem screen is lost while the user reads the help screen. Especially if the help screen is complex and detailed, it is not unusual for users to forget important details of the problem they are trying to solve while they navigate through the help system. If help is presented in a window, then the context of the problem screen can remain at least partially visible. This can greatly reduce the burden on short-term memory, significantly facilitating problem solving.

There are four major **types** of windowing systems, as follows:

1. System controlled, tiled
2. System controlled, overlapping
3. User controlled, tiled
4. User controlled, overlapping

Thus there are two main dimensions on which windowing systems differ. They are either *system controlled* or *user controlled,* and they are either *tiled* or *overlapping*.

In a **system-controlled** windowing system, the system controls when windows are opened, closed, moved, resized, and activated. These decisions are made based on user input and requests, but users cannot directly manipulate windows; they can only request certain general goals.

For instance, if two windows were currently open and the user asked to view a third file or open a third application, then a third window would be opened, but the system would determine how big it would be and where it would be positioned relative to the other two windows. Users would not be able to directly change the window configuration.

The *advantage* of *system-controlled* windowing systems is that they relieve the user of the burden of learning and executing window operations, thus allowing them to focus on the problem they are trying to solve. This can be important if users are unfamiliar with windowing systems and are infrequent, casual, novice users who will be unlikely to learn and remember the added complexity in the general interface of windowing operations.

The *disadvantage* of *system-controlled* windowing systems is that the system is less flexible and thus users cannot set up window configurations that are optimal for their particular needs or preferences. How serious a disadvantage this is depends on how easy it is to determine likely user needs and preferences and how well system choices for window configuration match these needs and preferences.

By contrast, in a **user-controlled** windowing system, the user has complete control over window configurations. The system might have defaults for initial window size and location, but the user can open, close, move, resize, and activate windows at will. Even the system defaults might be determined by previous user actions.

The *advantage* of *user-controlled* windowing systems is that they afford greater flexibility and power. Users can arrange windows in any manner that will best facilitate the task they are trying to accomplish. This can be important if tasks are highly variable and unpredictable, that is, unstructured, so that a single configuration that will support all users and all variations of a task does not exist.

The *disadvantage* of *user-controlled* windowing systems is the added complexity in the general user interface of window manipulation. Windows are really additional functionality that users must learn about. New users must now learn not only how to manipulate data, but also how to open, close, move, resize, and activate windows. How serious a disadvantage this is depends on such user characteristics as system experience, application (windowing) experience, attitude and motivation, frequency of use, use of other systems, and turnover rate (see Chapter 2).

Tiled and overlapping windowing systems are illustrated in Figure 13-5. In a **tiled** windowing system, windows are like tiles on a kitchen floor or in a mosaic. Each window (tile) fits snugly in a two-dimensional space surrounded by other windows (tiles). Each window is completely visible.

The main *advantage* of *tiled* windows is that all windows are completely visible at all times. The *disadvantage* of *tiled* windows is that, for a given screen size, only some number of windows can be opened before the size of each window becomes too small to be very useful. Thus, there is a definite limit to the practical number of simultaneously opened windows.

In an **overlapping** windowing system, windows are more like papers on a desktop. They are arranged in a simulated three-dimensional space and may be stacked up in piles, overlapping one another. Thus, at any point in time, a given window may be only partially visible or even totally obscured by other windows that are on top of it.

The main *advantage* of *overlapping* windows is that, because they can be overlapped, many can be simultaneously open without constraining the size of each. The *disadvantage* of *overlapping* windows is that, when many windows are

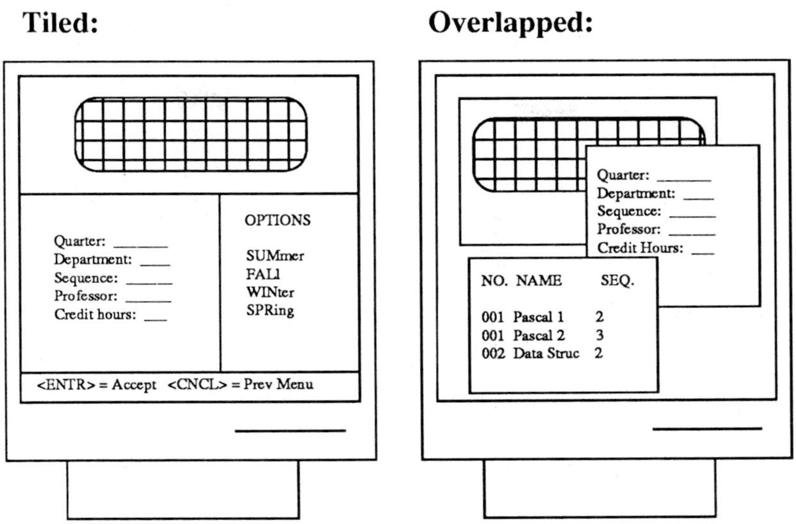

Tiled: Overlapped:

Figure 13–5   Windowing: uses and types.

opened, an individual window may be only partially visible and perhaps even totally obscured by other overlapping windows.

The *most common* systems are either *user-controlled/overlapping or system-controlled/tiled*. However, in theory, all combinations and variations are possible.

A *system-controlled/overlapping* system would arrange windows in an overlapping manner when this offered some important advantage, such as fitting many windows on a screen without making each window very small. Users could directly activate windows, but could not resize or move them. In a *user-controlled/tiled system,* the user would be constrained to tiled arrangements, but within this constraint, could open, close, move, and resize windows directly.

WINDOWING SYSTEMS: EXPERIMENTAL RESULTS

One study (Davies, Bury, and Darnell, 1985) asked the fundamental question of whether or not windowing makes a system easier to use or not. That is, does a system that allows windowing result in better performance than a system that does not?

Eight IBM employees, familiar with the hardware and application type (an editor) employed in the experiment, participated in this study. Each used both of two systems, one with windows and one without. Except for the presence or absence of windows, the two systems were comparable in functionality. After very thorough training on each system, each participant performed 12 editing tasks, 6 on each system. Participants used the two systems in different orders. The data collected included the time to perform each task and the number of errors made on each task.

The time and error data from the study are summarized in Figure 13-6. At first, the data suggest some rather surprising results. It actually took users of the windowing system longer, on average, to perform the tasks than users of the nonwindowing system. This was true even though users of the nonwindowing system made more errors. The time spent making and recovering from errors was included in the overall measure of task time, so it is a bit surprising that, in spite of making more errors, users of the nonwindowing system performed the tasks faster.

The authors were similarly a bit surprised at this finding, so they analyzed the data at a more detailed level to try to provide insight into their results. They divided the overall task time into four components:

i = time to initial keystroke: the time between the presentation of the first problem screen, and the users initial keystroke

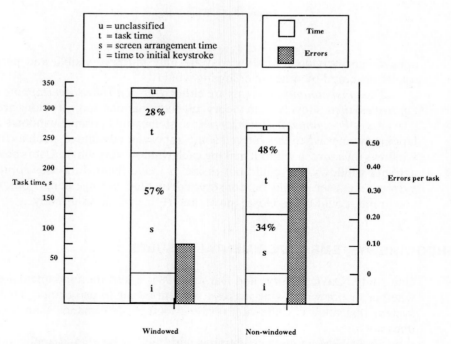

Figure 13-6 A Study of Windowing. From Davies, Bury and Darnell, "An Experimental Comparison of a Windowed vs. a Non-Windowed Operating System Environment," *Proceedings of the Human Factors Society 29th Annual Meeting,* 1985, 250–54. © 1985, by the Human Factors Society, Inc. Reprinted with permission. All rights reserved.

t = task time: time spent actually working on the editing problem (for example, reading, cutting, or pasting)

s = screen arrangement time: time spent opening and closing files, scrolling, and (in the windowing system) moving, resizing, and navigating between windows

u = unclassified: time that did not fit into any of the above categories

Looking at how overall task time was divided between these four components on the two systems, an interesting result emerges. While users of the nonwindowing system spent more *task* time and made more errors on the task, the reduced *task time* on the windowing system was canceled out by significantly more time spent on *screen arrangement*. That is, once windows were arranged on the screen, the task was accomplished in less time and with less errors. However, it took so long to get windows arranged on the screen that the *potential* benefit of the windowing system, reduced overall task time, was lost.

We should not conclude from this study that windowing systems in general will increase overall time to perform tasks. The important lesson to take away, however, is that windowing *in and of itself* does not guarantee better performance. The windowing capability must itself be carefully designed, or the added complexity of the windowing functionality may cancel out the potential benefits that windows offer, as it did in this study.

Windowing is additional functionality. It has its own user interface. Users must learn and be able to use a set of windowing operations such as moving, resizing, opening, closing, and navigating between windows. If these operations are cumbersome and difficult to learn or use, this will interfere with the task users are trying to accomplish.

Another thing to note about this study is that users were trained very thoroughly before any data were collected. That is, this study represents a test of *ease of use,* rather than *ease of learning.* The findings are even more powerful in this sense, because we cannot assume that the windowing system would afford superior performance once users became familiar with it. They *were* familiar with it. We might expect an even greater advantage to be shown by the nonwindowing system for first-time users unfamiliar with windowing systems.

On the other hand, we can easily imagine that a system with a windowing capability that was both more powerful *and* had a better user interface might result in superior performance compared to a nonwindowing system. The point to be made here is that the *details* of how the windowing capability is provided (that is, its user interface) will make the difference between improved or degraded performance relative to a nonwindowing system.

The potential advantages of windowing might also depend on the type of user and the type of task, as well as on the user interface of the windowing capability. This is suggested in another study (Bly and Rosenberg, 1986). The main focus of this study was a comparison of a *tiled* versus an *overlapping* windowing system, as defined in the previous section. Tiled and overlapped systems were compared on two types of tasks, regular and irregular. In a *regular* task, all necessary information can be viewed simultaneously in a configuration of tiled windows. In an *irregular* task, the windows must be overlapped in order to view all necessary information simultaneously. These two task types are illustrated in Figure 13-7.

Twenty-two Xerox employees with varying levels of experience with windowing systems participated in this experiment. They were given brief training on one of the two systems (tiled or overlapped) and then performed tasks that required them to search through four files and match text descriptions with graphic displays.

The main measure taken was time to perform the task, and these data are presented in Figure 13-8. In this graph, each user's data is represented as a dot, and the across-user median in each condition is represented by a horizontal line. The first thing to note in these data is that performance was, generally, better on *regular* than *irregular* tasks, regardless of the windowing system used. This makes sense, as we can imagine that, even though the overlapping system might make the irregular task easier than the tiled system, it will take some time for users to arrange windows on the screen to support the irregular task, as suggested by the Davies, Bury, and Darnell (1985) study.

The second thing to note is that the *tiled* system supported the *regular* tasks better than did the *overlapping* windowing system. This also is not too surprising, because less windowing operations are required in a tiled system, and as long as the tiled system accommodates the task, this should provide an advantage.

What is most interesting in these data is the performance of users in the fourth condition: an *irregular* task and an *overlapping* window system. We might have

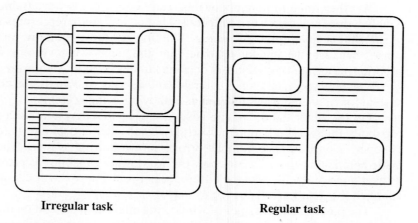

Irregular task   Regular task

Figure 13–7   A study of tiled versus overlapping windows. From Bly and Rosenberg, "A Comparison of Tiled and Overlapping Windows," *CHI '86 Proceedings*, 1986, pp. 101–6. With permission.

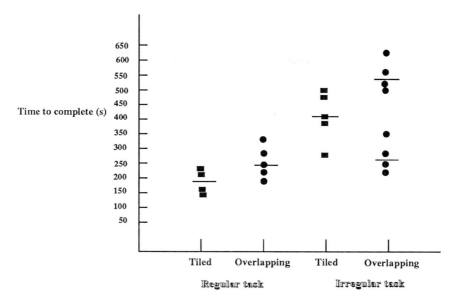

Time to complete (s)

650
600
550
500
450
400
350
300
250
200
150
100
50

Tiled   Overlapping   Tiled   Overlapping

Regular task   Irregular task

Figure 13–8 A study of tiled versus overlapping windows. From Bly and Rosenberg, ''A Comparison of Tiled and Overlapping Windows,'' *CHI '86 Proceedings,* 1986, 101–6. With permission.

expected that, while a *tiled* system would be better for *regular* tasks, *overlapping* systems would provide an advantage on *irregular* tasks. Here, however, the users seem to fall into two distinct groups. In one group, the users did perform better than users of the tiled system on irregular tasks, but in the other group performance was worse. This is somewhat unexpected. The explanation seems to lie in the characteristics of the two groups of users. As it turns out, those who performed better tended to be programmers with substantial *prior experience* with windowing systems, whereas those that performed worse tended to be nonprogrammers with *minimal prior experience* with windowing systems. That is, it seems that overlapping windows provide an advantage on irregular tasks only for more experienced users who understood the concept of overlapping windows and window operations. For those without experience, the potential benefits of the overlapping windows were not realized, probably due to the complexity of the windowing capability itself.

Unlike in the Davies, Bury, and Darnell (1985) study, here we may be observing an ease of learning effect. That is, with sufficient training the users who performed more slowly with the overlapped system on the irregular tasks might improve to the level of the group who performed more quickly.

This study suggests that the added power of overlapping windows may only be justified when *tasks are irregular* and when users can be expected to be or quickly become *experienced users*. Although less powerful and flexible, tiled windows may allow superior performance when tasks are regular and users are novice or casual users, because of the reduced complexity of the interface, and the lack of need for more flexibility and power.

Another study (Gaylin, 1986) investigated how users of an existing, in-use windowing system actually used its capabilities. Nine Digital Equipment Corporation employees were observed doing their normal daily work on a windowing system. Eight were programmers and one was a technical writer. All were high-frequency users of the system, using it an average of 5 or 6 hours per day. Each was observed during a 22.5-minute session in which they logged on and were asked to do their normal work. They were videotaped, and later their use of individual window operations was tallied.

Across the nine users, 254 windowing commands were used during the time of observation. The relative frequency of use of some of the available commands across all nine users is summarized in Figure 13-9. The data in the left column (total session) are summarized across the entire 22.5-minute sessions. The data in the right column (log in only) are from the first 2 minutes of the sessions only.

What is interesting to note in these data is that navigation (moving from window to window) is by far the most frequently used operation if we look across the total session. On the other hand, if we look at only the first 2 minutes of the session, the log in period, other commands that have to do with opening and arranging windows on the screen occur with a much higher frequency relative to other operations in the session as a whole. This suggests that, when users get on the system, they first open and arrange windows on the screen. After this, they do not

% Total commands

	Total session	Log in only
Navigate	59.5	32.4
Open	10.6	18.1
Create	7.5	17.1
Delete	8.3	2.9
Move	4.3	17.1
Resize	2.0	12.4
Other	7.8	

Figure 13–9   A study of window usage. From Gaylin, "How Are Windows Used? Some Notes on Creating an Empirically-Based Windowing Benchmark Task," *CHI '86 Proceedings*, 1986, 96–100. With permission.

make many changes to opened windows, but spend most of their time navigating among them.

These data are more than just interesting. They suggest some important goals for windowing user interface design. First, navigating among windows should be *easy to use,* even at the expense of being difficult to learn, since it is such a high-frequency operation. Many current windowing systems, however, do not provide easy to use and efficient navigation operations. Many early Apple Macintosh applications, for instance, required that a window be visible in order to select or activate it. This may mean that many other windows must be resized and moved around before the desired window can be selected. Later applications that allow a way to cycle among open windows, or call a window by name, make navigation easier. Given the high frequency of navigation operations, this seems important.

Second, the data suggest that operations that allow users to arrange windows on the screen should be *easy to learn and remember,* even at the expense of ease of use, because they are much less frequently used.

It should be pointed out that this study involved mainly one special type of user, a programmer, working on tasks that may be unique and unrepresentative of the tasks of other types of users. Use patterns for other types of users working on very different types of tasks may be very different. This would lead us to different conclusions regarding the goals of the design of individual windowing operations.

The studies cited so far deal with high-level aspects of window design. Although windowing systems have been implemented with a variety of user interfaces, studies have yet to be conducted comparing *specific designs* for *individual windowing operations.* Billingsley (1988) reviews a set of commonly included windowing operations and discusses alternative designs and design issues for each. Her discussion is paraphrased and summarized here.

Billingsley addresses the following windowing operations:

Create: Display an entirely new window.

Delete: Remove a window from the display.

Open: Replace an iconic window with the full-size window it represents.

Close: Replace a full-size window with an iconic representation of itself.

Bring-to-front: Move a window to the most forward plane of the display.

Push-to-back: Move a window to the most rearward plane of the display.

Move: Reposition a window in its two-dimensional plane.

Resize: Show more or less of the data in a window by expanding or contracting the window borders, up to the maximum size for that window type.

Zoom: With one action, expand a window to its maximum size.

Rescale: Show more or less of the data in a window by changing the scale of the image in the window.

Scroll: Select a different portion of the data for viewing, without resizing the window.

Name/rename: Define or edit the name of a window.

Make active: Designate a window as the one with which the keyboard (or other input device) can communicate.

Different systems include more or less than this set of operations, and some name these operations differently or use these names to refer to different operations. However, this is a fairly representative list of window operations. Some alternative designs for some of these operations are discussed next.

Opening and closing.   Closed windows are typically represented as icons or object names. Windows are typically opened by pointing to their iconic or name representation and selecting the "open" operation from a menu or by some keyboard or mouse shortcut, such as double-clicking. In some windowing systems, windows open to a default size and position; in others the user must specify these parameters as a part of the "open" operation. Some systems provide animation as a part of the open and close operations as visual feedback, showing the window expanding from and contracting to its iconic form.

Moving.   Typically, users may drag a window by pointing to an area or symbol on the window, clicking a mouse button and moving the pointer. In this case, usually a blinking outline of the window follows the pointer, rather than the whole window itself. When the operation is terminated, the whole window is redisplayed in the new location. Alternatively, users may initiate the move operation through a command or menu pick and then specify the new location in some manner.

Resizing.   Some systems offer this operation through a command or menu pick, followed by a specification of the new window size. Others allow the user to drag sensitive areas of a window's border either toward or away from some anchor point. Systems vary in the flexibility of the resize operation. Some only allow resizing from a single corner. Others allow resizing from any point on the entire border. Feedback during the operation is typically a blinking outline of the new window size and shape. The whole window is redisplayed upon termination of the operation. The effects of resizing the window on the data displayed within it vary across systems. In some, new data are revealed or existing data are obscured in the direction of the resizing. In others, the amount of data does not change, but the data are resized along with the window.

Scrolling.   Scrolling may be accomplished by selecting symbols on the window border, pressing keys, or choosing navigational commands from a menu. Systems vary in the unit of scrolling they allow. Possibilities include one line (for example, of text) at a time, one windowful at a time, one page at a time, to a particular location (for example, a page) and to the top or bottom of a file. Some applications allow only vertical scrolling, while others allow both vertical and horizontal scrolling.

Making active.   Possibilities here include moving the pointer into a window, pointing to and selecting a window, typing in a window name, and choosing a window name from a menu of currently open windows. In some systems, a window must explicitly be made active before other operations can be performed on it. In others, initiating some other operation (for example, resize) automatically makes the window active. In still other systems, performing some other operation such as a resize or move does not make a window active.

When a window is made active, it may or may not automatically "pop to the top" (in an overlapping windowing system). Systems vary in the way they designate the currently active window. This can be done by displaying control symbols in the window borders, highlighting some area of the window border, displaying a blinking cursor, or changing the window background color.

While we may all have intuitions about the best way to implement window operations, empirical data are needed that explicitly compare performance on alternative designs such as those described here. It is likely that there is no right way to design individual operations, but in fact they will interact with one another so that one *set* might be better than another *set*. Probably the best rule of thumb to follow at this time is to try to determine beforehand the likely ways users will be using windows, then to design to *minimize motor movements* for these tasks while striving for *consistency* across operations, and finally to test the set of operations before implementing them.

WINDOWING SYSTEMS: PRINCIPLES AND GUIDELINES

Several simple guidelines result from the studies cited. More detailed guidelines regarding the best way to actually design windowing operations will have to await additional research.

☞ **Design easy to use and learn window operations.**

As suggested by the Davies, Bury, and Darnell (1985) study, the complexity of the interface to the windowing capability of a system should not cancel out the potential advantages that windowing can provide. Thus windowing operations must themselves be carefully designed. Because more detailed guidelines cannot be offered at this time, testing design ideas for any new product is particularly important to ensure that the added power of windowing does not add undue complexity.

☞ **Minimize the number of window operations necessary to achieve a desired effect.**

A good rule of thumb is to consider the different window configurations users are likely to want and to minimize the number of operations that will be required to attain these configurations from any other. For instance, is a user likely to have many overlapping windows open at once and to want to activate an arbitrary one that might be obscured at the moment? If so, simple ways to cycle through open windows that do not require window visibility should be provided.

In general, *direct manipulation* methods for manipulating windows (for example, resizing by dragging a window corner with a mouse pointer) will be more efficient that nondirect manipulation methods such as cursor keys and menu selection of commands (Billingsley, 1988).

☞ **Make navigating between windows particularly easy and efficient to do.**

The Gaylin (1986) study suggested that simple navigation between windows may be the single most frequent windowing operation used. High-frequency operations should always be easy to use, even at the expense of being difficult to learn, if necessary.

☞ **Make setting up windows particularly easy to remember.**

The Gaylin (1986) study also suggested that window arrangement (for example, opening, closing, moving, and resizing) may be much less frequent an activity than might be imagined. Low-frequency operations should always be easy to learn and remember, even at the expense of being difficult to use, if necessary.

☞ **Provide salient visual cues to identify the active window.**

In an overlapping windowing system, the active window is often fairly easy to identify because it may be the only one that is completely visible; it is on top of the stack. However, on tiled windowing systems and on overlapping systems when users happen to have windows in a tiled arrangement, it is important to provide some other cue to indicate which window is currently active, that is, accepting keyboard input. Some possible techniques include a different color or gray shade for the window background, bolder borders, or symbols or icons in the border. Testing should be conducted to ensure that the technique chosen is salient enough to draw users' attention.

☞ **Allow overlapping when displays are unpredictable, screens are small, and users are fairly frequent and experienced.**

As suggested by the Bly and Rosenberg (1986) study, overlapping windowing systems add complexity and should only be used when they offer some significant advantage and when use is frequent enough that the added learning burden is justified by the added power. When no significant advantage is provided by overlapping windows or when users are casual and infrequent, a tiled windowing system, whose lack of power in turn means greater simplicity and ease of learning, should be employed.

☞ **In overlapping systems, provide powerful commands for arranging windows on the screen in user-tailorable configurations.**

When an overlapping windowing system is justified, every effort should be made to provide that power through easy to use operations that minimize time and steps in achieving desired windowing configurations. For instance, users should be able to create, name, and recall specific configurations of windows (Card and Henderson, 1987).

REFERENCES

BILLINGSLEY, PATRICIA A., ''Taking Panes: Issues in the Design of Windowing Systems,'' *Handbook of Human–Computer Interaction,* Martin Helander, ed. (Amsterdam: North-Holland, 1988), pp. 413–36.

BLY, S. A., and J. K. ROSENBERG, ''A Comparison of Tiled and Overlapping Windows,'' *CHI '86 Proceedings,* 1986, pp. 101–106, ACM.

CARD, S. K., and A. HENDERSON, JR., ''A Multiple, Virtual-Workspace Interface to Support User Task Switching,'' *CHI + GI '87 Proceedings,* April 1987, pp. 53–59, ACM.

DAVIES, S. E., K. F. BURY, and M. J. DARNELL, ''An Experimental Comparison of a Windowed vs. a Non-Windowed Operating System Environment,'' *Proceedings of the Human Factors Society 29th Annual Meeting,* 1985, pp. 250–54.

GAYLIN, KENNETH, ''How Are Windows Used? Some Notes on Creating an Empirically-Based Windowing Benchmark Task,'' *CHI '86 Proceedings,* 1986, pp. 96–100, ACM.

CHAPTER 14

Screen Layout and Design

There are two parties in any dialog, in our case, the human and the computer. Each party has a language form and, in our case, they are different. When two people converse, they use the same language. When a computer and a person converse, since they are different entities with different input and output devices, they "speak" different languages. When the user "speaks" to the computer, he or she does so (traditionally) through specifically designed sequences of keystrokes on a keyboard or movements of a cursor control device. When the computer "speaks" to the user, it does so (traditionally) by presenting information on the screen. A user interface designer designs the language of both parties. This chapter is concerned with the design of the computer "language": the design and layout of screens.

Whereas Chapters 4 through 10 covered some screen design issues relevant to particular dialog styles, this chapter covers screen design in general, including both *output* displays and *input* displays. The principles of screen layout and design offered here are general and apply to any kind of screen, such as a menu, a fill-in form, a display of database records or an iconically represented library index. The reader should refer to Chapters 4 through 10 for additional guidelines on designing specific types of screens.

The designer must work within the constraints imposed by the hardware and system software. These include screen size, screen orientation (horizontal or vertical), and available terminal capabilities, such as highlighting, reverse video, bit-mapped graphics, color, and sound.

Within these constraints, the designer must decide *what* to put on the screen, *where* to put things on the screen, and *how* to put things on the screen. These issues are addressed in the experimental studies and the principles and guidelines drawn from them which are presented below.

SCREEN LAYOUT AND DESIGN: EXPERIMENTAL RESULTS

The importance of screen design in usability is illustrated in a study by Burns, Warren, and Rudisill (1986). This study compared two existing screens from NASA's Space Shuttle Guidance, Navigation, and Control subsystem with two redesigned screens. Aspects of the original screens that were redesigned included the following:

1. Captions were provided for all data fields.
2. Related data were grouped together.
3. Consistency in the placement of certain items was introduced.
4. The menu selection technique was changed from number codes to cursor selection to avoid confusion between selection codes and other numerical fields.
5. Indentation and underlining were introduced to reinforce groupings.
6. Captions were changed to be more clear.
7. A consistent abbreviation scheme was introduced for captions.
8. Numerical data were decimal aligned.

These changes represent the wide variety of issues in screen layout and design. Data from a search task by *novice* users revealed a 31% improvement in search time and a 28% reduction in errors on the redesigned screens. These are striking results, indicating the importance of making the right screen design decisions. In addition, a set of *expert* users of the original screens was also tested. They also showed some improvement in performance on the redesigned screens, although not nearly such a dramatic one. Search times were comparable, but errors were reduced on the redesigned screens. This is a particularly interesting result, because it suggests that certain screen design techniques provide advantages upon first-time use over other techniques *even when those other techniques are already well learned*.

Tullis (1988) reviews a wide variety of additional studies, which also found performance improvements ranging from 25% to 78% and error reductions as high as 25% when comparing different formats and arrangements of a set of information on screens. Design variations in these studies included the use of grouping, indentation, abbreviations, and variations in information density, line length, message design, item alignment, and information structure. Clearly, all aspects of screen design have a measurable effect on usability.

A research program by Tullis (1983, 1984, 1986) has developed a model of the screen design parameters that seem to affect usability. Tullis (1983) first performed an extensive review of literature pertaining to screen design issues and from this review extracted a set of screen design parameters that met the following criteria:

1. Related to the *spatial* array of characters on a monochromatic alphanumeric display (*not* highlighting techniques, color, or legibility parameters)
2. Can be objectively defined (*not* "semantic relatedness" of items within groups)
3. Applicable to any alphanumeric display (*not* data-specific formatting techniques, such as date displays)

The parameters thus identified included:

Overall density: Number of filled character spaces as a percentage of total spaces available.

Local density: Average number of filled character spaces in a 0.088-radian (5-degree) visual angle around each character, expressed as a percentage of available spaces in the circle and weighted by distance from the character.

Grouping: (1) Number of groups of "connected" characters, where a connection is any pair of characters separated by less than twice the mean of the distances between each character and its nearest neighbor. (2) Average visual angle subtended by groups (as defined above), weighted by number of characters in the group.

Layout complexity: The complexity, as defined in information theory, of the distribution of horizontal and vertical distances of each label and data item from a standard point on the display.

Less formally, these parameters might be described as follows:

Overall density: How much information there is on the screen.

Local density: How tightly packed the information on the screen is.

Grouping: (1) Number of separate groups; (2) size of groups.

Layout complexity: (1) Number of items; (2) extent of item alignment and thus item position predictability (item uncertainty).

Tullis (1984) then developed a computer program that computed a numerical value for each parameter for a given screen and tested subjects on 520 different screens that varied systematically on these objective, measurable parameters. He then developed regression equations to fit the subjects' search times and ratings of ease of use to various subsets of these parameters. In other words, he analyzed the data to determine if some combination of the above parameters would serve as good *predictors* of search time and preference data. He found that *search times* were best predicted by an equation including the following four parameters:

Overall density
Local density
Number of groups
Size of groups

The latter two parameters, related to grouping, weighed most heavily. In particular, it appeared that minimizing the number of groups while keeping the maximum group size within 5 degrees of visual angle (approximately 12 to 14 characters wide and 6 to 7 lines high on a standard character-based screen) produced the fastest search times, that is, *performance*. *Preferences* were best predicted by an equation including all six parameters, in which *local density* and *item uncertainty* weighed most heavily.

Tullis (1986) then developed a computer program that would measure a given screen (represented as an ASCII file) on each parameter, compute *predicted* search times and preference ratings, and make suggestions for design changes that would improve search times. The general criteria the program uses for suggestions include the following:

Overall density should not exceed 40%.
Local density should not exceed 62%.
Group size should fall between 2.5 and 5 degrees of visual angle.
Number of groups should be between 19 and 40.

Tullis's work indicates that a small number of *spatial* layout parameters can significantly affect screen usability.

One counterintuitive finding in Tullis's work is that layout complexity, in particular the extent of alignment of data items, did not figure in the predictive equation for performance. Although it was the single most powerful predictor of *preference* data, it did not add any significant predictive power to the overall equation for *search times* made up of the other four parameters. This finding runs counter to the commonly cited guideline that recommends such alignment of data items. Fontenelle (1987) investigated this matter further. She collected empirical search time data on screens that varied systematically in layout complexity. In particular, she compared three screens that varied *only* on this dimension. One screen left justified data items ("left justified"), one did not left justify but did present data items in predictable positions ("predictable"), and one positioned data items randomly ("random"). Four different task types were assigned to subjects: find label, scan data, compare labels, and compare data.

The results were consistent with Tullis's model. Layout complexity did not affect search times for all except one task type: compare data. Layout complexity did affect preference data: subjects preferred the left-justified screens.

Although the *performance* data from this study are consistent with Tullis's findings, it is inconsistent with the commonly cited guideline to align data items in displays. However, no details about the actual displays used in this study are given, and minimal details are given about the actual tasks employed. Given the strong user preference for alignment, and the likelihood that, like everything else, the importance and effect of alignment will depend on the specific details of display and task types, it still seems advisable to strive for good alignment, that is, low layout complexity in screen design. More research is needed to shed further light on this issue.

Another study (Thacker, Tullis, and Babu, 1987) attempted to apply Tullis's predictive model to alphanumeric screens that included borders and lines. Tullis's original model interprets the ASCII characters that make up borders and lines just as any other character, counting them in the computation of density and grouping parameters. This resulted in predicted search times and preferences that did not fit the data empirically derived by Thacker and co-workers from real users. When the ASCII characters that made up the lines and borders were excluded from the parameter computations, the model predicted performance reasonably well.

Thus it seems that Tullis's model should be applied only to *actual information content* (for example, words and numbers), excluding any highlighting techniques such as lines, borders, and other special characters used for highlighting such as asterisks. It is known from other studies that such highlighting techniques do affect performance, however, and so it seems likely that Tullis's model will not predict performance as accurately for displays that use these techniques.

Schwartz (1988) noted that Tullis's work was all premised on a single task type: simple search tasks. He devised a study to see if the screen design dimensions identified by Tullis would bear the same or any relationship to performance in different task types.

Four task types were included:

1. *Scanning:* Subjects determined how many of a *fixed* (unchanging) set of data items had a given value.
2. *Pattern detection:* Subjects monitored a *dynamically changing* display and detected when a particular configuration of data items was present.
3. *Multiple cue judgment:* Subjects learned to associate *fixed* (unchanging) configurations of data items with conceptual states, in this case, safety levels.
4. *Energy allocation:* Subjects monitored a *dynamically changing* display of data items and had to make complex decisions based on the occurrence of certain configurations of data items.

These task types can be seen to vary on two dimensions. Displays are either fixed or dynamic, so the *monitoring* of changes is or is not part of the task. And tasks are either *simple or complex,* meaning that subjects either simply detected physical states or had to make conceptual decisions based on physical states.

Six screen formats were devised based on variations in four of Tullis's dimensions: local density, number of groups, size of groups, and item uncertainty.

Ten subjects performed all four task types on all six screen formats. Simply put, there did not seem to be any clear effects of Tullis's screen design dimensions on three of the task types: pattern detection, multiple cue judgment, and energy allocation. There *was* a relationship between screen dimensions and performance on the *scanning* task, but not the *same* relationship that occurred in Tullis's data from *search* tasks.

Thus it appears that different task dimensions will result in different requirements for screen design. Although Tullis's data can probably be safely generalized to screens involving other search tasks they may not generalize to other screens involving other types of tasks. Further research is necessary both to identify meaningful categories of tasks and then to determine screen design dimensions relevant to those task types. In the meantime, designers would be well advised to draw upon Tullis's work when searching is a main component in user tasks, but always to test screen designs empirically against acceptance criteria, especially when tasks involve monitoring and complex decision making.

Other limitations to Tullis's model are pointed out by Perlman (1987). He notes the following:

1. Tullis's model does not take into account the effects of quasi-graphic characters, such as lines and borders, and video highlighting techniques, such as reverse video, bold, blinking and color, whereas these are commonly used on modern displays.
2. The model does not consider the underlying structure of the information.
3. The model is only descriptive, not diagnostic or prescriptive.

The first point has already been covered in the foregoing discussion of other studies that looked at various quasi-graphic characters and highlighting techniques in the light of Tullis's model. The second point is very important. Although the number and size of groups is surely an important factor, Perlman points out that *how the information is divided into groups* is also most certainly important, and Tullis's model does not speak to this issue at all.

For example, in a form including personal information such as name, gender, birthdate, social security number, and the like, as well as home and work address information, there are some obvious ways to organize data items into meaningful groups. However, a screen that *organized the data items completely randomly,* but had a reasonable *number of groups* and the correct *group size,* would be predicted to result in optimal search times by Tullis's model. Both intuition and empirical results, however, point to the impact of data item organization on search times. Another study by Williams and Leaf (1986) found that predictions of search time by Tullis's model did not match judgments of ease of use made by application experts and screen designers who were considering the semantic as well as the spatial aspects of grouping and alignment.

Another important variable not addressed in Tullis's work or any of the related studies is user experience level. All the studies cited tested subjects on their first encounters with screens. It seems possible that different screen design parameters might differentially affect the performance of high-frequency, expert users versus low-frequency, casual, or novice users. This seems particularly likely in more complex tasks. More research is necessary to determine if different screen design principles and guidelines depending on user experience level and expected frequency of use should be developed.

Thus, while Tullis's model *highlights some important screen design parameters,* it is clearly *not a complete prescriptive design tool.* Designers must consider a number of other parameters in screen design beyond the simple spatial layout ones considered in Tullis's model, and the proper values of *all* parameters are likely to depend on both *user* and *task* characteristics.

One important aspect of screen design also not addressed in the previously cited studies is message design. Newsome and Hochlerin (1989) investigated two aspects of system messages: (1) affirmative voice ("Landing gear is up") versus negative voice ("Landing gear is not down") and (2) redundancy. They first reviewed a number of studies from the cognitive psychology literature that consistently found that messages in the affirmative voice resulted in faster response times than messages in the negative voice. The typical paradigm in these studies was to present a sentence paired with a picture and then to ask subjects whether or not the sentence was an accurate description of the picture. Subjects responded by pressing an appropriate button. Across these studies, the advantage of affirmative messages was both substantial and significant.

Newsome and Hochlerin also tested affirmative versus negative messages in a simple confirmation condition but in a more applied setting. Either the statement "Printer is now on" or "Printer is not off" indicated system readiness after a task had been set up, and subjects simply had to press a confirmation button. In this condition, it took subjects considerably longer to respond to the negative statement than to the affirmative. Accuracy was also higher for affirmative messages. This is consistent with the previous findings and suggests that affirmative messages are easier to comprehend and thus faster to respond to than negative messages.

However, another condition was also included in this study. Sometimes the message indicated that some action had to be taken before the system would be ready. These messages were also phrased affirmatively ("Printer is now off") or negatively ("Printer is not on"), but now subjects had to initiate an action by pressing an appropriately labeled key (for example, "on"). The negative messages now contained a word *redundant* with the required action (for example, "on"), while the affirmative messages did not. In this condition, the negative messages showed an equal response time but a much lower error rate as compared to the affirmative messages.

This suggests that building this sort of redundancy into messages is in general advisable. Often it is possible to design messages to be both affirmative and include redundant words. For example, instead of "Landing gear not down," "Put landing gear down" is both affirmative and includes words redundant with the required action. On the other hand, when redundancy can be built into a negative voice message but not into a positive voice message, the redundant negative voice message might be preferable.

SCREEN LAYOUT AND DESIGN: PRINCIPLES AND GUIDELINES

Screen layout and design principles fall into five categories:

General layout
Text
Numbers
Coding techniques
Color

General Layout

☞ **Include *only* information essential to decision making.**

Avoid overkill. Never put more than is necessary on a screen. Tullis (1988) cites studies that show clear decrements in performance as the amount of information increases. Unnecessary information includes full words when abbreviations will do, unuseful detail in decimal numbers and repeated captions and labels, as well as unnecessary prompts and instructions and nontask related information such as copyright notices. Knowing how much information users will need requires an understanding of both what the user will do with the information and how much the user understands about the information. Thus, what is insufficient and what is overkill will always be particular to the user and application. In general, be brief and concise, and tailor the level of detail to user knowledge and experience. For instance, high-frequency users of a fill-in form may not need on-screen instructions for cursor movement, while casual users probably will.

☞ **Include *all* information essential to decision making.**

Each screen should stand alone, containing one idea or one task. In addition, a user should never have to cross-reference one screen with another and should never have to remember data on one screen in order to complete another. For instance, if a user must fill in a file name on a print request screen, the designer should find a way to make the file names available with minimal screen flipping and human memory. Perhaps the file name can be selected from an index screen and be "remembered" by the system when the user goes to the print request screen. Thus the system remembers, rather than the user having to remember. Or perhaps there is a way to split the screen into two windows, one with the file name fill-in field and the other with a scrollable index listing.

Similarly, error messages should be complete and not require reference to manuals to decipher. "File name too long" requires a reference. Better to say, "File name should not exceed 8 characters."

How much to put on one screen again depends on the user and the application. Some users would prefer to have many selection items on one menu screen, rather than to have to go through several screens to find the desired items. Other users will find it easier to scan several screens, each presenting a small number of options. How the options can be logically organized into groups will also affect this decision.

The more information there is to be on a screen, the more important it is to consider the other guidelines offered here for layout and design.

☞ **Start in the upper-left corner.**

Eye-tracking studies indicate that the eye tends to go to the upper-left corner of a display. This is not too surprising, since the English language is written left to right and top to bottom. The studies also suggest that the eyes will move clockwise, influenced by the display's symmetry and other cues such as the balance of titles, graphics, and use of space. The mind will seek order and patterns in a display and follow them if they are apparent.

This does not mean that a display, no matter how simple or complex, should always start in the upper-left corner of the screen. Displays should be centered in the screen and laid out in a balanced, symmetrical manner. But the logical place to start reading a display, given its content, should be in the upper-left corner relative to other parts of the display body.

☞ **Design formatting standards and follow them consistently in all screens within a system.**

The related screens in a system should always have standard types of information located in the same part of the screen. For instance, screen titles, status messages, input fields, command input lines, and error messages should consistently appear in the same area of the screen throughout a system. These types of information should also be formatted consistently and employ other visual codes besides location, such as capitalization, underlining, or bold. It is a good idea to design one or more screen templates, which express these rules of screen layout and design, early in the design process so that individual designers can refer to them as they design particular screens. Figure 14-1 illustrates such a screen template for the menu screens of a system.

☞ **Group items logically.**

When many distinct items are to be displayed on a screen, it is helpful to organize them into semantically related groupings and to separate the groups by a minimum of three to five columns or one row. Figure 14-2 presents two screens,

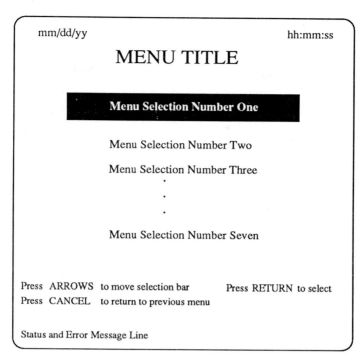

mm/dd/yy   hh:mm:ss

MENU TITLE

Menu Selection Number One

Menu Selection Number Two

Menu Selection Number Three
.
.
.

Menu Selection Number Seven

Press ARROWS to move selection bar   Press RETURN to select
Press CANCEL   to return to previous menu

Status and Error Message Line

Figure 14–1   Screen design template for menu screens.

one in which items are not well grouped and one in which they are. The groupings and spatial separation of groups will help users to learn where fields are and to easily find a particular field.

It appears that keeping *group size* within the 5-degree visual angle to which the eye is most sensitive enhances searching behavior, because the whole group can be taken in in a single eye fixation. This visual angle corresponds roughly to 12 to 14 characters wide and 6 to 7 lines high on a computer screen (Tullis, 1988).

The *number of groups* also affects search time, with increasing numbers of groups resulting in increasing search times, even when group size is small. Thus, minimizing the number of groups without exceeding the maximum recommended group size is suggested to facilitate searching.

Groups can be set off with white space or borders or through the use of color. There is some evidence that white space is a more effective grouping cue than color (Tullis, 1988).

☞ **Provide symmetry and balance through the use of white space.**

The term **white space** is used in this book as a general term to indicate blank space on the screen or in a window, that is, space not occupied by text or graphic

Poor:

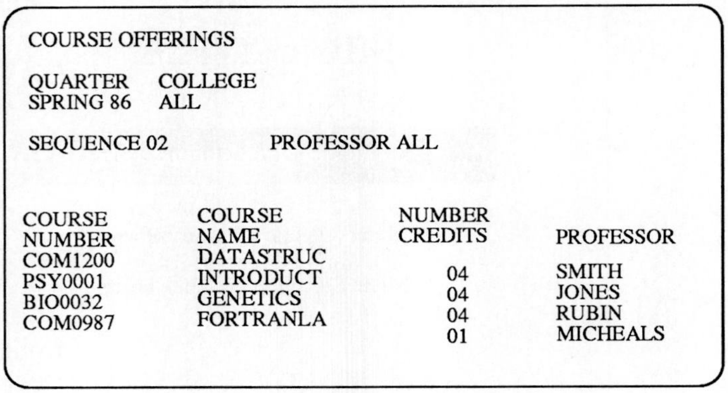

```
COURSE OFFERINGS

QUARTER    COLLEGE
SPRING 86  ALL

SEQUENCE 02            PROFESSOR ALL


COURSE        COURSE          NUMBER
NUMBER        NAME            CREDITS      PROFESSOR
COM1200       DATASTRUC
PSY0001       INTRODUCT       04           SMITH
BIO0032       GENETICS        04           JONES
COM0987       FORTRANLA       04           RUBIN
                              01           MICHEALS
```

Improved:

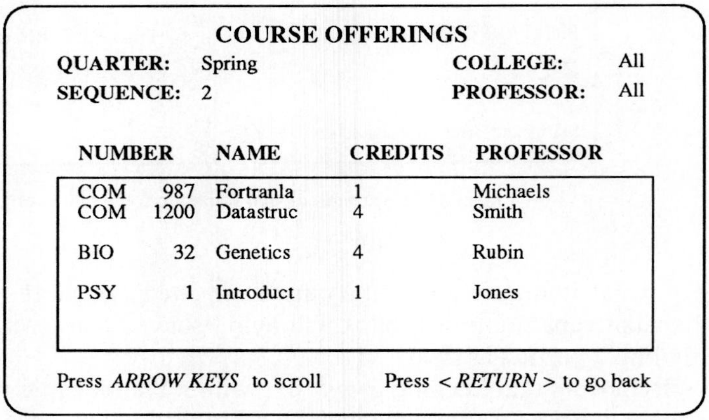

```
                COURSE OFFERINGS
    QUARTER:  Spring              COLLEGE:    All
    SEQUENCE: 2                   PROFESSOR:  All


       NUMBER      NAME      CREDITS    PROFESSOR
      COM   987  Fortranla   1         Michaels
      COM  1200  Datastruc   4         Smith

      BIO    32  Genetics    4         Rubin

      PSY     1  Introduct   1         Jones


   Press ARROW KEYS to scroll    Press < RETURN > to go back
```

Figure 14–2   Screen design examples.

objects. The blank space may in fact be black, white, yellow, or any other color, depending on the color of the screen or window background. Although inaccurate in these cases, white space is a term generally used to mean blank space in the screen design literature, and so is used here for consistency and simplicity.

Center titles and illustrations around vertical and horizontal axes. Use white space to separate logical groups of information and to lead the eye horizontally or vertically, as appropriate. Note that the "Poor" screen in Figure 14-2 is unsymmetrical. White space also creates the look of columns in the lower part of the screen, while the data are actually arranged in rows. This will mislead the eye. The "Improved" screen, on the other hand, uses white space to create both a sense of balance and to lead the eye across rows, as appropriate.

Tullis (1988) cites data that suggest that users perform better when searching through vertical, rather than horizontal, lists of data items. The same data showed the worst performance when data were laid out (through the use of white space) in several columns, but organized alphabetically by rows. In this case the use of white space led the eye in a direction opposite to the appropriate direction, given the organization of data items.

☞ **Avoid heavy use of all-uppercase letters.**

Text in all uppercase is more difficult to read than text in mixed case. Tullis (1988) reviews literature suggesting that people read mixed case text about 13% faster than uppercase. This is because lowercase letters look more different from one another than do uppercase letters, making it easier to determine a word in part by its overall shape. Note how much more difficult it is to read the "Poor" screen than the "Improved" screen in Figure 14-2. Uppercase letters should be reserved for captions, labels, titles, or other things that need to stand out in a display, because searching for a single uppercase item is about 13% faster than searching for one in many mixed case items. Thus, *ease of reading* is gained by mixed case, while *ease of finding* is gained by uppercase when it is embedded in otherwise mixed case text. There is some evidence (Williams, 1988) that uppercase is better for menu items, but it is not clear under what range of conditions this finding might hold up.

☞ **Distinguish captions and fields.**

A fill-in or display field should be easily distinguished from its caption, label, or title. Within a system, the style for differentiating captions and fields should be consistent. Spatial relationships and contrasting features, such as case, intensity, font, and reverse video, can be employed to make captions and fields stand out. Note how much easier it is to distinguish captions from fields in the "Improved" screen in Figure 14-2 as compared to the "Poor" screen. They are distinguished by both case and intensity.

Try to avoid stacking multiple-word captions on two or more lines. They are more readable on one line. For single item fields, the caption should be to the left of the field. For repeating, or list fields, a column format should be used, rather than a horizontal list format, with the caption at the top of the column. Note the violations of these rules in the "Poor" screen in Figure 14-2 and the correct application of these rules in the "Improved" screen.

Text

Three kinds of text may be present on a screen:

Messages
Instructional prompts
Instructions

Guidelines pertaining to each are given next.

Messages

☞ **Messages should be brief and concise.**

Avoid being unnecessarily wordy. Just enough words to get the point across is all that is required. See the first row in Figure 14-3 for "Poor" and "Improved" examples.

☞ **Design the level of detail according to users' knowledge and experience.**

The "Poor" message in the second row of Figure 14-3 would not be enough information for a user low in *semantic* and *syntactic* knowledge, although it might be for a high-frequency, expert user. The "Improved" message offers information appropriate for a user low in *semantic* information, although it too may be insufficient for a user low in *syntactic* knowledge. Some idea of the extent of user knowledge should drive decisions regarding the level of detail to be included in messages.

	Poor:	Improved:
(1)	The processing of the text editor yielded 23 pages of output	Output 23 pages
(2)	Error in DRESS SIZE field	Error: DRESS SIZE range is 4 to 16
(3)	Cannot exit before saving file	Save file before exiting
(4)	Bad/illegal/invalid file name	Maximum file name length is 8 characters
(5)	Syntax error 1542	Unmatched left parenthesis in line 210
(6)	Enter command	Ready for command

Figure 14–3 Messages.

☞ **Express messages in the affirmative.**

Most negative statements can be easily restated as affirmative statements. Rather than tell the user what they did wrong or what not to do, tell them how to do it right. See, for example, the third row in Figure 14-3.

☞ **Messages should be constructive, not critical.**

Avoid critical words such as those in the fourth row of the "Poor" column in Figure 14-3. The "Improved" message in the fourth row gives constructive advice in a nonjudgmental tone.

☞ **Messages should be specific and comprehensible.**

Give users precise information that they can act on, rather than vague and general information that requires looking for additional instructions. Note the examples in the fifth row of Figure 14-3.

☞ **Messages should imply that the user is in control.**

The whole tone of the interface should imply that the system is a passive tool and that the user is in control, rather than the other way around. Note the difference between the "Poor" and "Improved" messages in the sixth row of Figure 14-3. The former is a command from the computer to the user, while the latter suggests that the computer is a passive tool at the command of the user. Tone can intimidate or encourage the novice and may affect user satisfaction and comfort level (Shneiderman, 1986).

☞ **When messages imply a necessary action, use words in the message that are consistent with that action.**

For example, consider the following three messages:

Landing gear is up.
Landing gear is not down.
Put landing gear down.

The first is in the affirmative voice but does not contain the name of the required action ("down"). The second does contain the name of the required action, but is in the negative voice. Both action words and affirmative voice are desirable in messages, as both seem to contribute to speed and accuracy of response (Newsome and Hochlerin, 1989). Thus the third message is preferred over the first two.

Instructional Prompts

Instructional prompts include **prompts** following input fields and short navigational **instructions** on screens. The following guidelines apply.

☞ **Place prompts when and where they will be needed.**

Consider where the eye will be when the prompts are needed. For instance, put instructions on how to point to menu selections at the top of the screen and instructions on how to accept a menu choice at the bottom of the screen, as suggested in the "Improved" example in the first row of Figure 14-4. The user's eyes will likely be in the middle to bottom of the screen when the instruction on accepting is needed, and it is more natural to scan downward for this information than upward.

☞ **Design the level of detail according to the users' knowledge and experience.**

The "Poor" example in the second row of Figure 14-4 would not provide enough information for a user low in *semantic* and *syntactic* knowledge, although it might for a high-frequency, expert user. The "Improved" message offers informa-

	Poor:	**Improved:**
(1)	Position cursor and press return	Position cursor Press return to accept
(2)	SIZE: ___	SIZE: ___ (4 to 16)
(3)	The message is sent by pressing TRANSMIT	To send message, Press TRANSMIT
(4)	Do not return to menu before completing entry	Complete entry before returning to menu
(5)	Page forward after entering address	Enter address, then page forward
(6)	Press backtab to go up, tab to go down	To go *up*, Press BACKTAB To go *down*, Press TAB
(7)	Press U for up Hit D for down	For up, Press U For down, Press D

Figure 14–4 Instructional prompts.

tion appropriate for a user low in *semantic* and *syntactic* information. Some idea of the extent of user knowledge should drive decisions regarding the level of detail to be included in instructional prompts.

☞ **Phrase prompts in the active voice.**

Phrase prompts in the active, rather than the passive, voice. Note the difference between the "Poor" and "Improved" prompts in the third row of Figure 14-4. The active voice is a simpler grammatical construct and thus is easier to read.

☞ **Avoid negatives.**

Avoid negatives, and phrase prompts as affirmative statements. Note how much easier it is to understand the "Improved" message in the fourth row of Figure 14-4 compared to the "Poor" message. Again, the affirmative voice is a simpler grammatical form and thus is easier to understand.

☞ **Order prompts chronologically.**

Order parts of a prompt consistently with the order in which the user will carry them out. Note the examples in the fifth row of Figure 14-4. In the "Poor" example, the prompt refers to actions in the reverse order in which they are to be carried out. In the "Improved" message, prompts are given in the same order as they are to be carried out. This will be simpler to understand and less likely to be misread and cause errors.

☞ **Format prompts using white space, justification, and visual cues for easy scanning.**

The "Poor" prompt in the sixth row of Figure 14-4 is written in a straight prose format. Although it is readable to the novice, it is hard for the casual or expert user to scan quickly. The justification and use of uppercase, bold, and italics in the "Improved" prompt makes it much easier to scan.

☞ **Use consistent terminology.**

Natural language is very rich and redundant, and in conversation and prose we may use several synonyms interchangeably while discussing a topic. Our objective in system prompts and instructions is clarity, not style, however, and it is not appropriate to use synonyms. For each command, function, or object, a single consistent term should be used throughout the system. For instance, the terms "edit," "modify," "update," and "change" could all be used to refer to a single function. Rather than use them interchangeably, pick one and use it consistently. Note the examples in the last row of Figure 14-4. A user who encounters a different term may assume it has a different meaning.

The choice of terms should be made carefully to maximize the likelihood that the user will interpret the term correctly. For instance, the term "Type" is probably the best when the user is being instructed to type in a string, while "Press" is a better choice for using a function key. If used consistently, the user will come to know the difference and not type in "Return" in response to the instruction "Press Return."

Similarly, references to key labels should be exact. If the key is labeled "RTRN," don't say "Press Return"; say "Press RTRN." It might seem clearer to write out the full word that is abbreviated on the key, but it may mislead the user. When users don't find a key labeled "Return," they might try typing in the word.

Instructions

Occasionally, it is necessary to provide more extensive instructions on the screen than short, simple prompts. Help screens and tutorial screens are a case in point. The following guidelines refer to this type of instruction.

☞ **Make text simple and clear.**

Instructions, prompts, and other information expressed in prose should be simple, brief, concise, and clear. Rules of good prose, in most cases, do not apply. You are not writing a novel or a marketing brochure; you are simply trying to convey information. The user is more interested in quickly getting the information they need than in being entertained and challenged. A few rules for simplifying and clarifying text are given below (Galitz, 1985):

- Use short sentences and simple and familiar words. About a fifth-grade reading level is appropriate.
- Keep paragraphs short, and separate them by at least one blank line.
- Limit lines to 50 to 55 characters per line, or use two double columns, 30 to 35 characters per column.
- Avoid hyphenation.
- Avoid right justifying with unequal spacing.

Tullis (1988) adds some others:

- Space between lines should be equal to or slightly greater than character height (that is, approximately double-spaced).
- Avoid line lengths of less than 26 characters.

Tullis (1988) reviews several studies that show that right-justified, nonproportional text takes longer to read than text with ragged right margins. One study found an 11% difference. Trollip and Sales (1986) also found a reading time advantage for ragged right margin text over right-justified text when the latter resulted in uneven spacing between words, although no effect on comprehension was found.

Other studies cited in Tullis (1988) showed optimal performance on double-spaced as opposed to single-spaced text. Another study (Williams, 1988) found some evidence that double spacing is also faster and preferred for menu options.

Figure 14-5 presents "Poor" and "Improved" formatting of lengthy instructions according to these principles.

Numbers

Often, screen displays include numbers. The following guidelines apply.

☞ **Right justify integers.**

Integers in columns should be right justified, as in the "Improved" example in the first row of Figure 14-6. The "Poor" example is much harder to scan and read.

Poor:

Scrolling. There are a number of different ways you can peruse through text that is not currently visible on the screen, otherwise known as scrolling. First, the arrow keys are available for moving the cursor, and when the cursor reaches a border or edge of the screen, then the text will scroll in the appropriate direction, such as left from the right border, up from the bottom border etc. Alternatively, one can choose to scroll by pagefuls, and the next and previous keys are available for this purpose. Next takes you to the next pageful, and Prev

Improved:

SCROLLING

There are three ways to scroll.

FIRST,   move the cursor using the ARROW keys. When you reach any edge of the screen, the text will scroll.

If you reach the right edge, the text will scroll to the left. If you reach the bottom edge, text will scroll up, etc.

SECOND,   the NEXT and PREV keys scroll by page.

Figure 14-5   Instructions.

Poor: Improved:

10 100 1,000 10,00	10 100 1,000 10,000
100.00 25.2563 5,432.48 1.45491	5,432 .48 1.45491 100 .00 25 .2563
10:1 p.m 02/07/87 002 100 013	10:01 p.m. 2/7/87 2 100 13
6173954686 028405554 1234567890 135792468	617-395-4686 028-40-5554 1,234,567,890 135 792 468

Figure 14-6 Numbers.

☞ **Decimal-align real numbers.**

Decimal numbers in columns should be decimal-aligned, as in the "Improved" example in the second row of Figure 14-6. The "Poor" example is much harder to scan and read.

☞ **Avoid leading zeros when they are unnecessary and nonstandard.**

Note the examples in the third row of Figure 14-6. Expressions of time commonly use leading zeros for minutes and seconds, and this convention should be adhered to on computer displays. Dates, however, do not traditionally include zeros in the manual world, and so leading zeros should not be used in dates in computer displays. Leading zeros make lists of data harder to scan and read, as illustrated in the column of three numbers in the "Poor" example. The "Improved" column is much easier to read. If users have always included leading zeros in some corporate data, this convention should be carried over into on-line systems and reports. If not, it should be avoided to improve readability.

☞ **Break up long numbers into groups of three to four digits. Use standard separators when they apply; otherwise use spaces.**

Traditionally, phone numbers and social security numbers are broken up into specific groups separated by hyphens. Credit card numbers use spaces, and large numbers employ commas. These groupings make these data easier to read and transcribe, as can be seen in the examples in the last row of Figure 14-6. When displaying such data on a computer display, these conventions should be preserved. In addition, if the designer is in a position to format output data for which there are no established formats (for example, part numbers or employee numbers), similar conventions should be employed to improve readability.

Coding Techniques

A number of coding techniques are available on different workstations, including the following:

Blinking
Bold
Reverse video
Size
Font
Underlining
Shape
Special characters and icons
Proximity
Borders
Sound
Color

Guidelines for the use of these coding techniques are given next.

☞ **Use attention-getting techniques appropriately.**

Different terminals have different capabilities for providing contrast and formatting on the screen. These capabilities can be used in screen design to draw the eye to certain information. You might want to use contrast to distinguish an item from its background (such as making overlapping windows distinguishable from each other), to distinguish captions from fields, or to draw attention to urgent items such as warnings, directions, or error messages. Attention-getting capabilities are only effective if used sparingly. If they are overused, they lose their attention-getting value.

The following is a discussion of the common attention-getting attributes

Figure 14–7   Blinking.

available on many terminals, with guidelines for the application of each (see Rubinstein and Hersh, 1984, for a good discussion of visual attributes and more examples).

   Blinking.   Use blinking when you must get the user's attention and his or her eyes are likely to be directed elsewhere. People can easily perceive blinking in their peripheral vision, and it will involuntarily draw their attention. In many systems, the cursor blinks. This is helpful because the cursor is usually very small and would otherwise be hard to find on a very busy display. Urgent error messages that must be responded to are a good candidate for blinking, as illustrated in Figure 14-7. Use blinking with discretion, however, because it is hard to ignore and can be annoying if it is not really necessary to attend to the item. Also keep in mind that blinking reduces legibility. Lengthy text (more than a word or to) should not blink. Thus, in Figure 14-7, the label "Error" blinks but the error message itself does not. Smith and Mosier (1986) suggest a blink rate of 2 to 5 hertz, and a longer "on" interval than "off" interval.

   Bold.   Bold text is text constructed of letters that are heavier than normal intensity text. It can be an effective way to make something, such as a caption or

C O U R S E   O F F E R I N G S

NO.		NAME	SEC.	SEQ.	INSTR.
COM	1	Pascal 1	1	1	Smith
COM	1	Pascal 1	2	9	Mayhew
COM	**100**	**Artificial Int.**	**1**	**10**	**Jones**
COM	103	LISP	1	2	Hafner

Figure 14–8   Bold.

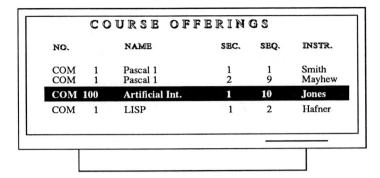

COURSE OFFERINGS				
NO.	**NAME**	**SEC.**	**SEQ.**	**INSTR.**
COM 1	Pascal 1	1	1	Smith
COM 1	Pascal 1	2	9	Mayhew
COM 100	**Artificial Int.**	**1**	**10**	**Jones**
COM 1	LISP	1	2	Hafner

Figure 14–9   Reverse Video.

title, stand out, as in Figure 14-8. Most systems have one level of bold. That is, there is a standard intensity to objects or text on the screen, and one option for making things high intensity, or bold. Some systems have more than one alternative level of bold, such as normal, medium, and bold. Any more than three different levels of bold should be avoided, as people may have difficulty perceiving and remembering the differences.

   Reverse video.   Reverse video is a reverse of normal video presentation. It is a relative, rather than absolute, attribute. If the terminal displays light objects on a dark background, then using reverse video means surrounding a dark object with a light background. If the terminal normally displays dark objects on a light background, then light objects on a dark background would be reverse video. Reverse video is another effective way to make something in a display stand out and draw the user's attention (see Figure 14-9). Like blinking, reverse video may reduce legibility (when the edges of the characters "bleed" into the screen background due to an inadequate space around the characters in the reverse video area) and should not be overused or used in lengthy text. On the other hand, evidence (Spoto and Babu, 1989) suggests that reverse video is a more powerful search cue than bold. Reverse video might be used to indicate that an item has been selected or to indicate an error field.

   Size.   Although inferior to color or shape for *search* tasks (Christ, 1975), the relative size of symbols is a good way to code for relative quantity or importance. Bar charts are an example. It is usually easier to interpret relative size than absolute size, and when only relative quantity is important, size can be a very effective cue. See, for example, Figure 14-10. But limit size codes to five or less levels, as people will have difficulty comparing and remembering more than this.

   Font.   Text items can be made to stand out and draw attention by using all-uppercase letters, double-sized characters, italics, or other different fonts (see

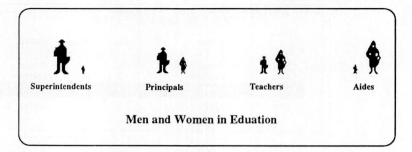

Figure 14–10 Size.

Figure 14-11). As in the case of color and highlighting, two to four different character types used in consistent ways are optimal. More become busy and hard to remember.

Underlining.   Most terminals allow underlining, and it is a simple way to make a text object stand out on a display. Underlining may reduce legibility, however, and should be used sparingly. Underlining might be used to draw attention to key words in instructions or to distinguish fill-in fields from other items on a display. Or it might be used as a pointer, as in Figure 14-12.

Shape.   Generally, shapes often have particular connotations for certain populations of users, and this can be exploited in screen design. For instance, consider road signs. In the United States, an octagon is always used for stop signs, and an upside down triangle for yield signs. A system might present error messages in an octagonal window and warning signs in a triangular window, as illustrated in Figure 14-13. The shape will thus communicate the relative urgency of the message to users even before they read it.

COURSE OFFERINGS

NO.		NAME	SEC.	SEQ.	INSTR.
COM	1	Pascal 1	1	1	Smith
COM	1	Pascal 1	2	9	Mayhew
COM	*100*	*Artificial Int.*	*1*	*10*	*Jones*
COM	103	LISP	1	2	Hafner

Figure 14–11 Font.

	COURSE OFFERINGS				
NO.	NAME	SEC.	SEQ.	INSTR.	
COM 1	Pascal 1	1	1	Smith	
COM 1	Pascal 1	2	9	Mayhew	
COM 100	Artificial Int.	1	10	Jones	
COM 103	LISP	1	2	Hafner	

Figure 14–12 Underlining.

Special characters and icons. Tags such as asterisks, arrows, and other graphic symbols, such as a small pointing hand (see Figure 14-14), can be used to draw attention to items on the screen. Unlike some other cues, such as bold and reverse video, however, they take up additional space on the screen.

Proximity. The proximity of items on a screen implies association and leads the eye to consider items as parts of a whole. White space can be used to correctly or incorrectly lead the user to associate items. For example, in the "Poor" screen in Figure 14-15, you may find that you try to read the numbers "4342 130 as the "Billing Date" because of the proximity of this caption to these numbers. In fact the number is part of the account number. This is much clearer in the "Improved" example, where the associated fields and captions are closer to one another than they are to other captions and fields.

Borders. Borders are very effective in identifying meaningful groups, creating a sense of closure, and focusing attention. Figure 14-16 offers an example

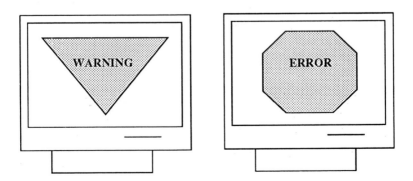

Figure 14–13 Shape.

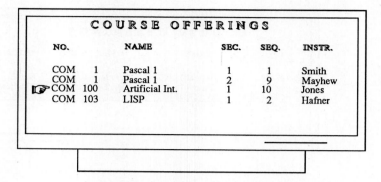

Figure 14–14 Special characters and icons.

of the use of borders to draw the eye in to the center of the important data on the display.

Sound.   Many terminals have the capability of making an audible beep under program control. Sound is a very effective attention getter. However, its use must be carefully considered. A terminal in a private office that beeps occasionally is one thing, while a room full of terminals that beep constantly can be aggravating for everyone. Often the beep is used to signal an error and the display of an error message. In an open area, users might object to having their every error announced to their peers. For these reasons, as effective as it is, the use of sound should be carefully considered, and users should have the option of turning it off.

Some terminals have several different tones available. A high tone might signal that additional input is required, while a low tone might signal that an operation has been successfully completed. This can be very useful, freeing the user's eyes for other tasks while waiting for system response.

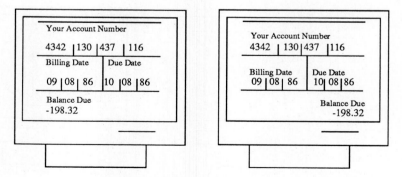

Figure 14–15 Proximity.

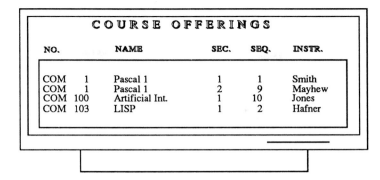

Figure 14–16 Borders.

In sum, a variety of attention-getting techniques are available depending on the capabilities of a particular terminal. They should be used sparingly to retain their attention-getting value. Too many different coding techniques (for example, bold, reverse video, and borders) should not be used in a single system, because people cannot easily remember more than about four or five different codes. In addition, the designer should consider how these techniques might appear in combination. For instance, an underline will be difficult to perceive in a reverse video field, and so these two attributes should not be used to code different information in the same display (Rubinstein and Hersh, 1984).

Color

The cost of color workstations is decreasing, and more and more designers have color available for the user interfaces they design. Color is a powerful cue, and is easy to misuse. It must be carefully considered in user interface design, and not applied just because it is available. This section first discusses pertinent aspects of human color vision. Then some experimental studies of the use of color on computer screens are reviewed. Finally, guidelines for the use of color in screen design are offered.

Color Vision

The human eye contains millions of **photoreceptors,** or sensory cells, selectively sensitive to light (Thompson, 1975). There are two main types of photoreceptor cells: rods and cones. **Rods** are sensitive to light across the full spectrum of visible light, but do not selectively mediate spectral values (that is, color). There are approximately 125 million rods in each eye, with the highest density in the periphery at about 20 degrees of visual angle, and none at all in the **fovea** or center of the eye. Rods are more sensitive, but less responsive to fine detail than cones. This is why flicker on a computer screen is more apparent in peripheral vision and why a dim star is more distinct when you look slightly away from it.

Cones are selectively sensitive to different light wavelengths. They mediate color perception. There are only about 6 million cones in each eye; most are in the fovea or center of the eye. The fovea contains only cones, no rods. Cones are less sensitive, but more responsive to detail and color than rods.

Perceived color corresponds to different light wavelengths. The visible spectrum of colors includes the following (Murch, 1987a; Galitz, 1985):

Red	Roughly 610 nanometers
Orange	600
Yellow	575
Green	505
Blue	470
Violet	380

Current theory (Thompson, 1975) holds that there are three types of photosensitive chemicals or pigments in the cones, which are responsive to red, green, and blue lightwaves. Red pigment is found in 64% of cones, green in 32%, and blue in about 2%. Given the way these pigments are distributed, we can detect yellows and blues farther out into our peripheral vision than reds and greens. There are no blue pigments at all in the center of the fovea, so small blue objects tend to disappear when fixated on.

Neurons at a higher level in the visual system respond in an opponent manner to two pairs of colors: red–green and blue–yellow. That is, some cells are excited by red and inhibited by green, while others respond in the reverse manner. The same is true of blue–yellow opponent cells. Other nonopponent cells are either excited or inhibited by all visible wavelengths of light. The collective response of these various kinds of cells results in the perception of color.

A simplified description of some principles of color perception is presented here, adapted from Murch (1987a). Objects do not have color. They selectively absorb or reflect different wavelengths of light, creating the perception of color. Pigment molecules in matter *selectively absorb and reflect* different wavelengths, so both the wavelengths present in the light source and the pigments present in the matter determine the perceived color. A surface appears white when the light source illuminating the surface contains all visible wavelengths and the surface *reflects* all those wavelengths equally. A surface appears black when the light source illuminating the surface contains all visible wavelengths and the surface *absorbs* all those wavelengths equally. In sum, the wavelengths that are *reflected* from a surface are perceived as color.

Color can be described along four dimensions: hue, saturation, lightness, and brightness. All are psychological, that is, subjective, variables, but they do correspond to physical variables in some relationship.

Hue is the visual sensation that varies according to light wavelength. Hue is the basic component of what we usually mean when we use the term color.

Saturation is a sensation related to the number of different wavelengths present and contributing to the sensation of color. Usually we do not receive a pure set of a single wavelength corresponding to a pure color. Instead we receive several different wavelengths simultaneously, and these are perceived as one unified color. A highly saturated color is made up of a very narrow band of wavelengths, for instance, a true red. A less saturated color is made up of a wider band of wavelengths, for instance, a bluish red or a yellowish red or a pink. In addition, adding achromatic light (for example, white or gray) to a color produces a desaturated hue.

Lightness refers to the range of achromatic colors ranging from white through gray to black. Achromatic color is produced when all wavelengths are equally reflected (white) or equally absorbed (black). Specific hues may be mixed with achromatic colors, and the lightness of the achromatic color will determine the lightness of the resulting mixture. For instance, white combined with red produces pink, a light color, while black combined with red produces a deep red that is not as light. Lightness is thus related to the reflectance of an object's surface.

Brightness refers to the dimension of dull to bright. Brightness is determined by the intensity of the light source illuminating the object. Thus, while lightness is a property of an object, brightness is determined by the amount of illumination cast on the object. The eye is differentially sensitive to different wavelengths; so as the intensity of illumination increases, different wavelengths in the reflected light become perceivable, thus causing the sensation of a change of color. It is important to note that, whereas lightness and brightness are distinguishable characteristics of a printed hard copy, the nature of a color display does not allow lightness and brightness to be varied independently.

When pigments are *mixed,* as when paints are mixed, the wavelengths that they individually absorb are combined; so only the wavelengths reflected by *both* are now reflected by the mixture and perceived. For instance, mixing cyan and yellow produces green. This is because yellow absorbs shorter wavelengths (blue and violet) and reflects longer ones, while cyan absorbs longer wavelengths (red, orange, and yellow) and reflects shorter ones. Together they absorb both longer and shorter wavelengths, and this leaves the middle range of wavelengths, that is, green, to be reflected and perceived. This process is known as **subtractive color mixing,** because the combined pigments together subtract (absorb) certain wavelengths from those reflected and perceived.

We also perceive color from light sources directly. A case in point is a computer screen. The screen contains hundreds of tiny dots of phosphor, which emit light when bombarded with electrons. On a color screen, the phosphors are arranged in groups of three, one emitting red, one green, and one blue. Each of these colors in its pure form is created by turning on just one phosphor (for example, red) in each triad. Other colors are created by turning on combinations of phosphors in the triads at varying intensities. Because the phosphor dots are so small, the brain perceives a single color rather than many tiny dots of different colors. The effect is similar to a light source hitting a surface and reflecting only certain wavelengths, which are also perceived as a unified, single color, rather than many colors together. For instance, yellow can be created by a combination of red and green phosphors. The exact color of yellow will depend on the relative intensities of the red and green phosphors. This is called **additive color mixing.**

As far as the way the eye perceives color is concerned, the main difference between *additive* and *subtractive* color mixing is that one creates brighter colors and the other creates darker colors. On the other hand, the eye receives the same wavelength combinations regardless of whether they come directly from a light source or are selectively reflected from an object. The two different processes account for the fact that mixing paints on an object's surface and mixing colored lights do not have the same effect on color perception. And other properties of an object's surface besides hue, for example, texture, contribute to the perception of color.

Color: Experimental Results

Lalomia and Happ (1987) tested 120 different color combinations to determine optimal foreground and background colors for text displays. They measured response time to recognize individual letters and preferences. The color combinations yielding the highest performance *and* preference scores were as follows:

Foreground	Black	Blue	Green	Background Cyan	Red	Magenta	Brown	White
Black				×		×		×
Blue								×
Green	×	×		×				
Cyan	×							
White	×							
Bold green	×							
Bold cyan	×	×		×	×	×		
Bold magenta	×		×					
Yellow	×	×		×		×		
Bold white	×		×	×				

Several generalities can be noted in the total data set. First, most good combinations included a bright color as the foreground color, and most poor combinations had poor contrast between foreground and background colors. The best overall background color was black and the worst was brown. Maximum flexibility in choosing a foreground color was afforded by the background colors black and cyan (half of all the good combinations included one of these two colors as a background). Brown and green were the poorest choices of background color (Galitz, 1989).

Recognizing a single letter on a small background area may or may not be the same as reading and scanning a lot of text on a whole screen. Thus, generalizations from these data should be made with caution. However, until further research confirms the advantage of these color combinations in a variety of contexts, they may be taken as *tentative* guidelines for optimal choices of foreground–background combinations of colors for text.

Another study (Matthews and Mertins, 1987) compared foreground–background color combinations for text using a different task and comparing a different combination of colors. In this study, 40 five-character strings were displayed in one color on a screen background of another color. Subjects had to search for a target string that started with a particular character (for example, an asterisk) and then compare it to another string. Subjects performed such tasks over an extended period of time (4 hours) to assess any fatigue effects. The color combinations compared included the following:

Foreground	Background
Green	Black
Red	Black
Blue	Black
White	Black
Red	Blue
Red	Green
Blue	Green

Accuracy was 10% lower for the red–green and red–blue combinations as compared to the others. No other differences in accuracy were significant. The green–black combination was about 7% slower than other combinations, and the red–black combination was about 3% faster than other combinations. No other differences in search time were significant. Fatigue effects increased over time, but did not differ across color combinations.

It is difficult to compare these data directly with the Lalomia and Happ (1987) data because the color combinations tested differed, as did the task. However, it is interesting to note that the two combinations showing the lowest accuracy in the Matthews and Mertins (1987) study, red–green and red–blue, also did not appear as one of the optimal color combinations in the Lalomia and Happ (1987) study. Also, nearly half the optimal color combinations in the Lalomia and Happ (1987) study involved either black or white in combination with a color, and the two combinations showing the lowest accuracy in the Matthews and Mertins (1987) study involved color on color combinations (as opposed to color with black or white). This suggests that combinations including black or white may be better than combinations of two colors.

Another study of 24 symbol–background color combinations (Pace, 1984) suggested that black text on blue backgrounds and blue text on white backgrounds resulted in fewer errors than magenta on green and green on white combinations (although the reader should keep in mind that blue for text is not recommended for other reasons discussed in the previous section and in the section on Principles and Guidelines). These findings are also consistent with the findings in other studies that color in combination with black or white is better than two colors for foreground and background and that colors contrasting in brightness as well as hue are better.

In sum, then, some tentative conclusions from these few studies can be drawn regarding optimal foreground–background color combinations *for text* as follows:

1. Display color images (text) on a black or cyan background.
2. Choose a bright foreground color for text (for example, white or bold green).
3. Avoid brown and green as background colors.
4. Be sure foreground colors contrast in both brightness and hue with background colors.

Besides foreground–background color combinations, another aspect of the use of color in screen design is *how many* colors are used and *which* colors are used in a set for coding objects or attributes. Luria, Neri, and Jacobsen (1986) measured the effects of set size and colors in the set in a color matching task. A color legend appeared on the screen. The legend included two to ten colors, arranged in a spatial layout that mapped to the numeric keypad layout on the keyboard. Thus the position of a color in the legend corresponded to a particular key on the numeric keypad. A target object (a vertical line) would appear on the screen below the legend. Subjects had to match the target line color to the corresponding color on the legend and then respond by pressing the corresponding key on the keypad. The task thus involved matching the color of the target to the correct color in a set of colors displayed elsewhere. This represents the way color legends might actually be used for color–coded information on computer displays.

The results indicated that, after subtracting out the motor response time for pressing the button, the time to match a color to the legend increased fairly linearly as the number of colors in the set increased from two to five. Then it increased by a smaller increment for each additional color between six and ten. In addition, error rates increased sharply with set sizes of more than seven. Of course, increases in both response time and errors as set sizes increase will undoubtedly be influenced by the particular colors in the set. The colors used in this experiment included the following:

Red	Aqua
Pink	Light blue
Orange	Dark blue
Yellow	Purple
Green	White

The colors with the shortest response times were dark blue, red, purple, and white. Those most slowly matched were yellow, orange, and aqua. It is interesting to note here that the colors most quickly matched were also the most *saturated* colors in the set, and the ones most slowly matched were the least saturated.

Certain confusions between colors were most common. These included orange with red and yellow with orange.

These results imply that increasing the colors used in a display will degrade performance when a task involves color matching and that the amount of the effect will depend partly on the particular choice of colors within a set. Choosing highly saturated colors seems advisable. Of course, it is undoubtedly true that set size will affect performance for *any* coding technique (for example, size or shape), and it is known that searching is faster for color than for other coding techniques. Perhaps the lesson to draw from this finding is simply that the number of color codes should be minimized as much as possible for a given task without sacrificing important functionality.

Different cultures have different color associations that can potentially be exploited in user interface designs employing color. Courtney (1986) surveyed a large sample (784) of Hong Kong Chinese to determine the strength of the associations between nine concepts and eight colors and then compared these data to a similar study of Americans (Bergum and Bergum, 1981). The percentage of subjects from the two studies associating each concept with the most frequently associated color are as follows:

	Chinese		American	
Concept	Color	%	Color	%
Safe	Green	62.2	Green	61.4
Cold	White	71.5	Blue	96.1
Caution	Yellow	44.8	Yellow	81.1
Go	Green	44.7	Green	99.2
On	Green	22.3	Red	50.4
Hot	Red	31.1	Red	94.5
Danger	Red	64.7	Red	89.8
Off	Black	53.5	Blue	31.5
Stop	Red	48.5	Red	100.0

It can be seen that there are some differences. In particular, while blue is most commonly associated with "cold" among Americans, among these Chinese white is more commonly associated with "cold." The Chinese more often associate green with "on," while red means "on" to most Americans. And the Chinese associate black most often with "off," while Americans more often associate this concept with blue. In addition, although there are agreements across cultures in the most frequently associated color for the other concepts, the associations are much stronger among Americans than among Chinese. Courtney points out that blue is the color of mourning among the Chinese and red means happiness, and that may be partly why these colors are not so strongly associated with the concepts "cold" and "off" and "danger," respectively. In general, these data point out the dangers of generalizing color associations across cultures, as well as the danger of assuming certain color associations among users in some cultures.

Color: Principles and Guidelines

Color is a very salient and powerful visual cue. It should not be used arbitrarily for esthetic value alone, because if used in non-task-related ways it can actually degrade performance (Christ, 1975). Used strategically to support a task and aid in decision making, it can enhance performance considerably (Christ, 1975). Color is now being used in computer systems to "monitor scientific and industrial processes, visualize and code functional relationships, evaluate medical conditions, image mathematical expressions and aid in business decisions" (Smith, 1988).

The following guidelines are offered for applying color to screen design. They represent an excellent starting point, but it should be kept in mind that a given color name, such as blue, cyan, or green, may apply to very different colors on different workstations. All blues, for example, are not equal, and so recommendations made here about certain color combinations must not be taken too literally. The designer should always test color design decisions on the particular workstation on which they are to be implemented before making final decisions.

☞ **Use color sparingly. Design first in monochrome and optimize other aspects of screen layout and design. Then add color only where it adds value.**

Color is still a novel capability for many designers. There is a tendency to use it just because it is available, to overuse it when it adds no particular value to a display, and to use it as a substitute for other design techniques that might actually be more effective in certain circumstances. The recommended approach, therefore, is to first design in monochrome, considering all the screen layout and design principles offered in this book. Then color can be considered and added only where it is needed and where it provides a more powerful coding technique than other alternatives. This approach will ensure that color is not used inappropriately and that it will be used where and how it can have the most benefit.

☞ **Use color to draw attention, to communicate organization, to indicate status, and to establish relationships.**

Color is very effective in *drawing attention*. Note the use of yellow for the menu selection input field in Figure 14-17 (see front endpaper). It contrasts highly in hue, brightness, and lightness with other colors in the display, and the eye is almost automatically drawn to it. This is appropriate in this display, because in fact the menu selection input field is probably the most important item on the screen.

Now look at Figure 14-18 (see front endpaper) and compare it to Figure 14-17. The two screens are very similar. In fact, Figure 14-17 is a screen for program execution and Figure 14-18 is a screen for program backup. The same programs are offered through a menu in each case, and the only difference is the function being executed: execution or backup. Because of the high degree of similarity in these two screens, it would be easy for users to confuse them and perform an execution or backup by mistake. Now note that the screen titles are in different colors: red or yellow. This use of different colors is intended to draw attention to the function being executed through the screen. It will help minimize confusion and errors.

Color can also help *communicate organization*. Figure 14-19 shows a screen of windows on a monochrome monitor. The screen is somewhat busy, and it is a little difficult to focus on one window.

Now compare this screen with Figure 14-20 (see front endpaper), which is the same screen except on a color monitor, where different colors are used for window backgrounds. With each window in a different color, it is much easier to focus on one window. The color helps communicate the organization of information into separate windows.

In Figures 14-21 (see front endpaper) and 14-22 (see front endpaper), color has been used to *indicate status*. Red is used for error messages, and yellow is used for warning messages. The user can determine the nature of the message even before reading it.

Finally, color can be used to *establish relationships* between distant items on the screen. For instance, in Figure 14-23 (see back endpaper), the use of yellow for

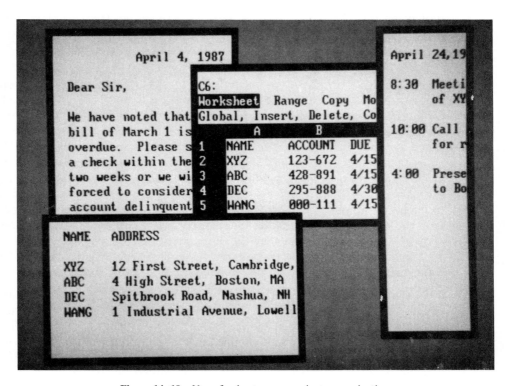

Figure 14–19   Use of color to communicate organization.

the input field at the current cursor location near the top of the screen and for the Microhelp line at the bottom of the screen helps to communicate to the user that the information in the Microhelp line refers to that fill-in field. Although the two items are distant from one another on the screen, the common color communicates the association between them effectively.

In contrast, look again at Figure 14-17. In this menu screen, there are two ways to make a choice: the user can enter the choice number in the fill-in field, which is in yellow. Alternatively, the user can move a cursor to the desired choice. The cursor consists of a little black arrow, and the use of black versus blue text on the current choice item. If the fill-in field and cursor were the same color, such as yellow, it might be clearer to new users that the cursor and the current number in the fill-in field were related. An opportunity to use color to help communicate this fact went unexploited here.

Color can also be used to communicate groupings of adjacent items when screen real estate is so scarce that using white space or borders to separate groups would pose serious trade-offs. Color-coded items with no white space between them will still clearly communicate groupings. Similarly, related screens can be grouped together by a common background color (Galitz, 1989). For example, all "Help" windows could have a blue background, distinguishing them from application windows. This would make it easy to identify the type of window quickly without reading any content.

☞ **Use color to support search tasks.**

Color is a more effective code for search tasks and symbol identification tasks than other cues, such as shape, size, or brightness (Christ, 1975). To get a feeling for this fact, look at the display in Figure 14-24 (see back endpaper). The objects in this display vary in four dimensions: shape, size, color, and brightness. If you were asked to count the number of *red* objects, you would find this easier to do than to count the number of *horizontal bars,* the number of *small* objects, or the number of *bright* objects. Color is a more salient cue than shape, size, or brightness; so when search and identification tasks are involved in the use of displays, it is desirable to use color to support them. The performance advantage of color coding increases with the density of the symbols in a display and when the number of nontarget symbols of a different color than the target increases (Christ, 1975).

☞ **Avoid using color in non-task-related ways.**

While color used appropriately can facilitate user tasks, color used inappropriately in displays can degrade user performance as compared to monochromatic displays (Christ, 1975; Green and Anderson, 1956). To get a feel for this, first look at Figure 14-25. This is a simplified display from an accounts receivable system on a monochrome screen. Accounts are identified by name and number, and the status of each account is indicated through the due date and payment status fields.

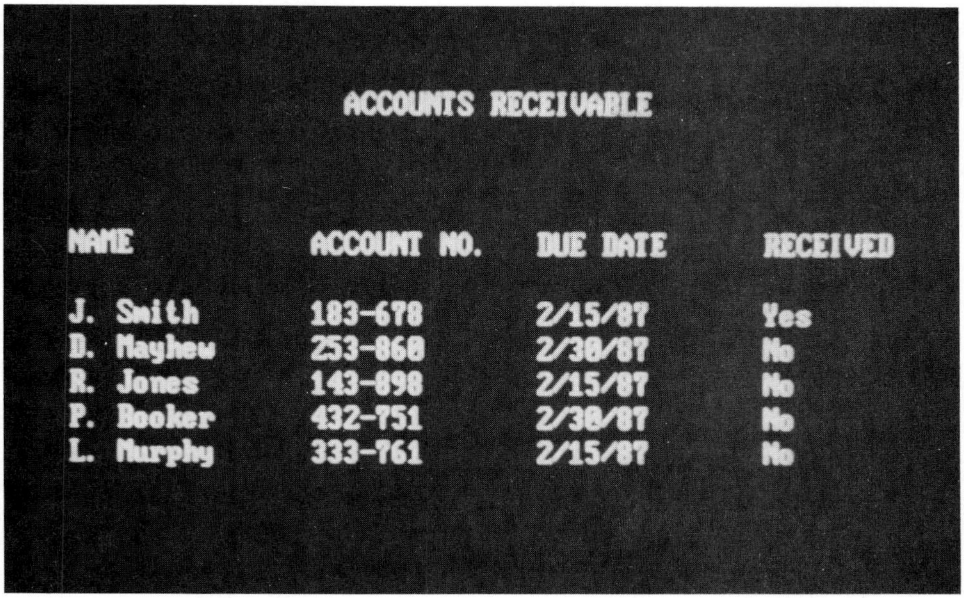

Figure 14–25   Using color in task related ways.

Suppose the user's task is to find all *past due accounts,* that is, all accounts whose *due date is in the past* and that have *not been paid* yet. To search for these accounts, the user first has to identify due dates in the past, scanning over those not yet due, and then check in the "Received" column for a "No." This will not be an easy task and, under time pressure, users are likely to make errors.

Now look at Figure 14-26 (see back endpaper). This is the same display on a color screen, and color has been strategically applied to support the task described. Past due accounts are displayed in red. Accounts not yet due are displayed in white. Accounts past due but already paid are displayed in green (Shneiderman, 1986). Now searching for past due accounts is trivial: the user need only pick out the accounts in red. This is an appropriate use of color to support a task.

Now consider another task. Suppose we ask the user to search for all accounts that are as yet *unpaid, regardless of whether or not they are past due.* This will be fairly easy to do on the monochrome display in Figure 14-25. The user need only scan for "NO"'s in the "Received" column. However, if users try to accomplish this task on the color display in Figure 14-26, they will find that the different colors of the data in the "Received" column will be distracting and may slow them down and cause errors (Shneiderman, 1986). Color is such a powerful cue that when used in non-task-related ways it can actually degrade performance. Thus it is important to avoid the arbitrary use of color.

☞ **Allow users to control color coding.**

Sometimes the user's task may vary so that is not possible to use color to code for one task without interfering with another, as in the example given previously. In such a case it is a good idea to give users control over color coding (Shneiderman, 1986). For instance, in the preceding example, it would be best if users could specify what they wish to search for and then have the system flag those items by applying color to them.

☞ **Do not use color without some other redundant cue.**

When color is used to convey important information to users, it should be supported by some other redundant cue. For instance, in Figure 14-27 (see back endpaper), both the color yellow and a rectangular border signal a warning message. Error messages might be another color, such as red, and also have a different kind of border around them (such as a thicker one) or be displayed in a different font.

There are three main reasons for this redundancy of coding. First, in many environments the designer cannot be sure that all users will have color workstations. Redundant coding *allows the interface to be ported to a monochrome workstation* without losing important user information. Second, in the total population of people, about 8% of males and 0.4% of females have some sort of color vision deficiency (Silverstein, 1987). Redundant coding will *assist users without color vision deficiencies while not depriving color vision deficient users of important information.* ("Color vision deficiencies" is preferred over the term "color-blindness" because most color vision deficient people have trouble perceiving only certain colors. True lack of any color vision at all is extremely rare. See Brown, 1988.) Third, it has been demonstrated (Christ, 1975) that *redundant coding enhances performance.* That is, it is faster, easier, and less error prone to search for, say, red squares than to search for objects that are just red or just square. The additional information in redundant coding seems to improve performance over color coding alone.

☞ **Ensure that colors differ in lightness and brightness as well as in hue.**

The most common types of color vision deficiencies are the inability to discriminate red from green and blue from yellow. However, all sighted people can discriminate differences in lightness. Thus, if colors differ in lightness as well as hue, even color vision deficient users will be able to discriminate between them (Smith, 1988).

Another reason to vary brightness as well as hue is that, when displaying color objects on a color background, edges will not be clear unless the colors contrast in brightness as well as hue. It is also true that the perception of brightness is mediated by the red and green photopigments, and thus colors differing only in the amount of blue will not produce sharp edges (Murch, 1987b).

☞ **Be consistent with color associations people have in their jobs and in their culture.**

Different cultures and subcultures have commonly accepted meanings for certain colors. In many Western cultures, the following associations are reinforced in traffic signals and consumer products:

Green:	go, on, safe
Red:	stop, hot, danger, on, loss, emergency
Yellow:	caution, warning, warm
Blue:	cold, off

These associations can be exploited in computer user interfaces. For instance, in Figures 14-21 and 14-22, note that red was used for error messages and yellow for warning messages. And in Figure 14-26 red was used for past due accounts and green for accounts already paid. Although any colors could have been used here to distinguish types of information, red, yellow, and green were specifically chosen because their common meanings in the culture matched the intended meanings on the screen. This will facilitate the users interpretation of colors and avoid interference between one set of common meanings and another arbitrary set of meanings.

On the other hand, designers for the international market should not assume that the color associations in their own culture will generalize to other cultures. Cultural stereotypes for a target culture should be determined before making design decisions regarding color.

☞ **Use color for a consistent purpose and with consistent meanings within one system.**

Just as with any other aspect of screen design, consistent conventions should be applied across screens in the use of color. For instance, red should not be used on one screen to signal an urgent error message and on another to group items together. Users will carry over their interpretations of color meanings from one screen to another and be misled.

☞ **Limit coding to eight distinct colors, spaced far apart along the visible spectrum. Four or less colors is preferred.**

Clearly, in a graphics display that is simply a picture, there is no reason to limit the number of colors. Often the more colors used, the more realistic the display is. However, when color is being used to *code* information, as in most of the examples offered here, it is important to limit the use of colors. All but highly trained users will not be able to reliably discriminate between and remember more than about four to five colors used for this purpose (ISO, 1988). They have difficulty absolutely identifying more than about four in the absence of comparisons (Silverstein, 1987). Colors are easier to discriminate between and remember the farther apart they are along the color spectrum (Silverstein, 1987). Often four or five colors are enough to communicate the necessary information, and this number is easy for people to learn and remember.

☞ **Provide a legend if color codes are numerous and not obvious in meaning.**

If it becomes necessary to use more than six to eight colors, and especially if colors are assigned arbitrarily and do not take on meanings already familiar to users in their everyday life, it is important to provide a color legend to assist users in learning and remembering color codes.

☞ **Avoid using saturated blues for text or other small, thin line symbols.**

Visual acuity is reduced for the shorter wavelengths in the visible spectrum, and some studies suggest that the human eye may not be able to bring saturated blues into clear focus, especially on a background of certain other colors (for example, red). Insensitivity to blue also increases with age (Murch, 1987b). Other studies show consistent, clear performance decrements in symbol identification tasks for blue symbols, as compared to symbols of other colors.

Most blues displayed on CRTs are low in luminance, and visual acuity also decreases with reduced luminance. For these reasons, the ISO (1988) recommends avoiding saturated blues for text on dark backgrounds and for stick fonts on light backgrounds. Desaturated blues, on the other hand, may be acceptable for symbols and may be useful when the common associations with blue (for example, cold and water) are appropriate. Also, blues make good background colors in the right combinations with other foreground colors.

Under normal lighting conditions, the eye is most sensitive to the middle of the spectrum (green and yellow), and symbol identification accuracy is greatest when white or colors close together and near the middle of the color spectrum (cyan, green, yellow) are used (Silverstein, 1987). It might be advisable, therefore, to use these colors for text displays and avoid colors at both ends of the color spectrum, especially when extended reading from the screen is expected.

☞ **Choose symbol and background color combinations carefully.**

In general, display *color images* on an *achromatic background* (black, gray, or white) or *achromatic images* on a *color background* (ISO, 1988). This allows better color discrimination and more contrast than color images on color backgrounds. Color images on color backgrounds do not create well-defined images unless the colors differ significantly in brightness as well as hue (Murch, 1987b). However, especially for thin line images, avoid gray on color backgrounds, as it tends to take on the appearance of a desaturated value of the color complement of the background color (color complements are colors that produce white or gray when mixed additively).

If color images *are* displayed on color backgrounds for some reason, then background and symbol colors should contrast in both brightness and hue to ensure legibility (ISO, 1988).

For some images, color discrimination is easier on a light background than on a dark background. On a light background, colors are perceived as more saturated and thus more dissimilar from one another. Light backgrounds not only facilitate color perception, but the color contrast between the light background and color symbol reduces the need for a luminance contrast between them (Silverstein, 1987).

On the other hand, there are some disadvantages to a light background (Smith, 1987). Flicker is usually more apparent, and glare may be more of a problem. Characters and other thin line images look smaller on a light as opposed to a dark background, because of the blooming effect of light colors on a dark background. Characters may thus be less readable at a distance if they appear on a light background. If these factors can be reasonably controlled, however, the advantages of a light background are significant. Thus it appears that *dark backgrounds are better for color text, while light backgrounds may be better for larger graphical symbols.*

Enough color and brightness contrast between symbol and background colors is important for legibility. Yellow on white or blue on black will be difficult to read. One study of 24 symbol–background color combinations (Pace, 1984) found that black text on blue backgrounds and blue text on white backgrounds resulted in fewer errors than magenta on green and green on white combinations. Because many other studies suggest that saturated blue text is less legible than other colors (Silverstein, 1987), it is not recommended.

Some foreground–background color combinations recommended for text displays are given next (from Lalomia and Happ, 1987):

				Background				
Foreground	Black	Blue	Green	Cyan	Red	Magenta	Brown	White
Black				×		×		×
Blue								×
Green	×	×		×				
Cyan	×							
White	×							
Bold green	×							
Bold cyan	×	×		×	×	×		
Bold magenta	×		×					
Yellow	×	×		×		×		
Bold white	×		×	×				

In three-dimensional displays, it should also be kept in mind that color in and of itself creates depth effects. For most people, reds appear closer and appear to advance forward, while blues appear more distant and appear to be receding (Murch, 1987b).

It should also be kept in mind that some colors that are legible in normal video (colored characters on a black background) are less legible in reverse video (black characters on a colored background). In these cases, legibility may be improved by defining reverse video as a white (rather than black) character on a colored background (Brown, 1988).

☞ **Consider viewing angle and distance in assigning symbol colors.**

Viewing angle and distance influence color perception. The ISO (1988) recommends the following guidelines:

Avoid red and green beyond 40 degrees of viewing angle.

Avoid yellow beyond 50 degrees of viewing angle.

Avoid blue beyond 60 degrees of viewing angle.

Use highly saturated colors and colors with high luminance contrast for viewing distances beyond 60 centimeters.

Avoid saturated colors on dark backgrounds for viewing distances beyond 60 centimeters.

☞ **Heavy use of highly saturated colors, opposing colors, or colors far apart on the color spectrum may cause afterimages, shadows, and depth effects.**

Opposing colors (yellow and blue or red and green), highly saturated colors, and colors far apart on the spectrum (for example, yellow and purple) used heavily on the same display or across displays may cause after-images and shadows (Galitz, 1985; ISO, 1988). The heavy use of colors far apart on the color spectrum also requires constant refocusing of the eye. Although no evidence exists that this will cause eye fatigue (Smith, 1987), it does result in visual discomfort, and it seems a good idea to avoid this possibility when no particular purpose is accomplished by the use of colors far apart on the color spectrum.

☞ **To express contrast or difference, choose high-contrast colors. To express similarity, choose low-contrast colors.**

In spite of the preceding guideline, when the task depends on discriminating between types of information, colors that are high contrast, that is, farther apart on the color spectrum and/or very different in brightness, are appropriate (Galitz, 1985). For instance, in Figure 14-26, red and green were chosen partly because they are fairly far apart on the color spectrum, and the task required quick and accurate discrimination between items coded in those colors. (Choosing reds and greens that contrast in saturation and lightness–brightness will ensure that users with red–green color blindness will still be able to discriminate between them.) Examples of other color combinations with high contrast include red–turquoise (or cyan), blue–yellow, green–pink (or magenta), red–green–blue, and red–green–blue–white (Brown, 1988).

On the other hand, when the task simply involves focusing attention on one rather than another type of information, rather than discriminating between them quickly and reliably, or when similarity is meant to be conveyed, then low-contrast colors are appropriate (Galitz, 1985). For instance, in Figure 14-28 (see back endpaper), white is used to display data from a file, while yellow is used for borders and instructions. The color difference, although slight, is enough to help the user focus on the data and tune out the "noise" of the instructions, or vice versa. An example of exploiting similarity in colors to communicate similarity in data would be to use red for accounts 60 days past due and pink for accounts only 30 days past due (Brown, 1988). Both are past due and differ only in degree. The similarity in *hue* signals this relationship, while the contrast in *saturation* differentiates the degree of lateness.

Other color combinations that appear to be similar include red–pink, yellow–orange, red–orange, blue–violet, and blue–turquoise (Brown, 1988). Keep in mind the preceding guideline to avoid the heavy use of opposing or high-contrast colors, and only do so when in fact discrimination is the key task being supported by color. The ISO (1988) recommends some color combinations that provide high and low contrast, as follows:

High Contrast	
Symbol	Background
White	Black
Green	Black
Cyan	Black
Yellow	Black
Blue	White
Black	White
Yellow	Blue
Red	Cyan
Magenta	Green

Low Contrast	
Symbol	Background
Blue	Black
Blue	Yellow
Red	Black
Red	Yellow
Cyan	White
Cyan	Green
Magenta	Red

☞ **Use light and bright, saturated colors to emphasize data, and use darker and duller, desaturated colors to de-emphasize data.**

In Figure 14-28, white was assigned to data and yellow to instructions for a particular reason. The white is a "lighter" color (see the definition of *lightness* earlier in this section) than the yellow in this display, and the intent was to draw the users' attention to the data. The lighter color accomplishes this. Often in displays we see lighter colors applied to such things as screen titles, copyright notices, and time and date fields. Usually these are the least important data on the screen, yet the eye is drawn to them because of their lightness. Reserve lightness for items that require user attention.

Use brightness (see the definition of *brightness* earlier in this section) in the same way. Brighter colors should be reserved for calling attention to special items.

☞ **Use colors consistently to code physical expressions, continuums, and states.**

The ISO (1988) recommends the following guidelines for using color to code physical impressions, continuums, and states:

Larger size:	Saturated or bright colors
Smaller size:	Desaturated or dark colors
Equal size:	Colors equal in brightness
Heaviness:	Saturated, dark colors
Lightness:	Desaturated, light colors
Depth:	Saturated, dark colors
Closeness:	Saturated, bright colors
Height:	Desaturated, light colors
Low-end continuum:	Short-wavelength dark colors
High-end continuum:	Long-wavelength bright colors

Also, colors with high contrast in both hue and brightness should be used to indicate state changes (for example, off–on and active–nonactive) and discrete indicators (for example, start–stop).

☞ **Use different colors for different fill patterns.**

When symbols have a fill pattern rather than a solid color, the ISO (1988) recommends the following use of colors in combinations with different fill patterns, depending on the screen background color:

BLACK BACKGROUND:

Widely spaced dots:	Yellow
Widely spaced diagonals:	Green
Widely spaced crosshatch:	Cyan
Closely spaced dots:	Magenta
Closely spaced diagonals:	Red
Closely spaced crosshatch:	Blue

WHITE BACKGROUND:

Widely spaced dots:	Red
Widely spaced diagonals:	Magenta
Widely spaced crosshatch:	Cyan
Closely spaced dots:	Green
Closely spaced diagonals:	Blue
Closely spaced crosshatch:	Yellow

☞ **Color discrimination is harder if items are small, far apart in distance, and/or close together on the spectrum.**

When using color to assist users in discriminating between items, for example, in a search task, it is important to keep in mind that color discrimination is not absolute, but is affected by other aspects of the display. If two colors are close together on the spectrum, such as red and orange or green and blue, then it becomes harder to discriminate between them as they grow smaller (Silverstein, 1987) and as they are positioned farther apart. For instance, two large circles, one green and one blue, may be easy to tell apart, but two small circles of the same colors may look identical. Small objects tend to become desaturated and show a shift in hue. Blues and yellows are particularly subject to this effect (Murch, 1987b).

Similarly, two circles close together may look like different colors, but the same two circles farther apart may look identical in color. If you are using size or distance as well as color for coding, it is important to keep these facts in mind.

The ISO (1988) recommends a minimum size for color images. All images should subtend at least 16 minutes of arc. However, blue and yellow images should subtend at least 20 minutes of arc. For users over 60 years of age, images should subtend at least 30 minutes of arc, as color discrimination decreases with age.

☞ **Warm colors appear larger than cool colors.**

Warm colors such as red, yellow, and orange seem to appear larger than *cool* colors such as green, blue, and violet (Tedford, Berquist, and Flynn, 1977). This should be kept in mind if size is being used as a cue, as well as color. Two circles of the same size may actually be perceived as different sizes if one is red and the other is blue. If size is being interpreted by users in some important way, this effect of color could cause errors.

☞ **Color sensitivity changes under different lighting conditions.**

Environmental lighting is another factor to consider when designing the use of color on displays. Two colors that look different in normal or dim light might be indistinguishable in bright light. Bright light tends to make colors appear washed out or unsaturated. Extremely dim light will also alter color perception. Most of the guidelines for color combinations given previously only hold for lighting conditions between 200 to 500 lux (ISO, 1988; the lux is the international unit of measurement for illumination).

Reds and blues will not be as discriminable in dim lighting as will greens and yellows, because the eye is most sensitive to wavelengths in the middle of the visible spectrum, as opposed to the extremes.

☞ **The use of color can improve user satisfaction.**

Some studies, which included subjective measures of user preference and satisfaction as well as objective measures of performance, suggest that, even when *performance* is not significantly enhanced by the use of color in displays, users may *prefer* color displays over monochrome displays. Users suggest that color displays are less monotonous, more natural, and less fatiguing. There is in fact some evidence that color displays do result in less fatigue than monochrome displays; this seems to be due to the fact that, since color is such an effective cue, it actually reduces eye scanning movements in search tasks and mental exertion in identification and interpretation tasks (Smith, 1987). Users may also believe color enhances their performance even when no objective evidence of this can be found (Christ, 1975). When user satisfaction is just as important as user performance, it may be wise to use color in displays even when no significant performance improvement would be achieved. Color must still be used in task-related ways, however, so that it does not in fact degrade performance. The application of all the preceding guidelines will ensure this.

☞ **Color trades off against resolution.**

It is important to keep in mind that color monitors generally have lower resolution than their monochrome counterparts. This is due to the burden on computer memory of storing color information. Color should only be used if the benefits it provides outweigh the cost in loss of resolution. This will be determined by the nature of the tasks involved in the application.

☞ **Establish and follow simple rules for color coding.**

Using the previous guidelines to select appropriate colors for different purposes, establish some simple rules for the use of colors and then follow those rules consistently throughout the interface. Each color used should be assigned a single meaning. The same meaning should not be coded by different cues in different places, and different meanings should not be coded by the same color. Figures 14–29 and 14–30 offer a sample set of such rules. Figure 14–29 documents rules for background colors in a windowed interface, and Figure 14–30 documents rules for text colors on these background colors. This set of rules is based on a color palette available on some Sun workstations, and is designed to maximize overall legibility while drawing attention to key control objects (icons) and data fields.

BACKGROUND COLORS

BACKGROUND	COLOR
Screen	BG1 (Turquoise)
Windows	
Input e.g. Menu Options	Wheat

Output
 	
    e.g.   Static Data
              E-mail
              Help
	Light Gray

Active	White
Icons	
Application A	Cornflower Blue
Application B	Sky Blue
Application C	Aquamarine
Mail	
Contains Mail	White
Empty	Yellow-Green
Calculator	Med. Sea Green
Pointer	
Ready	Black
Waiting	Red/Bold

Figure 14–29   Sample color rules: background colors.

TEXT COLORS

TEXT	COLOR
Captions	
Uncoded	Black
Key	Black/Bold
Fields	
Uncoded	Forest Green
Key e.g. zip code Name	(Color)/Bold
Debits	Firebrick
Credits	Dark Orchid
Messages	
Prompts	Forest Green/Bold
Status	
Success	Forest Green/Bold
Error	Red/Bold
Warning	Red/Bold
Wait	Red/Bold/Blink

Figure 14–30   Sample color rules: text colors.

REFERENCES

BERGUM, BRUCE O., and JUDITH E. BERGUM, "Population Stereotypes: An Attempt to Measure and Define," *Proceedings of the Human Factors Society 25th Annual Meeting,* 1981, pp. 662–65.

BROWN, C. MARLIN, *Human–Computer Interface Design Guidelines* (Norwood, N.J.: Ablex Publishing Corporation, 1988), pp. 65–78.

BURNS, J. J., D. L. WARREN, and M. RUDISILL, "Formatting Space-related Displays to Optimize Expert and Nonexpert User Performance," *CHI '86 Proceedings,* April 1986, pp. 274–80, ACM.

CHRIST, RICHARD E., "Review and Analysis of Color Coding Research for Visual Displays," *Human Factors,* 17, no. 6 (1975), pp. 542–70.

COURTNEY, ALAN J., "Chinese Population Stereotypes: Color Associations," *Human Factors,* 28, no. 1 (February 1986), pp. 97–100.

DURRETT, H. JOHN, ed., *Color and the Computer* (Orlando, Fla: Academic Press, Inc., 1987).

FONTENELLE, GAIL A., "A Contrast of Guideline Recommendations and Tullis's Prediction Model for Computer Displays: Should Text Be Left-justified?" *Proceedings of the Human Factors Society 31st Annual Meeting,* 1987, pp. 1226–28.

GALITZ, WILBERT O., *Handbook of Screen Format Design* (Wellesley Hills, Mass.: QED Information Sciences, Inc., 1985), pp. 153–62.

—— *Handbook of Screen Format Design* 3rd ed. (Wellesley, Mass: QED Information Sciences, Inc., 1989), pp. 203–219.

GREEN, B. F., and L. K. ANDERSON, "Color Coding in a Visual Search Task," *Journal of Experimental Psychology,* 51 (1956), pp. 19–24.

ISO Draft Standard 924X, Computer Display Color, August 19, 1988.

LALOMIA, MARY J., and ALAN J. HAPP, "The Effective Use of Color for Text on the IBM 5153 Color Display," *Proceedings of the Human Factors Society 31st Annual Meeting,* 1987, pp. 1091–95.

LURIA, S. M., DAVID F. NERI, and ALAN R. JACOBSEN, "The Effects of Set Size on Color Matching Using CRT Displays," *Human Factors,* 28, no. 1 (February 1986), pp. 49–62.

MATTHEWS, MICHAEL L., and KARIN MERTINS, "The Influence of Color on Visual Search and Subjective Discomfort Using CRT Displays," *Proceedings of the Human Factors Society 31st Annual Meeting,* 1987, pp. 1271–75.

MURCH, GERALD, "Color Displays and Color Science," in H. John Durrett, ed., *Color and the Computer* (Orlando, Fla.: Academic Press, Inc., 1987a), pp. 1–25.

MURCH, GERALD M., "Colour Graphics—Blessing or Ballyhoo?" *Readings in Human–Computer Interaction,* Ronald M. Baecker and William A. S. Buxton, eds. (Los Altos, Calif.: Morgan Kaufmann Publishers, Inc., 1987b), pp. 333–41.

NEWSOME, SANDRA L., and MICHAEL E. HOCHLERIN, "When 'Not' Is Not Bad: A Reevaluation of the Use of Negatives," *Proceedings of the Human Factors Society 33rd Annual Meeting,* 1989, pp. 229–33.

PACE, BRUCE J., "Color Combinations and Contrast Reversals on Visual Display Units," *Proceedings of the Human Factors Society 28th Annual Meeting,* October 1984, pp. 326–30.

PERLMAN, GARY, "An Axiomatic Model of Information Presentation," *Proceedings of the Human Factors Society 31st Annual Meeting,* 1987, pp. 1229–33.

RUBINSTEIN, RICHARD, and HARRY HERSH, *The Human Factor: Designing Computer Systems for People,* (Burlington, Mass.: Digital Press, 1984), pp. 163–74.

SCHWARTZ, DAVID R., "The Impact of Task Characteristics on Display Format Effects," *Proceedings of the Human Factors Society 32nd Annual Meeting,* 1988, pp. 352–56.

SHNEIDERMAN, BEN, *Designing the User Interface: Strategies for Effective Human–Computer Interaction* (Reading, Mass.: Addison-Wesley Publishing Co., 1986), pp. 336–42.

SILVERSTEIN, LOUIS D., "Human Factors for Color Display Systems: Concepts, Methods, and Research," in H. John Durrett, ed., *Color and the Computer* (Orlando, Fla.: Academic Press, Inc., 1987), pp. 27–61.

SMITH, SIDNEY L., and MOSIER, JANE N., *Guidelines for Designing User-Interface Software,* The Mitre Corporation, 1986.

SMITH, WANDA, "Ergonomic Vision," in H. John Durrett, ed., *Color and the Computer* (Orlando, Fla.: Academic Press, Inc., 1987), pp. 101–13.

———, "Standardizing Colors for Computer Screens," *Proceedings of the Human Factors Society 32nd Annual Meeting,* 1988, pp. 1381–85.

SPOTO, CHERYL G., and A. J. G. BABU, "Highlighting in Alphanumeric Displays: The Efficacy of Monochrome Methods," *Proceedings of the Human Factors Society 33rd Annual Meeting,* 1989, pp. 370–74.

TEDFORD, W. H., S. L. BERQUIST, and W. E. FLYNN, "The Size–Color Illusion," *Journal of General Psychology,* 97, no. 1, (July 1977), pp. 145–49.

THACKER, PRATAPRAY, T. S. TULLIS, and A. J. G. BABU, "Application of Tullis' Visual Search Model to Highlighted and Non-Highlighted Tabular Displays," *Proceedings of the Human Factors Society 31st Annual Meeting,* 1987, pp. 1221–25.

THOMPSON, RICHARD F., *Introduction to Physiological Psychology* (New York: Harper & Row, Publishers, 1975), pp. 197–213.

TROLLIP, STANLEY R., and GREGORY SALES, "Readability of Computer-generated Fill-justified Text," *Human Factors,* 28, no. 2 (April 1986), pp. 159–64.

TULLIS, THOMAS S., "The Formatting of Alphanumeric Displays: A Review and Analysis," *Human Factors,* 25, no. 6 (1983), pp. 657–82.

———, "Predicting the Usability of Alphnumeric Displays," *Doctoral Dissertation, Rice University,* 1984, available from The Report Store, Lawrence, Kansas.

———, "A System for Evaluating Screen Formats," *Proceedings of the Human Factors Society 30th Annual Meeting,* October 1986, pp. 1216–20.

———, "Screen Design," *Handbook of Human–Computer Interaction,* Martin Helander, ed. (Amsterdam: North-Holland, 1988), pp. 377–411.

WILLIAMS, JAMES R., "The Effects of Case and Spacing on Menu Option Search Time," *Proceedings of the Human Factors Society 32nd Annual Meeting,* 1988, pp. 341–43.

———, and WILLIAM A. LEAF, "Subjective and Objective Judgements of Screen Formats," *Proceedings of the Human Factors Society 30th Annual Meeting,* 1986, pp. 689–93.

WILLIGES, BEVERLY, H., and ROBERT C. WILLIGES, "Dialogue Design Considerations for Interactive Computer Systems," in Frederick A. Muckler, ed., *Human Factors Review* (Santa Monica, Calif: Human Factors Society, 1984), pp. 167–208.

CHAPTER 15

Response Time

System response time is the one aspect of computer–human interfaces that has always been considered important. Vendor companies have long set up minimum acceptability criteria for *system performance* and tested this aspect of hardware and software design. It has always been an aspect of the competitive edge. This is in contrast to other aspects of software user interface design, such as dialog and screen design, which have only recently been considered aspects of the competitive edge and received any significant attention.

On the other hand, simple *computer* response time is not really the relevant measure, as far as usability is concerned. What will be considered acceptable computer performance by users will depend on a number of other interacting factors.

GENERAL OBSERVATIONS

Two general observations can be made regarding system response time:

1. Overall task time is the relevant measure.
2. Users will adapt to system response time.

These observations are discussed next. Then experimental results are reviewed, and principles and guidelines are offered.

Overall Task Time Is the Relevant Measure

Although system response time is certainly an important aspect of the software user interface, like everything else, it should not be considered in isolation. Overall **task time** is the relevant measure to users. If the *system* is fast in responding, but everything else about the software user interface design results in slow *user response time,* then the system will not be perceived by users as fast, easy to use, and efficient.

Overall *task time* (for example, the time to open an electronic mail box, scroll through entries, and select a piece of mail to be viewed) can be viewed as the sum of several *system* and *user* response time elements, as illustrated in Figure 15-1. **System response time** here refers to the time between user input and the onset of system output. **System display rate,** on the other hand, refers to the time it takes to complete the display of a screen, once the system has begun to do so.

User scan/read time refers to the time it takes users to read and recognize data on a new screen or scan through it to find something they are searching for. **User think time** is the time it takes users to interpret data in the context of their task, make decisions, and form intentions for subsequent actions. Finally, **user response time** refers to the time to execute motor actions (such as selecting a pick from a menu or pointing to an icon with a mouse) once the user has decided on them.

Time making errors and **time recovering from errors** are two additional aspects of overall user response time that must also be figured into any measure of overall task time. Their impact depends on both the probability of making errors and the recovery time per error.

Often, complex user interface code added to an application slows down a system. This may be appropriate, however, if the user interface results in less user read, scan, and think time and less time spent making and recovering from errors, because these reduced times may more than cancel out the increased system response time and thus result in an improvement in overall task time. This is why system response time should not be measured and evaluated in isolation from the

> Task Time = system response time
>
> + system display rate
>
> + user scan/read time
>
> + user think time
>
> + user response time
>
> + time making errors
>
> + time recovering from errors

Figure 15–1   Overall user task time as a function of system and user response times.

Fast RT, fast error recovery = low user think time
high user errors
high user satisfaction
low stress

Fast RT, slow error recovery = moderate user think time
moderate user errors
moderate user satisfaction
moderate stress

Slow RT, slow error recovery = high user think time
low user errors
low user satisfaction
high stress

Figure 15-2 Adaptive user strategies to varying system response (RT) and error recovery times.

other components of task time listed in Figure 15-1. Users do not care as much about the time it takes a computer to complete a given step as they do about the time it takes them to accomplish something useful.

Users Will Adapt to System Response Time

Generally, people perform tasks faster and express more satisfaction when system response time is fast. Instantaneous response times are extremely important for simple input operations such as echoing keystrokes in response to typing or moving the pointer in response to mouse movements. However, for more complex operations, people adapt to slower systems to optimize overall task time. Figure 15-2 summarizes how users adapt to systems that have different response times (RT) and error recovery rates.

When *system response time is fast and error recovery is easy and fast* (for example, there is an "undo" function available, which reverses any user action in a single keystroke), users may adopt a trial and error approach and spend less time thinking through their actions. With this approach they may make more errors, but errors provide them with concrete feedback. Acting hastily and making errors is not costly on such a system, and it is sometimes easier to simply see if something works than to try to reason abstractly through whether it will work or not, in the absence of feedback. Usually, user stress is low and satisfaction is high on a system with fast response time and easy error recovery.

When *response time is fast, but error recovery is not necessarily fast and easy* (no "undo" function), users tend to think through their actions a little more carefully, making errors where the consequences of errors are not too costly and avoiding errors where the consequences are more costly. Since some errors are costly and users must therefore be more careful and think through their actions, user satisfaction is a bit lower and stress is a bit higher compared to the response time situation described previously.

Finally, when *response time is slow and error recovery is not necessarily fast and easy* (no "undo" function), then users tend to think through their actions very carefully, avoiding errors at all costs. This is very stressful and results in low satisfaction, although it is an optimal strategy under the circumstances and results in the maximum overall throughput.

RESPONSE TIME: EXPERIMENTAL RESULTS

A number of studies have been reported on various aspects of response time. Some representative studies are discussed here.

One study (Barber and Lucas, 1983) explored how system response time affects overall task time, or general productivity. Real use of an interactive system was tracked by a software monitor, which provided data on the total number of transactions completed successfully, the total number of transactions in error, and the system response time associated with the transactions, which varied widely on the system. User tasks were very complex, involving several transactions with difficult decisions made among them. In Figure 15-3, the number of transactions is plotted against the different system response times that occurred in the sample. Three different curves are presented. The *total transactions* at each response time is a simple sum of the number of successful or error-free transactions (*productive transactions*) plus the number of transactions in error (*total errors*).

Although the total number of transactions generally decrease with increased response time, it can be seen that the *proportion* of the total transactions that are

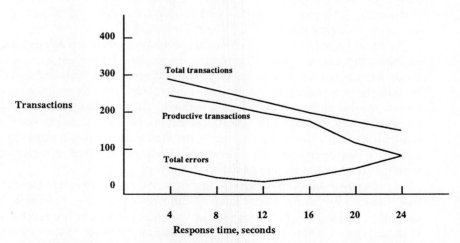

Figure 15–3 A study of system and user response time. From Barber and Lucas, "System Response Time, Operator Productivity, and Job Satisfaction," *Communications of the ACM,* 26, no. 11 (1983), 972–86. With permission.

successful versus in *error* changes significantly as response time increases, and the relationship is not a simple one. In particular, errors decrease between response times of 4 to 12 seconds and then steadily increase after 12 seconds.

One possible interpretation of these data is that, as response time increases from 4 to 8 seconds, users switch from a strategy of trial and error to a strategy of more deliberately thinking through their responses to avoid errors, because the increased response time means errors are more costly in terms of recovery time. At a certain point (roughly 12 seconds), however, longer response times start to interfere with human short-term memory limitations, and users start making more errors, not as a conscious strategy but because they lose track of what they are doing while waiting for the system to respond.

That is, while system response time places limits on the total number of transactions possible in a given time period, users can adapt to slower response times by increasing their own response time to minimize costly errors, thus optimizing overall throughput. At some point, however, when system response time starts taxing human memory, users can no longer adopt helpful strategies, and while overall transactions continue to decrease at a steady, gradual rate, many more of those transactions are errors, as opposed to successful transactions.

A second study (Tombaugh, Arkin, and Dillon, 1985) sought to determine how *system display rate* (characters displayed on the screen per second) affects reading and comprehension. The data from this study also suggest that users adopt different strategies to deal with different system response times.

Ninety undergraduate psychology majors participated in this study. Half had no prior computer experience at all, and another quarter had experience only with computer games. All users read single-spaced text from a screen of 24 rows and 80 columns. Their task was to read a single screen passage and answer four comprehension questions that were available on paper throughout the task. Different groups of users used systems with different display rates. The display rates corresponded to 150-, 300-, 1200-, and 9600-baud rate settings. The actual display rates in these conditions were measured at 15, 30, 133, and 860 characters per second (cps), respectively. A condition of instantaneous display rate was also included, in which all the text appeared on the screen simultaneously.

The average reading rate of people reading from a printed page is 25 to 30 cps. Thus the condition of 300 baud or 30 cps in this study most closely corresponds to the maximum reading rate of people. Other conditions displayed text either faster or slower than the eye typically reads.

Users performed on six passages with four questions each. They were told to work as quickly as possible, but also to answer questions correctly. They were measured for both time and errors.

Task time did not vary much across conditions (except that 15 cps, a rate below normal reading rate, slowed performance), and there did not seem to be any significant practice effects. However, the number of *errors* did vary with display rate, and these data are summarized in Figure 15-4. Here it can be seen that the highest comprehension scores were achieved on the display rates that were either

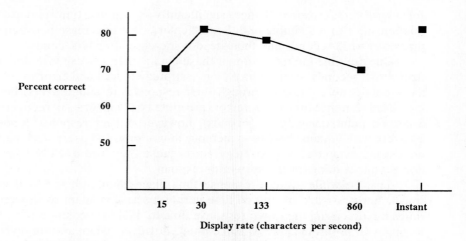

Figure 15–4 A study of system display rate and user reading performance. From Tombaugh, Arkin, and Dillon, ''The Effect of VDU Text-Presentation Rate on Reading Comprehension and Reading Speed,'' *Proceedings, CHI '85.* 1985, 1–6. With permission.

instantaneous or matched reading speed (30 cps). If the display rate was much slower or much faster than the reading rate, errors increased.

The authors' interpretation of these data is that users adopted different problem-solving strategies depending on display rate, and these strategies were more or less effective. For instance, a user might read the text while it is being displayed, or wait to read it until the whole screen is displayed. Or a user might read a passage, then read the questions and then scan back through the passage to confirm answers. Or the user might first read the questions and then only scan the passage to try to find answers.

At 15 cps, users cannot read or scan efficiently, so they might be encouraged to adopt the strategy of reading the questions while the text was being displayed and then scanning the text for answers under the time pressure of the experiment. Thus they could complete tasks efficiently, but perhaps at the expense of more errors.

At 30 cps, users could read but not scan the text efficiently while it was being displayed. Thus they might be encouraged to read the text first and then answer questions, scanning back to confirm only when necessary. This might also be efficient, but might result in less errors.

At 96 and 120 cps, on the other hand, the fact that display was fast but not instantaneous might encourage users to scan, trying to keep up with the display rate, and then answer questions. As with the 15-cps strategy, this might be efficient, but also more error prone.

Finally, when the display is instantaneous, users can choose the optimal strategy to minimize both task time and errors, as display rate is neither a constraint nor a distraction.

In sum, users might have been adopting different strategies to optimize task speed under the different display rate conditions, and the strategies may have varied in effectiveness, resulting in the different error rates observed.

We do not really know from this study *how* display rate affects performance in this task, only that it does. Nor do we know if this might be a temporary effect for new users unfamiliar with computer systems. It does seem plausible that, given display rates and task dimensions (such as pressure for speed and/or accuracy), users may adopt different problem-solving strategies to best accomplish the task. It is possible to imagine strategies (such as those described) that would produce the data observed in this experiment, although the data do not directly confirm these speculations.

What is clear is that reading comprehension by computer novices can, under some circumstances, be affected by the display rate of information on the screen. Since the mechanism responsible for this is not clear, it is not advised to reduce the display rate unless more is understood about the conditions giving rise to the results. Instead, it is advised that in situations where accuracy in reading comprehension is critical the reading material should be displayed instantaneously, or user testing should be conducted, using the reading material of the application and members of the user group, to make sure that reading comprehension is not adversely affected by the display method and rate.

Another study (Butler, 1983) investigated the effects of *response time* and *response time variability* on user performance.

Five typists with little or no computer experience participated in this study. They performed tasks that involved going back and forth between two screens, transcribing data from one to the other. They were told to be as fast as possible, but also as accurate as possible.

Each of the five users performed the task under ten different response time conditions. These ten conditions consisted of five different response times (2, 4, 8, 16, and 32 seconds), each at two rates of response time variability (high and low). The five different response times represented *average* response times. In the high-variability conditions, *actual* response times varied very noticeably from the average, both faster and slower; in the low-variability conditions, response times varied only a little from the average, both faster and slower.

These experimental conditions did not have any significant effects on such aspects of user performance as number of errors made or typing time. They did, however, have some effect on user response time (the time from the display of a screen to the initial user response), and these data are presented in Figure 15-5. The effect of system response time on user response time was, statistically significant. Generally, the longer the average *system* response time was, the longer the initial *user* response time. Variability had a small but not statistically significant effect. User response times were slightly longer when variability was high. Other studies

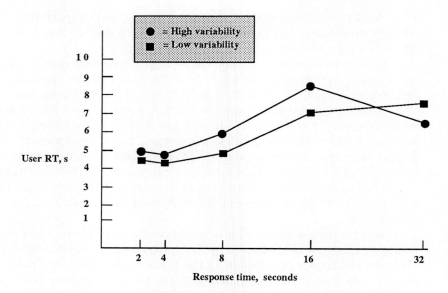

Figure 15–5 A study of system response time variability and user performance. From Butler, "Computer Response Time," *Proceedings, CHI '83,* 1983, 58–62. With permission.

have found response time variability to have a significant effect on user perform-ance.

It is interesting that the Butler study did not find an effect of response time on user errors, while the Barber and Lucas study did. This may be because the task in the Butler study was relatively simple, so that even with longer response times, human memory was not overtaxed, while the task in the Barber and Lucas study was much more complex, taxing short term memory to a greater degree. That is, it may be that longer response times will have more pronounced effects on the performance of more complex tasks.

While all these studies shed some interesting light on the user *performance* effects of different system response times, they do not comment on the *psychologi-cal* effects on users of longer system response times. Even when different user strategies allow them to maintain an optimal level of overall task time, it is possible that some strategies are more taxing than others, and thus more stressful and frustrating. It is also likely that even when longer response times do not seriously cut into overall accuracy or speed the sensation of being mentally idle may simply be frustrating.

At any rate, it is clear from these studies that system response time does not have a simple, clear relationship to general measures of human performance such as speed and accuracy. Rather, people are highly adaptive and will assume differ-ent problem-solving strategies to best cope with variations in system performance.

These intelligent adaptations obscure the meaning of the data we obtain from such studies as these and make interpretation somewhat speculative.

RESPONSE TIME: PRINCIPLES AND GUIDELINES

Based on the general observations and experimental studies discussed and reasoning from principles of human cognition, several guidelines can be offered for designing system response times when this is within the software designer's control.

☞ Optimal display rate depends on the user's task.

Based on the Tombaugh, Arkin, and Dillon (1985) study, it is recommended that, if the user's task is best accomplished by scanning (as opposed to reading), then an instantaneous (or close to instantaneous) display rate is desirable. Probably, most tasks on interactive applications, in fact, involve scanning and searching, as opposed to reading. The main exception to this would be text manipulation applications such as word processing and electronic mail systems.

If the user's task requires mainly reading rather than scanning or searching (for example, word processing), then an instantaneous rate or at least a rate comparable to the reading rate (25 to 30 characters per second, or 300 baud and up) is recommended. Rates slower than reading rates (for example, 150 baud) are not recommended in this case. Slower rates will impede user productivity.

☞ Response time for intermediate steps in a process should not exceed 2 seconds.

The Barber and Lucas (1983) study suggested that long response times may disrupt problem solving by taxing human short-term memory. Recall that the capacity of human working or short-term memory is only 7 ± 2 items, and the duration of information in working memory is only a few seconds unless the items are rehearsed repeatedly. In addition, the contents of working memory are erased by new input. If users must hold information in memory for more than a few seconds, they will start having problems remembering. Thus, when the user is waiting for feedback on some intermediate step on a task and holding context information in memory, response times that do not exceed a few seconds will keep errors due to memory loss at a minimum.

For example, when users are moving blocks of text from one document to another in a nonwindowing system, the intermediate steps between copying and pasting (that is, closing the source file and opening and scrolling the destination file) should each take no more than 2 seconds, because users must hold in memory what they have copied and where they want to copy it to while they are performing these operations.

☞ **Keep response time variability at less than ±50% of the mean.**

Although studies on the effects of response time variability are conflicting and inconclusive (Myers, 1985), response time variability of less than ±50% of the mean seems unlikely to affect performance significantly. Until more definitive research is reported, it seems safe to suggest that moderate variations will not significantly degrade user performance.

On the other hand, variations in response time may affect user satisfaction. Geist, Allen, and Nowaczyk (1987) found that users did not accurately perceive response time variations, and in fact their perceptions were heavily influenced by their most recent experience. And, human nature being what it is and given response times that vary around a mean, users will probably assume the best response times as the norm and be frustrated with slower ones, rather than assume the worst response times as the norm and be pleased with faster ones.

☞ **Make the sources of response time variability visible.**

Predictable variability is more acceptable to users than unpredictable variability. Users form mental models to predict system behavior. If they can find explanations for varying response times, and especially if variations are predictable, variable response times will be more psychologically acceptable than if response times seem random and unpredictable. For instance, if users understand that response time variations depend on the number of users currently on their time-sharing system, the variations will seem more acceptable than if the source of the variability is completely invisible to them. Furthermore, if they can predict the times of day that usage will be low and therefore response times will be faster, they will find this even more acceptable, because they might be able to plan their work around this predictable variation.

☞ **Make ease of learning and use versus response time trade-offs based on user experience and expectations.**

The desire for speed depends on experience level and frequency of use. *Fast* and *slow* are subjective, relative qualities. What one user considers slow, another user might consider fast. In general, computer novices are more accepting of slower response times because they have little to compare computer response times to, except doing comparable things in the manual world. Experts, on the other hand, prefer and perform better with faster response times. Experience with other systems creates expectations, and, generally, as computers become faster and faster, users' expectations simply rise along with them. Thus, a lot of complex code that makes a system easier to learn but slower may be preferable for novices. Experts may prefer a system that is faster, although less helpful.

☞ **Response times should be consistent with user expectations.**

All operations are not considered equal by users, and in fact they expect different kinds of operations to take varying amounts of time. They will have

Input: **instant response**

> Character echo
> Direct manipulation

Simple commands: **< 2 seconds**

> Paging
> Simple error checking
> Open file

Complex commands: **< 12 seconds**

> Load application
> Move across files
> Search

Complex processes: **12 seconds to many hours**

> Spelling checker
> Batch transaction processing

Figure 15–6 Suggested response time ranges for operations of varying perceived complexity.

simple models of what is a trivial versus a complex operation and will expect response times to be consistent with these models (Shneiderman, 1980). Figure 15-6 suggests response time ranges that might be consistent with user expectations for different operations.

Generally, users will expect instant feedback from simple input, such as typing, selecting, or dragging objects across the screen. Note here that what the user considers to be a trivial operation is not necessarily trivial for the computer. Dragging a window across the screen might seem simple enough to the user, but making this happen in real time is no simple matter from a technical viewpoint. Nevertheless, user expectations for response time will be based on their *perception* of the relative complexity of the operation, and they may have no insight into the technical underpinnings of the operation.

At the other end of the spectrum, users will expect slow response times for operations that seem complex and labor intensive to them. For instance, if a batch spell-checker gave a "no errors detected" message for a 300-page document after only 2 seconds, users might be doubtful and suspicious and not believe that the operation was actually carried out. They might rerun the spell checker several times "to be sure." Again, they do not understand the technical underpinnings of such operations and will base their expectations on the relative times analogous operations take in their manual world. Designers should *strive to provide fast response times where users expect them* and *provide informative messages when users are likely to be expecting long response times.*

☞ **Manage user expectations with feedback.**

As stated previously, users will have expectations that may or may not be met by a system's response times. Often, software designers cannot achieve the levels

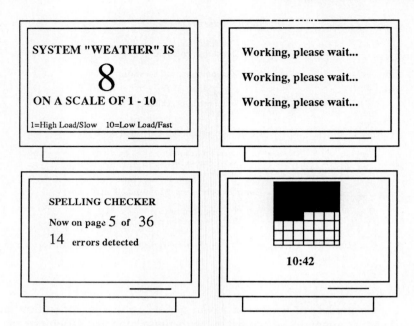

Figure 15-7 Status reporting techniques for delayed system response times.

of response time that would meet these expectations. When this is the case, the next best thing is to try and manage user expectations. This can be done in several ways, some of which are illustrated in Figure 15-7.

First, *make sources of variability visible*. That is, give information such as the relative or actual number of users currently on a time-sharing system (for example, the "system weather" message in Figure 15-7) to give users an understanding of the *sources* of slower response times and a general idea of the *level* of response time that they can currently expect.

When possible, *give estimates of expected delays*. The first and last examples in Figure 15-7 do this. The first gives the user an overall picture of system response times at the current time. In the last example, the response time of a particular, current operation is represented as an area that is gradually filled in, indicating the relative proportion of the overall operation that has currently been completed. The time clock below tells users how long the currently completed portion of the task took, allowing them to estimate the time left before the whole operation will be complete.

Provide status on progress. All but the first example in Figure 15-7 do this. The example in the upper-right simply assures people that progress is being made, and the system in fact has not crashed. Even this is reassuring. The bottom two examples, on the other hand, provide more detailed status information, which is constantly being updated as the operation is carried out. Myers (1985) found that users consistently preferred a system with progress indicators to one without. He suggests that novices will prefer progress indicators because it reassures them that their request has been accepted, and experts will prefer such indicators because they help them to plan their time more effectively.

While not actually improving the response time itself, these various kinds of feedback will give users more of a sense of control and satisfaction, because they will be able to manage their own time better with the information provided. If they can tell that the spell-checker is only processing about 1 page every 30 seconds, and they have submitted a 300-page document, they may choose to make a phone call or go get a cup of coffee. This will feel a lot different to them than sitting with their eyes glued to the screen, waiting and wondering what is going to happen when, even though the response time is the same. In general, as much specific information as can reasonably be provided should be whenever response times are expected to exceed around 15 seconds.

REFERENCES

BARBER, RAYMOND E., and HENRY C. LUCAS, JR., "System Response Time, Operator Productivity, and Job Statisfaction," *Communications of the ACM,* 26, no. 11 (1983), pp. 972–86.

BUTLER, T. W., "Computer Response Time," *Proceedings, CHI '83,* 1983, pp. 58–62, ACM.

GEIST, ROBERT, ROBERT ALLEN, and RONALD NOWACZYK, "Towards a Model of User Perception of Computer System Response Time," *CHI '87 Proceedings,* May 1987, pp. 249–54, ACM.

MYERS, BRAD A., "The Importance of Percent-done Progress Indicators for Computer–Human Interfaces," *CHI '85 Proceedings,* April 1985, pp. 11–18, ACM.

SHNEIDERMAN, BEN, *Software Psychology: Human Factors in Computer and Information Systems* (Cambridge, Mass.: Winthrop Publishers, Inc., 1980).

TOMBAUGH, JO, MICHAEL D. ARKIN, and RICHARD F. DILLON, "The Effect of VDU Text-Presentation Rate on Reading Comprehension and Reading Speed," *Proceedings, CHI '85,* 1985, pp. 1–6, ACM.

CHAPTER 16

Error Handling

One goal for a software user interface is to *minimize user errors*. To do this, a designer must understand the different types of errors that users might make and why they make them. Different kinds of errors can be prevented or at least reduced through different design techniques. Another goal for a user interface is to provide *easy recovery from errors* when they are made, because it will most likely be impossible to eliminate all errors.

This chapter presents an analysis of error types, some experimental data, guidelines for *preventing errors,* and guidelines for *facilitating error recovery*.

ERROR TYPES

User errors can be classified in several ways. One way is to consider errors in terms of the human information processing subsystem (or the user response phase) involved.

Referring back to Figure 2-2 (see Chapter 2), remember that the human side of the dialog can be thought of as occurring in three successive phases: the *read–scan* phase, the *think* phase, and the *respond* phase. These phases correspond to three subsystems of the human information processing system: the *perceptual* system, the *cognitive* system, and the *motor* system, respectively, as described in Chapter 2.

Users can make errors in each of the three phases of response, and the errors can be explained by the characteristics of the information processing subsystem associated with each phase. Thus, users can be said to make **perceptual errors, cognitive errors,** and **motor errors.** These three error types are explained and discussed next.

Perceptual Errors

Perceptual errors are caused by *insufficient perceptual cues* (for example, visual, auditory, and tactile), resulting in a failure to detect important information or discriminate correctly between display objects or types of feedback. For instance, *display objects that are visually similar* might be mistaken for one another. Two examples of this are offered here. In the first, characters that are visually similar, when presented on a low-resolution screen, might be mistaken for one another.

B/8   Z/2   I/1

In the second example, which follows, words are used to distinguish different objects. In this display of accounts, past due accounts (those whose due date is in the past, but that have not yet been paid) must be identified by words alone. Users who are scanning and trying to work quickly might make errors identifying past due accounts, making both false hits and misses, because words are simply not that easily discriminable when scanning. Color, capital letters, reverse video, or other equally salient visual cues could be used here to tag past due accounts, and this would greatly minimize searching errors.

Account	Due Date	Paid
A345	2/15	Yes
A410	2/15	No
B541	2/28	No

Another type of perceptual error results from *invisible modes* or states. If the system can be in different states and similar user actions have different effects in different states, then a lack of perceivable cues identifying states will result in "mode errors" (Norman, 1983).

For example, old-fashioned text editors used to have a command mode, in which users entered commands to operate on text, and a text mode, in which users entered text into a file. Often there was insufficient information to easily determine which mode one was in, and so users often entered commands in files and typed text intended for the file in the command line. Some sort of noticeable change in the appearance of the screen or different cursor areas for the two types of inputs could have prevented these errors.

Modern word processors also often have invisible modes, such as an insert mode or a caps lock mode. Users often forget they are in one of these modes and take actions that are inappropriate. For instance, they may type several paragraphs of capitalized text when they did not mean to, because they failed to detect that they were still in caps lock mode. Often designers in fact do provide perceptual cues for modes, but they turn out to be inadequate. Having a cue available is not sufficient. It must be an *effective* cue.

Another type of perceptual error is caused by a *failure to capture the user's attention*. For instance, important messages or data may be missed because they are visually indistinct from other parts of the display. Or instructions may be misread because they are poorly formatted.

Finally, perceptual errors include errors due to a *lack of perceivable feedback*. For instance, keys may be pressed in error or may not register when pressed due to a lack of auditory or tactile feedback from the keys.

Cognitive Errors

Cognitive errors are caused by *taxing the memory and problem-solving capabilities* of the human mind. For instance, some user interfaces *tax recall memory*. A command language with a positional syntax requires users to remember the proper order for specifying arguments. If they misremember, they will make an error. Insufficient instructions on a fill-in form may result in errors for infrequent users, who cannot remember between uses how to move the cursor from field to field or which function key to press to restore all the fields to their default values.

Another type of cognitive error results from a *lack of or poor mnemonic aids*. For instance, arbitrary function key assignments such as CMD/SHIFT/PF1 for moving a cursor to the bottom of the file will be hard to remember and result in errors. Menus using letter selection codes that are unassociated with the menu choice labels, as in the following example, may cause errors because people will have a tendency to press the first letter (which would be a mnemonic code) of the menu choice label.

> A. Create
> B. Delete
> C. Append
> D. Backup

Another type of cognitive error is caused by *inconsistencies*. Inconsistency can induce errors in almost all aspects of user interface design. For example, a command language syntax may have inconsistent argument order rules or inconsistent abbreviation rules (Norman, 1983). Instructions may use inconsistent terminology to describe the same operation on different screens. A different key may be used for the same function on different screens. Common menu choices may appear in different positions on different menus. In all these cases, users cannot learn one simple rule. They must rote memorize and then recall correctly the particular rules for each command, abbreviation, instruction, key, or menu screen.

Other cognitive errors result from a *lack of context or status information.* For instance, menus that do not include context information regarding where the user came from and what choices were made on the way may cause users to become disoriented and make errors, such as performing calculations on the wrong data. Command languages that do not provide feedback regarding the results of command execution may cause errors such as repeating commands or executing subsequent commands inappropriately.

Finally, cognitive errors may result from requiring users to perform *mental calculations and translations,* processes of the human mind that are quite error prone. For example, an interface that requires users to compare two lists and find items in common, translate inches into centimeters, or add numbers in their heads will likely produce a significant rate of errors. The system could easily perform these calculations and translations instead, and no errors would occur.

Motor Errors

Motor errors are caused by *taxing the eye–hand coordination and level of motor skill* of the users. For instance, requiring *awkward motor movements,* such as quick transitions between the fourth and little fingers or movement of one hand back and forth across the keyboard, may cause users to strike the wrong key.

Another type of motor error results from *highly similar motor sequences.* These are sometimes called "capture errors" (Norman, 1983). If the motor sequences of two operations are very similar, one sequence may be executed in place of the other by mistake. This will be especially true if one sequence is much more frequently executed than the other. For example, on the Macintosh, you click a mouse button once to select an object, but twice in rapid succession to "open" it. Users who frequently use the double click to open find that when they wish to only select an object they often double click and open by mistake.

In a command language, users who frequently use the command "sea" or "search" may type it by mistake when they mean to use the "sen" or "send" command. It would be much less likely that users would make this error if the "search" command were renamed "fnd" for find. It is the similarity of the motor sequences for typing "sea" and "sen" that induces the error.

Another type of motor error is caused by *pressure for speed.* Users make more errors in motor responses if they are pressured to perform quickly. For instance, if the interface has any timed sequences and users must make a motor response within a given time period in order to correctly execute an operation, users will make more errors if the time period is too short. Typists make more errors when they are pressured for speed.

Other motor errors result from *requiring a high degree of eye–hand coordination.* For instance, many pointing devices require a certain amount of learned eye–hand coordination. If targets are too small, users will make errors trying to hit them.

Finally, motor errors may result from *requiring other types of motor skills*. One estimate has it that 30% of all errors made on interactive systems are simple typos. Not all users have a high degree of typing skill. Users low in required motor skills will make more errors.

ERROR HANDLING: EXPERIMENTAL STUDIES

As we have seen in the previous discussion of error types, certain aspects of user interface design may induce certain types of errors. One study (Kraut, Hanson, and Farber, 1983) documented user errors on a system and found evidence of these different types of errors. In this study, usage data were collected by a software monitor from 170 expert, frequent users of a UNIX operating system over a period of 9 days. The users included office workers, programmers, managers, and technical staff performing their normal daily work. Among other things, the data collected allowed the tallying of errors. Error rates ranged from 3% to 50% for individual commands. That is, for some commands, users made errors one out of every two times they used the command. This is a high error rate indeed. In addition, error rates were often higher *after* an initial error. That is, the probability of making an error on a given command was higher after having just made one than for making one the first time. This indicates a serious problem with error handling. Clearly, users were not receiving adequate feedback to help them correct their errors.

The authors identified several sources of the errors made in their sample. In terms of the foregoing analysis of error types, four types of *cognitive errors* were identified: errors due to deviations from syntactic rules (inconsistencies), errors due to the need for nonvisible status information, such as a filename (lack of context or status information), lack of feedback after command execution (lack of context or status information), and poor error messages (lack of context or status information).

Mosteller and Ballas (1989) also collected error frequency data from real users of a security system through a software monitor that recorded and time stamped all system messages during interaction. Data were collected from 300 users over a 20-month period. Several observations were made. First, 12,117 error messages were recorded. The eleven most common error messages accounted for 65% of all error messages. Two thousand five hundred and seventeen of the 12,117 error messages involved identical messages repeated within a 10-minute period with no nonerror messages intervening. That is, these messages represented unsuccessful attempts to correct an initial error condition. In addition, the number of error messages did not change significantly from the first half of the 20-month period to the second half, suggesting that users did not learn to decrease their errors with practice. Mosteller and Ballas suggest that clearer and more constructive error messages could eliminate some of the repeated errors, and other techniques such as displaying valid options could help minimize errors in the first place.

Another study (Shneiderman, 1982) directly explored the effects of error message wording on error recovery. Forty undergraduates in an introductory programming course (novice COBOL programmers) tried to correct syntactic errors in a program based on diagnostic messages from a compiler. The messages were varied along two dimensions: *tone* and *specificity*. Examples of the four types of error messages included in the study are shown in Figure 16-1.

Three measures were taken. A *performance* measure (the number of successfully corrected errors) served as an objective measure of error message quality. In addition, two *satisfaction* measures were taken. Users were asked to rate the "comfort" and "helpfulness" of error messages on a scale of 1 to 5, where 1 was high and 5 was low.

Generally, it was found that more *specific* error messages resulted in significantly more successfully corrected errors. *Tone* had a small but statistically insig-

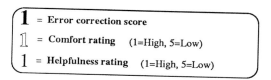

1 = **Error correction score**

1 = **Comfort rating**   (1=High, 5=Low)

1 = **Helpfulness rating**   (1=High, 5=Low)

S p e c i f i c i t y

	Normal	Improved
Normal	**10.7** 3.4 3.2 Illegal repeat count: character ignored	**15.3** 2.8 2.2 Nonnumeric picture-clause value: value ignored
Improved	**13.3** 3.3 2.7 Computer cannot recognize repeat count character; item not used	**15.4** 2.7 2.2 Computer only recognizes a numeric picture clause value; item not used

Tone

Figure 16–1 A study of error message design. From Shneiderman, "System Message Design: Guidelines and Experimental Results," in Badre and Shneiderman, Eds., *Directions in Human Computer Interaction.* (Norwood, NJ:Ablex Publishing Corp., 1982), 63–66. With permission.

nificant effect on corrected errors. Similar results were found on the satisfaction measures. Users rated more specific messages and messages with improved tone as more helpful. They also indicated they were generally more comfortable with them.

ERROR HANDLING: PRINCIPLES AND GUIDELINES

Guidelines for error handling can be divided into two categories: guidelines for **error prevention,** and guidelines for **error recovery.** A designer's first goal should be to minimize the number of errors that users will make. A second goal should be to make recovering from errors as easy and fast as possible.

Guidelines for Error Prevention

Guidelines for preventing errors are specific to the different error types described previously: perceptual errors, cognitive errors, and motor errors. Understanding how these errors occur provides some insight into how to design to prevent them.

☞ **Minimize perceptual errors.**

As discussed in the section on perceptual errors, *invisible modes* can be a source of errors. If certain actions or commands have different effects depending on the current mode, and the current mode is not readily apparent through perceptual cues, users are likely to assume they are in one mode when in fact they are in another and make errors as a result. One way to avoid this type of error altogether is to *eliminate modes*.

If eliminating modes altogether is not possible, then mode errors can at least be minimized by *providing salient, visible cues for modes* (see Norman, 1983). This will make it less likely that users will forget what mode they are in.

Other types of perceptual errors can be minimized by *using coding techniques* effectively to make different objects look more dissimilar. For instance, color, shape, reverse video, bold, and other visual codes can be used to facilitate search tasks and data interpretation and capture the users attention when necessary, thus reducing errors in these kinds of tasks. See Chapter 14 for a discussion on using visual coding techniques.

☞ **Minimize cognitive errors.**

Cognitive errors can be minimized in a number of different ways. *Maximizing recognition* versus *recall tasks* will reduce errors because recognition memory is less error prone than recall memory (Norman, 1983). Thus, for example, menus are less prone to cognitive errors than command languages.

Providing mnemonic aids will improve both recall and recognition memory.

Users will be better able to remember codes if they are closely associated with the object they code for. For instance, "M" is a more mnemonic code for "married" than "1" is. Whether the user is recalling the code to enter it in a field or recognizing the code in a display, the mnemonic will aid memory and reduce errors.

Building *consistency, rules, and patterns* into the interface will reduce the learning burden and thus reduce errors. For instance, a command language with command abbreviations that are always formed by truncating the command to the first three letters will produce less errors than a language that has no consistent rule for forming abbreviations.

Providing context and status information to orient users will prevent errors caused by misunderstanding the current context or status. For instance, if the current file name is not always displayed, users may perform an operation intended for another file by mistake. Always displaying the current file name will prevent this.

Minimizing mental calculation and transformations will reduce the errors associated with those processes in users. Human calculation and problem solving are quite error prone, especially when performed under pressure for speed. Computers, on the other hand, do not make these kinds of errors. Shifting from users to the computer whenever possible the burden of tasks such as translating inches to centimeters, comparing two lists for similarities, or adding numbers will reduce errors of this kind.

☞ **Minimize motor errors.**

Motor errors are caused by taxing the eye–hand coordination and level of motor skills of users. Minimizing the need for high skill levels will reduce motor errors. Errors brought about by awkward motor movements can be reduced by *careful key placement,* designing for the use of *alternate hands for common key sequences,* and *minimizing the use of SHIFT, CMD,* and other qualifier keys. *Home row indicators* will help reduce errors caused by misaligning the fingers before typing.

Errors due to highly similar motor sequences can be reduced by designing *nonsimilar motor sequences* (Norman, 1983). For instance, instead of the two commands "sea" for "search" and "sen" for "send," "srch" and "send" or "fin" for "find" and "sen" are less similar and thus may result in less errors.

Large targets and clear visual feedback will reduce errors due to poor eye–hand coordination. So will *cursor movement by meaningful units.* For instance, tabbing from icon to icon from the keyboard will be less error prone than selecting icons with a mouse, especially if the icons are small. Tabbing requires no eye–hand coordination, while pointing with a mouse does.

Minimizing the need for typing (for example, menu selection rather than fill-in, automatic command completion) will reduce errors associated with typing skill level.

☞ **Test and monitor for errors and "engineer" them out.**

Careful thought in the initial design, based on the guidelines given here, will go a long way toward minimizing user errors on a system. Even expert designers, however, will not anticipate all the errors users are likely to make in a given user interface design. There is no substitute for testing. Many common errors can be detected in prototype testing, and the interface can be redesigned to reduce or eliminate them. Systems in production can also be monitored for errors through software, human observation, or user reports so that later releases can be redesigned to eliminate common errors.

Testing to eliminate errors need only be done once by one engineer. But errors that are not eliminated may be committed over and over again by hundreds or even thousand of users. Usually the testing effort is easily cost justified.

Guidelines for Error Recovery

Even when a system has been designed and tested to eliminate common, serious errors, other errors will occur. It is impossible to design a truly error free user interface because users will always make simple motor errors such as typos or striking the wrong function key. Thus, besides minimizing errors, a good user interface must provide fast and easy error recovery. The following guidelines apply.

☞ **Provide the appropriate type of response.**

Lewis and Norman (1986) define six different types of possible system response to a user error.

Gag: Prevent the user from continuing, for example, lock the keyboard until the user takes some specific required action.

Warn: Note the occurrence of a potentially dangerous situation, but leave it to the user to decide how to respond.

Do nothing: Simply do not respond to an erroneous user action; for example, do not change the attributes of an object that the user has assigned an invalid attribute to.

Self-correct: Infer the intentions of the user and take appropriate action even if the action is not correctly specified; for instance, assume the user means "delete" when they type "delate."

Let's talk about it: Initiate a dialog with the user to clear up the problem.

Teach me: Query users to determine their intentions, and thereafter accept their previous action as legitimate; for example, accept "Exit" as a synonym for "Quit."

Lewis and Norman point out that these various responses are appropriate in different circumstances. For instance, the *do-nothing* response might be appropriate in a graphic, direct manipulation interface where the current state is always visually clear to the user, and error messages might simply add unnecessary clutter and interaction to the interface. However, it would not be very helpful in a command language environment where there are few other cues to the current state of the system.

The *self-correct* approach might be very useful in handling simple typos. However, in some situations where users intentions are more ambiguous, it might cause problems by resulting in erroneous assumptions by the system about what the user really intended, and would simply create additional errors that might be harder to diagnose and recover from.

The *gag* approach might be appropriate for preventing serious user mistakes, but it might be viewed as an unfriendly, brute-strength approach when consequences are less serious and a simple friendly warning would do. It also tends to discourage learning through experimentation.

It is important to consider the seriousness of the potential error, the complexity of the situation, and the availability and need for supporting information, as well as the more practical concerns of cost of implementation, when choosing between these possible types of system response to user errors.

☞ Provide an "undo" function.

Even the simplest of "undo" commands goes a long way. Most systems that provide "undo" do so through a single keystroke or menu pick. Most provide only for "undoing" the very last operation, although some provide more levels of "undo." Even "undoing" only the last operation can be very powerful if, for instance, that operation was deleting a 300-word passage in a document or throwing away a large file.

Besides greatly simplifying error recovery, an "undo" function also increases overall productivity. Users work faster because they are less concerned about the consequences of making an error. A system that is well designed to prevent errors and has an "undo" function is also much less stressful to use.

☞ Provide a cancel function for operations in progress.

Some operations take a long time to complete. Examples might be batch spell checking, repaginating, or printing or saving a very large document. Users may initiate these operations in error or simply change their mind after starting one. They should be able to cancel these operations, rather than having to wait for them to complete before "undoing" them.

☞ Require confirmation for commands with drastic, destructive consequences.

Even with an "undo" function, users should be asked to confirm a request if it has drastic, destructive consequences. For instance, if users ask to erase a diskette, reformat a hard disk, or rename a file to a name already taken by another file, they should be asked to confirm this request with a message such as "Do you really wish to reformat the hard disk?? ALL FILES WILL BE ERASED!" and perform an additional operation such as a keystroke or menu pick. Make confirmation messages very explicit. A message such as "Are you sure?" does not make it clear to the user what they are being asked. Tell the user exactly what will be done if they answer in the affirmative or negative.

☞   **Conduct error checking in context, but without interrupting work flow.**

When the inputs to fields on a fill-in form are interdependent, it makes sense to check for errors on a field by field basis, as the user leaves each field. For example, the valid dollar amounts a user may enter in one field might depend on the date information they may enter in another field, which might in turn depend on status information entered in a third field. If the status information is incorrectly entered, then this will affect valid dates and dollar amounts. If the user does not find out that the status input is incorrect until all three fields are filled in, then he or she may have to go back and reenter all fields. Alternatively, if error checking was executed immediately after the user entered status information, it should be less likely that the user will make associated errors in the dates and dollars fields.

On the other hand, expert data entry users and typists often do not want to be interrupted by error checking as they work. This would slow them down, and it would probably be more efficient to work quickly, making errors, and then to request error checking for all the input at once. Thus, when error checking should be done depends partly on the task and partly on user preference.

☞   **Return the cursor to and highlight the error field.**

Do not require users to interpret messages such as "error in date field" and then search for and move the cursor to the field in error. Place the cursor on and highlight (for example, with bold, reverse video, or color) the first error position and additional error positions as errors are corrected.

☞   **Allow editing of error fields.**

Do not require users to reenter whole fill-in fields, whole fill-in forms, or whole command strings when one part of one field or one part of a command string is in error. Allow users to delete and insert on a character basis and resubmit forms and command strings. This will be much more efficient and minimize additional input errors.

☞   **Provide intelligent error checking and recovery.**

An *intelligent* interface might, like another human being, make an intelligent guess at what the user meant when an error is made. For instance, a command language might guess at the intended meaning of misspelled commands, giving a message such as "DELATE: do you mean DELETE? Y or N:," rather than a message such as "Invalid command." Not only is the former error message more informative, but it provides a faster way to recover from the error.

As another example, a command language might prompt for missing parameters. If the user entered "Copy FileA," instead of responding "missing parameter," the system might respond "please enter destination file:" and accept the input as if it were entered in the original string.

☞ **Provide quick access to context-sensitive HELP.**

Even when error reporting is well designed, some users may need more detailed information than can or should be fit on the display where the error occurred. More detailed error assistance should be provided through *context-sensitive* help, so that a single keystroke or menu pick provides this detailed information on the error field that currently contains the cursor. Help can be presented in pop-up boxes, windows, or separate screens. It should also be easy to return from the Help display to the field in error.

☞ **Design effective error messages.**

As suggested in a study (Shneiderman, 1982) cited in the previous section, the quality of error messages can effect error recovery. Figure 16-2 gives examples of the error message design principles given next.

Be descriptive but concise.   The "Poor" message in the first row of Figure 16-2 is too general and vague, while the "Improved" message provides more specific information. This will aid error recovery. Notice that there are no more words in the "Improved" message; it is just as concise, but more descriptive.

Don't mislead.   If the error was failing to specify a file extension in a file name, the "Poor" message in the second row of Figure 16-2 would be misleading. The user might assume that a file had been deleted or moved to a different directory, when in fact it still existed. The proper message in this case would be the "Improved" one.

Be prescriptive.   The "Poor" message in the third row of Figure 16-2 is *descriptive* but not *prescriptive*. That is, it tells the user what is wrong, but not what to do about it. The "Improved" message helps the user determine how to recover from the error.

Design detail according to user knowledge and experience.   For users low in *semantic* and *syntactic* knowledge (see Chapter 2), the "Poor" message in the fourth row of Figure 16-2 is too vague. These users need the additional semantic information ("range is 4 to 16") and syntactic prompting ("no leading zeros") provided in the "Improved" message. Users high in *semantic* or *syntactic* knowl-

Poor: Improved:

	Poor:	Improved:
(1)	Filing error	Disk full
(2)	File not found	Missing filename extension
(3)	Disk full	Disk full. Use "Save As" command to save to another disk
(4)	Error in DRESS SIZE field	Error: DRESS SIZE range is 4 to 16. No leading zeros
(5)	Bad input	Unrecognizable command
(6)	Unrecognizeable command!!	Unrecognizable command.
(7)	Disastrous Fatal Abandoned Illegal Catastrophic Invalid Terminated Bad Aborted Killed Failed	Halted Unrecognized Cannot accept Could not execute
(8)	Unacceptable Cannot recognize Run canceled	Cannot accept Cannot recognize Cannot run
(9)	(bottom of screen)	(in window) (on top of screen) (next to error field)
(10)	Sorry, I can't accept that command	Cannot accept command

Figure 16–2   Error messages.

edge would not need one or both of these types of information. Error messages should be designed to match user knowledge and experience.

Take the blame.   The "Poor" message in the fifth row of Figure 16-2 implies that the user has made an error. The "Improved" message implies that the computer is at fault instead. This message will be less intimidating to novices and, in general, is less offensive. No one likes a machine to be critical of them.

Avoid exclamation points.   Exclamation points are unnecessarily dramatic. As in the "Poor" message in the sixth row of Figure 16-2, they imply that the error is inexcusable, surprising, stupid, and more serious than it usually is. They can be alarming to novices and offensive to experts.

Avoid violent and hostile words.   The "Poor" message terms in the seventh row of Figure 16-2 are typical of computer error messages. They are violent, melodramatic and hostile. They can be intimidating to novices and offensive to nontechnical experts. Other words, such as those in the "Improved" example, can express the same semantics in a more benign, less threatening tone.

Use consistent grammatical style.   Each of the three "Poor" messages in the eighth row of Figure 16-2 is grammatically different, while the grammatical structure of the three "Improved" messages is the same. The meanings, on the other hand, are the same in the two sets of messages. Grammatically consistent messages will be easier to read and understand.

Place in context.   As suggested in the ninth row of Figure 16-2, messages should be placed where the eye is likely to notice them. On screens of a traditional size, always placing the error message at the bottom of the screen may be appropriate, since it will always be well within the peripheral vision. On larger screens, however, the bottom of the screen may be outside peripheral vision, depending on where the eye is focused. In this case, it might be more noticeable if error messages appeared closer to the current focus of attention, such as in the current window or next to the field in which the error occurred.

Don't anthropomorphize.   To *anthropomorphize* means to attribute human qualities to nonhuman entities. In the case of a computer, this might mean phrasing messages in the first person, as in the "Poor" message in the tenth row of Figure 16-2, addressing users by name, or being humorous or conversational in messages. Although designers might be amused by designing humanlike qualities into a user interface, the result can often deceive, confuse, and mislead users. It can give a very untoollike flavor to a system and may weaken a user's sense of responsibility for intelligent use of the tool.

REFERENCES

KRAUT, ROBERT E., STEPHEN J. HANSON, and JAMES M. FARBER, "Command Use and Interface Design," *Proceedings, CHI '83,* 1983, pp. 120–24, ACM.

LEWIS, CLAYTON, and DONALD A. NORMAN, "Designing for Error," in Donald A. Norman and Stephen W. Draper, eds., *User Centered System Design* (Hillsdale, N.J.: Lawrence Erlbaum Associates, 1986), pp. 410–32.

MOSTELLER, WILLIAM S., and JAMES BALLAS, "Usability Analysis of Messages from a Security System," *Proceedings of the Human Factors Society 33rd Annual Meeting,* 1989, pp. 399–403.

NORMAN, DONALD A., "Design Rules Based on Analyses of Human Error," *Communications of the ACM,* 26, no. 4 (1983), pp. 254–58.

SHNEIDERMAN, BEN, "System Message Design: Guidelines and Experimental Results," in Albert Badre and Ben Shneiderman eds., *Directions in Human Computer Interaction* (Norwood, N.J.: Ablex Publishing Corp. 1982), pp. 63–66.

CHAPTER 17

User Documentation

User documentation is part of the user interface. Often it is a user's first encounter with a system. Users may form impressions of the usability of a system by reading the manual or accessing the on-line help or tutorial. If the manual or tutorial is easy to use, users will assume the system will be easy to use. When customers are deciding whether or not to buy software packages by scanning through the manual, the quality of the manual can influence their decision. The quality of the user documentation thus determines in large part both the perception of and the actual ease of learning and use of the system.

On the other hand, good documentation and/or a good on-line Help are no substitute for a poor user interface. Designers often give up grappling with difficult design issues, thinking that the interface will, after all, be explained in the manual. But describing operations clearly does not necessarily mean they will be easy to remember or that errors will not occur in executing them. These things are determined by the design of the interface itself. Good documentation cannot be expected to make up for a poor interface.

Nevertheless, for a system that is at all rich and powerful in functionality, even a good interface may not be totally self-explanatory. The quality of the user documentation will therefore either enhance or degrade the overall usability of the product.

User documentation should be started early in the software development life cycle. Writing a good manual requires a considerable effort, with many drafts. And writers should be closely involved in user interface design. They can provide valuable input to design, because as they document parts of the system they must struggle to find simple ways of explaining how to use it. A system that is difficult to describe and teach is probably going to be difficult to learn and use.

It is a good idea to develop a *style guide* for user documentation. A **style guide** is a set of design standards and conventions that provides for consistency in style, terminology, and organization within and across documents associated with a product or product line. In the same way that consistency and standardization in user interfaces make products easier to learn and use, consistency in documentation makes manuals and help systems easier to use.

User documentation should be *debugged* and tested for usability. A number of testing techniques are available, including automated indexes of reading difficulty, walkthroughs with users, and comprehension tests. Tests of documentation are also good pilot tests of interface design. If something is difficult for users to understand, it may be a flaw in the manual or it may be a flaw in the user interface itself.

There are two major types of user documentation: **user manuals** and **on-line help** systems. These are discussed in separate sections next.

USER MANUALS

User manuals are a part of the user interface to a computer system. They are often the user's first encounter with the system and, in many cases, the only training support the user receives. They are also often the only support the user has for troubleshooting.

Unfortunately, user manuals are typically poorly designed. They are intimidating, full of technical jargon, hard to navigate in, and difficult to read. They simply do not support the natural learning and problem-solving processes of people.

User manuals can be dramatically improved by following practical design principles drawn from learning theory, psycholinguistics, and graphic design. In the next section, different types of manuals are identified and discussed, and in subsequent sections, experimental results and design principles and guidelines are presented.

Manual Types

Although user expertise can in fact be divided into many independent types (see Chapter 2), for our purposes here it is useful to consider three categories of user expertise, each defined *relative to a particular system*.

True novices are users who have little or no experience with computers in general and little or no training on the system at hand. **Experts** are users who are very experienced with a particular computer system. They may or may not have wide experience with computers in general. **Intermediate users** fall somewhere in between. They might have considerable computer experience and may even have used other systems like the one they are about to learn. However, they are using the new system for the first time. They bring considerably more knowledge to the learning task than do true novices, but they are far from being experts on the new system. *Each of these types of users needs a very different kind of manual.*

Tutorials are best for *true novices.* These users know little about the *semantics* of the application (what the system can do), let alone the *syntax* of the human interface (precisely how to do anything in particular on the system). Tutorials are meant to be read from cover to cover, and they are organized as a course or training program would be.

Reference manuals are aimed at *experts.* A reference manual is organized to allow quick retrieval of specific *syntactic* information. A reference manual provides complete information on all system functions, while a **quick reference** summarizes information on a small subset of the most important or most frequently used functions.

A third type of manual, which we will call the **user guide,** is necessary as well. This type of manual is aimed at *intermediate users.* Intermediate users know something about the *semantics* of the application, but not necessarily all aspects of it. They may be at some intermediate stage in the learning process and know the *syntax* for some functions, but not all. That is, they may be experts in some aspects of the system, but novices in others.

An example of intermediate users might be users who have used many word processors before and are just beginning to learn a new one. These users are very familiar with what word processors can do. They may even be able to make correct guesses as to how to do things on the new system if the new system is similar to others they have used. In addition, these users may have already learned some basic functions of the system, but might be inexperienced in using more advanced features.

The *intermediate user* does not yet know how to accomplish many things on the new system. However, a *tutorial* is too basic and rudimentary. These users would have to wade through too much information that they are already familiar with. A *reference manual* assumes that these users know more than they do. It is not organized in a way that is useful for these users.

Thus, the user guide must simultaneously address the needs of all classes of users. It must allow users to easily skip over information that is already known, but not require that the user be already familiar with details of the syntax of the system.

Figure 17-1 summarizes the different kinds of experience users may or may not have and indicates the appropriate manual type accordingly. *Task* knowledge refers to general knowledge of the problem domain. *Application* knowledge refers to experience with other but similar applications (for example, other word processors or other spreadsheets). *System* knowledge refers to knowledge of how to use

User knowledge level

	Task	Application	System
Tutorial	Low	Low	Low
User guide	High	Low	Low
Reference	High	High	Low
Quick reference	High	High	High

Figure 17–1   Different types of manuals for different types of users.

the particular system at hand. These three types of knowledge are explained in more detail in Chapter 2.

Packaging Manuals

Usually, it is a good idea to provide all four types of manuals with any given system, as novices eventually become experts. Packaging them as separate documents makes each smaller and therefore less intimidating. In addition, a separate paper or brochure should describe the purpose of each manual. This communicates the fact that it is not necessary to read all four to become productive and also directs users to the proper manual, depending on their expertise.

USER MANUALS: EXPERIMENTAL STUDIES

One study (Foss, Rosson, and Smith, 1982) investigated the effects of broad design differences on the usability of manuals. Two manuals for a line-oriented text editor were compared. One was a traditional, *standard* manual, in that it was organized according to system functions and presented in terse technical prose with abstract formal notation. The other was a *modified* version of the manual that organized information around user tasks, presenting basic information followed by more advanced information in a layered approach. The prose was reworded to be simpler and less technical and plenty of examples were provided. The main characteristics of the two manuals can be summarized as follows:

Standard manual	Modified manual
Full details on each command	Layered approach to detail
Abstract formal notation	Examples
Terse technical prose	Less technical, more readable

Forty-four college undergraduates with no computer experience participated in the study, half with each manual. They were allowed to study their manual for 15 to 30 minutes and then were given a set of simple editing tasks through a marked up paper copy of a document that was on line. They were allowed to consult the manual while performing the editing tasks.

Data were collected by a software monitor, and four measures of performance were calculated: (1) the number of tasks successfully completed in a given time period, (2) the average number of minutes spent on each task, (3) the average number of individual commands used to accomplish a task, and (4) the number of requests made to an available on-line help system.

The data from this study are summarized in Figure 17-2. Here it can be seen that those subjects working with the *modified* manual performed better on all measures than did those working from the *standard* manual. They completed slightly more tasks, spent much less time and far fewer commands in completing each task, and made less calls to the help system. The time measure is particularly striking. Subjects using the modified manual spent an average of 10 minutes less on each task, a considerable time period indeed.

This study suggests that the quality of the user manual can have a significant

	Standard manual	Modified manual
Tasks completed	7.36	8.77
Minutes per task	26.63	16.00
Commands per task	23.63	13.04
Help requests	5.50	2.55

Figure 17-2 A study of user manual design. From Foss, Rosson, and Smith, "Reducing Manual Labor: An Experimental Analysis of Learning Aids for a Text Editor," *Proceedings, Human Factors in Computer Systems*, 1982, 332–36. With permission.

effect on the ease of learning of a system. It also suggests some of the design techniques that can contribute to the usability of a manual: organization, language, and the use of examples.

Some studies have been concerned with what characteristics of manuals facilitate *navigation* to desired information. Rowland and Williams (1989) report the experimental use of a computer program that allows the testing of the *organization* (that is, ease of navigation) of user manuals before they are written. The program takes as input skeletal versions of planned manuals, including title pages, table of contents, indexes, tab dividers, and chapter and section headings, and allows a test subject to navigate through these elements through a mouse-driven user interface intended to stimulate the use of hard-copy manuals. The program records how users navigate through such skeletal manuals in response to specific tasks presented to them, which allows researchers to evaluate how efficiently users will be able to find desired information, given a particular organization across and within a set of planned manuals.

An initial assessment of a set of manuals using the program resulted in a number of redesign recommendations, including renaming manuals, renaming sections headings, and cleaning up inconsistencies of various sorts. Although the utility of the program in identifying organizational flaws has yet to be validated, the authors point out that these preliminary results seem promising, and that being able to identify and redesign flaws in manual organization well before manuals are written has obvious benefits.

The Rowland and Williams (1989) study provides an example of collecting *performance* data on the usability of manuals. Another study (Comstock and Clemens, 1987) reports user *satisfaction* data on a set of manuals. On-site interviews were conducted with 15 technical users at ten locations. Users were asked open-ended questions and also asked to rate a variety of aspects of the current set of manuals on a rating scale. Both positive and negative aspects of the manual set were thus identified, including the following:

Positive	Negative
Style and format are good	Finding information is sometimes difficult
Tab dividers, spine labels, page headers, illustrations are good and heavily relied on	Identifying the right manual is sometimes difficult
Good consistency in organization across manuals	Hard to tell what the total set of available manuals is
Accuracy and clarity are good	Indexes should be included in all volumes of a set
Good use of examples, illustrations, tables and highlighting	Indexes should include more industry-standard terms
Liked small binders (easier to carry and use while standing)	Too much jumping required between manuals and sections
	Need more examples
	Content is not complete

Positive	Negative
	Prefer three-ring binders to bound manuals (easier to update)
	Prefer more detailed labeling on spines and tabs
	Prefer more durable manuals
	Would like to see color on covers used to help distinguish manuals in a set

Although these data are collected from a small number (15) of a particular type of user (technical) of a specific set of manuals, they shed light on the types of design issues that influence user satisfaction with user manuals.

The studies cited above are concerned primarily with manual *organization*. Other studies have investigated different ways of *presenting information*. Billingsley (1982) compared two methods of presenting information regarding a menu hierarchy. A *data index* presented an alphabetized list of target items, each followed by the sequence of menu choices that would lead to that target item. A *data map* showed the overall tree structure of the menu system with all choices labeled. Search time and search efficiency on retrieval tasks were compared for subjects who had one or the other of these learning aids. The more spatial presentation, the data map, resulted in a better overall performance.

Bauer and Eddy (1986) compared a graphical and a text presentation method for documenting a different kind of user interface, a command language. Backus normal form (BNF) was compared to flow-chart-like graphics for representing command language syntax. Examples of each presentation method are given in Figure 17-3.

Subjects familiar with computers but not with either presentation method for documenting command syntax first studied eight syntactic rules, half represented by each method. They then were shown actual commands and had to judge whether they were valid or invalid, given the syntax described by the two presentation methods they had studied. When they made errors, they received feedback in the form of a review of the relevant syntactic rule presented in its original format (BNF or graphical).

Although there was no difference in initial performance immediately following study, over time and with practice and feedback, subjects using the graphical representation method did better than those using BNF. That is, while simply studying the manual produced no difference in learning, practicing with the feedback showed that the graphical format resulted in faster learning and better retention of the syntactic rules over time. The advantage held for simple syntactic rules, but was even greater for more complex rules. Although this study and the Billingsley (1982) study differed in what was being learned (a menu hierarchy versus a command language syntax), both revealed an advantage of spatial over certain kinds of textual representations of relationships between interface elements.

Webb and Kramer (1987) compared a *spatial map* (similar to Billingsley's

BNF:

FIND [{[{[<SIGN>]<NUMBER>}|ALL]"<TEXT>"}|*]

Graphical:

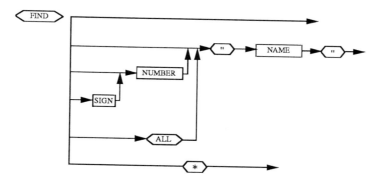

Figure 17–3 A study of information presentation in user manuals. From Bauer and Eddy, "The Representation of Command Language Syntax," *Human Factors*, 28, no. 1 (February 1986), 1–10. © 1986, by the Human Factors Society, Inc. Reprinted with permission. All rights reserved.

data map) to the use of an *analogy* as a learning aid to the menu interface to a database. In one analogy, navigating through a shopping database was likened to shopping in a department store. In another more distant analogy, searching in a database listing university courses was likened to shopping in a shopping mall. In both cases, subjects learned to use the menu hierarchy more quickly with the analogy learning aid as compared to the spatial map learning aid, suggesting the usefulness of analogies even when they are somewhat distant in content from the application. The performance advantage of analogies increased as the size of the hierarchical database and the time elapsed from initial training increased. Although it is difficult to compare these three studies directly because they differ in so many aspects, together they begin to suggest that perhaps spatial representations are useful to a point, but when the information space becomes too rich and complex to allow for manageable spatial representations, the use of analogies may be appropriate. In general, these three studies suggest that there is a variety of ways to present concepts and information in manuals, and that they may be differentially appropriate depending on such variables as concept complexity and frequency of use.

Another variation in presentation method was investigated by Black, Carroll, and McGuigan (1987). Four versions of a manual for the IBM Displaywriter were studied. They can be described as follows:

Skeletal: Contains all essential information stated explicitly but tersely.

Lengthy: Adds descriptive, explanatory, and summary information to the skeletal manual and is about 50% longer.

Rehearsal: Includes information that leads users to think again about information already presented. Same length as skeletal.

Inferential: Guides the user to infer some information about the system by asking questions, rather than explicitly stating all information. For example, users are given a general procedure and asked to infer a specific one. Or users are given a specific procedure and asked to infer another specific procedure *by analogy.* Same length as skeletal.

Four different groups of users, all naive with respect to the IBM Displaywriter, were given time to study (self-paced) one of the four manuals and then were asked to do a set of tasks. Data analysis revealed that the *Rehearsal* and *Lengthy* manuals were studied longer than the Inferential and *Skeletal* manuals. The difference was over 10 minutes. In addition, when asked to do realistic tasks such as editing a letter (as opposed to simply executing individual commands correctly), users of the *Inferential* manual performed significantly faster than the users of any other manual. The difference was 1 to 7 minutes per task.

The authors interpret these data to mean that users of the *Inferential* manual formed a better, more complete mental model of the system than did users of other manuals, and that this in turn helped them to perform new tasks more efficiently. They speculate that the inferences they were led to draw made them more aware of the general concepts around which the system was organized.

Although the details of this study differ significantly from the Webb and Kramer (1987) study, making any direct comparisons impossible, it is interesting that one aspect of the Inferential manual in this study is the use of analogies, which was the primary point of interest in the Webb and Kramer study. Taken together, these studies suggest that *analogy* may be a useful technique for teaching in manuals.

A follow-on study (Black and others, 1989) compared four different kinds of *inferences* to see if some were more effective than others. A different application was also used to see if the results from the previous study would generalize beyond word processing applications. The application in this study was a database, and subjects learned through one of four on-line tutorials to create files, declare fields and enter data. The four different types of inferences that characterized each tutorial were as follows:

General to specific: The instructions stated a general procedure or rule, and the user had to infer how it applied to a specific context. For example, users were told that field length should be large enough to allow for most values that could go in the field, but not larger than necessary. Users would have to infer from that how many spaces to reserve for a particular field.

Explanation to specific: The instructions gave information about the functional and conceptual organization of the system. For example, users were told that the field length declaration tells the computer how much space to reserve for the information that will be entered, allowing the efficient use of computer memory. This was expected to encourage users to form a *mental model* from which they could infer specific requirements. Some general information, of necessity, was also included.

Specific to specific inferences: The instructions give an example of a command's use, and the user must infer how to apply the command in a different context. For instance, the user is told that a zip code field should be declared with a length of five characters. From this they must infer how to declare the field length for other fields.

Explicit instructions: This was a control condition. Instructions explicitly stated everything that was to be typed into the computer.

Forty-two teen-aged subjects with minimal computer experience participated. They first studied one of the four tutorials at their own pace and then were tested through tasks on the database system to measure how well they had learned the material. Although the *Explicit Instructions* manual took the least time to study, it produced the longest test times and one of the highest error rates as compared to the other manuals. This finding is consistent with the previous study, which showed an advantage of manuals using inferencing. Of main interest, subjects using the *General to Specific* inferences manual performed the test tasks faster and with fewer errors than subjects using the other manuals. The *Specific to Specific* manual took the longest time to study and produced the most errors.

It is interesting that the *Explanation to Specific* manual, which differed from the *General to Specific* manual mainly by the inclusion of functional and conceptual information, did *not* produce the best performance. The authors acknowledge that the material to be learned was simple and brief and that such functional and conceptual information could possibly play a more important role in later stages of learning in more complex systems. In fact, it does seem likely that users will be most comfortable with simple procedural information initially, but that they will want to enhance their understanding at a later phase in the learning process through functional and conceptual explanations (Wright, 1988). The results suggest, however, that brief, simple, but general rules (without lengthy explanations of internal computer functions) from which users can infer correct command structures in specific cases provide a good presentation method for user manuals aimed at novices.

USER MANUALS: PRINCIPLES AND GUIDELINES

This section focuses on the design of the *user guide,* although many principles will also be applicable to tutorials and reference manuals. The design principles offered address three major design goals:

> Ease of navigation
> Ease of learning
> Ease of reading

Ease of Navigation

Intermediate users rarely sit down and read a manual from cover to cover. Perhaps they do once when they first acquire a system. But as they become more experienced, they only need to refer back to certain parts of a manual to refresh their memory or to learn more advanced features. Thus, it is always important that it be *easy to navigate* within the user guide and to quickly find a particular section or topic.

Principles for designing good *navigation* aids address how well the documentation is organized to facilitate finding a particular section or topic. Design issues here include the organization of topics, the wording and terminology used in the table of contents, and the structure and content of the index.

☞ **Organize and label chapters and sections according to users' goals.**

Generally, *intermediate users* have considerable *semantic* knowledge, but little or no *syntactic* knowledge of the system. Too often, user guides are organized according to system architecture, according to the particulars of the system's user interface, or according to some other logic and jargon that is meaningful to the developer, but obscure to the user who is trying to learn the system.

For *expert* users, this organization might be useful. Reference manuals are often organized around aspects of the system architecture or user interface. However, *intermediate users* have in mind what they want to accomplish, but are not yet familiar with system architecture or the user interface. That is why they are referring to the manual. Thus, the table of contents and other section headings in the user guide should be phrased in terms of *user goals*. This will help users find the part of the manual they need. The following are examples of poor and improved organization and labeling of topics in a programming language manual.

Examples of *poor chapter and section headings* that reflect system architecture, user interface, and developer jargon include the following:

Itinerary World
Listener Levels
System Variables for Tracking Listener Actions

Examples of *headings that better communicate the topic* in terms of user goals might be, respectively,

Getting a Menu of Tutorial Topics
Errors and Debugging
Shortcuts for Referring to the Results of Past Calculations

Examples of *poor organization of topics* might be

Keychord Commands to the Interpreter
Dot Commands

Keychord and dot commands in this example refer to aspects of the *syntax* of a group of commands. *Keychord commands* are those invoked by pressing multiple keys simultaneously. *Dot commands* are commands invoked by typing a command name preceded by a period. Perhaps tables of keychord and dot commands will be useful for *expert* users, but as the primary organizational theme in a user guide they are a problem. *Intermediate users* need to be able to find out how to accomplish tasks, and have no idea whether the way to do so is through a keychord or dot command. Commands should be organized according to likely user goals, not according to the conventions of the user interface.

Note that this is *not to say that introducing and teaching new jargon, architecture, and user interface conventions are wrong*. The point here is that *users should not have to know these things in order to navigate* to the part of the manual that will teach them what they need to know.

☞   **The table of contents should present a high-level overview, not an exhaustive list.**

There should be enough detail in the table of contents for a user to easily locate the chapter or section in which the desired information can be found, but not so much that the table of contents becomes cluttered and unwieldy, making search tedious and difficult. Examples of poor and improved levels of detail for a table of contents for a word processing manual are given next.

Poor:	Improved:
Editing	Editing
Selecting text	Selecting text
Regions	Inserting text
Words	
Sentences	
Paragraphs	
Inserting text	
New text	
From clipboard	

☞   **Provide an index, with entries for both user goals and tasks and operation names.**

A complete and well-organized index is critical for ease of navigation in a manual. All entries should be indexed twice: once under an operation or command name, and once in the form of a user goal. Here are some examples.

Command name	User goal
Renumber, 334–338	Paragraphs
	numbering paragraphs, 334–338
New, 14–16	Documents
	creating a new document, 14–16

☞   **Separate different types of information, and use a consistent visual cue for each type.**

There are at least four different types of information we might want to include in the description of any feature or function of the system:

Motivational
Conceptual
Procedural
Examples

Motivational information explains why a feature is useful and in what situations it might be useful. **Conceptual** information explains what the feature actually does, what the end result of using it will be. **Procedural** information tells what actual steps are necessary on the system to use the feature. **Examples** make *procedural* information more concrete. Good examples have *motivational* content as well; an example should describe a typical, useful, and high-frequency application of the feature being taught.

In most manuals, these four types of information are not consistently present in all sections. At least in the user guide, they should be. Usually, even if they are, they are somewhat arbitrarily intermixed with each other in straight prose format. Thus users who are scanning for some detail of *syntax* or trying to find a feature to accomplish a certain goal must wade through all four types of information to find what they are looking for. This is inefficient and frustrating.

Assigning each type of information a particular format and general location in a section or on a page will make it easier for users to scan for what they need. For example, *motivational* information might always be the first part of a section in some distinctive font. Uses for the function could be presented in list format, which is easier to read than prose. *Conceptual* information could appear next, in a different font and in prose. *Procedural* information could be illustrated through *examples*, with *syntactic* details described in blocks of text that are connected to the *example* by arrows.

Figure 17-4 gives an example of documentation that fails to use these techniques. Figure 17-5 shows how to improve the documentation using these techniques.

Ease of Learning

Learning new ideas can be facilitated if information is presented in a way that matches the natural learning and problem-solving strategies of people. Good teaching techniques include the use of examples are highlighting and the consistent assignment of spatial and locational cues to different types of information.

☞ **Provide a foundation and build on it.**

People need some underlying structure on which to base new ideas, concepts, and procedural information. New ideas are more easily learned and remembered if they can be related to already familiar ideas. The thing that users are already familiar with is the general type of tasks that the system can assist them with. Thus, it is helpful to first present a familiar problem and then to teach system features in the context of solving that problem.

For instance, many programming language manuals simply list the different logical elements of the language (for example, looping, if tests, and string manipulation) and provide exhaustive information regarding the use of each. It would be better to present a small, but interesting programming problem, and then start

Poor:

COPY

The Copy command allows the duplication of files. Files can be
copied from one volume and/or library to another, or copies can
be made within a library. Copy is useful for making backup
versions of files. When Copy is used, an exact duplicate of the
source file is made, and the copy is then independent of the
original. The syntax of the copy command is as follows:

```
*COPY
FROM:  [/VOL/LIB/]FILE.EXT
TO:    [/VOL/LIB/]FILE.EXT
*
```

The volume name (/VOL/) and library name (/LIB/) are optional
in both arguments. If they are omitted, the current volume
and library will be assumed as defaults. The COPY command
must be typed in all capital letters. File names, however, are
case insensitive.

Figure 17–4   Poor user documentation.

teaching the language through this example. People find it hard to remember lists of
unassociated facts. It is easier for them to learn information when some familiar
structure and organization is provided.

☞ **Teach in layers and in small, independent units of information.**

Organize information in the manual so that in a small number of pages, the
user has learned how to do something useful. Then start adding more advanced
features to the user's repertoire in small, independent units. This will help maintain
motivation, as well as facilitate learning.

Many programming language manuals are organized in such a way that the
user has to read most of the manual to learn how to write a very simple program.
This is because the organization is based on a logic that neatly categorizes different
linguistic or conceptual components of the language, but has little do with user

Improved:

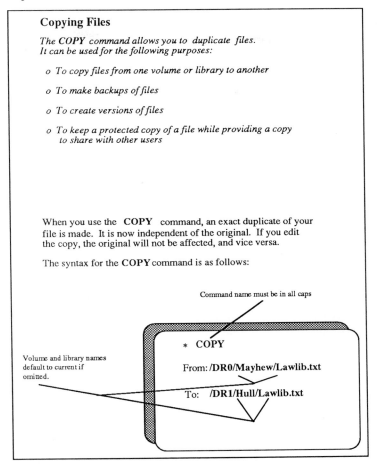

Figure 17–5   Improved user documentation.

tasks. Instead, for example, the user guide might first teach the most basic things a user needs to know in order to create a simple program, edit it, compile and run it, and debug it. Then advanced features and capabilities could be introduced in small units of information that would allow the user to learn new features at his or her own pace.

☞ **Teach in a logical sequence. Avoid forward references. Provide complete information to accomplish a task.**

Although it might be appropriate in a reference manual to present functions in alphabetical order, or even in logical order according to level of detail and interrelationships among functions, this would be inappropriate in a user guide. Present topics in the order in which users need to learn them and use them.

For instance, in a word processing manual, it makes sense to first teach about logging in, creating a new document, typing and basic editing, saving and logging off, in that order. This is enough information to allow the user to accomplish a very simple, basic task: create a simple document. It would not make sense to locate information about saving and logging off at the very end of the manual, after all the advanced editing and formatting functions, even if the user were referred to those sections in the earlier sections.

The sequencing of information in the manual should correspond as much as possible to the sequence in which users will need and want information as they learn to use the system to accomplish their goals. They should not have to flip back and forth among nonadjacent sections to find this information. If a piece of information might be needed in the description of several user tasks, it is appropriate to be redundant and provide it more than once. This will make the manual easier to use.

☞ Give examples.

People vary in their ability to process abstract information. Often a concrete example will serve better than an exhaustive description or a formal expression such as BNF (BNF is a formal symbolic language for expressing the syntax of a programming or command language). Examples should at least always accompany formal expressions. If the examples are good and meaningful, they will also help to maintain motivation. See Figure 17-5 for an illustration of the use of examples.

☞ Provide illustrations.

Instructions are always easier to follow when there is a picture to refer to. When instructing a user how to do something which requires a dialog with the system, pictures of the screen are always helpful. See Figure 17-5 for an example of the use of illustrations.

For instance, screens can be represented by a rectangle with rounded corners, and user input and system output can be represented by different fonts or colors (upper- and lowercase letters for this purpose are not salient enough). Instead of straight prose above or below the screen illustration, small rectangles of text, with arrows drawn to the lines on the screen that the text describes, make it easier to relate the screen illustration to the descriptive text.

☞ Make consistent use of spatial, visual and locational cues.

Use space, location, and other visual cues, such as highlighting, color, font, borders, symbols, and underlining, to tag different kinds of information, such as examples, syntactic rules, warnings, and special notes. (See Chapter 14 for guidelines on the use of these visual coding techniques.) This will make different kinds of information stand out and thus make it is easier to scan and find things. The key point here is to use visual cues consistently so that users will come to learn their meanings and be able to use them as aids in their search for information.

☞ **Avoid abstract, formal notation.**

Although precise and thorough for describing syntax, abstract notational descriptions are not necessarily good teaching mechanisms. They may be appropriate in a programming manual, but they should not appear in manuals intended for nontechnical users, except perhaps in a reference section or appendix. They should not be the primary mechanism for teaching. Examples and prose descriptions are much easier to understand quickly.

Consider the following examples. The "Copy" command in a command language is being described. Look at the "Poor" example. Note how difficult it is to translate this formalism into a proper command string. Compare this with the "Better" example, which is a set of representative examples rather than a formal description. Note how much easier it is to understand. Finally, in the "Best" example, again an example is given, this time for a system that prompts for parameters, thus not even requiring that the user know the argument order and separator syntax.

Poor:
>   COPY,[space],{[RETURN]!([volname!null],[:],[filename])},
>   {[RETURN]!([/],[volname!null],[:],[filename!null])}

Better:
>   COPY DJM:Version1/DJM:Version2
>   COPY DJM:Version1/DTH:
>   COPY Version1/Version2

Best:
>   COPY
>   from: DJM:Version1
>   to: :Version2

It's easier for most nontechnical users to infer rules from examples, rather than to translate rules into examples. And the abstract formalism is something additional to learn. The user is already trying to learn to use the system. The user should not have to learn how to use the manual as well. Abstract formalisms are good for expressing knowledge with precision, but not good for teaching or learning new information.

☞ **Use visual, spatial representations and analogies.**

Evidence suggests (Billingsley, 1982; Bauer and Eddy, 1986) that providing *maps* (see, for examplem Figure 4-29) and *spatial representations* (see, for example, Figure 17-3) for such interface components as menu hierarchies and command language syntax facilitates learning as compared to text-based explanations and descriptions. Other evidence (Webb and Kramer, 1987; Black, Carroll, and Mc-Guigan, 1987) suggests that drawing an analogy between the application and some other familiar task domain can be even more useful than spatial representations when the information space is large and complex. For example, navigating through a menu hierarchy can be likened to shopping in a shopping mall.

☞ **Lead users to draw inferences.**

Evidence suggests (Black, Carroll, and McGuigan, 1987; Black and others, 1989) that leading users to draw inferences rather than stating information explicitly can enhance learning, because it helps users to form a *mental model* of the system. Novice users will find the following kind of inference most useful:

General to specific: The instructions state a general procedure or rule, and the user must infer how it applies to a specific context. For example, users are told that field length in a database should be large enough to allow for most values that could go in the field, but not larger than necessary. Users must infer from this how many spaces to reserve for a particular field.

It is likely that the following kind of inference will enhance later learning as well:

Explanation to specific: The instructions give information about the functional and conceptual organization of the system. For example, users are told that the field length declaration tells the computer how much space to reserve for the information that will be entered, allowing for the efficient use of computer memory. This is expected to encourage users to form a *mental model* from which they can infer specific requirements. Some general information will of necessity also be included.

Since these two kinds of inferences are useful at different stages in the learning process, it might be advisable to include both in a *layered* approach. The first type might appear in the "Getting Started" chapters of a manual, while the second type might appear in the "Advanced Functions" chapters.

☞ **Avoid anthropomorphism.**

In a manual, just as in an interface, it is advisable to avoid *anthropomorphism*. To anthropomorphize means to attribute human qualities to nonhuman entities. In the case of a computer manual, this might mean using phrases such as those in the "Avoid" column below:

Avoid	Teaching	Reference
The computer:	You can:	
knows	ask for	to request
understands	request	
will solve	get a solution	to get
can tell you	find out	to get a listing
will teach you	learn	to learn

Although writers might use these phrases without thinking, the result can often be to deceive, confuse and mislead users. It can give a very untoollike flavor to a system and may weaken a user's sense of responsibility for the intelligent use of the tool.

Instead, present the user as the active, decision-making party in the interaction by using the alternative phrases presented in the "Teaching" column. That is, instead of saying "the computer will solve the equation when you press F5," say "you can get a solution by pressing F5." Instead of saying "the computer knows the phone number," say "you can get the phone number."

In the *teaching* sections (prose descriptions) of the manual, addressing the user in the first person ("You can request . . .") is appropriate. It is preferred to the more impersonal "To request . . ." because, again, it imparts to the reader a sense that they are in control and are responsible for the outcome of their actions. On the other hand, in the *reference* sections of a manual (procedure lists, appendix, and index), the use of the infinitive form, as in the "Reference" column above, is appropriate. For example:

You can ask for a phone number by pressing F5 and entering the name of the person whose number you want.

To request a phone number: 1) Press F5
                                         2) Enter name
                                         3) Press ENTER

This is better than:

The computer knows your phone numbers. To request a phone number, press F5 and enter the name of the person whose number you want.

The latter implies that the computer is intelligent, and the user must learn how to tap its knowledge. The former implies that the computer is a tool, and power is at the fingertips of the user.

☞ **Provide a section on troubleshooting. Provide a list of error messages with detailed explanations and suggestions.**

A good manual includes a list of common error conditions and a diagnosis and prescription for each. For instance:

Problem	Solution
The printer is on but won't respond to a print request.	Make sure the "select" button is depressed and lit up.

It also provides more detailed information corresponding to specific error messages. For instance:

"Disk is full. Save to another disk."   This means the file you are trying to save will not fit on your current diskette. You can use the "save as" command to save the file to another diskette. The "save as" command will prompt you to eject the current disk and insert the new one. No data will be lost.

☞ **Documentation should be consistent in style and terminology with on-line help, prompts, instructions, and messages.**

For instance, if the on-screen instructions use the term "Press" to refer to the use of special function keys and "Enter" to refer to typing from the alpha keys, then the manuals and on-line help system should also use these terms consistently in the same way. If the manual uses the form,

To request a phone number: 1) Press F5
                               2) Enter name
                               3) Press ENTER

to describe procedures, then the on-line help system should use the same form, rather than something like:

You can ask for a phone number by first pressing F5, then entering the name and pressing ENTER.

Ease of Reading

A manual should be clearly and simply written. It should be possible to quickly *read* and understand any explanation and description of system features and functions. The clarity of a manual depends on aspects of the prose style, including such things as length of paragraphs and sentences, familiarity of terms, and simplicity of words and grammatical structures.

☞ **Make use of white space.**

Dense text is difficult to read, especially when the content is complex and abstract. Liberal use of *white space* (that is, blank space) makes a manual look less intimidating and facilitates reading.

☞ **Write at the fifth-grade reading level.**

Studies show that people prefer that instructional text be written at a lower grade level than they are actually capable of reading. Contrary to what some designers believe, users do not find this condescending and insulting. They are trying to understand instructions, not enjoy great literature.

Reading levels are operationally defined by a number of elements. The fifth-grade level means roughly the following:

> Short, simple sentences
> Short, familiar words
> Short paragraphs
> Active voice
> Avoid negatives
> Order instructions chronologically
> Avoid hyphenation
> Do not right justify
> 50 to 55 characters per line, or multiple columns

An excellent reference for simple, clear writing techniques is Strunk and White, (1979).

☞ **Avoid unnecessary jargon.**

The key word in this principle is ''unnecessary.'' Often, learning the jargon of a *profession* is necessary and desirable. And often no ordinary words exist to describe a computer concept or function.

When introducing jargon in a manual, it should never appear in the table of contents or section headings. It should be defined the first time it appears in the text and flagged there and everywhere else it appears with some visual cue, such as bold or underlining. Jargon should always appear in the index, and a glossary is desirable when jargon is heavily used in the manual.

Do not, however, use jargon just because it exists. Often developers force users to learn their jargon when it is totally unnecessary for learning the system. The user already has enough to learn, and unnecessary jargon only adds to the burden and makes the system seem more complex than it is. Examples of computer jargon include the following:

buffer	syntax	server
port	boot	byte
volume	node	handler
pathway	block	module

Note that using *user* jargon is appropriate and desirable. Using jargon outside the user's area of expertise is usually not.

In sum, following the preceding principles and guidelines will result in better, more usable user manuals. Writing a good user manual takes a lot of time, thought, and effort. However, a good job done by one writer can save hundreds or thousands of users a lot of time and frustration. Considerable effort is usually easy to cost justify.

ON-LINE HELP

As computer power becomes cheaper and faster, an alternative to traditional hard-copy user manuals becomes more and more feasible: on-line help systems. Shneiderman (1986) offers a good discussion of the general advantages and disadvantages of on-line help systems, relative to traditional hard-copy documentation.

One *advantage* of on-line documentation is that, unlike hardcopy, it *can't be lost or damaged.* Another is that it *does not require desk space and place holding.* It is *faster and cheaper to update* than hard-copy documentation. It is also *potentially faster to access and navigate in,* although the word "potentially" is important here. Paging through a book is faster than paging through computer screens. Powerful search capabilities, however, could make navigation in an on-line help system faster and easier than in a manual. Unlike hard-copy manuals, on-line documentation *allows interactive teaching.* And, finally, in a well-designed help system, the *user can control the level of information detail,* while this is not true in a manual.

On the other hand, on-line help systems have some general *disadvantages* when compared to hard-copy manuals. Usually, text on the screen is *not as legible* as printed material due to the lower resolution of most computer screens. *Small computer screens* show less than an $8\frac{1}{2}$ by 11 inch page, and so more "pages" are required to display the same amount of information online as compared to a manual. *Paging is slower*. Understanding and remembering how to navigate in the help system adds an *additional learning burden*. And, finally, the help panel either takes up the entire screen (in a nonwindowing system) or *obscures part of the screen* (in a windowing system) and interrupts the user's primary task, causing the user to loose context.

Other *advantages* of hard-copy manuals as compared to on-line help include that they can be *left open at a particular page, markers can be inserted* in them, they can be *annotated* in the margins, and they can be *highlighted* (Wright, 1988).

There are many design issues to be determined in any on-line help system (Houghton, 1984; Relles, Sondheimer, and Ingargiola, 1981; Sondheimer and Relles, 1982). Some of these issues are discussed next.

Context sensitive versus one point of entry. Many help systems are **context sensitive;** that is, the user need not explicitly specify the topic on which help is required. The user simply issues the help command, usually by pressing a special key, and the system takes the current context of user activity and assumes that help is requested on the details of that context. Alternatives to this are to have the user either specify what sort of help is required (**keyword**) or simply enter the help system and navigate through it to the desired information (**single entry point**).

Obviously, an intelligently context sensitive help system would be optimal, because users would not have to take their mind off the immediate task to concentrate on how to navigate in the help system, thus risking the possibility that they might lose sight of their task. There is some evidence that this does indeed happen (Clark, 1981) and that on-line help systems that are not context sensitive actually degrade performance.

However, it is also unclear how successful context-sensitive help systems really are. If the system is not correct in its assumptions about what users have in mind when they press the help key, this may actually be more confusing than helpful. Users may get irrelevant information, which they must make sense out of, and then must have a way to navigate to the information actually desired. Unless the system is intelligent enough to have a very high hit rate, trying to be context sensitive may do more harm than good.

Even if the system can make unambiguous sense out of the present context, there is an implicit assumption that when users decide to ask for help it will always be on the topic that is implied by the current state in their interaction. If this is not the case, the user must then have some way of requesting the desired information.

In sum, both research that reveals when and what kinds of help are typically required by users and the demonstration of a context-sensitive help system that has an acceptable hit rate are needed to cast light on the pros and cons of help systems that vary on this dimension.

Independent versus integrated help frames. In some systems, when a user requests help, a single frame or screen of help information is presented, and the only option then available is to back out of the help system and possibly reenter from another context or specified point. That is, each help frame is independent, and users cannot scroll through to other parts of the help system from the point at which they entered.

In other systems, once the user has entered the help system, whether it is context sensitive or not, the user can scan and scroll through totally unrelated help information by navigating through the structure of the system, which might be *sequential, hierarchical,* or *networked* (see page 560).

The latter method seems desirable, but it is also more complex to implement; and it is unclear, in the absence of any data on user behavior and preferences, whether it is desirable enough to merit its relative expense. If it is desirable, there are many options for structuring the help information, each with implications for exactly how the user would navigate the structure. There are also no data that indicate which kind of structure and associated navigational operations would be easiest for users.

Windowing versus single screen.   In systems that do not allow windowing or split screen capabilities, any help information that is displayed must, by definition, replace and obscure the task the user is requesting help on. This potentially produces the same problem suggested in the discussion of context sensitivity: users will forget or lose track of what they were doing when help was requested, ultimately degrading overall performance.

Windowing systems, on the other hand, provide the possibility of viewing both the task screen and the help screen simultaneously. Intuitively, it seems that this is desirable and that performance degradations would not occur in windowing systems. Some anecdotal evidence supports this claim, but there is not enough hard data to justify the expense of windowing for the sole purpose of help systems.

Single versus multiple levels of detail.   Most systems provide only one level of detail. That is, when the user asks for help on a given topic, a single frame is presented, which represents the whole extent of the information that is available on that topic. This approach assumes that all users will want the same level of informational detail on a given topic. In fact, however, sometimes the user will be a novice, requiring full descriptive information on a topic, and other times the user will be an expert who has simply forgotten the exact syntax of a command and needs a quick, brief reminder.

An alternative provided by some systems is to make multiple frames available for each topic, which vary in how detailed they are or in what kind of information they contain. The user indicates which level of detail is desired. For instance, the first press of a special help key might give a terse, syntactic description of a command, while a second press might bring up a more detailed, semantic explanation of the command and when it might be used. A single, multilevel assistance program might be more effective than two separate systems, one for novices (an on-line tutorial) and one for experts (an on-line quick reference systems). It would recognize the fact that a given user is an expert in some applications and commands and a novice in others and provide a single system for both, which is simpler than navigating between two different systems. Unfortunately, sufficient data do not exist to guide us confidently in structuring different types and levels of help information.

Fixed versus user modifiable. A given, closed help system can provide a fixed, unmodifiable set of information, and this will probably be sufficient. However, we can imagine that it might be useful to allow users to edit help texts, that is, to add bits of information that are particularly relevant to their organizational unit.

There are potential disadvantages to offering editing capability to users, of course. Vendors would not want maintenance responsibility for a system that users could tinker with. And it is actually debatable whether or not it would be desirable to allow users the ability to alter their help system, because it is unclear that they would always do something constructive. Beyond editing rights to vendor-supplied help, however, we conceivably would like to give users the capability of adding their own help text to a system when they add their own specific applications. And, in an open system that accommodates third-party software, we would like to offer the mechanisms for third-party applications developers to add help texts relevant to their applications.

In a context-independent system, this is relatively simple, because it involves only the addition of text. In a context-sensitive system, things get more complex, however, because we must provide a way for developers to create the links between the help text and the contexts of the application. Surely this is desirable, because the user would want the help system to always be complete and system-wide. The expense and complexity of an open yet context-sensitive help system may, however, prevent it from becoming the norm.

Access methods. How the system provides access to help information determines how many steps the user must go through to obtain the desired information, how much the user must know to request the desired information, how much text must be stored in the help database, and how complex the help processor must be.

In *context-sensitive* systems, theoretically, the user pushes a single key and the system must figure out what is being requested. In *single-entry point* systems, there practically is no help processor, and users must know what they are looking for and how to navigate through the system to find it. In systems where the user enters a *keyword* to indicate the desired information, the burden is more or less shared between user and system. Although the user must actually know quite a bit to obtain the desired information, the system takes care of accessing and displaying the target information, thus freeing the user of navigational operations.

Of course, combinations of these access methods might be desirable. For instance, in a semi-context-sensitive system, the system might respond to the user's press of a help key by presenting a menu of topics in which the default selection is the system's best guess as to the desired information. Or the system might give the user the option of pressing a help key, followed by a terminator, such as "Execute", thus causing the system to determine the help text from the context. Or the user might press the help key, followed by a keyword, to obtain information on a specific topic unrelated to the current context.

More than one access and navigational method would probably be optimal, because users will undoubtedly use a help system in different ways for different purposes over time. Sometime in the future we may see natural language as an access method to help systems, although it is unclear whether this would actually be superior to context-sensitive or well-designed menu-driven systems (see Chapter 10).

Sequential versus hierarchical versus networked. In systems where navigating elsewhere from the entry point is possible, at least three structures that have implications for navigational ease are possible. Most simply, there could be a *sequential* structure in which the help system was structured like a word processing document that could be scrolled up and down in a linear fashion. Or the system could be organized *hierarchically,* so that users proceeded up and down branches of a tree structure, like traditional menu systems. Or the system could be *networked,* so that the user could somehow get from one help screen or frame to any other directly, without backtracking through a menu hierarchy or smooth scrolling in a linear fashion. Systems that provide access through user-entered keywords are an example of the latter type.

The trade-off between the three types of organization seems to be between ease of learning and ease of use. Documents and menus might be tedious and inefficient to navigate through, but they do not require that the user know the exact name or syntactic structure of the information desired. Keyword systems allow fast movement between frames, but they require that users know how to express what it is they are looking for. Probably some combination is optimal. The user could navigate through the menu hierarchy, but also specify a particular screen by name or keyword if they knew how to, thus bypassing the menu.

Navigation is a particularly important issue in help systems, because it is likely that, unless it is relatively easy and nondisruptive to access help information, help will not be regarded as helpful and will be underused.

User versus system initiated. Probably most help systems that currently exist at the time of this writing are *user initiated;* that is, the user must make an explicit request for help. A possible alternative is to have a system that, besides responding to specific user requests, also makes decisions based on user behavior to offer help information that it determines would be relevant and useful.

These two types of systems imply somewhat different underlying philosophies of the role of the computer system (Sondheimer and Relles, 1982). One view holds that the computer is a tool and that, as such, it should be passively responsive, easy to wield, reliable, and powerful. The other view is that the computer can be an intelligent assistant, with more active intelligence and a more natural communication mode in which the user expresses broadly what is desired, and the computer figures out what is necessary, does it, and reports the results.

This latter view implies that the initiative for user assistance may indeed reside in the system. To do this, the help system must be both *user* and *context* sensitive. That is, it must monitor the behavior of an individual user to determine what might be useful information for that user.

As a simple example, the system might tally the number of times the user executes a "Delete" and "Insert" command sequentially; if this was done very frequently, the system could suggest that the user use the "Replace" command and give instructions on the use of this command. Such intelligence in the system is of course costly, and it is debatable whether or not people would perceive this sort of active help as intrusive and offensive (that is, that the computer is measuring performance and passing judgment) rather than helpful. However, if users had the option of turning the active aspect of the system off and on, this might alleviate any negative reaction, and some users might perceive such a system as extremely helpful. As systems become more complex and functionally rich and as technology advances, enabling more capacity and power for less cost, such systems may begin to appear.

Literature is available that gives examples of existing help systems that vary on these dimensions (See Borenstein (1988) and Kearsley (1988)).

ON-LINE HELP: EXPERIMENTAL STUDIES

A number of studies investigating various aspects of on-line help systems are available in the literature. One group of studies, although not directly concerned with help systems, is nonetheless relevant. The studies compare reading performance on CRTs with reading from paper.

In a study by Muter, Latremouille, and Treurneit (1982), 32 users read 47 short stories either from a book or from a computer screen. In the book, the text was formatted in 40 rows and 60 columns per page. There were roughly 400 words per page. Text was black on a white background.

On the computer screen, text was formatted in 18 rows and 39 columns per page. There were approximately 120 words per page. Characters were white on a blue background. Only paging (versus smooth scrolling) was allowed, and paging took about $\frac{1}{2}$ second. The angle, height, and position of the computer screen were not adjustable.

Participants spent 2 hours reading the stories. After 1 hour, they were stopped and given 25 multiple-choice comprehension questions taken from all stories (some of which may have not yet been read). Then they were given another hour to read and received a second set of 25 comprehension questions. After this test, they were asked to rate their discomfort on a number of dimensions.

Book and computer screen users reported no significant differences in sub-

	Video	Book
Reading speed (words per minute)	158.95	222.30
Comprehension (out of 8)	6.22	5.97

Figure 17-6 A study of user performance reading from computer screens. From Muter, Latremouille and Treurniet, "Extended Reading of Continuous Text on Television Screens," *Human Factors*, 24, no.5 (1982), 501-8. © 1982, by the Human Factors Society, Inc. Reprinted with permission. All rights reserved.

jective ratings of dizziness, headache, nausea, fatigue, or eyestrain after two hours of reading. This is a bit surprising, given all the discussion in the popular press concerning the effects of prolonged use of computer screens. However, perhaps 2 hours is not long enough to produce any of the commonly cited effects.

Performance data from this study are summarized in Figure 17-6. Here it can be seen that, while reading *speed* was significantly higher reading from a book than from a computer screen, there were no significant differences in *comprehension*. One implication of these data is that reading *tutorials* from a manual rather than on line might be more efficient. *User guides* and *references,* on the other hand, which do not as a rule require extended periods reading lengthy passages, may not suffer from being presented on line, at least in terms of simple reading speed and basic comprehension.

On the other hand, these results must be cautiously interpreted, because the two conditions differed in color of foreground and background, column width, page length and viewing angle, as well as in presentation medium. All these factors are known to affect reading rate, and so it is not clear whether they, or the difference in presentation medium, is responsible for these results. That is, if the screen and paper presentations were equal in color, column width, page length, and viewing angle, it is possible that the difference in reading rate would not have occurred.

Gould and others (1987a,b) report on a series of studies that attempted to pinpoint the source of the apparent advantage of paper for reading. Studies that controlled all but one variable (for example, character size, font, polarity, contrast, and user experience with CRTs) failed to find any single variable that could account for the differences in reading speed found in other studies, such as that just cited. On the other hand, studies that matched CRT and paper displays as closely as possible on all variables (for example, polarity: black characters on a white background) and optimized CRT parameters such as resolution and perceivable flicker essentially eliminated any performance differences between reading from paper and CRTs. The authors conclude that the image quality of the characters themselves are the key factor in determining reading speed, rather than any inherent aspects of CRTs or users.

Thus, it would seem that a designer should take into account the image quality of the intended workstation as well as the importance of reading speed in choosing between on-line and hard-copy presentation of user manuals and learning aids. An on-line help system that is nothing more than a hard-copy manual put on line on a low-resolution screen will clearly not add anything over and above the hard-copy manual and may even degrade simple reading time. An on-line help system that is cleverly designed to provide increased power (for example, increased flexibility and more efficient navigation) as compared to a hard-copy manual and that is implemented on a high-resolution screen with high image quality will not only equal a manual in reading speed but may provide increased usability.

A number of help systems are implemented in current systems, and one interesting question is whether or not users actually use them. One researcher (Ross, 1987) conducted a *usage study* of an implemented help system to answer this question. A software monitor was installed in the application, and it tallied all accesses to help. Two kinds of help were available: help on fill-in fields and help on error messages.

The data thus collected revealed several interesting findings. First, help was being used. Across approximately 1000 users, it was accessed 800 to 1200 times per week on average. Second, usage increased by as much as 200% to 250% when major changes were made to the system and when new users got on the system. In these situations, usage peaked in about 7 to 10 days and then returned to normal within another week. From these two observations it would seem that users resort to help both as a training tool and as an ongoing reference tool.

Finally, explanation of error messages was the motive in 53% of all help calls. Those error messages for which help was most frequently accessed were analyzed. This revealed several things. First, some error messages were too vague. When they were rewritten, access to help from those messages decreased. Second, help did not exist for some error messages, because designers had thought they would be self-explanatory. About 7% of the time that users asked for help on an error message, no help message was available. Help messages were added for error messages that did not have them but from which help was frequently accessed. Third, some help messages did not add any information over the error message itself. These were rewritten. These data confirm in at least one case that help systems are actually used, that they are used during training and as a reference, and that they can be improved by an analysis of usage data once they are in production.

Another study (Cohill and Williges, 1982) compared the performance of novices using a system depending on whether they had access to a manual, an on-line help system, or no documentation at all. A number of different measures of performance were taken, including time to completion, errors, number of com-

Available Help

	Manual	Online	None
Time to completion	**293.1**	350.9	679.1
Errors	**0.4**	2.0	5.0
Number of commands used	**8.4**	13.5	20.2
Completed tasks	**5.0**	5.0	3.4

Figure 17–7   A study of on-line versus manual help systems. From Cohill and Williges, "Computer-Augmented Retrieval of HELP Information for Novice Users," *Proceedings of the Human Factors Society 26th Annual Meeting*, 1982, 79–82. © 1982, by the Human Factors Society, Inc. Reprinted with permission. All rights reserved.

mands used, and number of successfully completed tasks. These data are summarized in Figure 17-7.

Interestingly enough, the data showed significant advantages on most measures of performance for *manual users over on-line help users*. This contradicts the common assumption that on-line is always better than hard copy. The conclusion to be drawn from this study, however, is not that manuals are better than on-line help systems in general, but that being on-line is not, in and of itself, an advantage. As was revealed in a previously cited study, reading may take longer on line. And, unless the power of the computer is exploited in intelligent ways in designing an on-line help system, it may provide no particular advantage and may in fact result in a disadvantage, as compared to traditional hard-copy documentation. Some of the details of the help system used in this study, given in a later paper (Cohill and Williges, 1985), are revealing. The important characteristics were the following:

No browsing from initial help frame
Slow paging
Access by keyword
Help screen completely obscured problem screen

It is not too surprising that using a manual was easier in this case, because the manual provided easier access and more flexible navigation and did not obscure the problem screen. We can imagine a help system, however, with powerful and flexible access and navigation, presented in windows that did not obscure the problem area. A help system designed with these characteristics would possibly prove superior to a manual in a similar test.

Another study (Magers, 1983) makes this point more directly. Two on-line help facilities to the same electronic mail system were designed and compared. A *standard* or traditional help system was organized like a reference manual, made heavy use of technical jargon and mathematical notation, and required users to request help on specific topics by typing in keywords. The *modified* help system provided context-sensitive help through a special help key, was organized more like a tutorial, used simplified language, and included many examples. The differences between the two systems can be summarized as follows:

Standard help system	Modified help system
Command access only	HELP key access
Keyword access	Context sensitive
Reference	Tutorial and reference
Heavy use of jargon	Reduced use of jargon
Mathematical notation	Examples
Computer-oriented screens	Task-oriented screens
Precise command names only	Dictionary of synonyms
Oversized help panels	Screen-sized help panels

Thirty computer novices participated. Their task was to create two new reports from short notes and send them to specified recipients. Thus they had to learn to use the editing and sending capabilities of the electronic mail system. They were given brief verbal instructions, encouraged to use the hard-copy manuals that were provided, told how to use the help system, and given 1 hour to complete their task. A variety of performance measures was taken. The data are summarized in Figure 17-8.

Half the 30 participants were given each of the two help systems. Fourteen of the 15 modified help system users completed the task within the allotted hour. By contrast, only three of the standard help system users did so. They took an average of 75.6 minutes to either complete the task or give up. Those who completed the task took an average of 84 minutes.

Modified help users also scored higher, made less errors, used help more, and used manuals less than standard help users. In spite of the fact that modified help users used help more often and spent more time in the help facility, it is interesting that they still took less time overall to complete the task. Clearly, the particular design of the help system had a significant effect on user performance.

The two help systems in Magers's study (1983) varied on many dimensions, and it is not clear exactly how each contributed to the observed performance differences. Elkerton and Palmiter (1989) investigated one primary aspect of help systems: information organization. They compared performance navigating

Help system

	Standard	Modified
Time (min)	75.6	**52.0**
Score	43.0	**90.6**
% Errors	55.2	**19.7**
References to HELP	22.4	**60.8**
References to manual	11.1	**1.8**
Time in HELP	18.3	**24.6**

Figure 17–8   A study of on-line help system design. From Magers, "An Experimental Evaluation of On-Line HELP for Non-Programmers," *Proceedings, CHI '83*, 1983, pp. 277–81. With permission.

through two help systems with the same content and access mechanisms, but different organizations. In the *original* help system, information was organized in rather abstract categories, such as "Reference," "Closer and farther," and "Creating/modifying fields." In addition, all operations needed to accomplish a task were not always described in a single location. In the *GOMS* help system, information was organized in more user-task-oriented categories, such as "Create," "Delete," "Fields," and "Buttons," and all operations needed to accomplish a task were described in a single location (*GOMS* refers to the method used to design this help system). A measure of retrieval time to find the required information in the help system showed the GOMS help system to be twice as fast initially (in the first 14 of 56 trials), although there was no difference in later trials. This indicates that the organization of the GOMS help system allowed users to more quickly learn the location of information in the help system. Users also rated the GOMS help system as superior to the original help system on a subjective rating scale.

In a paper expanding on the GOMS approach to designing help, Elkerton (1988) offers a number of guidelines, summarized and paraphrased here:

1. Describe what can be done in task-oriented terms.
2. Provide an adjustable level of detail for a wide range of users.
3. Provide procedurally incomplete advice to encourage active learning.
4. Provide feedback on appropriate procedures after errors.
5. Describe simple actions common to many procedures.
6. Provide detailed knowledge of procedures.
7. Monitor user actions to provide context-sensitive help.
8. Present step-by-step procedures.
9. Provide procedural demonstrations.
10. Provide context-sensitive advice.
11. Help users select among interface methods.
12. Help users learn when to apply specific interface methods.

Another study (Clark, 1981) reported on problems encountered in prototyping and experimenting with the panels of an on-line help system for a business graphics system. A number of users were brought in to use a prototype of the system and its help panels; their performance was observed and conclusions were drawn. Some of these observations and conclusions are summarized next.

The system was not a context-sensitive or windowed system, so the help panels replaced and obscured the problem display. This was a problem for many users. They had trouble finding the part in the help panel that was relevant to their particular problem. This was solved by placing a marker in the help panel that pointed to the part of it that contained information relevant to the user at the time of the request. Thus, context sensitivity was presented and was determined to be very helpful. Of course, a windowing system might also have helped simply by not obscuring the problem display.

Presenting the help text as a solid block of text also made it difficult for users to scan and find what they were looking for. This was solved by stylizing the text with visual cues that made it easier to home in on parts that the user was looking for. Consistency of style was observed to facilitate scanning and finding, in particular.

An initial prototype appeared to have a reading level that was pitched too high. Experimentation suggested that a six- or seven-year-old reading level was optimal, with one sentence presented per line. Although it was obvious that users could understand much more complex language, the author noted that it was difficult for them to do so while keeping the details of their problems, as well as other rules for interacting with the system, in mind.

Inappropriate and vague "voice" in the instructions also seemed to present problems. For instance, "To draw the picture, press the PF5 key" was found to be a better choice of voice than "Pressing the PF5 key will cause the picture to be drawn." Users seemed to prefer the former because it stood out unmistakably in all the "noise" of the new material in the help panel. One related problem, however, was that users then expected instructions to work while they were still in the help system panel; they did not understand that they must first exit and return to the application itself. This was so hard to explain that the author suggested actually having the system behave according to these expectations, that is, to not require exiting explicitly from the help panel.

Finally, it was found that "Help" itself was a poor choice of a word for the assistance program, because it seemed to carry a connotation of distress or emergency use only, causing users to hesitate to use it as it was intended. A better term was not suggested, however.

All the previous studies focused on user *performance* with help systems. One study (Keister, 1989) looked at *preference* data. Drawing on the help literature, Keister drew up a questionnaire to determine what aspects of a help system were considered most important. Thirty-four different items were included. Examples include the following:

Restore original screen
Switch between screens
Step by step instructions
Help is automatic after errors
Access to all help screens
Does not interfere with task

Questionnaire respondents rated each item for importance on a scale from 1 to 5, where 1 was "Not Important" and 5 was "Very Important." Keister found a different pattern of responses when he administered the questionnaire to *users* as opposed to *developers*. In general, *users* seemed most concerned that the help system make their primary job easier and not interfere with it, while *developers* seemed more concerned with technical issues, such as consistency and whether screens were restored exactly. The two items that there was most disagreement on were the need to access all help screens and the need for step by step instructions. Users rated these as high in importance, while developers rated them quite low. These data provide insight into what users consider important in a help system and also highlight the often different agendas of users and developers, reinforcing the need for user input during design.

These studies taken together suggest two important points. First, on-line help systems are not necessarily always better than traditional hard-copy manuals. Hard copy may be superior for certain kinds of documentation, such as tutorials, because reading may be faster from paper than from many existing computer screens. Second, the *particulars of the design* of an on-line help system will determine how it compares to a hard-copy manual and how effective it is in general. This is consistent with the finding that the design of hard-copy manuals affects performance (Foss, Rosson, and Smith, 1982) and with the many studies cited in earlier chapters of this book that indicate that user interface design alternatives profoundly affect usability. After all, on-line help is just another application, with its own user interface, and so most of the design issues discussed in previous chapters apply to the design of on-line help systems as well.

One striking thing about a survey of the current literature on help systems is what is missing, rather than what is available. In particular, no paper or study surveyed here directly addresses the basic question of what the *content* or *subject matter* of a user assistance program should be. Few researchers seem to have posed and answered the question, "What kind of questions do novice and expert users actually ask when using a system?" All the fancy formatting, navigational ease and ease of access in the world will not be of much use if the information contained in the help system is not the information that users seek. Clearly, basic research into help *content* is required.

Simple studies applying a protocol analysis methodology would be useful here. A "human help system," that is, an expert in a particular application who works with a novice and responds to and records the kinds of questions asked could yield data that, if collected across a number of users and a number of applications, could be analyzed to reveal the general nature of help required by such users. Similar techniques could be applied to different classes of users (for example, technical experts on a new application or experts who are infrequent users) to observe how their requests for information differ from those of novices. Many questions regarding the type of help to provide on particular systems could be answered or suggested by such data.

Some initial thoughts on different types of questions that might be asked by users of interactive systems include the following:

> What do I do next?
> What did I do wrong?
> How do I . . . ?
> Can I . . . ?
> Where am I?
> Where is . . . ?
> Why did this happen?
> What will happen if . . . ?
> What can I do from here?
> Give me the big picture.

Different possible referents for these sorts of questions might include data fields, tasks (an answer here may cut across application boundaries), system objects (such as commands, files, or programs), applications, and concepts (for example, windows). It is not clear what referents and question types will most frequently be asked by different types of users. Without these data, it is impossible to design the content for an effective help system.

One study has made a foray into this aspect of help. Hill and Miller (1988) conducted a preliminary study to provide input to the design of intelligent advisory systems. They used a *Wizard-of-Oz* technique (see Chapter 10) in which users of an experimental graphical statistics program typed in natural language advice requests in the course of trying to accomplish some predefined tasks. A "wizard" in another room intercepted their requests and replied to them in natural language text which was sent back to their screen. Users believed they were interacting with an experimental advisory system and were unaware that they were actually interacting with another human being. In addition, the "wizard" gave advice under two different conditions. In one, the "wizard" had access to the user's screen at all times, and in the other the "wizard" could not see the user's screen and relied totally on typed natural language interaction with the user to understand the user's goals and problems. Thus, analyses could be conducted on both the kinds of advice users requested and the kinds of advisory strategies used by human advisors.

A number of interesting trends were revealed. First, user requests fell into several categories, as follows:

Give plan or next step:	61%
Describe or identify object:	20%
Verify action as proper:	8%
Other:	9%

Thus, the majority of requests involved the need for help with *high-level planning* for *specific tasks*. This type of help is characteristic of an intelligent advisory system and is not a capability of most help systems.

Second, advisors were much more effective when they could see the user's screen. Less interaction with the user was required to understand their request. Knowledge of both past interactions and the current screen state played heavily into the advice given when the user's screen was available to the advisor. Heavy clarification dialog was necessary when the user's screen was not available to the advisor.

Third, thinking-aloud protocols collected from advisors while they were giving advice revealed the following general strategies:

1. If a query presupposes dysfunctional ideas about the system, counter the wrong ideas with correct information.
2. When not answering a query literally, let the client know what the next right step is.
3. If the client's presumed reasons for using requested information are potentially harmful or not related to the client's current goal, warn the client or withhold the requested information.
4. If it can be confidently believed that the client already knows something, do not include that thing in the advice.
5. If particular concepts or skills are prerequisite to making use of some advice and it is

unlikely that the client has those prerequisite concepts or skills, include them in the advice.

6. When needed information is missing, assume a likely case and conditionalize the advice on that case.

7. If there is basis for assuming the client knows some critical but missing fact, ask the client for it. (Hill and Miller, 1988)

It can be seen here that what distinguishes intelligent advice from simple question answering is the monitoring of the client's high-level goals and the verification that their questions involving low-level subgoals are compatible with their higher-level goals. Successful advising thus requires that the advisor be able to track the clients goals and task states. The authors note that when users are most in need of help they are least able to form valid requests for help. These points are illustrated in the following example:

Student: What's my next step if I want to use a correlated t-test to compare these two groups of cars on the mpg?

Advisor: Since the groups contain no common members, you really want to use the independent t-test. Go to the *Procedures menu* to get the independent t-test icon. Then link to it the icons containing the grouped data. If you don't remember how to do the linking, call me over again. (Hill and Miller, 1988)

Here it can be seen that a simple question-answering help system would have taken the question literally and given procedural information on an inappropriate subgoal (the correlated t-test). The intelligent advisor, on the other hand, was aware of the high-level goal and provided a more appropriate subgoal (the independent t-test), as well as procedural information.

Thus, this study indicates that users may often want help with high-level planning, as well as with simple syntax, and may need advice on appropriate subgoals even when they are not aware of this. A simple question-answering help system will not meet these needs. An intelligent advisory system is required. Such systems are in the experimental stages of development, however, and developers must await more research and experimentation before such systems become generally feasible and practical. In the meantime, studies using a similar methodology could be used to provide input to the design of more traditional help systems.

ON-LINE HELP: PRINCIPLES AND GUIDELINES

☞ **Make help visible: "advertise."**

The fact that help is available should be made visible to users. They should not have to read about it in a manual and remember a command to invoke it. There might be a Help key on the keyboard, clearly labeled and distinctive in size or color from other keys. Or Help might be an always available option in a menu interface.

☞ **Make it complete and accurate.**

Nothing will discourage a user from asking for help faster than too many messages such as "Help not implemented for this function," or actual inaccuracies in the help screens and discrepancies between on-line help and manuals. One or two experiences of this sort will result in an underutilized help system that does not pay for its development in terms of increased user productivity.

☞ **Provide multiple access methods.**

There is no one right or best way to provide access to a help system. There are several ways, each of which is best for different users in different situations. *Context-sensitive* access is best for assistance in executing a system function, such as entering a command or filling in a fill-in field. *Key-word* access might be better, however, when users want syntactic information on a function they know the name of but that they are not currently executing. Finally, *single entry point* access might be best for a user trying to determine how to accomplish some general goal that might require the execution of a number of different functions. A given user may have these different needs at different times. Thus, it is best to provide all types of access in a help system.

☞ **Organize help around user tasks and goals.**

Often help users have considerable *semantic* knowledge, but little or no *syntactic* knowledge of the system. Too often, help is organized according to system architecture, according to the particulars of the system's user interface, or according to some other logic and jargon that is meaningful to the developer, but obscure to the user who is trying to learn the system.

For *expert* users, this organization might be useful. Reference manuals are often organized around aspects of the system architecture or user interface. However, *intermediate users* have in mind what they want to accomplish, but are not yet familiar with system architecture or the user interface. That is why they are referring to the help system. Thus, the organization of help topics should be structured and labeled in terms of *user goals*. This will help users navigate to the help information they need. The following are examples of poor and improved organization and labeling of topics within a help system.

Examples of *poor organization and labeling of help menu choices* that reflect system architecture, user interface, and developer jargon include (Elkerton and Palmiter, 1989)

Reference
Closer and Farther
Creating/Modifying Fields

Examples of *headings that better communicate the topic* in terms of user goals might be, respectively (Elkerton and Palmiter, 1989),

Create

Delete

Buttons

Fields

☞ **Provide different levels of detail under user control.**

When users ask for help, they may be interested in anything from the proper spelling or syntax of a command to a mini-tutorial on how to accomplish some general task. If they want simple *syntactic* information, they should not have to wade through tutorial-like discussions. If they want a tutorial, simple *syntactic* help will not help them. Again, a given user may want one level of help at one time and another level at another. Thus, it is a good idea to provide multiple levels of help information and allow users to specify the desired level of detail.

There are any number of different ways to do this. In some systems, selecting the help option several times in succession takes the user through successive levels of detail. In others, a parameter is specified along with the help command. It is best to allow specification of the level of detail on a case by case basis rather than as a user–session default, because a given user may need simple help on one function, but full help on another.

☞ **Provide powerful but easy to learn and use navigational aids.**

Once in a help system, it must be easy to navigate and find the information desired. A help system that is difficult to learn and use will not be helpful. A help system that is less easy to navigate through than a manual will not be used. Easy to learn and use functions such as cross referencing, browsing, expanding and contracting the level of detail, and searching should be provided.

☞ **Write at the appropriate reading level.**

Evidence suggests (Clark, 1981) that help text should be cast at a very low reading level, regardless of the reading level of the user. It will be comprehensible to users with lower reading levels and easy to read by higher-level users. Since help is always a secondary task, which the user must comprehend and manipulate while keeping the main task in mind, simplicity of language will facilitate the use of help with minimal interruption of the main task.

☞ **Provide a well-designed visual layout.**

The actual format of help screens or frames should not only be consistent, but should be designed to facilitate scanning and reading so that users can find what they are looking for as quickly and easily as possible. For instance, a solid block of text is quite unhelpful, whereas spatial cues such as columns, groupings, and different fonts, if used in a consistent manner, can give users at-a-glance information about where to look on a screen for what they are after. Similarly, do not put too much information on a single help screen. As a general rule of thumb, no more than about seven concepts should be included on a single screen. On screens with graphics capabilities, illustrations can also add to the readability of help information.

☞ Use windowing.

Help is best presented in a window or pop-up panel so that the help information does not obscure the context for which help is being requested.

☞ Make it simple and easy to return to the problem context.

It should not take more than a single keystroke or mouse click to return from help to the exact screen from which help was requested, regardless of where in the help system the user might be. Users must hold in short-term memory the details of the problem they are trying to solve and the information they have found in help. They should not be distracted by complex navigational operations just to return to the problem screen.

☞ Make it fast.

Using a help system must be faster than looking up the same information in a manual or it will not be used. A help system that takes a long time to load or page is not helpful.

☞ Make it user modifiable.

This is a controversial recommendation, because issues arise when many users share a workstation or help system or when help vendors are held responsible for quality and content. However, there are various ways to provide users with the ability to tailor their help systems in useful ways without creating problems. For instance, users may be allowed to *annotate* help panels, rather than *edit* them. Or users may be allowed to make copies of a help system and specify which copy is to be read whenever help is requested. They can then be allowed to modify their copies and share their copies with other users. Since help systems never provide all the information users may want, it can be useful to allow users to add to and improve their help systems. User organizations often publish hard-copy or on-line documents of helpful hints and procedures for commonly executed tasks. A good help system should support this need.

☞ Make tutorials interactive.

One advantage of an on-line tutorial over a hard-copy tutorial is the possibility of interaction with the tutorial. An on-line tutorial can give the user practice using the system in the process of teaching. For instance, an on-line tutorial on how to use a mouse could allow the users to practice basic operations such as moving the mouse, selecting a target, and learning the meanings of different buttons. Practice reinforces learning significantly.

☞ **Make it active ("suggestions").**

Most help systems are passive; that is, users must decide when they need help and then specifically ask for it. A help system could be active. The system could monitor the user's usage of the system and determine when help might be useful. For instance, if a user continuously scrolled through many pages of a document in a word processing application, the system might "notice" this and "suggest" the use of the paging or search commands. The power of many systems is underutilized because users simply do not discover or remember the more powerful commands or functions. User productivity may be less than optimal. An active help system could help users become more efficient without requiring their own initiative to do so.

An active help system must accomplish four main tasks (Fischer, Lemke, and Schwab, 1985):

1. *Recognize* what the user is doing or wants to do
2. *Evaluate* how the user is trying to achieve a goal
3. *Construct a model* of the user based on the evaluations
4. *Decide* when and how to interrupt with suggestions

One active help system is described in Fischer, Lemke, and Schwab (1985).

Of course, an active help system must be carefully implemented. Users must be able to turn the suggestions off and on. Some users may simply not like the idea of their system monitoring their behavior and offering advice. And there will always be some cases where the system misinterprets the user's behavior and offers inappropriate advice. This would be annoying, and users must be able to prevent it. An active help system as a user option, however, would probably be well received and could contribute to overall user productivity and satisfaction with a system.

☞ **Make it consistent in style.**

Consistency of style in the help system is just as important as consistency in the user interface for other aspects of the system. The access method, navigational operations, and presentation style of the help system should be the same across and within the help system to different applications and different functions. Designers should make decisions on the characteristics of a help system and then adhere to these decisions consistently throughout the help system. The user interface to the help system should also be as consistent as possible with the user interface to other parts of the system. If, for instance, the system in general is menu oriented, then perhaps the help system should be too.

☞ **Follow general guidelines for interface design and documentation design.**

A help system is, after all, just another interactive software system. It also has a user interface. Users must learn how to invoke it, how to navigate in it, how to turn options on and off, and so on. In addition, they must be able to get the information they want from it efficiently and effectively. Thus, most of the other guidelines offered in this book for good user interface and good documentation design apply to the design of on-line help systems.

REFERENCES

BAUER, DAVID W., and JOHN K. EDDY, "The Representation of Command Language Syntax," *Human Factors,* 28, no. 1 (February 1986), pp. 1–10.

BILLINGSLEY, PATRICIA A., "Navigation through Hierarchical Menu Structures: Does It Help to Have a Map?" *Proceedings of the Human Factors Society 26th Annual Meeting,* 1982, pp. 103–107.

BLACK, JOHN B., JOHN M. CARROLL, and STUART M. McGUIGAN, "What Kind of Minimal Instruction Manual Is the Most Effective?" *CHI '87 Proceedings,* May 1987, pp. 159–162, ACM.

———, and others, "Online Tutorials: What Kind of Inference Leads to the Most Effective Learning?" *CHI '89 Proceedings,* May 1989, pp. 81–84, ACM.

BORENSTEIN, NATHANIEL S., "On-line Help Systems: A Taxonomy, Survey and Research Review," in Greg Kearsley, *Introduction to the Design and Implementation of Online Help Systems,* CHI '88 Tutorial Notes, ACM/SIGCHI, 1988.

CLARK, I. A., "Software Simulation as for Tool for Usable Product Design," *IBM Systems Journal,* 20, no. 3 (1981), pp. 273–93.

COHILL, A. M., and R. C. WILLIGES, "Computer-augmented Retrieval of HELP Information for Novice Users," *Proceedings of the Human Factors Society 26th Annual Meeting,* 1982, pp. 79–82.

———, "Retrieval of HELP Information for Novice Users of Interactive Computer Systems," *Human Factors,* 27, no. 3 (June 1985), pp. 335–44.

COMSTOCK, ELIZABETH M., and ELIZABETH ANN CLEMENS, "Perceptions of Computer Manuals: A View from the Field," *Proceedings of the Human Factors Society 31st Annual Meeting,* 1987, pp. 139–43.

ELKERTON, JAY, "Online Aiding for Human–Computer Interfaces," *Handbook of Human–Computer Interaction,* Martin Helander, ed., (Amsterdam: North-Holland, 1988), pp. 345–64.

———, and SUSAN L. PALMITER, "Designing Help Systems Using the GOMS Model: An Information Retrieval Evaluation," *Proceedings of the Human Factors Society 33rd Annual Meeting,* 1989, pp. 281–85.

FISCHER, GERHARD, ANDREAS LEMKE, and THOMAS SCHWAB, "Knowledge-based Help Systems," *CHI '85 Proceedings,* April 1985, pp. 161–68, ACM.

FOSS, D., M. B. ROSSON, and P. SMITH, "Reducing Manual Labor: An Experimental Analysis of Learning Aids for a Text Editor," *Proceedings, Human Factors in Computer Systems,* 1982, pp. 332–36.

GOULD, JOHN D., and others, "Why Reading Was Slower from CRT Displays Than from Paper," *CHI '87 Proceedings,* May 1987a, pp. 7–12, ACM.

———, and others, "Reading Is Slower from CRT Displays Than from Paper: Attempts to Isolate a Single-variable Explanation," *Human Factors,* 29, no. 3 (June 1987b), pp. 269–300.

HILL, WILLIAM C., and JAMES R. MILLER, "Justified Advice: A Semi-Naturalistic Study of Advisory Strategies," *CHI '88 Proceedings,* May 1988, pp. 185–90, ACM.

HOUGHTON, RAYMOND C., "Online Help Systems: A Conspectus," *Communications of the ACM,* 27, no. 2 (1984), pp. 126–33.

KEARSLEY, GREG, *Online HELP Systems: Design and Implementation* (Norwood, N.J.: Ablex Publishing Corp., 1988), pp. 27–43.

KEISTER, RICHARD S., "The Content of Help Screens: Users versus Developers," *Proceedings of the Human Factors Society 33rd Annual Meeting,* 1989, pp. 390–93.

MAGERS, CELESTE C., "An Experimental Evaluation of On-line HELP for Non-Programmers," *Proceedings, CHI '83,* 1983, pp. 277–81, ACM.

MUTER, PAUL, SUSANE A. LATREMOUILLE, and WILLIAM C. TREURNIET, "Extended Reading of Continuous Text on Television Screens," *Human Factors,* 24, no. 5 (1982), pp. 501–8.

RELLES, N., N. K. SONDHEIMER, and G. P. INGARGIOLA, "Recent Advances in User Assistance," *Proceedings of the Conference and Easier and More Productive Use of Computer Systems,* SIGSOC Bulletin (ACM), 13, no. 2–3 (1981), pp. 1–5.

ROSS, EUGENE H., "Findings in Measuring the Usage of Online Documentation," *Proceedings of the Human Factors Society 31st Annual Meeting,* 1987, pp. 224–27.

ROWLAND, LAWRENCE R., and EVELYN L. WILLIAMS, "A Computer-aided Method for Assessing Accessibility of Information in Technical Documentation," *Proceedings of the Human Factors Society 33rd Annual Meeting,* 1989, pp. 394–98.

SHNEIDERMAN, BEN, *Designing the User Interface: Strategies for Effective Human–Computer Interaction* (Reading, Mass.: Addison-Wesley Publishing Co., 1986), pp. 336–42.

SONDHEIMER, N. K., and N. RELLES, "Human Factors and User Assistance in Interactive Computing Systems: An Introduction," *IEEE Transactions of Systems, Man and Cybernetics,* Vol. SMC-12 (March–April 1982), pp. 102–7.

STRUNK, WILLIAM, JR., and E. B. WHITE, The *Elements of Style* (New York: Macmillan Inc., 1979).

WEBB, JAYSON M., and ARTHUR F. KRAMER, "Learning Hierarchical Menu Systems: A Comparative Investigation of Analogical and Pictorial Formats," *Proceedings of the Human Factors Society 31st Annual Meeting,* 1987, pp. 978–82.

WRIGHT, PATRICIA, "Issues of Content and Presentation in Document Design," *Handbook of Human–Computer Interaction,* Martin Helander, ed. (Amsterdam: North-Holland, 1988), pp. 629–52.

CHAPTER 18

Design Methods

INTRODUCTION

Chapters 3 through 17 offered currently available principles for good software user interface design. These principles can be helpful guidelines for designers. However, even if every software developer and designer was well versed in these design principles, this would not be enough to ensure good interface design. There are several reasons for this. First, some of the available design principles are based on experts' experience and logical deduction from related fields such as cognitive psychology, rather than on hard data. Second, when directly related research is available to back up a design principle, the context the research was conducted in may not match the context of the designer's design issue, thus limiting the general applicability of the guideline. Third, for any given design problem, guidelines will usually come in direct conflict with each other, and there are no algorithms for making the trade-offs. In sum, design principles mainly bring the designer's attention to the issues that should be considered. This is extremely important. However, there is no "cookbook" approach to applying these principles to ensure good interface design.

User interface design is a matter of compromise and trade-off. We want powerful functionality, but a simple, clear interface. We want ease of use, but also ease of learning. We strive for consistency across all aspects of the interface, but also to optimize individual operations. We want an intelligent and sophisticated interface, but also good performance and low cost. Interface designers find themselves constantly confronted with these kinds of conflicting goals. They need methods and techniques to help them effectively manage the design of the user interface and make good design decisions for a given product with its particular set of end users.

This chapter introduces a general methodology for software user interface design, including specific management, design, and testing methods and techniques, in the context of a typical software development life cycle. Practice, rather than theory, is the main focus in this methodology. This chapter can only provide an overview of the methodology. Principles and guidelines, rather than methods, are the main focus of this book.

OVERVIEW OF THE METHODOLOGY

The methodology consists of a set of user interface design tasks applied in a particular order at specified points in the overall system development life cycle. Figure 18-1 through 18-5 depict this methodology. All tasks (that is, not just user interface tasks) in a typical system development life cycle are presented in the order that they would be carried out, according to the responsible organization. Each task is represented as a box enclosing the task name. User interface tasks are

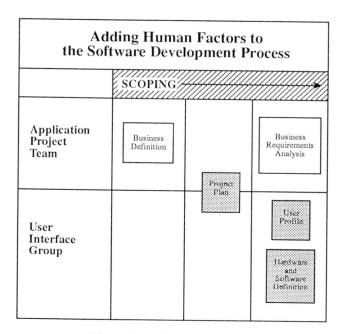

Figure 18–1 The scoping phase.

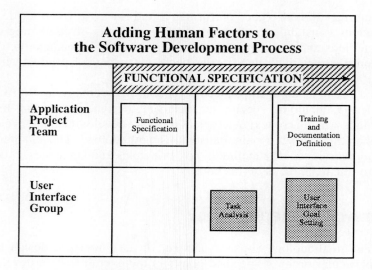

Figure 18–2 The functional specification phase.

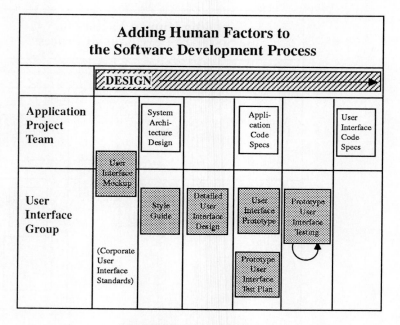

Figure 18–3 The design phase.

Adding Human Factors to the Software Development Process			
	DEVELOPMENT ▶		
Application Project Team	Coding	System Test Plan	Develop Training and Documentation
User Interface Group	User Interface Test Plan		

Figure 18–4   The development phase.

presented as dark gray boxes. Tasks for which the application project team has primary responsibility are shown in white. The horizontal dimension represents time. Each Figure in the sequence covers one phase in the typical software development life cycle.

The user interface tasks, listed in the proper order of their application during development life-cycle phases, are briefly defined next. They are described in more detail in the following sections of this chapter.

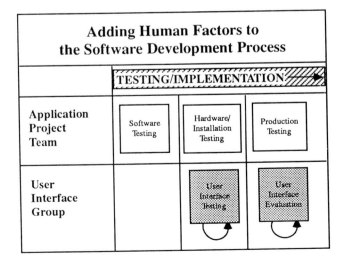

Adding Human Factors to the Software Development Process			
	TESTING/IMPLEMENTATION ▶		
Application Project Team	Software Testing	Hardware/ Installation Testing	Production Testing
User Interface Group		User Interface Testing	User Interface Evaluation

Figure 18–5   The testing and implementation phase.

Phase 1: Scoping

1. Project plan. A particular scope and schedule for each of the remaining tasks is determined and integrated with the overall project plan.

2. User profile. A description of the user characteristics relevant to user interface design is obtained.

3. Hardware and software definition. The user interface techniques (for example, windowing, reverse video, and color) made possible by the hardware and software platform chosen for the application are documented.

Phase 2: Functional Specification

4. Task analysis. A study of users' tasks, work-flow patterns, and conceptual frameworks is made, and this drives a very high level conceptual design of the user interface.

5. User interface goal setting. Specific, quantitative goals defining minimal acceptable user performance are defined. These focus later design efforts and form the basis for the test plan developed later.

6. Training and documentation definition. The various forms of hard-copy documentation, training materials, tutorials, and other on-line user aids that will be provided with the application are decided on. Key staff members who will be responsible for developing these materials and facilities are identified and participate in all later tasks.

Phase 3: Design

7. User interface mockup. Based on the high-level conceptual design generated in the task analysis and any existing corporate user interface standards, initial design ideas are generated and implemented in storyboard form or on a rapid prototyping tool. Several alternative designs may be mocked up.

8. Style guide. The high-level design (overall structure, specific implementation of corporate user interface standards, and navigational pathways) determined in the previous two tasks is documented in a user interface spec called a *Style Guide*.

9. Detailed user interface design. Detailed user interface design (for example, screen design and error message design) is conducted and documented.

10. User interface prototype. The detailed design is implemented in full prototype form on a rapid prototyping tool.

11. Prototype user interface test plan. A plan is developed for a testing procedure that will reveal any major flaws in the initial design.

12. Prototype user interface testing. High-level testing of the user interface prototype is conducted iteratively until all major identified problems are eliminated.

Phase 4: Development

13. Develop training and documentation. User manuals, on-line help, tutorials, and training materials are designed and developed.

14. User interface test plan. A plan for formal testing of the full system against the *ease of use* and *ease of learning* goals identified during the definition phase is designed.

Phase 5: Testing/Implementation

15. User interface testing. Testing and redesign are conducted iteratively until the *ease of use* and *ease of learning* goals are met.

16. User interface evaluation. After the application has been in production for 3 months or more, feedback is gathered to feed into enhancement design and/or new application design.

Where each of the preceding tasks is to be applied in the context of other software development activities is illustrated in Figures 18-1 through 18-5.

It is important to note that the user interface design methodology and the system development life cycle in which it is based are described in this overview as if they consisted of a neat set of nonoverlapping, linearly applied tasks, where each does not proceed until the previous is complete. This is not really the case, nor even the goal. Many tasks overlap or can actually be carried out in parallel. For example, functional specification, carried out by the application project team, and task analysis, conducted by the user interface group, are interrelated tasks that can be carried out more or less in parallel. On the other hand, user interface goal setting cannot proceed until task analysis is complete.

Such interdependencies among tasks are noted in the task descriptions that follow and are reflected in Figure 18-1 through 18-5 by the order in which tasks are presented: tasks in the same column can be conducted in parallel; tasks that must be completed before other tasks begin appear in the column to the right of them. That is, the horizontal dimension represents a time line.

The focal point of the whole procedure is the development of the *style guide* (task 8). The style guide documents the results of all other tasks. It is a dynamic, evolving document that is developed during the course of the scoping, functional specification and design phases and changed repeatedly during the iterative testing and redesign tasks in the testing and implementation phases.

The remaining sections of this chapter describe each task in more detail.

PHASE 1: SCOPING

In a typical software project life cycle, two general activities occur within phase 1, resulting in two work products: a business definition and a business requirements analysis. An **business definition** document results from the activities that precede a decision to initiate development of a new product. A high-level product description is developed based on input from a marketing organization (in the case of a vendor company) or a user organization (in the case of a data processing department of a business). Additional information is then gathered from marketing or users to further define the product, resulting in a **business requirements analysis** document. Then, a project team is assembled, and a **project plan** is drawn up complete with schedule and budget.

The user-interface-related tasks that should be carried out in this phase include the following:

Project plan
User profile
Hardware and software definition

These are described next.

Project Plan

Three important user interface tasks should be incorporated in the project-wide project plan:

1. Staffing and Organization
2. Cost–benefit analysis
3. Planning

Staffing and organization.   Having a skilled user interface designer on the project team will not ensure a good user interface. Designers must be strategically placed in the organization and their responsibilities and authority carefully designed and communicated to the rest of the project team. A few key points can be made here.

First, there should be a *single decision maker* for user interface design, with *final authority* for all user interface design decisions. Typically, each programmer designs the user interface to the module of code they have responsibility for. The programmers do not necessarily consult with one another nor are they commonly familiar with the kinds of research data and guidelines presented in this book. The result is suboptimal design with inconsistencies across the user interface to different parts of the system, which costs users in ease of learning and ease of use. One *decision maker* with the right set of skills, background, and expertise ensures quality and consistency, even if many designers have *input* into the design process.

Second, on large project teams where it can be cost-justified, it is important that this single user interface *designer* be a separate person from the user interface *implementer,* but with equal rank to the implementer in the organization. This ensures that one person can objectively promote usability without being biased by other conflicting goals such as ease of implementation and schedule and budget pressures. Placing the designer on a peer level with the implementer ensures that they will negotiate with one another and find reasonable compromises to these conflicting goals.

Cost–benefit analysis. Time, personnel, and equipment are all required to do a good job of user interface design. They all cost money. The importance of user interface design is often seriously underestimated by management, and too little resources are allocated to it. A justification for the expenditure of significant amounts of money on the kinds of user interface design tasks described in this methodology is very easy to develop and should be used to decide exactly how to allocate human factors resources to a project in a way that will result in a maximum payoff.

The costs and benefits of human factors tasks can be calculated very specifically. For instance, one cost category might be conducting user interface testing to evaluate a prototype. The time, personnel, and equipment costs for such a test can be easily estimated. Similarly, benefits can be estimated. Benefit categories include improved user productivity, decreased user errors, decreased user training time, decreased design changes after implementation, increased sales, and reduced customer support costs. The dollar amounts of these benefit categories can be estimated by making assumptions about the expected number of users of the system, the frequency of use of certain features of the system, and the cost of the users' time.

For example, the cost of running a usability test on a prototype might be calculated as follows:

Task	Hours	Cost
Determine testing issues:	24	
Design test and materials:	24	
Test 20 users:	48	
Analyze data:	48	
Prepare and present results:	16	
Total HF hours:	160	
160 Human factors hours @ $45 =		$7200
48 Assistant hours @ $20		960
48 Cameraman hours @ $30		1440
Video tapes:		120
Total cost:		$9720

Establishing the costs of adding human factors activities to a development effort is thus a simple matter of adding up the number of hours required for all planned tasks, multiplying this by the appropriate hourly rates, and adding in other expenses. The subtasks will vary depending on the task type. The number of hours for a given subtask will depend on the scope of the task (for example, testing 5 rather then 20 users), and the hourly rates will depend on the particular salaries of employees in a particular company. However, the preceding example can be taken as a general formula for computing the cost of any human factors task.

The key to a cost–benefit analysis is quantifying the expected *benefits* so that these can be compared directly to the costs. This is also fairly straightforward. Different types of benefits are most relevant in different organizations. *Vendor* companies care most about:

Increased sales
Decreased cost of providing training
Decreased customer support costs
Decreased development costs
Decreased maintenance costs

Data processing departments serving internal users are more concerned with:

Increased user productivity
Decreased user errors
Improved quality of service
Decreased training time
Decreased user turnover

Each of these types of benefits can be quantified and estimated in terms of time and money.

To estimate expected benefits, certain *assumptions* are required, such as the expected time to process screens developed *without* the benefits of human factors activities as compared to the time to process alternative screens developed *using* human factors techniques.

For example, one category of benefits is *user productivity*. Supposing the expected number of users for a system being developed is 250 and that their hourly rate is $15. Suppose further that two or three major fill-in form screens in this system (each containing many fill-in fields) are expected to be used 60 times a day, 230 days a year by each user. Now make the *assumption* that these screens can be improved by decreasing throughput time by 3 seconds per screen as a result of applying human factors techniques such as prototype testing. These facts and assumptions result in the following estimated benefit:

250 users

× 60 screens per day

× 230 days per year

× processing time reduced by 3 seconds per screen ÷ 3600

× hourly rate of $15

= $43,125 savings per year

A *complete* cost–benefit analysis involves adding up the costs of *all* planned tasks and adding up the expected benefits in *all* relevant categories in a fashion similar to the preceding two examples and comparing these two sums. Planned tasks can then be added or deleted, depending on the outcome of the analysis.

For a more detailed discussion of applying cost–benefit analysis to human factors activities, the reader is referred to Mantei (1986) and Mantei and Teorey (1988). For a case history of cost-justifying human factors activities, see Karat (1989).

Planning.   Each user interface design task and activity should be explicitly written into the overall project plan. It is not sufficient to simply assign a user interface designer to the project team. User interface tasks require not only the user interface designer's time, but also equipment, the time of other project team members, and time added onto the project schedule. If these latter resources are not explicitly planned for and committed to as part of the project plan, they will be very hard to negotiate for in the middle of the project when schedules and budgets are tight, as they always are. Thus the user interface designer should work closely with the product or project manager in the initial stages of the project to ensure that the necessary user interface design tasks are planned for and committed to. As described previously, all planned activities should and can be cost justified.

The project plan should be completed before any other task is begun. It may be revised at any time along the way as the project progresses.

User Profile

As described in Chapter 2, designers tend to make two assumptions that can seriously mislead their design efforts: (1) all users are alike, and (2) all users are like me, the designer. These assumptions might have been reasonable in the 1970s when most users of interactive computer systems were other programmers, but it is not at all true today. Users are almost never like designers in technical education and sophistication, and they vary from each other in important ways that should directly influence design decisions. It is extremely important that all design decisions be driven by a thorough knowledge of such user characteristics as job experience level, expected frequency of use of the system, level of computer literacy, typing skill, turnover rate, expected training methods, and level of motivation.

For instance, if the intended users of a product can be described as *low* in computer literacy, motivation, experience, and frequency of use and as having a *high* turnover rate, then *ease of learning and remembering* become very important. Such design techniques as menu systems, icons, touch screen input, heavy prompting, and on-line help make software systems easy to learn.

On the other hand, if users can be described as *high* in computer literacy, motivation, experience, and frequency of use and as having a *low* turnover rate, then *ease of use* is probably more important than ease of learning. Appropriate techniques in this case might include command languages, keyboard input, minimal keystrokes per command, and prompting only on request.

When users are expected to be very diverse, then several user definitions might be developed and prioritized so that when conflicts arise and trade-offs must be made it is clear how to make them. A thorough discussion of relevant user characteristics and how they should drive design decisions is provided in Chapter 2.

The user profile can be developed in parallel with the hardware and software definition. It should precede task analysis.

Hardware and Software Definition

Even on many development projects within vendor companies, and almost always on projects within data processing or information systems departments, the hardware and software platform for a new software package is predetermined. The software user interface must be designed within the constraints of what is and is not possible given this platform. Interface techniques that may or may not be available include the following

> Visual cues (for example, reverse video, blinking, color, fonts, borders, and bold)
>
> Input devices (mouse, touch screen, or function keys)
>
> Interaction techniques (windowing, pull-down menus, or direct manipulation)

The capabilities and constraints of the platform should be determined and documented as input to the design of the user interface.

The hardware and software definition can be conducted in parallel with the user profile. It must follow the project plan and precede task analysis.

PHASE 2: FUNCTIONAL SPECIFICATION

The major work of this phase is the **functional specification,** a detailed description of product functionality (what the product will do). In addition, a high-level **training and documentation definition** is developed to identify the types of training and documentation that will be developed to support the product.

The user-interface-related-tasks that should be carried out in this phase include the following:

Task analysis
User interface goal setting
Training and documentation definition

These are described next.

Task Analysis

Task Analysis involves observing and interviewing end users to obtain an understanding of how users currently accomplish the task(s) to be automated in the planned application. Users are asked to describe their relevant work activities. "Why?" questions get at the major goals. "How?" questions get at the details of actions that accomplish goals. In particular, users' work-flow patterns, users' conceptual frameworks, and the interrelationships between user objects and tasks are studied.

A task analysis differs from traditional systems analysis in its goals, output, focus and objectives, as follows:

	Systems analysis	Task analysis
Goal	Input to design of software processes and data structures	Input to design of user interface
Output	Functional spec and system architecture spec	User interface spec (style guide)
Focus	Technical information processing limitations, data characteristics, and system architecture considerations	Human information processing limitations, user characteristics, and task considerations
Main objects of analysis	Data and functions	User tasks

A task analysis reveals the specific requirements for particular products. For instance, what do users of a legal bibliographic search system need to be able to specify as search criteria? What patient and scan information do physicians need to see on the image displayed on a magnetic resonance imaging system? What functions would users of a new word processor like to have? What windowing capabilities are and are not important in a given application? The answers to questions such as these cannot be found by sitting in an office speculating. They must be extracted from the users themselves. Several techniques are available to conduct a task analysis.

Interviews are an excellent way to gather information as input to the design of a new application area that has not previously been implemented in automated form. Information can be gathered from a representative set of potential users regarding how they perform the function of interest in the current manual world and what they consider important and desirable in automated support for the function. The interviewer must be skilled in uncovering general needs, because users are not generally very good at suggesting particular solutions to their own problems and needs. They do not understand the capabilities of the technology well enough to do this. For instance, computer users in 1985 may not have been able to specify a need for windowing, but a skilled interviewer would have been able to discover that users often need to directly compare two pieces of information that reside in different files, but can never see them simultaneously on the screen. It is the job of the interviewer to uncover the need and the job of the designer to create a technological solution. (For an example of an interview study, see Malone, 1983.)

Questionnaires are another requirements analysis technique that is effective in getting *subjective* feedback on existing systems in use, for the purpose of designing a new release or competitive product. Users can be polled in large numbers for their subjective opinions and level of satisfaction with current features or functions, thus allowing designers to discover problem areas and opportunities for improvement.

Usage studies are a technique for *objectively* measuring the actual usage of current systems to gain insight into user needs for new or enhanced products. The frequency of use of particular commands in a word processing system could be measured to decide which commands to include in a future system and which to make most easily accessible based on relative frequency of use. The frequency of different types of errors could be collected to identify common errors that might be prevented through redesign. (For an example of a usage study, see Good, 1985).

A high-level conceptual model for the user interface is designed based on the outputs of the task analysis, which describes how the interface will present objects, relationships between objects, attributes of objects, and actions.

The task analysis can be conducted in parallel with the functional specification. It must follow the user profile, hardware and software definition, precede goal setting, and user interface training and documentation definition.

User Interface Goal Setting

User interface goals can be stated in a concrete, objective, quantitative, measurable form, just like any other engineering goal, such as performance or reliability. This should always be done at the beginning of the project for two reasons: (1) If you do not know what your goals are, you will never know if you have achieved them, and (2) stating clear goals for acceptance testing up front and gaining commitment from management at that point helps to ensure that unacceptable products will not be released until further work is done to improve them.

User interface goals can be stated in relative or absolute terms. An example of an **absolute goal** might be "error-free performance on task X in 30 minutes by a first-time user without reference to a manual or training." This might be a meaningful goal if it was known through market surveys that users' tolerance for the learning effort is low, and they will not buy the product if they think it will take more than 30 minutes to learn.

An example of a **relative goal** might be "Expert time to perform task Y on the system must be at least 30% faster than on any competitive product." This might be appropriate if customers were expected to make buying decisions based on the relative ease of use of competitive systems, and it was known that a 30% difference in performance time was the minimum that would be perceived as significant by buyers.

Appropriate goals for a particular product will depend on the needs of the intended users, and this is another reason why knowing who the users are is important. Goals are commitments to a certain level of quality and form the foundation for a test plan. They also help designers focus their design efforts, as they are agreed-on criteria for product release.

User interface goal setting must follow task analysis. It can proceed in parallel with the training and documentation definition.

Training and Documentation Definition

Based on the user profile, the high-level conceptual design arising from the task analysis, and the identified ease of learning goals, decisions regarding which training and documentation tools will be provided with the system are made. Possibilities include, but are not limited to, the following:

> Formal training class (live instructor in classroom)
> Video training program (self-paced learning from video tape)
> Training manual (hard-copy tutorial)
> On-line tutorial
> User guide
> Reference manual
> Quick reference
> On-line help

All project team members should have input into tool selection. Staff should then be assigned responsibility for managing the development of each selected learning tool. These individuals should participate in all subsequent user interface tasks. The project plan should be revised to accommodate the development and testing of the specific set of chosen learning tools, and to reflect any changes in the level of effort or schedule for later tasks as a result of this task. The resources required for ongoing maintenance of each of the selected learning tools should be assessed and planned for.

The training and documentation definition must follow functional specification and task analysis. It can, however, occur in parallel with UI mockup.

PHASE 3: DESIGN

Figure 18-3 shows the activities associated with the design phase in a typical development project: system architecture design, application code specs, and user interface code specs.

System architecture design refers to the overall structure of the code, including major subsystems, input and output files, data types, data flow through the subsystems, and so on. System architecture design also includes such basic hardware decisions as what input devices will be offered (mouse, lightpen, keyboard, touch screen) and whether screens are full page or standard size, bit-mapped or not, color or monochrome, and so on. Hardware choices should be driven by software interface design decisions, which in turn should be determined according to user requirements. Application code specs refers to the design of the flow of logic and data within particular modules of application code. User interface code specs refers to the logic design of modules that control the user interface.

User interface design methods that should be employed in the design phase of a software project are illustrated in Figure 18-3, and described next. They include the following:

> User interface mockup
> Style guide
> Detailed user interface design
> User interface prototype
> Prototype user interface test plan
> Prototype user interface testing

User Interface Mockup

Based on the user profile, the hardware and software definition, the task analysis, the goals, and any corporate user interface standards, *tentative* high-level design decisions are made regarding how objects, attributes, relationships, and actions will be presented. Taking one or more representative task scenarios, these design ideas are mocked up in storyboard fashion, including the primary screens the user would navigate through to accomplish each task. A rapid prototyping tool can be used for this purpose, but paper and pencil will suffice. It is not necessary on an automated mockup to make it interactive; it is only necessary to be able to demonstrate screens in a particular order. Several mockups representing alternative designs may be generated.

The purpose of the mockup is to provide something that other team members and users can react to. Although in order to mock up screens low-level design details (for example, exactly how pull-down menu choices will be displayed) must be included, these are not important at this point and need not represent final or even serious design decisions. The main point is to represent the high-level design ideas in order to solicit feedback on them in the next task.

The mockup(s) should demonstrate how the interface will present:

Different classes of objects
Different classes of actions
Different types of object attributes
Different types of relationships between objects

The mockup(s) will also demonstrate the high-level structure of the interface and how the user navigates through it.

The user interface mockup should not commence until all functional specification phase user interface tasks are complete except the training and documentation definition. It must be complete before any later tasks begin.

Style Guide

A *style guide* is a high-level design document describing the generic (module independent) user interface standards, rules, guidelines, and conventions for a product or family of products. It should be written by one author, the user interface designer, although the design decisions it contains may have been arrived at by the joint efforts of many designers consulting with the designated user interface designer. The style guide serves as a specification document to interface software developers and application designers.

The style guide includes descriptions of design standards and conventions for such things as the layout of screens, standard uses for keyboard keys, location and style of error messages, standard uses of terminology, guidelines for the use of color, and standard mechanisms for certain generic operations. These standards and conventions are to be followed during detailed design to ensure consistency in the user interface across subsystems or functions of the system. A sample table of contents for a style guide is offered next.

Introduction
Overview of Functionality
User Profile
Hardware and Software Constraints and Capabilities
Statement of Usability Goals
Training and Documentation Definition
Conceptual Design

Dialog Styles
Input and Output Devices
Organization of Functionality
Screen Layout and Design
Feedback
On-line User Aid

Development of the style guide should not proceed until after the User Interface mockup. Detailed user interface design should not proceed until this task is complete. (For more detail on writing style guides, see McCormick and Bleser, 1985).

Detailed User Interface Design

Once the conventions and standards to be followed have been documented in the style guide, it is time to proceed to the detailed design phase. Here, actual screens, user input formats, error messages, and the like are designed for all functions and features of the system, based on and adhering to the standards, conventions, and guidelines specified in the style guide.

In many organizations, it is not sufficient to publish and distribute a style guide. Developers may simply not get around to reading it given the pressure of deadlines and schedules. Or they may scan it, but not absorb its detail. Or they may simply not understand it. There need to be organizational structures and processes in place that ensure that the standards and guidelines documented in the style guide actually get implemented in the detailed design.

A couple of strategies will help here. First, find ways to effectively *communicate* the standards. Assume that no one will read the style guide. Present the standards in an oral presentation to which all designers are required to come. Demonstrate the guidelines with examples, either on paper or using the rapid prototyping tools available. Videotape the demo and presentation so it can be reviewed by designers repetitively at their leisure and by newcomers to the design team.

Second, create an organizational unit, such as a user interface steering committee, with the authority to approve or disapprove all design documents as conforming to the standards. Require approval before coding can commence. Explicitly build a review process into the project plan. Provide organizational incentives for designers to adhere to the standards. Management support for the standards is key here. *Communicating* the guidelines is the first step. *Enforcing* them is the second. Perhaps the best way of all to both communicate and enforce Style Guide rules is to build them into development toolkits.

Detailed user interface design should not proceed until the style guide is complete. It can go in parallel with system architecture design.

User Interface Prototype

A full-blown prototype is built that represents the core functionality of the application. The prototype should be fully interactive in that users can enter data in fill-in fields, look up sample information, and navigate through functionality via menu choices, function keys, and so on. However, the prototype need not be functionally complete in that it need not have complete files associated with it or process data. Exactly which functions to prototype should be driven by a variety of factors, including the following:

> Those functions considered to be "core," that is, most important
> Those functions whose interface is considered most likely to be problematic
> Those functions considered to be most representative of the full functionality
> Functions most likely to be executed in a sequence

With the right prototyping tool, the prototype, as it evolves, is in fact the implemented user interface code. That is, the right tool allows the interface built with the tool to be integrated directly with application code.

The user interface prototype should not proceed until detailed user interface design is complete. The next task, usability testing, can be in the planning stages while this task is underway. Application code specs can be developed in parallel with this task.

Prototype User Interface Test Plan

A plan for conducting usability testing to reveal any major problems in the initial design should be designed at this point. Core, high-frequency user tasks should be identified as the basis for the test. The test plan consists of the following:

> A set of specific user tasks with supporting test materials
> A definition of types of data to be collected on those tasks
> The number and types of test users to be run
> A schedule for the first iteration of testing

Developing the test plan can proceed in parallel with detailed user interface design or user interface prototyping. The project plan should be revised to reflect any changes in the level of effort or schedule for later tasks as a result of this task.

Prototype User Interface Testing

Just as code can be tested for "bugs," the user interface can and should be tested for "bugs." The notion of prototyping and iterative design and testing is a new one to the software industry, but it is a definite trend. Whenever a software organization builds a prototype, there is an opportunity for user interface testing and redesign that can greatly improve the success of the product once it is released.

The steps for each iteration of testing include the following:

Define usability issues to be tested

Design a test that will produce data relevant to those issues

Select, solicit, and schedule test users

Run test users and collect data

Analyze data and formulate redesign recommendations

Modify prototype according to recommendations

Several prototype testing techniques are available.

Structured observation.   A simple and powerful technique for revealing major flaws in the design of the user interface is to conduct *structured observations* of typical users attempting to execute typical tasks on the prototype system and to note their errors, confusion, frustrations, and complaints. Usually only six to eight users are required before patterns in behavior become apparent. Errors that five or six out of eight users make are indications that redesign is necessary. For example, when most users misunderstand an error message, it is clear that it needs to be redesigned. When most users take the same wrong turn in a menu hierarchy, it is clear that a menu label is misleading. When it takes most users several tries to successfully select an icon with a mouse, it is obvious that the icon should be bigger. These kinds of problems quickly reveal themselves in a structured observation study. (For an example of the structured observation technique, see Lund, 1985.)

Benchmarking.   Benchmarking is more specifically oriented toward testing the interface against the performance goals that were specified early on in the project (see "User Interface Goal Setting"). Specific tasks are constructed and representative users are brought in to test the system against the stated goals. If, for instance, the goal was established that it should take no longer than 30 minutes to attain error-free performance on a benchmark task without reference to a manual, a task can be devised to test the system against this criterion. Six to 10 users can be tested, and if the average learning time is less than or equal to 30 minutes, the interface can be declared acceptable. If the average learning time exceeds 30 minutes, redesign and retesting are indicated. (For an example of a benchmarking study, see Roberts and Moran, 1982.)

Classic experiments.   Yet another technique for prototype testing is based on classic experimental design. Two or more user interface design alternatives to the same functionality can be directly compared, and the one that results in superior performance can be selected for the final product. For instance, designers might be trying to decide whether to use a mouse or a touch screen as the input device to a system. Two prototypes could be constructed, where the task (selecting menu items) is the same, but the device (mouse or touch screen) is different. Representative users could be brought in and asked to perform representative tasks on the two prototypes. Speed and accuracy measures of performance could be collected, and preferences could be polled. Based on such *objective* measures of user performance and *subjective* measures of user satisfaction, a more rational choice between competing design alternatives could be made. (For an example of a classic experimental design, see Miller, 1981.)

The style guide should be updated at the completion of the cycle of iterative testing and redesigned to reflect the final design at this point.

Although *application* code specs can be developed during prototype usability testing, development of *user interface* code specs should not begin until prototype usability testing is complete. The first two steps of this task can begin during the UI prototype task.

PHASE 4: DEVELOPMENT

Typical software development tasks in this phase include **coding, system test plan,** and **developing training and documentation.** User interface tasks for this phase are illustrated in Figure 18-4 and described next. They include the following:

> Develop training and documentation
> User interface test plan

Develop Training and Documentation

Each learning tool specified in the training and documentation definition is completed when the design phase is complete and while the application is being developed. The user profile, task analysis, goals, and documentation standards should feed into tool design.

Possible learning tools include the following:

> Formal training class (live instructor in classroom)
> Video training program (self-paced learning from video tape)
> Training manual (hard-copy tutorial)
> On-line tutorial
> User guide
> Reference manual
> Quick reference
> On-line help

Training and documentation implementation cannot be completed until detailed user interface design is complete, but can proceed in parallel with all other development phase tasks except the training and documentation test plan.

User Interface Test Plan

Usability tests are designed to compare the performance of users on the application to the *ease of use* and *ease of learning* goals laid out in the goal setting task. The test plan follows in a fairly straightforward way from the goals definitions. The test plan consists of the following:

A set of specific tasks with supporting test materials

A definition of types of data to be collected on these tasks

The number and types of test users to be run

A schedule for the first iteration of testing

The development of this test plan can proceed in parallel with any other development phase tasks. The project plan should be revised to reflect any changes in the level of effort or schedule for later tasks as a result of this task.

PHASE 5: TESTING/IMPLEMENTATION

After the system is designed and the code written, there is usually a procedure in place for testing the system for bugs, performance, and reliability. Testing is often done in phases, starting with **software testing,** in which individual modules of code are debugged. Often a testing organization conducts **hardware testing,** a test of the whole software system on all anticipated hardware platforms. Sometimes **installation testing** is performed to test the procedures users will use to install the software on their workstations and networks. Finally, **production testing** continues after implementation.

During this phase, a number of user interface tasks are carried out. These are illustrated in Figure 18-5, and described next. They include the following:

User interface testing

User interface evaluation

User Interface Testing

Using the benchmark testing technique (see ''Prototype User Interface Testing''), 6 to 20 representative users are run through the planned tasks. Minimal instruction should be given, or a 1- or 2-page manual provided. Videotaping should be used for data collation. Data are taken as defined in the UI test plan. These data are compared against goals, and any areas where minimal performance goals are not met are noted. The interface is then redesigned to engineer these identified problems out of the interface. Testing and redesigning should be conducted iteratively until all goals are met.

The steps for each iteration of testing include the following:

Run test users and collect data

Analyze data and formulate redesign recommendations

Modify application according to recommendations

The style guide should be updated at the completion of this cycle of iterative testing and redesign to reflect the final design at this point. The project plan should be revised to reflect any changes in the level of effort or schedule for later tasks as a result of this task. User interface testing should occur after software testing but can go on in parallel with hardware installation testing.

User Interface Evaluation

User testing should not stop after implementation. Once a system has been installed for some time and there are a good number of *expert* users available, continued feedback can be collected to feed into enhancements, new releases, and future products. The same techniques applied in earlier phases of the project are appropriate again: interviews, questionnaires, usage studies, structured observation, and benchmarking.

SUMMARY

Design and development are never really a linear process, as might be implied in Figures 18-1 through 18-5 and in the foregoing discussion. There is no point in testing if you do not intend to go back and redesign in response to feedback. And we can never assume that the solution implemented for one problem has not introduced new ones. It is important to retest as well. Thus, just as with any other aspect of software design, user interface design is an iterative process with feedback loops between phases.

Finally, the design philosophy inherent in the methodology presented in this chapter can be summarized by the following points:

1. The quality of software user interfaces has a real, direct impact on a company's bottom line.

2. Successful user interface design requires not only the application of design principles and guidelines, but also appropriate managerial and organizational techniques and design, testing, and evaluation methods.

3. User interface design tasks start when the project starts, not late in the design phase.

4. Usability can be engineered through objective goal setting and quantitative testing.

5. Iterative testing and design are essential.

6. Planning and budgeting for user interface design tasks and resources at the beginning of the development project are essential.

REFERENCES

GOOD, MICHAEL, "The Iterative Design of a New Text Editor," *Proceedings, Human Factors Society 29th Annual Meeting,* September 1985, pp. 571–74.

JACOB, ROBERT J. K., "Using Formal Specifications in the Design of Human–Computer Interfaces," *Proceedings, Human Factors in Computer Systems,* March 1982, pp. 315–21, ACM.

KARAT, CLARE-MARIE, "Iterative Usability of a Security Application," *Proceedings of the Human Factors Society 33rd Annual Meeting,* 1989, pp. 273–77.

LUND, MICHELLE A., "Evaluating the User Interface: The Candid Camera Approach," *CHI '85 Proceedings,* April 1985, pp. 107–13, ACM.

MALONE, THOMAS W., "How Do People Organize Their Desks? Implications for the Design of Office Information Systems," *ACM Transactions on Office Systems,* 1 (1983), pp. 99–112.

MANTEI, MARILYN, "Techniques for Incorporating Human Factors in the Software Lifecycle," *Proceedings of STA-III Conference: Structured Techniques in the Eighties: Practice and Prospect,* Chicago, June 1986.

———, and TOBY J. TEOREY, "Cost/Benefit for Incorporating Human Factors in the Software Lifecycle," *Communications of the ACM,* April, 1988, Vol. 31, No. 4, pp. 428–39.

McCORMICK, KATHLEEN, and TERRY BLESER, "Developing a User Interface Styleguide," *Proceedings National Computer Graphics Association,* 1985.

MILLER, DWIGHT P., "The Depth/Breadth Tradeoff in Hierarchical Computer Menus," *Proceedings of the Human Factors Society 25th Annual Meeting,* October 1981, pp. 270–300.

ROBERTS, TERESA, and THOMAS P. MORAN, "Evaluation of Text Editors," *Proceedings, Human Factors in Computer Systems,* March 1982, pp. 136–41, ACM.

SHNEIDERMAN, BEN, *Designing the User Interface: Strategies for Effective Human–Computer Interaction* (Reading, Mass.: Addison-Wesley Publishing Co., 1986).

Recommended Reading

GENERAL GUIDELINES REFERENCES

BADRE, ALBERT, and SHNEIDERMAN, BEN, eds., *Directions in Human Computer Interaction* (Norwood, N.J.: Ablex Publishing Corp., 1982).

BAECKER, RONALD M., and WILLIAM A. S. BUXTON, eds., *Readings in Human–Computer Interaction* (Los Altos, Calif.: Morgan Kaufmann Publishers, Inc., 1987).

BAILEY, ROBERT W., *Human Performance Engineering: A Guide for Systems Designers* (Englewood Cliffs, N.J.: Prentice-Hall, 1982).

BROWN, C. MARLIN, *Human–Computer Interface Design Guidelines* (Norwood, N.J.: Ablex Publishing Co., 1988).

CARD, STUART K., THOMAS P. MORAN, and ALLEN NEWELL, *The Psychology of Human Computer Interaction* (Hillsdale, N.J.: Lawrence Erlbaum Associates, Publishers, 1983).

CARROLL, JOHN M., ed., *Interfacing Thought: Cognitive Aspects of Human–Computer Interaction* (Cambridge, Mass.: M.I.T. Press, 1989).

———, *Designing Interaction: Psychology at the Human Computer Interface,* (Cambridge, England: Cambridge University Press, 1991).

DUMAS, JOSEPH S., *Designing User Interfaces for Software* (Englewood Cliffs, N.J.: Prentice Hall, 1988).

DURRETT, H. JOHN, ed., *Color and the Computer* (Orlando, Fla.: Academic Press, Inc., 1987).

GALITZ, WILBERT O., *Handbook of Screen Format Design,* 3rd ed. (Wellesley, Mass.: QED Information Sciences, Inc., 1989).

GARDINER, MARGARET M., and BRUCE CHRISTIE, *Applying Cognitive Psychology to User-interface Design* (New York: John Wiley & Sons, Inc., 1987).

HECKEL, PAUL, *The Elements of Friendly Software Design* (New York: Warner, 1984).

HELANDER, MARTIN, ed., *Handbook of Human-Computer Interaction* (Amsterdam: Elsevier Science Publishers, 1988).

MEHLMANN, MARILYN, *When People Use Computers* (Englewood Cliffs, N.J.: Prentice-Hall, Inc. 1981).

MONK, ANDREW, ed., *Fundamentals of Human–Computer Interaction* (New York: Academic Press, Inc., 1985).

MOSIER, JANE, and SIDNEY SMITH, "Application of Guidelines for Designing User Interface Software," *Proceedings, Human Factors Society 29th Annual Meeting,* September 1985, pp. 946–52.

MUCKLER, FREDERICK A., ed., *Human Factors Review: 1984* (Santa Monica, Calif.: Human Factors Society, 1984).

NIELSEN, JAKOB, *Coordinating User Interfaces for Consistency* (San Diego: Academic Press, 1989).

———, *Designing User Interfaces for International Use* (Amsterdam: Elsevier Science Publishers, 1990).

NORMAN, DONALD A., and STEPHEN W. DRAPER, eds., *User Centered System Design* (Hillsdale, N.J.: Lawrence Erlbaum Associates, 1986).

RUBINSTEIN, RICHARD, and HARRY HERSH, *The Human Factor: Designing Computer Systems for People* (Burlington, MA: Digital Press, 1984).

SALVENDY, GAVRIEL, ed., *Advances in Human Factors/Ergonomics, Volume 1, Human Computer Interaction* (Amsterdam: Elsevier, 1984).

SHNEIDERMAN, BEN, *Software Psychology: Human Factors in Computer and Information Systems* (Cambridge, Mass.: Winthrop Publishers, Inc., 1980).

———, *Designing the User Interface: Strategies for Effective Human–Computer Interaction* (Reading, Mass.: Addison-Wesley Publishing Co., 1986).

SMITH, SIDNEY L., and MOSIER, JANE N., *Guidelines for Designing User-interface Software* (Bedford, MA: Mitre Corporation, 1986).

WILLIGES, BEVERLY H., and ROBERT C. WILLIGES, "Dialogue Design Considerations for Interactive Computer Systems," in Frederick A. Muckler, ed., *Humand Factors Review* (Santa Monica, Calif.: Human Factors Society, 1984), pp. 167–208.

OTHER INFORMATION SOURCES

Conference Proceedings

ACM SIGCHI Annual Conference on Human Factors in Computer Systems
Human Factors Society Annual Meeting
IFIP Conferences on Human–Computer Interaction
Interact

Journals

ACM Transactions on Office Information Systems, ACM
Behavior and Information Technology, Taylor and Francis
Communications of the ACM, ACM
Human–Computer Interaction, Lawrence Earlbaum Associates, Publishers
Interacting with Computers, Butterworth Scientific Ltd.
International Journal of Man–Machine Studies, IEEE
Journal of the Human Factors Society, HFS

Index

Figure 14–23 Use of color to establish relationships.

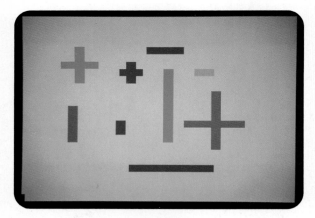

Figure 14–24 Use of color as a search cue.

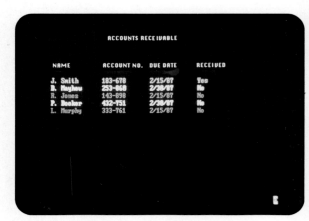

Figure 14–26 Using color in task related ways.